West Virginia

West Virginia

Leonard M. Adkins

The Countryman Press ✳ Woodstock, Vermont

FIRST EDITION

Explorer's Guide West Virginia

978-0-88150-947-2

Interior photographs by the author unless otherwise specified
Maps by Erin Greb Cartography, and Mapping Specialists Ltd. Madison, WI,
© The Countryman Press
Book design by Bodenweber Design
Composition by PerfecType, Nashville, TN

Published by The Countryman Press, P.O. Box 748, Woodstock, VT 05091

Distributed by W. W. Norton & Company, Inc., 500 Fifth Avenue, New York, NY 10110

Printed in the United States of America

10 9 8 7 6 5 4 3 2 1

*To all of my relatives and friends who understand what it means
to be a West Virginian.*

EXPLORE WITH US!

Welcome to the second edition of *West Virginia: An Explorer's Guide*, the state's most comprehensive travel companion. All attractions, lodgings, and restaurants are chosen on the basis of merit, not paid advertising. The organization of the book is simple, but the following points will help to get you started on your way.

WHAT'S WHERE

In the beginning of the book is an alphabetical listing with thumbnail sketches of special highlights, important information, and advice on everything from finding the best art galleries to attending a festival celebrating one of the state's finest natural delicacies, the ramp.

LODGING

Lodging establishments mentioned in this book are selected on the basis of merit; no innkeeper or business owner was charged for inclusion. When making reservations, which almost all B&Bs require, ask about the policy on children, pets, smoking, and acceptance of credit cards. Many B&Bs do not accept children under 12, and some places have a minimum-stay policy, especially on weekends, holidays, and during special events.

Rates: The rates are for two people to stay in one room for one night and are weekend rates during what the establishment considers its high season. Weekday and off-season rates may be lower. However, please do not hold the respective innkeepers or the author responsible for the rates listed as this book went to press. Changes are inevitable. State, local, and room taxes (which can be above 10 percent) have not been included.

RESTAURANTS

Please note the distinction between *Dining Out* and *Eating Out*. By their nature, restaurants in the *Eating Out* section are less expensive and more casual. Many restaurants change their menus often; the specific dishes mentioned in this book may not be available when you dine. They are cited to give you a general idea of the cuisine offered. Like the lodging rates quoted in this book, menu prices were current when it went to press. However, as we all know, prices never go down; be prepared for them to have risen somewhat.

KEY TO SYMBOLS

- ❧ **Special value.** The special-value symbol appears next to lodgings, restaurants, and other attractions that offer a quality not often found at the price charged.
- ✍ **Child-friendly.** The crayon symbol appears next to places or activities that accept and/or appeal to young children, or have a children's menu.
- 🐾 **Pets.** The pet symbol appears next to places, activities, and lodgings that accept pets. Almost all lodging accommodations require that you inform them of a pet when you make a reservation and often request an additional fee.

 ♿   **Handicapped access.** The wheelchair symbol appears next to lodgings, restaurants, and attractions that are partially or completely handicapped-accessible.

☂   **Rainy-day activity.** The rainy-day symbol appears next to places of interest and things to do that are appropriate for inclement-weather days.

⚭   **Weddings.** The wedding-ring symbol appears next to establishments that specialize in weddings.

🍸   **Bars.** The martini glass symbol appears next to establishments that have choice selections of beers, wines, and other alcoholic beverages.

✪   **Don't miss this.** The don't-miss-this symbol appears next to places, activities, and sights that you will remember a long time after you return home.

CONTENTS

Also by Leonard M. Adkins

50 Hikes in West Virginia: From the Allegheny Mountains to the Ohio River

50 Hikes in Northern Virginia: Walks, Hikes, and Backpacks from the Allegheny Mountains to the Chesapeake Bay

50 Hikes in Southern Virginia: From the Cumberland Gap to the Atlantic Ocean

50 Hikes in Maryland: Walks, Hikes, and Backpacks from the Allegheny Plateau to the Atlantic Ocean

Maryland: An Explorer's Guide

The Appalachian Trail: A Visitor's Companion

Images of America: Along Virginia's Appalachian Trail

Postcards of America: Along Virginia's Appalachian Trail

Wildflowers of the Appalachian Trail

Wildflowers of the Blue Ridge and Great Smoky Mountains

Best of the Appalachian Trail: Day Hikes (with Victoria and Frank Logue)

Best of the Appalachian Trail: Overnight Hikes (with Victoria and Frank Logue)

Walking the Blue Ridge: A Guide to the Trails of the Blue Ridge Parkway

Seashore State Park: A Walking Guide

Adventure Guide to Virginia

The Caribbean: A Walking and Hiking Guide

ACKNOWLEDGMENTS

I am not exaggerating when I say hundreds of people had a hand in helping me put this book together. Many spent multiple hours setting up efficient itineraries for me; others spent days driving me around; some unselfishly gave of their historical and natural-history knowledge; and quite a number took time out of busy schedules to open museums, historic sites, and other establishments during off hours. I was generously granted places to stay; dozens of people spent evenings looking over portions of the manuscript; and many others were consistently patient and polite even when I pestered them time after time. Every entry in this book represents hours that someone was willing to help me. Without the assistance of all of them, this book would still be but an idea.

Heartfelt thanks goes to Bob Anderson, South Charleston Convention and Visitors Bureau; Christy Bailey, Coal Heritage Highway Authority; Twila Clark, Denny Bellemy, and Jacob G. Hill, Mason County Tourism Center; Bonnie Branciaroli, Potomac Highlands Travel Council; Stacey Brodak and Jack Thompson, Greater Morgantown Convention and Visitors Bureau; Linda Bush, Putnam County Convention and Visitors Bureau; Joe Cardullo, Summersville Chamber of Commerce; Susan E. Church, Lewis County Convention and Visitors Bureau; Mallie Combs-Snyder, Hardy County Rural Development Authority; Shannon Dean, Southern West Virginia Convention and Visitors Bureau; Sandra Dionne, Martinsburg-Berkeley County Convention and Visitors Bureau; Cindy Dragan, New River Convention and Visitors Bureau; Tim Brady, Gabe Feist, and Cynthia Hunter, Greater Bridgeport Convention and Visitors Center; Helen Graves, Monroe County Tourism; Sheila Haney, Preston County Visitors Center; Paul Zuros, Top of West Virginia Convention and Visitors Bureau; Belinda Metheney, Preston County Chamber of Commerce; Michelle M. Blumhagen and Janet Harlow, Hampshire County Convention and Visitors Bureau; Marvin Gelhausen, Grafton/Taylor County Convention and Visitors Bureau; Betty B. Carver and Tricia Sizemore, Department of Commerce; and Mel Hobbs and Gail Hyer, Pocahontas County Convention and Visitors Bureau.

Thanks also to Amy Kaczynski and Kelly Tucker, Greenbrier County Convention and Visitors Bureau; David Knuth, Marshall County Tourism and Chamber of Commerce; Gerry Krueger, Cabell-Huntington Convention and Visitors Bureau; Marianne Moran and Sharon Kay Phillips, Convention and Visitors Bureau of Marion County; Jeanne Mozier and staff, Berkeley Springs Visitors Center; Cleta Mullins, Coalfield Convention and Visitors Bureau; Frank O'Brien, Wheeling

Convention and Visitors Bureau; Bob O'Connor, Jefferson County Convention and Visitors Bureau; Brenda Pritt, Randolph County Convention and Visitors Bureau; Carolyn Simmons, Pendleton County Chamber of Commerce; Andrea Smith, Snowshoe Mountain; William Smith, Tucker County Convention and Visitors Bureau; Kent Spellman, Ritchie County Economic Development Authority; Kari Thompson and Steve Nicely, Greater Parkersburg Convention and Visitors Bureau; Kathryn Titus, Greater Clarksburg Convention and Visitors Bureau; Judy Ward, Patricia Bradley Pitrolo, and Eddie Canaday, Charleston Convention and Visitors Bureau; and Beverly Weilman, Mercer County Convention and Visitors Bureau.

Caryn Gresham, West Virginia Division of Tourism—may the quality of this book reflect the high caliber of assistance you provided me. Dr. Stephen Lewis, Caroline Charonko, Terry Gumming, and Susie Surfas—West Virginia is a wonderful state, isn't it? Thank you for enabling me to enjoy it all these years. Kathleen, John, Tim, and Jay Yelenic—who would have ever thought that you would move back to West Virginia while I was researching this book? Thanks for letting me use your home as a base in the Northern Panhandle. Laurie—I love you!

INTRODUCTION

Is it any wonder then,
That my heart with rapture thrills,
As I stand once more with loved ones,
On those West Virginia Hills?
—Part of the official West Virginia state song

Montani Semper Liberi
(Mountaineers Are Always Free)
—State motto

Welcome to my native state of West Virginia and the second edition of *West Virginia: An Explorer's Guide.* You are about to find out what many residents of the state have known for decades: In addition to being America's best outdoors amusement park, West Virginia is a travel destination with something worth seeing or doing tucked into every little nook, cranny, and hollow of its convoluted mountainous scenery. From the waters of the Potomac River flowing beside the Eastern Panhandle to the heights of the Allegheny Mountains shadowed by a setting sun to the rolling hills of the Mid-Ohio region dropping into the Ohio River, all areas of the state hold treasures waiting for you to discover.

As you head to Berkeley Springs in the Eastern Panhandle to enjoy a massage at a centuries-old spa, you could stop to take a fishing trip on the Potomac River, visit Harpers Ferry National Historical Park to relive John Brown's raid and the tumultuous days of the Civil War, learn who was really the first person to successfully build a steamboat, hike a portion of the multistate Appalachian or Tuscarora trails, and have your choice of fine-dining restaurants whose reputations rival the best of those found in cosmopolitan centers throughout the world.

If the state is an outdoors amusement park, then the Potomac Highlands region is the main attraction—the grand roller coaster that will bring oohs, aahs, and shouts of sheer enjoyment. Here you can drive to the state's highest point, hike between two state parks in a landscape more akin to New England than West Virginia, stay in luxury accommodations after swooshing down your choice of dozens of downhill ski runs or gliding along cross-country trails, watch bald eagles fly overhead as you negotiate the rapids of a narrow gorge, and look at the stars from a backcountry campsite located miles from any annoying lights or other signs of civilization. You're not done yet. You can also be awed by the staggering beauty of the fall colors on a scenic train ride to the state's second-highest point, ride a horse to the top of some of West Virginia's most spectacular rock formations (or take a course that will teach you how to safely climb them), or attend the state's largest heritage festival.

A tour of Southern West Virginia can introduce you to the 77-mile Greenbrier River Trail, world-class whitewater rafting on the New and Gauley rivers, or the state's coal-mining industry by driving through dozens of coal-mining towns. You can even go underground in an exhibition coal mine. You could also hobnob with the world's rich and famous by staying at the Greenbrier or purchase a thing of beauty from a concentration of private galleries in Lewisburg.

In two of the state's largest cities, Charleston and Huntington, you can take in the exhibits at renowned art museums, enjoy a large-format movie, attend a radio music program that is broadcast internationally, watch minor-league baseball players hone their skill in hopes of making it to the majors, and lick superpremium ice cream while strolling along a tree-lined downtown street.

Within a 30-minute drive of this cosmopolitan atmosphere, you could be mountain biking more than 20 miles of rugged trails, slipping money into slot machines and betting on dog races, or motorboating on a lake that attracts more than a half-million visitors per year.

In the more northern part of the state, you can cheer on the West Virginia University Mountaineers as they play a game in their modern facility, take another whitewater rafting trip on the Cheat River or an easy guided canoe trip on the Monongahela River, watch reenactors bring the Civil War Battle of Philippi back to life, drive over the state's oldest and longest remaining covered bridge, or trace the routes of more than 50 miles of interconnecting rail trails.

Another rail trail runs along the Ohio River and through Wheeling's original neighborhood in the Northern Panhandle, where you also have your choice of betting on horses or dogs. Oglebay Resort, one of the country's largest municipal parks, is a wonderland for children, with playgrounds, picnic areas, a zoo, a planetarium, a miniature train ride, and a $2 million environmental-education center.

By traveling to the Mid-Ohio Valley region you can walk, hike, horseback ride, or experience what it is like to be in a covered wagon on the 70-mile North Bend Rail Trail. A paddleboat ride on the Ohio River takes you to an island that was the scene of an American tragedy, and a visit to a multistory museum can enlighten you as to how the fortunes amassed in the rich oil fields fueled the movement for West Virginia statehood.

To facilitate your explorations, this guide, the most comprehensive of its kind, has been divided into broad geographic regions. Individual chapters then cover areas that can easily be explored from their listed overnight accommodations.

Each chapter begins with an overview of the area, taking in its geographic features, historic aspects, and attraction highlights. There are listings on how to obtain further information, how to get to the area and get around once there, and places to obtain emergency help should the need arise.

Following those are the *To See* and *To Do* sections, which provide you with enough information to decide if a particular museum, historic home or site, family attraction, guided tour, golf course, hiking trail, lake, or other place or activity should fit into your travel plans.

I then give descriptions of places to stay, including B&Bs, inns, resorts, cabins, vacation rentals, and a few motels and hotels. Having stayed in them, or at least visited, I have based my descriptions on firsthand experiences and a propensity to snoop into hidden areas and out-of-the-way places. I try to be as honest as possible in my appraisals. What I saw and experienced is what I wrote about.

The same is true for the dining options provided. I gained quite a few pounds sampling the fare of the upscale restaurants (*Dining Out*) and that of the everyday places (*Eating Out*), in addition to bakeries, candy shops, ice-cream parlors, and coffeehouses.

Listings of entertainment venues, outstanding businesses worthy of some of your shopping time, and special events that take place annually round out each chapter.

Within all of these hundreds of listings and descriptions you will find very few negative remarks (and those are usually small comments about something trifling). The reason is that I visited and dined in a few places that I simply did not include in the guide. If I was uncomfortable in a place or found it lacking in cleanliness, I felt that other lone travelers, couples, or families would be, too. If a meal was not worth the calories consumed, or the atmosphere made for an unpleasant dining experience, the restaurant was not included. (I felt it was not even worth listing the B&B that had long, dirty spider webs hanging from the ceiling fan and dust bunnies that scooted across the floor when I walked around. I also did not include the restaurant whose restroom appeared to have not been cleaned for decades, plates that had bits of the previous diner's meal stuck to them, and signs insulting customers plastered all over its walls.)

This does not mean that an inn had to be palatial or a restaurant serve five-star cuisine. It just means that you should get a good and fair experience for the money you spend.

Please remember: I confirmed that all of the listings in this book were correct before the second edition of *West Virginia: An Explorer's Guide* went to press. However, all of us know that businesses come and go, opening times and days are altered, and admissions and fees inevitably change. It is always a wise idea to call ahead to make sure things are as you hope they will be. So, if the Web site for a restaurant is no longer on the Internet and the only answer you get when you call the restaurant is an answering machine for a different business, don't hold me or the publisher responsible if you then drive five hours to find the business closed (as one reader animatedly wrote me).

I was born, raised, and spent most of my life in West Virginia, and, I have to admit to you, I had fun doing the field research for this book. I had already experienced many wonderful adventures in the state, but the need for current, firsthand knowledge set me off on new explorations. I revisited places from my childhood and had the perfect excuse to go to new places and engage in activities I had always wanted to explore but lacked the time. From a horseback ride to the top of Seneca Rocks to a tour of the hallowed halls of the capitol building in Charleston, from a weekend hike in the wilds of the Cranberry Wilderness to admiring the handiwork of dozens of artists and craftspersons on display at Tamarack in Beckley, I was privileged to spend months experiencing all that the state has to offer. In addition, I was able to sample the sumptuous offerings of some of the world's most innovative chefs and engage in intriguing conversations with the guests and hosts of the state's relaxing and historically rich B&Bs.

I had fun getting to intimately know my native state. You will, too. Happy exploring.

17

INTRODUCTION

A BRIEF HISTORY OF WEST VIRGINIA

Archaeological digs have uncovered artifacts to suggest that what is present-day West Virginia was inhabited as early as 12,500 years ago, but very little is known about these people. On the other hand, the Adena Indians, who lived in the area about 3,000 years ago and built burial mounds (thus, they are also known as "the mound builders"), left ample evidence of their lives, with two of the largest mounds being found in South Charleston and Moundsville. By the time the first European explorer, Joseph Lederer, arrived in 1669, the mound builders were long gone, and various Indian tribes, such as the Shawnee, Mingo, Delaware, and Cherokee, were using the land as a hunting area.

In 1671, Thomas Batts and Robert Fallam passed through the New River Gorge to arrive at the Kanawha River on the confluence of the New and Gauley rivers, thereby giving England a claim to lands stretching to the Ohio River. Soon afterward, the French claimed these same lands, setting the stage for many years of conflict, which culminated in the French and Indian War of the mid-1700s. Both sides enlisted the aid of various Indian tribes, pitting them against one another and the area's early settlers.

Chief Logan, a leader of the Mingo tribe, had lived peacefully with the settlers until a drunken crowd murdered his entire family. Logan, joined by Shawnee Chief Cornstalk, sought revenge and fought and lost a battle against 1,000 militiamen led by Andrew Lewis at Point Pleasant on the Ohio River in 1774. Many historians mark this as the first battle of the Revolutionary War, as the Native Americans gave up claims to land east of the Ohio River and moved westward, preventing them from forming alliances with the British during the war.

After independence from Great Britain, settlers moved into the western frontier in large numbers, and hostilities with the Native Americans came to an end near the turn of the 19th century.

As the economy of the eastern part of Virginia prospered and became dependent on slave labor to work on large plantations, many inhabitants of western Virginia lived on small farms that they worked themselves. John Brown's raid on a federal arsenal in Harpers Ferry in 1859 turned the entire nation's attentions to the issue of slavery. Other matters, involving voting rights, political apportionment, taxation, and public spending grew so severe for the inhabitants of western Virginia that, by the time Virginia

A FEW LITTLE-KNOWN FACTS

Forget the lofty mountains of New Hampshire or the 6,000-foot peaks in North Carolina. West Virginia's nickname, the Mountain State, is justly deserved: It has the highest mean altitude of any state east of the Mississippi River. It is said that if its 24,232 square miles of mountainous terrain could be made perfectly flat, the land would cover most of the United States. Also, if its twisting and winding border were straightened out, it would stretch from New York City to almost El Paso, Texas.

seceded from the Union in 1861, representatives met in Wheeling and formed the Restored Government of Virginia.

During the first two years of the Civil War, Virginia's western counties, especially those in the Eastern Panhandle and Potomac Highlands, were the site of many battles. Once Union forces were victorious at the 1863 Battle of Droop Mountain, their supremacy in the region was established. Recognizing the need for a truly legitimate government, the western counties applied for statehood, and on June 20, 1863, West Virginia became the country's 35th state—the only state born of the Civil War and by presidential proclamation.

The state was primarily agrarian when it was admitted to the United States, but things started to change in the late 1800s with improved railroad transportation. Timber was harvested from nearly every inch of the state, and coal production increased dramatically. At the same time, oil was discovered in the Northern Panhandle and Mid-Ohio Valley, and boomtowns—such as Burning Springs, whose population increased from fewer than 100 to 6,000 in less than six months—dotted the landscape.

The oil boom went bust around 1915, but jobs in the coal industry continued to increase, attracting thousands of Scots-Irish, Welsh, Italian, Polish, and other European immigrants, as well as African Americans from the rural South. Despite the promise of good wages and living conditions, coal miners and their families found themselves living in squalid company homes and always being in debt to the company because they were paid in "scrip," which could only be spent at over-priced company stores.

Although it was successful in organizing and addressing the plight of miners in Illinois, Indiana, Ohio, and Pennsylvania, the United Mine Workers of America's efforts were stymied in West Virginia by mine owners who hired armed guards to intimidate union organizers and members. In 1912, miners and their families who went on strike in Paint Creek and Cabin Creek were evicted from their homes. Forced to live in tent villages, the families were harassed by the guards, and tensions flared, with people being killed on both sides.

THE FLOATING STATE CAPITOL

The state capitol was housed inside the Linsly Institute in Wheeling when West Virginia became a state in 1863. In 1870, the legislature designated Charleston as the state capital, and all state records and properties were placed on a small barge and floated down the Ohio River and up the Kanawha River to Charleston. Just five years later, the legislature reversed its decision, and state records and properties took a return trip along the waterways.

Yet, in 1877, the legislature ordered that the citizens of the state should be able to vote for the location of the state's capital city. The result was that, in 1885, state records and properties once again floated down the Ohio and up the Kanawha to Charleston, where they have remained—albeit in a number of different buildings—until the present capitol was completed in 1932.

For the next several years, strikes, tensions, ill feelings, and murders escalated to the point that the era came to be known as the West Virginia Coal Mine Wars. After a couple of especially egregious murders by company-hired men on the McDowell County courthouse steps in 1921, thousands of miners assembled to march on Logan, and they were met on Blair Mountain by an opposing force of mine guards, deputies, and state police. A three-day battle ensued and was only brought under control when President Harding ordered federal troops into the area. Not wanting to fight against their country's government, most of the miners laid down their arms. This defeat effectively put an end to union organizing until federal legislation in 1933 protected the rights of unions to organize.

(I highly recommend you do more reading about the Coal Mine Wars to gain a better understanding of West Virginia. What happened during this time shaped and affected nearly every aspect of life in the state—in the past and into the present day.)

Following World War II, coal production plummeted to one-third of what it once was, and hundreds of thousands of West Virginians left the state in search of jobs. Soon afterward, modern machinery was able to do the work of many miners, so even though production went up, the number of jobs never rebounded. Additional new methods, such as strip mining and mountaintop removal, have not only further reduced the need for employees, but have also destroyed tens of thousands of acres of once pristine mountain landscapes.

As the number of industrial jobs has continued to decline in West Virginia, the state is being discovered by more and more travelers who have found the state to be a mecca for hiking, biking, canoeing, kayaking, climbing, whitewater rafting, fishing, hunting, caving, and other outdoor pursuits. Others come to seek out the handiwork of master artists and craftspersons, enjoy the rich culture of the people, or merely revel in the state's scenic beauty. Tourism is now West Virginia's leading industry.

WHAT'S WHERE IN WEST VIRGINIA

AREA CODES A number of area codes exist in West Virginia, with the possibility of new ones being added in the future. You must dial the area code on all phone calls, including local calls. This means that making a call will always involve dialing at least ten numbers.

ADMISSION FEES Admission fees of less than $10 per person are simply listed as "small admission fee." The actual cost is provided if higher. Please keep in mind that, as this book went to press, the rates quoted were accurate, but they are always subject to change.

AFRICAN AMERICAN HERITAGE Unbeknownst to many Americans, West Virginia has been the site of key events in the history of the country's African Americans. The first blacks in what would become West Virginia arrived as slaves in the 1780s. By 1830, close to 20,000 African Americans lived in the area, most of them working as slaves in the coal, salt, and iron industries. With the outbreak of the Civil War—and Pennsylvania and Ohio representing freedom to a slave who could make it across the states' bor-

ders—West Virginia was used by many a slave as an escape route. Since the Underground Railroad was operated in secrecy, it is hard to know exactly how many sites there were in West Virginia. However, located directly on the Ohio River, Ceredo and Parkersburg were definitely places where slaves made daring crossings of the water, while local lore says the stone **Dunbar Wine Cellars** were used as a hiding place. When West Virginia abolished slavery in 1865, many former slaves left in the hope of finding long-lost relatives and obtaining a greater sense of security in the more northern states. Conversely, some, like the family of **Booker T. Washington**, came into the state to work for the wages they could never have received as slaves.

Parkersburg's **Sumner School** opened in 1862 as the nation's first free African American school south of the Mason-Dixon Line, while **Storer College**, established in Harpers Ferry soon after the Civil War, was one of the country's first institutions of higher learning dedicated to the education of former slaves. The Niagara Movement, founded by W. E. B. Dubois and other African Americans as a civil rights organization, met at the college in 1906. At about the same time, more blacks were moving into the state to work in the booming oil, gas, timber, and coal industries and came to make up close to one-quarter of the coal-mining work force. Thousands of African American West Virginians answered the call to arms in World War I, and the **Kimball World War I Memorial** is believed to be the country's only monument dedicated to black veterans. Like thousands of other West Virginians who departed after huge job losses in the coalfields—and further economic hardships brought about by the Great Depression and World War II—African Americans left West Virginia in such large numbers that they now comprise only about 3 percent of the population.

A brochure available from the Division of Tourism (see *Information*) directs you to three dozen sites along the state's **African American Heritage Trail**.

AIR SERVICE West Virginia has airports in its larger cities, but all are off the main routes of the major airlines and are serviced by shuttle or commuter flights. In the more southern part of the state, **Yeager Airport** (304-344-8033; www.yeagerairport.com) in Charleston is the state's largest and receives more flights in one day than many of the others do in several days. **Tri-State Airport** (304-453-6165; www.tristateairport.com) in Huntington is also one of the state's busier airports. Both of these (usually) have the lowest fares of all the state's airports. Also in the more southern part of West Virginia are **Greenbrier Valley Airport** (304-645-3961; www.gvairport.com) in Lewisburg and **Raleigh County Memorial Airport** (304-255-0476; www.flybeckley.com) in Beckley.

You can fly into Parkersburg via the **Mid-Ohio Valley Airport** (304-464-5113; www.flymov.com). Clarksburg and Fairmont are serviced by the **North Central West Virginia Airport** (304-842-3400; www.flyckb.com), and the **Morgantown Municipal Airport** (304-291-7461; www.morgantown airport.com) is the gateway to Morgantown and the Mountaineer Country region.

Often it is easier and more cost-effective to fly into an out-of-state airport and drive into West Virginia. **Pittsburgh International Airport** (412-472-3525; www.pitairport.com) is within an hour's drive of many sites in the Northern Panhandle and Mountaineer Country regions, and it's only a bit more than an hour away from some places in the more northern portions of the Potomac Highlands or the western part of the Eastern Panhandle.

Also somewhat close to the Eastern Panhandle and the Potomac Highlands are the three large airports clustered around the Washington, DC, area: **Washington Dulles International Airport** (703-572-2700; www.metwash airports.com/dulles), **Reagan Washington National Airport** (703-417-8000; www.mwaa.com/reagan), and **Baltimore/Washington International Airport** (1-800-I-FLY-BWI; www .bwiairport.com).

ALLEGHENY TRAIL For approximately 300 miles, the **Allegheny Trail** traverses some of eastern West Virginia's most inspiring scenery. Stretching from the state's southeastern border with Virginia to the Pennsylvania line near Morgantown, it passes through national forests, numerous state parks and forests, and—with owner cooperation—across an assortment of private lands.

Nick Lozano, Bob Tabor, and

Charley Carlson, all from the Charleston area, are generally acknowledged as having advanced the idea of a long-distance hiking trail through the state. Along with Dr. Bob Urban, Fred Bird, Shirley Schweizer, and Doug Wood, they established the West Virginia Scenic Trails Association in the early 1970s. The association is a grassroots organization, with the trail route being identified, built, and maintained almost exclusively by volunteers.

My wife, Laurie, and I were recognized by the WVSTA as being the first people to walk the trail's entire length in 1983, and we repeated the trip in 1985.

By design, the Allegheny Trail can be a rugged hike. Do not expect Appalachian Trail–level maintenance. There are a number of places where there is no dug treadway to delineate the route, and the yellow blazes that mark the way may be faded or have disappeared. Many miles are across steep, rocky terrain where footing is unsure and vegetation may overtake the pathway, despite the best efforts of volunteers. Yet, the rewards are many.

Unlike the Appalachian Trail, which seeks the high ground as much as possible, the Allegheny Trail parallels scenic rivers for miles at a time, traverses virgin red spruce forests, rises onto ridgelines for pleasing views, wanders along sidehill pathways, drops into isolated mountain valleys, and goes beside thousands of acres of West Virginia farmlands.

More information and a guidebook for the entire trail may be obtained from the West Virginia Scenic Trails Association, P.O. Box 4042, Charleston, WV 25364; www.wvscenictrails.org.

AMTRAK Despite its critics and detractors, AMTRAK (1-800-872-7245; www.Amtrak.com) service to the southern part of West Virginia is fairly extensive. Three times a week a westbound train originating from New York and a different eastbound train coming from Chicago make stops in White Sulphur Springs, Alderson, Hinton, Prince (near Beckley), Thurmond (this is a flag stop), Charleston, and Huntington. Eastbound and westbound trains pick up and discharge passengers daily at Harpers Ferry and Martinsburg in the Eastern Panhandle.

ANTIQUES Old Central City in the western part of Huntington has so many antiques shops that it has dubbed itself the "Antiques Capital of West Virginia." Other areas with heavy concentrations of dealers include **Lewisburg**, **Nitro**, **Morgantown** and the **Mountaineer Country** region, and the three towns of **Buchanan**, **Sutton**, and **Weston**, which are just a short drive from one another. Quite a number of shops may also be found throughout the **Mid-Ohio Valley** region.

APPALACHIAN TRAIL The **Appalachian Trail** follows the crest of the Appalachian Mountains for more than 2,000 miles from Georgia to Maine, but there are only two short sections of the route in West Virginia. The pathway runs along the West Virginia/Virginia border for more than a dozen miles in Southern West Virginia a short distance east of Peterstown. It also runs along the West Virginia/Virginia border in the Eastern Panhandle for close to 5 miles before passing through Harpers Ferry National Historical Park and crossing the Potomac River into Maryland.

The Appalachian Trail Conservancy (304-535-6331; www.appalachiantrail.org); (mailing address: P.O. Box 807, Harpers Ferry 25425), is the source for the 11-book series of trail guides, *The Appalachian Trail: A Visitor's Companion*, *Wildflowers of the Appalachian Trail*, and other publications and information.

ART GALLERIES The **Huntington Museum of Art** (304-529-2701; www.hmoa.org) is the state's largest art gallery, and the quality of its collections and exhibits has earned it a world-class reputation. The 9,000-square-foot **Juliet Museum of Art** (304-561-3570; www.theclaycenter.org) is a state-of-the-art gallery located in Charleston's impressive Clay Center. The **Parkersburg Art Center** (304-485-3859; www.parkersburgartcenter.org) can stand up to comparison with other such places found in much larger cities, while Wheeling's **Stifel Fine Arts Center** (304-242-7700; www.oionline.com) has works of art both inside a historic mansion and on the grounds.

Smaller in size but still worth visiting is Chief Logan State Park's **Museum in the Park** (304-792-7229), which showcases items borrowed from the state museum. A component of West Virginia University in Morgan-

town, the **Monongalia Arts Center** (304-292-3325; www.monarts.bizland.com) is a 1913 stone and marble neoclassical building with Doric columns and pilasters. Located next to a municipal park in Hurricane, **Museum in the Community** (304-562-0484; www.museuminthecommunity.org) is a modern building that is an architectural attraction unto itself.

Charleston is blessed with a plethora of quality privately owned galleries, such as the **Callen McJunkin Gallery** (304-342-5647; www.mcjunkingallery.com) and **The Art Store** (304-345-1038). Many of West Virginia's smaller cities and towns, such as Berkeley Springs, Elkins, and Lewisburg, have so many artists and privately owned galleries that they are consistently included on lists of America's best small art towns.

ARTS AND CRAFTS Since the earliest settlers moved westward from North America's east coast, the area that would become West Virginia has been known for the artists and craftspersons that produce items that are both aesthetic and functional. Today's practitioners, whose numbers are increasing, continue the tradition and are gaining more national and international exposure through places such as **Tamarack** (304-256-6843; 1-888-262-7225; www.tamarackwv.com) in Beckley and **Mountainmade.com** (304-463-3355; 1-877-686-6233; www.mountainmade.com) in Thomas. Potters, blacksmiths, painters, sculptors, basket weavers, quilt makers, glassblowers, woodworkers, and other creative types may be found working in studios across the state. Numerous festivals, including the **Mountain State Art and Craft Fair** in Ripley, **Mountain Heritage Arts & Crafts Festival** in Charles Town, **Berkeley Springs Studio Tour**, and

Charleston's **Rhododendron State Arts and Crafts Festival** feature the works of scores of artists and craftspersons.

BALLOONING Hot-air balloon rides are available from **Mountain Air Balloons** (304-472-0792; www.mountain airballoons.com) in Buckhannon and **Foxfire Resort** (304-743-4588; www .foxfirewv.com) in Milton. There are sometimes more than 50 balloons aloft at one time during October at the **Mountaineer Balloon Festival** in Morgantown.

BED & BREAKFASTS I don't list every one that is in operation, but I have stayed in more than 50 B&Bs in West Virginia and visited and inspected scores more. The selection ranges from modest homes to palatial mansions, historic houses in busy downtown areas to rustic lodges in isolated woodlands.

Each B&B is different, and it is this diversity that makes each place a new experience. As opposed to staying in a hotel or motel, a visit at a B&B is a much more personal way to get to know the locals and the area in which they live. Although you can make reservations by other means, I like making mine over the phone, as it gives me a chance to chat with the host and establish a relationship before I arrive.

Rates were current when this book went to press, but as in all things monetary, they will probably be a bit higher by the time you visit. Be aware that a number of B&Bs do not accept credit cards or children and some may require a stay of a minimum number of nights.

BICYCLING West Virginia has embraced mountain biking in a big way. So much so, that the International Mountain Biking Association declared that the state is the country's best mountain biking destination, and *Mountain Biking Magazine* placed it within the top five. Hundreds of miles of trails in Monongahela and George Washington national forests, as well as state forests, are open to bicycle riders. Unlike many other states, bicycles are permitted on many pathways in West Virginia's state parks. In fact, a number of the parks, including Canaan Valley and Blackwater state parks, will rent you a bike if you did not bring along one of your own. In addition, check the *Hiking, Kayaking & Canoeing*, and *Lodging* categories for other places that rent bikes or arrange shuttles and guided rides. Several of the state's cross-country and downhill skiing destinations become mountain biking meccas during the warmer months.

The West Virginia Mountain Biking Association's (www.wvmba.com) Web site has a thorough overview of places to ride, while *Mountain Biking in West Virginia* by Frank Hutchins gives details on 17 rides in various parts of the state.

Look through the *Rail Trails* listing found in many of the chapters for easier, more level routes. Many of the state's roadways would make great road-biking trips; however, the twisting routes are often narrow and have no shoulders. Yet, where possible, I describe enjoyable road rides, such as a designated route in Charleston, the state capital. The Philippi Convention and Visitors Bureau has a brochure extolling several rides in Barbour County, and *Best Bike Rides: Delaware, Maryland, Virginia, Washington, D.C. and West Virginia* by Trudy Bell has details on a few rides in the state.

Elk River Touring Company, Inn, Restaurant, and Guide Service (304-572-3771; 1-866-572-3771; www

.ertc.com), **Free Spirit Adventures** (304-536-0333; 1-800-877-4749; www .freespiritadventures.com) and **New River Bike & Touring Company** (304-574-2453; 1-866-301-2453; www .newriverbike.com) offer guided rides in numerous parts of the state.

BIRDING The ridgelines of the Eastern Panhandle, Potomac Highlands, and Southern West Virginia make great seats from which to watch the annual raptor migration in the fall. Heated air from rays of the sun striking cliffs and rock outcroppings couples with warm air rising from the lowlands to create forceful drafts, or thermals, that the birds use to soar upward. In addition, by gliding near the crest of the ridges, they are able to take advantage of the northwesterly winds striking the Alleghenies, where air currents are forced across the mountain crests, providing more uplift.

Sometimes as early as mid-August, ospreys, American kestrels, and a few bald eagles begin the procession southward. The migration begins in earnest in the middle of September as broadwinged hawks take to the skies. Peak daily sightings of several thousand are not uncommon. In the early weeks of October, peregrine falcons join the movement; later in the month, one of the smallest hawks, the sharp-shinned, becomes the dominant migrant. Joining the procession at this time are the larger but fewer-in-number Cooper's hawks. Making use of the cold winds of November, red-tailed hawks, northern harriers, and red-shouldered hawks zip by leafless trees. Soaring over a West Virginia that could be covered by December snows, northern goshawks and golden eagles bring the migratory season to a close.

Just about any ridgeline will let you watch this phenomenon, but for one of the best seats in the state, and one that lets you join other people who are as interested in spotting the birds as you are, head to **Hanging Rock Raptor Migration Observatory** near Gap Mills in Southern West Virginia.

Bald eagles have become year-round residents along the hillsides bordering the **South Branch of the Potomac River** near Romney and Petersburg, while the wetlands of the **Canaan Valley National Wildlife Refuge** attract birds rarely seen in West Virginia, such as common loons, cormorants, plovers, and greater and lesser scaups.

The **New River Birding & Nature Festival** near Fayetteville features multiple days of bird-watching field trips, lectures, and classes. Pricketts Fort State Park near Fairmont features an **Annual Bird Walk** in the spring, and bird walks are also a part of the spring **Annual Wildflower Pilgrimage** at Blackwater Falls State Park.

Be sure to check the *Birding* section in each chapter for other hot spots that will enable you to observe more of the state's flying fauna.

BOOKS It is always a good idea to read a few books to help you gain a greater awareness, enjoyment, and understanding of your surroundings.

West Virginia: A History for Beginners by John A. Williams takes an original approach to providing an in-depth survey of the state's history. For a shorter, albeit less detailed account, consult Ann Smuckers's *A History of West Virginia. Rebels at the Gate* by W. Hunter Lesser may be the best way to learn about the state during the Civil War without having to read multiple volumes. William J. Switala's *Underground Railroad in Delaware, Maryland, and West Virginia* is a look at the same time period in our nation's history, but, obviously, from a different perspective.

Born in Charleston, Mary Lee Settle is a recipient of the National Book Award. Among her many novels are the five Beulah Land books, which chronicle the history of the state from when white settlers first arrived to the present. The second book in the series, *O Beulah Land*, describes the establishment of Canona (her fictionalized name for Charleston), while the fourth, *The Scapegoat*, is an accounting of West Virginia's early-20th-century coal mine wars. Two of American Book Award Winner Denise Giardina's books, *Storming Heaven* and *The Unquiet Earth*, are novels that entertainingly, vividly, and accurately portray the struggles of coal-mining families during the same period. John Knowles's *A Vein of Riches* is a fictionalized account of coal mining in the northern part of the state, near Fairmont. Although not set in West Virginia, his most noted book, *A Separate Peace*, is a coming-of-age novel that is often required high school and college reading.

Homer Hickam's story of growing up in McDowell County, *Rocket Boys: A Memoir*, was turned into the hit movie *October Sky*. Fiction writer Stephen Coonts was born in Buchanan and is probably most known for his first novel, *Flight of the Intruder*, which was also made into a major motion picture. *Night of the Hunter* and *Fools' Parade* are two novels by Moundsville-born Davis Grubb that became box-office hits when they were released as movies in the mid-1900s.

The comments of the great West Virginia newspaper owner Jim Comstock and other authors have been gathered into the *Best of Hillbilly: A Prize Collection of 100-Proof Writing*, which should be looked over for the caustic wit and astute observations it contains.

If planning outdoor activities, I recommend you consult my guidebook *50 Hikes in West Virginia* (The Countryman Press), as well as *Circuit Hikes: In Virginia, West Virginia, Maryland, and Pennsylvania* by the Potomac Appalachian Trail Club; *Birding Guide to West Virginia*; and *Flora of West Virginia*, which contains close to 2,200 plants found throughout the state. Although it is beginning to get a bit outdated, *The Appalachians* by Maurice Brooks is considered one of the best introductions to the natural history of the mountains of West Virginia and the entire Appalachian range.

Michael J. Pauley and Pat Love are not mainstream poets, so you may need to search to find any of their published works, but once you do, you will find their words to be evocative of West Virginia.

BUS SERVICE Greyhound (1-800-231-2222; www.greyhound.com) makes stops to pick up and deliver passengers in Beckley, Bluefield, Charleston, Huntington, Parkersburg, and Wheeling.

CAMPING Reservations for campsites and cabins in state parks may be made by dialing 1-800-CALL-WVA or online at www.wvstateparks.com. A few are open year-round, but most of the parks' campgrounds are open from early spring to late fall. Backcountry camping is permitted almost anywhere in the national forests— more information than could be included in this book about these sites and the forest service's developed campgrounds may be found on the Web sites www.fs.fed.us/gwj and http://fs.usda.gov/mnf.

The largest percentage of commercial campgrounds listed in this book have hookups and other facilities for those traveling and camping with trailers or RVs.

CHILDREN, ESPECIALLY FOR

The crayon symbol ✐ identifies activities and places of special interest to children and families.

CIVIL WAR Born of the Civil War, West Virginia was the site of many battles between Union and Confederate armies. Even before the war, John Brown's raid on what is now **Harpers Ferry National Historical Park** foretold of the struggles that were to come, while many historians consider the **Battle of Philippi** to be the war's first land battle. **Rich Mountain Battlefield Civil War Site**, west of Beverly; **Droop Mountain Battlefield State Park**, north of Hillsboro; and **Carnifex Ferry Battlefield State Park**, close to Summersville, preserve the sites of just a few of the many battles fought in the state. A short drive north of Harpers Ferry is **Antietam National Battlefield** in Maryland, where more soldiers lost their lives in a single day than in any other place during the war.

The trenches that men built to protect themselves may still be seen at the **Confederate Overlook**, close to Burnsville Lake; **Fort Mill Ridge Trenches**, near Romney; and **Fort Mulligan**, on the west end of Petersburg. Other sites, battles, and museums of Civil War significance are detailed in their respective sections of each chapter.

The **Civil War Discovery Trail** has hundreds of sites, including parks, cemeteries, battlefields, and homes, in more than a dozen states. The state of West Virginia is investing heavily in the trail by placing hundreds of markers at various sites throughout the state. Details about the trail may be obtained from the Division of Tourism (see *Information*) and at www.civilwartrails.org.

COAL The **Coal Heritage Trail National Byway** (304-256-6941; www.coalheritage.org) in Southern West Virginia is one of the best ways to introduce yourself to the industry that has shaped and affected nearly every aspect of life in West Virginia—in the past and into the present day. If you can't drive the entire route, visit the **Coal Heritage Trail Interpretive Center** in Bramwell.

The **Bituminous Coal Heritage Foundation Museum** (304-369-5180) in Madison and the **Matewan Depot Replica Museum** (304-426-5744; www.matewan.org) have exhibits and displays concerning the subject, while Bluefield's **Eastern Regional Coal Archives** (304-325-3943) is a repository of materials for those who are doing research about the industry.

If you can only visit one place devoted to coal, make it the **Beckley Exhibition Coal Mine** (304-256-1747; www.beckleymine.com), where you will have an eye-opening experience going underground into a mine that was in operation until the 1950s.

COVERED BRIDGES Of the many covered bridges that once dotted the state's landscape, only 17 survive. The most famous is the **Philippi Covered Bridge**, the oldest in the state and the site of the Civil War's first land battle. The others are: **Locust Creek Covered Bridge**, north of Hillsville; **Hern's Mill Covered Bridge**, constructed in 1884 west of Lewisburg and reconstructed in 2001; **Hoke's Mill Covered Bridge**, south of Ronceverte, also rebuilt in 2001; **Laurel Creek Covered Bridge**, south of Union, the state's shortest (24 feet); **Indian Creek Covered Bridge**,

south of Union; **Walkersville Covered Bridge**, built in 1903 for $567; and **Dent's Run Covered Bridge**, still in use over its namesake stream south of Westover.

The **Barrackville Covered Bridge** is the state's second-oldest existing covered bridge and is still in use northwest of Fairmont; **Simpson Creek Covered Bridge** is only 0.2 mile from an interstate exit near Bridgeport; **Carrollton Covered Bridge** was an important link on the Middle Fork Turnpike south of Philippi; **Center Point Covered Bridge** was reconstructed in the late 1900s west of Wolf Summit; **Fletcher Creek Covered Bridge** has not been significantly altered since it was built in 1891; **Mud River Covered Bridge** is more than 100 feet long and located close to Milton; 97-foot **Staats Mill Covered Bridge** is open to pedestrians in Cedar Lakes Conference Center at Ripley; **Sarvis Fork Covered Bridge** was dismantled and moved to its present location north of Sandyville in 1924; and **Fish Creek Covered Bridge**, renovated in 2001, is east of Hundred.

DRIVING TOURS, SCENIC & HISTORIC Through the grassroots efforts of historians, community leaders, tourism officials, naturalists, and others, the federal and state governments have identified a number of scenic and historic driving routes that have been designated National Byways, State Byways, or State Backways. **Byways** are scenic routes that introduce you to historic sites, eye-pleasing vistas, and people and places that exemplify the history, culture, and recreational opportunities of an area. A **Backway** is a more rustic experience, often following the route of one-lane or dirt roads, so they are not recommended for RVs.

I have given you brief descriptions of all of these routes within their respective chapters. More information may be found in the *West Virginia Byways & Backways* brochure available from the Division of Tourism (see *Information*).

However, don't limit yourself to these identified routes. Almost every drive in West Virginia will turn out to be a scenic journey. To help you get started, you will find descriptions of some of my favorite drives in several of the chapters.

EMERGENCIES Hospitals with emergency rooms are noted near the beginning of each chapter. In an emergency, you should first try calling 911, but because the number is not in operation statewide, you may need to dial the operator and ask for the state police. They may also be reached from a cellular phone by dialing °SP.

EVENTS County fairs, arts-and-crafts demonstrations, nature walks and festivals, skill competitions, historical reenactments, music concerts, ramp festivals: Some kind of distinctive event or celebration takes place almost every day of the year. Leading annual events are noted in the *Special Events* section at the end of each chapter. A brochure available from the Division of Tourism (see *Information*) lists hundreds of events that occur within the calendar year.

FALL FOLIAGE Autumn brings bright, clear days to West Virginia, and the brilliant and varied colors of the turning leaves easily rival those of New England. Many B&Bs, state parks, and other lodging facilities offer fall "leaf peeping" specials, while scenic train rides, understandably, have their busiest season. Just about any countryside drive will be a thing of beauty at this time of year, but the **Highland Scenic Highway** near Marlinton will be one of the most spectacular. For a longer drive that takes in much of the Potomac Highlands region, follow **WV 92** north from Lewisburg to Bartow and then take **WV 28** north to Petersburg. Allow most of the day so that you can stop many times to enjoy nature's displays.

To make sure you will see the most colors as possible, consult the Division of Forestry (304-558-2788; www.wvforestry.com), which posts peak leaf-color information on its Web site.

A few of the many famous West Virginians:

Pulitzer and Nobel Prize winner **Pearl S. Buck**, most known for her novel *The Good Earth*, was born in Hillsboro. One of the Confederacy's most revered generals, **Thomas "Stonewall" Jackson** was born in Clarksburg and raised nearby at a place that would become the state's first 4-H camp. **Don Knotts**, who played Barney Fife on *The Andy Griffith Show*, was born and raised in Morgantown. **Little Jimmy Dickens**, most noted for his country song "Take an Old Cold Tater and Wait," was born in Bolt. Country singer **Kathy Mattea** is a native of Cross Lanes; **Brad Paisley** grew up in Glen Dale. Noted third-baseman **George Brett** was also born in Glen Dale. **John Forbes Nash Jr.** was born in Bluefield, received the 1994 Nobel Prize, and was the subject of the 2002 movie *A Beautiful Mind*.

Astronaut **Jon A. McBride**, pilot of the space shuttle *Challenger* in 1984, was born in Charleston. Olympic gold medalist **Mary Lou Retton** is from

---

WHY DO LEAVES CHANGE COLOR?

The absence of chlorophyll plays the major role in the look of the woods in the fall. Not only does the substance give the leaves their green color, but it also produces simple sugars to nourish the trees. The leaves also contain yellow pigments—carotenoids—that are masked by the chlorophyll. Cooler temperatures and less daylight signal the leaves to quit making the sugars, and as the chlorophyll breaks down, the green fades and the yellows, browns, and oranges emerge. Autumn's reds and purples come from other pigments called anthocyanins, which develop in the sap of leaves as a result of a complex interaction between sugars, phosphates, and other chemicals. An early fall of bright, sunny days and cool nights (but not below freezing) will produce the most brilliant colors.

Fairmont. Comedian **Soupy Sales** grew up in the Huntington area. Born in Clarksburg, **Cyrus R. Vance** was secretary of state for President Jimmy Carter. An inductee into the Basketball Hall of Fame, **Jerry West** was born in Cabin Creek. Born in Myra in Lincoln County, **Charles (Chuck) Yeager** was the first person to fly faster than the speed of sound (and was a boyhood acquaintance of my father).

FARMERS' MARKETS Farmers' markets may be found in every region of the state and are listed in the *Selective Shopping* section of each chapter. I love going to them, but be aware that the locations and operating days and times of farmers' markets have been known to change frequently.

FERRIES The **Sistersville Ferry** is the last of many such boats to cross the waters of the Ohio River between West Virginia and Ohio.

FISHING The **Division of Natural Resources** (304-558-2754; www.wvdnr .gov) can supply the information you need about regulations and licenses, and they have free publications that provide regulations and tips on the best places to go for the type of fish you would like to catch. Within the *Fishing* section of the chapters are places to fish on your own, or companies and individuals who provide guided trips.

GAMING *Gaming* is the industry's polite word for gambling. The palatial places to engage in the activity are **Hollywood Casino at Charles Town Races** (1-800-795-7001; www.holly woodcasinocharlestown.com), **Mardi Gras Casino and Resort** (304-776-1000; 1-800-224-9683; www.tristate racetrack.com) in Cross Lanes near Charleston, **Wheeling Island Hotel-Casino-Racetrack** (304-231-1831; 1-877-943-4536; www.wheelingisland .com), and the **Mountaineer Casino Racetrack and Resort** (304-387-8300; 1-800-80-40-HOT; www.mtr gaming.com) south of Newell in the Northern Panhandle. In addition, the state permits restaurants and other establishments to have a few slot machines, and you will find that, until you learn to identify them, you will walk into a place indentified as a coffeehouse or simply as "Jane's" or "Mary's" and be surprised that it offers very little in the way of nutritional sustenance.

GOLF The courses listed under the *To Do* section in each chapter are public courses that do not require payment of a membership fee. *The Mountain State Golf Guide*, available from the Division of Tourism (see *Information*), outlines a number of public, semiprivate, and private courses.

GREAT EASTERN TRAIL The Great Eastern Trail is an exciting long-distance trail project that is currently under construction. Stretching for close to 2,000 miles, the route runs from Alabama to New York. Much of it is already in place, but there are currently a number of gaps, such as where the trail is planned to enter West Virginia from the south at Matewan. Heading to the northeast, it is thought the trail will go through R. D. Bailey Wildlife Management Area, Twin Falls State Park, the town of Mullens, Camp Creek State Park and State Forest, Pipestem Resort State Park, Bluestone State Park, and Bluestone Lake Wildlife Management Area, and follow the Appalachian Trail atop Peters Mountain on the Virginia/West Virginia border to meet up with the Allegheny Trail. Following that pathway for about 60 miles, the Great Eastern Trail would enter Virginia to eventually follow the Tuscarora Trail and reenter West Virginia on that trail's route through the Eastern Panhandle. More information may be obtained in the Web site www.greateasterntrail.net.

HANDICAPPED ACCESS The wheelchair symbol ⅋ appears next to lodgings, restaurants, and attractions that are partially or completely handicapped accessible.

HATFIELD-MCCOY ATV TRAILS The more than 500 miles of Hatfield-McCoy ATV Trails are located within the Southern West Virginia and Hatfield-McCoy Mountains regions. The first few miles were opened in 2003, and the plan is to eventually have a network of more than 2,000 miles of trails coursing through the southern part of the state (and maybe even going into neighboring states).

Administered by a statutory corporation created by West Virginia legislation for the purpose of economic development through tourism, the trails system is fulfilling its purpose. The routes see more than a million visitors a year, rejuvenating many business that were having a hard time staying open and encouraging other people to create companies geared specifically to those riding the trails.

Named a National Recreation Trail, the trails system is on private and corporate-owned lands, with many miles of the pathways traversing former coal mine areas. Payment of a fee is required to ride, and law-enforcement officials patrol the routes to ensure safety and compliance with rules. Each trail is numbered and rated according to difficulty: Green is easiest, blue is more difficult, and black is most difficult. Orange designates a narrow, single-track pathway. Hikers, bikers, and equestrians are also permitted on the trails (although I can't imagine trying to compete with the ATVs).

Trails, outfitters, and other businesses related to ATV riders are described within their respective chapters. More information may be obtained from **Hatfield-McCoy Trails** (304-752-3255; 1-800-592-2217; www.trailsheaven.com; mailing address: P.O. Box 539, Lyburn 25632).

HIGHWAY TRAVEL The speed limit on interstates is 70 miles per hour unless otherwise noted. Driver and passengers are required to wear safety belts, and children less than 4 feet tall must be in approved child-safety seats. Driving lights must be on during adverse conditions, inclement weather, and when daylight conditions restrict visibility to less than 500 feet. You may make a right turn at a red signal light after coming to a complete stop unless posted signs prohibit doing so.

Call the **West Virginia Department of Transportation's Road Conditions Hotline** (1-877-WVA-ROAD) to obtain weather-related road conditions, and consult www.wvdot .com for the latest information on construction projects that may impact your travel plans. This Web site also contains a wealth of road-travel information.

The official state-highway map may be obtained from the **Division of Tourism** (see *Information*). Available at bookshops and many convenience stores, the *West Virginia Atlas and Gazetteer* (published by DeLorme) is an invaluable navigation tool.

HIKING West Virginia is, without a doubt, one of America's finest hiking destinations, and I have included the state's best hiking excursions under the *Hiking* section of each chapter; look at information in the *Arboretum, Bicycling, Birding, Gardens, National Forests, Nature Preserves, Parks, State Forests, Walks, Wildlife Management Areas*, and *Wildlife Refuge* sections for additional opportunities to walk outdoors.

One of my own books, *50 Hikes in West Virginia* (The Countryman Press), covers the entire state, with outings ranging from easy jaunts to multiday backpacking treks.

HORSEBACK RIDING Places to ride your own horse and businesses offering guided rides are listed under the *To Do* section of a chapter; additional places to ride can often be found by looking in the *Bicycling, Hiking, National Forests, Parks, State Forests*, and *Wildlife Refuges* sections.

HUNTING A comprehensive booklet, *West Virginia Hunting and Trapping*, may be obtained from the **Division of Natural Resources** (304-558-2754; www.wvdnr.gov). If you like the outdoors but are not a hunter, be aware that hunting is permitted in wildlife management areas, state forests, and some state parks. Also, be aware that Sunday hunting is permitted on private lands in some counties.

INFORMATION Regional information sources are described under the Guidance section near the beginning of each chapter. The **West Virginia Division of Tourism** (304-558-2200; 1-800-CALL-WVA; www.wvtourism .com), 90 MacCorkle Ave. SW, South Charleston 25303, publishes *West Virginia Wild and Wonderful*, an annual guide to many attractions, outdoor opportunities, and lodging facilities throughout the state. The office can also be the source for numerous brochures on specialized topics such as the Civil War, festivals, golfing, biking, antiques, canoeing, fishing, and more.

INSECTS Warm weather brings no-see-ums, gnats, fleas, deerflies, mosquitoes, ticks, and more. Although the lower elevations of the state may have the largest population concentrations, the mountains have their fair share of insects, too. Bring repellent on any outing from late spring through mid-fall. (And remember that one of the pleasures of travel during the colder months of the year is the absence of insects.)

KAYAKING AND CANOEING Kayakers and canoeists, like whitewater rafters, have discovered that West Virginia has some of the best streams in the country. Many are challenging and should only be run by those with experience, while others can be easy float trips suitable for novices and everyone in the family.

Included in the *Kayaking & Canoeing* and *Whitewater Rafting* sections of the various chapters are guided trips by outfitters as well as places to paddle on your own or rent a watercraft. A *Canoeing & Kayaking Guide to West Virginia* by Charlie Walbridge and Ward Eister can provide additional information. See *Whitewater Rafting* for a discussion on stream difficulty ratings.

MOTELS AND HOTELS For the most part, chain motels and hotels have not been listed because information about them is easily obtained from many sources and because their architecture and amenities tend to have a cookie-cutter sameness. Those that are included are in areas where lodging options are few, are in a desirable location, are outstanding places to stay, or permit pets.

PARKS AND FORESTS, NATIONAL West Virginia does not have vast acreages of national parks like the 200,000-acre Shenandoah National Park or 520,000-acre Great Smoky Mountains National Park. What it does possess are a number of significant components of the national park system. The 72,189-acre **New River Gorge National River** was authorized in 1978 to protect a 52-mile section of New River between Hinton and Fayetteville, and it has become a major whitewater rafting, kayaking, mountain biking, hiking, and rock-climbing destination. It also preserves an area rich in coal-mining history. The **Gauley River National Recreation Area** encompasses 26,607 acres where 25 miles of the Gauley River and 6 miles of the Meadow River pass rugged gorges. The Gauley is considered by many to be the premier whitewater rafting experience in the East, if not the entire country. Within the 4,310 acres of the **Bluestone National Scenic River** are 10.5 miles of the Bluestone River flowing through a thousand-foot-deep gorge. A 10-mile pathway provides access for hikers, mountain bikers, equestrians, and anglers.

The **Harpers Ferry National Historical Park** may only be a bit larger than 2,000 acres, yet it preserves one of the most historically rich towns in the country. In addition to being well known for John Brown's raid on a federal arsenal, the town has played pivotal roles in the nation's history since Colonial times.

There are nearly 1 million acres of land on which to roam in the state's three national forests. Centered primarily in the Potomac Highlands region, **Monongahela National Forest** is the largest with more than 800,000 acres. Most of the **George Washington National Forest** is in Virginia, but more than 100,000 acres are located in West Virginia east of Romney, Moorefield, and Franklin. A little more than 18,000 acres of the **Jefferson National Forest** are within Monroe County in the Southern West Virginia region.

PARKS AND FORESTS, STATE With almost 50 of them scattered through the state, there is a state park or forest within a 30-minute drive of any location in West Virginia. Many of them have campgrounds and cabins for rent, so consult the *Bicycling, Hiking, Kayaking & Canoeing*, and *Parks* sections in each chapter to find what is available in each region.

Are you a goal-oriented person? Do you like to be able to mark your progress as you work toward a goal, and then be given a something-you-can-actually-hold-in-your-hands reward once you achieve it? If so, you should know about two programs offered by the West Virginia Division of Natural Resources.

A one-time registration fee of $10 is

required to join the Hiking West Virginia program. After that, simply go out, hike in any state park, forest, wildlife management area, or state park rail trail, and keep track of your mileage on a record log. You could easily get the first, and major, award in only one weekend's outing. All it takes is 25 miles for you to be given a nicely turned and polished wooden walking stick. Another 25 miles brings you a 50-mile shield to attach to the stick, and additional miles reward you with different shields to commemorate your accumulated mileage.

While doing all of this, you can also be participating in the Very Important Parks Person program. Enrolling is absolutely free, and all you do is have the program card officially stamped each time you go to a state park or forest. After visiting 15 mandatory parks and forests and five of the 21 elective parks and forests, you will be rewarded with an embroidered windbreaker jacket and be invited to special Very Important Parks Person events, such as an annual picnic lunch and entertainment in a state park.

Both programs are ongoing—get everything done in just a few months, or use your vacation time over the next several years to finish visiting the facilities and racking up the hiking miles.

The **Division of Natural Resources** (304-558-2754; www.wvdnr .gov) can send you a packet brimming with all kinds of information.

PETS The dog-paw symbol 🐾 appears next to places, activities, and lodgings that accept pets. Always inform a hotel, motel, B&B, or other lodging that you will be traveling with your pet; payment of an additional fee is required in some places.

PICK-YOUR-OWN PRODUCE
There is just something about a straw-

berry, tomato, or peach that is picked ripe off the plant that grocery-store produce can't match. Farms and orchards that invite the public into their fields and orchards are listed in a number of the chapters. Unless you don't mind just taking a drive in the country, it is a wise idea to call ahead to confirm what is ripe and at what time and day you may come out to pick.

POPULATION The state's population was 1,859,815, according to the 2010 United States Census Bureau Population Division's official count.

RAILROAD RIDES AND MUSEUMS **Cass Scenic Railroad** (304-456-4300; www.cassrailroad.com, the state's longest-running train excursion, rises to West Virginia's second-highest point, Bald Knob. The adjacent **Railroad & Logging Museum** provides background to the scenic ride. The ***Durbin Rocket*** (304-456-4935; 1-877-686-7245; www.mountainrail.com) takes passengers on journeys along the scenic Greenbrier River. There is a choice of several excursions on the diesel-powered, climate-controlled ***New Tygart Flyer*** (304-456-4935; 1-877-686-7245; www.mountainrail.com), based in Elkins. More than 90 percent of the ***Potomac Eagle*** (304-424-0736; www.potomaceagle.info) passengers have seen bald eagles soaring over the South Branch of the Potomac River near Romney. The C. P. Huntington Railroad Historical Society sponsors scenic **New River Train Excursions** (1-866-639-7487; www.newrivertrain .com) on two weekends in October every year.

There is no fee to walk through the small museum in the **Parsons Railroad Depot** (304-478-2402) or the **Hinton Railroad Museum** (304-466-5420), which pays tribute to the early

A number of rail trails in the **Mountaineer Country** region connect with each other to total more than 50 miles. Other rail trails are described in their respective chapters.

The **West Virginia Rails-To-Trails Council** (www.wvrtc.org; P.O. Box 836, Morgantown 26507) is a nonprofit organization that can supply you with maps and other information.

RAMPS Growing beneath the canopies of southern and cove hardwood forests is a plant that has played an important role in the lives of southern Appalachian inhabitants. It was not that long ago that preserving vegetables by canning or freezing was unknown; by the time winter was ending, people were craving fresh green foods. To the rescue came ramps, which appear in early spring as (usually) a pair of lilylike leaves growing in the rich cove soils, often beside creeks and small streams.

Sometimes referred to as a wild leek, the underground portion of a ramp is a small onion containing allyl sulfate, the ingredient that gives garlic its taste. Gathered when the plants are young, the strong-tasting ramps have a loyal following to this day, with ramp festivals held annually throughout the state. The plant is cooked as a vegetable, served in salads, added to soups, used as a seasoning, and, most popularly, fried and mixed with ham and/or eggs.

To enjoy this delicacy, attend the **Annual Ramp Festival** in Elkins or the **Feast** of the Ramson in Richwood, both held in April. An assortment of dishes incorporating ramps appear on the menus of a number of state restaurants, including **Bright Morning Inn Restaurant** (304-259-5119; www.brightmorninginn.com) in Davis, **Lot 12 Public House** (304-258-6264; www.lot12.com) in Berkeley Springs,

days of the C&O Railroad. The **Martinsburg Roundhouse Center** (304-269-4141; www.martinsburgroundhouse.com) was a major railroad service center in the Eastern Panhandle and is in the process of being restored. In addition to looking over the model train layouts at the **Harpers Ferry Toy Train Museum** (304-535-2521), visitors can take a short ride on a miniature railroad route. You can operate a wood-frame handcar in **Huntington's Railroad Museum** (304-736-7349; www.newrivertrain.com).

RAIL TRAILS There were nearly 400 miles and close to three dozen rail trails in the state (and many more in the planning stage) when this book went to press. Many are in remote or rural areas, while quite a number are urban in nature. All are excellent pathways on which to get into the outdoors without having to worry about route finding or traversing precipitous or rugged terrain.

The two longest are the 72-mile **North Bend Rail Trail** in the Mid-Ohio Valley and Central West Virginia regions, and the 77-mile **Greenbrier River Trail** in the Southern West Virginia and Potomac Highlands regions.

and **Smokey's on the Gorge** (1-800-252-7784; www.class-vi.com) in Lansing.

Insider's tip: The strong odor of ramps can linger for a long time on your breath, and some people say even exude from skin pores, so don't be surprised if people avoid you for a day or two!

SKIING, CROSS-COUNTRY West Virginia has an almost endless number of places to cross-country ski. In addition to all of the downhill skiing resorts (see *Skiing, Downhill*) that have routes designated for cross-country skiers, you can also engage in the sport in the Mountaineer Country region at **Coopers Rock State Forest**, **Alpine Lake Resort**, and **Big Bear Lake Campland**; in the Northern Panhandle at **Grand Vue Park**; and in Southern West Virginia in **Twin Falls Resort State Park**. In the **Potomac Highlands** region, head to **Blackwater Falls State Park**, **Canaan Valley National Wildlife Refuge**, and just about any trail in the vast **Monongahela National Forest**. In addition, do not overlook the state's many **rail trails**, which can provide some easy, almost level gliding across the ground when enough snow falls to cover the pathways' roots, rocks, and gravel.

The **Whitegrass Ski Touring Center** in Canaan Valley and the **Elk River Touring Company, Inn, Restaurant, and Guide Service** close to Snowshoe Mountain provide groomed trails, equipment rentals, and instruction.

SKIING, DOWNHILL Canaan Valley Resort State Park, **Timberline Four Seasons Resort**, **Snowshoe Mountain**, and **Silver Creek** are in a part of the Potomac Highlands region where 150–200 inches of fluffy frozen precipitation fall from the sky each year. **Winterplace Ski Resort** is in Southern West Virginia not far from Beckley. All of these resorts have extensive snowmaking capabilities just in case Mother Nature slips up on providing enough. Snowboarding, cross-country skiing, tubing, night skiing, and children's programs are also available.

SNACKS & GOODIES One of the fun things about traveling is being able to enjoy a few guilty pleasures by finding out and sampling what sweet treats are produced locally. (And I expect you to utter a word of thanks to me for gaining quite a number of pounds just to be able to provide you with this information.)

Ellen's Homemade Ice Cream (304-343-6488) in Charleston claims its product is "super premium." Ceredo's **Austin's Homemade Ice Cream** (304-453-2071) has been producing ice cream for more than five decades.

Holl's Swiss Chocolatier (304-295-6576; 1-800-842-4512; www.holls .com) in Vienna hand makes all of its items, produced with chocolate created specifically for them in Switzerland. **DeFluri's Fine Chocolates** (304-264-3698; www.defluris.com) in Martinsburg was proclaimed the "Best Candy/Confection in the Americas" at an international trade show competition.

Of the many bakeries in the state, seek out the **Shepherdstown Sweet Shop Bakery** (304-876-2432; www .wvbakery.com) for holiday stollen, an old-world baked loaf with rum-soaked raisins, dates, and pecans combined with sweet butter and spiced flour. Lewisburg has **The Bakery** (304-876-2432; www.wvbakery.com), with rich brownies and the state's best pizza, and the **Greenbrier Valley Baking Company** (304-645-6159), serving artisan breads and first-class tiramisu. You would have to take a trip to Europe to find pastries on par with those made in Huntington's **Francois Pastry Shop** (304-697-4151).

SNOWMOBILING There are multiple miles of trails available for snowmobile riding in **Big Bear Lake Campland** east of Morgantown. If you have never been on a snowmobile and would like some instruction or just want someone to go with, guided tours traverse the backcountry areas of **Snowshoe Mountain**.

SWIMMIN' HOLES Having a picnic beside a free-flowing mountain stream, cooling off in its refreshing waters, and soaking up some rays on a sun-warmed rock is one of the best ways to spend a hot summer day. Within the various chapters are descriptions of some of the state's best and most glorious swimmin' holes, many known only to locals. Be sure to devote at least one day to this activity—or you will miss one of West Virginia's most enjoyable (and free) attractions.

A few words of caution: Always scout out a swimmin' hole before wading in. Never take a swim during times of high water or if the current appears to be beyond your swimming capabilities. Always wear some kind of foot protection—you never know what some unthinking, or uncaring, person has tossed into the water. And, of course, never dive into a stream unless you want to run the risk of injury or even death.

TAXES The state sales tax is 6 percent; lodging, meals, and amusement taxes can sometimes be 10 percent or more.

TUSCARORA TRAIL Concern in the 1960s that the Appalachian Trail (AT) might become impossible to maintain

due to closings by private landowners led volunteers from Pennsylvania's Keystone Trails Association and the Potomac Appalachian Trail Club, based in Vienna, Virginia, to develop a route to the west.

Leaving the AT in Shenandoah National Park, the **Tuscarora Trail** runs for 250 miles through Virginia, West Virginia, Maryland, and into central Pennsylvania, where it rejoins the AT. Guides to the entire trail may be obtained from the Potomac Appalachian Trail Club (703-242-0315; www.patc.net), 118 Park Ave. SE, Vienna, VA 22180.

WATERFALLS Mountainous terrain ensures a wealth of waterfalls. Dramatically tumbling **Blackwater Falls**, in the state park that bears its name, is justifiably one of the most photographed scenes in the state. A short trail makes it one of the state's most accessible, too. While in the park, be sure to also seek out **Elakala Falls**. The easiest way to reach **High Falls of Cheat** is to take a scenic train ride on the New Tygart Flyer from Elkins. You can reach three impressive falls on one hike via a number of staircases, observation decks, bridges, and board-

walks at the **Falls of Hills Creek** near Cranberry Glades.

Just north of Hinton are three waterfalls along WV 20 you should not miss: **Brooks Falls**, **Big Branch**, and **Sandstone Falls**, which is the state's widest. You don't have to get out of the car to see **Cathedral Falls** and **Kanawha Falls**; they are visible from US 60 at Gauley Bridge. **Moatsville Falls** is a scenic 18-foot drop in the Tygart Valley River.

Numerous other waterfalls are noted throughout the book.

WEATHER West Virginia can have a wide range of temperatures and conditions. Winters can be unpredictably cold or relatively mild, while summers can become hot and humid or may be rather temperate. Spring and autumn can be the most pleasant times of the year, as days warm up to a comfortable degree, nights cool down for easy sleeping, and crowds are fewer.

Snow is common in the Potomac Highlands, Mountaineer Country, and Southern and Central West Virginia; moderate in the Metro Valley, Hatfield and McCoy Mountains, and Northern Panhandle; and quite infrequent in the Mid-Ohio Valley. When heat and humidity have taken the joy and fun out of the state's lower elevations, the mountains will beckon with temperatures that can be 10 or more degrees lower. Exploring West Virginia can be a year-round activity.

WHITEWATER RAFTING Many people consider West Virginia to be the East's (if not the country's) premier whitewater rafting destination, and the epicenter of the activity is along the **New and Gauley rivers** near Fayetteville in Southern West Virginia. The upper New River is quite gentle with only Class I and II rapids and can easily be rafted or kayaked by just about

anyone. With Class III to V rapids, the lower New River is certainly more challenging, but most rafting companies have guides with enough expertise that the general public can safely run it. When the Summersville Dam is releasing water in the fall, the upper Gauley has 60 rapids that include five consecutive Class V rapids, while the lower Gauley is only slightly less demanding.

Farther north in the Mountaineer Country region, the **Cheat River** does not receive as much press coverage as the New and Gauley rivers, but it can have Class IV to V rapids when the water is running high. Along the edges of the Eastern Panhandle, the **Potomac and Shenandoah rivers** are certainly not rip-roaring whitewater streams, but there are enough Class II to III rapids to make for some exciting trips.

Companies that provide guided trips are highlighted in the respective chapters.

Keep in mind what these difficulty ratings mean when you are trying to decide if you have the skill to safely undertake a particular whitewater rafting trip:

Class I: Easy, with small waves and riffles. There are few obstructions, and self-rescue is easy.
Class II: There are more easy rapids and a number of low ledges. Although there are more obstructions, figuring a way around them is easy.
Class III: For those with intermediate skills. Waves, long rapids, and obstructions require the ability to maneuver quickly. Open canoes could be swamped.
Class IV: Advanced. You need good boat-handling abilities and may still end up in unavoidable waves, eddies, and crosscurrents. You should scout a Class IV (and above) stream if it is

your first time running it. (It's always a good idea to scout it every time.)

Class V: Experts only. There will be long, continuous, and obstructed rapids on an extremely complex course. Rescue spots, if any, are few and far between. Every skill of paddling will be needed.

Class VI: Extreme. Errors could result in loss of life.

WILDFLIFE MANAGEMENT AREAS

With 51 of them spread throughout the state, wildlife management areas (WMAs) are probably West Virginia's most often overlooked parcels of public backcountry lands. (An additional 30 WMAs are located on national forest land in the state.) Except during hunting season (usually late October to early January and again in early spring), when it might be best to avoid them, many of the areas can go for weeks on end without anyone visiting their inner reaches.

While state parks were primarily established to provide outdoor recreation and state forests founded for silviculture, WMAs were created with the emphasis on protecting and harvesting game animals. Habitat for waterfowl, white-tailed deer, ruffed grouse, fish, rabbit, squirrel, and others are often artificially created and maintained.

Within the last few decades, many people have come to view these areas also as places of conservation for nongame species and recreation for the general public. In many ways, WMAs can't be beat if you are looking for an uncrowded and primitive experience. Amenities such as picnic areas, restrooms, and the like are usually nonexistent, and trails are sometimes nothing more than informal, unmarked pathways created by the footsteps of occasional hunters.

Consult the **Division of Natural Resources** (304-558-2754; www.wvdnr.gov) for more information.

WINERIES

West Virginia boasts more a dozen wineries; most grow their own grapes, and some supplement their harvest with purchased grapes. You will also find that a large variety of other fruits, such as apples and strawberries, are also turned into delectable beverages. The **Department of Agriculture** (304-558-2200; www.wvagriculture.org), 1900 Kanawha Blvd. E, Charleston, has a small brochure describing each winery and a list of wine-tasting events and festivals. Wineries of note are described in their respective chapters.

Eastern Panhandle 1

WHERE THE POTOMAC
AND THE SHENANDOAH MEET—
HARPERS FERRY, CHARLES TOWN,
AND SHEPHERDSTOWN

SOUTH OF THE POTOMAC—
MARTINSBURG, BERKELEY SPRINGS,
AND THE CACAPON RIVER AND
MOUNTAIN

EASTERN PANHANDLE

The Eastern Panhandle was the first area of West Virginia to be settled and, as such, retains reminders of its earlier days. Many of the towns still look as they did more than a hundred years ago, with their historic districts composed of buildings from the 1800s, and even a few from the 1700s. The mark of a young George Washington is here, from homes he and his family owned to a resort town he helped establish.

John Denver was singing about the Eastern Panhandle when he mentioned, "Blue Ridge Mountains, Shenandoah River," in "Country Roads, Take Me Home." He was right. A little bit of West Virginia extends across the Shenandoah River and into the Blue Ridge Mountains. However, most of the Eastern Panhandle is sandwiched between the Blue Ridge Mountains and the Allegheny Plateau, with a topography that is one of rolling hills mixed with alternating long, narrow ridgelines and valleys. There are still large expanses of rural countryside, but the area was discovered in the 1980s by people wishing to escape living in Washington, DC, and housing developments crop up on a regular basis, turning many parts of the region into a bedroom community for the metro area, with large shopping malls and other modern contrivances.

All of this makes for an interesting place to visit. The West Virginia of old is still here, with its mountain traditions of country cooking, crafts developed from a history of being useful items and not just for decoration, and open countryside in which to hike, bike, paddle, and fish. Yet, the Eastern Panhandle is one of the state's most cosmopolitan places, with world-class restaurants, fine-art galleries, and performing-arts venues.

WHERE THE POTOMAC AND THE SHENANDOAH MEET— HARPERS FERRY, CHARLES TOWN, AND SHEPHERDSTOWN

Harpers Ferry had its beginning in 1733, when Peter Stephens established a ferry service at the confluence of the Potomac and Shenandoah rivers. Recognizing that passengers and the flow of commercial goods would grow as settlers moved westward, Robert Harper purchased the business in 1747. Soon afterward, he constructed a gristmill on low-lying land, later known as Virginius Island, at the western bank of the Shenandoah River.

From those humble origins, Harpers Ferry has been the scene of many major and pivotal events throughout the history of the United States.

On his way to Philadelphia to serve as a Virginia delegate to the Continental Congress in 1783, Thomas Jefferson gazed upon the meeting of the Potomac and Shenandoah rivers and proclaimed the scene to be "worth a voyage across the Atlantic." In 1794, George Washington convinced the U.S. Congress to establish a federal arsenal and armory on a site close to where Harper had built his gristmill.

Thomas Jefferson and Meriwether Lewis were so impressed with the arsenal's quality munitions that Lewis traveled to Harpers Ferry in 1803 to obtain rifles and related supplies for his upcoming expedition into the newly purchased Louisiana Territory. Around 1820, John Hall opened his rifle works, which manufactured rifles with interchangeable parts, a new and innovative feature.

Yet, the small town's fortune soon changed. John Brown's failed raid on the federal arsenal in October 1859 was an attempt to seize the 100,000 muskets and rifles stored there. Brown had intended to turn the arms over to slaves, hoping to inspire an insurrection against their owners.

Strategically situated as it was near the border between North and South, the town exchanged hands eight times during the Civil War. By the time the hostilities ended, much of the town and most of the factories had been burned and the railroad bridge destroyed. Massive floods in 1870 and 1889 damaged almost everything that the war had not. Floods in the 20th century completed the job, and by 1936, Virginius Island was abandoned.

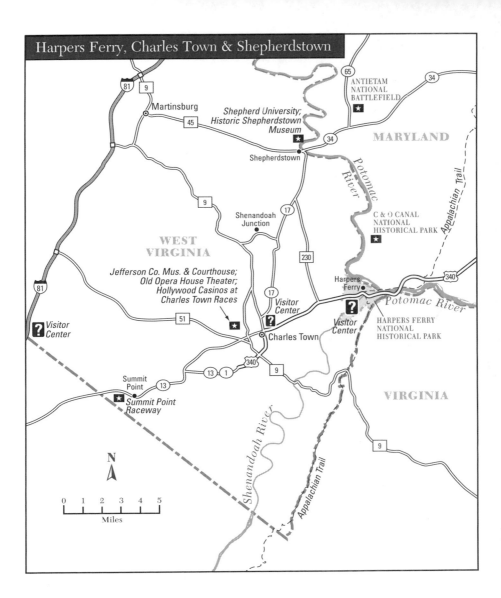

ANTIETAM
NATIONAL
BATTLEFIELD

MARYLAND

Martinsburg

Shepherd University;
Historic Shepherdstown
Museum

Shepherdstown

Potomac River

C & O CANAL
NATIONAL
HISTORICAL PARK

Appalachian Trail

WEST
VIRGINIA

Shenandoah
Junction

Jefferson Co. Mus. & Courthouse;
Old Opera House Theater;
Hollywood Casinos at
Charles Town Races

Visitor
Center

Harpers
Ferry

Potomac River

Visitor
Center

HARPERS FERRY
NATIONAL
HISTORICAL PARK

Visitor
Center

Charles Town

VIRGINIA

Summit
Point

Summit Point
Raceway

Shenandoah River

Appalachian Trail

N

0 1 2 3 4 5
Miles

In 1963, much of the town was incorporated into the Harpers Ferry National Historical Park and the lower part of town restored to its appearance in the 1800s.

A few miles south, John Brown was tried for treason and hanged in Charles Town, originally established by George Washington's brother, Charles. The downtown has a historic district, but the small city has now developed into the area's commercial center, complete with a horse racetrack and shopping centers edging their way toward Harpers Ferry along US 340.

On a rocky bluff overlooking the Potomac River, Shepherdstown is the oldest incorporated town in West Virginia, site of James Rumsey's successful demonstration of a steamboat in 1787, and home of Shepherd University. Its little downtown area is an attractive place of about three square blocks of well-kept, 1800s brick buildings occupied by some of the region's best restaurants, coffee-houses, galleries, and interesting shopping experiences.

GUIDANCE Charles Town Visitors Center (304-728-3939) is downtown at 108 North George St., Charles Town 25414.

The **Jefferson County Convention and Visitors Bureau** (304-535-2627; 1-866-HELLO-WV; www.hello-wv.com; mailing address: 37 Washington Court, Harpers Ferry 25425), at the corner of US 340 and Washington St. in Harpers Ferry, provides information on Harpers Ferry and the entire county.

In the middle of the historic part of Shepherdstown, the **Shepherdstown Visitors Center** (304-876-2786; www.shepherdstownvisitorscenter.com), 136½ East German St., Shepherdstown 25443, can direct you to historic sites, lodging, and dining.

GETTING THERE *By air*: **Hagerstown Regional Airport** (240-313-2777) is the closest air facility, and there is scheduled passenger commuter service to and from **Baltimore/Washington International Airport** (1-800-I FLY BWI; www.bwiairport.com).

Washington Dulles International Airport (703-572-2700; www.metwashairports.com/dulles) is less than an hour's drive away. About an hour away is **Reagan Washington National Airport** (703-417-8000; www.mwaa.com/reagan), and located a little more than an hour away between Baltimore and Washington, DC, is the **Baltimore/Washington International Airport** (1-800-I-FLY-BWI; www.bwiairport.com). It is possible to take public transportation from all three of the DC-area airports to Union Station in Washington, DC. From there you could take rail transportation into Harpers Ferry.

By car: **US 340** is the area's only major four-lane highway, entering West Virginia at Harpers Ferry and continuing on to Charles Town. I-81 is a bit farther to the west and connects to this area via WV 51, WV 9, and WV 45.

By rail: Harpers Ferry is lucky enough to be one of the dwindling number of small towns in America that can still be reached by passenger rail service. **AMTRAK**'s (1-800-872-7245; www.Amtrak.com) Capitol Limited arrives from Chicago in the morning. A westbound train makes a stop in town in the evening. On weekdays, commuter trains run by **MARC**—the Maryland Rail Commuter service (1-800-RIDE-MTA; www.mtamaryland.com)—have two eastbound runs headed to Washington, DC, that stop in Harpers Ferry in the morning, and three that stop in town in the evening. Adding a bit of pleasantry to all of this is the **Harpers Ferry Train Station** (304-535-6346) on Potomac St., which has been restored to look as it did in the 1930s.

GETTING AROUND *By bus*: **Eastern Panhandle Transit Authority** (304-263-0876; www.pantran.com) is the local bus company; it enables you to take public transportation between the three largest towns in the area and other points in the Eastern Panhandle.

A LITTLE-KNOWN FACT
On October 6, 1896, Charles Town became the site of the first rural free mail delivery, which eventually spread throughout the entire country.

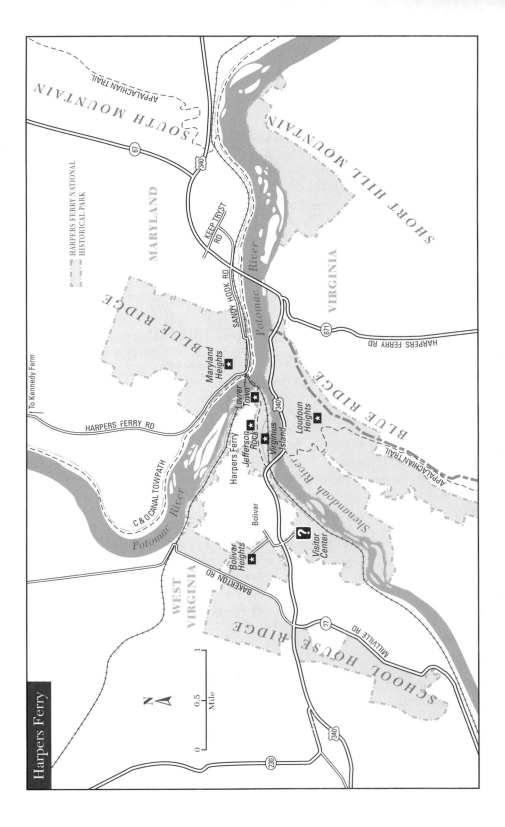

Harpers Ferry

N

0   0.5   1
Mile

SOUTH MOUNTAIN

APPALACHIAN TRAIL

MARYLAND

VIRGINIA

SHORT HILL MOUNTAIN

67

340

KEEP TRYST RD

SANDY HOOK RD

Potomac River

671

HARPERS FERRY RD

BLUE RIDGE

HARPERS FERRY RD

To Kennedy Farm

C & O CANAL TOWPATH

Potomac River

Maryland Heights ★

Lower Town

Harpers Ferry

Jefferson Rock ★

Virginius Island

340

Loudoun Heights ★

BLUE RIDGE

APPALACHIAN TRAIL

Shenandoah River

Bolivar

Visitor Center ?

Bolivar Heights ★

BAKERTON RD

WEST VIRGINIA

SCHOOL HOUSE RIDGE

77

MILLVILLE RD

230

340

HARPERS FERRY NATIONAL HISTORICAL PARK

By taxi: **Community Taxi** (304-725-3794) is headquartered in Charles Town and will take you to most of the closest outlying villages and towns.

PUBLIC RESTROOMS Restrooms for the **Harpers Ferry National Historical Park** are located on Shenandoah St. in the lower part of town.

MEDICAL EMERGENCIES Jefferson Memorial Hospital (304-728-1600; www.jeffmem.com), 300 South Preston, Ranson. (Ranson is on the western edge of the Charles Town city limits.)

If you are in the western part of this area, it might be closer and faster for you to go to **City Hospital** (304-264-1000; www.cityhospital.org), Dry Run Rd., Martins-burg.

✳ To See

COLLEGES Shepherd University (304-876-5000; 1-800-344-5231; www.shep herd.edu), P.O. Box 5000, Shepherdstown 25443. The school can trace its origin back to 1871, when the state legislature established a normal school at Shepherds-town. Today the university has close to 4,000 students and adds much to the cultural life and activities of the area through art exhibits, concerts, and theater and dance presentations. It's also the host of the internationally acclaimed Contemporary American Theater Festival (1-800-999-CATF; www.catf.org) held every July.

DRIVING TOURS, SCENIC & HISTORIC The **Washington Heritage Trail** (www.washingtonheritagetrail.com). As much a scenic drive as it is a trip through history, the 137-mile heritage trail loops around the entire Eastern Panhandle, bringing you past just about everything mentioned in this book for the region. It's a good way to get around without really having to think on the logistics of doing it. A brochure is available from the trail's Web site, or from any of the places mentioned in *Guidance*.

HISTORIC SITES

Charles Town

Jefferson County Courthouse, Washington and George streets. Originally constructed in 1837, the courthouse was bombarded during the Civil War and reconstructed in 1872. Its national claim to fame is that it was the site of the trial in which John Brown and six of his raiders were convicted of treason. Inside are a number of drawings and documents pertaining to the events. The courthouse was also the site of another famous trial when 1922 proceedings against William Blizzard, a leader of striking coal miners who was accused of treason and murder, were moved from Southern West Virginia.

Docents give guided tours of the courthouse on some weekends.

Sharpsburg, Maryland

Antietam National Battlefield (301-432-5124; www.nps.gov/anti). The visitor center is off MD65, a few miles north of Sharpsburg. Open daily. Small admission fee. Antietam is not in West Virginia, but it is so close (just a few miles north of Shepherdstown) that you should take the time to visit.

I was impressed with the way the park service had organized visitors' experiences

⚓ **Harpers Ferry National Historical Park** (304-535-6029; www.nps.gov/hafe; mailing address: P.O. Box 65, Harpers Ferry 25425). There is much to see and do here, and the best place to start is the visitor center on US 340, a short distance south of town. Displays and videos help put the history of the place, and your visit here, in perspective. It is also where you will park (small fee for a three-day pass) and take the shuttle into town. (There are a few free parking sites in town, but with residents and commuters vying for them, good luck finding one.) Ask personnel if there will be any living-history demonstrations occurring during your visit. It's possible you may get to watch soldiers march through town, walk among reenactors camped on the square, see John Brown and his raiders in action, or listen to speeches made at the 1906 establishment of the Niagara Movement, which was a cornerstone of the modern civil rights movement in America. As far as historic parks or sites go, Williamsburg in Virginia may be bigger, but Harpers Ferry is a much more manageable place to get a handle on the big picture—and its admission fee is much less.

Lower Town contains the many restored buildings and is where living-history demonstrations take place. Here you'll get to explore the John Brown Fort, a blacksmith shop, Mrs. Stripes' Boarding House, Funkel's Clothing Store, and more. Hand-carved steps lead uphill (on what is the Appalachian Trail) to the oldest structure in town, the Robert Harper House (constructed between 1775 and 1782); St. Peter's Catholic Church; and Jefferson Rock. From this rock, Thomas Jefferson proclaimed the view of the confluence of the Potomac and Shenandoah rivers was "worth a voyage across the Atlantic" and "perhaps one of the most stupendous scenes in Nature."

A few steps beyond the rock are the Harper Cemetery and the site of Storer College, established soon after the Civil War as one of the country's first institutions dedicated to the education of former slaves.

Virginius Island was the town's industrial center, with waterpower from the Shenandoah attracting mills, machine shops, and various other manufacturers. By the mid-1800s, the island had close to 40 factories and a popu-

when I first came here many years ago. It was the first Civil War battlefield I had ever visited, and I have never failed to learn something new on subsequent visits. A driving tour takes you by significant battle sites, rangers lead guided walks, and a couple of trails take the more inquisitive into hidden areas of the battlefield's 3,000 acres.

The **Antietam National Cemetery** is off MD 34 in Sharpsburg. Grand old maple, oak, and Norway spruce trees provide shade for the graves set out in a cir-

lation of more than 180. Today, maple, sycamore, and box elder trees stand where brick walls once enclosed cotton and flour mills. The songs of wood thrushes, cardinals, and blackbirds have replaced the whine of turbines and saw blades, and ducks float peacefully in the waters of the old canal. A moderately easy walk of less than a mile affords the opportunity to relive history while taking in the island's natural beauty.

Across the Potomac River in Maryland is a not-so-easy hike. On an inspection tour of federal forces stationed on **Maryland Heights**, Abraham Lincoln gave up before reaching any of the fortifications, saying the trip was just too strenuous. If you make it all the way, you'll be rewarded with a grandstand view of Harpers Ferry and the two rivers. Also in Maryland is the 184.5-mile **C&O Canal National Park**, an almost level biking and hiking route that runs along the Potomac River from Georgetown in Washington, DC, to Cumberland, Maryland. (More information on these two attractions may be found in two of my other books, *Maryland: An Explorer's Guide* and *50 Hikes in Maryland*.)

ST. PETER'S CATHOLIC CHURCH

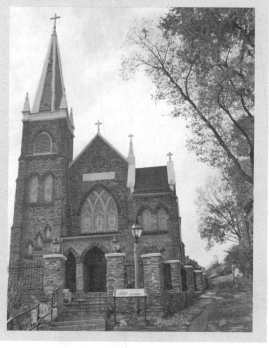

A little longer hike, this one on the Appalachian Trail and a side route to **Loudoun Heights** in Virginia, is not quite as strenuous and provides a different perspective on the same scene from a spot known as Split Rocks.

Bolivar Heights has a short, easy trail looping around sites from which Robert E. Lee's army fired artillery shells into the lower part of town.

cular fashion. It is mind-boggling to walk through here and realize that this is just a portion of those killed during the battle.

MUSEUMS

Charles Town
Jefferson County Museum (304-725-8628; www.JeffCtyWVmuseum.org), 200 East Washington St. Open mid-Mar.–mid-Dec., Tue.–Sat. 11–4. Small admission

fee. Like many county museums, this one contains a number of items of local interest. However, unlike those other museums, the items here are of national significance. The sheer number of pieces relating to the John Brown raid and the Civil War is quite surprising, especially since this museum is contained in one room. There's a collection of rifles from the federal armory Brown tried to capture, the wagon that delivered him to the gallows, the frame of the gurney that he sat on during the trial, and even his personal copy of his Provisional Constitution. Going back even further into national history are the original 1748 land transfer papers of the Washington family, who owned many acres of land in this area.

Harpers Ferry

✍ **Harpers Ferry Toy Train Museum** (304-535-2521), on Bakertown Rd. (WV 27), just south of Harpers Ferry. Open Apr.–Oct., Sat. and Sun. 9–5. Small admission fee. Sometimes a hobby collection outgrows a person's room and ends up being a museum. Robert E. Wallach began collecting trains as a child and opened his collection to the public in 1970. Now operated by his sons, it has model trains of just about every size ever made and, just for kids, antique handcars they can ride. Everyone can get on board the 1950s Joy Line Railroad, a miniature train that departs from an original B&O Railroad section car house.

John Brown Wax Museum (304-535-6342; www.johnbrownwaxmuseum.com), 168 High St. Open mid-Mar. to mid-Dec., daily 9–5. Small admission fee; children age 5 and younger are free. I probably visited Harpers Ferry at least 10 times before I went inside this museum. Don't make the mistake I did, thinking it is some kind of Ripley's Believe It or Not–type of place. There are three floors of dioramas and wax figures (some with audio information) that provide detailed information on what really happened, and why, in Harpers Ferry. Besides history, you can also appreciate the talent and work that went into making the figures. By today's electronic technological standards, the displays here may seem a bit dated, but that just adds to the historical nature of the place.

Shepherdstown

Historic Shepherdstown Museum (304-876-0910; www. historicshepherdstown .com), German and Princess streets. Dates have changed, but most years open Apr.–Oct., Sat. 11–5 and Sun. 1–4. Donations accepted. The museum is located in the Entler Hotel, which was one of the area's most luxurious places to lodge when it was built in 1809. Through the years, the building served as a number of establishments, including a dormitory and faculty residence for the nearby college.

THE REPLICA OF RUMSEY'S STEAMBOAT

Don't be dismayed by the sparseness of the downstairs when you first walk in, for upstairs you'll find enough to keep you busy for hours. Items like an early 1800s clock that still works, 1800s Weiss pottery made from Potomac River clay, and information on the C&O Canal tell the story of the town's past residents.

Housed in a small outbuilding is a half-scale replica of James Rumsey's steamboat, amazingly built by present citizens of the town. It actually works and is often exhibited steaming under its own power on special occasions. A few blocks away is the Rumsey Monument, a stone spire overlooking the river that should have made the man famous, but he was overshadowed by Robert Fulton's steam-powered *Claremont*—23 years after Rumsey's successful demonstration of his invention in 1787.

✸ To Do

AUTO RACING ✍ **Summit Point Motorsports Park** (304-725-8444; www .summitpoint-raceway.com), Summit Point. You can be witness to all manner of auto racing—sports car, motorcycle, and go-cart—on a 2-mile course every weekend Mar.–Oct. However, what makes this a really special motor sports place is that, during certain weeks, you can get out on the track yourself and be taught how to race, or just be a better driver on today's busy highways.

BICYCLING The **C&O Canal National Historical Park** is in Maryland, not West Virginia, but it is easily accessible by a footbridge from Harpers Ferry across the Potomac River and is, without a doubt, the best bicycling opportunity in the area.

Originally projected to extend 360 miles, the canal never lived up to its investors' dreams. Mounting costs, coupled with other problems, caused financial backers to decide in 1850 that enough was enough, and that Cumberland was the farthest west the canal would be constructed—a distance of 184.5 miles from Washington, DC.

The canal was proclaimed a national monument in 1961 and named a national historical park in 1971. Today, the towpath is opened to hikers, bikers, and (except for a short section) horseback riders, and camping is permitted at designated sites. The park service has an abundance of informational handout sheets at its Great Falls Visitor Center (301-767-3714; www.nps.gov/choh), 11710 MacArthur Blvd., Potomac, MD 20854, while Mike High's book, *The C&O Canal Companion*, covers the subject in great detail.

FISHING The **Shenandoah** and **Potomac rivers** are both known for the quality of their fishing and, in what seems to be nature's nod to anglers, the rivers come together at Harpers Ferry. Just upstream from the confluence, the Shenandoah is often shallow enough to permit wading far out into the water. It's also possible to wade into the Potomac, but usually not as far out and not on as regular a basis as you can in the Shenandoah. Bring tackle and lures appropriate for catching largemouth and smallmouth bass, channel catfish, rock bass, walleye, and tiger muskie—and be ready to contend with quite a bit of aquatic vegetation in the summer.

If you'd like to have the knowledge of a local, contact **Bryan Kelly** (304-535-1239; www.theanglersinn.com), operator, along with his wife, Debbi, of the Angler's Inn (see *Bed & Breakfasts*). He was once a tournament angler, but now he guides. Besides being an expert fisherman, Bryan hand built the wooden McKenzie River drift boats that he uses to bring clients to places that are inaccessible to other outfitters.

GOLF Locust Hill Golf Course (304-728-7300; www.locusthillgolfcourse.com), 1 St. Andrews Dr., west of Charles Town. The 18-hole, semiprivate course has been ranked number five in the state by *Golf Week* magazine.

Sleepy Hollow Golf and Country Club (304-725-5210; www.golfsleepyhollow .com), on WV 24 east of Charles Town. Built in the 1990s using the natural lay of the land as much as possible, the semiprivate course has 18 holes with tees from 5,776 to 6,815 yards.

HIKING The Maine-to-Georgia **Appalachian Trail** enters West Virginia from Maryland by crossing the Potomac River, winds its way through the sites of Harpers Ferry National Historical Park, crosses the Shenandoah River, and ascends Loudoun Heights to continue southward into Virginia.

West Virginia may have only a few miles of the world-famous pathway, but the umbrella organization that oversees the route of the trail is located in Harpers Ferry. The **Appalachian Trail Conservancy** (304-535-6331; www.appalachian trail.org; mailing address: P.O. Box 807, Harpers Ferry 25425) can be visited at 799 Washington St.

Harpers Ferry
The Outfitter at Harpers Ferry (304-535-2087; www.theoutfitteratharpersferry .com), 36 High St. Located just a few feet from the Appalachian Trail, the Outfitter's personnel are well acquainted with the needs of serious backpackers and campers.

Also see the "Harpers Ferry National Historical Park" sidebar earlier in the chapter, and *Bicycling*.

HORSE RACING & GAMING & **Hollywood Casino at Charles Town Races** (1-800-795-7001; www.hollywoodcasinocharlestown.com), US 340 on the north side of Charles Town. Horse racing was started here in 1933, and although the track may not have the Kentucky Derby or the Preakness, Charles Town is home to the prestigious West Virginia Breeders' Classic, held every fall with $1 million in purses. Live thoroughbred racing occurs on Wed.–Sat. evenings and on Sunday afternoon. Simulcast wagering is available seven days a week, as is the opportunity to feed close to 4,000 slot machines or play table games.

KAYAKING, CANOEING & RAFTING ✍ **River Riders** (304-535-2663; 1-800-326-7238; www.riverriders.com), 408 Allstadts Hill Rd. (on US 340 , a short distance south of Harpers Ferry). The Potomac and Shenandoah rivers are certainly not rip-roaring whitewater streams like the New and Gauley rivers, but you will still find enough Class II–III rapids to provide good thrills. River Riders is a full-service outfitter that offers raft/canoe/kayak/ducky (inflatable kayaks) tours and instruction on both rivers. When the waterways get too low to really enjoy paddling, rent a tube and take a lazy float trip downstream. Shuttles and bicycle rentals are also available.

River and Trail Outfitters (1-888-446-7529; www.adventurecentral.com), located next to the Shenandoah River in Millville. Founded in 1972, this family-owned outfitter has more than 80 professional guides and staff members who provide rafting, tubing, biking, hiking, and cross-country skiing trips.

WALKING TOURS

Charles Town

Downtown Charles Town boasts more than 40 homes, churches, government buildings, and other sites of historical significance within a few blocks of one another. These sites are described in two brochures, *Walking Tour of Historic Charles Town* and *Black History Tour of Charles Town*. Both are available from the Jefferson County Convention and Visitors Bureau in the Charles Town Visitors Center (see *Guidance*). Pick up copies and take an easy stroll into the city's past.

SHEPHERDSTOWN

Harpers Ferry

♪ **Ghost Tour** (304-725-8019; www.harpersferryghost.20m.com). Dressed (usually) in period costume, a guide will take you through dark streets and alleyways to relate paranormal happenings and stories based on historic fact. Learn about the doctor who was buried standing up, or the man who looked like John Brown and took one of the tours in 1974, but didn't show up in any photographs taken of the trip. Trains whistling their way through the tunnel across the Potomac River add a feeling of eeriness to the walk. A fun way to spend 60–90 minutes.

Shepherdstown

A brochure available from the Shepherdstown Visitors Center (see *Guidance*) provides an amazing amount of detail on more than 50 places in a five-block area. You will learn tidbits of history, such as Shepherdstown is where the screw lock—used as switch locks by railroads—was invented, and that Newton Diehl Baker Jr., who was President Wilson's secretary of war, was born here. Although it is not described in the brochure, one of my favorite parts of walking in Shepherdstown is to go into the alleyways to enjoy some of the meticulously tended backyard gardens.

✳ Green Space

PARKS Bolivar Nature Park (304-728-3207; www.jcprc.org), Primrose Alley, Harpers Ferry. It is only 7 acres, but this little park makes a nice, quick escape from the hustle and bustle of the national historical park. A gazebo, picnic tables, and short nature trail offer a quiet respite.

Have you ever wondered what pawpaw, black locust, box elder, black cherry, sugar maple, red oak, and black locust trees look like? These, and others, are marked and keyed to a brochure available at the trailhead of the short 0.3-mile pathway, permitting you to make close-up observations of the texture of their barks, shapes of leaves, kind of seeds or flowers, and other identifiable characteristics.

✱ Lodging

INNS

Charles Town 25414

Hillbrook Inn (304-725-4223; 1-800-304-4223; www.hillbrookinn.com), 4490 Summit Point Rd. Check into the Hillbrook Inn and experience what it must feel like to be the lord of an English manor. Located 6 miles southwest of Charles Town, the European country home has 15 levels that look like they grew out of the ground, as they so much resemble the levels of rocks upon which the house is built. The interior's polished brass, rich wood, and Oriental rugs are highlighted by sun shining through 2,000 panes of glass. Libraries, fireplaces, artwork, and a stream gliding through tended gardens all add to the sumptuous ambience. All six guest rooms have private baths, and each is decorated in its own style. Be sure to also make reservations for the seven-course dinner served Thurs.–Sun. (see *Dining Out*). $275–325; includes breakfast.

Shepherdstown 25443

♿ **Bavarian Inn** (304-876-2551; www.bavarianinnwv.com), 164 Shepherd Grade Rd. German immigrants Carol and Erwin Asam inspired construction of their Bavarian Inn by showing workers photographs of Bavarian postcards. The result is a 12-acre inn/resort of chalets and a lodge with turrets, frescoes, and rich woodwork, all sitting on the lip of a low gorge overlooking the Potomac River. Rooms are large, and most feature a private balcony, whirlpool tub, and, for a bit more of the European flavor, a bidet. There's also a swimming pool, tennis court, and putting green. For the best view of the river, ask for a room numbered 53 or above. For me, the most enjoyable part of staying here was the chance to eat three German-inspired meals a day at the inn's Greystone Mansion (see *Dining Out*). $109–359.

BED & BREAKFASTS

Charles Town 25414

The Carriage Inn (304-728-8003; 1-800-697-9830; www.carriageinn.com), 417 East Washington St. Located within a couple of blocks of the downtown business district, the Carriage Inn was used by Gen. Ulysses S. Grant and Gen. Philip Sheridan to plan their Shenandoah Valley campaign during the Civil War. The 1836 home has been restored and furnished to reflect the times. However, just because there are high ceilings and canopied beds, don't think you have to give up modern niceties, such as a Jacuzzi and a private porch in the Copper Beech Suite or a sunken bathroom in the Mary Rutherford Room. $135–250.

❀ **Cottonwood Inn Bed & Breakfast** (1-800-868-1188; www.mydestination.com/index.html), Mill Lane. As you turn into the long driveway, you receive the first hint that you are arriving at a special place. The Cottonwood Inn sits on 6 acres of bottomland surrounded by cornfields. Built at the turn of the 19th century, the inn retains many of its features (original flooring and bricks are exposed throughout the house) and is one of few B&Bs in the area that made me feel that I was staying in a truly historic home.

Room 2 faces the east so that you are warmed by the morning's rising sun, while the room at the top of the stairs overlooks the countryside and has a private bath with a pocket door. I like my B&Bs to have a rural setting, and this one has one of the best. Next visit I intend to do nothing more than sit on a porch rocker and watch the creek flow by. $95–135.

Washington House Inn (304-725-7923; 1-800-297-6957; www.washingtonhouseinnwv.com), 216 South George St. Owner/hostess Nina Vogel has seen to every little detail in her inn, which was built in 1899 by descendents of George Washington's brother. The large rooms are wonderfully decorated and, because each has a private bath, air-conditioning, TV, and phone, many of her guests are business travelers. In fact, you never know who you might share breakfast with. My morning companions were NFL Hall of Famer Sam Huff and a number of recently retired and current Washington Redskins football players. In addition to pleasant conversation, we all enjoyed the abundance of raspberry and cream cheese–stuffed French toast. $149–225.

Nina also has a number of separate houses she rents by the week, if you will be in the area for an extended period of time.

Harpers Ferry 25425

The Angler's Inn (304-535-1239; www.theanglersinn.com), 867 Washington St. Like many current residents of the Eastern Panhandle, Debbie and Bryan Kelly moved here from the Baltimore/Washington, DC, metro area. In a departure from usually telling you about the rooms of a B&B (the Angler's Inn's are nice, spacious, and inviting, and I enjoyed the one with the sunporch overlooking the yard), I feel the need to tell you about the aromas of this place. Step through the front door and be greeted by a whiff of fresh to-die-for chocolate chip cookies. Wake up in the morning to the smells of balsamic-glazed plum-chocolate zucchini bread, spiced bacon, and toasted almond French bread drifting into every corner of the house. What a perfect way to start a day of fishing

with Bryan out on the Shenandoah and Potomac rivers (see *Fishing*). $165.

Harpers Ferry Guest House Bed & Breakfast (304-535-2101; www.harpersferryguesthouse.com), 800 Washington St. Despite having been built in 1992, the Harpers Ferry Guest House was designed in such a way that it fits in well with the historic homes of the neighborhood. Being a modern building, it is also bright and roomy, especially the open dining and kitchen area where guests can easily interact with the hosts. There's off-street parking, with a handicapped-accessible ramp leading to first-floor accommodations. Children over age 12 are also welcome. $115.

The Jackson Rose Bed and Breakfast (304-535-1528; www.thejacksonrose.com), 1167 Washington St. Built around 1795, once owned by the Lee family, and used as Stonewall Jackson's headquarters during the Civil War, the B&B has only three guest rooms, so stays here are peaceful and quiet. I thought the "cubbyhole" bathroom of the upstairs Garrett Room was more quaint than confining. The restored Federal-style home has the original

THE JACKSON ROSE BED AND BREAKFAST

heart of pine floor and gas fireplaces, and breakfasts always include entrée, homemade jams and breakfast breads, fresh fruit, and local ingredients. Relax in the backyard herb garden on sunny days, or stay in bed and listen to the rain dropping on the tin roof on inclement ones. $135–150.

Shepherdstown 25443

Thomas Shepherd Inn (304-876-3715; 1-888-889-8952; www.thomas shepherdinn.com), German and Duke streets. You are right in the middle of things when you stay at the Thomas Shepherd Inn, built in 1868. A multitude of shops, restaurants, and Shepherd University are all within two blocks. The guest rooms in the front of the house overlook the main street, while those in the back have easy access to the porch above the small backyard. Fresh biscotti and coffee are available for early risers, and the gourmet breakfasts range from a mushroom-cheese omelet accompanied by local sausage and sour cream coffee cake to blueberry-pecan French toast and hot apple soup. $160–195.

CAMPGROUNDS

Harpers Ferry 25425

Harpers Ferry KOA (304-535-6895; www.harpersferrykoa.com), on US 340 between Charles Town and Harpers Ferry. All of the amenities this national chain is known for.

✳ Where to Eat

DINING OUT

Charles Town

Hillbrook Inn (304-725-4223; 1-800-304-4223; www.hillbrookinn.com), 4490 Summit Point Rd. Lunch and dinner served Thurs.–Sun. by reservation only. Some restaurants are known as "special occasion" establishments. The Hillbrook Inn qualifies as "the absolutely very special occasion" place.

Three-course lunches ($35) and seven-course dinners ($65 plus 20 percent gratuity, with house wines) are served by the fireplace or in the garden. Some of those courses have included spinach timbale, velvet onion soup, penne with saffron cream, salmon en papillote, quail, and chocolate-pecan pâté. Low-fat, vegetarian, and low-carbohydrate options are available. You may not feel like leaving after such a wonderful meal, so make a room reservation (see *Inns*) at the same time you reserve your mealtime.

Shepherdstown

& **Bavarian Inn** (304-876-2551; www .bavarianinnwv.com), 164 Shepherd Grade Rd. Open daily for breakfast, lunch, and dinner. I will admit right off that I am not a big fan of German cooking. Having said that, the delicious and eye-pleasingly presented meals at the Bavarian Inn went a long way in changing my mind. The traditional Bavarian entrées include Wiener schnitzel ($21), sauerbraten ($18), and a schweinebraten ($18), but you also have the choice of contemporary items such as Kona coffee–encrusted lamb ($34) and scotch-scented New York strip steak ($29). Visit in the fall, and you get to take part in the Wild Game Festival, when items such as wild boar, rabbit, and venison are on the menu. The wait staff are attentive but not annoying, and the extensive wine list contains almost as many $300 bottles as $35 ones. You have a choice of four differently decorated dining rooms in the 1930s Greystone Mansion, but to put you in the most appropriate Bavarian mood, ask to be placed in the Hunt Room, complete with a huge stone fireplace and antler chandeliers.

Three Onions (304-876-8000; www .threeonions.com), 117 East German St. Open for lunch Sat.–Sun. and dinner Wed.–Sun. Bright interior walls, fresh flowers, linen tablecloths and napkins, and glass stemware all set the mood for the elegant meals served here. Wood-fired halibut ($28), spicy citrus-glazed pork tenderloin ($25), vegetable lasagna ($25), and rack of New Zealand lamb have all been on the menu at one time or another, along with some wonderful gourmet pizzas—Mediterranean, roasted veggie, and four cheese—for $13–15. Lunch features salads and sandwiches, and the martini bar has plush sofas and tapas selections.

Yellow Brick Bank (304-876-2208; www.yellowbrickbank.com), 201 East German St. Sadly, the Yellow Brink Bank was closed for vacation on the night I had planned to eat here. I'm breaking my rule of including in this book only places I have been to because I was told by a number of people that I had missed out on a special Northern Italian and Continental dining experience. They make their own bread, mozzarella, pasta, sausage, and desserts. Let me know how your experience was. Entrées $22–31.

EATING OUT

Charles Town
La Mezzaluna Café (304-728-0700), in the Somerset Village shopping center on US 340 between Charles Town and Harpers Ferry. Once you start eating, you will forget that La Mezzaluna is located in a strip mall. (The quality of food is so good that this place should be in the *Dining Out* category, but its reasonable prices and casual atmosphere made me decide to put it here in the *Eating Out* section.) The owner is from El Salvador, and he made his way to the Eastern Panhandle after learning his craft in numerous New York restaurants. Almost all of the Italian dishes are slight variations on traditional recipes (my chicken Mode-

na was like chicken Marsala, but the broth was beef based), making the offerings fresh, different, and appealing. Entrées start at $10.95; most expensive item is around $20.

Harpers Ferry
❧ **The Anvil Restaurant** (304-535-2582; www.anvilrestaurant.com), 1270 Washington St. Open for lunch and dinner Wed.–Sun. The Anvil, in business since 1985, is located a few blocks from the historic part of town, so its clientele is a mix of travelers and locals. The pub serves more than 20 brands of beer, yet the restaurant retains a family atmosphere. Seafood is the specialty, and my dining companion enjoyed her crab cakes, while my serving of shrimp and artichokes with fresh tomatoes was so large I had to ask for a doggie bag. Other entrées include filet mignon, pasta, chicken Parmesan, and veal. Entrées $12.95–22.95.

Shepherdstown
Blue Moon Café (304-876-1920), Princess and High streets. Open daily for breakfast, lunch, and dinner. The Blue Moon is popular with the university students and has a bit of a bohemian atmosphere, but don't let that stop you from dining on the many fresh and healthy items offered. Some of the best salads in the region and inventive sandwiches (such as the chicken Charmaine—roasted chicken breast with roasted pepper and fresh spinach, served on a ciabatta roll topped with herbed cream cheese) are nice for lunch, while caramelized onion pork loin with poached pear and sesame stir-fry are found on the dinner menu. Dinner entrées $10.95–15.95.

Stone Soup Bistro (304-876-8477; www.stonesoupbistro.com), 118 West German St. Open for lunch and dinner; closed Tue. Within the confines of their small establishment, owners Liz

Gallery and Greg Joyce use as many locally grown organic items as possible in their offerings, which have just a bit of Southern chic to them. The soups and salads are, of course, fresh and refreshing, while the pleasant blend of spices and other ingredients in the main dishes makes them that way, too. You will leave here feeling healthy and satisfied. This is the kind of place you might expect to find in the trendy Georgetown section of Washington, DC. Entrées $15–29.

♪ Tony's Pizza and Stonewalls Underground Pub (304-876-2720; www.tonysstonewalls.com), 126 East German St. Open daily for lunch and dinner. Tony's is the place to go if you get a hunger attack late in the night. They serve pizza, sandwiches, subs, burgers, and calzones until 3 AM. Almost all items, including large pizzas are less than $20.

SNACKS & GOODIES Shepherds-town Sweet Shop Bakery (304-876-2432; www.wvbakery.com), 100 West German St., Shepherdstown. Nationally known for holiday stollen, an old-world baked loaf with rum-soaked raisins, dates, and pecans combined with sweet butter and spiced flour. Also a place for cappuccino and a muffin for breakfast, and soup, sandwiches, and a pastry for lunch.

✳ Entertainment
DANCE, MUSIC, AND THEATER
Charles Town
♪ The Old Opera House Theatre (304-725-4420; 1-888-900-SHOW; www.oldoperahouse.org), 204 North George St. In a lovingly renovated 1910 opera house, year-round entertainment ranges from Broadway musicals and concerts to dance and programs for children.

Shepherdstown
Contemporary American Theater Festival at Shepherd University (304-876-3885; 1-800-999-CATF; www.catf.org; (mailing address: P.O. Box 429, Shepherdstown 25443). Since 1991, the festival has been presenting new American plays, lectures, and postshow discussions. There have been world premieres by playwrights such as Lee Blessing, Keith Glover, Sam Shepard, and Richard Dresser. Held over the course of about three weeks in July, the festival has gained such renown that it turns what could be a quiet period on campus, between the spring and fall semesters, into a time when scores of visitors excitedly attend one performance after another.

Shepherd University (304-876-5000; 1-800-344-5231; www.shepherd.edu; (mailing address: P.O. Box 5000, Shepherdstown 25443). The school is the place to attend a wide variety of performing-arts presentations. The music department hosts concerts and events, plays are presented by the Shepherd Theater, and the university's Performing Arts Series brings in a wide variety of programs throughout the year. Past performances have included professional dance troupes, comedy teams, and gospel quartets.

✳ Selective Shopping
ART GALLERY
Charles Town
Washington St. Gallery & Gift (304-724-2090; www.wstreetgallery.com), 235 W. Washington St. Open Wed.–Sun. A juried gallery of 40 artisans whose work is displayed in a 2,000-square foot gallery within an historic building. Some of the outstanding items include furniture, pottery, paintings, textiles, and sculptures.

BOOKSTORES

Harpers Ferry

Harpers Ferry Books (304-535-1862; www.harpersferrybooks.com), 170B High St. You will find an extensive selection of used books, especially historical and local items, in this bookstore, located within the historic part of town.

✍ **Harpers Ferry Historical Association** (304-535-6881; www.HarpersFerryHistory.com; mailing address: P.O. Box 197, Harpers Ferry 25425), Shenandoah St. Located within Harpers Ferry National Historical Park, the association's bookstore is a treasure trove of books, audio, video, and artwork for anyone interested in the 19th century; the Civil War; history; and hiking, walking, and the natural history of the region. Most national park gift shops or visitor centers have just a small selection of such materials, but this shop contains hundreds, if not thousands, of items. It's also a good place to pick up material that will help spark your child's interest in these subjects.

Shepherdstown

Four Seasons Books & Café (304-876-3486; www.fourseasonsbooks.com), 116 West German St. A complete selection of new and used books.

FARMERS' MARKETS Little **Shepherdstown** has very active farmers' markets, with three of them in different locations and open on different days. Information on all three may be obtained by calling 304-725-3149.

On Sunday, you can find produce in the parking lot behind the public library at King and German streets 9:30–1 during Apr.–Nov. On Wednesday, drive a short distance to One Valley Bank on WV 45 to find the farmers' market in operation 4–6:30 PM in July and Aug. The farmers' market at the post office on Washington St. is in operation 9:30–noon on Sat. year-round.

PICK-YOUR-OWN PRODUCE FARMS

Harpers Ferry

Ridgefield Farm and Orchard (304-876-3647; www.ridgefieldfarm.com), 840 Kidwiler Rd. Strawberries, apples, pumpkins, and Christmas trees in their respective seasons. Corn maze and hayrides in the fall.

SPECIAL SHOPS Dickinson & Wait Craft Gallery (304-876-0657), 121 East German St., Shepherdstown. Quality jewelry, textiles, papers, wood, silver, and copper items are marketed by Dickinson & Wait, named a top 100 retailer of American crafts.

✍ **O'Hurley's General Store** (304-876-6907; www.ohurley.com), 205 East Washington St., Shepherdstown. Open daily. "Strangers visiting our friendly town are respectfully solicited to examine our assortment, which will be found very attractive, comprising all the best to be found in large cities at much lower prices, goods warranted in cases as represented." This quote

O'HURLEY'S GENERAL STORE

from their brochure lets you know that you are stepping back in time and into an establishment whose proprietor, Jay O'Hurley, has a good sense of marketing and humor. You could spend quite a bit of time here just purveying the décor—such as stained-glass windows, musical instruments, and the fireplace, which was hand-made by Jay and his friends. Items for sale include Bulgarian pottery, rustic furniture, cast-iron cookware, pocket watches, swage blocks, clothing, dolls, toys, and candy. Kids will enjoy looking for "Rufus" in the fireplace mantle and saying hi to the store cat. Also, be sure to make a visit to the restroom to pull the chain on the old-style water closet.

On the Wings of Dreams (304-876-0244; www.wingsofdreamsshop.com), 139 West German St., Shepherdstown. Celebrating the spirit of the earth, owner Laura E. Rau presents an assortment of crystals, books, and Native American, Southwestern, and Celtic art objects.

✳ Special Events

March: **Annual Upper Potomac Dulcimer Fest** (304-876-2786), Shepherdstown.

April: **Annual House and Garden Tour** in Jefferson and Berkeley counties (304-263-9606).

June: **Mountain Heritage Arts & Crafts Festival** (304-725-2055; 1-800-624-0577; www.jeffersoncounty.com /festival), Charles Town. One of the largest and best-regarded festivals of its kind, with more than 200 artists/craftspersons, who must pass stringent judging to get in. A second such festival is held in Sept.

August: **Annual African American Cultural & Heritage Festival** (304-725-9610; www.harpersferrywv.net /naacp.htm), Charles Town. **Annual Jefferson County Fair** (304-724-1411), Jefferson County Fairgrounds.

September: **Mountain Heritage Arts & Crafts Festival** (304-725-2055; 1-800-624-0577; www.jeffersoncounty .com/festival), Charles Town. (See *June*.)

September/October: **Annual Appalachian Heritage Festival** (304-876-2786), Shepherdstown. One of the Eastern Panhandle's best mountain music festivals.

November: **Over the Mountain Studio Tour** (304-725-0567). A special driving-tour weekend when artists and craftspersons welcome visitors into their studios and homes. There's always something new—and the possibility of winning a one-of-a-kind item.

SOUTH OF THE POTOMAC— MARTINSBURG, BERKELEY SPRINGS, AND THE CACAPON RIVER AND MOUNTAIN

Martinsburg was chartered in 1778, but it did not really grow until the Baltimore and Ohio Railroad arrived in 1837. It had gained such importance by the Civil War that North and South both coveted it, with so many skirmishes in and around the town that it changed hands dozens of times during the course of the conflict.

With America's reduced reliance on railroads, Martinsburg slipped from importance, and its fortunes began to decline until the construction of I-81. Today, the town is the economic hub of the entire Eastern Panhandle, with malls, shopping centers, restaurants, and other commercial enterprises lining the land close to the interstate.

Yet, the inner part of town has been able to keep much of its character, with more than a half-dozen distinct historic districts and the core downtown area dominated by buildings of Federal and Greek Revival architecture. Most heartening is the fact that citizens and the government recognize what they have and are working to keep it, and even improve it, as evidenced by the restoration of the B&O Railroad Roundhouse.

Across two major ridgelines to the west is Berkeley Springs, whose restorative spring waters were a gathering place for Native Americans long before settlers began to move into West Virginia. George Washington visited often in the mid-1700s. In 1776, he and his family and friends established the town of Bath as the country's first spa. Bath is still the municipality's official name, despite being known to the world as—and having the U.S. Postal Service's name of—Berkeley Springs.

Modern Berkeley Springs is a small town with many of its historic structures intact, but it is thriving as it never has. Numerous spas cater to travelers, providing stress relief through therapeutic soaks in the mineral waters, skin treatments, and massages of every known kind. (It is said that there are more certified massage therapists in town than there are lawyers.) Along with this renewed popularity have

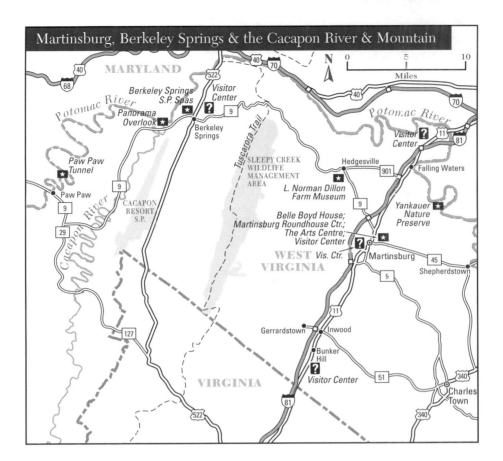

come some of the state's finest restaurants and a reputation as one of the best small art towns in America.

For escapes into the natural world, there's the 6,000-acre **Cacapon** (pronounced *kuh KAY pun*) **Resort State Park**, 23,000-acre **Sleepy Creek Wildlife Management Area**, and the Potomac and Cacapon rivers.

COMMUNITIES Bunker Hill is near the site of where the first settler in what became West Virginia, Morgan Morgan, built his log cabin. It's now a small community along US 11, just a couple of miles north of the Virginia border.

Gerrardstown was established in 1784 and contains many of its original buildings, including the 1743 Hays-Gerrard House.

The small village of **Paw Paw**, named for the fruit that grows on the hillsides around it, is located along the bends of the Potomac River and was where the C&O Canal met the B&O Railroad in 1850. Today, WV 9 provides the only highway crossing of the Potomac River between Hancock and Cumberland in Maryland.

GUIDANCE Berkeley Springs Visitors Center/Travel Berkeley Springs (304-258-9147; 1-800-447-8797; www.berkeleysprings.com), 127 Fairfax St., Berkeley Springs 25411. Located a block away from Berkeley Springs State Park, this is by far one of the most complete and organized visitor centers in the state. Ask about a topic, and not only can they tell you about it personally, but most likely they will have a pamphlet describing it in detail. Among the pamphlet topics available are outdoor recreation, boating, driving tours, walking tours, spas, and arts and culture.

Martinsburg–Berkeley County Convention and Visitors Bureau (304-264-8801; www.travelwv.com), 115 N. Queen St., Martinsburg 25401. The visitors center has an active staff able to provide needed information.

Two **West Virginia Welcome Centers** are located on I-81. The center for northbound travelers (304-229-8836) is 2 miles north of the Virginia line, while the one for southbound lanes (304-272-2281) is 1 mile south of the West Virginia–Maryland border.

GETTING THERE *By air*: **Hagerstown Regional Airport** (240-313-2777) in Maryland is the closest air facility and provides scheduled passenger commuter service to and from **Baltimore/Washington International Airport** (1-800-I FLY BWI; www.bwiairport.com).

Washington Dulles International Airport (703-572-2700; www.metwashair ports.com/dulles) is a little more than an hour's drive away. A bit farther away is **Reagan Washington National Airport** (703-417-8000; www.mwaa.com/reagan), and between Baltimore and Washington, DC, is the **Baltimore/Washington International Airport** (1-800-I-FLY-BWI; www.bwiairport.com). It is possible to take public transportation from all three of the DC-area airports to Union Station

ENJOY A PAWPAW

Found in many places in West Virginia, the pawpaw tree is usually a large shrub, but it can grow to 40 feet tall. The pawpaw's triangular flowers are green when they first open, but they turn to deep red and brown as they grow. Some people say they have a fragrance akin to wine. The 4- to 5-inch fruit, which resembles a short, fat banana, follows the same pattern. At first green, it ripens to a purple-brown from mid-Aug. to Oct. At one time it was a food source for rural families and is still considered somewhat of a delicacy by many people.

The best way to enjoy a pawpaw is fresh off the tree. Cut it open, scoop out the flesh, and be sure to discard the seeds, which are poisonous. Some people say the creamy white to orange flesh has the consistency of custard or yogurt and tastes like a very ripe banana, with hints of mango and pineapple. Enjoy, and eat away. Pawpaws contain three times as much vitamin C as an apple, twice as much riboflavin as an orange, about the same potassium as a banana, and lots of amino acids.

in Washington, DC. From there you could take rail transportation into Martinsburg (see *By rail*).

By car: **I-81** is the major four-lane highway that brings you into the area from the north or south. You could also arrive from Hancock, Maryland, by way of **I-70** and **US 522** or Winchester, Virginia, via **US 522**.

By rail: On weekdays, commuter trains run by **MARC**—the Maryland Rail Commuter service (1-800-RIDE-MTA; www.mtamaryland.com)—have eastbound runs that stop in Martinsburg in the morning on the way to Washington, DC, and trains that return from the nation's capital in the evening.

AMTRAK's (1-800-872-7245; www.Amtrak.com) *Capitol Limited* arrives from Chicago in the morning. A westbound train makes a stop in town in the evening.

GETTING AROUND *By bus*: **Eastern Panhandle Transit Authority** (304-263-0876; www.pantran.com), the local bus company, enables you to take public transportation to major points in the Eastern Panhandle. A complete schedule is available on their Web site.

By car: Running in an east–west direction along the length of the Eastern Panhandle, **WV 9** is the route that you will use to explore much of the area.

By taxi: **Courtesy Cab** (304-267-8294) services Martinsburg and the surrounding area.

MEDICAL EMERGENCIES

Berkeley Springs
War Memorial Hospital (304-258-1234; www.warmemorialhospital.com), 109 War Memorial Dr.

Martinsburg
City Hospital (304-264-1000; www.cityhospital.org), Dry Run Rd.

✳ To See

DRIVING TOURS, SCENIC & HISTORIC The **Washington Heritage Trail**. As much of a scenic drive as it is a trip through history, the 137-mile heritage trail loops around the entire Eastern Panhandle, bringing you past just about everything mentioned in this book for the region. It's a good way to get around without really having to think on the logistics of doing it. A brochure is available from any of the places mentioned in *Guidance*.

A small pamphlet available from the **Martinsburg-Berkeley County Convention and Visitors Bureau** (see *Guidance*) describes a historical driving tour of the county that takes in more than 25 sites and is so extensive that it may take most of a day to accomplish. Even if you don't have the time or inclination to do the entire tour, at least take a look at the stone **Vanmetre Ford Bridge** (on WV 36, 2.6 miles east of Martinsburg), which looks very much like the more famous Burnside Bridge at Antietam National Battlefield in Maryland. Built in 1832, it is the oldest intact bridge still in use in West Virginia. Also consider the short drive north to the spot where the Potomac River flows beside the **Dam No. 4 Hydroelectric Plant**. This is not a modern, imposing structure, but a small brick building built in 1909 that leaves the area looking quite scenic and inviting for picnicking and fishing. The plant is the only known rope turbine electric generator plant in the world.

HISTORIC CHURCHES The small village of Hedgesville was established at a well-traveled gap in North Mountain in 1832 by Josiah Hedges. Amazingly, much of the town is still comprised primarily of the original log buildings that were built between 1832 and the Civil War. Of particular interest are three churches: The brick **Mount Zion Episcopal Church** (304-702-7111; www.mtzionhedgesville .com) on WV 9 was built in 1818 and is still used for Sunday services. At 200 East Main St., the **Hedgesville Presbyterian Church** (304-754-3039; www.hedges villepres.org) is noted for its Carpenter Gothic architecture. The **Hedges Chapel** (304-754-8258) at 668 Mountain Lake Rd. is a log church built in 1859.

HISTORIC SITES **Morgan Cabin** (304-229-8946). Drive US 11 less than 2 miles south of Inwood, turn right onto WV 26, and come to the cabin, in Bunker Hill, about 2.5 miles later. Usually open June–Aug., Sun. 2–4. Donations accepted. Morgan Morgan was the first European settler in what was to become West Virginia, and this cabin is a testament to how hearty our ancestors were. He built a crude cabin when he first arrived in 1728 and, during the next three years, sifted sand from Mill Creek, cut trees, saved hair from animals, and quarried stone to build this cabin for his family. Remember, this was in addition to the usual chores of everyday life. On your way back to US 11, stop at the 1851 Greek Revival **Morgan Chapel** (also on WV 26) to visit the site of the first Episcopal church in West Virginia and Mr. Morgan's final resting place.

MUSEUMS

Berkeley Springs

⚓ **Museum of the Berkeley Springs** (304-258-9147; 1-800-447-8797; www .museumoftheberkeleysprings.com), on the second floor of the Roman Bath House, Fairfax St. Open Sat.–Sun. Closed Jan. Donations accepted. A small museum that explores how the springs affected the development and growth of the town. Most interesting to me was the display about the tomato industry that made use of the water and flourished for a while.

Hedgesville

✎ **L. Norman Dillon Farm Museum** (304-267-7519), intersection of Ridge Rd. and WV 9. Open Apr.–Oct., Sat. and Sun. 1–5. Donations accepted. Founder L. Norman Dillon worked the soil for many years and wanted to make sure that people did not forget their connection to the land. The museum has plans to greatly expand,

MORGAN CABIN

but even now you could spend a few hours perusing the hundreds of farm implements (some older than the Civil War), viewing the blacksmith shop, or watching the cultivation of the 8-acre wheat field. Special events are geared toward the kids.

Martinsburg

⊤ **Belle Boyd House Museum** (304-267-4713; www.bchs.org), 126 East Race St. Open weekdays (except Wed.) and Sat. Donations accepted. Belle Boyd and her family moved into this Greek Revival home in 1853. For nearly two years during the War Between the States, Belle (described in one tourist pamphlet as a beautiful Southern aristocrat) stayed in the home of her aunt in nearby Front Royal, Virginia, and used her charms to extract military secrets from Union forces. Local lore says she invited Gen. Nathaniel Banks to the home one evening and overheard him discussing upcoming maneuvers with his officers. That night she rode horseback 15 miles to apprise Stonewall Jackson of the situation. Marching through a gap in Massanutten Mountain, Jackson's troops surprised the Union forces on the morning of May 23, 1862, capturing nearly every soldier of the garrison.

In addition to retaining the original floors, staircase, and pocket doors, the museum contains multiple rooms of artifacts pertaining to the Boyd family, the Civil War, and the history of Martinsburg.

This is quite an impressive museum, especially in light of the fact that it is operated by the local historical society, which only asks for donations from visitors. Next door is the **Archives and Research Center**, whose vast collection of historical and genealogical information, with documents going back to the original land grants for the three Eastern Panhandle counties, is available to anyone. (Also see *Gardens.*)

SCENIC VIEWS ✪ It is just a 3-mile drive from Berkeley Springs on WV 9 to take in one of the most stirring views in the Eastern Panhandle—one that so impressed George Washington and his contemporaries that they rode many miles on horseback numerous times just to see it. **Panorama Overlook**, once known as Prospect Peak, sits at the northern end of 30-mile-long Cacapon Mountain. No matter the name, this is a soaring viewpoint. From hundreds of feet above the valley floor, you look onto three states—Pennsylvania, West Virginia, and Maryland—and the meeting of the Cacapon and Potomac rivers.

In 1796, Lawrence Augustine Washington, George's nephew, was moved to write that it was "one of the wildest, sublimest and most interesting views of mountain country interspersed with cultivated valleys and rivers." The Museum of Natural History in New York says it is the fifth-best view in the United States, and another organization rates it the 10th finest in the world.

All you have to do to enjoy this is make a short drive—do not miss it. Besides, after enjoying the view, you can dine at one of the area's best restaurants, Panorama at the Peak (see *Dining Out*).

OTHER SITES Berkeley Castle, WV 9. Perched on the hillside overlooking Berkeley Springs, the Berkeley Castle, complete with battlements and a three-story tower, may make you think you have been transported to medieval Europe. The sandstone structure was built in the 1880s as a wedding gift from Col. Samuel Taylor to his bride, Rosa Pelham. The castle is privately owned (visitors were once

THINGS TO LOOK FORWARD TO—OR TO DO NOW

Martinsburg Roundhouse Center (304-269-4141; www.martinsburground house.com), 100 East Liberty St., Martinsburg. Please call as the restoration is going slowly and regular tours have been temporarily suspended. For more than 100 years, 1848 to 1988, the roundhouse served the railroad industry in West Virginia. In 1990, vandals burned the East Roundhouse, and the entire complex fell into disrepair.

The Berkeley County Roundhouse Authority has plans to preserve and rehabilitate the complex, bringing much of it back to its original look while turning the facility into a center for commercial and artistic endeavors.

Yet you can visit today and have a guided tour, walking through the cavernous buildings, marveling at the architectural beauty of the roundhouse's dome rafters and imagining giant locomotives being turned around on the roundtable, which still works.

𝕋 **The Arts Centre** (304-263-0224; www.theartcentre.org), 229 East Martin St., Martinsburg. In 2005, the Arts Centre moved from small facilities in the Boarman Building to expansive spaces in the historic Federal Building. It will take years of work and many dollars to bring the center up to what supporters envision it will one day be. In the meantime, they are making use of what they can, and art exhibits, classes, and performances are presented as time and space permit. Like the Martinsburg Roundhouse, it's worth a visit just to take a look at the historic architecture and aspects of the place.

INSIDE THE MARTINSBURG ROUNDHOUSE CENTER

permitted to take tours), but that can't stop you from admiring it as you walk around town.

✳ To Do

BICYCLING The **C&O Canal** across the Potomac River in Maryland has the best biking in the area, and it can be accessed from WV 9 at Paw Paw or US 522 at Hancock, Maryland, a few miles north of Berkeley Springs. For more information see *Hiking—Paw Paw Tunnel* in this chapter and *Bicycling* in the "Where the Potomac and Shenandoah Meet—Harpers Ferry, Charles Town, and Shepherdstown" chapter.

BIRDING See *Green Space—Nature Preserve* and *Green Space—Wildlife Management Area.*

BOAT RENTALS ✍ **Cacapon Resort State Park** (304-258-1022; www.cacapon resort.com), 818 Cacapon Lodge Dr., on US 522 approximately 10 miles south of Berkeley Springs. Rowboats and paddleboats are available for rent by the half hour for excursions on the park's lake.

BOWLING

Berkeley Springs
✍ **Berkeley Springs Bowlerama** (304-258-1815; www.bsbowlerama.com), 4909 Valley Rd., 7 miles south of Berkeley Springs on US 522. Open daily. Fourteen lanes of 10-pin bowling.

Martinsburg
✍ **Pikeside Bowl** (304-267-2042), 3485 Winchester Ave. Ten-pin and duckpin lanes, with laser bowling and a live DJ on Sat. evening.

FAMILY ACTIVITIES ✍ **Timber Ridge Go-Karts** (304-258-4888), 11180 Valley Rd., on US 522 a short distance south of Cacapon Resort State Park. Old tires line the track to make sure everyone stays on course while going as fast as possible in the go-carts.

Wonderment Puppet Theater (304-258-4074; www.wondermentpuppets.com, 412 West King St., Martinsburg. Shows every Sat. and Sun at noon and 2. With close to two decades of experience as a puppeteer, Jeff Santoro entertains the family with puppet shows of his own creation, often based on traditional fairy tales and stories that the children are familiar with. If the kids really get into it, they may purchase finger and hand puppets in the theater's gift shop.

FISHING The **Potomac** and **Cacapon rivers** are the major streams to head for in this area, with bass being what most anglers are looking to catch. However, you may be pleasantly surprised at the numbers of channel catfish, rock bass, walleye, and tiger muskie, too. One of the easiest access points for the Potomac is at the Dam No. 4 Hydroelectric Plant on WV 5/7 close to a small community known as Scrabble (northeast of Martinsburg). For the Cacapon River, try the low-water bridge on WV 7, south of Great Cacapon.

The 205-acre lake in **Sleepy Creek Wildlife Management** Area is a quiet place (only paddle and electric motor–powered boats are permitted) to cast for bluegill, crappie, and largemouth bass. On many days, especially in the middle of the week, you may be the only person on the entire lake.

Serious anglers will probably forego **Cacapon Resort State Park**'s small lake, but families looking to have a little fishing fun might enjoy dropping a line into the water in the hope of catching some of the stocked trout and bass.

GOLF

Berkeley Springs

Cacapon Resort State Park (304-258-1022; www.cacaponresort.com), 818 Cacapon Lodge Dr., on US 522 approximately 10 miles south of Berkeley Springs. With some holes set in front of the park's lodge, the 18-hole course was designed by Robert Trent Jones Sr. and has 72 sand traps to test your skill.

Martinsburg

Stonebridge Golf Club (304-263-4653; www.stonebridgegolfcoursewv.com), 1959 Golf Course Rd. With a yardage of 6,253, the course has a history dating from the 1920s. Wide, open meadows and rolling hills look up to the surrounding ridges.

Woodbrier Golf Course (304-274-9818), 250 Topflite Dr. A nine-hole public course.

HIKING Traversing the 30-plus miles of the **Tuscarora Trail** (see "What's Where in West Virginia" at the front of this book for background information) in the Eastern Panhandle is like going back in time to like the Appalachian Trail before it became world famous and crowded with people. It can seem as if the forest is yours alone as you walk for hours and sometimes days, without meeting other people.

The pathway enters the state at the southern end of the **Sleepy Creek Wildlife Management Area** (see *Green Space—Wildlife Management Area*), which it passes through for 20 miles by going by Sleepy Creek Lake and four designated campgrounds. The last 10 miles are on a combination of private lands and public roadways before the route crosses the Potomac River and enters Maryland.

Paw Paw

The **Paw Paw Tunnel** is along the C&O Canal in Maryland, but it's just across the Potomac River, and it is such a good attraction that to leave it out of this book would have been a disservice to you.

Like so many other things associated with the canal, construction of the 3,118-foot tunnel faced difficulties and miscalculations from the onset. Intense friction among camps of Irish, English, and German laborers—in conjunction with a cholera epidemic—compounded the problems. Originally estimated to be built within two years at a cost of $33,500, it took 14 years and more than $600,000 to complete. Once finished, though, the tunnel—lined with close to 6 million bricks in layers of seven to 11 deep—was used from 1850 to the canal's demise in 1924.

Drive to the tunnel from Paw Paw by taking WV 9 across the Potomac River (the road becomes MD51) and continuing about 0.5 mile to the C&O Canal parking area. Hike 0.5 mile along the canal towpath and break out your flashlights as you enter the 0.6-mile-long tunnel. The pathway is usually wet and slippery, so use the provided handrail. Some of the boards are the original lumber, and your hand can feel the grooves worn into it from years of towropes sliding across.

Once on the other side, you can either retrace your steps through the tunnel or, for a bit of variation, consider hiking the Tunnel Hill Trail up and over the ridgeline the tunnel passes through.

HOW DO YOU SPELL THAT?
Through the centuries, the Cacapon River has had numerous variations on its name. Historians have found at least eight: Calapechan, Cape-cape-pe-hon, Cape Caps, Caor-Capon, Cacapahaowen, Cape-Capon, Cacapehon, and Cacapetion.

Also see Cacapon Resort State Park under *Lodging* and *Green Space—Parks*.

HORSEBACK RIDING 🐎 **Cacapon Resort State Park** (304-258-1022; www .cacaponresort.com), 818 Cacapon Lodge Dr., on US 522 approximately 10 miles south of Berkeley Springs. From stables close to the golf course, you can take guided rides of one, two, three, and six hours on trails that are separate from the park's hiking trails. Minimum age is 10, and reservations a day in advance are requested.

KAYAKING & CANOEING From a put-in at Paw Paw, you can paddle the **Potomac River** downstream for 50 miles or more, most of the time on easy flat water, or, at the most, encountering Class I challenges. Old dams may be the most dangerous things, so always be on the lookout for them. However, this is a nice stretch of river, with high cliffs coming down to the water in some places, while other areas are wide and sunny.

Driving from Largent to Great Cacapon on WV 9 is less than 15 miles, but a float trip along the twisting and winding **Cacapon River** from an informal put-in on WV 9 at Largent to Great Cacapon lasts close to 22 miles. Miles of the river pass through high, narrow gorges, with never more than Class II water to face.

Head to the 205-acre lake in **Sleepy Creek Wildlife Management Area** (see *Green Space—Wildlife Management Area*) if you want a peaceful, easy day, or are taking out a novice friend to help him or her get the feel of paddling without facing any hardships.

SPAS 🌿 **Atasia Spa** (304-258-7888; 1-877-258-7888; www.atasiaspa.com), 41 Congress St., Berkeley Springs. The atmosphere is one of the most important aspects of a spa, and owner Frankie Tan, a Malaysian native who studied massage at a Buddhist temple in Thailand, has converted one of the town's historic homes into one of its most pleasant spas. Chinese scrolls on the wall, terry-lined robes, and restful music blend to create a relaxing environment for whirlpools, wraps, exfoliations, and a variety of massages. Before starting my reflexology treatment, which is a type of hand and foot massage, my therapist claimed I would become more relaxed than if I had a full body massage. How right he was.

⬩ **The Bath House** (304-258-9071; 1-800-431-4698; www.bathhouse.com), 21 Fairfax St., Berkeley Springs. Open daily. Besides being a retail establishment that sells oils, salts, gels, and locally made soaps, The Bath House has certified and licensed therapists providing shiatsu, Reiki, Swedish, and deep muscle massage, along with aroma steam cabinets and soakings in the town's famed mineral water. A specialty here is LaStone massage, a type of thermal therapy where warm and cool basalt rocks are placed on the body.

Upstairs is the spa's **Park View Suite**, a large suite with TVs, full kitchen, bath, and living room overlooking the springs of Berkeley Springs State Park. $189; special massage packages available.

⬩ **Five Senses Spa** (304-258-2210; 1-866-458-2210; www.thecountryinnat berkeleysprings.com), 110 S. Washington St., Berkeley Springs. The Five Senses Spa, a part of The Country Inn at Berkeley Springs (see *Lodging*), is a labyrinth of floors, stairs, and elevators perched on the hillside overlooking the town. This is a plus, as I learned when I opened the door to my private hydrotherapy room. Giant picture windows let the sunshine in and allowed me to purvey the scenery while relaxing in a huge whirlpool mineral bath. Other treatments include various massages, body treatments, and skin and nail care. Special day packages, as well as overnight ones, are available.

Also see Berkeley Springs State Park under *Green Space—Parks*.

SWIMMING Lifeguards watch over swimmers taking advantage of the small beach on **Cacapon Resort State Park**'s lakeshore. There's also a bathhouse with showers and a snack bar. The pool in **Berkeley Springs State Park** is filled with the town's famous mineral springs water and is open during the summer months.

TENNIS Courts are available to the public in **Cacapon Resort State Park**.

WALKING TOURS

Berkeley Springs

You are going to be walking around town visiting all of the spas, shops, art galleries, and restaurants, so why not pick up free copies of *Walking Tour of Berkeley Springs* and *The Town of Bath* at the visitors center (see *Guidance*) and learn about history and architecture while you're wandering around? The walking tour describes many of the buildings along the main streets, while the town brochure provides short biographies of the owners of every one of the town's original 131 lots. You'll find out things such as George and Sally Fairfax served tea to George and Martha Washington in the house on Lot #55, and that Washington owned the two lots on the corner of Fairfax and Mercer streets.

Martinsburg

A small pamphlet available from the **Martinsburg–Berkeley County Convention and Visitors Bureau** (see *Guidance*) describes a tour of five of the town's seven historic districts. Most brochures of this kind focus on either history or architecture; this one provides a bit of both. Among the 24 sites are the Berkeley County Courthouse, where Belle Boyd was held after her arrest as a Confederate spy; an ornate Queen Anne house complete with pedimented dormers and rounded corner towers; and an 1883 High Victorian Gothic high school. (They don't build them like that anymore.)

✳ Green Space

GARDENS Belle Boyd House Museum (304-267-4713; www.bchs.org), 126 East Race St., Martinsburg. Open weekdays (except Wed.) and Sat. Donations accepted. (See *To See—Museums* for more information.) The rose was Belle Boyd's favorite flower, and museum curator Don Wood (who has also been responsible for having 3,000 sites placed on the National Register of Historic Places!) has cultivated more than 150 rosebushes in the museum's courtyard. With new and old varieties, something is always in bloom May–Nov. There is also a small herb garden with plants that were used medicinally and in cooking during the 1800s.

NATURE PRESERVE Yankauer Nature Preserve (304-676-3397; www .potomacaudubon.org). From Martinsburg, follow Berkeley Station Rd. for 6.3 miles and turn left onto Whitings Neck Rd. for 0.5 mile. Open dawn to dusk daily. Managed by The Nature Conservancy of West Virginia and the Potomac Audubon Society, the 104-acre preserve borders the Potomac River and has about 2 miles of trails (open only to foot travel). The pathways wind through a landscape that is recovering from past agricultural use with a diversity of wildflowers and more than 116 species of birds. Among those that have been identified are pileated and hairy woodpeckers, warblers, scarlet tanagers, wood thrushes, and yellow-billed cuckoos. About the only other people you encounter may be a few local neighbors out for a morning stroll.

PARKS ♪ **Berkeley Springs State Park** (304-258-2711; www.berkeleysprings sp.com), 2 South Washington St., Berkeley Springs. Berkeley Springs State Park is unlike any other state park you will visit in West Virginia, and possibly in the country. There are no trails, campgrounds, lodges, golf courses, horseback rides, or even woodlands. Located in the center of town, the 5-acre park is a health spa whose origins can be traced to 1776, when George Washington's family and friends established a business of using the mineral springs that flow from Warm Springs Mountain. None of the original buildings still stand, but visitors can soak in 102-degree water in 750-gallon sunken tile tubs in the 1815 Roman bathhouse, or receive massages, infrared heat treatments, and other forms of physiotherapy in the 1929 main bathhouse. (Call 304-258-2711 for reservations.)

At the base of the mountain, the springs flow from five principal sources into wide, stone-lined races that attract children and adults alike to wade in the constant 74.3-degree water. The public swimming pool, which is open during the summer, is also filled with the spring water. Proving that this is a state-operated facility and not a for-profit corporation, you can fill up jugs of water—for free—from the public tap in a pavilion next to the Roman baths.

♪ ᴋ **Cacapon Resort State Park** (304-258-1022; www.cacaponresort.com), 818 Cacapon Lodge Dr., on US 522 approximately 10 miles south of Berkeley Springs. Just as the federal government had purchased land for Shenandoah National Park in Virginia and Catoctin Mountain Park in Maryland, the state of West Virginia obtained land for Cacapon State Park in 1934, in part to demonstrate how parks for recreation and conservation could be created from worn-out lands. Earlier owners and settlers had, for more than a century, clear-cut many acres of forest for timber, stripped oak trees of their bark for tanning, and employed farming practices unsuited to the region's terrain and soil.

Men of the Civilian Conservation Corps (CCC), camped in what is now the main picnic area, busily built trails, shelters, fire roads, and various visitor attractions. Many of the facilities they constructed, such as the Old Inn (check out the hand-wrought-iron chandeliers in the lounge to appreciate the quality of CCC craftsmanship), hand-cut stone walls, and a few guest cabins, are still in use.

So many other amenities have been added through the years that the park is now known as Cacapon Resort State Park, complete with a large lodge, restaurant, rental cabins, swimming and boat rentals in a small lake, horseback riding, picnic and playground areas, tennis courts, nature center, and an 18-hole golf course designed by Robert Trent Jones Sr. There is no campground, and backcountry camping is not permitted. The park does have one of the most active nature and recreation programs I have ever come across in a state or national park. The schedule for just one week during the summer can list as many as 24 different activities. Among other things, you may find yourself wading a stream in search of crayfish and salamanders, identifying birdsongs while on a morning stroll, or roasting marshmallows around an evening campfire.

Yet, all of the facilities, and many of the activities, are concentrated on just a few hundred acres, which enables hikers to use more than 20 miles of trails (one walking path is handicapped accessible) to explore the remainder of the park's 6,115 acres, which have been left in a natural and lightly visited state.

A very special hike to a view overlooking the Cacapon River follows a grassy fire road along the top ridge more than 12 miles to Prospect Rock, where George Washington and other 18th- and 19th-century visitors often rode on horseback. The fire road begins at the spectacular Cacapon Mountain Overlook, which provides a panoramic view of the entire Sleepy Creek Mountain to the east and is accessible by automobile from late spring to early fall. Although the hike is on relatively easy terrain, remember it is 12 miles one way, and no camping is permitted in the park.

WILDLIFE MANAGEMENT AREA Sleepy Creek Wildlife Management Area (304-822-3551; administered by the West Virginia Division of Natural Resources office at 1 Depot St., Romney). Stretching for 16 miles along two parallel ridgelines and encompassing close to 23,000 acres, the wildlife management area is home to wild turkeys, bear, deer, Carolina chickadees, tufted titmice, northern mockingbirds, and several species of warblers. In the valley between the two mountains is a 205-acre lake that has been producing some state-record bass in the last few years. Four primitive designated campgrounds (with pit toilets) are spread out along the eastern side of the lake, which has had pairs of nesting osprey in recent years. The long-distance Tuscarora Trail (see *To Do—Hiking*) passes through the length of the area and connects with a few other pathways that see very little use (or maintenance, so be prepared). Come here anytime other than hunting season, and you may be the only person on the lake or the entire 23,000 acres.

✳ Lodging

RESORTS

Berkeley Springs 25411

& **Cacapon Resort State Park** (304-258-1022; www.cacaponresort.com), 818 Cacapon Lodge Dr., on US 522 approximately 10 miles south of Berkeley Springs. Motel-type rooms (some quite small by today's standards), cottages with kitchens, and log cabins enable you to enjoy the park without having to leave in the evening. (Also see *Green Space—Parks*.)

INN

Berkeley Springs 25411

The Country Inn at Berkeley Springs (304-258-2210; 1-866-458-2210; www.thecountryinnatberkeley springs.com), 110 S. Washington St. The antebellum look of two-story columns, brick exterior, and multiple flagpoles make The Country Inn at Berkeley Springs one of the first buildings to catch your eye as you enter the main part of town. Offered are a number of suites and more than 60 guest rooms, and while the rooms in the newer part are nice enough (modern motel setup with oak furniture), try to reserve one in the original 1933 structure. You may have to share a bath, but these rooms have character, each one being different and decorated with its own blend of antiques and reproductions, and giving easy access to the inn's **West Virginia Room** (see *Eating Out*). With such a wide range of accommodations, the rates go from $79–289. Special packages are also available that include treatments at the inn's Five Senses Spa (see *To Do—Spas*).

BED & BREAKFASTS

Berkeley Springs 25411

Inn on Fairfax (304-258-2210; www .theinnonfairfax.com), 151 Fairfax St. This B&B is just one block from the center of town, has hosts that have been in the hospitality business for years, and four guest rooms and a suite. I liked the back room with its sunporch, and the fact that each bath has a 10-inch showerhead. $125–200.

The Manor Inn (304-258-1552; 1-800-974-5770; www.bathmanorinn .com), 234 Fairfax St. Huge old trees, a mansard shingled roof, dormer windows, and lush paint colors all make for an appealing greeting when you first drive up to The Manor Inn. Walk inside the 1870s Second Empire Victorian home, and you find 12-foot ceilings, original floors, a curved staircase, and French doors opening onto the wide, gingerbread-trim porch. Ellen and Wesley Lewis obviously enjoy their home and the fact that they are able to share it with others. Guest rooms are furnished in antiques, and a bountiful breakfast is served in the morning—on the porch if weather conditions are good. Only two blocks from the center of town. $95–140.

Sleepy Creek Mountain Inn (304-258-0234; 1-877-258-0234; www .sleepycreekmountaininn.com), 877 Winstead Rd. Located east of town. Dale Winstead, retired from the Army Corps of Engineers, invites guests into the home where he was raised. The outside has been covered with aluminum siding, but inside are the original 1800s walls of long, huge logs, and a stone fireplace that provides the inn with a homey and inviting atmosphere. In addition to enjoying my morning breakfasts and conversations with Dale, I especially liked being able to wander around on his 128-acre farm (half in meadow, half in forest) and sit on the porch rocker or the patio to gaze at the Sleepy Creek Mountain ridgeline. This is a wonderfully quiet respite from a noisy and busy world. $130–175. A carriage house ($175) is available for those who prefer complete privacy.

🐾 ✎ 🌿 **Sleepy Creek Tree Farm Bed and Breakfast** (304-258-4324; 304-275-8303; www.virtualcities.com /ons/wv/p/wvp6801.htm), 37 Shades Lane. Surround by an 8-acre tree farm, and almost looking like a modern cottage you would find in the English countryside, Kerry Noon's home has two guest rooms that share a bath, and a sitting area with large windows to gaze upon the small pond and out to Sleepy Creek Mountain. Kerry is a resourceful type who did all of the interior finishing of the house herself. The B&B is just a few yards from Sleepy Creek, where you can fish, tube, or swim. Rates start at $80.

Hedgesville, 25427

Cider Mill House Bed and Breakfast (304-754-6643; www.cidermill house.com), 130 Fourth Bridge Rd. Located on acres of a working farm, whose grounds and trails are open to guests for wandering and relaxation; you might even be invited to experience some of the farmwork, such as sheep shearing and produce harvesting. Many of the farm items end up on the breakfast table. The stone home, built in the 1800s, is furnished with items reflecting the period. $95–125.

Martinsburg 25401

Aspen Hall Inn (304-260-1750; www .wvbnbs.com/inns/44.html), 405 Boyd Ave. The only B&B-type accommodation in Martinsburg is the 1750s Aspen Hall Inn. Designed by the owners for extended corporate stays, they will accept one-night guests if their schedule permits. Hopefully, it will, because you are in for a pleasant stay. Innkeepers Rebecca Frye and Charles Connolly are interpreters at nearby Fort Frederick in Maryland, and their

regard for history is evident throughout the house. In fact, the antiques portraits of former owners, and original 40-inch boards and batten doors make it feel as if you are staying in a historic home that people would pay to take tours of. In the front yard there is even the shell of Menhenhall's Fort, where George Washington stationed troops during the French and Indian War. The home sits on 7 acres, and a short trail takes you over Tuscarora Creek (stocked with trout) to the ruins of an old mill. $115–170.

Also see Maria's Garden and Inn and Grandma's Country Kitchen and Inn under *Eating Out.*

SUITES AND HOUSES

Berkeley Springs 25411

Bathkeeper's Cottage (304-258-1088; www.virtualcities.com/vacation /wv/b/wvb12v1.htm), 146 South Washington St. The little Bathkeeper's Cottage is located within a block of

ASPEN HALL INN

Berkeley Springs State Park and is on the home grounds of John Davis, who was bathkeeper from 1849 to 1896. The cottage is set back from the main road by several hundred feet and has gardens that grow beside softly flowing Warm Springs Run, making it a nice choice for honeymooners or couples who want to feel they are separated from everyone else, but still have quick walking access to the town's spas and restaurants. $125.

🐾 ❦ **Berkeley House** (304-947-7314; www.berkeleyhousewv.com), College Ave. A home built at the turn of the 20th century and located three blocks from the center of town, the Berkeley House has simple accommodations and welcomes children and pets. There's a kitchen, sunporch, pool table, piano, Jacuzzi, and video player. Provisions for a continental-style breakfast will be in the home when you arrive. $190 for one couple, $280 for two couples, and $310 for three couples.

Also see The Bath House (see *To Do— Spas*).

VACATION RENTALS There are so many rental homes in the Berkeley Springs area—more than 100—that descriptions of them would fill several books. Everything from small, rustic cabins dating from Civil War days to multiple-bedroom luxury homes are available. Some are located in town, while others are nestled in quiet, out-of-the-way places beside creeks or on mountains with nice views. In a sign of the times, some include free computer and Internet access. Information on most of the individually rented places may be obtained from the Berkeley Springs Visitors Center (see *Guidance*). However, a couple of companies manage the bulk of the rentals:

Berkeley Springs 25411
Berkeley Springs Cottage Rentals (304-258-5300; 1-866-682-2246; www .berkeleyspringscottagerentals.com), 120 Independence St.

Mountain Morning Vacations (304-258-1718; www.mountainmorning.net), 867 Libby's Ridge Rd.

CABINS

Berkeley Springs 25411
Gobblers' Knob (304-258-3605; www .virtualcities.com/vacation/wv/p/wvpa8v 10.htm), 2442 Creek Rd. *Mid-Atlantic Country* magazine devoted six pages to extolling the qualities of this log cabin, so I'm just going to be able to touch on highlights in a couple of paragraphs.

Richard and Sylvia Thomas have loving restored the four-room 1820s log cabin, which now has a covered porch, soapstone wood-burning stove, and an addition with a kitchen, mud room, bathroom, and whirlpool tub. The couple spent days removing whitewash from the logs, so the interior walls show the original beauty of the wood. Spinning wheels, pierced tin lampshades, old tools and rifles, antiques appropriate to the period, and fireplace tools made by local blacksmith Glenn Horr all come together to create a rustic, but pleasurable and pampered, atmosphere. The cabin sits a few hundred feet from the Thomases' home, but no other houses are in sight, so enjoy the quiet seclusion. $250 for two for the evening; a group of six could stay for $1,015 a week.

Also see Cacapon Resort State Park under *Green Space—Parks*.

CAMPGROUNDS

Falling Waters 25419
Falling Waters Campsite (304-274-2791; 1-800-527-4902; www.falling

waterscampsite.com), 7685 Williamsport Pike. A small family-owned campground located close to I-81, exit 20, that caters primarily to RV travelers along the interstate.

Hedgesville 25427
Lazy A Camping (304-229-8185; www.lazyacamping.com), 2741 Back Creek Valley Rd. Pull-in sites with some tent sites available.

For more primitive tent camping, see **Sleepy Creek Wildlife Management Area** under *Green Space— Wildlife Management Area.*

✳ Where to Eat
DINING OUT
Berkeley Springs
✪ **Lot 12 Public House** (304-258-6264; www.lot12.com), 117 Warren St. Open Thurs.-Sun. for dinner; closed Jan. Reservations strongly suggested. I almost melted into the chair the moment the toasted gnocchi passed by my lips. How could something so simple as a ball of flour taste so wonderful? The same was true with the coq au vin, chicken in red wine with cremini mushrooms. And even the mashed potatoes—mashed potatoes, mind you—were simply divine.

Obviously, I could go on and on, but suffice it to say that chef-owner Damien Heath makes everything about Lot 12 perfect, from the honeydew melon sorbet intermezzo and the local art on the walls to the knowledgeable wait staff. The menu changes seasonally to make use of fresh items from the local area. Look for crisp roasted duck, pecan-crusted trout fillet, grilled spice-rubbed pork chop, herbed goat cheese, and sautéed wild ramps to show up from time to time. A nice wine list, microbrews, and cognacs add to the experience.

This is dining you should not miss; Lot 12 is currently my favorite West Virginia restaurant. If the weather is nice, reserve one of the few outdoor tables. Entrées $23–30.

⌗ **Panorama at the Peak** (304-258-0050; www.panoramaatthepeak.com), on WV 9, 9.3 miles southwest of Berkeley Springs at the Panorama Overlook. Open for dinner Thurs.–Sun. Proprietors Leslie Hotaling and Patti Miller spent close to three decades in private business and civil service, and they told me they knew almost nothing about restaurants before opening this one. That may be, but what little knowledge they had has gone a long way in making this an extremely popular establishment. I strongly recommend reservations on Fri. and Sat. nights.

Everything was just right with my salmon bisque ($5.99) and broiled trout ($20.99). Even the rice pilaf (which is often dry and boring at other places) was moist and flavorful. The menu is always evolving, but other entrées have included salmon with red pepper pesto, eggplant lasagna roll, and filet mignon. It's also worth it to pay the couple of extra dollars to substitute the toasted walnut–watercress salad for the garden salad. Entrées $12.99–27.99.

Make sure you allow enough time before or after your meal to take in the magnificent scene across the road (see *To See—Scenic Views*).

EATING OUT
Berkeley Springs
⌗ ⅙ **Cacapon Resort State Park** (304-258-1022; www.cacaponresort .com), 818 Cacapon Lodge Dr., on US 522 approximately 10 miles south of Berkeley Springs. The park's dining room serves breakfast, lunch, and dinner daily and is known for its weekend seafood buffet.

Tari's Café and Inn (304-258-1196; www.tariscafe.com), 123 North Washington St., Berkeley Springs. Open daily for lunch and dinner.

Tari's is exceptional food served in a stylish atmosphere. There really is a Tari, and she is an imaginative and creative person who uses fresh ingredients—as many from local sources as possible—in her original offerings. The tomato-arugula bisque I started my meal with was perfect, not like other, heavier bisques that can ruin an appetite. The horseradish-Dijon sauce on the cedar-planked salmon came with a roasted corn–pimiento succotash. The pork in Jamaican marinade is glazed with mango barbecue sauce, topped with fruit salsa, and served with ginger-smashed sweet potatoes. The other steak, chicken, and pasta offerings sound just as mouthwatering. Tari's tiramisu is better than any other I've had; the filling was wonderfully thick, like that found in a cannoli or cheesecake. Entrées $15.95–26.95. Lunch has many of the same items at a lower price—and the Blue Plate Specials at $5.99 are a real deal. (Tari sold her restaurant to a longtime employee in 2006, but things have remained pretty much the same—especially since Tari checks in every once in a while.)

Tari's is the place to go for music and a night on the town. Next door to the café, Tari's brings local and regional acts to the tavern, which has its original wood floor and pressed tin ceiling. Together, the café and the tavern are the draws that bring dozens of people downtown in the evening.

Tari's is a gourmet food shop. A number of Tari's creations, such as her salsa and bean soup mix, along with a few select other West Virginia food products, are for sale.

Tari's is an art gallery. In between the café and tavern is the **Wild Women Gallery**, showing the works of area artists and crafters. Some of the art spills over into the café and the tavern, with stained glass highlighting the windows and paintings adorning the walls.

Tari's is accommodations at low cost. Four rooms above the restaurant have private baths, TV, and air-conditioning. As Tari told me when she showed me the rooms, "People shouldn't expect fancy surroundings, and you have to park on the street and climb a flight of stairs, but the rooms are clean, comfortable, and only $59 a night." I concur.

Habenero Mexican (304-596-5667), 100 North Queen St. Open for lunch and dinner; closed Sun. In a Gothic Revival corner building that has been an open-air market, hotel, and jail, the grill's large windows provide a view onto the street and allow sunlight to illuminate the entrées, including traditional Mexican offerings of burritos, tacos, fajitas, and nachos. As the waiter told me, everything is made from scratch daily—the establishment has no freezer, microwave, or can opener! Most entrées are less than $10.

Maria's Garden and Inn (304-258-2021; 1-888-629-2253; www.marias garden.com), 201 Independence St. Open for breakfast, lunch, and dinner daily. The entranceway's image of Our Lady of Guadeloupe sets the stage for the rest of the décor in Peg Perry's restaurant. Religious icons, relics, sculptures, and artwork from around the world, much of it presented to the restaurant by former patrons, adorn walls, tables, and outside grottoes. Peg will be happy to talk with you about her faith, but if you are not so inclined, she will be just as happy to serve you her well-regarded Italian cooking. Whatever you decide on, make sure it contains some of her red sauce, which is heavy and thick from having cooked all day. Seafood and American fare are also available. Entrées $9.95–21.95.

The religious theme is carried onto the second-floor chapel, and the guest rooms on the third floor named for archangels. The rooms are large, nicely furnished, and have TVs, and some have private baths with a Jacuzzi; others share a bath. $75–150; includes a full breakfast in the restaurant.

Mi Ranchito (304-258-4800), 87 North Washington St. Like Chinese restaurants, Mexican restaurants in America are starting to become all the same—same food, same taste, nothing special. Mi Ranchito seems to be working hard not to be that way. The salsa is fresh and spicy, and the veggie burrito I had was better than average. Language barriers with the servers can sometimes lead to amusing misunderstandings. Entrées $7.95–16.95.

West Virginia Room (304-258-2210; www.thecountryinnatberkeleysprings .com), 110 S. Washington St., inside The Country Inn at Berkeley Springs (see *Lodging*). Open daily for breakfast, lunch and dinner. If you are staying at the inn or have just had a massage, this is a convenient choice for sandwiches and a menu of American fare that supports local framers and uses as many organic and all-natural products as possible.

Martinsburg

La Trattoria (304-262-6925), 148 Lutz Ave. Open daily for lunch and dinner. The most popular Italian restaurant in Martinsburg. Business people come here for sandwiches for lunch during the week, families dine on traditional dishes in the evening, and the local teens flock here for the pizza on the weekends. Entrées $8.95–16.95.

Martinsburg Asian Garden Restaurant (304-263-8678), 748 North Foxcroft Ave. Open for lunch and dinner; closed Mon. In the complex of businesses clustered around the mall off I-81, you will find what a number of locals told me is the area's best sushi, made fresh when you order it ($4–12.95). Also on the menu are traditional Japanese and Chinese meals. Entrées $10.95–23.95.

Peking Restaurant (304-263-6544), 139–141 South Queen St. Open daily for lunch and dinner. They offer the

GRANDMA'S COUNTRY KITCHEN AND INN

usual Chinese dishes—moo goo gai pan, egg foo yong, and the like—but do it in a place that is tastefully decorated, not the usual run-of-the-mill Chinese-restaurant décor. With its downtown location, the Peking Restaurant is often packed with workers coming in for the lunch buffet. Entrées $6.95–12.95.

Paw Paw

✎ **Grandma's Country Kitchen and Inn** (304-947-7751), 103 Winchester St. Open daily for breakfast, lunch, and dinner. There are a couple of restaurants in Paw Paw, and this is certainly the better of the two. Nice breakfasts and country cooking, with good homemade desserts, especially the apple dumplings.

If you are biking or hiking on the C&O Canal or paddling the Potomac River, the rooms Grandma's has upstairs would make convenient places to spend the night. Each room is large and has three windows, making it feel bright and airy. The guest washer and dryers might also come in handy after a day outdoors, and you get a full breakfast at the restaurant. $95; children under age 18 stay free.

Grandma's also operates the **Heritage Trail Bed & Breakfast** next door. The four rooms are on the second floor and share a bath. The rate of $78 for two people is a good deal because breakfast at Grandma's is included.

COFFEE BARS Fairfax Coffee House (304-258-8019; www.fairfax coffeehouse.com), 23 Fairfax St., Berkeley Springs. Open daily. There are just a few wooden booths in this small coffeehouse, which also offers lunch items and some baked goods.

SNACKS & GOODIES

Berkeley Springs

Creekside Creamery (304-258-4271), 123 Congress St. Open daily (weekends only Jan.–Feb.) for hand-dipped ice cream and soda-fountain creations.

Heaven Sent Cakes and Sweets (304-258-5429; www.heavensentcakes nsweets.com), 114 North Mercer St. Closed Sun. and Mon. Jane Younker started in the baked-goods business by accident. Thinking she had no real talent for it, she baked a cake for her husband one year, and everyone was so pleased that they made requests for more, and she baked and cooked at home for years before opening her retail business. Her pies, cakes, cookies, and other sweets have now developed into a full-time occupation.

Martinsburg

DeFluri's Fine Chocolates (304-264-3698; www.defluris.com), 130 North

FAIRFAX COFFEE HOUSE

STAR THEATRE

Queen St. Take a look into the production area, and you'll see three lines of chocolatiers busy making truffles, chocolate-covered cherries, caramels, fudges, butter crunches, and more. They must know what they are doing, as DeFluri's was proclaimed the "Best Candy/Confection in the Americas" at an international trade show competition.

Patterson's Old Fashioned Drug Store (304-267-8903; www.pattersons drugstore.com), 134 South Queen St. Stop in on a hot day to sit down at the soda fountain and cool off with a sundae or handmade milk shake. The homemade salads and sandwiches bring in workers looking for a good, quick lunch.

Sweet Inspirations (304-263-0050; www.sweet-inspirations-bakery.com), 531 W. King St. A family-operated business that opened in 2003, Sweet Inspirations serves an array of fresh-baked goods including pies, cookies, muffins, turnovers, tarts, sticky buns, and more. Known far and wide for the

artistry of the chef in creating wedding and other special occasion cakes.

✷ Entertainment
FILM

Berkeley Springs
Star Theatre (304-258-1404; www .starwv.com), Congress and Washington streets. Jeanne Mozier (author of *Way Out in West Virginia—A Must Have Guide to the Oddities and Wonders of the Mountain State*, a most amusing and recommended book about the state) and her husband, Jack Soronen, restored the 1928 theater (originally a brick car garage) in 1977. The cost of a ticket is several dollars lower than other first-run theaters, and the popcorn is cooked in peanut oil in a 1949-model popper and served with real butter. Jeanne picks the films with families in mind. On the occasion when an R-rated film is shown, she makes sure that children under age 17 have a note from their parents. Be sure to stop by at 8 PM on Fri., Sat., or Sun. Meeting affable Jeanne is enough of a reason to visit the theater.

Martinsburg
Martinsburg Cinema 10 (304-264-4037), 950 Foxcroft Ave. First-run movies and some of the most expensive concessions I've ever come across. Last time I was there it was more than $10 for a small popcorn and small drink.

NIGHTLIFE The Troubadour Lounge (304-258-9381; www.trouba dourlounge.com), 25 Troubadour Lane, Berkeley Springs. Closed Mon. The Troubadour is the area's country-music bar, and it serves a full menu as well as drinks. Karaoke is on Fri. nights, with live bands on Sat. evenings. Special weekend events feature well-known acts and pay tribute to some of country music's finest, such as Patsy Cline and Ernest Tubb. One room contains the West Virginia Country Music Hall of Fame, filled with memorabilia, photos, and videos.

THEATER ♪ ⊤ **Apollo Civic Theatre** (304-263-6766; www.Apollo-The atre.org), 128 East Martin St., Martinsburg. Reginald Geare, architect of the Knickerbocker Theater in Washington, DC, designed the early-1900s Apollo Civic Theatre. It retains so much of its original look that it was used for several scenes in the Civil War movie *Gods and Generals*, and it stood in for the Ford's Theatre in a documentary about Abraham Lincoln on the Discovery Channel. Will Rogers and Tex Ritter graced the stage during the days of vaudeville.

So many performing-arts venues are presented here that rarely a week goes by without something happening. Professional tour companies present Broadway plays and musicals, local groups give concerts, and an active children's theater has puppet programs, haunted theater, and more.

✷ Selective Shopping
ANTIQUES
Berkeley Springs
Berkeley Springs Antique Mall (304-258-5676), 100 Fairfax St. A rather large establishment for being in the center of town, the mall has stalls of furniture, art, books, glass, dolls, and, most of all, a sizable amount of collectibles.

Bunker Hill
Bunker Hill Antiques (304-229-0709), 144 Runnymeade Rd. More than 35,000 square feet of coins, glass, memorabilia, furniture, and collectibles inside a restored 1800s woolen mill.

ART AND CRAFTS GALLERIES
Berkeley Springs
Frog Valley Artisans and Forge (304-258-3541; www.frogvalley.com), 82 Powerline Lane. The artists here have decades of combined experience producing stained and fused glass, pottery, and metalwork.

Heath Studio Gallery (304-258-9840; www.jheath.com), 327 North Washington St. Jonathan Heath's paintings are almost always an amusing look at the characters and incidents that pass through our lives, while Jan Heath's printmaking has received numerous honors.

Ice House Artists Co-Op Gallery (304-258-2300; www.icehouseartists co-op.com), Independence and Mercer streets. Open Sat. and Sun. 11–5.

ARTWORK AT THE ICE HOUSE ARTISTS CO-OP GALLERY

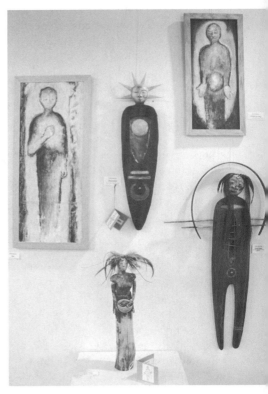

Local artists are represented, with some whimsical and interesting pieces—especially the sculpture and pottery work—not found elsewhere. Shares space with rotating gallery exhibits curated by the Morgan Arts Council, owner of the Ice House.

Mostly Woven (304-258-5276; www.kimpotter.com), 19 North Washington St. Englishman Kim Potter was introduced to weaving in Norway and became so enamored that he went to school for it. The jackets, coats, vests, and other clothing he makes from wool and other natural fibers are in such high demand that there is a waiting list to get something custom made. However, there are items always on the rack for sale, and even if you're not really planning on getting anything, you should stop in to watch this master at work.

Mountain Laurel Gallery (304-258-1919; 1-888-809-2041; www.mtn-laurel.com), 1 North Washington St. In a town known for its galleries, Mountain Laurel is one of the best. Owner Chuck Wheeler and staff travel the region and throughout the United States and Canada to bring back quality pieces from more than 50 artists. Browse multiple rooms for candles, fine art, glass, pottery, wearable fibers, jewelry, metals, pictures, wood, leather, and furniture.

Martinsburg

Crafters Gallery (304-262-4300), 617 West King St. At first glance, it looks like what is here could be found in many other such stores throughout the country—Boyds Bears, Thomas Kinkade prints, and the like—but wander around, and there are a few treasures, such as West Virginia–made jams and jellies, prints by local artists, and even a few Civil War prints.

Queen Street Gallery (304-263-9495; www.queenstreetgallery.com), 213 North Queen St. A bit of everything, including local and regional artists' works, pottery, glass, posters, sculptures, and Russian and African art pieces.

West Virginia Glass Outlet (304-263-1224), 148 North Queen St. This is just a small storefront, but you won't find any place in the state that has merchandise from more West Virginia glass producers. Last time I was there, there were items from 18 different manufacturers, from the large (such as Fenton Art Glass) to the small, single-artist company (such as Sam Hogue). It is also the largest reseller of Blenko glass, with pieces that can only be found here.

FARMERS' MARKETS

Berkeley Springs

Berkeley Springs Farmers' Market (www.berkeleyspringsfarmersmarket.com), Washington and Fairfax streets. Open May–Oct., Sun. 10–2; late June–early Oct., Thurs. 2-5. Pick up fresh produce from local farmers, in addition to baked goods, flowers, herbs, and other products.

Inwood

Inwood Farmers' Market (304-229-5011), 1 mile east on Pilgrim St. from I-81 exit 5. Open Mon.–Sat. May–Dec. and Mon.–Fri. Jan.–Apr. Operated by the West Virginia Department of Agriculture, the indoor market has some fresh produce, but it showcases packaged food and beverages—jams, maple syrup, apple butter, wine, pasta, and other items—from state producers.

PICK-YOUR-OWN PRODUCE

FARM Nob Hill Orchards (304-229-8495), Union Corners Rd., Gerrardstown. Pick your own apples in the cool autumn breezes.

✳ Special Events

January: **Spa Fest** (304-258-9147; 1-800-447-8797), Berkeley Springs. Free Saturday-morning spa services along with a products show.

February: **Annual Berkeley Springs International Water Tasting Festival** (304-258-9147; 1-800-447-8797; www.berkeleysprings.com/water), Berkeley Springs. More than 100 waters from around the world are judged in a festive atmosphere.

April: **Uniquely West Virginia Wine and Food Festival** (304-258-9147; 1-800-447-8797), Ice House, Berkeley Springs. **West Virginia Book Festival** (www.wvbooks.org), Martinsburg. Author readings and book signings, entertainment, and workshops.

May: **Berkeley Springs Studio Tour** (304-258-3541; www.berkeleysprings studiotour.com), Berkeley Springs and Morgan County. Artists and craftspersons open their studios to a driving tour. Another tour takes place in Oct. **West Virginia Wine and Arts Festival** (304-263-0224; www.theartcentre .org), The Art Centre, Martinsburg.

September: **West Virginia State BBQ and Bluegrass Festival** (www.pan handlepickin.com), Martinsburg/ Hedgesville. Food and music, along with BBQ and music competitions.

October: **Annual Apple Butter Festival** (304-258-9147; 1-800-447-8797), Berkeley Springs. Copper-kettle apple butter making, crafts, food, music, turtle races, hog-calling contest, and a quilt raffle. **Berkeley Springs Studio Tour** (304-258-3541; www.berkeley springsstudiotour.com), Berkeley Springs and Morgan County. (See *May*.) **Mountain State Apple Harvest Festival** (www.msahf.com), Martinsburg. A celebration of the apple harvest in the Eastern Panhandle. Parade, crafts fair, pageants, food, and apples, apples, apples.

Potomac Highlands

2

POTOMAC HIGHLANDS

I n a state known as an outdoors destination, the Potomac Highlands region reigns supreme. This is where the Mountain State truly lives up to its name. Unlike the Blue Ridge region far to the east, which attained its appearance through pressure and heat, or the Ridge and Valley Province, shaped by being folded and angled, the Potomac Highlands, which is a part of the Allegheny Plateau, was lifted up as one continuous mass when Africa collided with North America 250 million years ago. The northern part of the highlands, in places such as Dolly Sods and Canaan Valley, has remained essentially a plateau, while water and wind have cut valleys and eroded softer rock to leave behind higher parallel-running ridges in the highlands' central region. In the very southern portion, the ridgelines are no longer parallel but rise from the narrow valley floors as a jumbled mass of knobs and knolls.

Elevations above 4,000 feet are common, with the state's highest point, Spruce Knob, rising 4,861 feet above sea level. Even lowlands are high—at 3,200 feet, Canaan Valley is the loftiest valley east of the Mississippi River. Plants more often associated with the cool temperatures of New England and Canada thrive here.

Four-lane highways are few and far between, while scenic two-lane roadways snake over heavily forested ridgelines, beside swiftly moving mountain streams, and along the edges of narrow valleys and fields of cattle to connect one sparsely populated community with another.

Two national forests encompass nearly 1 million acres and close to 1,000 miles of trails, with a major percentage of the pathways open to hikers, bikers, and horseback riders. A multitude of state parks, wildlife management areas, and federal wilderness areas add thousands of more acres and miles of pathways to explore.

The state's premier ski resorts are located here, while rock formations that rise hundreds of feet attract climbers from around the world. The fresh coldwater streams that flow down these mountainsides are home to native and stocked trout, smallmouth bass, and so many other species that many anglers consider this area to have some of the best fly-fishing and boat-fishing spots in the eastern part of the country. These same streams are an exhilarating challenge to paddlers in some places, while other spots are peaceful and placid enough for families to leisurely tube down or splash into a favorite swimmin' hole.

SOARING WITH EAGLES ALONG THE POTOMAC'S SOUTH BRANCH— ROMNEY AND MOOREFIELD

Okay, let's see if you can keep all of this straight. The Potomac River defines the West Virginia–Maryland border as it flows eastward to pass Washington, DC, and empty into the Chesapeake Bay. The Potomac is formed when the North Branch of the river meets the South Branch several miles east of Cumberland, Maryland. The North Branch of the Potomac is considered one stream from its source, which is a spring next to the Fairfax Stone Monument in Tucker County, West Virginia. However, three streams make up the South Branch of the Potomac River. The South Fork of the South Branch of the Potomac River rises in Virginia and flows northward to meet the South Branch of the Potomac River at Moorefield. The South Branch of the Potomac River (which, if it followed form, should really be called the Middle Fork of the South Branch of the Potomac River) also begins in Virginia and flows northward along the eastern side of North Fork Mountain. The North Fork of the South Branch of the Potomac River forms in West Virginia at the confluence of Straight Fork and Laurel Fork, and it runs below the western side of North Fork Mountain before meeting the South Branch of the Potomac River near Petersburg, West Virginia.

Got it? Well, don't worry, you don't really need to have it all make sense to enjoy this area. All you need to know is that many people consider this to be one of the best parts of the state in which to travel. You are definitely in mountains, but they are lower and gentler than those of the Allegheny Plateau to the west. Driving is at a slower pace and is through a decidedly rural landscape of rolling terrain ringed by rising ridgelines.

The many rivers and streams beckon paddlers onto waters that pass through narrow gorges, home to the state's largest resident population of bald eagles, while George Washington National Forest and Lost River State Park reward hikers with wide-reaching vistas.

History is here, too. George Washington (who sure seems to have gotten around at a time in history when travel was slow and laborious) surveyed these lands as a young man and returned as a leader of troops during the French and Indian War.

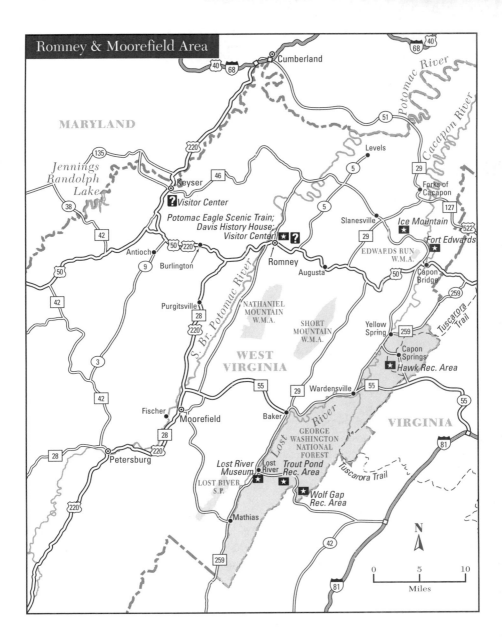

The area was so important during the Civil War that Romney is said to have changed hands at least 56 times during the conflict.

A major highway project that has been in the planning stages for decades is now under way. Known as Corridor H (it will be designated US 48 when completed), it enters the state near Wardensville, moves on to Moorefield, and will continue westward to pass close to Davis, Thomas, and Canaan Valley (see "The Land of Canaan—Canaan Valley, Blackwater Falls, and Dolly Sods" chapter). As all major highways do, it will have an impact on the natural and human world through which it passes. Visit here as soon as possible to experience the area before these changes occur.

COMMUNITIES Located along the South Branch of the Potomac River and incorporated in 1762, **Romney** lays claim to being the oldest town in West Virginia. (Shepherdstown in the Eastern Panhandle states it is the oldest "incorporated" town in the state.) As an important crossroads, Romney was hotly contested during the Civil War. Today, it is a county seat and home to the *Potomac Eagle*, a scenic train whose route takes in the "Trough," home to bald eagles.

Although **Moorefield** is a working town processing poultry and beef, it has an attractive historic district and serves as a gateway and supply point for those setting off to explore the surrounding mountains.

GUIDANCE The **Hampshire County Convention and Visitors Bureau** (304-822-7477; www.cometohampshire.com), located at 426 E. Main St., Romney 26757, is able to provide information about Romney, Hampshire County, and the surrounding area.

Information concerning Moorefield and the lands around it may be obtained from the **Hardy County Convention and Visitor's Bureau** (304-89-8700; www.visit hardy.com), P.O. Box 797, Moorefield, 26836.

The **Mineral County Convention and Visitors Bureau** (304-788-2513; www .mineralchamber.com), 1 Grand Central Park, Keyser 26726, is in Suite 2081 of the Grand Central Business Center.

West Virginia Mountain Highlands (304-636-8400; 1-877-WVA-MTNS; www .mountainhighlands.com), P.O. Box 1456, Elkins 26241, is an umbrella organization that helps supply information about the entire Potomac Highlands region.

GETTING THERE *By air*: There is really no easy way to fly into this area. **Hagerstown Regional Airport** (240-313-2777) in Maryland is the closest air facility. **Washington Dulles International Airport** (703-572-2700; www.met washairports.com/dulles) is another possibility, but it is close to 100 miles away.

By bus: See *Getting Around—By bus*, below.

By car: **I-81** runs in a north–south direction in Virginia and gives the easiest access to the area by leaving it at Winchester, Virginia, to take **US 50** west to Romney. You can also exit the interstate at Strasburg, Virginia, and drive west on US 48 (which becomes **WV 55** in West Virginia) to Moorefield. From the north, exit **I-68** at Cumberland, Maryland, and follow **US 220** into the area. Be sure to allot plenty of time because, no matter which way you come from, you will be driving almost exclusively on two-lane roadways.

GETTING AROUND *By bus*: For such a rural locale, **Potomac Valley Transit** (304-257-1414; 1-800-565-7240; www.potomacvalleytransit.org) is a far-reaching public-transportation system. In addition to having stops in all of the major towns and many of the small communities in this area, it also connects to Cumberland and Oakland, Maryland, and Winchester and Harrisonburg, Virginia.

By car: The major east–west routes are **US 50** and **WV 55**. Permitting travel in a north–south direction are **US 220/WV 28**, **WV 259**, and **WV 29**. As noted in the chapter introduction, **Corridor H (US 48)** is currently under construction or in the planning stage and will be a major east–west route when completed.

By taxi: **Yellow Cab** (304-788-3531) is headquartered in Keyser.

MEDICAL EMERGENCIES

Keyser
Potomac Valley Hospital (304-597-3500; www.potomacvalleyhospital.com), 100 Pin Oak Lane.

Romney
Hampshire Memorial Hospital (304-822-4561), 549 Center Ave. Drive west from Romney on US 50 to WV 28 North, go six blocks, turn left on Depot St., go to Center Ave., and turn right.

If you are in the southern part of this area, you may find it faster and more expedient to go to **Grant Memorial Hospital** (304-257-1026; www.grantmemorial.com) on WV 28/WV 55 in Petersburg.

✳ To See

DRIVING TOURS, SCENIC & HISTORIC

As you have seen in other regions, the state of West Virginia has developed a number of scenic drives known as Byways and Backways. There are no "official" drives in this area, but that hasn't stopped me from enjoying the scenery and putting together my own circuit route that, during the course of a leisurely day, takes in some of the best sites, sights, and delights.

Drive US 50 east from Romney, soon crossing the North and South Forks of the Little Cacapon River and coming into Augusta. (Side trips from here could take you to North River Mountain Ranch for a horseback ride or shopping on US 50 at Dan's Antiques.)

Continuing eastward on US 50, pay attention after you pass through the small settlement of Hanging Rock, for you want to pull over at the top of Cooper Mountain for an Olympian view of ridgeline after ridgeline receding to the east into Virginia. Descend to Capon Bridge (stop at the Capon Bridge Public Library & Doctor Gardner Museum if it's open) and turn right onto WV 14 (River Rd.). This is a wonderfully winding road along the Cacapon River past small cottages, youth camps, and farms, one of which has meadows dotted by buffalos, miniature horses, emus, and llamas. Ducks and herons ply the river, while gnawed trees along the shore are testament to the industry of resident beavers.

Bear right on WV 259 in Yellow Spring (there's a little general store here that's good for a snack and drink and a historic perspective on country stores) and continue along the river. Bald eagles are often seen soaring over the valley. South of Wardensville, the Lost River disappears under Sandy Mountain and emerges on the other side as the Cacapon River.

Near Mathias, turn right onto WV 12 and maybe stop to take a hike to Cranny Crow Overlook in Lost River State Park. Beyond the park, the road may test whether you are a true explorer or not, as there are many miles of dirt road twisting and winding up and over South Branch Mountain before dropping to a right turn onto WV 7.

Grab a snack or meal in Moorefield, drive north on US 220/WV 28, make a right onto WV 15, and a left onto WV 6 (which becomes WV 8 once you cross a county line). This country road takes you along the hillside above the South Branch of the Potomac River, where once again bald eagles live, and returns you to US 50 and Romney.

HISTORIC SITES

Capon Bridge

Fort Edwards (304-856-2356; www.fortedwards.org; mailing address: P.O. Box 623, Capon Bridge 26711), on WV 15 (Springfield Grade/Coldstream Rd.), 0.5 mile north of US 50 in Capon Bridge. Open late June through mid-Oct., Sat. and Sun. Small admission fee. A string of forts protected the frontier in Virginia, (what would become) West Virginia, and Pennsylvania during the time of the French and Indian War. A young George Washington came here in 1748 to aid in the surveying of Lord Fairfax's land, and he returned a few years later in command of forces stationed at Fort Edwards along the Cacapon River.

There is very little physical evidence of the fort today, but under the auspices of the Fort Edwards Foundation, archaeological digs have unearthed thousands of artifacts and helped establish the size and location of the fort. A small visitor center displays some of the artifacts, shows a short video, and has storyboards portraying the fort and its significance. Outside is a colonial kitchen garden with medicinal, culinary, and dying herbs and vegetables.

Romney

Fort Mill Ridge Trenches (304-822-4320), 3 miles west of Romney off US 50. Open sunrise to sunset. Fort Mill Ridge contains some of the best-preserved Civil War trenches in West Virginia. Built by Union troops in 1863, the trenches overlook the South Branch of the Potomac River and the roadways that were strategic transportation routes during the war. An easy gravel pathway works its way around the trenches, with interpretive panels providing an overview of the fortifications and their history. This historic site is located within Fort Ridge Wildlife Management Area, so use caution when visiting during hunting season.

INDIAN MOUND CEMETERY

Indian Mound Cemetery, on US 50 at the west end of town. It is amazing how such a small piece of ground can have had so many significant events occur upon it. An unopened Indian burial mound, believed to date from AD 500 through 1000, sits at the western edge of the cemetery (and must be searched for as it is only a few feet high). Fort Pearsall, which was manned by soldiers commissioned by George Washington, is believed to have been near this site during the French and Indian War, and both attacking Native Americans and the settlers they killed are buried here. Soldiers from both sides of the conflict during the Civil War are also buried in the cemetery. Sadly, many of them are unidentified. What is believed to be the first monument to fallen Confederate soldiers was erected in the cemetery in 1867.

LAKES Jennings Randolph Lake (304-355-2890; www.nab.usace.army.mil /recreation/jenran.htm) is more than 5 miles long and is located on the North Branch of the Potomac River, which separates Maryland from West Virginia. Scenically sandwiched in by high ridges, the lake is one of the area's least used for powerboating, skiing, and fishing. The fly-fishing tailwater area regularly yields brown, rainbow, and brook trout. Picnic areas, a campground, swimming beach, and an overlook are spread around the shore of the lake.

Trout Pond (see *Green Space—National Forest*) is the only naturally occurring pond in the entire state. Thankfully, it was decided to call it a pond and not a lake, for this little body is only 1.5 acres in size and was formed when a sinkhole appeared on the limestone topography. Still, it's a unique and scenic place, worth the short walk from the parking area.

MUSEUMS
Capon Bridge
🛉 **Capon Bridge Public Library & Doctor Gardner Museum** (304-856-3777; www.youseemore.com/caponbridge), on US 50 in Capon Bridge, next to the First National Bank of Romney. Open Mon., Wed., and Thurs. 11–6; Tue. 2–8; Fri. 11–5; and Sat. 9–1. Free; donations accepted. Blink and you may miss this cute, tiny building that was once a medical office. Besides being a library, there is also a small museum that, given the limited amount of space, does a good job of painting the story of the local area. Stop by just to take a look at the building.

Lost River
🛉 **Lost River Museum** (304-897-7242; www.lostrivercraft.com; mailing address: P.O. Box 26, Lost River 26810), on WV 259, halfway between Baker and Mathias. Closed Tue. through Thurs. Memorial Day through late Oct.; open weekends mid-April to Memorial Day and Nov. and Dec. Donations accepted. The museum is housed in the lower portion of a refurbished 1845 barn and features rotating loan and permanent exhibits that most often focus on the lifestyles and crafts of rural life. Almost always on display is one of the most complete collections of spinning and weaving equipment you'll find anywhere, and if you're lucky, there will be demonstrations by nationally acclaimed weavers taking place when you visit. The Lost River Craft Cooperative (see *Selective Shopping*) occupies the barn's upper floor.

Romney
Davis History House (304-822-3185), beside the library on Main St. Open on special occasions, but the key is at the library, and it will be opened upon request. As far as records can determine, this log home, the only one still standing on its original lot in Romney, was built before 1798. The house came into the Davis family in 1849 and was a meeting place for Confederates during the Civil War. Two sisters, born in the late 1800s, lived in the house their entire lives and donated the home (and the land for the county library) upon their death in the 1970s. The

museum contains some of the sisters' furniture, as well as Civil War memorabilia, including the flag that the women of the county painted and McNeil's Rangers carried throughout the Civil War.

Taggart Hall Museum (304-822-7221), 91 High St. (Usually open Mon.–Sat. 9–4, Sun. noon–4. Donations accepted. Inside a historic 1795 building, the Taggart Hall Museum devotes the small space it has to portraying the area's role in the Civil War.

Also see Lost River State Park under *Green Space—Parks*.

DAVIS HISTORY HOUSE

✳ To Do

BICYCLING Lost River State Park (304-897-5372; www.lostriversp.com), 321 Park Dr. On WV 12 (Howards Lick Rd.), 4 miles from WV 259 at Mathias. Two of the park's trails are open to mountain bikes. The **East Ridge Trail** is 2.5 miles long and connects with the 0.5-mile **Covey Cove Trail**. Both routes have trailside shelters to duck into in case of rain or other inclement weather.

Also see *Green Space—National Forest*.

BIRDING Quite a number of bald eagles have taken up residence along this area's waterways, especially in an area known as the "**Trough**," on the South Branch of the Potomac River between Romney and Moorefield. I have witnessed eagles soaring above the Cacapon River along WV 259 between Baker and Mathias. Osprey, wood ducks, and blue and white herons are also seen along the streams.

BOWLING

Keyser
 Rainbow Lanes (304-788-3574; www.rainbowlanesbowl.com), 1575 Cornell St.

Moorefield
 Potomac Lanes (540-538-8140; www.wvafun.com/pl-files/pl-html/PLindex .html), 185 Hyde St. Open daily.

Romney
 Wilson Lanes Bowling (304-822-4100), on US 50 a short distance east from the center of Romney.

FAMILY ACTIVITIES **John Arnold Farm Corn Maze** (304-822-3603; www.arnoldfarmwv.com), 7.5 miles south of Romney on WV 8 (South Branch River Rd.). See who can be first in the family to find the way out of the cornfield (Sept.–Oct.).

FISHING Head to the **Potomac**, **South Branch of the Potomac**, and **Cacapon rivers** for smallmouth bass, bluegill, redeye rock bass, catfish, carp, and a few trout. **Mill Run** at Grayson Gap near Antioch is known for muskellunge and trout. Tiny **Warden Lake** is the place to go for northern pike and catfish, while **Waites Run** has brook, brown, and rainbow trout; both are near Wardensville.

Also see *Green Space—Wildlife Management Areas.*

GOLF Valley View Golf Club (304-538-6564; mailing address: Rte. 220, Box 61, Moorefield 26836), 4 miles south of Moorefield on US 220. On flat river bottom-land, water figures into nine of the 18 holes in the par 71, Russell Roberts and Bill Ward–designed course.

HIKING The **American Discovery Trail**, a route that runs more than 6,800 miles from the Atlantic Ocean to the Pacific shore, enters this area after crossing the Potomac River at Green Spring. From there it follows country roads as it climbs a ridgeline close to the Springfield Wildlife Management Area and passes through the Patterson Creek Valley to leave the area south of Burlington.

For more information about the American Discovery Trail, write to P.O. Box 20155, Washington, DC 20041; call 540-720-5489 or 1-800-663-2387; or log on to www.discoverytrail.org.

The 50,000 acres of the **George Washington National Forest** (see *Green Space—National Forest*) have close to 100 miles of interconnecting pathways that enable you to do multiple days' worth of trekking and backcountry camping. However, if you only have time for one hike, go to **Big Schloss**, which sits high atop the ridgeline that marks the border of Virginia with West Virginia. A moderate 4.4-mile round-trip hike from the Wolf Gap Recreation Area (see *Green Space—National Forest* for driving directions) along the Mill Mountain Trail will bring you to this sandstone outcropping that juts upward from the mixed hardwood forest, rising above the trees to permit a superb view of the surrounding countryside. Luckily, because most of the land surrounding Big Schloss is national forest, the scenery remains somewhat the same as it appeared back in the settlers' days. There are not many places like this left in the eastern part of America—your eyes can gaze out upon ridgelines, forests, and valleys that show remarkably few signs of the 21st century.

Lost River State Park (304-897-5372; www.lostriversp.com), 321 Park Dr. On WV 12 (Howards Lick Rd.), 4 miles from WV 259 at Mathias. *Bucolic*: It's such a mellifluous-sounding word. The dictionary defines it as "pastoral," suggesting an idyllic rural life. Taking that into account, there is certainly no better word than *bucolic* to describe the scenery as seen from the park's **Cranny Crow Overlook**.

There are a couple of ways to get to the viewpoint, but by using a gravel service road (0.4 mile from the park entrance), and Shelter Oak, Millers Rock, Virginia View, and Big Ridge trails, you can do a 4.1-mile circuit hike on a relatively moderate route, with just a few short, steep sections.

About 1,000 feet below the Cranny Crow Overlook is a narrow valley with hemlock-bordered Howards Lick Run flowing down the middle of it. The lowing of livestock is carried on the wind as your eyes are drawn to the 180-degree view that takes in the mountains and ridgelines of Shenandoah and Rockingham counties in

Virginia, and Pendleton, Grant, and Hardy counties in West Virginia. The farm-steads on the mountaintop directly in front of you may make you envy the folks who get to enjoy this scenery from their homes every day.

The nice thing is that after you finish this hike, there are about 15 more miles of trails to explore in the park.

Also see *Green Space—Nature Preserve*.

HORSEBACK RIDING

Mathias

🔹 **Lost River State Park** (304-897-5372; www.lostriversp.com), 321 Park Dr. On WV 12 (Howards Lick Rd.), 4 miles from WV 259 at Mathias. Horseback rides for children and adults are available for a half hour, hour, or longer. Reservations should be made by calling 304-897-5621.

Romney

🔹 **Crystal Valley Ranch** (304-822-7444; www.crystalvalleyranch.com; mailing address: HC 65, Box 1350, Romney 26757), 3 miles north of Romney on WV 28. Trail rides by the hour are available on the 800-acre property. You can either ride one of their horses or your own.

KAYAKING & CANOEING All of this area's large north-flowing streams are worthy of dipping a paddle into. South of the small town of Forks of Cacapon, the **Cacapon River** can be shallow and most often run only in the spring, but north of the public access point on WV 127, the stream develops some nice Class II and III rapids. The **Potomac River** along the West Virginia–Maryland border becomes a whitewater-rafting experience when the dam at Jennings Randolph Lake releases water. The West Virginia Division of Natural Resources (304-558-3380; 304-558-2754; www.wvdnr.gov; State Capitol Building 3, Charleston 25305) publishes a small pamphlet detailing 17 public access points on the **South Branch of the Potomac River**. Without a doubt, its most popular stretch is the "Trough," an iso-lated 6-mile part of the river between Moorefield and Romney.

Romney

Trough General Store (304-822-7601; www.wvcanoerentals.com; mailing address: P.O. Box 357, Romney 26757), on WV 8 south of Romney. Open Apr.–Oct.; closed Tue. You can park your automobile at the general store, and they will shuttle you and your canoe, either your own or one rented from them, to the head of the "Trough." Paddle downstream and end the trip back at the store and your car.

SWIMMING The town park swimming pools in **Moorefield** and **Wardensville** are open from Memorial Day through Labor Day. For a rustic swimmin' hole, drive to what I call "The Bridge to Nowhere" at the intersection of WV 259 and WV 16, 2 miles south of Capon Bridge. This historic Whipple truss bridge was built on US 50 near Romney in 1874, moved to this site in 1934, and used until 1991. It is the oldest of the few remaining Whipple truss bridges in the state. Just below the structure, the Cacapon River makes a nice pool that is a favorite local swimming spot.

A SCENIC TRAIN EXCURSION

⚓ *Potomac Eagle* (304-424-0736; www.potomaceagle.info; mailing address: P.O. Box 657, Romney 26757), at the Wappocomo Station on WV 28, north of Romney. Sat. late May–late Sept.; daily during most of Oct. and first week of Nov. Fare for the three-and-a-half-hour trip on coach is $48 for adults, $45 for seniors, $20 for children ages 6–16, free for children under age 6, Classic Club class (includes lunch) $90 for everyone; special all-day trips are $80 for adults, $75 for seniors, $30 for children ages 6–16, free for children under age 6, Classic Club class $125.

The *Potomac Eagle* scenic train, hauled by mid-1900s locomotives, takes passengers through the "Trough," an isolated 6-mile canyon of the South Branch of the Potomac River. More than 90 percent of passengers have had the good fortune of witnessing bald eagles soaring over the steep mountainsides here. One of my complaints about other scenic train rides is the lack of commentary provided as you travel along, but not with the *Potomac Eagle*. A running narration gives proficient information about Civil War, Native American, and natural history along the route, with tidbits on the state's history and sites you pass along the way.

The excitement and anticipation builds as the train travels farther into the "Trough." People start pointing and moving from their seats to the outside open car, where children switch from one side to the other to get a better look. Soon, there's oohing, aahing, and squeals of delight as the great white-headed birds soar overhead on 7-foot wingspans. The last trip I was on, we spied a half dozen bald eagles swooping down to the water or perching atop tall trees.

POTOMAC EAGLE

⚓ **Lost River State Park** (304-897-5372; www.lostriversp.com), 321 Park Dr. On WV 12 (Howards Lick Rd.), 4 miles from WV 259 at Mathias. The park's outdoor swimming pool, located next to the rental cabins, is open from Memorial Day through Labor Day. Be sure to make use of it if you're staying in one of the cabins, as there is no extra fee for you.

Also see Trout Pond Recreation Area under *Green Space—National Forest*.

✳ Green Space

NATIONAL FOREST More than 50,000 acres of the **George Washington National Forest** spill across the border from Virginia into West Virginia. A few paved roads, close to 80 miles of forest service roads, and approximately 100 miles of interconnecting trails, including a portion of the long-distance **Tuscarora Trail** (see "What's Where in West Virginia" at the front of this book for background information), provide easy access for you to explore and backcountry camp. This is a land of long narrow mountains, intersecting cross ridgelines, and isolated valleys full of mountain laurel, meadow rue, wild geraniums, and dozens of other spring and summer flowers. (All of the trails are open to hikers and mountain bikers.) Because this is a disjunct part of the national forest, miles removed from other parts of the federal land, it receives less attention, which translates into more solitude and an improved chance of observing wildlife. Three forest service recreation areas increase the opportunity to linger and explore:

To reach the **Trout Pond Recreation Area** (also see *To See—Lakes*) from the small settlement of Lost River on WV 259, drive 4.5 miles on WV 16 (Mill Gap Rd.), turn right onto FSR 500, and continue another 1.7 miles. This is the most developed of the three areas, with 16-acre Rock Cliff Lake available for swimming, boating, and fishing, and a campground with a dumping station, bathhouse, and modern toilets. More rustic, with just a few campsites, a hand pump, and vault toilets, the **Wolf Gap Recreation Area** is located on WV 23/10 right on the West Virginia–Virginia border, almost 13.5 miles from Wardensville. Also on the rustic side, the **Hawk Recreation Area** may be reached by driving east from Wardensville on WV 55 for 4.2 miles, turning left onto dirt FSR 502, continuing another 2.9 miles to make a left onto FSR 347, and coming to the area in an additional 0.7 mile.

More information may be obtained by contacting the Lee Ranger District, 95 Railroad Ave., Edinburg, VA 22824; 540-984-4101; www.fs.fed.us/r8/gwj/lee.

NATURE PRESERVE Ice Mountain, preserved by The Nature Conservancy and located on WV 45/20 between Slanesville and Capon Bridge, is named for the phenomenon that causes ice to form and linger late into the year. Recent warm summers have melted the ice earlier than in the past, but it's still quite eerie to be hiking in 90-degree weather and walk by one of the natural vents at the base of the mountain blowing out 38-degree air. The cooler environment permits plants not usually seen this far south, such as bunchberry, to cling to the hillside. In addition, the moderately strenuous hike to the mountain's rocky crest provides an exhilarating view. There is no fee, but arrangements to visit Ice Mountain, usually on a Saturday morning, must be made two weeks in advance (304-496-7359; www.steve bailes.org). Pets not permitted.

PARKS ✍ **Lost River State Park** (304-897-5372; www.lostriversp.com), 321 Park Dr. On WV 12 (Howards Lick Rd.), 4 miles from WV 259 at Mathias. Lost River State Park takes in 3,712 acres of long and level Big Ridge, a portion of East Ridge, and narrow Howards Lick Run valley sandwiched in between the two.

The park takes its name from the nearby river that disappears underground for 3 miles, where it flows under Sandy Ridge to reemerge as the Cacapon River near Wardensville. What is now state park land was once a part of the vast holdings of Lord Fairfax, but it was later given to "Light Horse Harry" Lee in appreciation of his military service during the Revolutionary War. Lee built a cabin, and his family used it as a summer retreat during the early 1800s. The dwelling is now on the National Register of Historic Places and is open as a museum from Memorial Day to Labor Day.

A naturalist is on staff during the same period, and you can join in on hikes, stream wadings in search of aquatic life, campfire activities, evening programs, and more. The park has no campground or areas for backcountry camping, but a commercial site, Big Ridge Campground (open May–Oct.; see *Lodging*), is located just a short distance away on WV 14.

Situated along the main road beside Howards Lick Run and its smaller tributary, Cabin Run, are the park's game courts, riding stables, a swimming pool, an activities building, picnic areas, a gift shop, and rental cabins. Close to 20 miles of hiking trails (two are also open to mountain bikes—see *To Do—Bicycling*) emanate from these points and rise onto the park's more elevated and isolated area. The moderate trek to Cranny Crow Overlook is highly recommended (see *To Do— Hiking*).

WILDLIFE MANAGEMENT AREAS Information on the wildlife management areas (WMA) in this area may be obtained from the West Virginia Division of Nat-

ONE OF THE VENTS AT ICE MOUNTAIN

ural Resources District II, 1 Depot St., Romney 26757; 304-822-3551. Remember that these areas are primarily managed for game (so it's best to avoid them during hunting season), but they are good places to hike and camp if you are prepared for primitive campgrounds (no backcountry camping permitted) and rudimentary trails.

The 10,600 acres of the **Nathaniel Mountain Wildlife Management Area** are laced with 21 miles of pathways and 4 miles of Mill Run populated by small native brook trout. The primitive campground has hand pumps and vault-type toilets. The entrance road is off WV 10 (Grassy Lick Rd.) east of Romney. **Short Mountain Wildlife Management Area** has 15 miles of trails on 8,000 acres of oak and pine forest. Beaver ponds punctuate portions of Meadow Run, which has small native brook trout, while the North River is stocked with trout. Primitive camping areas are located along dirt roads. The WMA is located off WV 7 (Ford Hill Rd.) south of Augusta.

Edward's Run Wildlife Management Area is about 400 acres with a spring-fed trout stream, stocked 2-acre trout pond, and a primitive camping area with pit-type toilets. It is off WV 15 (Springfield Grade Rd.) north of Capon Bridge.

✳ Lodging

RESORTS

Romney 26757

Avalon (304-947-5600; www.avalon -resort.com; mailing address: P.O. Box 369, Paw Paw 25434), Critten Owl Hollow Rd., off WV 29 northeast of Romney. A 250-acre, clothing-optional family recreation facility that is open to the public year-round. There are modern motel rooms with private baths, camping sites for RVs and tents, a swimming pool, volleyball and other game courts, fishing pond, playground, restaurant, and spa facility with several different types of massage. Also, one of the East Coast's best annual folk festivals is held here in August (see *Entertainment—Music*). If you have never been to a nudist camp, this may be the one to go to; they welcome first-timers and work with making you feel comfortable. Note that the operative phrase is "clothing optional," meaning you can keep your clothes on if it makes you feel better. My bet is that you'll decide to shed them once you see just how innocent an atmosphere a nudist camp is. $60.

MOTELS & HOTELS

Lost River 26810

Lost River Motel (304-897-6482; www.lostrivergrill.com), on WV 259. The motel was built in the mid-1900s, and its design and wood paneling reflect the era. The owner has kept the place in good repair, replacing furniture as needed and keeping things clean and orderly. The rooms may feel small by today's standards, but open the curtain and they'll feel bigger as you take in the view across the lush farmland of the Lost River Valley. There is also a restaurant on the premises (see *Eating Out*). $75.

Moorefield 26836

♿ **South Branch Inn** (304-538-2033), 1500 US 220/WV 28. A multistory Colonial-style motel with the feel of a small hotel. There are 100 rooms and suites, some with refrigerators and microwaves. Also available to guests are an exercise room and laundry. $85–120.

Romney 26757

Koolwink Motel (304-822-3595; www

.koolwinkmotel.com), on US 50 East. The Koolwink started as a tourist home in the 1930s, and has been a family-owned business ever since. Today, the motel rooms have the look of the 1950s, yet the owners have worked hard to keep the place modernized, clean, and in good repair. Rooms are large for having been built in the mid-1900s and have refrigerators, microwaves, and coffeemakers—even wireless Internet. Rates are $69.

BED & BREAKFASTS

Lost River 26810
The Inn at Lost River (304-897-7000; www.theinnatlostriver.com), 7015 State Road 259. Open mid-Apr.—mid-Dec. Three bedrooms and two cottages (all with private baths) provide guests with reasons to linger on the grounds on the late 1800s farmland. A three-course dinner, afternoon hors d'oeuvres and wine, and an evening snack are additional enticements. $95–115.

Yellow Spring 26865
The Asa Cline House Bed & Breakfast (304-874-4115; 1-866-665-4115; www.asaclinehouse.com; mailing address: P.O. Box 177), on WV 259. My multiple stays here have been made memorable by the easy conversations—some of them late into the evening—that I have shared with John and Merrie Hammond. When you stay in as many B&Bs as I do, you are able to discern between hosts who are just being polite and those who truly take pleasure in meeting and interacting with their guests. There is no doubt the Hammonds are in the latter category.

The Asa Cline House is more than 200 years old, and tall, stately maple trees shade the front porch while 23 acres of vegetable gardens, pastures, ponds, and hillside invite leisurely wanderings.

THE ASA CLINE HOUSE BED & BREAKFAST

The three guest rooms have antique and locally crafted furnishings, private baths, and porches overlooking the grounds. The large breakfasts include homemade bread and jams, such as blackberry and pear preserves, made from fruit grown on the property. $95–105.

The Hammonds are also experts at organizing weddings, reunions, and other special occasions. A modern carriage house apartment above the garage is available for those who want complete privacy and comes equipped with a full kitchen and washer and dryer. $150.

CABIN AND HOUSE RENTALS

Augusta 26704
Just Far Enough Getaway (304-496-8002; www.justfarenough.com; mailing address: HC 71, Box 139A), Hoy Rd. On a ridgeline 4 miles east of Romney, the three-bedroom, two-bath home was originally built in the 1990s for the owner's mother-in-law. You can now take advantage of the back deck overlooking the woods or relax in the hammock in the yard. It's not isolated, but the neighborhood is quiet and con-

conducive to relaxing, reading, or playing one of the many provided board games. $90; special $500-a-week rate.

Fisher 26818

⚓ **Riverside Cabins** (304-538-6467; www.riversidecabinswv.com/contact .htm; mailing address: P.O. Box 61). A few miles south of Moorefield, the small, simple, two-bedroom cabins sit side by side in an open field next to a bend in the South Branch of the Potomac River. Everything is provided, except linens. The same people own the adjacent campground, and you are permitted to use its swimming pool. For larger parties and those wanting more privacy, make a reservation for the "Log Cabin in the Sky." It accommodates nine and has a hot tub, television, and large stone fireplace.

⚓ **Lost River State Park** (304-897-5372; www.lostriversp.com), 321 Park Dr. On WV 12 (Howards Lick Rd.), 4 miles from WV 259 at Mathias. The park's modern cabins, with forced-air heat, stone fireplace, bath, kitchen, and linens, are open year-round. The standard cabins, which only lack the forced-air heat and supplied linens, are available for rent from Apr. to the fourth Mon. in Oct. Although somewhat close together, the cabins are in a wooded setting apart from the park's main activity areas.

CAMPGROUNDS

Mathias 26812

Big Ridge Campground (304-897-6404; www.bigridgecampground.com), 6547 Dove Hollow Rd. (WV 14). The closest campground to Lost River State Park. Open May–Oct.

Romney 26757

Middle Ridge Campground (304-822-8020; www.middleridgecamp ground.com). Drive US 50 5 miles west of Romney, turn right onto Fox

Hollow Rd. (WV 50/4), and continue for another 7 miles. Open year-round. Only 21 large wooded campsites, with water, sewer, and electric hookups. In-ground swimming pool, two ponds (catch-and-release fishing), hiking trails, and play areas.

🐾 **Wapocoma Family Campground** (304-822-5528; www.wapocomacamp ground.com; mailing address: P.O. Box 1004), 5 miles south of Romney on WV 8 (South Branch River Rd.). There's close to 300 sites in an open field (ask for a site with shade or you will surely get hot in summer) and only one bathhouse to service all of the campers. The advantage of staying here is direct access to 2,000 feet of the South Branch of the Potomac River shoreline.

Springfield 26763

🐾 **Milleson's Campground** (304-822-5284), on WV 28/5, 3 miles from WV 28. Open Apr.–Oct. Milleson's has dozens of shaded sites on an oxbow bend of the scenic South Branch of the Potomac River, with direct access to the water for boating, fishing, and swimming. Modern bathhouse, full hookups, store, and game fields. Pets permitted with proof of shots.

RIVERSIDE CABINS

✷ Where to Eat

EATING OUT

Capon Bridge

Anthony's Jr. Pizzeria and Family Restaurant (304-856-3027), Blue Marlin Plaza, off US 50. As some people refer to such places, Capon Bridge is "just a wide spot in the road," so it's nice that you're able to stop and have a pizza, sub, or pasta. Unless you are really, really, really hungry, order the small calzone and not the large. When my small one arrived, the people at the next table looked over and said, "Are you really going to eat that all by yourself?" Entrées $7.50–19.50.

Greg's Restaurant (304-856-2445), on US 50. Breakfast, lunch, and dinner daily. Home-cooked meals served in a place that was obviously once a fast-food restaurant. Breakfast served anytime. Entrées $4.50–12.

Lost River

Lost River Grill (304-897-6482; www.lostrivergrill.com), on WV 259. Lunch and dinner daily; breakfast on Sat. and Sun. Owner Tim Ramsey has spent many years in the hospitality business, so he knows how to cater to his customers. In a rural area far removed from other eating establishments, he serves country-cooking favorites such as meat loaf, roast beef, and pork chops, but you will also find char-grilled salmon marinated in Bloody Mary sauce (all seafood is brought in fresh from Washington, DC) and roast duck. Steaks of various cuts and sizes are a specialty, and the selective wine list has bottles approximately priced $12–60. Entrées $7.99–22.99.

Mr. Ramsey is supportive of local artists, whose works are displayed on the pine-paneled walls that evoke the mid-1900s when the restaurant was built. (Parts of the building have been a gas station, garage, and grocery store.) The adjoining motel (see *Lodging*) has the same feel and décor.

Moorefield

O'Neills (304-530-2727), 614 North Main St. Breakfast, lunch, and dinner; closed Sun. In a heavily commercialized part of town with nondescript buildings and small strip malls, O'Neill's is inside a quaint little wooden cottage set back from the road a few feet. When I asked Moorefield native Jamie O'Neill how she comes up with menu items, she replied, "It's just things me and my family like to eat." Maybe so, but they are things that you wouldn't expect to find in an otherwise meat-and-potatoes town, such as vegetarian omelet, homemade chips, tomato and fresh mozzarella salad, or steamed spiced shrimp. This is also the place to get your specialty-coffee fix. Entrées $9–16.

Romney

☙ **Mario's** (304-822-7776), 33 South High St. Lunch and dinner; closed Sun. Amedeo Lumado is from Naples and came to Romney after owning restaurants in New York and Pennsylvania. The wonderful pasta sauce, full of spices but not heavy, is his recipe, and his wife, Helen, and her sister, Lillian, do most of the cooking. They make their own pizza dough (also used for the garlic bread), and the chicken and veal are pounded fresh daily. It's an interesting atmosphere—there's an intricately designed pressed tin roof and an etched glass chandelier matched with vinyl chairs and table-cloths. The last Friday evening I dined here, there was a steady stream of customers, but my food arrived quickly, and the wait staff remained efficient and friendly. My favorite Romney restaurant. Entrées $7–16.

☙ **Mountain Top Truck Stop** (304-822-5918), east of town on US 50. Breakfast, lunch, and dinner daily. The

Mountain Top is always busy, serving a good breakfast and conventional truck-stop fare for lunch and dinner. Entrées $7.25–12.25.

✦ **Shirley's Diner** (304-822-3904), 44 Marsham St. Breakfast and lunch Sat., Mon., and Tue.; breakfast, lunch, and dinner Wed.–Fri. Inside a small building on a side street, Shirley Hott serves home-cooked meals to a loyal clientele, many of whom show up for breakfast every day she is open. Soups and sandwiches for lunch, and a limited number of items for dinner. Entrées $6.50–9.50.

Wardensville

✦ **Kac-Ka-Pon Restaurant** (304-874-3232), 295 East Main St., at the intersection of WV 55 and WV 259. Breakfast, lunch, and dinner daily. Current owners Doug and Diana Coffman have a real interest in the Kac-Ka-Pon—they grew up nearby, ate here with their families, and one of them even worked here as a dishwasher when a teenager. They put a lot of work into refurbishing the building, which was built in the 1960s, and they serve what I call honest country cooking: liver and onions, hot roast beef sandwich with mashed potatoes and gravy, country ham, and grilled trout. Finish your meal with a slice of homemade pie. Entrées $5–14.50.

✷ Entertainment

FILM

Moorefield

✦ **South Branch Cinema 6** (304-538-8100; www.wvafun.com), 100 Hyde St. The area's only movie theater.

MUSIC Avalon (304-947-5600; www.avalon-resort.com), Critten Owl Hollow Rd., off WV 29 northeast of Romney. If the usual music venues are too conventional and diffident for you, shed your inhibitions and head to the **Annual Music, Arts, and Crafts Festival** at the clothing-optional Avalon Resort (see *Lodging*) in August. Naturist groups may be the butt of many jokes, but the folks that run this festival are serious about their music and book some big names. Previous lineups have included nationally known performers such as songwriter John Gorka, Celtic band Big Agnes, and guitarist Carla Ulbrich.

✦ **Potomac Music** (304-822-6021), 152 East Main St., Romney. Inside you will find new, used, and vintage instruments, but even if you aren't a serious musician, you should show up for the Fri.- and Mon.-evening jam sessions. Starting about 6:30–7, local musicians gather on the sidewalk (or inside during cold weather) and play some of the most authentic and sincere mountain music you are likely to hear anywhere. They are really playing only for themselves, but you are invited to pull up one of the chairs or sit on the steps and enjoy what transpires. A highly recommended, priceless experience that won't cost you a penny.

THEATER

McCoy's Grand Theatre (304-530-7115; www.mccoysgrand.com), 121 N.

A JAM SESSION AT POTOMAC MUSIC

Main St., Moorefield. Locally produced plays (such as *Harvey* and *How to Succeed in Business Without Really Trying*) and others are presented in the refurbished 1920s theater.

✳ Selective Shopping

ANTIQUES Antiques, Etc. and Main St. Espresso (304-874-3300; www.antiquesandespresso.com) 295 E. Main St., Wardensville. With more than 20 dealers and consigners located in a former Southern States Feed Store, there's a little bit of everything here. The proprietors also support local artisans, so you'll find a nice array of jewelry, handmade soaps, wood works, and other pieces of art. In addition, there is a café that offers a full coffee bar and a lunch menu that has featured items—such as shrimp wraps, crab chowder, and gazpacho—not often found in this part of the state. Open hours have been known to change, so it may be wise to call ahead.

Dan's Antiques (304-496-8187), US 50, Augusta. Open daily. More than 10,000 square feet of furniture, clocks, glassware, toys, and other items offered by multiple dealers.

CRAFTS Lost River Craft Cooperative (304-897-7242; www.lostriver craft.com; mailing address: P.O. Box 26, Lost River 26810), on WV 259, halfway between Baker and Mathias. Closed Tue. through Thurs. from Memorial Day to late Oct.; open weekends mid-Apr. to Memorial Day and Nov. and Dec. The handcrafted products you will find in this cooperative have been placed here only after having been selected by jury, so the woven items, wood-turned bowls, pottery, and the like are much higher in quality than you will find in other shops. The pieces of wood furniture were some of the nicest I've seen, and they would have gone home with me if had not been traveling for another month.

The cooperative is on the floor above the **Lost River Museum** (see *To See—Museums*).

FARMERS' MARKETS Hampshire County Farmers' Market (304-822-3603). Pick up fresh produce at the Bank of Romney Community Building, Romney, on Sat. July–Oct.

White Barn Farm Market (304-257-3353), on US 55 across from the South Branch Inn. Open June–Dec. Not a farmers' market per se (there are not multiple stands here), but still some great produce and other locally made items and gifts.

PICK-YOUR-OWN PRODUCE FARMS

Levels
Ken Ruggles Orchard (304-492-5181; 492-5751). Call for directions. Sweet corn and sour cherries are available for picking from mid-June into July; apples, peaches, and plums will be ripe in August.

Romney
Gary Shanholtz Orchard (304-822-5827), Jersey Mountain Rd. Cherries and raspberries are usually ready to pick the last part of June and the first week in July.

SPECIAL SHOPS

Romney
Anderson's Corner (304-822-4285; www.andersonscorner.com), 8 West Main St., Romney. Stop in to take a look at new and antique jewelry and some clever locally produced handcrafted items.

✐ **Gourmet Central** (304-822-6047; www.wvgourmetfoods.com/gourmet central), 47 Industrial Park Rd., Romney. Open Mon.–Fri. Inside an industrial park, Harvey Christie, a.k.a. "Chef Harv," oversees a food-processing business that prepares and packages food for a wide range of other businesses, including the Homestead and Stonewall Jackson Resorts, and The Greenbrier in White Sulphur Springs. All of the products that he makes, from gourmet spaghetti sauce to hot pepper jelly to barbecue sauce, are for sale. Best of all—especially for the kids—if things are not too busy, Chef Harv or an employee will take you through the manufacturing process and maybe even let you participate. The day I was there, they were making a health fruit drink (that was going to Indonesia!), and I rolled labels onto the bottles.

Lost River
Lost River General Store (304-897-6169; www. thelostrivergeneralstore .com), 7015 State Rd. 259, Lost River. Adjacent to the Inn at Lost River (see Lodging), the general store is located in a late 1800s buildings that has been serving the local (and now traveling) community for more than 100 years. Filled with items you would expect to find, as well as many unexpected folk art, gourmet foods, collectibles, and West Virginia wines. A small café serves coffee, pastries, and light lunches.

WINERY Robert F. Pliska and Company Winery (304-289-3493; 1-877-747-2737; www.vineyardhome .org), 101 Piterra Place, Purgitsville, which is off WV 28/US 220. Ruth and Robert Pliska planted their first grapes across an isolated mountaintop in 1974 and bottled their first wine in 1983, making them one of the earliest wineries in West Virginia. The three fruit and six grape wines gained national

attention when Julia Child used them in her television cooking show over the course of five years. It's a long dirt-road drive to the winery and the top of the mountain, so it is best to call ahead, especially if you are hoping to take a tour of the facility.

Incidentally, your wine purchase supports a good cause. For more than three decades, the Pliskas have teamed with Homes for the Mentally Handicapped by having four residents live on their property and help with the wine-making.

✳ Special Events
April: **Annual Barbershop Quartets on Parade** (304-874-3950), Wardensville, Songs sung in four voices all over town.

June: **Annual Strawberry Festival** (304-492-5073), Hampshire County Fairgrounds. **Fort Edwards Farm Days** (304-496-7218; www.fortedwards .org), Fort Edwards Visitor Center, Capon Springs. **South Branch Bluegrass Festival** (304-822-7300), Wapocoma Family Campground south of Romney. Music, children's activities, and fireworks.

September: **Hampshire Heritage Fest** (www. hampshireheritagefest .com), multiple sites Hampshire County. Crafts, artwork, Civil War reenactments, music, and living-history demonstrations.

October: **Hampshire County Arts Council Fall Fine Art & Photography Show** (www.hampshirearts.org), Romney. **Old-Fashioned Apple Harvest Festival** (304-289-3511), Burlington. Apple-butter making, crafts, music, flea market, and apples turned into a multitude of foods.

THE LAND OF CANAAN—
CANAAN VALLEY, BLACKWATER
FALLS, AND DOLLY SODS

When glaciers advanced from the Arctic during the last ice age, the only way many plants and animals were able to survive was to "migrate" southward. Once the ice floes receded, some of these plants and animals were able to take up permanent residence by clinging to the Allegheny Mountains' higher elevations, where conditions closely resemble that of their original habitats much farther north.

Canaan Valley is such a place. At an elevation of 3,200 feet and above, it receives 150 to 200 inches of snow annually and looks more like New England and Canada than West Virginia. In this highest large valley in eastern America—which is close to 14 miles long—grow spruce, balsam fir, bigtooth aspen, sphagnum moss, snowberry, and cranberry tree. Here is the land of the snowshoe hare, beaver, mink, and endangered West Virginia flying squirrel. About 9,500 acres of wetlands, the largest such complex in West Virginia, attract shorebirds not often found anywhere else in the state. Solitary and spotted sandpipers are often seen darting about in the bogs, muskegs, spirea thickets, and shrub swamps. Bobolink and Savannah sparrow wing their way through the swaying vegetation of extensive grasslands. Ferns and running cedar grow on bumpy hummocks, and mountainsides rise up to meet the sky.

There are many stories as to how Canaan Valley was named. The most widely circulated one says that an early explorer in the mid-1700s was so moved by the scene he saw from a mountain overlook that, in reference to biblical passages, he proclaimed, "Behold, the Land of Canaan!" (Be sure to pronounce this as *kuh-NANE*, or locals will immediately recognize you as a visitor.)

Canaan Mountain rises close to 4,000 feet in elevation to the northwest, separating the valley from the Blackwater River and the deep and narrow canyon the stream has carved into the Allegheny Plateau. The dramatically tumbling Blackwater Falls is justifiably one of the most photographed scenes in the state.

Cabin Mountain forms the valley's southeastern border. This is the Allegheny Front, the eastern rampart of the Allegheny Plateau that rises quickly and sharply from the South Branch of the Potomac River Valley, and a part of the so-called

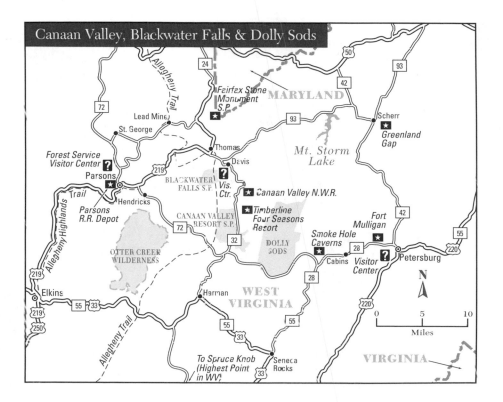

Eastern Continental Divide. Raindrops that happen to fall on the eastern side of the divide will flow to the Atlantic Ocean, while those that fall to the west will eventually reach the Gulf of Mexico. Something to ponder as you stand upon this windswept topography: It is possible that a small grain of sand that is washed into a stream on top of this mountain may one day add just a bit more mass to the delta at the mouth of the Mississippi River.

All of this is spectacular country and, in my opinion—along with the rest of the Potomac Highlands—possesses the most sensational scenery in the entire state.

COMMUNITIES In the late 1800s, when Henry Gassaway **Davis** paid less than $20 an acre for the land around the town that bears his name, the area was a vast forest of hardwoods and spruce. During the lumber boom (from about 1880 to the 1920s), the town had a population of 3,000 and was a bustling place with boardinghouses, banks, hotels, sawmills, and restaurants. With most of the timber removed, the area fell into a depression, but today Davis is on the rise again. Making use of many of the original buildings (so there is still the feel of a mountain lumber town), B&Bs, restaurants, outfitters, and gift shops are catering to the thousands of tourists—including hikers, bikers, equestrians, skiers, anglers, hunters, and sightseers—who flock here year-round. (By the way, you will notice that Davis and Canaan Valley have the same zip code. Davis is the town, and the valley is a place name.)

Located at the meeting place of the Cheat River, Shavers Fork, and Black Fork, **Parsons**'s early economic base was a tannery. Somewhat removed from the tourist areas of the land of Canaan, the town is still primarily industrial in nature, with the Kingsford Charcoal company producing more than 1 billion charcoal briquettes annually. (It's quite a shock to drive northward on US 219, go around a curve, and suddenly see the factory, with roaring flames shooting out of its tall smokestacks.)

Sited along the North Fork of the Blackwater River, the small town of **Thomas** owes its existence to the area's coal mines, whose product was shipped by rail to the town and turned into coke by the hundreds of small beehive coke ovens that lined the tracks. Like Davis, Thomas was a boomtown in its heyday, with a population of 3,000 living on terraces that progress up the hillside above the river. The hotels, opera houses, and saloons of the former days are being turned into art galleries, restaurants, and antiques shops.

GUIDANCE The **Grant County Chamber of Commerce** (304-257-2722; www .gowv.com), 105 Virginia Ave., Suite 1, Petersburg 26847, maintains a Chamber of Commerce Travel Information Center inside the South Side Depot (see *Selective Shopping*) at 126 South Main St.

There is a small information center (304-478-2402) in the historic 1888 Parsons **Railroad Depot** on US 219 near the southern end of Parsons. Also inside is a small railroad museum and arts-and-crafts co-op.

The **Cheat Ranger District** (304-478-3251) on US 219 east of Parsons can provide you with maps and other information about the Monongahela National Forest areas in the Land of Canaan.

Tucker County Convention and Visitors Bureau (304-259-5315; 1-800-782-2775; www.canaanvalley.org; mailing address: P.O. Box 565, Davis 26260), on WV 32 in downtown Davis. I've always envied the employees of this agency. Not only

A major highway project that has been planned and contested for decades is now under way. Known as **Corridor H** (it will be designated US 48 when completed), it will be a fast-track route for people from the northern Virginia–Washington, DC, area to reach the Land of Canaan. It enters the state near Wardensville, moves on to Mooorefield, continues westward by way of Mount Storm Lake, and cuts between Thomas and Davis (within almost a stone's throw of Canaan Valley) before meeting up with US 219 near Elkins. One of the reasons the project has taken so long is that many local people (along with others) recognize the profound changes the highway will bring. Years of challenges and court battles have led to minor alterations in the highway's location, but as is so often the case in our modern world, prodevelopment and business interests have won out. There is no doubt that some good things will come from it, but those who value the quiet atmosphere of this area will have to make adjustments. My advice? As I said in the previous chapter, visit as soon and as often as possible to experience the Land of Canaan before these changes occur.

do they live in one of the best parts of the state, but they also get to share with visitors all of the good things to do here.

West Virginia Mountain Highlands (304-636-8400; 1-877-WVA-MTNS; www .mountainhighlands.com; mailing address: P.O. Box 1456, Elkins 26241) is an umbrella organization that supplies information about the entire Potomac Highlands region.

GETTING THERE *By air:* The Land of Canaan is a long way from any major airport. Whichever you choose, you have to be prepared for many miles of driving to reach here.

To the east, you could fly into **Washington Dulles International Airport** (703-572-2700; www.metwashairports.com/dulles) in northern Virginia and drive close to 150 miles. The other major airport, also about 150 miles away, is **Pittsburgh International Airport** (412-472-3525; www.pitairport.com) in Pennsylvania.

If you don't mind making connections and flying commuter and shuttle flights (and the extra expense they entail), you could fly into **Morgantown Municipal Airport** (304-291-7461; www.morgantownairport.com) or **North Central West Virginia Airport** (304-842-3400; www.flyckb.com) near Clarksburg. Both are 70–80 miles away.

One additional choice is **Yeager Airport** (304-344-8033; www.yeagerairport.com) in Charleston. It's almost 200 miles away, but you'll be driving exclusively through West Virginia, giving you the opportunity to see different parts of the state—and make use of even more of the information found in this book.

By car: From the north, leave **I-68** at Keysers Ridge in western Maryland and follow **US 219** to Thomas. Coming from the east, exit **I-81** at Strasburg, Virginia, and drive west on **US 48** (which becomes **WV 55** in West Virginia) to Petersburg. (This route will change substantially when Corridor H [US 48] is completed.) The best approach from the west is to take **I-79** exit 99 (near Weston), follow US 33 to Elkins, and continue on **US 219** to Parsons and Thomas.

My favorite approach is from the south; it's a long drive on two-lane country roads, but you get to pass through the length of the Potomac Highlands. Take **I-64** exit 175 at White Sulphur Springs, drive east through town on **US 60**, turn north on **WV 92**, and follow it north to Petersburg. There is the option of turning onto WV 55 at Seneca Rocks and continuing northward on **WV 32** to Canaan Valley. All in all, this is one of the most scenic drives in the entire state.

By rail: The closest you can get to this area by **AMTRAK** (1-800-872-7245; www .amtrak.com) is its station in Cumberland, Maryland.

GETTING AROUND *By bus:* **Potomac Valley Transit** (304-257-1414; 1-800-565-7240; www.potomacvalleytransit.org; mailing address: P.O. Box 278, Petersburg 26847) is a far-reaching public-transportation system that will take you to a number of small towns and settlements in and around Petersburg—and as far away as Cumberland and Oakland, Maryland, and Winchester and Harrisonburg, Virginia. Unfortunately, there is no public-transportation service to Thomas, Davis, Canaan Valley, and other locales in the western part of the Land of Canaan.

By car: It's all two-lane driving until Corridor H (US 48) is completed.

MEDICAL EMERGENCIES Grant Memorial Hospital (304-257-1026; www.grantmemorial.com), Hospital Dr. on WV 28/WV 55, on the west side of Petersburg.

✷ To See

CAVERN TOURS ✎ **Smoke Hole Caverns** (304-257-4442; 1-800-828-8478; www.smokehole.com; mailing address: HC 59, Box 39, Seneca Rocks 26884), on WV 55/WV28 in Cabins, less than 10 miles west of Petersburg. Adults $13, children (ages 5–12) $8, age 4 and younger free. The 45-minute guided tours take you deep into the caverns, where the temperature is 56 degrees year-round and the sound of flowing or dripping water is a constant. As is done in other commercial caverns, you will be directed to gaze upon interesting formations with fanciful names like "The Capitol Dome" and "Queens Canopy," but you will also get to see what is believed to be the world's longest ribbon stalactite (it's more than 16 feet long and weighs 12,000 pounds), one of only two known cavern coral pools, and unusual sideways-growing helectites. The accompanying gift shop has a surprisingly good selection of local-interest books.

DRIVING TOURS, SCENIC & HISTORIC

A circular route of 100 miles takes you by just about everything the Land of Canaan has to offer. It's a full day of sight-seeing; maybe plan two days so that you can get out of the car and experience the places firsthand. There's more than 15 miles of driving on dirt forest service roads, but don't worry, the roads are in good shape—attested to by the fact that I traveled them in a Honda Civic sedan.

Begin the trip by driving westward from Petersburg on WV 55/WV 28 for 10 miles, passing through scenic North Fork Gap and by Smoke Hole Caverns (see *Cavern Tours*). Turn right onto what some maps show as WV 4, but the roadway sign says is Jordan Run Road (WV 28/7). Make a left in another 7.9 miles onto FSR 75, which will soon turn to dirt. Reach the top of the mountain and a parking area for Bear Rocks and the Dolly Sods North area 4.8 miles later (see the "Dolly Sods" sidebar later in this chapter). Another 3 miles brings you to the trails in the upper part of Dolly Sods Wilderness and the Red Creek Campground. Close to 3 miles beyond it, bear right onto FSR 19 to drive by trailheads for the Flat Rock/Roaring Plains Area and the lower portions of the wilderness.

SMOKE HOLE CAVERNS

FSR 19 becomes paved WV 45/4, which takes you through farmland to a right turn onto WV 32 and the wonderful traverse of Canaan Valley, where you have the options of visiting Canaan Valley Resort State Park, Timberline Four Seasons Resort, Canaan Valley

BLACKWATER FALLS

National Wildlife Refuge, and other attractions. At the northern end of the valley, WV 32 climbs Canaan Mountain, passing through a forest of spruce before delivering you to the small town of Davis. Shopping and good restaurants may slow your progress a bit, but when you are ready to leave, continue on WV 32 to make a right onto WV 93. (You have the option of visiting Blackwater Falls State Park and Thomas before leaving the Davis area.)

WV 93 rises onto the high plateau of the Allegheny Front. Along the way, you will pass reclaimed strip mines and a couple of active ones before driving around Mount Storm Lake (see *Lake*), joining up with WV 42, and making a rapid and exhilarating descent down the face of the front.

When WV 42 and WV 93 split at Scherr, make a left onto WV 93, but almost immediately make a right onto WV 1, and a short distance later, another right onto WV 3/3 to pass through attractive Greenland Gap (see *Green Space—Nature Preserve*). At the far end of the gap, a right onto WV 3 and a left onto WV 42 will take you through the farmland of the South Branch of the Potomac River valley before returning you to Petersburg.

HISTORIC SITES

Petersburg

&. **Fort Mulligan**. Follow directional signs from WV 55 on the west side of Petersburg. On a knoll with a sweeping view of the valley of the South Branch of the Potomac River, Fort Mulligan was constructed by Union troops in 1863 as a place to try to stem the movement of agricultural supplies to Confederate forces. Interpretive panels along a short pathway, most of which is accessible to wheelchairs, provide a great amount of detailed information. The breastworks and trenches are still very much in evidence and are some of the best preserved I've seen. The impressive 360-degree view of the valley and the abrupt rampart of the mountains of the Allegheny Front to the west make this a place to visit even if you are not interested in the Civil War.

Thomas

In 1681, Lord Hampton received a grant of 6 million acres, which was inherited by Lord Fairfax in 1722. Marking the boundary of his land, the **Fairfax Stone** (which some historians believe was placed here by the young surveyor George Washington) is most significant today because it sits at the small spring that is the very source of the Potomac River. Fairfax Stone State Park, located off US 219 about 4 miles north of Thomas, provides 4 acres of protection for the stone and the spring.

LAKE Mount Storm Lake is one of the most interesting bodies of water you will come across in the state. Unlike most artificial lakes that were constructed to create hydroelectric power, 1,200-acre Mount Storm Lake is here to provide cooling water to the coal-fired power plant that sits on its western shore. The resulting discharged warm water usually keeps the lake at 60 degrees or above during the winter, making it a favorite of scuba divers who use it to keep in practice during the colder months. The water gets to about 90 degrees during the warmer months, so it's also great for swimming (if you don't mind looking at the massive power plant looming on the horizon) when nearby mountain streams are way too cold to even think of wading in. The lake sits high on the Allegheny Plateau and receives near steady winds for sailboarding or sailboating. Sadly, there are no rental facilities, so you will have to bring your own. The best access for swimming or boating is the ramp off WV 93 at the eastern end of the lake's dam.

MUSEUMS

Parsons
𝄢 ⚸ **Parsons Railroad Depot** (304-478-2402), Main St., on the southern end of town. In addition to a small visitor center supplying tourist brochures, inside the refurbished 1888 depot is a small museum with railroad memorabilia and a surprising model train layout that will entertain you and the kids. This is also the home of the **Heritage House Fine Arts and Crafts Co-op**, with some quality items worth making a stop here even if you have no interest in the museum.

Petersburg
Top Kick's Military Museum (304-257-1392; mailing address: P.O. Box 152, Petersburg 26847). About 1.5 miles west of Petersburg, turn into Ridgeview Estates and follow signs to Maple Dr. Free; donations accepted. Gerald Bland spent 20 years as an army combat engineer, and this museum is a result of his passion for military vehicles. He began collecting in the 1980s and opened the museum in 1995, with more than 50 vehicles and a building overflowing with weapons, field and mess gear, radios, and uniforms. Mr. Bland does all of the restoration himself and, amazingly, almost all of the vehicles are in running order. His knowledge and the stories he relates are reason enough to make a visit.

WATERFALLS See Blackwater Falls State Park under *Green Space—Parks*.

OTHER SITES It's quite disconcerting—and almost appears like a scene from a science fiction movie—when you're driving northward toward Thomas on US 219 and go around a curve to have 350-foot-tall windmills suddenly appear on the ridgeline in front of you. With 100-foot blades (creating a 200-foot circle) slowly turning in the mountain breezes at 17 revolutions per minute, the tips of the blades are moving at 114 miles per hour. The 44 windmills of the **Mountaineer Wind Energy Center** stretch for 6 miles along the top of Backbone Mountain and produce the electricity needed to power 22,000 homes. There's a parking area at the base of the windmill nearest to the road, and it's quite an experience to be so close to something so massive that responds to something so ethereal as the wind. You can find out more about them by contacting Mountaineer Wind Energy Center, HC 60, Box 292, Thomas 26292; 304-463-3341.

✳ To Do

BICYCLING Blackwater Bikes (304-259-5286; www.blackwaterbikes.com), on WV 32 in downtown Davis. Blackwater Bikes was one of the first places to recognize the vast opportunities for road and mountain biking in this area. To help you discover these places on your own, the shop rents all manner of bicycles, will service yours, or will sell you a new one. They will be happy to tell you about many miles of single and double track or quiet country lanes to ride.

For other bicycling opportunities, also see Canaan Mountain under *Hiking*; *Rail Trails*; *Green Space—Parks*; and the Highland Inn under *Lodging*.

BIRDING See *Green Space—Wildlife Refuge*.

FISHING In and around the Canaan Valley area, the West Virginia Division of Natural Resources stocks **Clover Run, Horseshoe Run, Dry Fork, Red Creek, Red Run**, and the **Blackwater River. Mount Storm Lake** is stocked with large-mouth bass, channel catfish, and sunfish. A bit more to the east, the **South Branch of the Potomac River**, which has yielded a number of state-record catches, offers good fishing for smallmouth bass, catfish, eel, carp, and a variety of trout. At the **South Mill Creek Dam**, 14 miles south of Petersburg on South Mill Creek Rd., a boat ramp along with a fishing pier for the handicapped lets you fish for crappie, trout, largemouth bass, sunfish, and catfish in the small lake. Also available are a picnic area, restroom, and an easy walking trail along the shoreline.

Scherr

✍ ♿ **Mountain Meadow Farm** (304-749-8049; mailing address: HC 72, Box 7168, Scherr 26726), on WV 93, 2 miles north of the WV 93 intersection with WV 42 in Scherr. In a family-friendly atmosphere, the Ours family has several ponds in which you can fish (for a fee) for stocked trout. Other facilities are rather limited, but what you pay by the inch for what you catch is unbelievably low.

GOLF

Canaan Valley

✍ ♿ **Canaan Valley Resort State Park** (304-866-4121; 1-800-622-4121; www .canaanresort.com; mailing address: HC 70, Box 330, Canaan Valley 26260), on WV 32. The park's 18-hole, par 72 course is on nearly level ground and has 65 sand bunkers and numerous water hazards. Open Apr.–Oct. Rates are highest during the usual tourist time and drop by several significant dollars in the off-season.

Parsons

✍ **Holly Meadows Golf Course** (304-478-3406), WV 72 at the end of County Farm Rd. The nine-hole public course is located in a rural setting with an undulating landscape. Lots of trees will make you alter your shots, fairways are narrow, and the greens are small. Children age 12 and under play for free with a paying adult.

HIKING The **Allegheny Trail** (see "What's Where in West Virginia" at the front of this book for background information) enters the Land of Canaan area from the south as it leaves its route along Glady Fork to pass through Canaan Valley Resort State Park, over Canaan Mountain, into Blackwater Falls State Park, and continue northward close to the Cheat River.

The **American Discovery Trail**, a route that runs more than 6,800 miles from the Atlantic Ocean to the Pacific shore, enters this area on country roads near the

DOLLY SODS

DOLLY SODS

✪ The land that came to be called **Dolly Sods** was once the domain of loggers who, from the mid-1800s to the early 1900s, cut almost all of the trees (which averaged 4 feet in diameter) growing on the mountain's broad plateau. The amount of slash left behind, along with the dried-out soil, was perfect tinder, and massive fires repeatedly swept across the land. The rich humus layer, which some sources say was more than 6 feet deep, was completely burned away. Near the end of the logging era, settlers, such as the Dahle family, burned the land even more to create open meadows, or "sods," on which to graze livestock. They obtained a good grass cover by doing this, but it only lasted a short while as the soil was too nutrient-poor to support the luxuriant growth. Disillusioned, the Dahles moved on, but the land has borne the Anglicized version of their name ever since.

Heath vegetation, such as blueberry and teaberry, can tolerate such poor soil and soon thrived. In addition, it is theorized that, with no large trees to draw moisture, the water table rose, thereby restricting the growth of new forests and expanding the bogs. Dolly Sods has evolved into a windswept landscape of rocky plains, heath barrens, sphagnum bogs, stunted spruce trees with limbs growing on just one side, and wide vistas in all directions.

This eerily beautiful landscape is now a part of the Monongahela National Forest and one of the Mountain State's most popular hiking destinations. The centerpiece is 10,215-acre **Dolly Sods Wilderness**, where the mountain plateau has been cut into a deep gorge by the erosive action of Red Creek. Close to 28 miles of interconnecting trails drop from the plateau to Red Creek, forming a network of routes through open plains and dense forest. Red Creek is a popular trout stream with crashing waterfalls and deep pools for summertime swimming. The forest service maintains the Red Creek Campground on FSR 75, but it's so small and popular that you would be lucky to find an open space from spring to fall. Don't worry, though, as backcountry camping is permitted throughout this area. Adjacent to the campground is the North-land Loop Trail, an easy 0 3-mile pathway whose interpretive signs provide excellent information about the area's flora, fauna, and history.

In the 1990s, the forest service purchased 6,168 acres of land north of the wilderness that has come to be known as **Dolly Sods North**. It is a land of bogs, heath, insectivorous plants, and small stunted spruces growing a scant few feet up from the ground, meaning the views are nearly continuous and far reaching. For a while, hikers had to find their own way among the maze of old logging routes, but the forest service has now named and signed these pathways, making it easy to navigate and plan your hike. Without a doubt, this can be one of the most magnificent hiking experiences in the Mountain State. Not to be missed at the very northern end of this area are Bear Rocks, whose spectacular views to the east are just a short five-minute walk from a parking area off FSR 75.

Adjoining the Dolly Sods Wilderness to the south are the 17.4 square miles of the **Flat Rock/Roaring Plains Area**. The vegetation and scenery are very much like that found in the wilderness, but unlike the pathways of the wilderness, all of the 17 miles of trails are signed and blazed, welcomed assurances for those just beginning to hone their outdoor abilities. It is also a good place to escape the large numbers of people drawn to Dolly Sods. The forest service says that hiker traffic is on the rise, yet I have seen few people each time I have been here. In fact on an overnight journey I took here on a beautiful Labor Day weekend, I did not see anyone on the pathways.

You can reach all of these areas from the east by driving westward from Petersburg on WV 55/WV 28 for 10 miles. Turn right onto what some maps show as WV 4, but the roadway sign says is Jordan Run Rd. (WV 28/7). Make a left in another 7.9 miles onto FSR 75, which will soon turn to dirt. Reach the top of the mountain and a parking area for Bear Rocks and the Dolly Sods North area 4.8 miles later. Another 3 miles brings you to the trails in the upper part of Dolly Sods Wilderness and the Red Creek Campground. Close to 3 miles beyond it bear right onto FSR 19 to drive by trailheads for the Flat Rock/Roaring Plains Area and the lower portions of the wilderness.

Coming from the west and Canaan Valley on WV 32, turn left onto WV 45/4 (about 12 miles south of Davis), which eventually brings you to the lower portion of the Dolly Sods Wilderness and graveled FSR 19.

town of Scherr, passes through Greenland Gap (see *Green Space—Nature Preserve*), climbs a forest road beside the Dolly Sods Wilderness area, follows the Allegheny Trail into Canaan Valley Resort and Blackwater Falls state parks, and passes through Blackwater Canyon on its way to Hendricks. The Dry Fork Rail-Trail and country roads take the pathway out of the area as it continues westward.

More information about the American Discovery Trail may be obtained from P.O. Box 20155, Washington, DC 20041; 540-720-5489 or 1-800-663-2387; www.discoverytrail.org.

Canaan Mountain, a 19,000-acre area of the Monongahela National Forest, is on a high mountain plateau ringed on three sides by high cliffs that separate Canaan Valley from the Blackwater Falls area. Covered by young spruce trees and vast boggy areas drained by tannin-stained streams, the mountain was logged around the turn of the 20th century, and the former railroad grades provide more than 20 miles of routes on which to explore by foot, horseback, mountain bike, or cross-county skis. These routes connect with those in Blackwater Falls and Canaan

THE INCIDENT AT RED CREEK

I'd like to tell you a story about something that happened to me in the Dolly Sods Wilderness a number of years ago. Friends I told about it dubbed it "The Incident at Red Creek," but I simply think of it as "My First Bear Encounter."

I was on only the second solo backpacking trip of my life and had spent a wonderful day walking Rohrbaugh Plains to Red Creek, where I set up camp. Being a city boy, I was unaccustomed to the sounds of the wilderness, but I was enjoying the gurgling of the creek and chirping of birds. However, just as darkness approached, there was a heavy rustling, followed by a sepulchral *haruumph* that echoed off the hillside above. I listened attentively. The rustling got closer, the *haruumphs* louder.

Bear! With that much noise and guttural reverberations, it had to be a bear. The sounds moved from the hillside into the valley. What should I do if it comes out of the woods and into the clearing? I know. I'll climb a tree (this was before I knew bears were excellent tree climbers). I've never had much upper body strength—I was the kid in high school gym class that couldn't scale the rope—so I don't know what made me think I could climb a tree. Yet, for practice, I grabbed a low hanging branch, and, walking up the trunk with my feet, wrapped by legs around the limb, ending up looking like a dangling sloth. Glancing down, I thought, "Well, that's just great!" My rear end was closer to the ground than if I was standing up, and my body swayed back and forth as if it was a piñata waiting to be split open by a bear claw.

"Okay, okay, that won't work," I thought. "I know, I know—I'll build a fire. That's what they always do in the movies to keep wild animals away."

Valley Resort state parks and are most easily accessed from gravel FSR 13 off WV 32, a few miles east of Davis. (The gravel road is a good, moderate mountain bike ride that takes you along the crest of this wonderful mountain, without forcing you to pedal through the bogs' muck and ooze.)

This is an excellent area to bring friends who are just learning about the outdoors. The trails, including a portion of the Allegheny Trail, are at a fairly easy grade, and they are signed at intersections, so navigation is no problem. Camping is permitted anywhere, and water is abundant. So abundant, in fact, that there is no way you can hike here without getting wet and muddy feet.

The state parks on both sides of the mountain sponsor a special Walk Between the Parks at least two (often four) times a year. The nice thing about the 9.7-mile journey is that you can do it as a lodge-to-lodge hike by staying at Blackwater Falls on the night you arrive in the area and spending the evening after the hike in Canaan Valley Resort State Park.

Just as the fire got some good, roaring flames, several loud *haruumphs* erupted in the woods only a few feet behind the tent.

"Well, crap! So much for animals being afraid of fire. I'm out of here!" After I hastily threw all my belongings in the tent, I took the aluminum poles out of their sleeves and gave the tent one good yank upward, sending several stakes flying into the darkness. Everything jammed into the pack and the fire doused with the contents of my canteen, I was ready to leave.

However, the coals were still smoldering, and to be a good camper, as Smokey says, the fire has to be "dead out." "Oh man, what to do, what to do? I need to get out of here now, but I don't have any more water. Wait. Wait. Yes, I do. There's still the liquid inside of me!"

So, conscientious camper that I am, I sidled up to the fire ring and relieved myself. Hoooo, weeee! What a lesson I learned! The stench of that serous fluid steaming up from hot embers was unbelievably foul and is an odor that, unfortunately, I can recall to this day.

Fire finally out, I grabbed the flashlight and walked the 3 miles out to the forest road where my car was parked. It was 2 o'clock by that time, so I dropped off into a fitful sleep, curled up in the backseat of my Volkswagen Beetle.

Early-morning sun rays had just hit the car, when *haruumph, haruumph*. In my slumber I thought, "Oh man, is that sound going to haunt me in my dreams, too?" *Haruumph*, again. "Crap. It's not in my dreams. Can it really be? Did that thing follow me all of the way out here?" Slowly, I open one eye. All I can see through the back window, blocking out any scenery, is a huge patch of fur. "Oh, man. It really did. It really did. It followed me. Okay. Okay. So, let's at least get a good look at it." I opened the other eye, and there . . . just on the other side of the glass and looking in at me . . . was the biggest buck deer I've ever seen in my life.

Almost as popular as the Dolly Sods Wilderness, **Otter Creek Wilderness** is a land of coves, hillsides, and ridgelines covered by northern hardwood and red spruce woodlands, with lush thickets of rhododendron spread across miles of forest floor. Otter Creek drains the 20,000 acres and has carved a deep basin that forms the heart of the wilderness. The 45 miles of trails primarily follow the routes of old logging railroads. The pathway along Otter Creek is one of the easiest, while those that branch off can be rather steep as they climb the surrounding mountainsides. All of the trails connect in one way or another, so hikes of just about any length are possible. Remember, this is a wilderness—trails are not marked or blazed, and they may rarely be maintained. Fording is the only way to get across streams. The northern, and most accessible, trailhead is on WV 72, 2 miles south of Hendricks.

Insider's tip: If you're feeling lazy but still want to make it to the top of one of the mountains surrounding Canaan Valley, **Timberline Four Seasons Resort** and **Canaan Valley Resort State Park** (see *Skiing, Downhill*) operate their chairlifts during the summer months. Either one will deliver you to Olympian views of the entire valley. You then have a choice of hiking some of the trails along the ridge-lines, walking a descending pathway back down the mountain, or, being lazy once again, taking the chairlift for the return trip.

For more hikes, also see *Green Space—Parks*, and for information about possible shuttles for many of the area hikes, see *Kayaking & Canoeing* as well as Highland Inn and Spa under *Lodging*.

HORSEBACK RIDING

Canaan Valley

🐎 **Mountain Trail Rides** (304-866-4652; www.mountaintrailrides.com; mailing address: HC 70, Box 311, Canaan Valley 26260), on Freeland Rd., 0.25 mile from WV 32. Experienced guides take adults and children as young as 6 years of age on one-hour to all-day rides through woodlands and open meadows. Pony rides for those 8 years old and younger are also available, as well as tack supplies if you own your own horse.

KAYAKING & CANOEING

St. George

Blackwater Outdoors Adventures (304-478-3775; www.blackwateroutdoors .com), located on the Cheat River in St. George. For more than 25 years, this family-owned company has taken guests for guided rafting, kayaking, and canoeing on the Cheat, Tygart, and North Fork of the Potomac rivers. They also offer tubing on the Blackwater River and guided fishing trips on a number of streams. Ask about the "duckies," inflatable kayaks that are a nice choice when the waters are running low.

Eagle's Nest Outfitters (304-257-2393; http://wvweb.com/eaglesnest; mailing address: P.O. Box 731, Petersburg 26847), 1 mile north of Petersburg on US 220/WV 55. Open Apr.–Oct. Arvella and John Zimmerer have decades of experience on the South Branch of the Potomac River and other nearby streams. They will rent you canoes, kayaks, duckies, or rafts, and provide gear, a safety lecture, maps, and a shuttle to and from the river. There are eight trips already mapped out, or the couple will tailor a journey of a few hours to a few days (letting you know the best places to camp) based on your skill level and time. Camping at the facility lets you get an early start the day of your trip. If their schedule permits, they are also available for shuttles if you have your own canoe, and they will even do shuttles for hiking trips into the surrounding areas.

If you are an angler and want to take advantage of some local knowledge, Eagle's Nest conducts guided fishing trips and a fishing school to introduce you to the sport or improve your skills.

Also see Blackwater Falls State Park under *Green Space—Parks*.

MINIATURE GOLF ♫ **Deerfield** (304-866-2127; 1-866-438-7259; www.deerfield wv.com), on WV 32, Canaan Valley. This course, in the Deerfield Village Resort, is open to the public.

RAIL TRAILS ♿ When completed, the **Allegheny Highlands Trail**, which follows the route of the former West Virginia Central and Pittsburgh Railway of the late 1800s, will be more than 40 miles long and extend from Elkins to Mount Storm Lake. At present, there are approximately 25 miles of the pathway from Highland Park (north of Elkins) to Hendricks (with a short section that needs to be ridden on highways). Unlike many rail trails that are perfectly flat, this one is fairly level for 13 miles north of Highland Park, then makes a stiff, short climb before descending quickly into Parsons and rising just as quickly to Hendricks. An additional 10 miles of trail in the Blackwater Canyon from Hendricks to Thomas is not officially a part of the trail—yet. Although those 10 miles are a great ride that you can currently do, there was some controversy about them being closed by a logging company. However, proponents of the trail won a legal victory just as this book went to press and it looks like those miles will remain open to the public. Check with the Highlands Trail Foundation (www.highlandstrail.org; P.O. Box 2862, Elkins 26241) for the latest information.

SAILING See *To See—Lake*.

SKATING ♫ **Canaan Valley Resort State Park** (304-866-4121; 1-800-622-4121; www.canaanresort.com; mailing address: HC 70, Box 330, Canaan Valley 26260), on WV 32. In the winter you can glide around on the covered outdoor ice-skating rink, while the skate park is the place to go in summer with your board or in-line skates.

SKIING, CROSS-COUNTRY White Grass Ski Touring Center (304-866-4114; www.whitegrass.com; mailing address: Rte. 1, Box 299, Canaan Valley 26260), on Freeland Rd. (WV 37), 1.3 miles from WV 32. Open daily during the snow season. White Grass (along with the Elk River Touring Center in the southern part of the Potomac Highlands) popularized the idea of cross-country skiing in West Virginia. In business for decades, they have 30 miles of trail on the side of Bald Mountain, with at least half of those miles groomed at all times. Rentals and lessons are available. The café serves some of the most delicious and innovative organic breakfasts, lunches, and dinners, as well as baked goods, to be found in the Land of Canaan. Come here to eat even if you have no plans to put on a pair of skis. Too bad it's not open year-round.

For other cross-country skiing opportunities, also see Canaan Mountain under *Hiking*; *Skiing, Downhill*; *Green Space—Parks*; and *Green Space—Wildlife Refuge*.

SKIING, DOWNHILL ✧ **Canaan Valley Resort State Park** (304-866-4121; 1-800-622-4121; www.canaanresort.com; mailing address: HC 70, Box 330, Canaan Valley 26260), on WV 32, Canaan Valley. Bald Mountain rises 4,300 feet above sea level, and the park's ski lift takes you almost to the summit, giving you access to dozens of routes with 850 feet of drop and a run of 6,000 feet. In addition to downhill (night skiing, too), the resort has facilities for air boarding, snowshoeing, cross-country skiing, tubing, and ice skating. Snowboarders can test their skills on rails, mailboxes, and other events in the Terrain Park. Lessons and equipment rental available.

✧ **Timberline Four Seasons Resort** (304-866-6326; 1-800-766-9464; www .timberlineresort.com), 488 Timberline Rd., Canaan Valley. Rising to the top of Cabin Mountain at 4,200 feet, two lifts deliver skiers to more than 30 runs, the longest of which is almost 2 miles. Canaan Valley gets an average of 150–200 inches of snow a year, but just in case Mother Nature fails to deliver, snowmaking equipment pretty much ensures good skiing for the entire season, Dec.–Mar. The lifts will also bring you to the beginning of a 10-mile network of cross-country ski trails. Timberline is the area's largest housing development, so you have a wide choice of accommodations to choose from—condos, duplexes, cabins, and private homes—if you wish to spend the night close to the slopes.

SLEDDING ✧ **Blackwater Falls State Park** (304-259-5216; www.blackwater falls.com; mailing address: P.O. Box 490, Davis 26260), on WV 29, 1 mile west of WV 32 in Davis. For those who want to zoom across snow but don't have any skiing abilities, the park has a groomed and maintained 0.25-mile-long sledding run. There is almost no effort involved in this activity, as you get to the top of the hill by way of a rope tow, which operates on weekends when snows are sufficient. Sleds are available for rent from mid-December through March 15.

SPA Massage Therapies of Davis (304-259-2255), WV 32 in the downtown Davis area close to the post office. Closed Tue. Massage therapies include neuromuscular pain relief, facials, reflexology, and a variety of massage techniques.

Also see Highland Inn and Spa under *Lodging*.

SWIMMING ✧ The swimming pool in **City Park**, Petersburg, is open during the usual summer season.

Also see *Green Space—Parks*.

SWIMMIN' HOLES ✧ Drive 2 miles northeast of Petersburg on US 220 to **Vernon W. Welton Park**, where you can take a swim in the South Branch of the Potomac River while looking up at interesting rock formations—some people call them the "Fox and Ox Rocks." The park is a nice location for a family outing as it also has picnic pavilions, restrooms, a playground, ball fields, boat ramps, and a walking track.

Also see *To See—Lake* and Horseshoe Run Recreation Area under *Lodging*.

TENNIS Four lighted tennis courts located in the Petersburg **City Park** are open to the public, as are the courts at **Blackwater Falls** and **Canaan Valley Resort state parks**.

WHITEWATER RAFTING *&* **Blackwater Outdoors Adventures** (304-478-3775; www.blackwateroutdoors.com; mailing address: Rte. 1, Box 239, St. George 26290), off WV 72, St. George. Whitewater rafting trips on the Cheat and Potomac rivers. Canoe, kayak, and ducky rentals in addition to providing shuttles for those who have their own watercraft.

✳ Green Space

NATURE PRESERVE The construction of four-lane Corridor H (US 48) is sure to change the landscape and character of the Land of Canaan, so it's gratifying to know that The Nature Conservancy has preserved at least a little piece of it. **Greenland Gap** (304-637-0160; www.nature.org), an 800-foot-deep gorge, was created by the erosive powers of diminutive Patterson Creek. The walls of the gap (about 1 mile east of the WV 42/WV 93 intersection at Scherr) rise at such a steep, 65-degree angle that sunlight reaches the forest floor only during the midday hours. Paved WV 3/3 will take you through the gap for an opportunity to observe the interesting vegetation and watch Patterson Creek tumble down one small waterfall after another. The conservancy has constructed trails to the ridgelines on both sides of the gaps, but make sure you're really ready to tackle them. The routes, which are hard to discern in some places, ascend the steep slopes on loose rock scree, making a hike that would be strenuous with good footing even tougher to accomplish.

PATTERSON CREEK IN GREENLAND GAP

PARKS

Canaan Valley
& ⅙ **Canaan Valley Resort State Park** (304-866-4121; 1-800-622-4121; www.canaanresort.com; mailing address: HC 70, Box 330, Canaan Valley 26260), on WV 32. Canaan Valley Resort State Park occupies more than 6,000 acres of this grand valley. It is one of West Virginia's resort parks, with an 18-hole championship golf course, tennis courts, a heated outdoor pool as well an indoor pool, a restaurant and lodge with more than 200 rooms, rental cabins, and a campground. The park's abundant snowfall makes it an obvious choice for skiing, and lifts take visitors to more than 30 runs with an 850-foot drop from atop

4,250-foot Bald Knob. The park also rents equipment for cross-country skiing, and a naturalist program operates year-round.

In recent years, the park has endeavored to update itself and appeal to a younger crowd, or families with children, by offering miniature golf, a skate park, climbing wall, Eurobungy, paintball, and mountain bike rentals. One of the newest offerings, and one that appeals to those with a sense of adventure and/or kids who like to treasure hunt, is geocaching, where you are given a GPS unit and instructions, and set off in search of the hidden cache.

There are close to 20 miles of hiking trails (many of which are also open to mountain bikes) that follow boardwalks into wetland areas, wander through open meadows, and rise onto the hillsides. For the most part they are easy to moderate in difficulty and provide a great way to see the various parts that make up the interesting Canaan Valley environment. If you have time for only one trail, make it the easy 1.5-mile Deer Run Trail, which starts at the lodge and goes through meadow, woods, and wetlands on its way to the park's nature center.

Davis

✿ & **Blackwater Falls State Park** (304-259-5216; www.blackwaterfalls.com; mailing address: P.O. Box 490, Davis 26260), on WV 29, 1 mile west of WV 32. Blackwater Falls State Park was established in 1937 to highlight and protect the falls and the land around it. Depending on what source you consult, the falls drop 63 feet, five stories, 57 feet, almost six stories, 65 feet, or 59 feet. No matter the height, the falls are an inspiring sight. Throughout much of the year, it is split into three by a jutting rock that sends one part of the river down the precipice as a long cascade, while another portion seeks various paths as it washes over dozens of layers of rock. The third runnel tumbles straight down for close to 30 feet before breaking apart near the base of the falls. The swell from spring rains overwhelms the jutting rock, and water roars down the falls in one crashing stream, wider than the length of the drop. The scene can become suspended in time when the falls freeze solid in winter.

Two trails lead to views of the falls. The paved 0.25-mile wheelchair-accessible Gentle Trail stays high above the falls. The slightly longer trail from the park's trading post descends into the gorge to an observation deck so close to the falls that visitors often get soaked from spray.

Insider's tip: Blackwater Falls may be the park's namesake, but don't do like most people do and overlook Elakala Falls. It's only a five-minute walk from the lodge to the 20-foot falls, which drop through a rich green landscape of rhododendron thickets and moss-covered rocks.

Within the 1,688-acre state park are more than 12 miles of trails (including a 3-mile stretch of the Allegheny Trail), rental cabins, guest rooms in the lodge, a campground, restaurant, tennis and game courts, and an indoor pool. Additional swimming, as well as boating (rentals available), is permitted in Pendleton Lake. Bicycles are rented from Memorial Day to Labor Day. About 10 miles of the trails are groomed for cross-country skiing (equipment may be rented from mid-Dec. through mid-Mar.), while there is a sledding course for those who want to glide across the snow without having to put forth any physical effort. Bicycles are permitted only on about 1 mile of trails, but the park's main road connects with FSR 13 (see Canaan Mountain under *To Do—Hiking*), opening up almost unlimited dirt road and single-track adventures. Nature programs, such as the Astronomy Weekend, Wildflower Pilgrimage, or Walk between the Parks (see Canaan Mountain under *To Do—Hiking*), are held throughout the year.

If you want to be lazy, almost all of the park's best features can be accessed from the main roadways with just easy short walks from where you park your car.

WILDLIFE REFUGE Canaan Valley National Wildlife Refuge (304-866-3858; www.fws.gov). The headquarters/visitor center is on WV 32, a short distance north of Canaan Valley Resort State Park. Canaan Valley contains 40 percent of the wetlands in the state, and the 15,000-acre Canaan Valley National Wildlife Refuge was established in 1994 as the nation's 500th such sanctuary to protect this intriguing environment. With the rapid development of private lands, which will surely only increase when Corridor H (US 48) is completed, it's nice to know that the essential core of the valley is protected.

More than 20 percent of the plants that grow here are normally found much farther north, while close to 200 species of birds have been seen winging their way over these lands. Mallards and black and wood ducks nest in the marshes, solitary and spotted sandpipers wander the wetlands, and hermit thrush, ovenbirds, and woodland warblers fly through the forest. Rarely seen in West Virginia are the common loons, cormorants, plovers, and greater and lesser scaups that ornithologists have identified here.

Within three far-flung tracts are more than 30 miles of trails open to hikers, with bicyclists and horseback riders permitted on more than 20 of those miles. An additional 10 miles are open in the winter for cross-country skiing. If time constraints keep you from exploring far afield, I suggest you walk the 0.25-mile Freeland Trail. It's a good introduction to the refuge, with a boardwalk winding over a wet field to a beaver pond and into a stand of balsam fir.

There are quite a number of rules, regulations, and restrictions about activities that may be done in the refuge, so it is a good idea to stop at the visitor center to get a clear picture of what you can or cannot do.

✻ Lodging

RESORTS

Canaan Valley 26260
& **Canaan Valley Resort State Park** (304-866-4121; 1-800-622-4121; www .canaanresort.com; mailing address: HC 70, Box 330), on WV 32. More than 200 guest rooms are located in several two-story wings that fan out from the main part of the lodge, which overlooks the wide expanse of the Canaan Valley. They are typical motel-like rooms, but the main reason for staying here is that you are in the middle of the state park, with all of its amenities, ski runs, and hiking and bik-

ing trails. *Insider's tip*: When making reservations, be sure to ask for a room with a valley view. You're in some of the state's most spectacular scenery, so why end up with a window overlooking the parking lot? $101–129.

Davis 26260
& **Blackwater Falls State Park** (304-259-5216; www.blackwaterfalls.com; mailing address: is P.O. Box 490), on WV 29, 1 mile west of WV 32. The park's lodge, close to the lip of Blackwater Canyon, has rooms that are somewhat small, standard motel-type accommodations. This is a spectacular

setting, but it's a real bummer to be here and get stuck in one of the rooms overlooking the parking lot; be sure to ask for a canyon-view room. A favorite pastime of guests is to sit on the lawn chairs along the edge of the canyon and watch the sun turn everything to a golden glow as it drops behind the ridge to the west. $94–125.

MOTELS & HOTELS

Canaan Valley 26260
Windwood Fly-In Resort (1-888-359-4667; www.windwoodresort.com), Cortland Lane, off WV 32. This is the place for you if you own an airplane. There's a 3,000-foot paved runway with pilot-activated lights and a motel-like inn adjacent. Those of you who do have your own planes will know what the following means: Identifier WV 62; elevation 3220 MSL; latitude 39 deg 03.03 N; longitude 79 deg 25.9 W; lights work on 123.0.

Petersburg 26847
✐ **Fort Hill Motel** (304-257-4717; www.forthillmotel.com; mailing address: HC 59, Box 99), on WV 55/28 on the west end of Petersburg. Petersburg native Sarah Moomau has owned this motel for more than two decades, and the property shows the care she pours into it. Everything is in working order, neat as a pin, and, unlike some places, she has the air-conditioning or heat on in advance of your arrival. Rooms have TVs, refrigerators, and microwaves. This is a nice family gathering place with an outdoor pool, sandbox, game courts, and no smoking anywhere on the entire property. The wonderful view of the farmlands of the South Branch of the Potomac River Valley is just one more reason to stay here. $60–110.

♨ **Homestead Inn** (304-257-1049; mailing address: HC 59, Box 146), on WV 55/28, 1 mile west of Petersburg.

Like the Fort Hill Motel, the appearance of the Homestead Inn is evidence that it has an owner—children's book author Helen Groves Hedrick—who cares. The small rooms are clean, in working order, and have TVs and refrigerators. The Hedrick family owns the adjacent dairy farm, and you can sit on benches at the back of the motel and observe the goings-on of daily rural life. $65; includes a continental breakfast of fruit, cereal, and packaged pastries.

INN

Canaan Valley 26260
Highland Inn and Spa (304-866-4455; 1-877-223-5388; www.highlandinnandspa.com; mailing address: HC 70, Box 291), on WV 32. The proprietors of the Highland Inn have turned their business into a one-stop shop for just about everything you could ever want to do in the Land of Canaan. The evening you arrive, they'll have your guest room, with one or two beds and private bath, ready. Rent a mountain bike or kayak and head out on your own adventure, or arrange to have them take you on a scenic driving, nature, or ecology tour. After a hard day outdoors, get a relaxing massage and/or facial in the spa. These folks will be of help even if you don't stay there or rent a piece of equipment from them. With advance reservations, they will shuttle you and your own equipment to local trailheads or waterways—a most valuable and time-saving service. $85–115.

BED & BREAKFASTS

Davis 26260
✐ ♨ **Bright Morning Inn & Guest House** (304-259-5119; www.brightmorninginn.com; mailing address: P.O. Box 576), on WV 32 in the downtown area. The tidy little flower garden that

greets you at the front door is an indication of how neat, clean, and well kept the interior of the Bright Morning Inn is. The inn was built in 1896 as a boardinghouse for lumberjacks, and the seven guest rooms and one suite (all have private baths) are furnished simply—fixtures from the 1800s, rag rugs, and quilts on the beds—in keeping with the building's history. The hosts have a vast knowledge of, and are enthusiastic about, the area, so the inn makes a great base from which to go hiking, biking, skiing, or paddling. The rate also includes a breakfast from the inn's delectable restaurant downstairs (see *Eating Out*). $110; suite is $135.

Doc's House, built in the 1920s, is behind the inn on one of the town's quiet side streets. With accommodations for a dozen people, it is a good choice for large groups or an extended stay. Much of the history of the doctor's family that lived in the house is still here, while some of the furniture came from the Jefferson Hotel in Richmond, Virginia. $250.

Petersburg 26847
Breath of Heaven Bed and Breakfast (304-257-4971; www.breathof heavenbb.com), 215 Dawn Lane. A swing on the deck, where breakfast is served in nice weather, gives you a chance to enjoy views of the 12 acres and surrounding Allegheny Mountains. Three guest rooms, each with a private bath, and a separate cottage that may accommodate up to four people, enable you stay overnight to enjoy the mountain breezes. $89–119

Thomas 26292
🐞 **The Lady Bug Bed and Breakfast** (304-463-3362; www.ladybug bandb.bizland.com; mailing address: P.O. Box 441), Bowery Ave. Extension. Janie Smith is an award-winning artist (mostly oils and watercolors), and the first things to greet you as you come

through the door are her art supplies and easels scattered about the first floor. The home was built around 1900 for a mine superintendent, but don't expect a stuffy Victorian atmosphere. Janie's paintings are found throughout the house, and furnishings are modest, giving you the feel of being family friends rather than paying guests. I like the guest rooms' large, bright windows, from which you can watch birds flit from branch to branch in the yard's tall evergreens as you relax in bed. Shared bath and continental breakfast, and an easy walk to MountainMade.com (see *Selective Shopping*). $60.

Upper Tract 26866
🐾 🐕 🐾 **Wildernest Inn** (304-257-9076; www.wildernestinn.com; mailing address: HC 32, Box 63 V), on South Mill Creek Rd., approximately 12 miles south of Petersburg. This is one dramatic place. You have to drive a 1-mile, steep, and narrow dirt road to reach the modern house perched on the lip of Spring Mountain. The wooden deck juts into space, while a spiral staircase twists upward into the air. Sunset's glow glistens on Mill Creek Lake hundreds of feet in the valley below, moonlight shines on the outdoor sunken hot tub, and 80 acres of mountaintop land invite secluded wanderings.

The six guest rooms have private baths, and the spacious home is furnished with pieces the hosts have acquired on their travels throughout the world. Stewart and Kathy Hornby are from southern Africa and bring a distinctive perspective to the B&B. Also, be sure to take them up on the optional dinner offer. Not only will you enjoy superb cooking, but you'll also experience dishes you may have never even heard about. They also make sure the food is plentiful at all dinners and breakfasts; their motto is, "There are no calories above 2,000 feet." $125–135.

CABINS AND VACATION RENTALS

Davis 26260

There are hundreds of rental homes, condominiums, cabins, and cottages located throughout the Land of Canaan. So many, in fact, that the listings for them take up page after page of advertisement booklets published by the agencies. The "Big Three" companies are **Canaan Realty** (304-866-4400; 1-800-448-0074; www.canaanrealty.com; mailing address: HC 70, Box 171), **Timberline Four Seasons Realty** (304-866-4777; 1-866-438-7259; www.t4sr.com; mailing address: HC 70, Box 475), and **Mountain Top Realty and Rentals** (304-866-4300; 1-800-624-4341; www.mountaintoprealty.com; mailing address: HC 70, Box 196).

Cabins 26855

Harman's North Fork Cottages (304-257-2220; 1-800-436-6254; www.wvlogcabins; mailing address: HC 59, Box 1412), on WV 55/28, approximately 7 miles west of Petersburg. Location, location, location. That old real estate adage could certainly apply to Harman's North Fork Cottages. Not only are they within a few minutes' drive of a number of the area's best attractions—Smoke Hole Caverns,

HARMAN'S NORTH FORK COTTAGES

Dolly Sods, Seneca Rocks, and others—the log buildings are on the banks of the North Fork of the South Branch of the Potomac River. Some look directly at an imposing rock wall rising dramatically from the water, while others are in Hopeville Canyon, secluded from the main highway. Fishing (great trout spot), swimming, hiking, and mountain biking are as simple as walking out the cottages' front doors.

These are not rustic. Each modern, attractive cottage (from one to four bedrooms) has a kitchen, laundry, full bath, satellite TV, linens and towels supplied, and a Jacuzzi or hot tub, either indoors or outside. Harman's offers guests different daily itineraries, including hunting and fishing, woodland Jeep tours, and canoe trips. One of my favorite places to stay in this area. $139–279; special rates available for stays of five nights or more.

Smoke Hole Family Log Cabins and Motel (304-257-4442; 1-800-828-8478; www.smokehole.com; mailing address: HC 59, Box 39, Seneca Rocks 26884), on WV 55/WV 28, less than 10 miles west of Petersburg. The modern one- and two-bedroom log cabins are clustered around an open field with a swimming pool and scenic trout stream (no fishing). Each cabin has a kitchen, fireplace, and cable TV. The honeymoon cabins have a Jacuzzi. $169–209.

Also available are rooms, with satellite TVs, in the log motel. $57–89.

Canaan Valley 26260

🐾 ♿ **Black Bear Resort** (304-866-4391; 1-800-553-2327; www.blackbearwv.com; mailing address: HC 70, Box 55, Davis 26260), Northside Cortland Rd., off WV 32. Black Bear Resort is spread across many acres of the gently sloping land that rises above Canaan Valley. This gives nearly every one of the rental properties—single houses, duplexes, small condo complexes, and a main, motel-like inn—sweeping views of the wide, open lowlands and surrounding ridgelines. A fitness trail, swimming pool, miniature golf course, and tennis court are available to all guests. There is a two-night minimum for all of the properties, except the lodge. Rates vary widely from property to property and season to season.

  Canaan Valley Resort State Park (304-866-4121; 1-800-622-4121; www.canaanresort.com; mailing address: HC 70, Box 330), on WV 32. The park's 20-plus cabins (officially they are cottages) are on a small, wooded knoll set a good distance away from the main lodge. With two to four bedrooms, they come completely equipped with all kitchen amenities and linens, and they are open year-round with heating and air-conditioning. $165–250.

  Deerfield Village Resort (304-866-4698; 1-800-342-3217; www.deerfieldwv.com; mailing address: HC 70, Box 152), on WV 32. The Deerfield is a tastefully constructed and decorated community located a short distance from the main highway and all of the attractions of Canaan Valley. There are two-, three-, and four-bedroom luxury homes and villas, with tennis, fishing pond, and pool available to all guests. The restaurant (see *Dining Out*) is popular with locals, too. Rates vary widely depending on the accommodations and the season.

The Golden Anchor Cabins (304-866-2722; www.goldenanchorcabins.com), WV 32 South (in the southernmost part of Canaan Valley). Several cabins, located next door to the Golden Anchor restaurant (see *Dining Out*), have soaring views of the western slope of the Dolly Sods Wilderness. All have hot tubs and other luxury amenities, but the one that struck my fancy has a tree growing

right through the outside deck. $185–250; two-night minimum on weekends.

Davis 26260

  Blackwater Falls State Park (304-259-5216; www.blackwaterfalls.com; mailing address: P.O. Box 490), on WV 29, 1 mile west of WV 32 in Davis. The park's deluxe year-round cabins are in a quiet wooded area about a mile from the lodge; have wood-paneled walls, stone fireplaces, and forced-air furnaces; and are in sizes that can accommodate up to eight people. Minimum rental periods are in effect during certain times of the year. $150–235.

CAMPGROUNDS

Canaan Valley 26260

  Canaan Valley Resort State Park (304-866-4121; 1-800-622-4121; www.canaanresort.com; mailing address: HC 70, Box 330), on WV 32. The small, wooded campground—less than 40 spaces—is set several hundred yards from the park's entrance and overlooks some of Canaan Valley's prettiest meadows and mountain ridgelines. It is open year-round and has a central bathhouse with hot showers. It's a great deal in winter: The rate is cheaper than staying at any indoor lodging, and you are just a short distance from the park's ski slopes.

Davis 26260

  Blackwater Falls State Park (304-259-5216; www.blackwaterfalls.com; mailing address: P.O. Box 490), on WV 29, 1 mile west of WV 32 in Davis. The park's campground, most popular with those with RVs, has two loops. One encircles a large, open field with little shade or privacy, while the other contains a forested area for more of a woodlands experience. Each loop has a central bathhouse with modern toilets and hot showers. Usually open from mid-Apr. through Oct.

Lead Mine 26290

The forest service's **Horseshoe Run Recreation Area**, 1.3 miles south of Lead Mine on WV 9, has a small campground with water from a spigot and a pump, vault and flush toilets, and a couple of trails. It is usually open from late May to early Sept. Best thing about staying here? Good swimming in Horseshoe Run.

✳ Where to Eat

DINING OUT Deerfield Restaurant (304-866-4698; 1-800-342-3217; www.deerfieldwv.com; mailing address: HC 70, Box 152, Canaan Valley 26263), on WV 32, Canaan Valley. The Deerfield is a popular place with locals, who come here knowing that whatever they choose will be well prepared and fresh tasting. My Pine Ridge chicken, with goat cheese, spinach, and pine nuts, was the perfect end to an active day in Canaan Valley. My dining companion thoroughly enjoyed the orange roughy stuffed with crabmeat. Next time we'll sample the steaks that the people at the next table praised. Entrées $13.99–27.99. (Also see *Lodging*.)

✐ **The Golden Anchor and Port Side Pub** (304-866-2722; www.golden anchorcabins.com), WV 32 South (in the southernmost part of Canaan Valley). Dinner daily. The restaurant was once a barn but has been completely redone, with the hickory boards having been removed, replaned, and replaced, creating a historic and polished interior. The large windows and dining porch overlook the western slope of the Dolly Sods Wilderness.

The menu offers pasta, chicken, and beef, but come here for the seafood, such as oysters, crabs, and flounder, which is delivered fresh from Maryland's Eastern Shore. Entrées $13.95–34.95. (Also see *Lodging*.)

EATING OUT

Canaan Valley

✐ **Big John's Family Fixin's** (304-866-4418; www.wvpizzacompany.com), on WV 32. Open for lunch and dinner daily. It seems as if a little bit of everything is served at this family-friendly place, where you walk in the door, pick up a menu, order at a central counter, and have the food delivered to your table. Sandwiches, soups, steaks, fish, chicken and dumplings, pizza, pasta, and more range from $2.99–7.99.

When the kids start squirming in their seats, send them off to play the many arcade games, from which they can win tickets to claim a number of small prizes. Children too small to play the games can be entertained by the model train that encircles the dining area on an elevated track.

Davis

✐ 🍴 ✿ **Bright Morning Inn Restaurant** (304-259-5119; www.bright morninginn.com; mailing address: P.O. Box 576, Davis 26260), on WV 32 in the downtown area. Open for breakfast daily in summer, Mon.–Fri. the rest of the year. When I think of breakfast in this area, I only think of the Bright Morning Inn Restaurant. Where else can you get a wholesome, hearty breakfast burrito of scrambled eggs, garlic potatoes, and cheese smothered in homemade chipotle sauce? Or how about scrambled eggs loaded with spinach, feta cheese, red peppers, and ramps? If you have never had biscuits and gravy, this is the place to try them as everything is made from scratch. Make sure that at least one of your meals while visiting this area is eaten here. Stay at one of the inn's rooms upstairs (see *Lodging*), and you will be guaranteed to do so—your choice of any breakfast is included in the room rate. $3.50–6.95.

Muttley's Downtown Soup Kitchen and Steakhouse (304-259-4858), on WV 32. Open for lunch and dinner. Muttley's is a casual steakhouse/tavern so popular—especially during the ski season—that there is often a long line snaking outside the door and along the street. Steaks are the specialty, but there's also chicken, pork, and seafood on the menu. Speaking of the menu, be sure to trade them around with other members of your party; the front cover of each has different, and often entertaining, photos. Pass up the other desserts in favor of the house-made cheesecake. Entrées $12.95–29.95.

Sirianni's (304-259-5454), on WV 32 in the downtown area. Open for lunch and dinner. You could spend half a day looking over all the photographs on the wall in this popular, and often crowded, Italian eatery. The owner's family came to America in the early 1900s, and the food reflects that heritage with pasta dishes—sautéed portobellos over linguine, squash pasta, mussels linguine, and puttanesca pasta—not often found in West Virginia restaurants. Order the "extreme garlic chips" (pizza dough topped with tremendous amounts of garlic) if you want people to avoid you for the next several hours. $9.25–15.95.

Petersburg

✒ **Family Tradition** (304-257-5305), 21 Virginia Ave. Open for breakfast, lunch, and dinner Mon.–Fri., breakfast Sat., and breakfast and lunch Sun. A native of Petersburg, Tonya Ketterman worked here for a few years before buying the restaurant. Don't come here for the décor—it's typical country restaurant with vinyl tables and chairs, dropped ceiling, and linoleum floor— but for the tasty homemade sausage gravy, brown beans and corn bread, and pies. $6.50–10.

✒ **Hermitage Inn Restaurant** (304-257-4800; www.hermitageinn.net), 203 Virginia Ave. The original Hermitage was built by slave labor in the 1840s as a private home, and it opened its doors as an inn in 1881. Today, the décor reflects the earlier days, and the cuisine is a blend of the old and new, with fried bread and apple butter being offered along with bruschetta topped with mozzarella and dried tomatoes. The potato soup I had for lunch was creamy and full of potato chunks. Dinner entrées include steak, pork, salmon, and rainbow trout, and there is a nice selection of imported and domestic beers and wines. $9.95–18.95. *Please Note*: Hermitage Inn Restaurant was still open, but for sale as this book went to press.

Also see *Entertainment—Music*.

MUTTLEY'S DOWNTOWN SOUP KITCHEN AND STEAKHOUSE

A VERY SPECIAL SHOPPING EXPERIENCE

☂ **MountainMade.com** (304-463-3355; 1-877-686-6233; www.mountainmade .com), Buxton and Landstreet Building, Douglas Rd., Thomas. West Virginia has become known to artists and craftspersons as a pleasant place to live. Those of us who appreciate what they create have learned that West Virginia is the place to come to browse for fine handcrafted items, and MountainMade.com is one of the companies that have helped establish this reputation. The main gallery is within a residential area. What was once an extravagant coal company store is now refurbished with gleaming hardwood floors, pressed tin ceiling, and large picture windows that bathe the artwork in natural light. This is a good place to spend a rainy day, as you could browse for hours, taking in 3,000 square feet of handmade jewelry, pottery, wood, glass, textiles, furniture, sculpture, and an extensive offering of books and music produced by more than 600 West Virginia artists. Every one of them had to pass a stringent juried process, so the items all exhibit a mastery of the artist's craft and, often, a wonderful range of originality. The gallery also presents a rotating exhibit of two-dimensional works.

Although many pieces are reasonably priced, you may experience a bit of sticker shock at some of the gallery's more elaborate objects. If so, head to downtown Thomas and MountainMade.com's **Country Store** on Front St. It is a little more down-home, with items that are still of high quality, but more along the lines of candles, food, and smaller works of art.

MountainMade.com is not just about selling. The nonprofit organization also wants to help you release your inner artist by offering a wide range of classes and workshops, usually held on Sat. from June through Nov. Past subjects have included weaving, jewelry, stained glass, papermaking, spinning, basketry, and hat making.

MICROBREWERY

Davis

🍺 **Blackwater Brewing Company** (304-259-4221; www.blackwater -brewing.com), William Ave. (WV 32), Davis. Lunch and dinner daily. Brewmaster Debbie Sampson has been making small batches (maximum of 24 kegs a month) here since 1998. Usually six brews are available every night, including her award-winning stout, porter, and wheat. None of the beers have additives, and all are cold filtered and nonpasturized to retain peak flavor. Arrive early for lunch, and you may get to witness the brewing process—the vats are located just a few feet behind the bar.

Appetizers, soups, sandwiches, and German and Italian entrées, such as Wiener schnitzel and manicotti, complement the beers. The place has been known to get crowded (and a bit rowdy) on Fri. and Sat. nights Entrées $8.99–22.50.

Thomas

Mountain State Brewing Company
(304-463-4500; www.mountainstate
brewing.com). Open Thurs.–Sat. Mountain State Brewing Company opened in
2005 and serves pints of their ales and
stouts across a handbuilt stone and copper bar located next to the brewery. A
very popular place, especially on the
weekends, when you can catch a wide
variety of live musical acts.

✳ Entertainment

**MUSIC The Purple Fiddle Coffee-
house & Mountain Market** (304-
463-4040; www.purplefiddle.com), 21
East Avenue (WV 32), Thomas. West
Virginian John Bright and his wife,
Kate, have turned the Purple Fiddle
into a household name for people who
enjoy music, especially mountain,
string band, and bluegrass music.
Thurs. is open mike night (no cover
and half-price beer), and Fri., Sat., and
Sun. feature local and regional talent
so good that national acts are starting
to ask to appear here. Even with all
the music and 50 different beers, the
Purple Fiddle remains a family-oriented place, with no cover charge ever for
children. This is my pick for the best
place in the state to just show up without having any idea who is performing
and know that you will get to hear
some quality music in an atmosphere
that is not rough and rowdy, but actually conducive to listening.

The Purple Fiddle is more than music,
though. Breakfast, lunch, and dinner
are served daily using local items,
there's homemade ice cream, and Kate
makes the home-baked goodies. She
also produces most of the wearable
fiber art that hangs on the walls and is
for sale.

✳ Selective Shopping

ART AND CRAFTS GALLERIES

Canaan Valley

Ben's Old Loom Barn (304-866-
2732; mailing address: HC 70, Box
139). Turn off WV 32 onto Cortland
Lane, go 0.4 mile, and turn right onto
Cortland/Thompson Rd. The shop is
on the right. Quite unpretentious, this
shop is recognized as one of the East
Coast's premier businesses in which to
purchase handwoven items. Local artisans, who may be at work when you
stop by, make most of the pieces.

Petersburg

Water Street Gallery (304-257-
4095), 5 Water St. Open Thu.–Sat.
11–4. Inside a small cottage on a side
street, Mary VanMeter has a continuously changing array of paintings, photographs, sculpture, pottery, and other
items by area and West Virginia artists.

For other art and crafts galleries, also
see *Bookstore*.

**BOOKSTORE The Davis House
Bookstore and Upstairs Gallery**
(304-257-2144), 105 North Main St.,
Petersburg. There are not many bookstores in the Potomac Highlands
region but Nancy D. Cooley's shop,
though small, is one of the best. In
addition to bestsellers and mainstream
books, she has one of the finest offerings of regional-interest and West Virginia books you are likely to find.
Upstairs are used books and a small
gallery with seasonal shows by local
artists.

SPECIAL SHOPS

Davis

**West Virginia Highlands Artisans
Group** (304-259-5411), on WV 32 in
the downtown area. A cooperative of

local and regional artists and craftspersons in a variety of media.

Petersburg

🐾 ⚡ **South Side Depot** (304-257-9264), 126 South Main St. The South Side Depot could have just as easily been placed in the Art and Crafts Galleries category as it was here. Housed in a former hardware store, the shop is full of arts, crafts, and an extensive offering of West Virginia–produced foods, such as honey, apple butter, salsa, jams, cider, chocolates, and relishes. I was impressed that most things, including the artwork, were more reasonably priced than similar items found in other shops like this.

Thomas

🏷 ⚡ **Colabrese Old General Store** (304-463-4240), Front St. You step back in time when you walk through the door. Established in 1932, making it the oldest business in town, the general store has shelves jammed with toys from yesteryear, collectibles, and furnishings not seen in other establishments for decades.

Also see the Parsons Railroad Depot under *To See—Museums*.

✳ Special Events

April: **Spring Mountain Festival** (304-257-2711), Petersburg City Park. Rides, games, children's activities, arts and crafts, and helicopter rides.

May: **Annual Wildflower Pilgrimage** (304-259-5216; www.blackwaterfalls

.com), Blackwater Falls State Park. Wildflower hikes, bird walks, nature programs, beginner wildflower- and bird-identification workshops.

June: **Southern Boreal Birding Festival** (304-866-4121; www.canaan valley.org), Canaan Valley State Park. Walk, hikes, discussions and more concentrating on the large variety of birds found in the valley, including more than 20 species of warblers.

July: **Celebration of the Arts** (304-259-5315; 1-800-782-2775), various area locations. Weekend family fun, hayrides, games, and a free concert by the Wheeling Symphony Orchestra. Fireworks follow in nearby Thomas. **Walk Between the Parks** (304-259-5216; www.blackwaterfalls.com). An organized hike from Blackwater Falls State Park to Canaan Valley Resort State Park.

August: **Annual Pickin' in Parsons** (304-478-3515), Parsons. A celebration of bluegrass and hillbilly music. **Tri-County Fair** (304-257-2711), Petersburg.

September: **Annual Astronomy Weekend** (304-259-5216; www.black waterfalls.com), Blackwater Falls State Park. Stargazing and other celestial-oriented events.

October: **Walk Between the Parks** (304-259-5216; www.blackwaterfalls .com). An organized hike from Blackwater Falls State Park to Canaan Valley Resort State Park.

REACHING FOR THE SKY— SPRUCE KNOB, SENECA ROCKS, AND CRANBERRY GLADES

W hat is now West Virginia was at the bottom of a vast inland sea about 500 million years ago. Erosion from a mountain chain to the east, believed by some to be as high as the present-day Andes, washed onto the floor of the sea for millions of years, depositing layer upon layer of sand, rock, and silt thousands of feet thick. The massive weight of these layers compacted and cemented them into various types of rock.

When ancient continents collided a little less than 300 million years ago, the earth folded and buckled upward, creating the Appalachian and Allegheny mountains. Millions of years of erosion stripped away the softer rock, exposing the harder rock, such as Tuscarora limestone, of which Seneca Rocks is made. Looking like a fin on the spiny back of a shark, the rocks rise close to 900 feet above the North Fork of the South Branch of the Potomac River, attracting climbers from around the world.

Across the valley, Spruce Knob soars to 4,861 feet above sea level. It's a wild, and some say eerie, place, with the broad, level ridgeline buffeted by near constant winds and cool temperatures. Stunted, one-sided red spruce trees grow above sods of grass and heaths of huckleberry and blueberry bushes. America's western states may be known for their "big skies," but to stand atop Spruce Knob, especially at sunrise or sunset, and gaze to where receding ridgelines meet earth's canopy is to be filled with a sense of immense space.

Farther south, the Cranberry Glades Botanical Area and Cranberry Wilderness harbor plants and animals more commonly found in New England and Canada.

More than 500,000 acres of George Washington and Monongahela national forests are laced with scores of trails most of them open to hiking, mountain biking, horseback riding, and cross-country skiing. There are hundreds of campsites, some in commercially developed campgrounds, others rustically situated in a state forest. Backcountry camping is permitted on almost every acre of national forest land.

Four different scenic trains take passengers on excursions along flowing mountain streams or up to precipitous heights, while the world's largest radio telescope listens to the heavens from a lush rural valley.

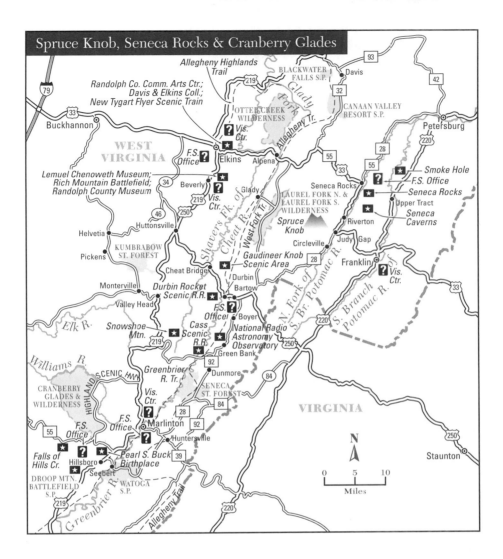

Spruce Knob, Seneca Rocks & Cranberry Glades

Twisting mountain roads leading to soaring vistas and into wide, open valleys of undulating farmlands invite explorations by automobile, motorcycle, or bicycle, and small towns and roadside establishments provide uniquely West Virginia places to rest, dine, and relax.

COMMUNITIES There are many small towns as rich in history as **Beverly**, but as soon as you drive into it, you know this is a place that cares about its past. Older homes are well cared for, streetside placards describe events of days gone by, and museums preserve the items and heritage of those days. Other localities would do well to emulate this example. The town was founded as a county seat in 1790 and thrived with the arrival of the Staunton-Parkersburg Turnpike in 1847. When Union troops won the Battle of Rich Mountain nearby, they occupied the town, which remained a federal stronghold throughout the conflict.

Cass was a boomtown around the turn of the 20th century, when millions of board feet of timber were being extracted from the Allegheny Mountains. Much of the town is now a state park and on the National Register of Historic Places. This is also where you can take a ride on the state's longest running scenic train.

Durbin is another town that owes its existence to railroads, and still does. It is home to the Durbin-Greenbrier Valley Railroad, the company that operates three different scenic train excursions. Of course, there's not much else here—a small grocery, a campground, and an inn.

Elkins sits beside the Tygart River along the western edge of the Potomac Highlands and is named for Stephen B. Elkins, a U.S. secretary of war and senator around the turn of the 20th century. Railroading, timbering, and coal mining were the town's main businesses, but today Davis and Elkins College, along with the Augusta Heritage Center and numerous shops and galleries, help the town to consistently be named one of the best small arts towns in the country.

A town of less than 1,000 and chartered in 1794, **Franklin** is the county seat of Pendleton County and is, more or less, the economic center for the Spruce Knob–Seneca Rocks area. A walking tour brochure available from the Pendleton County Convention and Visitors Bureau (see *Guidance*) directs visitors to dozens of Queen Anne, Greek Revival, Italianate, Colonial Revival, and Folk Victorian buildings from the 19th century. Franklin gained a degree of national fame with the publication of John O'Brien's nonfiction book *At Home in the Heart of Appalachia*, a bestseller that describes life in the town.

Marlinton is a former railroad town that is slowly making a change into the center of services for the thousands of outdoors enthusiasts flocking to the area. Motels were the only places to stay not that long ago. Now B&Bs and vacation rentals are flourishing, new restaurants are opening, outfitters are multiplying, and you can even get a cup of espresso after a day's ride on the Greenbrier River Trail, which passes through the middle of town.

Pickens is reached by driving many miles of winding mountain roads. A town whose primary business pursuits are lumber and coal, it reached its zenith in the 1930s and is now a sleepier village than it once was. However, it attracts scores of visitors to the annual West Virginia Maple Syrup Festival, held annually on the third full weekend in March.

GUIDANCE Greenbrier Ranger District (304-456-3335), US 250/WV 92, Bartow 24920, on the eastern edge of town. They can provide information on the central area of the Monongahela National Forest.

The **Marlinton Ranger District** (304-799-4334), Cemetery Rd., Marlinton 24954, off WV 39 at the eastern edge of Marlinton, has information about the southern portion of the Monongahela National Forest.

For details on every aspect of the **Monongahela National Forest** (304-636-1800; www.usda.govmnf), head to its headquarters at 200 Sycamore St., Elkins 26241.

The **Pendleton County Convention and Visitors Bureau** (304-358-3884; www.visitpendleton.com), 605 North Main St., Franklin 26807, is active in promoting the attractions of the county and maintains a visitor center in its office.

Housed in the restored 1901 Marlinton C&O Railroad Station and next to the Greenbrier River Trail, the **Pocahontas County Convention and Visitors**

A BIT OF THE ALPS IN THE ALLEGHENIES

Tiny **Helvetia** (*Hel-vay-sha*) was established by Swiss immigrants in 1869. The population of about 150 people, spread out over many acres, retains the traditions and heritage of their ancestors by farming the land, producing cheeses renowned for their taste and authenticity, and celebrating old-world traditions with fairs and festivals that attract hundreds of visitors. *Fasnacht*, celebrated on the Saturday before Ash Wednesday, is a Swiss ritual in which Old Man Winter is hung in effigy, everyone dresses up in scary costumes for a ball, and foods of Swiss origin are consumed in a feast whose breadth covers the entire community.

This is not an alpine theme town like Helen, Georgia. Don't come here looking for Swiss-chalet façades, expansive gift shops, or fancy dining places. Helvetia is a quiet working community that simply celebrates its way of life.

So what is there to do here on nonfestival days? Walk the quiet streets. Swim with the locals in the Buckhannon River under the shadow of the wooden-railed, flower-boxed bridge. Visit the small museum and library in the 1800s log cabins. Stop by the church with its handmade pews and stained glass. Eat, and eat some more, at the authentic Swiss Hütte Restaurant. And just appreciate a place removed from many of the ill effects of the modern world.

Bureau (1-800-336-7009; www.pocahontascountywv.com; mailing address: P.O. Box 275, Marlinton 24954), Eighth St. and Fourth Ave. near the center of town, is one of the state's most active sources of information. Personnel are knowledgeable about their county, and, if you happen to stump them, the CVB publishes a plethora of brochures on every imaginable subject. Open daily except Easter, Thanksgiving, Christmas, and New Year's Day.

The **Randolph County Convention and Visitors Bureau** (304-636-2780; 1-800-422-3304; www.randolphcountywv.com), 1302 North Randolph Ave., Elkins 26241. There is also information available downtown, inside the historic Elkins Depot at 315 Railroad Ave., but it is only open on Sat. and Sun.

The Rich **Mountain/Historic Beverly Visitor Center** (304-637-RICH; www.historicbeverly.org), 4 Court St., Beverly 26253, is in the historic Bushrod Crawford House, built around 1850.

In the shadow of Seneca Rocks, the forest service's **Seneca Rocks Discovery Center** (304-567-2827) is the best place to learn about outdoor adventures in this area of the Monongahela National Forest. Exhibits and interactive displays explain the geology and history of the region and provide good introductions to the many area attractions. Telescopes let you zero in on climbers, who look like little dots inching their way along the immense rock formation. The center is usually open daily 9–4:30 Apr.–Oct., and 10–4 on Sat. and Sun. in Nov. and Mar. Closed Dec.–Feb.

West Virginia Mountain Highlands (304-636-8400; 1-877-WVA-MTNS; www .mountainhighlands.com), P.O. Box 1456, Elkins 26241, is an umbrella organization that supplies information about the entire Potomac Highlands region.

In addition to all of the above, I suggest you make a stop at the forest service's **Cranberry Mountain Nature Center** (304-653-4826; at the intersection of WV 39/WV 55 and Scenic Highway 150, a few miles west of Mill Point). You may obtain free trail maps and information about the national forest and look over exhibits concerning local history, wildlife, plants, forestry, and mining, which will provide knowledge and add depth to your travels. Best of all, a diorama gives an excellent three-dimensional image of the terrain you are about to immerse yourself in. Open Thurs.–Sun. Apr.–Nov.; open daily May–Oct.; closed Dec.–Mar.

GETTING THERE *By air*: The closest large airport, about 165 miles from Elkins, is **Pittsburgh International Airport** (412-472-3525; www.pitairport.com) in Pennsylvania.

By making several connections, taking shuttle flights, and paying a few dollars more, you could fly into the **North Central West Virginia Airport** (304-842-3400; www.flyckb.com), near Clarksburg and about 60 miles from Elkins. You could also take shuttle flights into the **Greenbrier Valley Airport** (304-645-3961; www.gvairport.com), which is 3 miles north of Lewisburg and only about 20 miles from the very southern portion of this area.

Many people arrive by way of **Yeager Airport** (304-344-8033; www.yeagerairport .com) in Charleston and drive about 140 miles on I-79 and US 33 to reach Elkins.

If you have your own airplane, you can fly into the **Elkins–Randolph County Airport** (304-636-2726; www.elkinsairport.com), located just 2 miles south of town.

By car: From the east, it is best to exit I-81 in Harrisonburg, Virginia, and follow **US 33 West** into this area. From the west, take **I-79** exit 99 (near Weston) and follow **US 33 East**. For an interesting and scenic ride from the north, leave **I-68** at Keysers Ridge, Maryland, and follow **US 219 South**. Just as interesting is following **US 219 North** from **I-64** in Lewisburg.

By rail: The closest you can get to this area by **AMTRAK** (1-800-872-7245; www.amtrak.com) are its stations at White Sulphur Springs, West Virginia, or Cumberland, Maryland.

GETTING AROUND *By bus*: **Potomac Valley Transit** (304-257-1414; 1-800-565-7240; www.potomacvalleytransit.org; mailing address: P.O. Box 278, Petersburg, 26847) is a far-reaching public-transportation system that primarily services places farther north and east in West Virginia, but it does have a line that comes into the northern part of this area and makes stops in Upper Tract and Franklin. Making use of this, you could take a bus from this area to places as far away as Cumberland and Oakland, Maryland, and Winchester and Harrisonburg, Virginia.

By car: **US 33**, which is four-lane for just a short distance east of Elkins, is the major east–west route. **US 250** and **US 219** will take you southward from Elkins, while **US 220** is the north–south route in the northeastern part of this area. You are in the mountains, so expect to spend more time than usual traveling from place to place. That's good, because every inch of this area is worth taking your time to enjoy, study, and revel in.

PARKING It's often hard to find a parking space on Main St. in Franklin, so go one block over to South Branch St., where there are almost always spaces across from the post office.

MEDICAL EMERGENCIES

Buckeye
Pocahontas Memorial Hospital (304-799-7400; mailing address: Rural Rte. 2, Box 52W, Buckeye 24924) is located a few miles south of Marlinton on US 219/WV 55.

Elkins
Davis Health Systems (304-636-3300; www.davishealthsystem.org), Reed St. and Garman Ave.

If you have an emergency and are in the northeastern part of this area, it may be quickest to go **Grant Memorial Hospital** (304-257-1026; www.grantmemorial .com), Hospital Dr., Petersburg.

✳ To See

ART GALLERY ⷍ **Randolph County Community Arts Center** (304-637-2355; www.randolpharts.org), Randolph Ave. and Park St., Elkins. Open Mon.–Fri. 9–4:30, Sat. 10-4. Donations accepted. The community arts center is housed in the old St. Brendan Catholic Church, built with hand-hewn limestone in 1926. The building's 4,280 square feet retain the original bell and pipe organ, carvings, and murals, making it an impressive hall for classes, changing exhibits, and performing-arts presentations.

MUSIC TO YOUR EARS
A radio station is usually not something you will find in a travel guide, but WVMR 1370 AM (304-799-6004; 1-800-297-2346; www.alleghenymountain radio.org), **Allegheny Mountain Radio**, is such a special experience that I wanted to make sure you tuned in while traveling through the area. It is a cooperative venture in which most of the on-air personalities are volunteers who play music that is near and dear to them, often bringing in albums and CDs from their home collections. What I like is the great variety of music. During the course of a typical day, you will be treated to country, bluegrass, gospel, jazz, classical, Celtic, rock, acoustic, blues, big band, folk, and more. Because of power limitations placed on it by being located so close to the National Radio Astronomy Observatory, you will probably only be able to pick it up in Pocahontas County, but you may also be able to listen to it on WVLS 89.7 FM, WCHG 107.1 FM, WVMR 91.9 FM, or Radio Durbin 103.5 FM.

SENECA CAVERNS

CAVERN TOURS ✎ ⊤ **Seneca Caverns & Gemstone Mining** (1-800-239-7647; www.senecacaverns .com; mailing address: HC 78, Box 85, Riverton, 26814), located on WV 9, about 3 miles from Riverton. Open daily year-round; tours leave every 20 minutes. Adults $13, children $8. Native Americans used these caverns for centuries, and guides on the 50-minute cavern tours point out places where smoke marks are still visible. Along with natural formations of cave coral, flowstone, and calcite crystal, the caverns have what is believed to be the world's second-largest underground room.

The children who were on the tour with me seemed to enjoy the caverns well enough, but they got really excited while panning for gemstones outside the caverns. The bags you purchase ($5.50–9) and empty into the water raceway are laced with sand and stones from North and South Carolina, Arizona, Mexico, and South America, so the kids are guaranteed of finding some kind of gemstone or fossil. You and the children may also enjoy a game of miniature golf while you're here.

Opened to the public in 2006, the Stratosphere Cavern is for the adventurous. It's not the typical commercial caverns tour, but one that more resembles caving, in that there is no electricity (the only light is from headlamps participants wear), and you will probably get muddy and dirty (so dress accordingly). Children under 12 years of age are not permitted. Cost of a guided tour of the Stratosphere Cavern is $13 per person. A more ambitious and strenuous tour of the cavern in about 2.5 hours and is $45 per person.

COLLEGE Davis & Elkins College (304-637-1900; www.davisandelkins.edu), 100 Campus Dr., Elkins. Davis & Elkins College was established in 1901 as an academy associated with the Presbyterian Church. Today it is a coeducational liberal arts college and the cultural center of Elkins. The 170-acre campus is a historical district with a mix of modern and 1800s buildings, including Graceland, the 1893 stone mansion summer home of Henry Gassaway Davis (see *Lodging* and *Dining Out*); the 1890 native hardwood and stone Hallihurst Hall; and the cylindrical, late-1800s Ice House. The modern Hermanson Center–Auditorium hosts sporting events, concerts, theater performances, and art exhibits. In 1981, the college became the sponsor and principal site of the Augusta Heritage Center, which helps preserve traditional regional cultures.

COVERED BRIDGE The **Locust Creek Covered Bridge** was built in 1888 and is Pocahontas County's only surviving covered bridge. In a pleasing rural setting, it may be reached by turning onto Locust Creek Road (WV 20) a short distance south of Hillsboro.

SPECIAL CLASSES AND FESTIVALS PRESERVE TRADITIONS

Augusta Heritage Center (304-637-1209; 1-800-624-3157; www.augusta heritage.com), 100 Campus Dr., Elkins. Begun in 1973, the Augusta Heritage Center was established to help preserve Appalachian heritage and traditions, and has become known nationally and internationally for its activities relating to the folk life and folk arts of many regions and cultures. Its week-long workshops attract more than 2,000 participants annually, and thousands attend its public concerts, dances, and festivals.

Augusta's full-time staff, volunteers, and work-study students produce a variety of events, including the spring dulcimer week, October old-time week, and summer workshops in everything from fiddle and Cajun to Irish and blues. Other classes teach participants how to weave baskets, hand-make musical instruments, and dye batik fabrics.

The center's yearly highlight is the Augusta Festival in August, which caps off the summer session of classes and workshops. You could get lost amid the juried crafts fair, quilt show, dances of all kinds, and concerts that feature newly graduated workshop participants alongside some of the country's best-known traditional performers. If you can't make it to a specific event, you can always show up for the weekly Pickin' in the Park informal old-time and bluegrass jams held every Wednesday throughout the year.

DRIVING TOURS, SCENIC & HISTORIC The **Highland Scenic Highway** extends for close to 46 miles, from Richwood to US 219 about 7 miles north of Marlinton, but my favorite portion is the 22-mile stretch on Scenic Highway 150 from the Cranberry Mountain Nature Center (see *Guidance*) to US 219. This is one of the most spectacular drives in the state and reminds me of a miniature Blue Ridge Parkway. Winding along the crest of a 4,000-foot ridgeline, the roadway runs through an area of spruce and fir trees, passing numerous access trails that would take you into the Cranberry Wilderness (see *To Do—Hiking*), and going by a couple overlooks into the Williams River Valley. Making a dramatic drop to the Williams River (giving access to the Tea Creek and Dry Run Campgrounds and the Williams River Backway), it then rises dramatically to about 4,500 feet and wends its way past two more overlooks, one that provides a sweeping vista of the ridgelines to the east. By far one of the best drives in the entire state.

The **Williams River Backway** intersects the Highland Scenic Highway at the Williams River and parallels the meandering stream for 28 miles of wooded slopes, water rushing over huge boulders, and dozens of inviting fishing spots and swimmin' holes.

The state-designated **Staunton-Parkersburg Turnpike Byway** runs for more than 40 miles on US 250 from the West Virginia–Virginia border and follows the route of one of the first major thoroughfares into the Allegheny Mountains. Almost exactly at the state line, turn onto WV 3 (the **Camp Allegheny Backway**) and follow it to the remains of Confederate fortifications and the forest service's interpretive signs. Down from the mountain near the intersection of US 250/WV 92 and WV 28/WV 92, look for the earthworks of a former Confederate camp.

Continue into Bartow and stop at the ranger station, where there is a small Civil War museum and forest service information center. A bit farther west is the small town of Durbin and the opportunity to take a ride on the *Durbin Rocket* (see *To Do—Train Excursions*). Beyond Durbin, the byway rises to the top of Cheat Mountain at the Pocahontas–Randolph County line. Here you could turn onto FSR 27 to visit the towering trees of the Gaudineer Scenic Area (see *Green Space—Nature Preserves*). Farther down the western side of Cheat Mountain, a turn onto Red Run Road provides access to the **Cheat Mountain Backway** and the interpretive signs and short trails of the Civil War Union Cheat Summit Fort.

Dropping off the mountain, the byway passes through Huttonsville and the historic town of Beverly, where a turn onto the **Rich Mountain Backway** (WV 37/8) takes you onto a winding gravel route to the Rich Mountain Battlefield Civil War Site (see *Historic Sites*). Returning to US 250, the tour comes to an end in Elkins.

You may obtain more information about the byway from the Staunton-Parkersburg Turnpike Alliance (304-637-2474; www.spturnpike.org), P.O. Box 227, Beverly 26253.

Insider's tip: **WV 9/5** (turn left off US 33 a short distance east of Judy Gap) in Germany Valley is not an officially designated byway, backway, or scenic highway of any kind, but it is one of the prettiest drives to be taken in this area. Cattle grazing in lush rolling meadows broken by small bits of woodlands, and neat farm buildings bordered by Spruce and North Fork mountains paint a picture of beauty and serenity that make you want to stop and take pictures every few feet.

The **Pendleton County Convention and Visitors Bureau** (see *Guidance*) has produced a set of four CDs that take you on a guided tour through some of the most scenic and historic portions of the county. The CDs direct you from place to place, and local residents recount stories that have been passed down from generations of ancestors.

The Potomac Highlands' twisting, two-lane highways may be frustrating for those who are trying to make good time, but they are custom made for those who enjoy **motorcycle touring**. A free brochure from the Pocahontas County Convention and Visitors Bureau (see *Guidance*) details eight popular circuit routes, ranging from 119 to 220 miles.

HISTORIC HOME Pearl S. Buck Birthplace (304-653-4430; www.pearl sbuckbirthplace.com; mailing address: P.O. Box 126, Hillsboro 24946), on US 219/WV 55 at the north end of Hillsboro. Open May 1–Nov. 1, Mon.–Sat. Small admission fee. Pearl S. Buck, probably most noted for her book *The Good Earth* (winner of the Pulitzer Prize in Literature), was born in this home, which belonged to her grandparents, in 1892. The stately house

BEAUTIFUL GERMANY VALLEY

PEARL S. BUCK BIRTHPLACE

contains many family items (such as the chair used to rock her to sleep) and most of the 107 books that Miss Buck wrote. The home that her father was born in, 40 miles away, was moved to this site and provides additional understanding into her life.

HISTORIC SITES

Beverly

Rich Mountain Battlefield Civil War Site (304-637-RICH; www.rich mountain.org), 5 miles west of Beverly on Rich Mountain Rd. (WV 37/8). On July 11, 1861, Union troops led by Gen. William S. Rosecrans overwhelmed Confederate soldiers at Rich Mountain pass, enabling the federal government to control the Staunton-Parkersburg Turnpike and the northwestern portion of Virginia. Many historians maintain this was the event that paved the way for West Virginia statehood two years later. A few interpretive signs provide details of the battle, while 1.5 miles farther west on WV 37/8 is a short walking trail that goes by breastworks and other reminders of Confederate Camp Garnett. A reenactment takes place on the two sites in July of every odd-numbered year.

Seneca Rocks

Located just below Seneca Rocks, and accessed from WV 55/WV28 or by a short walking path from the forest service's Seneca Rocks Discovery Center (see *Guidance*), the **Sites Homestead** helps paint a picture of what life was like for local residents in the early 1800s. The log cabin, which has influences of German, French, and English architecture, was built in 1839, and an adjoining garden has vegetables and herbs popular in those days. You'll understand some of the hardships faced back then when you read the interpretive sign that states, FENCES HAD TO BE PIG TIGHT, HORSE HIGH, AND BULL STRONG to protect the garden.

You are permitted to wander around here on your own during daylight hours, but to get the best understanding of what you are seeing, take part in one of the guided tours. Check at the Discovery Center for dates and times.

Also see Droop Mountain Battlefield State Park under *Green Space—Parks*.

MUSEUMS

Beverly

⚓ **Lemuel Chenoweth House Museum** (304-636-2650; mailing address: P.O. Box 239, Beverly 26253), Georgetown Rich Mountain Rd., one block west of US 250/US 219. Open daily, but for a limited time each day so call ahead. Small admission fee. Lemuel Chenoweth was a self-educated architect of the 1800s who gained fame by designing and building some of the state's most famous covered bridges. He built his Beverly home in 1856, and it retains the original redwood and yellow poplar floors and is filled with Indian and Civil War artifacts. I call it "the museum that sells itself" because present owner Randy Allen has furnished the house with antiques from the early 1700s to late 1800s—and put a price tag on every piece in the hope that you may decide to take a bit of the museum home with you.

☂ **Randolph County Museum** (304-637-7424; www.richmountain.org/beverly /museum.htm), corner of Main and Court streets. Hours and days have been known to change, but at press time the museum was open Memorial Day–Labor Day, Wed.–Sat. 10-noon and 1–4, Sun. 1–4; May, Sept., and Oct., Sat. and Sun. only. Small admission charge. The small museum is housed in the old Blackman-Bosworth Store. Built by slave labor during the early 1800s, it has served as a general store, print shop, and post office. The collection is a broad-based one, taking in early farm tools, Civil War artifacts, old store items, and clothing belonging to the early settlers. Behind the museum are an original subscription school from the late 1800s that has a collection of one-room-school items, and the Stalnaker Cabin, one of the area's first homes that was moved here from another site.

Helvetia

The tiny **Helvetia Museum**, in the town square, is housed in the home of one of the town's original settlers and is crammed full of artifacts of local interest, such as surveying equipment and oompah band instruments. Most amazing is the Swiss flag carried across the ocean by the town's first arrivals in 1869. There are no regular hours, but ask at the library (almost a museum itself), and someone will open it for you.

Marlinton

☂ **Pocahontas County Historical Museum** (304-799-6659 during the summer; 799-4973 in the off-season), on US 219/WV 55. Open daily from mid-June to Labor Day. Very small admission fee.

There is more inside than what it looks like there would be when you first drive up to this small museum, housed in a 1904 home. The many rooms are filled with items pertaining to Native Americans, the Civil War, local lumber history, tools, weaving implements, and other objects used by early settlers. Make sure you walk around back, which is really what the front of the house was once. This side is a bit grander as it faces the Greenbrier River, once the area's most important thoroughfare.

LEMUEL CHENOWETH HOUSE MUSEUM

SCENIC VIEWS There are very few places where you can get such a stupendous view while putting forth so little effort as the scene available from the forest service's **Bickle Knob Tower**. The tower, which is just a few hundred feet from the parking area, can be intimidating to those afraid of heights, but even just going up the first flight or so will provide a 360-degree vista of the surrounding countryside, including the ridges of Otter Creek Wilderness to the north and some of the state's highest peaks to the east. Don't want to go up the tower at all? You'll still get a great view to the north just a few steps from the parking area.

From Elkins, go east on US 33 for 4 miles, turn north on WV 33/8 (old US 33), and travel approximately 2 miles. Turn north on WV 6, continue another 0.5 mile, and turn right onto FSR 91. Go approximately 4 more miles, and then turn left onto FSR 91A to the parking area.

✪ At 4,861 feet above sea level, **Spruce Knob** is the state's highest point. The low-growing vegetation provides 360-degree views, but climb the observation tower for an even loftier perspective.

More than 70 miles of intersecting trails, open to hikers, mountain bikers, and horseback riders, wander through the 20,000 acres of land surrounding the knob, where you could spend days wandering this glorious backcountry. If your time is limited, take the easy 0.5-mile Whispering Spruce Trail. Interpretive signs along the way provide an understanding and appreciation of the high country vegetation, geology, and animal life.

From Riverton, go south for 2 miles on US 33/WV 28, turn right onto WV 33/4, and follow the signs to Spruce Knob. It's many miles of dirt mountain roads, so allow ample time.

You don't even have to get out of the car to enjoy the view of **Germany Valley** from the designated pullout on US 33 as it climbs eastward from Judy Gap onto North Fork Mountain. This is one of the state's best, and most easily reached, vistas. The fertile, green valley stretches out far below, while soaring Spruce Knob and the Allegheny Mountains form the backdrop to the west. My mother was so moved by this majestic scene that she said, "Now I know what 'How Great Thou Art' means."

Also see Droop Mountain Battlefield State Park under *Green Space—Parks*.

WATERFALLS The **High Falls of Cheat** is one of the state's most spectacular falls. At about 15 feet in height, it's certainly not one of the highest, but it sits in a horseshoe bend, which makes it a bit wider than the rest of the river. Rocks above and below it let you walk into the stream to get a variety of perspectives, and the pool at the base is pretty hard to resist plunging into on a hot summer day.

You could take a long, strenuous hike to the High Falls of Cheat, but the easiest way is to climb aboard the ***Tygart Flyer*** or the ***Cheat Mountain Salamander*** (see *To Do—Train Excursions*) and let either one of the railroads take you there.

♿ The **Falls of Hills Creek** is the showpiece pathway of the Gauley Ranger District. The forest service has lavished much attention on the route, keeping it well maintained and building a number of staircases, observation decks, bridges, and boardwalks—both simple and complex—to enable you to hike with greater ease and enjoyment.

The attention is well deserved, for the 114-acre area is one of the prettiest waterfall settings in the state. Hemlock and rhododendron adorn the sides of the narrow gorge, creating shadows upon the dozens of wildflower species springing up from the forest floor, and letting in bits of sunlight to highlight the sparkling water of three separate falls. That's right—you can visit three waterfalls in just one short outing. The first, which is reached by a paved accessible route of 0.3 mile, is about 25 feet in height; Middle Falls drops 45 feet into a narrow grotto; and Lower Falls, reached after 0.75 mile, rushes over a crescent-shaped wall, dropping unimpeded for 63 feet.

This is not a hard walk, but you do descend hundreds of feet, and coming back up may be difficult for those not accustomed to climbing steps. Just take your time and make as many rest stops as needed on the benches provided. It might be a good idea to stop at the **Cranberry Mountain Nature Center** (see *Guidance*) to check on the condition of the trail, for, time and again, landslides and fallen trees have caused the lower portions to be closed

H'GH FALLS OF CHEAT

until the route can be reconstructed. From the nature center, drive west for 5.4 miles on WV 55/WV 39 and turn left onto the road marked for the falls.

Also see *Green Space—State Forests*.

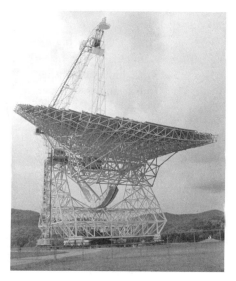

ROBERT C. BYRD GREEN BANK TELESCOPE AT THE NATIONAL RADIO ASTRONOMY OBSERVATORY

OTHER SITES 🐾 𝄢 **National Radio Astronomy Observatory** (304-456-2150; www.gb.nrao.edu; mailing address: P.O. Box 2, Green Bank 24944), on WV 28/WV 92 in Green Bank. Open daily from Memorial Day weekend through Labor Day; closed Mon and Tue. from the day after Labor Day to the day before Memorial Day weekend. Free admission. The National Radio Astronomy Observatory would be the perfect setting for a science-fiction movie, only what is going on here is science *fact*. The huge dishes of the radio telescopes that are spread across hundreds of acres are studying the heavens by listening to the radio magnetic radiation emitted by celestial bodies.

Free guided tours have a short introduction before taking visitors into the field for a close-up look at the telescopes. Standing under the Robert C. Byrd Green Bank Telescope can be both intimidating and awe-inspiring.

It is 30 stories tall, the dish has a surface area of 2.3 acres, and the entire thing weighs close to 17 million tons. Yet, tracks enable it to be turned and tilted at will, making it the largest movable structure on earth. The visitor center contains the Science Center museum, where you can learn more about the work that goes on here. Hands-on exhibits instruct you on the finer points of laser beams, radio waves, and other aspects of radio astronomy. The Galaxy Gift Center has science kits to help keep the kids interested long after you leave here, and, amazingly, the little Starlight Café serves some pretty good food.

All in all, this is a special place to visit, and it's all free!

✳ To Do

BICYCLING At one time, railroads wound into nearly every valley and hollow of the Allegheny Mountains, carrying out the riches of timber, coal, and iron ore. They were also like the metropolitan bus systems of today, running on a schedule several times a day to transport passengers and goods between small settlements and commercial centers.

Construction on a line of the C&O Railroad along the Greenbrier River began in 1899, with the first train chugging into Marlinton in the fall of 1900. Mirroring the experiences of most small rail lines, this one was profitable for many decades, but it fell into disfavor as Americans turned to highways for their transportation needs. Soon after the line was abandoned in 1978, the company donated the right-of-way to the state to develop as the **Greenbrier River Trail**, which runs for more than 70 miles between Cass and North Caldwell.

Never far from civilization, yet with long periods of detachment from the humanized world, this is a great place to introduce someone to the joys of mountain biking without subjecting them to the rigors, and fear, of a harsh or isolated terrain. The pathway is level (even with a slight downhill trend if ridden from north to south), while the historic aspects of the railroad are a bonus. Mile markers help keep track of your progress, and camping is permitted at designated sites, which often include a water source and pit toilets.

The Web site www.greenbrierrivertrail.com contains a wealth of information on mileage distances, equipment rental and shuttle services, and dining and lodging options. This is a multiuse trail, also open to hikers and equestrians, so be ready for possible frequent encounters.

A bit more rustic than the Greenbrier River Trail, the **West Fork Trail** is also a good route to bring novice mountain-biking friends who are not in the best of shape, but who still want to experience some backcountry riding. Once you head south from the trailhead parking on WV 27 in Glady, you will follow a former railroad grade for close to 22 miles, leaving behind most signs of civilization and never crossing a paved road as you travel in the deep gorge of the West Fork of the Greenbrier River. It is only slightly uphill for the first 3 miles, then it's a gradual downhill grade all of the way to the southern terminus in Durbin. You are on forest service land, so you could make this an overnight trip by camping anywhere along the route you can find a flat spot.

In addition to these rail trails, bicycles are permitted on the gated roads and many of the trails in **Monongahela National Forest**. Contact the main office in Elkins or any of the ranger stations (see *Guidance*) for further information. The Pocahontas County Convention and Visitors Bureau (see *Guidance*) produces a free pamphlet detailing popular road and mountain biking routes near Marlinton.

Cass
Rte. 66 Outpost (304-572-2200; www.route66snowshoe.com), on WV 66. Bicycle, canoe, tube, and snowboard rentals, along with shuttle services.

Elkins
Fat Tire Cycle (304-472-5882; www.fattirecycle.com), 33 Main St. The employees of this bike shop have a wealth of knowledge about local riding areas and trails, and they can service your bike or sell you a new one.

Marlinton
Appalachian Sport (304-799-4050; www.appsport.com), 3 Seneca Trail (on US 219/WV 55 at the intersection with WV 39). Open daily. Appalachian Sport rents (at reasonable rates) bicycles, canoes, and kayaks by the day or half day, as well as providing shuttles to those who do, or do not, rent from them. If time and employee numbers permit, they may also be able to shuttle hikers to trailheads.

Seebert
Jack Horner's Corner (304-653-4515), located next to the Greenbrier River Trail in Seebert. Jack offers bike rentals and repairs.

Slatyfork
Elk River Touring Company, Inn, Restaurant, and Guide Service (304-572-3771; 1-866-572-3771; www.ertc.com; mailing address: HC 69, Box 7, Slatyfork 26291), on US 219/WV 55. It could easily be claimed that Gil and Mary Willis almost single-handedly made West Virginia the worldwide mountain-biking mecca that it has become. They opened their cross-country skiing operation in 1980 and soon expanded into mountain biking during the summer. The inn property has more than 4 miles of trails (groomed in winter for cross-country skiing) that connect with multiple miles of pathways in the Monongahela National Forest. Other services include bicycle, ski, and snowboard rentals, along with lessons available for each of the activities. They also provide guided mountain biking and fly-fishing trips (they are an Orvis-endorsed guide company), and a shuttle service is available to the general public. See *Lodging* and *Dining Out* for more information about this company.

Also see *Hiking, Green Space—State Forests*, Monongahela National Forest Service Campgrounds under *Lodging*, and Dirtbean Halé under *Coffee Bars* in this chapter, and Allegheny Highlands Trail under *To Do—Bicycling* in "The Land of Canaan—Canaan Valley, Blackwater Falls, and Dolly Sods" chapter.

BIRDING See *Green Space—Nature Preserves* and *Green Space—Something for Everyone*.

CLIMBING

Judy Gap
Nelson Rocks Preserve (304-567-3169; 1-800-729-2930; www.nelsonrocks.org),

on Nelson Gap Rd., which is off WV 28 just 0.25 mile south of the intersection of US 33 and WV 28 in Judy Gap. Like Seneca Rocks, Nelson Rocks are fins of rock rising high above a valley floor. The 140-acre preserve is privately owned and features the Via Ferrata, a most interesting system of steel cables, metal rungs, and bridges, making it possible for those without prior climbing experience to ascend vertical rock that is usually the domain of technical rock climbers. It's a great experience, but, even with these aids, the course is not for those who are out of shape or have a fear of heights. If you want to find out if you are up to it or not, hike up to the Via Ferrata swinging bridge, 200 feet long and suspended 150 feet in the air. If you feel confident walking across it, you will probably be okay on the course. If you decide it's not for you, you will still have been able to get a great view of the rocks from the beginning of the bridge.

It is possible to do the Via Ferrata on your own, or the preserve can arrange for someone to guide you.

Seneca Rocks

Soaring 900 feet above the North Fork of the Potomac River, **Seneca Rocks** has been attracting rock climbers from around the world since the early 1900s, including the U.S. Army's 10th Mountain Division, which trained here during World War II. The rocks are a staggered set of smaller peaks leading to the summit of the South Peak, which is all of 10 feet wide. Depending on the source you consult,

THE SWINGING BRIDGE AT THE BEGINNING OF THE VIA FERRATA IN NELSON ROCKS PRESERVE

there are anywhere from 100 to 400 vertical routes, all with great degrees of exposure. Regardless of the difficulty, more than 3,000 climbers scale the rocks every year. The rocks are all on forest service land, and there are no permits, fees, or registration required. On belay! Although open to climbers year-round, most people, including the two guide services listed below, consider the season to be Apr.–Oct.

The forest service has built a moderately easy, 3-mile round-trip hiking trail that will deliver those of us who are not climbers to an observation platform close to Seneca Rocks' North Tower for grand views across the valley and overlooking some of the state's highest land masses.

Seneca Rocks Climbing School (304-567-2600; 1-800-548-0108; www .seneca-rocks.com; mailing address: P.O. Box 53, Seneca Rocks 26884), at the main intersection in Seneca Rocks. Just as Gil and Mary Willis of the Elk River Touring Company, Inn, Restaurant, and Guide Service in Slatyfork could be credited with making West

Virginia a mountain biking destination, so could John Markwell be considered the one person who focused the attentions of rock climbers on the state. My wife attended John's school in the 1980s not long after he established it and climbed the rocks. John is now retired, but the school continues with basic, intermediate, and safety classes, along with providing guides for private (up to three people) climbs on the rocks.

The school's climbing shop, The Gendarme, is the place to pick up gear as well as meet other climbers, who often spend hours on the wooden benches of the covered porch talking about their exploits.

Seneca Rocks Mountain Guides (304-567-2115; www.senecarocks.com; mailing address: P.O. Box 223, Seneca Rocks 26884), at the main intersection in Seneca Rocks. Located across the street from Seneca Rocks Climbing School, Seneca Rocks Mountain Guides—it's the place with the outside climbing wall—provides basically the same type of classes and guide services.

FISHING

The **South Branch of the Potomac River**, especially the portion that flows through the Smoke Hole area (see *Green Space—Something for Everyone*), teems with stocked trout. Locals say to look for the golden trout, as they are a good indication that other fish will be hanging in that area, too. Use nymphs in the many spots of pocket water. The smallmouth and largemouth bass fishing is pretty good here, too. All of this is also true for the **North Fork of the South Branch of the Potomac River**.

If the easy access to the South Branch of the Potomac River makes fishing a little more crowded than you like, drive a little farther west to the **Glady Fork** and/or **Shavers Fork** of the Cheat River, both south of Elkins. You can only get to the streams via dirt forest service roads. The result is fewer people casting for the stocked brown, golden, and rainbow (as well as native brook) trout.

In the more southern part of this area, the **Cranberry**, **Williams**, and headwaters of the **Elk rivers** are known for their large populations of rainbow, brook, and brown trout, while anglers cast for smallmouth and rock bass in the Greenbrier River.

Consider 22-acre **Buffalo Lake** or the small lake in Watoga State Park for calm water angling. The former has a natural trout population, while trout, bass, and catfish make their homes in the latter. **Seneca Lake** in Seneca State Forest attracts those hoping to hook largemouth bass, bluegill, and stocked trout.

ELK SPRINGS FLY SHOP AND OUTFITTERS

🎣 **Elk Springs Fly Shop & Outfitters** (304-339-2359; 304-339-2347; 1-877-355-7774; www.elkspringsflyshop.com), #14 Dry Branch Rd., Monterville. Growing up in Charleston, I only knew the Elk River as the wide, muddy stream that met up with the Kanawha River on the west side of town. This shop and outfitters is located at the river's very source, where clear, cold springs burst forth from the ground, providing the perfect environment for trout (which were highly visible from the outfitters' rental cabin porch when I visited). The guides know the river well and can teach you how to fly-fish or improve on the skills you may have been relying on for years. The Orvis-endorsed shop has all the gear you'll need; the restaurant serves meals, so you never have to leave the grounds; and a lodge and rental cabins provide a place to swap tales at night.

Also see Elk River Touring Company, Inn, Restaurant, and Guide Service under *Bicycling*.

GOLF

Elkins
The Elks Golf Club (304-636-9704; www.elks.org), Country Club Rd. Open to nonmembers of the Elks Club, the nine-hole course is on 73 acres next to the Tygart River, has four sets of tees, 15 sand traps, and a total yardage of 6,100.

Marlinton
Pocahontas Country Club (304-799-7466; www.pccgolf.com), off US 219 about 2 miles south of Marlinton. This semiprivate nine-hole course was built on rolling hills in 1958. With open fairways, it has a number of blind approaches to the greens, with water coming into play on only one hole.

GOLF, MINIATURE See *To See—Cavern Tours*.

HIKING More than 100 miles of West Virginia's premier long-distance pathway, the **Allegheny Trail** (see "What's Where in West Virginia" at the front of this book for background information), pass through this area. It comes from the south (see *To Do—Hiking* in the "Old Towns, Surviving and Alive—Lewisburg, White Sulphur Springs, and Union" chapter) to pass through Calvin Price State Forest and Watoga State Park, before traversing national forest land to descend and join with the Greenbrier River Trail, which it follows, more or less, into Cass. From the small town, the pathway climbs to the Gaudineer Scenic Area (see *Green Space—Nature Preserves*) on Shavers Mountain, whose ridgeline it traverses for more than 10 miles. The trail then drops to the West Fork Trail (see *Bicycling*), a rail trail that it follows for 6 miles into Glady before it parallels the Glady Fork River for 25 miles. The pathway leaves this area by ascending into Canaan Valley Resort State Park (see "The Land of Canaan—Canaan Valley, Blackwater Falls, and Dolly Sods" chapter).

Designated USFS Wilderness by Congress in 1983, the **Cranberry Wilderness** encompasses 35,864 acres, making it the largest such preserve in West Virginia. That's more than 55 square miles of land on which no natural resource extraction or motorized vehicles are permitted. Add the 26,000 acres of the Cranberry Back-country, officially made a part of the wilderness in 2009 (see *To Do—Hiking* in the "Along the New and Gauley Rivers—Beckley, Fayetteville, and Summersville" chapter), that connect with the western edge of the wilderness, and you have close to 80 remote square miles in which to wander.

Situated near the southern end of the Allegheny Plateau, the land is broken up by deep and narrow stream valleys. The elevation ranges from 4,600 feet to 2,400 feet, with red spruce dominating the higher places and hardwood trees such as black cherry and yellow birch growing on the middle and lower elevations. Protected from the transgressions of the modern world, wildlife is varied and abundant. Hikers at one time or another have seen white-tailed deer, mink, bobcat, fox, snowshoe hare, cottontail rabbit, wild turkey, grouse, and several species of squirrels. This large expanse of land is also one of the best places in the state to possibly catch glimpses of black bears.

Although the 10 trails, close to 70 miles in length, are not blazed, most of them are signed at junctions and follow old logging roads, so route finding is usually not a problem. The area receives 60 inches of rain annually, however, so be aware that there are no bridges across the streams, and fording them can be dangerously difficult, if not impossible, in times of high water. Also, be prepared for temperatures that could be many degrees cooler than what they were when you left home. Storms that are dropping rain just a few miles away may be depositing a deep covering of snow on the wilderness.

The wilderness is located a few miles west of Marlinton, with trailheads situated along WV 55, Scenic Highway 150 (see *To See—Driving Tours, Scenic & Historic*), FSR 86 beside the Williams River, and FSR 102 (which also provides access to the not-to-be-missed Cranberry Glades—see *Green Space—Nature Preserves*).

Adjacent to the Cranberry Wilderness, the **Tea Creek Area** can be a botanist's dream. With elevations rising from 3,000 feet at the Williams River to more than 4,000 feet along the crest of Turkey Mountain, it is possible to pass through several different environments. The lower elevations contain maple, beech, birch, oak, locust, basswood, cherry, ash, and more. Witch hazel, hobblebush, and a variety of berry bushes make up a part of the understory. A quick glance at the ground near the Tea Creek Campground will reveal more than a dozen wildflowers, including monkshood, wood sorrel, goldenrod, white snakeroot, asters, phlox, chickweed, and wood betony. In the moist areas around streams, look for jewelweed, black snakeroot, Joe-Pye weed, and buttercup. What's more, the Tea Creek drainage receives 60 inches of rain annually, making it the ideal habitat for more than a dozen different mosses, more than 30 species of fungi, and luxuriant growths of ferns.

Be prepared for wet feet. The main route fords Tea Creek at least nine times. However, take heart. Except in times of high water, most crossings are easily accomplished, all trails are well blazed, and many of the ascents are done along gradually rising old railroad beds and logging roads.

Mountain bikers come here in droves because all trails are open to them, and many of the routes join with the pathways of the Elk River Touring Center (see *To Do—Bicycling*). Easiest access to trailheads is a few miles west of Marlinton along FSR 86 beside the Williams River.

A hike in the **Laurel Fork South** and **Laurel Fork North Wilderness** is for experienced hikers looking for a challenge. Trail signs and blazes are virtually nonexistent—the only ones still around were installed decades ago and are rotting and fading. Budget constraints keep the forest service from maintaining the trails on a regular basis, so expect faint routes and overgrown pathways through tall vegetation. Personnel with the forest service hope to rectify this someday, but that may be years in the future.

Nevertheless, the rewards are many if you are willing to face these hardships. This is the least visited wilderness in the state, so you may not run into anyone else throughout the hike, which adds to the overall sense of seclusion. Wildflowers abound within the confines of the valley and on the bordering hillsides. It's possible that you may see blue cohosh, Indian cucumber root, wood sorrel, lady's slipper, trillium, Canada mayflower, partridgeberry, cinquefoil, and skunk cabbage all on the same hike. Keep an eye out for the rare glade spurge in midsummer. Wildlife includes black bear, bobcat, deer, turkey, mink, squirrel, and an active beaver population. Sharpshinned and red-shouldered hawks have been seen flying overhead, and you should consider bringing along a fly rod, as the river contains native brook and stocked trout.

Campsites abound along the river, or you have the option of using the forest service's Laurel Fork Campground (see *Lodging*). If you set up in the campground, you could take day hikes of varying length. (One of my other books, *50 Hikes in West Virginia*, provides a detailed description of a 16-mile overnight journey in the wilderness.) Just be aware that the campground is popular and can fill up quickly in nice weather.

The wilderness is bordered by, and most easily accessed from, FSR 14, which intersects US 33 about 15 miles east of Elkins.

In one of its articles, *Backpacker* magazine claims **North Fork Mountain** possesses "classic eastern mountain scenery" and is "as good as mountain country gets in the East." *Outside* once described it as West Virginia's "most outstanding foot trail." The mountain rises sharply for more than 1,500 feet from the North Fork of the South Branch of the Potomac River to end in a ridgeline adorned by miles-long cliffs. Views, of which there are dozens, take in all points of the compass, while the strikingly upright fins of Seneca Rocks punctuate the mountain's lower flanks.

This is a moderate hike if done from the southern trailhead on US 33 between Judy Gap and Franklin to the northern terminus on WV 28/11 (Smoke Hole Rd.) southwest of Petersburg. The one downside of this hike is that there is no water available anywhere along the ridgeline. Luckily, there is an option if you don't want to carry the weight of extra water: A forest service road intersects the trail at the halfway point, enabling you to stash some water before beginning the hike. Again, my book *50 Hikes in West Virginia* provides all the details you need to complete the 23.9-mile trek.

Access to the 20,000-acre **Otter Creek Wilderness** (see *To Do—Hiking* in "The Land of Canaan—Canaan Valley, Blackwater Falls, and Dolly Sods" chapter) may be obtained by driving east from Elkins on US 33 for 11 miles, turning left onto FSR 91 for 1.3 miles, bearing right onto FSR 303, and continuing 0.6 mile to the Otter Creek Trailhead.

Also see *Bicycling*, Seneca Rocks under *Climbing*, *To See—Scenic Views*, *To See— Waterfalls*, *Green Space—Parks*, *Green Space—Something for Everyone*, *Green Space—State Forests*, and Monongahela National Forest Service Campgrounds under *Lodging*.

HORSEBACK RIDING Equestrians are permitted on many of the trails in **Monongahela National Forest**. Contact the main office in Elkins or any of the ranger stations (see *Guidance*) for further information. For a quick overview of what is available near Marlinton, the Pocahontas County Convention and Visitors

Bureau (see *Guidance*) produces a small pamphlet detailing popular equestrian routes.

✧ **Yokum's Seneca Rocks Stables** (304-567-2466; www.yokums-stables.com), located on WV 28/55 behind Yokum's Restaurant and Motel, a short distance north of Seneca Rocks. Open Apr. to mid-Nov. Rides leave at 10, 1, and 4. $35 per person. If you are not skilled or brave enough to climb Seneca Rocks or don't want to invest the energy to hike the trail to the top, the Yokum family, now in its third generation of doing so, will lead you to the same point on horseback. Best of all, the whole family can go, as children as young as 6 years of age are permitted. I would have liked a little more narration directed at the whole group I was with, but if you are able to ride close to one of the guides, I found them to be full of knowledge and lore about the area.

Also see Watoga State Park under *Green Space—Parks*.

KAYAKING & CANOEING The **Smoke Hole Canyon** portion of the **South Branch of the Potomac River** is generally regarded as this area's prettiest paddling trip. It's amazing to me that, as popular as this stretch of water is, the nearest outfitter to provide shuttles and equipment rentals is Eagle's Nest Outfitters in Petersburg (see *Kayaking & Canoeing* in "The Land of Canaan—Canaan Valley, Blackwater Falls, and Dolly Sods" chapter).

If you are looking for a challenging run, you can take the **Laurel Fork of the Cheat River** from a put-in where US 33 crosses the stream east of Wymer. The 13 miles of Class III–IV rapids through a remote valley include obstacles such as a 12-foot waterfall, bridge abutments, and strainers before you reach the take-out at Jenningston.

The **Greenbrier River** is one of the gentlest streams in the state and a good place to bring friends who are just beginning to dip paddles into water.

For totally flatwater paddling, head to the small lakes and ponds at the forest service's **Spruce Knob**, **Brandywine**, **Brushy Fork**, and **Buffalo lakes**.

Also see *Bicycling* and Watoga State Park under *Green Space—Parks*.

SKIING, CROSS-COUNTRY An abundance of winter snow blankets most of the forest service trails, especially those near **Spruce Knob** and **North Fork Mountain**, with enough of the powder to enable miles and miles of isolated backcountry gliding.

Also see Elk River Touring Company, Inn, Restaurant, and Guide Service under *Bicycling*.

SPA Locust Hill Bed and Breakfast and Day Spa (304-799-5471; 1-800-617-0530; www.locusthillwv.com), 1525 Locust Hill, Marlinton. How times have changed in West Virginia. When Dave and Paula Zorn became massage therapists in 1987, it would have been unimaginable that there would be a thriving day spa in the rural Marlinton area. Locals and visitors alike come here for massages, body treatments, paraffin dips, wraps, and facials. After your body has become so relaxed, you may not want to go anywhere else, so check into one of the spa's B&B rooms (see *Lodging*).

SWIMMIN' HOLES

Huntersville

Pretty much known only to locals, "Alec's Hole" is in **Knapp Creek**. Drive eastward from Huntersville on WV 39 for approximately 1 mile. A short distance after the road crosses a bridge over the creek, there will be a dirt parking area along the right shoulder. (There are sure to be cars parked here if it's a nice, warm summer day.) A classic mountain stream, Knapp Creek has deep pools to swim in, riffles to lay in and feel like you're in a whirlpool, and good-size rocks to laze about on.

Seneca Rocks

Close to the bridge over the **North Fork of the Potomac River** at Seneca Rocks (see *Climbing*) is a swimmin' hole popular with locals, rock climbers, and hikers. There's a gravel beach on one side of the stream and rocks on the other side that could be used for sunbathing.

Valley Head

There are two good swimmin' holes in the waters of the upper **Elk River**. At the intersection of US 219/WV 55 with WV 15 at Valley Head, follow WV 15 westward for 4 miles and turn left onto Valley Fork Rd. A little more than 5 miles later, there will be a pulloff. Walk down to the river and what the locals call "Elk Hole," a deep spot surrounded by flat rocks. If you want another good place to splash about, continue an additional 7 miles on Valley Fork Rd. to Whittaker Falls, where you can swim behind the falls and slide down a rock chute.

Also see *To See—Waterfalls*, Stuart Knob Recreation Area under *Lodging*, Watoga State Park under *Green Space—Parks*, and *Green Space—State Forests*.

TRAIN EXCURSIONS

Cass

✐ **Cass Scenic Railroad** (304-456-4300; www.cassrailroad.com; mailing address: P.O. Box 107, Cass 24927). The station is in the center of Cass. The Cass Scenic Railroad is not only the state's longest-running train excursion, it is also the longest and narrowest of the state parks. Shay locomotives take the 11 miles to the summit of Bald Knob on the same route they followed when the tracks were laid in 1901 to haul lumber out of the mountains. Cars are logging flatcars that have been refurbished into enclosed passenger cars.

There is a choice of three trips. A two-hour round-trip excursion takes riders to Whittaker Station, the site of a re-created logging camp of the 1940s. A five-hour round-trip takes you to Spruce, built in 1905 for lumberjacks cutting timber on Cheat Mountain. It was at one time the highest town in the East and accessible only by train. My favorite journey has always been the five-hour round-trip to Bald Knob, the second-highest point in the state. The spectacular view from here takes in two states, and the train stops at Whittaker Station, so you also have the opportunity to explore that site.

Whatever journey you decide to take, pick up a free copy of the Track Guide. The trips are only lightly narrated, so the guide will add a great deal of point-by-point information as you travel up the 11-percent grade. (A 2-percent grade is considered steep for conventional locomotives.) Also, bring along a warm outer layer—it's almost always cold on the mountain, and I have experienced upper 30-degree temperatures in July.

Excursions run from sometime in May to late Oct. It would take pages to describe the actual schedule, so visit the Web site or make a phone call. Weekend and holiday tickets for Whittaker Station are $21 for adults, $16 for children (ages 5–12); Spruce or Bald Knob are $27 for adults, $20 for children. Prices are about $3 less during the week; all prices increase about $5 in the fall. Special rates are available if you take multiple rides.

There's more to the state park than the trains. To gain a better understanding of what you are going to experience on the ride, visit the **Railroad & Logging Museum**, view the free *History of Cass* audiovisual show, and take one of the scheduled guided tours of the town. Also visit the **Cass Country Store**, at one time the world's largest company store. It's now a restaurant and gift shop with a good selection of material related to the area.

To really immerse yourself in the atmosphere of an early-1900s logging town, stay in one of the two-story cottages built by the company for its employees. These modest homes are sparsely furnished, but they have full kitchens, electric heat, woodstoves, and all linens. You can also rent a wilderness cabin on Bald Knob or stay on the mountain in the train's caboose (see the "A Caboose in the Wilderness" sidebar later in this chapter).

Durbin

✒ **Durbin Rocket** (304-456-4935; 1-877-686-7245; www.mountainrail.com; mailing address: P.O. Box 44, Durbin 26264). The station is in Durbin on US 250/WV 92. A 1910 Climax geared locomotive, one of only three in the world still operating, powers the *Durbin Rocket*. The engine takes an open observation car, a caboose, and passengers on a two-hour, 10.5-mile round-trip journey along the scenic Greenbrier River. This is the route of a line once used to haul timber out of the mountains, and, just as locomotives did more than a century ago, the train makes a pause along the way to suck water from the river to provide the steam power. As a reminder of the old days, telegraph lines are still strung along the route, while beaver dams and lodges dot the river, and wildflowers grow in profusion along its banks.

Like the *Cheat Mountain Salamander*, the *Durbin Rocket* has quite a complicated schedule, so it is best to check the Web site or make a phone call to see when it is operating. You can also call to make reservations 9–5 on weekdays. Its season is May–Oct. Adults $22, seniors $20, children (ages 4–11) $12.

You can also rent the caboose for an overnight stay in the woods (see the "A Caboose in the Wilderness" sidebar later in this chapter).

Elkins

✒ ***Cheat Mountain Salamander*** (304-636-9477; 1-877-686-7245; www.mountain rail.com; mailing address: P.O. Box 44, Durbin 26264). The station for this ride is the Elkins Depot at 315 Railroad Ave., Elkins.

The *Cheat Salamander* takes three different excursions. The 9-hour roundtrip begins in Elkins and goes upstream along the Shavers Fork of the Cheat River, passing through an isolated area of the Monongahela National Forest, around the two sharpest mainline railroad curves still in active use in the United States, and makes a stop at the High Falls of Cheat (see *To See—Waterfalls*) before continuing into a high-elevation spruce forest and to the ghost town of Spruce, more than 4,000 feet above sea level. This journey is on the highest standard-gauge mainline railroad east of the Mississippi River. A six-hour roundtrip has the same itinerary, but does not go to Spruce. A shorter 3-hour roundtrip begins at a boarding platform close to US 250 several miles west of Durbin, missing the High Falls of Cheat, but going to Spruce.

The *Cheat Mountain Salamander* has quite a complicated schedule, and one that has changed through the years, so it is best to give them a call or consult the Web site. There is usually some train running on weekend days, but there are also some scheduled for weekdays. The season usually starts in mid-May and runs into October.

Tickets for the 9-hour journey (includes two meals) are adults $85, seniors $82, and children (ages 4–11) $78. The 6-hour excursion (includes a sandwich buffet) is adults $58, seniors $56, and children $50. The shortest ride (includes lunch) is adults $34, seniors $32, and children $24.

ᴥ New Tygart Flyer (304-456-4935; 1-877-686-7245; www.mountainrail.com; mailing address: P.O. Box 44, Durbin 26264). The station is on 12th St. and Davis Ave. The 4-hour roundtrip excursion is on the diesel-powered, climate-controlled *New Tygart Flyer*. Large windows in each car allow passengers to enjoy the views of a deep canyon with densely forested slopes, the rushing waters of the Shavers Fork of the Cheat River, and the High Falls of Cheat. The train operates May–Oct., but because the schedule is more convoluted and complicated than that of the *Cheat Mountain Salamander*, I will instruct you to call or consult the Web site. You can also call for reservations 9–5 weekdays.

There is also a choice of seating. The coach cars (adults $40; seniors $38; children [ages 4–11] 30) have individual reclining seats or family-style table seating and includes a buffet lunch. The deluxe Pullman Palace cars, which cost $54 per person (children under age 12 not permitted), have individual cushioned armchair arrangements and includes a lunch ordered from a menu.

WALKING TOURS The ***Historic Beverly Walking Tour*** brochure, available from the Rich Mountain/Historic Beverly Visitor Center (see *Guidance*), directs you to more than 40 sites in the small town's central historic district. Unlike many such brochures, which leave you wondering what it means when a building is described as being designed in a certain architectural style, this one has a handy glossary that relates what those different terms and styles entail.

For the description of another walking tour, see Franklin under *Communities*.

✳ Green Space

NATURE PRESERVES ✪ **Cranberry Glades** is a not-to-be-missed place. A 0.6-mile, perfectly level boardwalk takes even the most out-of-shape visitors into four different bogs of the 750-acre glades. The plants and animals seen here are more commonly found in Canada and the northern parts of the United States, and several are at the southernmost point of their range. Those of you who enjoy birds should be on the lookout for ravens, purple finches, warblers, cedar waxwings, flycatchers, red-shouldered hawks, veeries, and northern water thrushes.

From the Cranberry Mountain Nature Center (see *Guidance*), drive west on WV 55/WV 39 for 0.5 mile and turn right onto FSR 102, which brings you to the parking area a little more than a mile later.

Walk onto the boardwalk and keep to the left, passing through rhododendron and hemlock, to enter the openness of Round Glade, where fiddleheads, which have unfurled a month ago in other places, are still tightly wrapped in late May. At the edge of the bog grow speckled alder, wild raisin, and long-fruited serviceberry. Stop for a few moments to let your eyes sweep across this inspiring landscape of open glades ringed by spruce-crowned ridgelines.

The boardwalk swings into a bog forest of false hellebore, monkshood, tall meadow rue, and marsh marigold before crossing over Yew Creek. Insectivorous plants, such as sundew and horned bladderwort, grow next to the boardwalk. The pitcher plants you see here are not native but are the descendants of some that were planted as an experiment in mid-1900s. A few additional feet of boardwalk over more glades will return you to your car. Do not miss this place!

The Monongahela National Forest's **Gaudineer Scenic Area** is a magical place. Spruce trees and moss-covered logs and rocks keep the area looking richly green throughout the year and provide the feel of a forest primeval. Approximately 50 acres of this small woodland were the lucky recipients of a surveying error that spared them from logging in the early 20th century. The area was designated an official forest service Scenic Area in the 1960s so that it could be managed and preserved for its special values. Some of the towering trees are 250–300 years old and have base diameters of more than 40 inches. Others are young and sprouting upon the fallen trunks of their ancestors. An easy 0.5-mile trail, which connects with the Allegheny Trail (see *To Do—Hiking*), has interpretive plaques describing the intricacies of an old-growth forest.

One additional attraction is the amount of bird life, especially from mid-May to July. You may see black-capped chickadees, chestnut-sided warblers, golden-crowned kinglets, dark-eyed juncos, winter wrens, and Blackburnian warblers, as well as wood, Swainson's, and hermit thrushes.

From the US 219/WV 55 junction with US 250/WV 92 in Huttonsville, drive east for 14 miles on US 250/WV 92, turn left on FSR 27, and come to the trailhead in another 1.5 miles.

PARKS

Hillsboro

Droop Mountain Battlefield State Park (304-653-4254; www.droopmountain battlefield.com; mailing address: HC 64, Box 189, Hillsboro 24296), on US 219/WV 55. Following the Civil War battle of Chickamauga in September 1863, Federal forces were being pushed farther westward by Southern troops. In the hopes of severing the Virginia/Tennessee Railroad that was the supply line for the Confederates, Federal Brig. Gen. William W. Averell marched his troops eastward from Beverly, West Virginia, toward the rail line in Salem, Virginia. On November 5, 1863, a skirmish at Mill Point, about 8 miles south of Marlinton, slowed the movement somewhat, but Averell's superior numbers caused the men under the command of Confederate Col. William 'Mudwall" Jackson to retreat.

Throughout the night, Jackson's army placed artillery, built trenches, and otherwise fortified a site atop Droop Mountain, a high point with a commanding view of the Greenbrier River Valley. Joined by troops under the command of Confederate Brig. Gen. John Echols, the smaller Southern army was able to withstand the first wave of attacks by Union forces. As the day of November 6 wore on, Federals in the 28th Ohio and 10th West Virginia under the command of Col. Augustus Moor attacked the Confederates' left flank.

On all sides, the Union army of about 4,500 continued assaulting the 2,500 men of the Confederate army, and by 4 PM the Southerners were in retreat, ending the state's largest Civil War battle. Encumbered by prisoners and captured livestock, Averell decided to return to Beverly, waiting until December to lead a successful attack on the Virginia/Tennessee Railroad.

LOOKOUT TOWER AT DROOP MOUNTAIN BATTLEFIELD STATE PARK

On July 4, 1928, 125 acres became West Virginia's first state-owned park when they were dedicated as the Droop Mountain Battlefield. An additional 139 acres were later acquired, and today the day-use state park has picnic shelters, play areas for children, and a small museum with items from, and displays about, the battle. A small network of trails that winds through open meadows and into deep forests not only lets hikers enjoy the natural beauty of the area, but also visit places that were important sites during the battle. As a bonus, visitors can climb the six-sided log lookout tower built by the CCC for an Olympian view of the Greenbrier River Valley and surrounding ridgelines.

Reenactments of the battle take place the second weekend of October in every even-numbered year.

Seebert

Watoga State Park (304-799-4087; www.watoga.com; mailing address: HC 82, Box 252, Marlinton 24954). Turn onto WV 27 barely a mile north of Hillsboro and follow it to the park. With more than 10,000 acres, Watoga is West Virginia's largest state park. A network of 13 trails wanders through the backcountry areas, allowing you to hike for more than 30 miles. A portion of the Allegheny Trail (see *To Do—Hiking*) goes through the park, while a number of miles of the Greenbrier River Trail (see *To Do—Bicycling*) run along the western border. From Memorial Day to Labor Day, you can rent paddleboats and rowboats, swim in the pool, or take guided horseback trail rides. Two campgrounds are open Apr.–early Dec., and cabins (the modern ones are open year-round) are available for rent.

Insider's tip: There is good swimmin' in the Greenbrier River next to the Riverside Campground.

Insider's tip for birders: Take a walk on the Black Oak Trail to maybe catch glimpses of a red-eyed vireo, least flycatcher, scarlet tanager, eastern wood-pewee, Blackburnian warbler, rose-breasted grosbeak, or American redstart. Hike a little farther afield on the Allegheny Trail, and you might be rewarded with sightings of ovenbirds, Cerulean warblers, hooded warblers, wood thrushes, eastern towhees, and eastern phoebes.

SOMETHING FOR EVERYONE For more than 20 miles, the South Branch of the Potomac River has carved a half-mile-deep gorge, known as **Smoke Hole Canyon**, between Cave and North Fork mountains. There are several theories as to the origin of the name. One says Native Americans used the many area caves to smoke meat, another claims smoke rising from moonshine stills gave the canyon its name, while a third alludes to the vaporous fogs that drift up from the cool waters of the river.

Anglers are attracted to the Smoke Hole by the golden and rainbow trout stocked by the state Division of Natural Resources, as well as an abundance of catfish and largemouth and smallmouth bass. Rafters, canoeists, and kayakers come here to ply the currents, while birdwatchers have hopes of catching glimpses of bald eagles.

All of this makes the Smoke Hole an excellent day destination for the entire family. Arrive early in the morning and let everyone go off to pursue his or her own activities. Meet back at the picnic area for lunch, and then spend the afternoon on a group circuit hike along the moderate 3.7-mile South Branch Loop Trail.

STATE FORESTS

Dunmore

Seneca State Forest (304-799-6213; www.senecastateforest.com), on WV 28 about 4 miles south of Dunmore. West Virginia's first state forest, 11,684-acre Seneca State Forest has one of the nicest of the state-operated campgrounds. There are only 10 sites (no hookups), but they are in a wooded setting and pleasantly secluded from each other. For a primitive indoor experience, you can rent one of the rustic cabins, built by the Civilian Conservation Corps in the 1930s. They have no running water or electricity but do have gaslights, wood-burning cookstoves, gas refrigerators, and cooking utensils, and they are open mid-Apr. to early Dec. I most enjoy the ones overlooking the Greenbrier River, as they provide immediate access to the stream and the Greenbrier River Trail (see *To Do—Bicycling*). There is a network of 23 miles of trails, including a portion of the Allegheny Trail (see *To Do—Hiking*). Some are open to mountain bikers, who also are permitted to ride many miles of gated roads. Canoes, rowboats, and paddleboats are available for rent on small Seneca Lake, which has largemouth bass, bluegill, and stocked trout.

Huttonsville

Kumbrabow State Forest (304-335-2219; www.kumbrabow.com; mailing address: P.O. Box 65, Huttonsville 26273). Turn onto WV 219/6 almost 7 miles south of Huttonsville and follow it into the state forest. Located on Rich Mountain at the western edge of the Potomac Highlands, 9,474-acre Kumbrabow State Forest offers a small campground (open mid-May through deer rifle season) with pit toilets and coin-operated showers and laundry, picnicking, and fishing in a native trout stream. Rustic cabins, available mid-Apr. through early Dec., have no electricity, but they do have gas lights and refrigerators. Restrooms are pit toilets, and water is drawn from a nearby well. A trail system of close to 12 miles that takes hikers into the more hidden parts of the state forest appears to be rarely used.

Insider's tip: Unknown to many people other than locals or those who happen to camp here, the state forest has two nice swimmin' holes. Just before the bridge to the cabin area is a parking lot and trail leading to the pool at the bottom of Mill Creek Falls. The second spot is also on Mill Creek and is accessed through the campground. What makes this one special is the smooth rock that you can slide down to the 6-foot-deep hole. A lot of fun—and well used during the summer camping season.

✳ Lodging

MOTELS & HOTELS

Bartow 24290

The Hermitage (304-456-4808; www .hermitagemotel.com; mailing address: P.O. Box 8), at the intersection of US 250 and WV 28/92. This older motel has been remodeled several times, and despite showing a bit of its age, the rooms are always neat and clean. It is popular with hunters in the fall and those who are looking for convenient and fairly low-cost accommodations close to the scenic trains in Durbin and Cass. $74–99. The adjoining restaurant is one of the nicest in the immediate vicinity (see *Eating Out*).

Bowden 26254

Alpine Lodge and Restaurant (304-636-1470; mailing address: HC 73, Box 3), 10 miles east of Elkins on US 33. The 18 rooms and two kitchenettes are what you would expect in a motel that has been in business for two full generations. Its location is surrounded by national forest land, making it a popular choice for hunters, anglers, hikers, and other outdoors types. The country-style restaurant downstairs serves breakfast and lunch daily, and dinner Wed.–Sun. $60.

Boyer

Boyer Motel (304-456-4667; mailing address: Rte. 1, Box 51, Arbovale 24915), on WV 28/WV 92 in Boyer. A well-kept, older establishment, this is the closest motel to Cass Scenic Railroad. It is also one of the lowest-cost accommodations in the area. $55. A campground and restaurant are located nearby (see *Campgrounds* and *Eating Out*).

Marlinton 24954

Marlinton Motor Inn (304-799-4711; 1-800-354-0821; www.marlintonmotor inn.com; mailing address: US 219 N, Box 25), on US 219/WV 55 a short distance north of Marlinton. The Marlinton Motor Inn, a standard motel built in the mid-1900s, has rooms that may be a bit small by today's standards, but its location close to outdoor destinations makes it a popular choice for hikers, bikers, paddlers, hunters, and anglers looking for a place to stay that has reasonable rates. The outdoor pool is a nice attraction, too. The adjoining Sixties Café is open for breakfast, lunch, and dinner. Rates are in the $70 range, but have been known to go below $40.

For additional hotels and motels, also see Yokum's Vacationland under *Cabins and Vacation Rentals* and Star Hotel and Restaurant under *Eating Out*.

INNS

Durbin 26264

The Greenbrier Suites (304-456-1004; 1-800-510-0180; www.green

brierinn.us), on US 250/WV 92 in Durbin. Directly across the street from the Durbin Train Depot, the Greenbrier Suite's two suites each have a kitchenette, private bath, dining room, and parlor with décor and furnishings that are sparse, but the rooms are clean, and the person who opened the Inn, Frank Proud, helped establish the West Fork Trail (see *To Do— Bicycling*). It's also on the route of the Allegheny Trail (see *To Do—Hiking*), so it's a convenient stop if you have been backpacking for days and seek the comfort of a bed and shower. $85–95.

Elkins 26241

Cheat River Lodge (304-636-2301; www.cheatriverlodge.com), on Old US 33 a few miles east of Elkins. On a narrow strip of land deep in the gorge formed by the Shavers Fork of the Cheat River, the lodge's efficiency rooms and suites have screened porches overlooking the waterway. Also available are a number of cabins (really full-size houses) spaced along 4 miles of riverfront. Some are next to the water, while others cling to the hillside. Each is different in style and furnishings, but all are equipped with kitchens, baths, linens, and daily housekeeping services. Lodge rooms are $88; cabins are $216.

The lodge also contains the Cheat River Inn (see *Eating Out*), one of the area's better dining options.

The Graceland Inn (304-637-1600; 1-800-624-3157; www.gracelandinn .com), on the Davis & Elkins College campus. Stay at The Graceland Inn and experience what it was like to live in the opulent style of a timber baron around the turn of the 20th century. Built in 1893 as the summer retreat of Henry Gassaway Davis, the sandstone Queen Anne mansion has turrets, a two-story great room, an oak-paneled billiard room, and a veranda with a sweeping view of the town. Guest rooms have private baths and period-appropriate furnishings. As grand and luxurious as this sounds, members of the staff (a number are students in the college's hospitality program) are down-to-earth and quite used to having gritty hikers, mountain bikers, and anglers show up from a long day in the woods. After a shower, head downstairs to the Mingo Room Restaurant (see *Dining Out*) for a satisfying meal. The $105–175 rate includes a continental breakfast.

Frost

🐾 **The Inn at Mountain Quest** (304-799-7267; 1-866-245-6494; www .mountainquestinn.com; mailing address: Rural Rte. 2, Box 109, Marlinton 24954), on WV 92 south of the WV 92 intersection with WV 84 in Frost. The Inn at Mountain Quest is one of the most unexpected pleasures to find in a very rural countryside setting. After careers in information technology, organizational development, and knowledge management, David and Alex Bennett purchased this 450-acre farm. A two-story wing off the original farmhouse has 12 uniquely decorated

THE GRACELAND INN

guest rooms. And when I say unique, I really mean it. In the Safari Room, a mural of a sunset over Africa serves as the backdrop for beds covered by mosquito nets. A large rosewood dollhouse filled with tiny furnishings runs the length of one wall in the Playhouse Room. As I was shown each room, all with different themes, I couldn't help but think how much fun Alex must have had. When you decorate your own home, you have to pick one theme. Here, Alex was able to let her imagination run wild.

Miles of trails wander over the 450 acres (be sure to take the one high onto the ridge for a soaring view of the farm) for hiking, biking, or cross-country skiing, and a two-story library, which has so many volumes it is now a part of the Pocahontas County library system, invites quiet hours. And then there is the food. A country breakfast starts the day, while lunch and dinner have featured items like glazed stuffed pork chops, seafood bisque, and honey bread pudding.

This is the place to come to relax and be pampered in luxury, while at the same time being immersed in the quiet retreat of a countryside landscape that, even in West Virginia, is disappearing and giving way to the modern world. $130–190.

Mingo Village 26294

 ♿ **The Brazen Head Inn** (304-339-6917; 1-866-339-6917; www.brazen headinn.com; mailing address: HC 69, Box 28-A), on US 219 almost 6 miles north of the turnoff to Snowshoe Mountain. Being in the southern portion of this area, The Brazen Head Inn is relatively close to Snowshoe Mountain (see the "Snowshoe Mountain" chapter) and is a popular choice for those not wanting to lodge at the resort. Named after Dublin, Ireland's, oldest pub (established in 1198), the

inn gets pretty lively, especially during the skiing season, when owner and instrument maker Will Fanning, a native of Dublin, invites friends over to play some music in his restaurant tavern (see *Eating Out*). Traditional Irish and mountain music gets many patrons on their feet, while others just enjoy watching and listening as they sip a pint of Guinness.

Will used his woodworking skills to design and build the inn with hardwood floors, dovetailed joints, and double-tongue and groove walls. The guest rooms have a homey feel, and each has a private bath. $119–149.

Slatyfork 26291

Elk River Touring Company, Inn, Restaurant, and Guide Service (304-572-3771; 1-866-572-3771; www .ertc.com; mailing address: HC 69, Box 7), on US 219/WV 55. After full days of hiking, mountain biking, cross-country skiing, or fishing (all on inn property if you wish—see *To Do— Bicycling*), check into one of the five guest rooms (each with private bath) in the main lodge ($90–130), or rent one of the cabins ($100–300) if you have a large group. They are equipped with fireplaces, full kitchens, TVs, phones, washer and dryer, and all linens. There's even a large farmhouse with five guest rooms and three baths available for rent. No matter which accommodation you choose, you're sure to meet many other like-minded outdoors enthusiasts and spend evening hours swapping tales, especially if you have dinner in the restaurant (see *Dining Out*).

Morning Glory Inn (304-572-5000; www.morninggloryinn.com), on US 219/WV 55 close to the turnoff for Snowshoe Mountain (see the "Snowshoe Mountain" chapter). Each of the seven large rooms has a vaulted wooden ceiling and skylight (making the rooms appear even larger and brighter). The entire place has the feel of an intimate ski lodge. Known for the quality and quantity of the full country breakfasts. $90–140.

BED & BREAKFASTS

Elkins 26241

The Post House Bed & Breakfast (304-636-1792; www.virtualcities.com /ons/wv/z/wvz7603.htm), 306 Robert E. Lee Ave. Usually only open July-Oct. Within a residential area, the B&B's three guest rooms (one with a private bath) provide a low-cost lodging option. A covered brick porch is a nice spot to enjoy evening breezes. A continental breakfast is served in the morning. $65–70.

Tunnel Mountain Bed & Breakfast (304-636-1684; 1-888-211-9123; www .bbonline.com/wv/tunnel; mailing address: Rte. 1, Box 59-1), on old US 33 a few miles east of Elkins. The hosts of this three-story, three-guest-room fieldstone home have been operating a B&B for decades, so you can be assured that they know a thing or two about hospitality. Set on 5 acres, the house's warm and inviting interior has pine and chestnut woodwork and is furnished with antiques and crafts. The pre–Civil War bed in the room I stayed in got me to thinking about its long history and service: How many people have slept in this bed; how many heads have leaned against the headboard? What were these people's lives like; were they happy/sad when they slept in this particular bed?

The B&B's location couldn't be any better. It's a short stroll to the Shavers Fork of the Cheat River, national forest land is a five-minute drive away, and the amenities of Elkins are close by. $89–99.

Also available is the **Riverside Retreat Vacation Cottage,** a small cottage accommodating up to six people that sits on the bank of the river. Linens, kitchen items, games, TV, and a DVD player are provided, so all you need to bring is food. $125 per night; a minimum stay may be required.

Hillsboro 24946

🐾 **Hillsboro House Bed & Breakfast** (304-653-4895; mailing address: P.O. Box 508), on US 219/WV 55 in Hillsboro. The Hillsboro House was built in 1891, and current owners Leah and Eugene Burford spent more than a year remodeling and renovating it before opening their B&B. This is not a fancy, palatial place, but one whose three guest rooms are tastefully decorated in simple and appealing furnishings, with family photographs on the walls adding the touch of a loving home.

In fact, that is the best way to describe my stay here—I (and you will, too) felt as if I had been invited into the Burford's home, as we spent several evening hours on the porch getting to know each other. After a full breakfast in the morning, it seemed as if I was saying goodbye to valued friends. My only regret is I didn't have enough time to relax and watch the sunset from the hammock in the backyard. It will be a priority on the next visit. $50–75.

Huntersville 24954

Carriage House Inn (304-799-6706; www.carriagehousewv.com; mailing address: HC 52, Box 56, Marlinton 24954), on WV 39 in Huntersville. The Carriage House Inn was built around 1852 and retains its country charm and appearance. Five guest rooms and an attic suite have private baths (check out the rain-barrel sink in the suite), while the herb garden is a quiet place to wander and relax. In fact, many of those herbs, along with other produce from the host's vegetable garden, find their way into the imaginative breakfast dishes. She also operates two small gift shops full of items from local artists and craftspersons. $95.

Marlinton 24954

Locust Hill Bed and Breakfast and Day Spa (304-799-5471; www.locust hillwv.com), 1525 Locust Hill. Paula and Dave Zorn totally renovated their 1920s home, which sits on a knoll just outside of Marlinton with an inspiring view of the surrounding ridgelines. All rooms have private baths; the third-floor suite struck my fancy, as it takes in the vistas from dormer windows. The B&B is situated on 20 acres, where you are encouraged to hike, or fish and rowboat on two different ponds. Dave is a trained baker, so don't hesitate to reach for the delicious rolls and breads at breakfast. Gourmet meals are also available to guests who make prior arrangements. Ninety percent of those staying here take advantage of Paula's day-spa treatments (see *To Do—Spa*). $75–95.

Old Clark Inn Bed & Breakfast (1-800-849-4184; www.oldclark inn.com), 702 Third Ave. The brick Old Clark Inn has been a guest house of one kind or another since its construction in 1924. Today, the 10 simply decorated guest rooms (some with

CARRIAGE HOUSE INN

shared bath) are available to families traveling with their children and pets. The owners are avid motorcyclists and provide a covered area for bikes, a compressor to fill tires, and other amenities that only those who ride would know to offer. They will even let you use the facilities late into the day after you have checked out of your room. $60–85.

Slatyfork 26291

Mount Airy Bed and Breakfast (304-572-5208; www.mtairybnb.com; mailing address: HC 69, P.O. Box 61, Mount Airy Lane), on US 219/WV 55 north of the turnoff to Snowshoe Mountain (see the "Snowshoe Mountain" chapter). The closest B&B to Snowshoe Resort, Mount Airy sits high on the hillside with a grand view of the mountain ridgelines to the southwest; the deck is an excellent place to enjoy sunsets. All rooms have waterbeds that are fully baffled (they don't toss you around like the waterbeds of old) and down pillows and comforters. $85–160.

Valley Head 26294

Hello House (304-339-6179; www .virtualcities.com/ons/wv/h/wvhc801.ht m; mailing address: P.O. Box 263). Miles out a dirt road—actually miles from anywhere else—Donald Morfitt and watercolor artist Grey Darden offer an entire house (with two bedrooms) for guests to enjoy the quiet of their hidden acreage adjacent to national forest land. What to do here? Harvest ramps in March, gather blueberries in July, enjoy vegetables from the garden during the summer, and feast on apples in the fall. Or maybe just sit on the porch watching the deer and wild turkeys while gazing up at the stars. $85 includes breakfast; extra charge to use the kitchen.

The Hello House is in the southern portion of this area, which makes it a popular choice for skiers not wanting to lodge at Snowshoe Mountain (see the "Snowshoe Mountain" chapter).

Nakiska Chalet Bed & Breakfast (304-339-6309; www.nakiska.com), HC 73, Box 24. Close to Snowshoe Mountain (see the "Snowshoe Mountain" chapter), Nakiska Chalet is popular with skiers and others who visit the resort but don't particularly enjoy its hustle and bustle. Miles out a country road, the B&B has only one guest room, so things will be as peaceful as you want them to be, and you will have the almost undivided attention of the hosts. $70–110.

✍ Adjacent to the B&B is the **Nakiska Lodge** (www.nakiskalodge.com), a modern, spacious, and luxurious vacation home with three bedrooms, two baths, and amenities galore. Families with children are welcome. $400 per night; $475 holidays—minimum stays are required.

CABINS AND VACATION RENTALS

Helvetia 26224

The Beekeeper Inn (304-924-6435; mailing address: Rte. 46), near the intersection of WV 45 and WV 46. You will be disappointed if you come here expecting modern luxury, as The Beekeeper Inn is one of the oldest buildings in Helvetia, built around 1870 for the village's original beekeeper. Keeping the age of the building and village in mind, look at your stay from a historical aspect, and, like me, you will appreciate the fact that each room's floor slopes at a different angle, the ceilings are low, and the front door has the appearance of having received dozens of coats of paint. Yet, everything you need to be comfortable is furnished—a complete kitchen, three bedrooms with private baths, and unpretentious antique furnishings appropriate to the home's past. Operat-

ed by the owners of the Hütte Restaurant and Alpine Penthouse (see *Eating Out*), this is one of the simplest, yet most authentic and enjoyable, places I have stayed in West Virginia. $90.

Laurel Fork South Wilderness

The three **Middle Mountain Cabins**, operated by the forest service, are located next to a small pond on the edge of the Laurel Fork South Wilderness. While they have no electricity, rented as a unit they can accommodate up to 10 people, with the main cabin having a gas refrigerator and stove, pots, dishes, and silverware. Going along with its rustic nature, you have to bring the flashlights, lanterns, bed linens, and anything else you think you may need. Water is from an outside hand pump; the bathroom is a vault toilet. A wonderfully isolated, primitive experience with direct access to the trails of the wilderness. Reservations must be made at least four days in advance through www.recreation.gov or by calling 1-877-444-6777. $75.

Marlinton 24954

The Jerico Pre–Civil War Log Cabins (304-799-6241; www.jericobb.com; mailing address: Rte. 1, Box 371-T), on Jerico Rd. off US 219/WV 55 in Marlinton. What an interesting thing—and a wonderful job of historic preservation—the owner of these cabins has done. The cabins, which have modern baths, complete kitchens, TVs, and all linens, truly were constructed before the Civil War and have been dismantled, moved, and reconstructed. Some are located in a narrow, shady hollow next to a babbling stream, while others are on high, open meadows with far-reaching views. Staying in one is an exceptional way to relive a bit of history. The $75–350 rates vary according to the cabin.

Seneca Rocks 26884

🐾 ✍ **County Line Guest House** (304-227-4455; www.countylineguest

house.com; mailing address: P.O. Box 41), on US 33/WV 55 on the Randolph/Pendleton County line between Harmon and Seneca Rocks. As a non-hosted B&B, this home is just right for family vacations. You can reserve the entire house, or just a room, and have access to all of the amenities. The early-1900s farmhouse (recently renovated and remodeled) with a wrap-around porch sits high on the same ridgeline as Spruce Knob, so you are exposed to all the wonderful vagaries that come with such an environment.

The night I arrived, the sky was brilliant with the stars of the Milky Way. By morning, the house and I were wrapped in a cloud, with the wispy vapors being swirled around by a soft mountain breeze. Things had cleared by early evening, just in time to watch the blush of a crimson sunset. Sunrise the next morning bathed everything in a deep, glimmering gold. What more could you ask of a place to escape from the concerns of your everyday life? Rates start at $70.

Yokum's Vacationland (304-567-2351; 1-800-772-8342; www.yokum .com; mailing address: HC 59, Box 3), at the main intersection in Seneca Rocks. With a view of Seneca Rocks from each one of the facilities, Yokum's offers log cabins (some newer, some showing a bit of their age; $80–200) fully equipped with kitchen, fireplace, linens, and cable TV. Also available at the same location are tent and RV campsites and, for a different experience, Indian tepees. Across the street are motel rooms above Yokum's store that start at $50. *Insider's tip*: Be sure to ask for one with a view of the rocks and not the parking lot.

Slatyfork 26291
🔊 **Pleasant Valley Farms** (304-572-2319; www.pvfarmsretreat.com; mailing address: HC 69, Box 96 South), off

US 219/WV 55 about 12 miles north of Marlinton. Sam Gibson and Gayle Boyette operate their cattle farm as environmentally responsibly as possible, trying to show their respect for land that has been in Sam's family for more than five generations. They invite guests to wander the property, learning a bit about farm life.

Several modern cottages (starting at $109) and rustic cabins (starting at $79) are spaced throughout the property, giving you privacy, while still enjoying what the farm has to offer.

For other cabin and vacation-rental options, also see Cass Scenic Railroad under *To Do—Train Excursions*, *Green Space—State Forest*, Tunnel Mountain Bed & Breakfast under *Bed & Breakfasts*, and Watoga State Park under *Green Space—Parks*.

CAMPGROUNDS ⅙ **Monongahela National Forest Service Campgrounds** (all with fees of varying rates and amenities that are at least partially handicapped accessible) are spread throughout this area. Some are quite primitive, others somewhat deluxe with dump stations, electric hookups, and modern restrooms. Almost all of them have hiking and mountain biking trails nearby. More information on these sites may be obtained from Monongahela National Forest (304-636-1800), 200 Sycamore St., Elkins 26241.

In the northwestern part of this area:

The **Stuart Knob Recreation Area**, located on the Shavers Fork of the Cheat River, is usually open from mid-May to mid-Oct. It's one of the forest service's more deluxe campgrounds, with dump station, modern restrooms and showers, electric hookups, and swimming in the river. From Elkins, go east on US 33 for approximately 4 miles, turn north on WV 33/8 (old US 33), and travel approximately 2 miles.

A CABOOSE IN THE WILDERNESS

Want to spend a night away from civilization, but don't want to hike for miles to reach a site and then set up a tent? Rent a caboose! The caboose of the **Durbin Rocket** (304-456-4935; 1-877-686-7245; www.mountainrail.com) is quite deluxe, with a modern bathroom and shower, refrigerator, heat, and all linens and utensils. At the end of the train excursion along the Greenbrier River, your private accommodations will be unhooked, and you can spend the night several miles from the nearest reminder of the modern world. At the end of your stay, the train will reconnect to the caboose and haul you back to Durbin. Make reservations early; the last time I checked, this interesting overnight accommodation was booked almost a year in advance. The caboose can accommodate up to six people, and the rate for four people is $260 for the first night, $180 for the second, and $150 for a third evening. This includes a round-trip fare on the train.

The caboose available for rent on the **Cass Scenic Railroad** (304-456-4300; www.cassrailroad.com) is a bit more rustic. Depending on which caboose you get, you may or may not have a gas refrigerator and only a coal stove for heat (coal and drinking water provided). You have the choice of having it dropped off at Whittaker Station, Spruce, or atop Bald Knob. Call for current rates as they have changed often. In addition, all patrons must purchase individual train-ride tickets.

See *To Do—Train Excursions* for more information.

Turn north on WV 6 and drive 0.5 mile to the recreation area entrance.

The **Bear Heaven Campground**, open year-round, is more rustic, with just eight sites placed among some interesting rock formations, vault toilets, and a hand pump. From Elkins, go east on US 33 for 11 miles, turn left onto FSR 91, and continue 3 miles to the campground. *Insider's tip*: There is no official trail, but if you scramble up the rocks beside the day-use area, you'll get a wonderful panoramic view of soaring peaks and deep valleys.

Located to the southeast of Elkins is primitive **Laurel Fork Campground**. Open Apr.–Oct., it is on the road that separates the Laurel Fork North Wilderness from the Laurel Fork South Wilderness (see *To Do—Hiking*) and has sites that are in an open area with little vegetation, vault toilets, and a hand pump. *Insider's tip*: Walk 0.2 mile south of the campground on the Laurel River Trail, and you'll find a cold spring whose gushing water is a nice alternative to that which comes out of the hand pump. From Elkins, take US 33 east for 15 miles, turn right onto FSR 14, continue another 12.3 miles, turn left onto FSR 423, and come to the campground a few minutes later.

Campgrounds located more to the east:

The **Spruce Knob Lake Campground** is the state's highest developed campground, being located just a few miles from the state's highest point, Spruce Knob (4,861 feet). There are the usual campsites you can drive up to, as well as a number of walk-in sites. Accessible vault toilets and a solar-powered water pump are the only amenities.

True to its name, the **Seneca Shadows Campground** sits just a mile from the base of Seneca Rocks. Open Apr.–Oct., it is the forest service's showpiece campground in this area. There are more than 20 drive-in sites (with hookups) large enough to hold eight people. More than a dozen walk-in sites have picnic tables, tent pads, and lantern poles. It's on US 33/WV 28, 1 mile south of Seneca Rocks.

Campgrounds more to the south and close to the Virginia border:

Island Campground has only six sites, pit toilets, and no source of water. However, the sites are large and spaced far enough apart to provide quite a bit of privacy. It is on WV 28 about 5 miles north of Bartow.

Rustic **Bird Run** has only a few primitive sites, a hand pump, and vault toilets. Its location is on WV 84 less than 2 miles east of Frost. Open year-round, but the pump will be out of operation in winter.

Also quite rustic is the **Pocahontas Campground**, situated on WV 92 close to 2 miles south of the WV 92 intersection with WV 39 east of Minnehaha Springs. It, too, only has a few sites with a hand pump and vault toilets. Open mid-Mar. to mid-Dec.

A number of camping options are close to the Cranberry Wilderness (see *To Do—Hiking*) in the southern portion of this area and are located along forest service roads beside the Williams River:

The **Tea Creek Campground** is less than a mile from the Highlands Scenic Highway 150. It is popular with anglers, hikers, mountain bikers, hikers, and families, so its 29 sites often fill up quickly on nice weekends. There are three sets of vault toilets and one hand pump. Open year-round.

The small **Day Run Campground** on the upper Williams River has only 12 sites, vault toilets, and a hand pump.

Also situated along FSR 86 and FSR 216 beside the Williams River are approximately 30 dispersed camping sites, each with picnic table and fire ring. Several pit toilets are at various locations along the roads. There is no fee to camp in any of these sites.

The **George Washington National Forest's Brandywine Recreation Area** is so far east, it is just a few miles from the Virginia border. With campsites in a wooded area, it has modern restrooms and showers, along with a small swimming lake. From the intersection of US 33 with WV 21 in Brandywine, drive east on US 33 for 2.7 miles to the recreation area entrance.

A sampling of the commercial campgrounds in this area include:

Bowden 26254

Alpine Shores Campground (304-636-4311; mailing address: HC 73, Box 3), off US 33 several miles east of Elkins. Open Apr.–Oct. Located along the Shavers Fork of the Cheat River, Alpine Shores is owned by the operators of the Alpine Lodge and Restaurant (see *Motels & Hotels*). With 150 sites, it has electric and water hookups, dump station, camp store, hot showers, and a restaurant.

Revelle's River Resort (304-636-0023; 1-877-988-2267; www.revelles.com; mailing address: Box 96), located several miles east of Elkins on Faulkner Rd. off US 33. Open year-round. One of the state's oldest privately owned RV camp resorts, Revelle's is situated along 1 mile of the Shavers Fork of the Cheat River, which is a trout-stocked stream. With scheduled activities, entertainment, hot showers, laundry, dump station, country store, playgrounds, tube and bicycle rentals, and cottages, cabins, and trailers for rent, you may never want to leave the property. A small restaurant serves breakfast, lunch, and dinner.

Shavers Fork Campground (304-636-0023; 1-877-988-2267; www.revelles.com), located several miles east of Elkins on East Faulkner Rd. off US 33. Situated along the Shavers Fork of the Cheat River and operated by the same people as Revelle's River Resort, the campground was formerly a Yogi Bear's Jellystone Park Camp-Resort and has many of the amenities associated with this national chain: heated swimming pool with kiddie pool, hot showers, laundry, camp store, hookups and dump station.

Boyer

Boyer Campground (304-456-4667; mailing address: Rte. 1, Box 51, Arbovale 24915) on WV 28/92 in Boyer. Open mid-Apr. to mid-Dec. One of the closest campgrounds to Cass Scenic Railroad (see *To Do—Train Excursions*), its amenities include full hookups, hot showers with private dressing rooms, and a playground.

Cass 24927

Whittaker Campground (304-456-3218; www.myspace.com/whittaker campground; mailing address: HC 61, Box 45), off WV 66 a short distance west of Cass. A large campground with more than 100 sites, the majority of which have electricity, water, fireplaces, firewood, and picnic tables. As large as it is, this is quite a bare campsite, with no recreational activities such as a pool, playground, or sports fields.

Durbin 26264

East Fork Campground (304-456-3101; www.eastforkcampgrounddurbin.com; mailing address: WV 92/US 250), along the East Fork of the Greenbrier River in Durbin. Open-field and shaded sites with municipal water, hot showers, hookups, and a dump station. A very short walk from the *Durbin Rocket* (see *To Do—Train Excursions*).

For additional campgrounds, also see Yokum's Vacationland under *Cabins and Vacation Rentals*, *Green Space—Parks*, and *Green Space—State Forest*.

✳ Where to Eat

DINING OUT

Elkins

☙ **The Mingo Room Restaurant of Graceland Inn** (304-637-1600; 1-800-624-3157; www.gracelandinn.com), on the Davis & Elkins College campus (see *Lodging*). Open for dinner Tue.–Sat. 5:30–9 and Sun. brunch 11:30–2. Lunch is served Tue.–Sat. 11:30–1:30 during the summer season. A menu of regional and Continental cuisine, featuring seafood, poultry, and meats, is served in Graceland's original dining room. Locals come here for special occasions and for the Sunday brunches (the blintzes are divine!), and dine on the veranda overlooking the town in good weather. (Sadly, a modern building has recently been constructed, blocking out many of the older, and lovelier, 1800s buildings.) Entrées $19–26.

Slatyfork

Ⓨ **Elk River Touring Company, Inn, Restaurant, and Guide Service** (304-572-3771; 1-866-572-3771; www.ertc.com), on US 219/WV 55. Open for dinner Thurs.–Sun. Because this restaurant is at the center of a business where people have spent the day hiking, biking, skiing, or fishing, the clientele is definitely relaxed and informal with each other. However, the atmosphere and food are of such exceptional quality that I just had to include it in the *Dining Out* category. There's also an extensive wine list and pub selections of domestic and imported beers. This is such a popular place that you should consider making reservations, especially during the skiing season.

All of the health-conscious entrées are made with organic produce when available, and the breads and desserts are homemade. Start the meal with chèvre and herbs baked in phyllo or try the West Virginia rainbow trout spread (local trout blended with cream cheese and spices). The Brazilian toasted coconut halibut with a sweet and spicy pepper coulis is my favorite entrée, but then again, the spicy Thai noodles, roasted pork with rum curry glaze, or duckling with blueberry barbecue sauce have never disappointed me. As you can tell, I come here as often as possible. After one visit, you will, too. Entrées $15–32.

EATING OUT

Bartow

The Hermitage (304-456-4808; www.hermitagemotel.com), at the intersection of US 250 and WV 28/92. Open for lunch and dinner Fri., Sat., and Sun. *Please note*: Hours of operation were changing and in state of flux as this book went to press. The Hermitage is the exception to most motel restaurants; it actually has good food, and as an exception to many other dining establishments in the area, it offers more than just country cooking. French onion soup is a nice meal starter, while the two crab cakes are available at an unheard-of price. My Allegheny Mountain trout fillets, which come from a freshwater trout farm just across the border in Virginia, were broiled with a seasoned lemon pepper sauce. Entrées $8.95–16.95. (Also see *Lodging*.)

Beverly

Mama's Kitchen (304-636-7672), north of Beverly on US 219/US 250. Open for breakfast, lunch, and dinner daily. The home-style food is so popular that the restaurant had to relocate to its current larger facilities on the north end of town. Their slogan is, "Food so good you'd swear we kidnapped your mother." Entrées $3.95–9.95.

Boyer

Boyer Restaurant (304-456-4667), on WV 28/WV 92 in Boyer. Open Fri.–Sun. A local family favorite for decades, the Boyer Restaurant is the best place to go for a good country breakfast ($2.50–6). Dinner ($6.50–15.75) is primarily country cooking, such as grilled pork chops, fried chicken, roast beef, and, a specialty, lasagna. Homemade strawberry shortcake is *the* dessert here.

For other amenities in Boyer, also see *Lodging*.

Brandywine

Fat Boy's Pork Palace (304-249-7025), on US 33. Open daily for breakfast, lunch, and dinner. Owned by sisters Melanie Ruddle and Ashley Holloway, Fat Boy's barbecue is so well thought of that residents of Virginia drive twisting US 33 over Shenandoah Mountain just to have lunch here. Sandwiches start at $1.70; dinner entrées $4.99–14.99.

Elkins

✿ **Cheat River Inn** (304-636-6265; www.cheatriverlodge.com), on Old US 33 a few miles east of Elkins. Open for dinner daily except Mon.; lunch is served during the summer. Reservations suggested. With outdoor seating overlooking the flowing waters of the Shavers Fork of the Cheat River, the Cheat River Inn has a reputation for first-rate dining. Originally a roadside tavern when Old US 33 was the main highway, the restaurant now serves a diverse menu of poultry, seafood, and beef prepared in ways not often seen in West Virginia. A good example is the Honey Hibiscus. It is jumbo shrimp and sea scallops grilled and served in a sweet and tart hibiscus-flower sauce. Whenever possible, the vegetable dishes are made with produce from local organic farms, and all salad dressings are prepared at the inn, which is a part of the Cheat River Lodge (see *Lodging*). The staff is knowledgeable about the best wines to pair with your meal. Entrées $16.95–27.95.

Franklin

✿ **Korner Shop Café** (304-358-2979), 100 North Main St. Open for breakfast, lunch, and dinner daily. There are just a few tables and counter stools, but sit here long enough and it is a good possibility you will see just about everyone who lives in Pendleton County come in for the homestyle food. The restaurant has been around since the 1960s, and current owner Craig Thompson took over when his father, "Peanut," retired from serving hand-dipped ice-cream milk shakes and hot turkey and roast beef sandwiches smothered in gravy. Dinner platters $5.95–9.95.

Star Hotel & Restaurant (304-358-3580; www.thestarhotelrestaurant.com), 200 North Main St. Open for lunch Mon.–Fri., dinner Fri.–Sat. Angela Miller, a native of the area, and her husband, Steve, from San Francisco, have turned the 1920s Star Hotel Restaurant into one of the Seneca Rocks–Spruce Knob area's most diverse dining spots. You can find country cooking favorites like pot roast, pork chops, chicken-fried steak, and meat loaf, but since you seem to find items like this in most of the area's other restaurants, order the shrimp and broccoli Alfredo, broiled fillet of trout, or lobster tail. Entrées $6.95–market price. Wine is available by the glass or bottle, but don't pass up the delicious fresh-squeezed lemonade.

Upstairs, the couple has also done a nice job renovating the hotel rooms

($65–75) and making them a pleasant place to stay. They are popular with business travelers, who enjoy the Internet access.

Helvetia

♪ **The Hütte Restaurant** (304-924-6435), at the intersection of WV 45 and WV 46. Open daily for lunch and dinner. The Swiss are hearty eaters, and Hütte Restaurant serves up meals true to that tradition. Choose from bratwurst, Zurich sauerbraten, or the house-made sausage. Whatever you get, be sure to ask for a plate of Helvetia cheese and homemade bread to go along with it, and top the meal off with the cherry tart or peach cobbler. There is a decidedly homey atmosphere about the place, with simple family furnishings (every piece has a history behind it) and an unpretentiousness that definitely reminded me of the small village restaurants that sustained me while hiking through the Alps. Lunch sandwiches $5.25–6.75; evening meals $10–16.50.

Upstairs is the **Alpine Penthouse**, simple bed and breakfast rooms that reflect the atmosphere of the dining room downstairs. They are a good

THE HÜTTE RESTAURANT

choice for families and groups. The owners also operate The Beekeeper Inn (see *Lodging*).

Marlinton

♪ **The River Place** (304-799-7233), 814 First Ave. Open daily for breakfast, lunch, and dinner. The owners opened this restaurant several decades ago because they thought Marlinton lacked a dining place with a family atmosphere. Sandwiches and country-cooking offerings, along with an extensive dessert menu, fill several menu pages. The best part is that the restaurant overlooks the Greenbrier River. Entrées $6.95–12.95.

Mingo Village

♿ **The Brazen Head Inn** (304-339-6917; 1-866-339-6917; www.brazen headinn.com), on US 219 almost 6 miles north of the turnoff to Snowshoe Mountain. Open for lunch and dinner daily; breakfast is served on Sat. and Sun. It's a diverse menu owner Will Fanning serves up. Some of the items you can choose include leg o' lamb roulade, roasted salmon, or penne pasta primavera. In keeping with the inn's atmosphere and Will's homeland, why not give the ham and cabbage or corned beef and cabbage a try? Freshly baked bread and desserts round out any meal. Entrées $8.95–16.95. If you consume too much of the Guinness, Bass, or Killians available on tap, you might want to think about checking into one of the guest rooms (see *Lodging*).

Seneca Rocks

Front Porch Restaurant (304-567-2555; www.harpersoldcountrystore .com), above Harper's Old Country Store (see *Selective Shopping*). Open daily for lunch and dinner. The Front Porch is a favorite of Seneca Rocks climbers (maybe because you can sit on the porch and look at the rocks) who come here for the fresh-dough pizza, pita pockets, and American lamb sandwiches. Subs, spaghetti, and salads round out the menu, which has items $1.50–11.25.

For an additional *Eating Out* option, also see Alpine Lodge and Restaurant under *Lodging*.

COFFEE BARS

Elkins

Highland Café (304-636-4197; www .rchawv.org/cafe), 1404 North Randolph Ave. Open Mon.–Fri. 7–2. The coffees, baked goods, and lunch items (like salmon turnovers and spanakopita) here do more than provide you with food and drink. The Highland Café is a project of the Randolph County Housing Authority's Youth-Build program. Working within a historic 1830s home, the employees are (mostly) young people acquiring workforce skills while being employed in a sustainable program that is not dependent on any outside funding sources. Enjoy a cup of coffee and let your money help someone succeed in life.

✿ ♿ **Kissel Stop Café** (304-636-8810; www.kisselstop.com), 23 Third Street. Open Mon.–Fri. 6:30–4 and Sat. 8–2. The model-train tracks; railroad photos under plastic on the tables; and painted scenes on the wall, which give the illusion of riding on a dining car through West Virginia, make this a fun place to sip a cup of coffee or tea and munch fresh baked goods or sandwiches.

301 Coffee Company (304-637-2300; http://sites.google.com/site/coffee301co mpany), 301 Third St. Open Mon.–Sat. 7–6 and Sun. 7–2. It is a sure sign of the times that a town the size of Elkins can support a third place where you can get your fix of espresso, cappuccino, or latte. Light sandwiches and salads are served, along with gelato and sorbet.

Marlinton

Dirtbean Halé (304-799-4038; www .dirtbean.com), 217 Eighth St. There's much diversity in this coffee-bar business. In the morning, you can sip a cup of gourmet coffee and enjoy a breakfast pastry. Come here for lunch or early dinner and have a sandwich or wrap (my bean burrito wrap was tasty and filling). Now here's where it gets different—want to rent a bike? They have a variety to fit all ages and sizes. Not getting enough exercise on your vacation because it's been raining too much? The back of the shop is a fitness center complete with stationary bikes, treadmills, elliptical machines, and free weights.

The owners also operate the **Dirtbean Halé Inn** at 707 Second Ave., which has four guest rooms (two shared baths) and is just two blocks from the Greenbrier River Trail. $85.

TAKEOUT ✿ ♿ **Double Play Pizza** (304-636-1000), 1313 Harrison Ave., Elkins. Open daily from 11. A good choice for those times when you feel like eating in your room. The pizzas are as good as you will find anywhere else in town, but it's the prices that are the real draw. Regular prices are always $7.49 for a large 15-inch cheese pizza; buy two for $13.49. However, always ask about specials before ordering. I've seen them offer large, one-topping pizzas for as little as $4.99.

✳ Entertainment

FILM Elkins Cinema 7 (304-636-3555; www.elkinscinema7.com), 1513 Harrison Ave., Elkins (in the Tygart Valley Mall). The only first-run movie theater in this area.

Elkins

♪ American Mountain Theater (304-630-3040; www.americanmoun taintheater.com), on US 129/US 250 on the south side of town. Home-grown musicians perform country, bluegrass, Cajun, pop, and gospel music along with lots of old-fashioned corny comedy.

Franklin

Country Store Opry (305-358-7771; www.countrystoreopry.com/), Pendle-ton County Middle/High School audi-torium. Call for schedule. For more than four decades, the two-and-a-half-hour shows have featured local musi-cians and singers re-creating the classic songs and singers of country music, such as Patsy Cline, Gene Autry, Con-way Twitty, Loretta Lynn, and others.

For other opportunities to hear live music, also see *To See—Art Gallery* and the "Special Classes and Festivals Preserve Traditions" sidebar earlier in the chapter.

THEATER

Elkins

♪ The Old Brick Playhouse (304-637-9090; www.theoldbrick.org), 329 Davis Ave. Inside what was once a bus station and garage, members of the community present programs, plays, musicals, and movies appropriate for children from prekindergarten through elementary school.

Franklin

The Pendleton County Committee for the Arts (304-358-2521; www .pendletoncounty.net/pcca) is a volun-teer organization that sponsors work-shops in crafts and fine arts, and presents theatrical and musical per-formances. Most of the productions take place in the Smith Creek Play-house, located 6 miles west of

Franklin. (At the courthouse, turn onto Walnut St., which eventually becomes Smith Creek Rd., and then turn right on Hartman Ln.)

Marlinton

♪ The Opera House (304-799-6445; www.pocahontasoperahouse.org), 818 Third Ave. An ornate pressed metal ceiling, a solid wood balustrade, and 32 huge windows that let in the light make for a surprisingly rich place in this small town to see musical concerts and live theatrical productions.

For an additional opportunity to see theater, also see *To See—Art Gallery*.

✳ Selective Shopping
ART AND CRAFTS GALLERIES

Beverly

The Goff House Antiques & Textile Studio (304-637-6702; www.appala chianpiecework.com), 2 Fountain St. Laurie Gunderson calls herself a utili-tarian folk artist, in that the rag weav-ings she dyes utilize the materials she has at hand. Stop in and watch her produce table linens, scarves, rugs, quilts, pillows, and more. Interested in making these heritage arts items your-self? Take one of her workshop classes inside the historic 1795 Goff House.

Elkins

Artists at Work Gallery (304-637-6309), 329 Davis Ave. Established as a cooperative gallery in 1993, this is one of the reasons Elkins is consistently ranked as one of America's best small art towns. You could spend quite some time looking over the paintings, pho-tography, sculptures, musical instru-ments, furniture, and other items made by talented locals.

Ceramic with Class (304-636-2903), 203 Davis Ave. Take classes to learn how to work with and decorate all manner of ceramic products.

Green Bank

The Pocahontas County Artisan Cooperative Gallery (304-456-9900; www.artisancoop.net), on WV 92/WV 28 one mile south of the National Radio Astronomy Observatory. Closed Tue. during the summer; call for hours in other seasons. Opened in 2007, the coop features the works of talented people from Pocahontas County and the local region. Since the artists and craftspersons devote time to working in the shop to keep it open, they are able to keep 100 percent of the sale—and this means you may get to watch them go about their creative process of painting, sculpting, blacksmithing, broom making, basketweaving, or woodcarving.

BOOKSTORES Main Line Books (304-636-6770), 301 Davis Ave., Elkins. I have found Main Line Books to be staffed by employees who are genuinely excited by books and reading. It also has a section that thoroughly covers local and regional interests, including the outdoors, travel, and history.

FARMERS' MARKETS

Elkins

Head to the **City Park Farmers' Market** (304-227-4427) on Wed. mornings during July, and Sat. mornings in Aug. and Sept., to enjoy the labors of local farmers.

Franklin

The **Pendleton County Farmers' Market** is held in the Fox's Pizza parking lot on Sat. mornings during July–Oct.

SPECIAL SHOPS

Hillsboro

MorningStar FolkArts (304-653-4397; www.morningstarfolkarts.com), on US 219/WV 55 just north of Hills-

boro. Elaine and Dwight Diller have searched West Virginia for artists and craftspersons whose work they feel is worthy to be in this shop. Honeys, jams, pottery, woodcarvings, folk toys, books, and candles are just of few of the items they feature. Dwight is recognized for his expertise in old-time mountain music and offers classes in banjo, fiddle, and voice.

Pickens

Richter's Maplehouse (304-924-5404; 1-877-986-2753; www.treewater.com; mailing address: HC 74, Box 7A). It's best to call ahead to make sure Mike or Beth Ritcher will be home to sell you some of the state's best maple syrup, used by places such as The Greenbrier and Stonewall Jackson resorts. From Helvetia, drive 4.3 miles on WV 45, make a left onto Turkeybone Rd., go another mile and turn left at the sign for Richter's, and continue an additional 3 miles on a dirt road to the Maplehouse. Come here in late winter/early spring, and the Ritchers will provide a 20-minute tour of the syrup-making process.

Seneca Rocks

Harper's Old Country Store (304-567-2586; www.harpersoldcountrystore.com), at the main intersection in Seneca Rocks. Built in 1902, the store retains its original floors, shelving, and ceiling. It's primarily a small grocery store now, but what makes it interesting to wander through are the West Virginia–made products, some books of local interest, and sheepskins from the flock of Joe Harper, who runs some of the state's largest agricultural and livestock concerns. Upstairs is the Front Porch Restaurant (see *Eating Out*).

✳ Special Events

March: **Maple Syrup Festival** (www.pickenswv.com), Pickens. Tours of a maple syrup camp, pancake feed, arts and crafts, and entertainment.

April: **Annual Ramp Festival** (304-636-2780; 1-800-422-3304; www .randolphcountywv.com), Elkins. Cook-off competition, entertainment, and public ramp food tasting.

May: **Spring Fest** (304-358-3884; www.visitpendleton.com), Franklin. Crafters, food, music, antique cars, comedy acts, and square dancing. **Annual Rails & Trails Festival** (1-877-686-7245), Durbin. Celebrating the arrival of the town's first steam train.

June: **Pendleton County Fair** (http://www.visitpendleton.com),

HARPER'S OLD COUNTRY STORE

Circleville. **Annual West Virginia Writers Fair & Pearl S. Buck Celebration** (1-800-336-7009), Hillsboro.

July: **Battle of Rich Mountain Reenactment** (304-637-RICH; www .richmountain.org), Rich Mountain Battlefield, Beverly. Takes place in odd-numbered years. **Durbin Days** (1-800-336-7009), Durbin. Primarily a celebration of the scenic railroad with rides on the train, but there's also a carnival for the kids, music for the adults, and food for everybody.

September/October: **Helvetia Fair** (www.helvitiawv.com), Helvetia. A celebration of local produce and flowers, with a parade of decorated farm wagons, farm animals, and homemade floats. **Mountain State Forest Festival** (304-636-1824; www.forestfestival .com), Elkins. About 200,000 people attend this oldest festival in West Virginia. Dances, a carnival, arts and crafts, weaving and quilt exhibits, woodchopping, archery and horse-pulling contests, gospel sings, and more. **Treasure Mountain Festival** (www.pendletoncounty.net), Franklin. Mountain man and woman contests, clogging, rifle demonstrations, children's games, guided historical walking tours, turkey calling and owl hooting contests, and Civil War reenactments.

SNOWSHOE MOUNTAIN

High atop Cheat Mountain is a place unlike any other in the state. There were many skeptics when plans were announced several decades ago to develop a major skiing destination in West Virginia. Today, having weathered a number of setbacks and financial difficulties, thriving 11,000-acre **Snowshoe Mountain** resembles ski resorts found in the western United States. A major resort and residential community has grown across the mountain's ridgeline, with a central village of shops and restaurants surrounded by thousands of guest rooms located in high-rise condominiums and lodges, palatial vacation homes, cabins, cottages, and even a backcountry cabin.

At an elevation of more than 4,800 feet, Cheat Mountain has an average annual snowfall of 180 inches. If nature does not drop enough of the fluffy frozen precipitation from the sky, snowmaking equipment is able to cover the dozens of runs on the more than 200 acres of skiable terrain, letting you head downhill from November into the first part of April. You can even do some night skiing on the lighted slopes adjacent to the Silver Creek Lodge, while cross-country routes, terrain or freestyle parks, and tubing runs enable every member of the family to engage in his or her favorite winter sport.

Like most other ski resorts, Snowshoe Mountain has expanded into a four-season destination with hiking, mountain biking, horseback riding, golfing, and more available when snow is not on the ground.

GUIDANCE The all-purpose phone number for Snowshoe Mountain (www.snowshoemtn.com; 10 Snowshoe Dr., Snowshoe 26209) is 1-877-441-4FUN. Operators at this number can help you make lodging reservations and/or connect you with other numbers throughout the resort area. Call 304-572-INFO for snow reports. Logging onto www.snowshoemtn.com could occupy hours as you look through page after page of lodgings, activities, and dining and shopping options.

GETTING THERE *By car:* From the south, leave **I-64** at White Sulphur Springs and follow **US 219 North**. From the north and west, take **I-79** exit 99 (near Weston), follow **US 33** to Elkins, and take **US 219 South**. From the east, leave **I-81** at Staunton, Virginia, follow **US 250** into West Virginia, and head south on **WV 28/WV 92**.

GETTING AROUND Shuttles run year-round throughout the Snowshoe Mountain area.

PARKING Parking is at a real premium, especially if you are here for the day and not staying overnight. Once you find a parking space, leave your car where it is and take advantage of the shuttle buses.

MEDICAL EMERGENCIES The **Snowshoe Health Center**, located on the lower level of the Shavers Centre, can take care of most minor emergencies. The nearest hospital (**Davis Health Systems**; 636-3300; www.davishealthsystem.org; Reed St. and Garman Ave.) with an emergency room is in Elkins, about an hour's drive from Snowshoe Mountain.

✳ To Do

BICYCLING Snowshoe Mountain has welcomed bicycling in all of its many forms. There are more than 100 miles of trails that can be accessed by the lifts or the shuttle buses. You can ride into the backcountry on single track; fly downhill on dirt routes; test your technical skills (and balance!) on the constructed wooden course with twists, turns, seesaws, and rails; catch air at the **Bike Park**; or become a better rider by taking some of the many classes offered. Rentals are available from the **Mountain Adventure Centre** (304-572-5917) in the Village at Snowshoe. Details for all of the biking activities can be found at http://ride.snow shoemtn.com.

CARRIAGE RIDES Feeling a bit romantic? Take your significant other on one of the horse-drawn sleigh rides offered every evening during the ski season, or a carriage ride at other times of the year.

CLIMBING See *Outpost Adventure Park*.

GOLF With the up-and-down terrain of Snowshoe Mountain, the **Raven Golf Course** (304-572-6500), designed by Gary Player, is sure to test your skills. Some holes vary 200 feet in elevation from tee to green.

HIKING The 11,000 acres of mountainous terrain contained within Snowshoe Mountain provide hiking opportunities that are pretty much endless. Dozens of designated hiking trails course through the backcountry, and you are permitted to use any of the ski routes during the warmer months. With so much to choose from, I suggest you consult personnel at the depot office. They can supply you with a detailed sheet of each route that includes a map, elevation profile, points of interest, and point-by-point descriptions.

HORSEBACK RIDING ✆ Rides of one and two hours depart daily from about mid-May to the end of warm weather. Children as young as 6 years of age are permitted; pony rides around a corral are available for those 8 years old and younger.

KAYAKING & CANOEING ✆ Kayaks, canoes, hydro bikes, and paddleboats can be rented at Shavers Lake during the warmer months.

A VIEW OF SHAVERS LAKE FROM HIGH ATOP SNOWSHOE MOUNTAIN

OUTPOST ADVENTURE PARK ✍ The **Shavers Lake Outpost Adventure Park** (304-572-5982) is a center of nonskiing activities, with a skateboarding park, climbing wall, Bike Park, Eurobungy, volleyball, horseshoes, and more. These are the folks who also arrange customized hikes, ATV tours, and many other outdoor activities

SKIING, CROSS-COUNTRY More than 25 miles of cross-country skiing and snowshoe routes course along the Cheat Mountain Ridge Trail and into the backcountry area. Rentals and guided tours are available.

SKIING, DOWNHILL, AND SNOWBOARDING Snowshoe and the Silver Creek area have 60 slopes and trails, with a vertical drop of 1,500 feet, which is the highest in the mid-Atlantic and southeast United States. A total of 14 lifts ensure that you won't have to wait long to get back to the top. Equipment rental and classes are available for children and adults, along with a wide array of package deals that include lodging and other activities. Unlike many other ski areas, snowboarders are permitted on every one of the ski slopes and trails. Four different terrain parks, complete with rails and a half-pipe, are for those looking to add different kinds of skills to their skiing or snowboarding. Lights stay on until 10 PM at most of the slopes and trails adjacent to the Silver Creek Lodge. Call 1-877-441-4FUN for information on passes and packages; call 304-572-INFO for a snow report.

SNOWMOBILE AND SNOWCAT TOURS Guided snowmobile and snowcat tours, from one hour to all day, take riders into the backcountry area during the day or evening.

SWIMMING The **Split Rock Pools**, indoor and outdoor places for watery fun with slides and fountains, are open year-round. Take a swim from the beach at **Shavers Lake** during the summer months.

TUBING Nonskiers, rejoice! You can join in the downhill fun by flying across the snow in one of six lanes on the 600-foot tubing hill at the Silver Creek Lodge area.

✳ Lodging

There are close to 2,000 different guest accommodations available at Snowshoe Mountain, including hotels, condominiums, vacation homes, lodges, town houses, efficiency units, and a backcountry cabin. Call 1-877-441-4FUN or consult www.snowshoe mtn.com to obtain the particulars and inquire about the many (almost overwhelming) choices of money-saving package deals that are offered throughout the year.

Insider's tip: No matter what accommodation you decide upon, make sure that you ask if it has a view of the mountains—and be willing to pay the few extra dollars for that view so that you don't end up overlooking the other buildings (like I did the first time I came here). Also, be ready to pay those annoying little extra fees that

A BACKCOUNTRY LODGE AT SNOWSHOE MOUNTAIN

businesses seem to enjoy tacking on to your bill—like 75¢ to $1 just to make a local phone call.

For lodging options off the mountain, see the *Lodging* section in the "Reaching for the Sky—Spruce Knob, Seneca Rocks, and Cranberry Glades" chapter.

✳ Where to Eat

DINING OUT ✂ ♿ **Foxfire Grille** (304-572-5555; www.foxfiregrille.com), Rimfire Lodge in the Village at Snowshoe. Open daily for lunch and dinner. The Foxfire Grille is known for its various barbecue dishes that are flavored with smoked fruitwoods, dry rubs, and homemade sauces. Barbecued burgers, salmon, pork chops, ribs, tuna, and sandwiches make up the bulk of the menu, which also includes pasta, an excellent fried green tomato and crab-cake appetizer, and vegetarian selections. Entrées $15.95–28.95.

✂ ♿ **The Junction Restaurant and Saloon** (304-572-5801), in the Village at Snowshoe. Open for breakfast, lunch, and dinner daily. You can always count on this railroad-themed establishment to be open when other resort restaurants may be closed during the off-season. Banana-nut French toast is a sweet way to start the day. Lunch and dinner menus change with the seasons, which is one of the reasons I like visiting in summer, when the refreshingly cold berry soup ($3.99) is available. Entrées include pecan-seared trout and a tasty blackberry chipotle barbecue-glazed pork chop. Rotisserie chicken is a staple year-round. Entrées $8.99–27.99.

EATING OUT ✐ ♿ **Brandi's** (304-572-6508), in the Inn at Snowshoe at the base of the mountain. Open for breakfast and dinner daily. Brandi's doesn't serve the bland restaurant fare usually found inside a motel. Instead, there's French toast and specialty omelets for breakfast, and a varied menu, including London broil, Yankee pot roast, and Cajun seared salmon, for dinner. Entrées $11.99–18.99.

♿ **Cheat Mountain Pizza Company** (304-572-5949), in the Village at Snowshoe. Open daily for lunch and dinner. There are other places to get pizzas on the mountain, but not like the gourmet pizzas—available with traditional tomato sauce or more exotic sauces such as basil pesto—made here. Salads and sandwiches also available. Prices start at about $5.

COFFEE BARS ♿ **Starbucks Coffee** (304-572-5747; www.starbucks.com), in the Village at Snowshoe. By now, everyone is familiar with the offerings of this national chain.

✳ Special Events

July: **Independence Day Celebration**. Arts-and-crafts show, bluegrass and folk music, children's activities, and, of course, fireworks. **"Fire on the Mountain" Chili Cook-Off**. Live entertainment and an arts-and-crafts fair are complements to the chili cooking contest that picks a winner to represent Snowshoe Mountain at the World Chili Cook-Off. **Freedom Fest Motorcycle Rally**. An all-brands rally with mountain road tour itineraries, activities, and live entertainment.

August: **Taste of the Mountains Wine and Jazz Festival**. The region's finest food, wine, and jazz. **Snowshoe Symphony Festival**. Themed dinners and concerts, along with performances by the West Virginia Symphony.

November/December: **Ski Free Weeks**. Book three or more nights' lodging and get free lift tickets. **New Year's Bash**. Ten different parties from which to choose.

Southern West Virginia

3

OLD TOWNS, SURVIVING
AND ALIVE—LEWISBURG, WHITE
SULPHUR SPRINGS, AND UNION

THE SOUTHERN BORDER—
BLUEFIELD, HINTON, PINEVILLE,
PRINCETON, AND WELCH

ALONG THE NEW AND GAULEY
RIVERS—BECKLEY, FAYETTEVILLE,
AND SUMMERSVILLE

SOUTHERN WEST VIRGINIA

Southern West Virginia is the most varied region of the state, both in topography and in the lifestyles of its inhabitants.

A lush, high mountain plateau characterizes the eastern edge, with green farmlands stretching out for acres that are grazed by the cattle and horses of a landed gentry whose wealth and lineage go back many generations. Flowing through this landscape is the gentle Greenbrier River, the longest untamed river in the eastern United States.

The region's northern portion is also a plateau, but this one is a bit more rugged, with one of the world's most acclaimed whitewater streams, the Gauley River, slicing through the middle of it. Along the river, Summersville Lake attracts boaters who are looking for more placid water on which to enjoy their days.

The central part is a transition zone. The land is still on a plateau of sorts, but here ridgelines rise more prominently, providing a more mountainous look to the terrain. Coal mining is still a way of life for a number of people, but that lifestyle is beginning to fade as younger generations and newer emigrants look at the region's natural resources in a different light—as a way to enjoy the outdoors. Paddlers are attracted to the New and Bluestone rivers for whitewater rafting, kayaking, and canoeing; hikers, mountain bikers, and rock climbers explore the region's gorges in ever increasing numbers. The populations of Fayetteville, Oak Hill, and Beckley have increased thanks to the influx of outdoors enthusiasts who have decided to stay here instead of just visiting on their vacations.

The southern portion of this region is definitely mountainous, but unlike the Potomac Highlands, which has long parallel ridgelines separated by broad valleys, the mountains here are a mixed jumble of ridgelines running in all directions. Valleys are often not much wider than the stream that flows through them. There is no doubt that coal is still king here, but due to mechanization, mining does not employ the numbers it once did. Yet, coal trucks and mile-long trains still carry tons of the black rock out of the region to fuel the world's power plants. The industry's boom and bust cycles have left mine owners with wealth in their pockets to weather the down times, while workers' families often endure economic struggles. Travel through here is a bit different than other parts of the state, but you get to meet the people who face hard times and survive. The Coal Heritage Trail National Byway takes you to many sites that provide insight into this rich culture as well as to a number of places for outdoor recreation that are far off the beaten path.

OLD TOWNS, SURVIVING AND ALIVE—LEWISBURG, WHITE SULPHUR SPRINGS, AND UNION

Early settlement in the area around Lewisburg came to a halt after a number of Shawnee Indian attacks. However, by 1764, so many people had moved back into the area that Andrew Lewis was able to raise a force of close to 1,000 men, whose war against the Native Americans culminated with the victory over Chief Cornstalk at the Battle of Point Pleasant. Chartered in 1782, the town prospered as traffic increased along the James River–Kanawha Turnpike (now US 60). The downtown area of Lewisburg has been able to maintain its heritage, with scores of 1800s buildings, stately Victorian mansions, and early-20th-century homes. The last few decades have seen a steady increase in the numbers of artists, craftspersons, and restaurateurs, so much so that the town has become a destination unto itself, with art galleries, antiques shops, and a number of the state's better dining and overnight establishments.

As they did in a number of the springs and resorts in this area, people have been coming to White Sulphur Springs since the late 1800s to "take the waters," which one early visitor claimed would cure every known ailment in the world, except "chewing, smoking, spitting, and swearing." The Greenbrier resort was established in the early 1900s to replace an earlier hotel. It is one of the most exclusive resorts for the world's rich, famous, and powerful, and it has made its owners millions of dollars. Unfortunately, much of that money stayed in the resort or the coffers of the corporation, with very little trickling into the town. That is beginning to change with The Greenbrier's decision to construct exclusive housing developments on a large portion of its property. As people move into these homes, they spend their money at local establishments, and the townspeople are responding by opening more and more restaurants, art galleries, antiques shops, and service businesses.

Retirees and other emigrants are coming here to live and create a more cosmopolitan atmosphere while working to retain the rural character of the area and preserve its history and culture. A walking-tour brochure available from the Monroe County Tourism (see *Guidance*) will take you by some of these historic sites, such as the 1846 Greek Revival home of Confederate Gen. John Echols and the frame structure that was built in 1849 as West Virginia's oldest Masonic Hall.

185

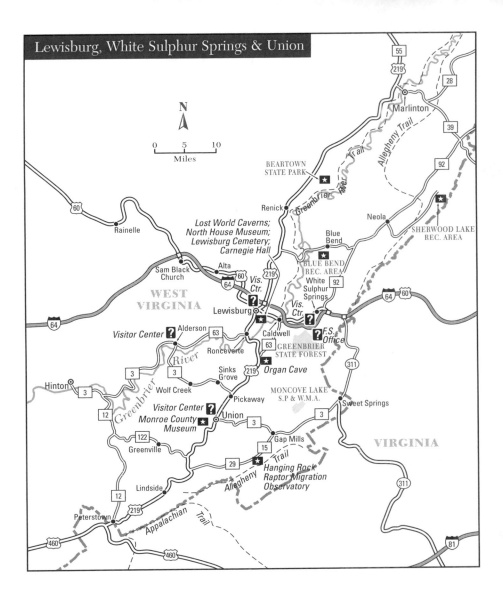

N

0   5   10
Miles

BEARTOWN
STATE PARK ★

Renick ●

Neola

SHERWOOD LAKE
REC. AREA ★

Rainelle

Lost World Caverns;
North House Museum;
Lewisburg Cemetery;
Carnegie Hall

Blue
Bend

Sam Black
Church

Alta

WEST
VIRGINIA

Lewisburg ●

BLUE BEND
REC. AREA ★

White
Sulphur
Springs

Vis.
Ctr. ?

Vis.
Ctr. ?

Visitor Center ? Alderson

Caldwell

F.S.
Office ?

GREENBRIER
STATE FOREST

Ronceverte

Sinks
Grove

Organ Cave ★

MONCOVE LAKE
S.P & W.M.A.

Sweet Springs

Hinton ○

Wolf Creek

Pickaway

Visitor Center ?
Monroe County
Museum ★

Union

VIRGINIA

Greenville

Gap Mills

Hanging Rock
Raptor Migration
Observatory ★

Lindside

Allegheny
Trail

Peterstown

Appalachian
Trail

Marlinton

Greenbrier River Trail

Allegheny Trail

Greenbrier River

COMMUNITIES Alderson has more than 160 structures of historic significance, many dating from the late 1800s. Located next to the Greenbrier River, it was once a regional transportation hub. It is a much quieter, and primarily residential, town today, with a restored train depot and the 1913 Alderson Memorial Bridge bearing witness to its past. The town gained national fame when Federal Prison Camp Alderson became home for Martha Stewart, who was serving a five-month term for lying to federal investigators about a stock sale. Of course, the prison had gained notoriety in the past by housing other notables such as Billie Holiday, Tokyo Rose, Axis Sally, and Charles Manson devotees Lynette "Squeaky" Fromme, Sandra Good, and Sara Jane Moore.

Gap Mills is just a few miles from the West Virginia–Virginia border and is not much more than a few homes and a couple of stores, but the quality of goods produced and sold by several Mennonite-run businesses has put it on the radar of an increasing number of travelers.

GUIDANCE The **City Hall** (304-445-2916) at 202 Madison St. in Alderson provides some visitor information.

Greenbrier County Convention and Visitors Bureau (304-645-1000; 1-800-833-2068; www.greenbrierwv.com; mailing address: Box 17, Suite N, Lewisburg 24910), 540 North Jefferson St., Lewisburg.

Monroe County Tourism (304-772-3003; 1-866-677-3003; mailing address: P.O. Box 341, Union 24983), at 261 Health Center Rd., maintains a detailed Web site at www.travelmonroe.com.

Southern West Virginia Convention & Visitors Bureau (304-252-2244; 1-800-847-4898; www.visitwv.com), 1406 Harper Rd., Beckley 25801. Not located within this area, this visitor center is an umbrella organization that provides information for the entire Southern West Virginia region.

A **West Virginia Welcome Center** (304-563-4553; mailing address: P.O. Box 550, White Sulphur Springs 24896), which has information about this area and the entire state, is on the westbound lane of I-64 near mile marker 179.

The office of the **White Sulphur Springs Ranger District** (304-536-2144), 410 East Main St., White Sulphur Springs 24896, can supply you with detailed information and brochures about the opportunities awaiting you in the Monongahela National Forest.

GETTING THERE *By air*: Shuttle flights from a couple of major carriers will deliver you to the **Greenbrier Valley Airport** (304-645-3961; www.gvairport.com), 3 miles north of Lewisburg. Many people fly into **Yeager Airport** (304-344-8033; www.yeagerairport.com) in Charleston and drive a couple of hours via I-64 or US 60. You might also consider the **Roanoke (Virginia) Regional Airport** (540-362-1999; www.roanokeairport.com). It is also about two hours away.

By bus: The closest **Greyhound** (1-800-231-2222; www.greyhound.com) will get you to this area are its terminals at 105 Third Ave. in Beckley or 514 Scott St. in Bluefield.

By car: **I-64** cuts right through the heart of this area.

By rail: An **AMTRAK** (1-800-872-7245; www.amtrak.com) train, *The Cardinal*, is an east–west train that you may take to White Sulphur Springs or Alderson from as far away as New York and Chicago.

GETTING AROUND *By car*: Four-lane **I-64** will take you on an east–west route, and two-lane **US 219** is the major north–south route.

MEDICAL EMERGENCIES **Greenbrier Valley Medical Center** (304-647-4411; www.gvmc.com), 202 Maplewood Ave., Ronceverte.

✳ To See

CAVERN TOURS

Lewisburg

✇ ↑ **Lost World Caverns** (304-645-6677; 1-866-228-3778; www.lostworldcaverns .com; mailing address: Rte. 6, Box 308, Lewisburg 24901). From I-64 exit 169, take US 219 South into Lewisburg; turn right onto Arbuckle Lane; make another right onto Court St., which becomes Fairview Rd.; and continue to the caverns. Closed Easter, Thanksgiving, Christmas, and New Year's Day. Adults $12; children (ages 6–12) $6; children under age 6 are free. The tours of Lost World Caverns, which stay at a constant 52 degrees year-round, take you into large rooms and passageways full of stalagmites rising up to 80 feet off the floor and some of the world's largest flowstone formations. An added attraction that I have seen children really get excited about is the Lost World Museum, possibly the only prehistoric natural-history museum in the entire state. There are fossils and replicas of dinosaurs, including the prehistoric cave bear that was discovered in the caverns.

Those looking for more of an adventure can sign up for the Wild Cave Expeditions ($70 per person) that take you into primitive passageways not open to the general public.

Ronceverte

✇ ↑ **Organ Cave** (304-645-7600; www.organcave.com), 417 Masters Rd. From I-64 exit 175 at White Sulphur Springs, drive west on US 60, turn left onto WV 63, and follow it to the cave. Closed Sun. Adults $14, children (ages 6–12) $7, children age 5 and under are free. A visit to Organ Cave will teach you one of the differences between a cave and a cavern. While it does have some calcite formations, Organ Cave is not awash with dozens of formations like Lost World Caverns. What it does have are huge passageways and rooms whose walls and ceilings are covered with fossils. Human history figures prominently into the cave's past, too: Thomas Jefferson discovered the bones of an ancient three-toed sloth, and hoppers from saltpeter mining operations during the Civil War are still in the cave. Also, be prepared to get a different take on the geological history of the earth you will hear at most caverns, colleges, and universities. In step with their religious viewpoint, the owners say, "We believe the cave was created by Noah's flood. We believe the world to be no more than 6,000 years old."

HERN'S MILL COVERED BRIDGE

COVERED BRIDGES

Lewisburg

The queenpost truss **Hern's Mill Covered Bridge**, restored in 2001, was originally constructed in 1884 to provide access over Mulligan Creek to the S. S. Hern's Mill. More than 53 feet long, it may be reached by driving US 60 West from the US 60 intersection with US 219 in Lewisburg. In 3.3 miles, turn left onto Muddy Creek Mountain Rd. (WV 60/11), make another left onto WV 40 in less than 0.2 mile, and come to the bridge 0.9 mile later.

Ronceverte

The **Hoke's Mill Covered Bridge** is 81 feet long and was constructed in 1899 (rebuilt in 2001) using the long variant type of truss. It crosses over Second Creek but is closed to traffic. From the south side of the Greenbrier River at Ronceverte, drive southwest on WV 48 for 3.8 miles, continue on WV 62, and arrive at the bridge in another 1.4 miles.

Union

Queen truss **Laurel Creek Covered Bridge** is only 24 feet long (the shortest in the state), was constructed in 1911 by Charles Arnott, and is still in use over its namesake creek. From the intersection of US 219 and WV 3 in Union, drive south on US 219 for 3.1 miles, turn right onto WV 219/7, go 2.7 miles, and turn right onto WV 219/11, which will bring you to the bridge.

Visiting the 51-foot **Indian Creek Covered Bridge**, built in 1898 by teenagers Ray and Oscar Weikel and restored in 2000, is much easier than finding the one over Laurel Creek. Travel south on US 219 for 4.8 miles from Union and you will see the bridge, closed to traffic, across the road from St. John's Church.

DRIVING TOURS, SCENIC & HISTORIC The 180-mile **Midland Trail National Scenic Byway** (304-343-6001; www.midlandtrail.com) follows the route of US 60 from White Sulphur Springs to a few miles west of Huntington. Before the completion of I-64, US 60 was the major east–west transportation route. For someone trying to get from point A to point B as quickly as possible, it can be quite frustrating. Yet, its two-laned, twisting and winding route over scenic mountains and through farmlands, river gorges, and small towns can be a pleasurable drive for travelers willing to take their time, stop to see the sites, and enjoy the journey and not the destination. In this area, I thoroughly enjoy the drive through the bucolic landscape from Lewisburg to Sam Black Church.

For more than 20 miles, the **Wolf Creek Backway** travels country roads (WV 3 and WV 43/WV 5), passing through a lush mountain farm landscape and giving access to small towns and settlements like Alderson and Pickaway.

The **Farm Heritage Road Byway** is a 59-mile trip that offers a view onto the rural and agricultural way of life in this area by traveling along Indian Creek, onto rolling plateaus of farmland, and through the Sweet Springs Valley. Highlights include the sites of old spring resorts, access to Moncove Lake State Park, Gap Mills, and the small town of Union. You can begin the trip by traveling westward on WV 3 from Gap Mills to Union. Follow US 219 south from Union, turn left onto WV 122, and make another left onto WV 12 to end in Peterstown.

Of the designated scenic drives in this area, my favorite is the 30-mile **Mountain's Shadow Trail Backway** from Peterstown to Gap Mills. Almost exclusively on one-lane or dirt roads, it passes through a varied and isolated landscape that is always in the shadow of 40-mile-long Peters Mountain. A homemade plaque I always stop at while driving here, which is signed simply "Old Monroe Farmer," evidences the love of the local residents for this land:

OLD PETERS MOUNTAIN HIGH AND GRAND
IN ALL YOUR BEAUTY THERE YOU STAND
FROM HERE TO FAR YOU CHANGE YOUR HUE
FROM EMERALD GREEN TO SAPPHIRE BLUE
I LOVE YOU NOW FROM OLDEN DAYS
WITH YOUR WILD WOODS, WINDING WAYS
WHEN LEAF WAS GREEN OR RED OR BROWN
OR WHEN THE SNOW WAS ON THE GROUND

The Monroe County Historical Society has produced a small pamphlet, *The Springs Trail* (available from Monroe County Tourism or Greenbrier County Convention and Visitors Bureau—see *Guidance*), which profiles a driving tour of historic springs and resorts in a three-county area.

Also see The Lower Greenbrier River Byway under *Driving Tours, Scenic & Historic* in the "Southern Border—Bluefield, Hinton, Pineville, Princeton, and Welch" chapter.

GARDENS

Renick

✪ **Sunshine Farm and Gardens** (304-497-2208; www.sunfarm.com), 696 Glicks Rd. Reaching this place may test if you are a true explorer or not. After turning off a major highway, the roads you follow becoming increasingly more rural, to the point that the final approach is on a one-lane dirt road winding its way up to the 60 acres of mountaintop property. However, once here, it's a feast for the eyes and the mind of anyone who is even slightly interested in flowers and horticulture. Barry Glick has been cultivating and propagating many kinds of plants (more than 10,000) for more than three decades, with an emphasis on hellebores. Although the business caters to plant wholesalers, Mr. Glick invites the general public to visit his 24-acre show gardens, with something in bloom almost year-round. As I said, it's a feast for the eyes and something not to be missed. You need to call to make reservations and for directions—and to make sure someone will be there after you invest the time in getting there.

HISTORIC CHURCHES

Lewisburg

John Wesley United Methodist Church (304-647-3123), 209 East Foster St. Built in 1835, the historic church has interior galleries and a slave entrance. What is most interesting, though, is that during the Battle of Lewisburg in 1862, a cannonball struck the southwest corner and is still visible.

Old Stone Presbyterian Church (304-645-2676; www.oldstonechurch wv.com), 200 Church St. Built of native limestone in 1796, this is believed to be the oldest church still in

OLD STONE PRESBYTERIAN CHURCH AND LEWISBURG CEMETERY

continuous use west of the Allegheny Mountains. It is certainly one of the prettiest
of Lewisburg's landmarks, while the adjacent cemetery (see *Historic Sites*) is one
of town's most visited sites.

Union

**Rehoboth Church—West Virginia's United Methodist National Historic
Shrine** (304-772-3518), off WV 3 about 3 miles east of Union. The log Rehoboth
Church is a small place, measuring only 12 by 29 feet, but its history goes back to
its construction in 1786, making it the oldest Methodist church west of the
Allegheny Mountains. Next door is a small museum with items of local interest,
including Native American artifacts, World War I memorabilia, early farm implements, and, and most interesting to me, amazingly small and intricately detailed
wood carvings by L. N. Bishop. The church and museum have a regular schedule
of open hours, but that often depends on who is available. It may be best to call
ahead.

HISTORIC SITES

Lewisburg

The **Lewisburg Cemetery**, adjacent to the Old Stone Presbyterian Church (see
Historic Churches), was established in 1797 and contains the graves of close to
2,000 individuals, many of them influential in shaping the history of the town and
area. The variety of headstones and the way the cemetery is laid out make for a
strikingly creepy place on a dark and stormy night. It figures prominently on the
Ghost Tours of Lewisburg (see *To Do—Walking Tours*). A few blocks away is the
cross-shaped common grave of the **Confederate Cemetery**, where lie the
remains of 95 unknown soldiers killed during the Battle of Lewisburg in 1862.

Union

Confederate Soldiers of Monroe County. A monument to Confederate soldiers stands in an open field on the south side of town. Carved in nearby Hinton of
Italian marble, it was placed here in 1901 by officials who anticipated the town
would grow in this direction, thereby having the monument be in the middle of
everything in a decade or two. Growth went in the other direction, keeping the
monument in this quiet and scenic setting.

MUSEUMS

Lewisburg

☂ **North House Museum** (304-645-3398; www.greenbrierhistorical.org), 301
West Washington St. Open 10–4; closed Sun. Small admission fee. The North
House Museum, operated by the Greenbrier Historical Society, is surprisingly
large and complete to be located in as small a community as Lewisburg. The 1820
building contains period furniture, textiles, Civil War items, historic wagons, and
decorative arts. Some of the more outstanding pieces are the first buggy used by
the Rural Free Delivery system and the saddle Robert E. Lee used to train his
beloved horse, Traveler, who came from a farm in Greenbrier County.

Union

Monroe County Museum (no phone), Main St. Open June–Sept.; closed
Sat.–Sun. Housed in the 1820 brick office of Allen Taylor Caperton, who was a
senator for both the Confederacy and the United States, the small museum is the

repository for the local historical society. Next door are two reconstructed log homes furnished exclusively with period pieces from Monroe County.

✳ To Do

BICYCLING

Caldwell

The southern terminus of the more than 70-mile **Greenbrier River Trail** (see *To Do—Bicycling* in the "Reaching for the Sky—Spruce Knob, Seneca Rocks, and Cranberry Glades" chapter for complete background information) is located a short distance from US 60 in Caldwell. There are more than 37 miles of the route in this area, which includes five designated campsites, several options for food and drink, and the 402-foot Droop Mountain Tunnel. A number of outfitters rent bicycles and provide shuttles or guided trips.

Free Spirit Adventures (304-536-0333; 1-800-877-4749; www.freespiritadventures.com; mailing address: HC 30, Box 183-C, Caldwell 94925), on US 60, 0.5 mile west of I-64 exit 175. Free Spirit Adventures will rent you a bike, repair yours, shuttle you to or from a hiking or biking trailhead (whether you rent from them or not), customize tours for you, take you on guided rides or hikes, or enroll you in a class to learn how to be a better road or mountain bike rider.

White Sulphur Springs

Outdoor Adventures (1-888-752-9982; www.wvoutdooradventures.com; mailing address: P.O. Box 535, White Sulphur Springs 24986). In addition to providing the same basic services as Free Spirit Adventures, Outdoor Adventures also rents canoes and kayaks, and runs guided canoe trips on a number of nearby rivers and streams.

For other bicycling opportunities, also see Moncove Lake State Park under *Green Space—Parks*, the "A Naturalist's State Forest" sidebar later in the chapter, and Lake Sherwood Recreation Area under *Lodging*.

BIRDING Hanging Rock Raptor Migration Observatory (www.hangingrocktower.org). From Gap Mills, take WV 15 to the southwest for approximately 4 miles to its intersection with WV 29. Keep to the left on WV 15 and continue another 1.7 miles to the top of the mountain. You will have to walk almost 1 mile on the Allegheny Trail (see *Hiking*) to reach the wooden tower of the observatory, but it is worth the moderate hike. Birdwatchers have been coming here for decades, as the Peters Mountain ridgeline produces perfect wind conditions for raptors and other birds as they travel along their long migration routes. It is not unusual for observers to see hundreds of hawks and eagles soaring by during peak seasons. Even if you don't see a single winged creature, you'll still be able to take in the magnificence of a 360-degree view of ridgeline after ridgeline in Virginia to the east and West Virginia to the west.

Also see *Green Space—Nature Preserve*.

BOWLING ⚲ Greenbrier Bowling and Recreation Center (304-645-3111), US 219 North, Lewisburg.

FISHING The **Greenbrier River** is probably this area's best-known fishing destination. However, in your quest for trout, do not overlook the southern portion of this area, which has **Potts Creek**, the **South Fork of Potts Creek**, and **Second Creek**. More to the west, head to **Big** and **Little creeks** and **Meadow Creek**, all located close to Rainelle.

Lewisburg

Serenity Now Outfitters (304-647-9779; 1-877-WV-FISHIN), 207 West Washington St. Guided wading fly-fishing trips for trout and smallmouth bass originate from this outfitters' retail shop, full of fishing and other outdoors equipment. Overnight trips are available.

Top Water Guide Service (304-645-3326; http://pages.suddenlink.net/topwater /index.html), 310 Echols Lane. Charlie Hughes has more than 40 years' experience fishing the waters of West Virginia and Virginia, and he will take you on guided wading or float trips.

White Sulphur Springs

✍ **White Sulphur Springs National Fish Hatchery** (304-536-1361; www.fws .gov), 400 East Main St. The visitors center is open Mon.–Fri. 8–3. No admission fee. If you catch a rainbow trout in West Virginia, chances are good it began life in White Sulphur Springs. In fact, that is true for just about anywhere in America. The White Sulphur Springs hatchery is one of only three of the country's primary broodstock stations. It produces millions of rainbow trout eggs annually and ships them nationwide to other federal, state, and tribal hatcheries. It also propagates freshwater mussels to replenish dwindling natural populations. A self-guided tour takes you by a display pool of trout 3 to 8 years old, raceways of eggs and juvenile trout, an incubation room, and ponds of freshwater mussels.

For other fishing opportunities, also see *To Do—Swimmin' Hole*, Moncove Lake State Park under *Green Space—Parks*, and Lake Sherwood Recreation Area and Greenbrier River Campground under *Lodging*.

GOLF

Lewisburg

Lewisburg Elks Country Club (304-645-3660; www.lewisburgelkscc.com; mailing address: HC 74, Box 284, Lewisburg 24901), on US 219 approximately 0.5 mile north of I-64 exit 169 at Lewisburg. On a rolling countryside terrain, the course's first nine holes were constructed in the 1930s, and the back nine were built in the 1960s. Water comes into play on five of the holes.

Peterstown

Fountain Springs Golf Course (304-753-4653), 93 Fountain Springs Dr. The public 18-hole course, designed by Robert F. Breedon and opened in 1998, is par 71 and has 6,278 yards.

Rainelle

Greenbrier Hills Golf Club (304-438-9050), 310 Sewell Mountain Rd. The nine-hole municipal course, built in 1933, is par 35 and has 2,631 yards. Open mid-Apr. through Oct.

White Sulphur Springs

Valley View Country Club (304-536-1600; www.valleyview.cc), Big Draft Rd. The public course, opened in the 1930s, is a nine-hole par 36 course with 3,446 yards.

For more golf, also see The Greenbrier under *Lodging*.

HISTORIC GOLFING

Oakhurst Links (304-536-1884; www.oakhurst1884.com), One Montague Rd., White Sulphur Springs. *Please note: As this book went to press, Oakhurst was for sale and closed to public play. I have left the listing here because the course is of such historical value that you should at least know about it.* Every golfer in the country should play a round at Oakhurst Links to learn something about the history of the game. Established in 1884, it is the site of the first golf club and tournament in America, and you play the course in the fashion of those days. Using replica equipment, you swing long-nose hickory-shafted clubs to hit gutta-percha balls, made out of a material as hard as billiard balls. You personally form the tees with water and sand. There are also some interesting hazards that come into play. As in the olden days, the course is kept mowed by a flock of sheep, which will be munching away as you play. And you must abide by the original rules: (1) If an opponent's ball gets in front of yours, you must play around (or over) it. (2) If your ball breaks in two (which gutta-percha balls are wont to do), you can't take another out of your bag. You must play the largest piece until holed out. (3) If your ball lands in sheep castings, you are allowed a free drop.

There surely can't be a more fun way for a dedicated golfer to spend the day—and get a history lesson in the process. The $75 fee for nine holes includes the use of the equipment. There are, of course, no carts available.

HIKING The **Appalachian Trail** comes in contact with southeastern West Virginia a few miles east of Peterstown. Traversing Peters Mountain along the West Virginia–Virginia border, it zigzags across the state line for close to 13 miles. At one moment you will be in West Virginia, another time in Virginia, and sometimes one foot will be in one state while the opposite foot will be in the other. Highlights are the commanding views overlooking waves of Allegheny Mountain summits and rural farmlands from Rice Field and Symms Gap Meadow.

For easiest access to the trail from West Virginia, drive US 219 North for 6.1 miles from its junction with WV 12 in Peterstown. Turn right onto WV 219/21 (Painter Run Rd.), go 1.3 more miles, turn left onto WV 219/24 (it may be unsigned), and continue for another 0.5 mile to the Groundhog Trailhead parking on the right. This pathway ascends the western slope of Peters Mountain to intersect the Appalachian Trail on the ridgeline. Once on the Appalachian Trail, a 3.9-mile hike to the north would bring you to the Allegheny Trail's southern terminus. A 13-mile hike southward takes hikers to US 460 on the western edge of Pearisburg, Virginia.

More than 50 miles of West Virginia's premier long-distance pathway, the **Allegheny Trail** (see "What's Where in West Virginia" at the front of this book for background information), pass through this area. The pathway's southern terminus is at a junction with the Appalachian Trail on Peters Mountain along the West Virginia–Virginia border a few miles east of Lindside. Whereas the Appalachian Trail drops off the mountain to the east, the Allegheny Trail begins by heading northward along Peters Mountain, sometimes slightly in West Virginia, sometimes a short distance across the border in Virginia. Passing by the Hanging Rock Raptor Migration Observatory (see *Birding*), the trail comes to a temporary end in Laurel Branch, 21 miles north of its southern terminus.(Volunteers are working hard to create trail on a 20- to 30-mile break in the route that has yet to be constructed.)

The Allegheny Trail begins again near the Jerry's Run Trail exit off I-64 in Virginia. Soon crossing back into West Virginia, it parallels pretty Laurel Run for a number of miles, crosses WV 92 north of Neola, and leaves this area as it enters Calvin Price State Park.

For other hiking opportunities, also see *Bicycling, Birding, Swimmin' Hole, Green Space—Parks*, the "A Naturalist's State Forest" sidebar later in the chapter, and Lake Sherwood Recreation Area under *Lodging*. In addition, see Free Spirit Adventures under *Bicycling* for guided hiking trips and/or possible shuttles to and from trailheads.

KAYAKING & CANOEING See Moncove Lake State Park under *Green Space—Parks* and Lake Sherwood Recreation Area and Greenbrier River Campground under *Lodging*. In addition, see Free Spirit Adventures and Outdoor Adventures under *Bicycling* for possible shuttles and guided trips.

SWIMMING See Moncove Lake State Park under *Green Space—Parks*, Lake Sherwood Recreation Area under *Lodging*, and the "A Naturalist's State Forest" sidebar later in the chapter.

SWIMMIN' HOLE For those who enjoy outdoor activities, the forest service's **Blue Bend Recreation** Area is hard to resist. It has a trail that has an amiable saunter into a stream valley, a climb of a bit more than a mile to provide a cardio-vascular workout, an easy ridgeline walk to a trailside shelter, and a quick but rather gentle descent with a succession of good views. Set among thick growths of rhododendron bushes, the developed campground, open year-round, has modern restrooms with running water (vault toilets only in winter) and picnic facilities with a large covered pavilion. Members of the family who are anglers will want to come here to fish for the stocked trout.

The real draw is the swimmin' hole. It's one of the best in the entire region. A constructed rock platform, located just below the picnic pavilion so parents can watch the kids, slopes gently into the deep waters of a wide bend of Anthony Creek. On bright, sunny days, the stream almost looks green as it reflects the leaves and needles of ash, poplar, sycamore, maple, beech, hemlock, and pine.

From I-64 exit 175 at White Sulphur Springs, turn right onto US 60 East, drive 4.8 miles, and turn left onto WV 92 North. Make a left on WV 16/2 in an additional 9.4 miles, and turn left into the recreation area in another 3.9 miles.

WALKING TOURS A *Walking Tour of Historic Lewisburg* (available from the Greenbrier County Convention and Visitors Bureau—see *Guidance*) is a multipage brochure that is one of the most complete and extensive of its kind I've ever used. In addition to identifying and providing detailed information on more than 70 sites, it presents a concise history of the town as well as a very thorough timeline. Pick this up, even if you don't intend to do the entire tour, and read it in your

HISTORIC LEWISBURG

room in the evening to gain a better understanding of the place you are visiting.

Ghost Tours of Lewisburg (304-256-TOUR) meets at the General Lewis Inn (see *Lodging*) in Lewisburg every Fri. and Sat. in the fall. Local resident John Luckton has put together candlelight tours that take you into the town's eerie past. Sometimes you will be walking by homes that have a horrible story to tell, other times you will take a stroll through the Lewisburg Cemetery (see *To See—Historic Sites*) to bear witness to the lives of those buried there.

✳ Green Space

NATURE PRESERVE Slaty Mountain Preserve (304-637-0160; www.nature .org). From Sweet Springs, drive west on WV 3/14 for 2.2 miles. After crossing a small bridge, stay left on a dirt road and follow it uphill to the preserve. Open year-round during daylight hours; pets are not permitted. Hiking is confined to the dirt road that crosses the property.

Owned by The Nature Conservancy, the 153-acre preserve is home to a number of rare shale barren species such as Kate's Mountain clover and Allegheny plum. Common birds include blue-head vireo, scarlet tanager, indigo bunting, rose-breasted grosbeak, and black and white warbler.

PARKS

Gap Mills
Moncove Lake State Park (304-772-3450; www.moncovelakestatepark.com; mailing address: Rte. 4, Box 73-A, Gap Mills 24941). From the intersection of WV 3 and WV 15 in Gap Mills, drive WV 3 northwestward for about a mile, turn right onto WV 8, and follow it 5.5 miles to the park. Located in a southeast corner of the state that is off the usual tourist track, 896-acre Moncove Lake State Park is one of the state's smallest and least visited. Even though it has a swimming pool (open Memorial Day–Labor Day), a good-size campground (usually open from mid-Apr. to late fall) with hookups and hot showers, and rowboat and paddleboat rentals to enjoy the 144-acre lake or fish for largemouth bass, bluegill, and catfish, the park always seems tranquil and quiet. A small network of trails (all but one open to mountain bikes) takes visitors onto remote ridgelines that provide a few scenic vistas.

Hillsboro
🐾 ♿ ✪ **Beartown State Park** (304-653-4254; www.beartownstatepark.com; mailing address: HC 64, Box 189, Hillsboro 24946). From I-64 exit 169 at Lewisburg, drive on US 219 North for 22 miles and turn right onto the road signed for Beartown State Park. Follow the road 1.5 miles to its end in the state park parking lot. (A 250-foot wheelchair-accessible walkway permits an overview of the forma-

tions and access to one of the major crevasses. Parking for it is on the service road, 700 feet east of the main parking area.)

Do not pass up the chance to walk through the fairy-tale landscape of Beartown State Park. It is such an easy walk that even those who are out of shape can handle it if they just take their time. This is also an excellent introduction for someone you are taking out on a hike for the first time. If you find the jaunt too short, you can always combine it with a walk on the trails of nearby Blue Bend Recreation Area (see *To Do—Swimmin' Hole*).

Beartown is an enchanted place. Atop the eastern summit of Droop Mountain, sandstone that formed during the Pennsylvanian age about 300 million years ago has weathered and broken off into huge boulders, protruding cliffs, long rock walls, and nature-sculpted rock formations. Ice and snow often remain in the resulting deep crevasses until midsummer, while lichens, mosses, and ferns cling to life in bits of soil that become trapped in tiny cracks on the rock. A lush forest of hemlock and yellow birch towers over all of this, letting in small bits of sun that look like spotlights purposely pointing out certain spots to be accentuated and admired. If approached with the right frame of mind, you can feel like a kid again, following the 0.5-mile wooden boardwalk and staircases through a giant outdoor maze of rock labyrinths.

The park is open daily during daylight hours Apr.–Oct. To preserve the natural features of the area, the West Virginia Division of Natural Resources has not developed the park, and the only facilities are a picnic table, outhouses, water pump, interpretive signs, and the boardwalk.

BEARTOWN STATE PARK

✳ Lodging
RESORTS

White Sulphur Springs 24986
✍ ♿ **The Greenbrier** (304-536-1110; 1-800-453-4858; www.greenbrier.com), 300 West Main St. Constructed by the Chesapeake and Ohio Railroad, which opened it in the early 1900s near the end of the "taking the waters" era, The Greenbrier has hosted generations of the world's powerful and elite—some of them rich and famous, others who have been able to live a Greenbrier lifestyle yet remain relatively obscure. The resort has approximately the same number of employees as guests, so pampering is a foregone conclusion. The 40,000-square-foot spa is one of the oldest in the country, plush fur-

A NATURALIST'S STATE FOREST

Greenbrier State Forest (304-536-1944; www.greenbriersf.com; mailing address: HC 30, Box 154, Caldwell 24925). Take 1-64 exit 175 at White Sulphur Springs, drive south on WV 60/14, and enter the forest in 1.2 miles.

It was in the warming temperatures of spring in the year 1892 that botanist John Kunkel Small, while exploring the environs of Kate's Mountain, came upon an unknown plant growing in a shale barren. With cloverlike leaves and white, round flower heads, the plant came to be known as Kate's Mountain clover, not only because it was discovered here, but also because for many years it remained the only place it was found.

The clover was not the only plant first discovered on the shale barrens of Kate's Mountain. About 15 years prior to Small's explorations, Gustav Guttenberg recorded finding a nodding flower that lacked petals but had thick, purple sepals, and it was later named white-haired clematis. In 1903, Kenneth M. Mackenzie found the mountain pimpernel, an upright plant with several terminal clusters of tiny yellow flowers.

For many years after their discovery, each of these plants was believed to exist only on Kate's Mountain and nowhere else in the world. It is now known that they are found in, and are endemic to, shale barrens in several Mid-Atlantic and Southern states. Yet, they grow in such small numbers that they are certainly not common plants, and, in fact, Kate's Mountain clover is listed as rare, threatened, or endangered in every state in which it is found.

nishings are found throughout the resort, and evening dances, concerts, and afternoon teas are daily events. In keeping with the atmosphere of gentility, a strict dress code is maintained, with guests receiving a list of what is appropriate in the various parts of the resort. A variety of shops carry the best of everything from around the world, as well as locally handcrafted items.

And then there is the food. The Greenbrier's Culinary Arts Center has trained chefs for decades and sent them out to the four corners of the earth. What they have learned, and the new innovations the center is constantly making are available in the resort's many restaurants, each of which has its own signature menu and atmosphere. Dinners in the Main Dining Room or Prime 44 West are elegant affairs, with jacket-and-tie attire. Other restaurants are only slightly more casual. Save up a few days' salary and treat yourself to a meal here; you may receive sticker shock, but you will have enjoyed one of West Virginia's finest dining offerings. Sadly, after decades of offering it to the general public, The Greenbrier has discontinued its Sunday brunch buffet. It was here that I was introduced to a wonderful array of entrées and the most delicious pastries this side of France that I have ever consumed.

The Greenbrier is not all sitting around and just thinking about how good life can

Much of Kate's Mountain is within the boundary of 5,130-acre Greenbrier State Forest. Unlike the state forests in many other states that are managed primarily for timber and have few amenities, a large percentage of West Virginia's state forests offer a variety of outdoor opportunities and visitor attractions. Greenbrier State Forest has a campground (hookups and hot showers), rental cabins, game courts, picnic areas, a seasonal nature program, and a swimming pool that is extremely popular with local children.

Almost all of the state forest's developed areas are located in the narrow valley of Harts Run, leaving the few people who hike along the trails with a good feeling of isolation. (Hunters use the pathways and surrounding forest during the various seasons, so take proper precautions.) All of the trails are well marked and signed at intersections, but many are not for those who are out of shape. They start in the valley and climb steeply for more than 1,000 feet to the ridgeline.

Yet, there are compelling reasons to put yourself through all of this. Botanists list 15 species of plants that are confined to shale barrens, and 14 of them grow upon the slopes and ridgelines of Kate's Mountain. Deer, opossum, raccoon, chipmunk, black bear, squirrel, woodpecker, turkey, grouse, quail, and close to 250 other species of birds have been seen here. In addition, there is a spectacular view that more than makes up for the huffing and puffing.

If you feel like you may have trouble identifying plants, consider visiting here in the spring when volunteers and park personnel conduct the annual Show-Me Wildflower Hike.

be. It offers more than 50 activities, including three 18-hole championship golf courses, horseback riding and hiking on the resort's 6,500 acres, and more esoteric things such as sporting clays and learning the art of falconry or how to drive your recently purchased $100,000 four-wheel drive vehicle down a steep and rocky mountainside. Parents are able to enjoy these outings on their own because The Greenbrier maintains a complete schedule of programs designed specifically for children.

Accommodations range from rooms and suites in the 1913 white-columned, Georgian Revival hotel to palatial luxury homes that will hold large groups of people. The rate for two people in a standard room, about the size of a typical motel or hotel room, starts at $309 per night during the high season (Apr.–Oct.). Rates go up from there.

One final note: At one time, the general public could wander around the resort, taking in the sites and enjoying many of the amenities offered. Soon after the tragedies of 9/11—and the resort's construction of private homes on some of its outlying properties—this practice was halted. If you are not a registered guest, you can still play golf or have dinner by making advance reservations. You can also participate in a scheduled tour of one of The Greenbrier's most interesting features:

During the cold war, the resort cooperated with the federal government by building a huge underground bunker that was designed to protect the entire U.S. Congress in the event of a nuclear attack.

MOTELS & HOTELS This area has such an abundance of B&Bs, inns, and other types of lodging that you really shouldn't have to stay in a motel—unless you have a pet, and that is why the following are included in this book.

Lewisburg 24901

🐾 **Quality Inn** (304-645-7722; www.qualityinn.com), 540 Jefferson St. Located just off I-64 exit 169, the Quality Inn has close to 200 rooms and an outdoor pool. There are also complimentary shuttles to and from Greenbrier Airport. Pets permitted with approval. $80–115.

🐾 **Relax Inn** (304-645-2345), 635 North Jefferson St. Close to the interstate, the Relax Inn has less than 30 rooms. It permits small pets for an extra fee. $70–140.

INNS

Greenville 24945

✒ 🐾 ✂ **Creekside Resort** (1-800-691-6420; www.creeksideresort.net; mailing address: P.O. Box 111). Take US 219 south from Union for 8 miles, turn right onto WV 122 toward Greenville, and continue another 3 miles to a gravel road where signs will direct you to the resort. A number of cottages and vacation homes are spaced throughout a 200-acre working farm; one is large enough for 12 people. The resort is a good choice for families, groups, or wedding parties looking for a quiet country retreat. Children can visit the barn to see the goats, horses, cats, and ducks, and everyone can hike or bike the miles of trails in woodlands and meadows.

There is a two-night minimum on the weekends. Nightly rates $129–389.

Lewisburg 24901

✒ **The General Lewis Inn** (304-645-2600; 1-800-628-4454; www.generallewisinn.com), 301 East Washington St. Portions of the General Lewis date from 1834, while the main section and west wing were constructed for the inn in 1928 by Walter Martens, architect of the Governor's Mansion in Charleston. I know it's a worn-out and trite phrase, but it really does seem like you have gone back in time when you stay here. Thomas Jefferson and Patrick Henry stood by the very same desk that you also use to check in, the rooms are furnished with antiques from the earliest days of Lewisburg, the more than 20 guest rooms all have beds that are at least 100 years old (mattresses are newer, of course), and drinking water flows from the antique original fountains. A hallway downstairs, known as Memory Hall, is chock-full of tools, weapons, household items, and musical instruments from earlier days.

There is an understated dignity about the General Lewis Inn, but the atmosphere is pretty laid-back. The resident

THE GENERAL LEWIS INN

dog and cat walk about at will, and, if the inn is not booked solid when you arrive, you may be invited to wander through the guest rooms to decide which one will be yours for the evening. The dining room (see *Dining Out*) specializes in Southern-style cooking (with a bit of a flair), and the decades-old gardens in the inn's backyard beckon as a place to stroll and relax after a meal. $120–145.

BED & BREAKFASTS

Lewisburg 24901

Church Street Bed and Breakfast (304-645-7014; www.bbonline.com/wv /churchstreet), 213 Church St. The three-story home was built by a successful coal miner around the turn of the 20th century and is on the National Register of Historic Places. Today, it welcomes travelers to its two guest rooms (private baths), each with a tiger maple fireplace and beds of solid wood created in nearby Monroe County. $100–115.

White Sulphur Springs 24896

James Wylie House (304-536-9444; 1-800-870-1613; www.jameswylie .com), 208 East Main St. Set back from East Main St. on a large lot, the 1819 brick James Wylie House (on the National Register of Historic Homes) looks inviting as soon as you drive up. Large trees shade the dormered gable and front porch, which you will soon find to be the place guests gather to socialize and sip lemonade or enjoy breakfast. Inside, the two parlors, guest rooms, and suite are filled with antiques. For a bit more privacy, you could check into the house's predecessor, a 1790s log cabin that has been converted into a one-bedroom, bath, and full-kitchen accommodation. The host has been bright and cheerful every time I have visited, welcomes children, and is considered an expert

quilter (she teaches classes if you are interested). Rooms $130; suite and cabin $180.

CABINS & VACATION RENTALS

Greenville 24945

Larew Cottage (304-832-6827; www.larewcottage.com; mailing address: HC 81, Box 33). From I-64 exit 169 at Lewisburg, drive US 219 South for 28 miles, turn right onto WV 122, go an additional 10 miles, turn left onto Hans Creek Rd., and come to the cottage 4 miles later. The Larew family built this simple farmhouse in 1920 using timber from their farm, and the spacious living area served the family well as they raised 10 children. It can accommodate up to 13 and sits wonderfully secluded on the working farm that the family has operated for more than 200 years. Going along with the nature of the house and property, it is sparsely furnished, but it does have all the amenities you need, including a washer and dryer. Rented by the weekend, three-day stay, or week. The weekend rate is $250 for two people.

Union 24983

Mountain Shadow Cabin (304-772-5382; http://wvweb.com/mountain-shadowcabin; mailing address: HC 76, Box 32A). Located on a narrow, one-lane back road that sits facing the western slope of Peters Mountain, this two-story cabin is constructed from logs hand-hewn in the 1800s. It accommodates up to six and has an early American tub to soak in. Rented by the weekend, three-day stay, or week. The weekend rate for two is $250.

Wolf Creek 24993

High Meadow Farm Lodge (304-445-7634; www.visitwv.com/high meadow; mailing address: General Delivery). Follow WV 3 from Alderson, cross the Greenbrier River

Bridge, drive 6.4 miles, turn left onto a secondary road just before the Wolf Creek Post Office, and continue 0.5 mile. High Meadows Lodge is one of the most secluded places you can rent in the southeastern part of West Virginia. Located on its own private road, it is constructed of logs hand-hewn by early settlers hundreds of years ago and can accommodate 12 people. The large deck, with a hot tub, has a soaring view of the mountains. There are two baths, an equipped kitchen, and two woodstove fireplaces. Rented by the weekend, three-day stay, or week. Weekend rates are $300 for two people.

For other cabin accommodations, also see the "A Naturalist's State Forest" sidebar earlier in the chapter.

CAMPGROUNDS The forest service's **Lake Sherwood Recreation Area** (304-536-2144) is so close to Virginia that hikers can reach the border in only 1.5 miles along the network of trails (also open to mountain bikers). This is, by far, one of the most deluxe recreation areas in the Monongahela National Forest. The 165-acre lake contains bass, bluegill, bullhead, catfish, tiger muskie, and stocked trout.

HIGH MEADOW FARM LODGE

Rowboats and canoes are available for rent, and there are three boat launches and a dock for public use. You can swim from two sand beaches, one of which is on an island connected to the mainland by a scenic footbridge. The campground, open year-round with close to 100 sites, has modern restrooms with hot showers (only vault toilets in winter), but no hookups.

From the intersection of WV 92 and WV 14 near Neola, follow WV 14 for 11 miles to the recreation area.

Ronceverte 24970
Greenbrier River Campground (1-800-775-2203; www.greenbrierriver .com; mailing address: P.O. Box 265), on the Greenbrier River. Open Apr. 15–Oct. 15. The 8-acre campground has wooded and riverside sites for tents and RVs with full hookups. They also rent a variety of paddle craft and tubes, and offer guided fishing and rafting trips.

For other campgrounds, also see *To Do—Swimmin' Holes*, Moncove Lake State Park under *Green Space—Parks*, and the "A Naturalist's State Forest" sidebar earlier in the chapter.

✳ Where to Eat
DINING OUT

Lewisburg
🍴 🍸 **Food and Friends** (304-645-4548; www.foodandfriendswv.com), 213 West Washington St. Open for lunch and dinner; closed Sun.–Mon. Reservations suggested for dinner. Paige and Bob Murphy started out by just serving sandwiches, but their fare proved so popular that they now offer an eight-page menu full of dining pleasures. The restaurant has its own smoker for the salmon, chicken, and ribs that are served alongside entrées such as shrimp New Orleans (barbecue-grilled bacon-wrapped jumbo shrimp),

seafood ravioli, pecan-crusted chicken, salmon basilica, and a variety of steaks. You know you are going to have a fine meal when something as commonplace as asparagus can be made extraordinary. The wine list features bottles from Europe, Africa, North and South America, Australia, and New Zealand. All desserts are made here, so save room for the pineapple cake or crunchy peanut butter pie (with enough calories and fat to supply an entire day's worth of recommended daily allowances of such things—but oh so yummy). Entrées $7.95–28.95.

I know it has nothing to do with the food, but I just have to say that Food and Friends has the most pleasant and appealing storefront in all of Lewisburg.

✎ **The General Lewis Inn** (304-645-2600; 1-800-628-4454; www.general lewisinn.com), 301 East Washington St. Open Mon.–Sat. for breakfast, lunch, and dinner; only breakfast and dinner (starting at noon) on Sun. The dining room of the General Lewis Inn (see *Lodging*) is on the first floor of the original 1834 home, so there is a bit of a rustic elegance to it. The fare has been described as Southern cooking with an epicurean touch. The fried chicken is known far and wide, the locally raised pork loin is seasoned with spiced apples, and the salt-cured Virginia ham is served with the traditional red-eye gravy. It's not all Southern, though. You can also choose from roast duck à l'orange, lamb chops, or a pasta du jour. All of the breads and desserts are homemade—the fruit cobbler brought to mind the ones my grandmother used to make. Entrées $13–22.95; a full complement of alcoholic beverages is served.

Julian's (304-645-4145), 102 South Lafayette St. Open for dinner Wed.–Sun. Reservations are recommended to ensure being seated at Julian's, selected as the finest restaurant in West Virginia by the Huntington Gourmet Society. Start your meal with sopressatta (dry cured Italian sausage) and move on to grilled chicken with peach chutney, paella, pepper-crusted salmon with honey mustard sauce, Angus sirloin topped with blue cheese sauce, or crispy veal sweetbreads. Entrées $12.50–28.

Tavern 1785 (304-645-1744), 208 West Washington St. Open for dinner Tue.–Sat. The twisting vines of a grape arbor welcome diners onto a brick dining area. Those who wish to eat inside can do so in the 1785 log house decorated with antiques and items from the Civil War. I got a big smile on my face as I took the first bite of the roasted tomato and crab Napoleon. My dining companion beamed when she tasted her miso-seared ahi tuna, and every-

FOOD AND FRIENDS

body at the table vied for the last of the profiteroles we had ordered as a group. Entrées $17.95–29.95.

EATING OUT

Charmco

Possum Holler Pizza (304-438-6622), on US 60. Open for lunch and dinner. Restaurants are few and far between once you leave Lewisburg driving west on US 60. This pizza place will serve to fill the empty spot in your stomach with pizza, sandwiches, and Italian dishes. Entrées $2.50–15.

Lewisburg

Jim's Drive-In (304-645-2590), approximately 1 mile west of Lewisburg on US 60. Open for lunch and dinner Mon.–Sat. Jim's is a local institution that has been around for decades, serving English-style hot dogs (with butter-toasted buns), hamburgers, homemade chili, and old-fashioned milk shakes brought to your car. Drive-in restaurants are an endangered breed, but Jim's is so popular that you may not be able to find a parking space. Entrées $1.50–8.95.

The Market (304-645-4084; www .foodandfriendswv.com), corner of Church and Washington streets. Open Mon.–Fri. 8–6, Sat. 10–5. Operated by the owners of Food and Friends (see *Dining Out*), The Market is more casual and serves breakfast and deli sandwiches. Judging from the crowd that was there when I went in to look around, the food results in happy diners. Prices are pretty reasonable, too. Entrées $2.50–5.25.

Stardust Café (304-647-3663; www .stardustcafewv.com), 102 East Washington St. Closed Sunday. One of the owners of the Stardust Café is a member of Poteen, one the state's best-known Irish music bands. (Pick up a CD if you can find one; you're sure to

enjoy it.) With the relaxed atmosphere of a coffeehouse, the café operates on an environmentally conscious basis by serving locally grown and organic products, brewing fair-trade coffee, and using recycled coffee cups. Sandwiches, subs, and panini are served on freshly baked breads. I often make a meal of the appetizers, such as the quiche or the freshly made soup. This is a place to enjoy good food in a casual setting. Entrées $12–28.

Union

Kalico Kitchen (304-772-3104), Main St. Open for breakfast, lunch, and dinner daily. The Kalico Kitchen is where local residents come for a low-cost breakfast. Where else can you get two eggs with a biscuit or toast for only $1.75? Lunch and dinner choices include subs, sandwiches, salads, and country-cooking items such as hamburger steak, fried chicken, and a vegetable plate. Entrées $3.50–5.99.

White Sulphur Springs

April's Pizzeria (304-536-1011), 709 East Main St. Open daily for lunch and dinner. Serves a variety of calzones, sandwiches, salads, pizzas, and other Italian dishes. Entrées $3.95–16.

✗ **Granny's House Restaurant** (304-536-2361), on US 60 adjacent to the I-64 White Sulphur Springs exit (exit 175). Open daily for breakfast, lunch, and dinner. Granny's has a home-cooking menu and is one of the best spots for a hearty breakfast. Be aware: This place can become very busy, making serving time slow down considerably. Entrées $4.95–13.95.

✪ **Rte. 60 American Grill and Bar** (304-536-4666), 12 West Main St. Open daily for lunch and dinner. It doesn't look like much from the outside, and it is definitely a bar atmosphere, but this restaurant, a favorite with motorcyclists, must be doing something right. It has been around for years, serving a host of fried appetizers, burgers, hot dogs, and specialty sandwiches. Entrées $3.50–7.95.

SNACKS & GOODIES

Gap Mills

The Cheese 'N' More Store (304-772-5211), 5521 Sweet Springs Valley (WV 3). Closed Sun. This little Mennonite-run shop has an amazing array of items that includes nuts, dried fruit, cooking and baking ingredients, spices and herbs, jellies, candies, and a deli with close to 50 kinds of cheeses and 15 different lunch meats. One of my fondest memories of traveling in this region is stopping here on a warm spring day, ordering a sandwich (made with bread from the Kitchen Creek Bakery across the street), and sitting on the storefront bench to soak up the sun and lots of local color.

Kitchen Creek Bakery (304-772-4253), on WV 3. Open Wed.–Sat.; only open Fri. and Sat. Feb.–Mar.; closed Jan. The logical thing to do after having a lunch sandwich at The Cheese 'N' More Store is to walk across the road to the Kitchen Creek Bakery, where white-capped Mennonite women have been working from the early-morning hours so that you can have your dessert choice of home-baked cookies, pies, or cakes. Just before leaving, purchase a loaf of fresh white, whole wheat, or sourdough bread to enjoy once you get back home.

Lewisburg

The Bakery (304-645-1106; www.thebakeryllcwv.com), 102 North Court St. Open Mon.–Fri. 7–4, Sat. 9–2. Freshly baked goods, including a variety of the most sinfully rich and calorie-laden brownies you will find anywhere. And, oh, those personal-size pizzas! Better than any you will find in a dedicated pizza shop.

Greenbrier Valley Baking Company (304-645-6159), 110 South Jefferson St. Open Tue. 7:30–5:30, Wed.–Fri. 7:30–8, Sat. 7:30–4. At a restored bakery building, Gina and Tod Lang (he has degree in specialty bread baking) arrive early in the morning to bake artisan breads, European pastries (first-class tiramisu!), cookies, and light lunches.

✳ Entertainment

DANCE See Carnegie Hall under *Theater*.

FILM

Lewisburg

Lewis Theater (304-645-6038), 113 North Court St. An experience missing in many places—movies on the big screen in a downtown location.

Marquee-Seneca Showplace (304-645-6033), Greenbrier Valley Mall. First-run movies.

Also see Carnegie Hall under *Theater*.

MUSIC See *Theater*.

THEATER

Lewisburg

☂ **Carnegie Hall** (304-645-7917; www.carnegiehallwv.com), 105 Church St. Exhibit space is open Mon.–Fri. 9–4:30, Sat. 10–1 from May–Oct. Yes, you read that right. There is a Carnegie Hall in West Virginia, and it is one of only four Carnegie Halls in the world built by Andrew Carnegie that are still in continuous use. The Greek Revival building was constructed in 1902 and is now operated by an active not-for-profit organization that sponsors an annual program of more than 100 events, including live theater, classes, dance, art and museum exhibits, films, lectures, and concerts. Be sure to check the concert schedule as there is almost always something going on, and the hall has hosted some of the world's best-known performers, such as Isaac Stern, Doc Watson, Tom Rush, and the Moscow Dramatic Ballet.

Greenbrier Valley Theatre (304-645-3838; www.gvtheatre.org), 113 East Washington St. Located in downtown Lewisburg, the Greenbrier Valley Theatre is the state's only year-round professional live theater. Productions range from the well-known, such as *A Christmas Carol*, to local stories such as *The Greenbrier Ghost*. The theater also sponsors an extensive series of music concerts, and the lobby serves as an art gallery.

Ronceverte
Riders of the Flood (304-645-2070; www.ridersoftheflood.com), in the Island Park Amphitheater, off US 219 in Ronceverte. Presented as an outdoor drama annually for two weekends in September, *Riders of the Flood* was written by Greenbrier County native Robert Tuckwiller (see Tuckwiller Gallery under *Selective Shopping—Art Galleries*). Set in the days of West Virginia's logging boom, it portrays the adventures of a young city man who finds adventure, romance, and success in the high mountains.

✳ Selective Shopping
ANTIQUES
Lewisburg
Brick House Antiques (304-645-4082), 123 East Washington St. Brick House is located in the oldest standing commercial building in Lewisburg and is set back a few feet from the street. It's always a treat to walk by the shop

because the owner has a way of arranging things in the small yard that is pleasing to the eye and draws you in to take a closer look.

Robert's Antiques (304-647-3404; www.robertsantiquesltd.com), 120 East Washington St. Early American and primitive antiques, along with paintings, books, wines, and specialty coffees. I found the furniture selection to be outstanding.

ART GALLERIES
Lewisburg
Cooper Gallery (304-645-6439; 1-888-868-5129; www.coopergallery .com), 122 East Washington St. The Cooper Gallery showcases many nice pieces of sculpture, furniture, art glass, and other items. However, what impresses me each time I walk in is the superiority of the painters and photographers represented here, including owner G. P. Cooper.

Harmony Ridge Gallery (304-645-4333; www.harmonyisle.com), 209 West Washington St. Usually open later into the evening when most of the town's other galleries have closed. While researching a book such as this one, I see gallery after gallery and can get jaded, so it sometimes takes a lot to really capture my interest, and Harmony Ridge Gallery succeeded in doing so. Monica and Aaron Maxwell owned a gallery in Florida before moving to Lewisburg, and they have brought a new level of flair to a town that was already awash with it. In displays that are eye-pleasingly arranged, their 5,000-square-foot gallery showcases some of the finest craftsmanship in American art pieces. Prices may have a tendency to reflect this, but you certainly can't deny the quality of the blown-glass vases, furniture, pottery, interesting jewelry, woodwork, and other items they continually find and bring into their store.

Tuckwiller Gallery (304-645-2070; www.tuckwillergallery.com), 102 West Washington St. A native of Greenbrier County, Robert Tuckwiller is one of the state's best-known painters of pastoral country settings and the natural environment. He is also the author of the outdoor drama *Riders of the Flood* (see *Entertainment—Theater*).

The Washington Street Gallery (304-647-4561; http://washingtonst gallery.com), 123 West Washington St. The Washington Street Gallery offers the works of a number of contemporary artists. However, owner Gary Roper has a master of fine arts degree in ceramics from West Virginia University, and what he is able to fashion out of a simple blob of clay is the real reason to stop by.

BOOKSTORES

Lewisburg

The Bookstore, 104 South Jefferson St. A hole-in-the-wall-size place (it does not even have a phone) crammed full of used scholarly, uncommon, and out-of-print books.

The Open Book (304-645-7331), 113B East Washington St., Lewisburg. The Open Book specializes in West Virginia books in addition to bestsellers and special orders.

Also see Alderson's under *Special Shops*.

FARMERS' MARKETS

Lewisburg

You can pick up the best of what local farmers produce at the **Lewisburg Farmers' Market** (304-653-4784) Sat. 9–1 (May–Oct.) at the parking lot behind the post office.

Union

Monroe Farm Market (304-772-3003), beside the Ames Clare Church. May–Oct., every Thurs. 11-3. A volunteer-run, open-air market where everything is grown or produced in Monroe County.

PICK-YOUR-OWN PRODUCE FARMS

Renick

🌱 **White Oak Blueberry Farm** (304-497-3577; www.whiteoakberryfarm), 418 Brownstown Rd. Closed Sun. Pick your own blueberries July–Aug.

Sinks Grove

Morgan Orchard (304-772-3638; www.morganorchardwv.com; mailing address: Rte. 2, Box 114). Call for directions. Pick-your-own berries, peaches, plums, grapes, corn, pumpkins, and apples in their respective seasons. A farm store is open for those who don't have the time or inclination to head out into the fields.

SPECIAL SHOPS

Alderson

Alderson's (304-445-2851; www.alder sonsstore.com), 203 South Monroe St. There are not many businesses like Alderson's that can claim to have been a family business since 1887. This small shop, with art deco architecture and fixtures from the 1930s, has an interesting mix of women's clothing, jewelry, gift items, antiques, and a good selection of local-interest books.

WINERY Wolf Creek Winery (304-772-5040; www.wolfcreekwinery.com; mailing address: HC 75, Box 36A, Wolf Creek 24993). From Pickaway, follow WV 3 west. The road signed for the vineyard is across from Flat Mountain Rd. The tasting schedule has been known to change from year to year; call ahead. The winery planted its first vines in 1991, and its wines, including Seyval, Foch, Chambourcin, Chancellor, and Vidal, have become so popular that more vines were planted around 2006. The tasting room and adjoining deck have a nice view of the vineyard and surrounding mountains.

✳ Special Events

April: **Annual Lewisburg Chocolate Festival** (1-800-833-2068; www.lewis burgchocolatefestival.com), various venues in Lewisburg. A variety of activities with everything focused on chocolate: music, chocolate themed dinners, chocolate tastings, chocolate bake-off, and chocolate mousse–eating contest.

June: **Farmer's Day** (304-772-5904; www.travelmonroe.com), Union. A small-town celebration where it seems everyone has a part in the parade, horse show, children's activities, and crafts. **Ronceverte River Festival** (304-647-7651), Ronceverte. The Great Rubber Ducky Race, in addition to a pet parade, car show, music, and river events.

August: **West Virginia State Fair** (304-645-1090), Fairlea.

September: **Autumn Harvest Festival** (304-772-3003), WVU Demonstration Farm, 4 miles south of Union on WV 13. Celebrates the end of the growing season with food, music, crafts, tractor pulls, apple butter making, and vegetable, flower, canned food, and art contests.

October: **Taste of Our Town** (304-645-7917), Lewisburg. Good food, concerts, games for the kids, and the fall foliage.

THE SOUTHERN BORDER—
BLUEFIELD, HINTON,
PINEVILLE, PRINCETON,
AND WELCH

There is no doubt about it: This is coal country. Located along the state's southern border, the area has only one major four-lane highway, making it almost one of those you-really-have-to-want-to-get-there types of places.

In fact, it is a world apart. Isolated from the rest of West Virginia, in this area things are still a little rough around the edges—and that is its allure. Malls and supersize discount stores are few and far between, large luxury resorts occupying thousands of acres are nonexistent, home-style cooking is what you will find in the restaurants, and mom-and-pop enterprises are the norm. The mountains are more rugged than those to the north, rising more in jumbles than in long ridgelines. As stated, this is West Virginia's coalfield, and while driving on the narrow roadways you may often look into the rearview mirror to see the grill of a heavily loaded coal truck barreling down the mountain just inches from your back bumper.

Much of this may change. Four-lane highways have been proposed (and are currently being constructed), and there are always ever-evolving plans for "economic development." The time to visit is now, before this place loses its rough edges, before roadsides are cluttered with fast-food restaurants instead of being bordered by modest homesteads. Visit now, before other people learn about the area's charms and while you can still explore in relative peace and quiet, delighting in the knowledge that you are experiencing a distinctive and different kind of place.

COMMUNITIES **Bluefield** and **Princeton** are anomalies in this area, in that they are large urban areas next to a major four-lane highway and have all of the services of the modern world, such as fast-food restaurants, shopping malls, discount stores, and movie theaters.

The arrival of the Norfolk and Western Railroad to ship coal out of the state in 1882 transformed farmland into the booming town of Bluefield. Unlike other rail towns that have since declined, Bluefield continues to have such an active rail yard

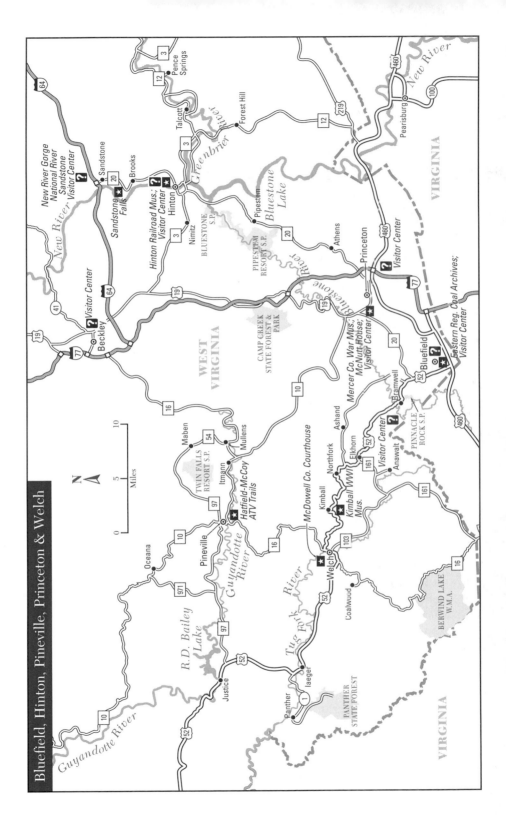

Bluefield, Hinton, Pineville, Princeton & Welch

VIRGINIA

New River

New River Gorge National River Sandstone Visitor Center

Sandstone

Brooks

Sandstone Falls

Hinton Railroad Mus.; Visitor Center

Hinton

Nimitz

Pence Springs

Talcott

Forest Hill

Greenbrier River

Pearisburg

BLUESTONE S.P.

Pipestem

Bluestone Lake

PIPESTEM RESORT S.P.

Bluestone River

Athens

Princeton

Visitor Center

Eastern Reg. Coal Archives; Visitor Center

Visitor Center

Beckley

WEST VIRGINIA

CAMP CREEK STATE FOREST & PARK

Mercer Co. War Mus.; McNutt House; Visitor Center

Bluefield

Bramwell

Visitor Center

PINNACLE ROCK S.P.

Maben

Mullens

TWIN FALLS RESORT S.P.

Itmann

Hatfield-McCoy ATV Trails

McDowell Co. Courthouse

Ashand

Northfork

Elkhorn

Anawalt

Kimball

Kimball WWI Mus.

Oceana

Pineville

Guyandotte River

Welch

Coalwood

BERWIND LAKE W.M.A.

R.D. Bailey Lake

Tug Fork River

Justice

Iaeger

Panther

PANTHER STATE FOREST

VIRGINIA

Guyandotte River

N

Miles

0   5   10

that there is a special automobile pullout on Bluefield Ave. for the multitude of rail fans that come here to watch coal cars be moved from one track to another. John Nash, winner of a 1994 Nobel Prize and subject of the film *A Beautiful Mind*, grew up in Bluefield, which now bills itself as "Nature's Air-Conditioned City." Sitting at 2,612 feet above sea level, where a cool breeze blows much of the time, Bluefield's chamber of commerce hit upon the idea of serving free lemonade whenever the temperature reaches 90 degrees. From 1960 to 1982, the lemonade was served only once. The offer is still good today, so be watching the thermometer and look for the "lemonade lasses" to get your complimentary refreshment.

As seen in many places throughout the world where pockets of super wealth have been accumulated from the labors of those who live next door in near abject poverty, **Bramwell** (www.bramwellwv.com) was settled by affluent coal mine owners in the late 1800s. Once thought to be the richest town in America, it was such a hub of activity that trains stopped here 14 times a day, often bringing the high society of the Northeast's elite for a summer visit. (There was a ticket window at Grand Central Station in New York just for Bramwell.) The prosperity came to an end during the Great Depression, but most of the town's ornate and beautifully designed homes have been maintained or restored to their original splendor. If nothing else, it is certainly worthwhile to visit just to see these grand old homes. A walking-driving tour pamphlet (available from the Coal Heritage Trail Interpretive Center— see *Guidance*) provides historical information on more than 20 of the buildings (but fails to make much mention of their architectural heritage). It may never gain its former glory, but a gallery or two, a B&B, and a few other businesses are instilling new life to the town. **Coalwood** was the boyhood home of Homer Hickam (www.homerhickam .com), the author of *Rocket Boys*, which was made into the movie *October Sky*. The town is still a small, sleepy little place that now has a municipal park and monument to its most famous son. It comes alive on the first Friday in October during the Annual October Sky Day Festival, when Hickam and many of the Rocket Boys sign copies of books; you can take tours of their original rocket site, see scale model rockets from NASA, and partake in the overall festive atmosphere.

Hinton is a narrow town whose homes and businesses cling to the hillside above Bluestone Lake and the New River. The Chesapeake & Ohio Railway Company established its maintenance complex here in the late 1800s and employed so many people that the monthly payroll was more than $80,000. The thriving economy spurred a boom in the construction of buildings that are interesting for their mix of architectural styles. Because of this, more than 200 buildings in the downtown district have been placed on the National Register of Historic Places. A self-guided walking-tour brochure available from the Summers County Convention and Visitors Bureau (see *Guidance*) takes you by American Gothic, Classical and Greek Revival, High Victorian, American Four-Square, and Second Empire styles. Befitting its railroading past, Hinton is one of the few towns left in the state that has AMTRAK passenger rail service (see *Getting There*).

First settled around 1840, **Pineville** is located at the junction of a number of old Native American trails. A water-powered gristmill was one of its first industries, soon followed by coal mining, which is still an important economic factor. Today, the town is seeing a major influx of visitors eager to ride the many miles of the Hatfield-McCoy ATV Trails. When there, take a look at the Greek Roman–style

Wyoming County Courthouse, built with native stone by Italian immigrant stone-masons in 1916.

Welch—whose location on a small piece of flat land next to a river is representative of so many communities in Southern West Virginia—boomed at the turn of the 20th century as its rail yards shipped thousands of tons of coal out of the state. Historians remember it as the site of the murder of two coal miner union supporters in 1921 (see McDowell County Courthouse under *To See—Historic Sites*). *Some obscure trivia*: Welch was the site of the nation's first multilevel municipal parking building.

GUIDANCE The **Bramwell Visitors Center** (1-866-858-5959) and the **Nick J. Rahall Coal Heritage Trail Interpretive Center,** open daily 9–5, are housed in a reconstructed railroad depot on Main St., Bramwell 24715.

You may obtain information about Mercer County from the **Mercer County Convention and Visitors Bureau** (1-800-221-3206; www.visitmercercounty .com), 704 Bland St., Bluefield 24701.

New River Gorge National River Sandstone Visitor Center (304-466-0417; www.nps.gov/neri), on WV 7 at I-64 exit 139. Visitor center personnel can provide you with information about the New River, but the real reason to visit is to take a look at the displays concerning the natural and human history of the area. Of particular note is the route of the New River and its tributaries, which are traced out on the floor.

The building and its landscaping are also interesting, as they were constructed using state-of-the-art green design. The building—which is south-facing for maximum sunlight, insulated with recycled paper products, and has a geothermal water system and a light-colored roof to reflect sunlight—uses an estimated 60 percent less energy than a standard design. The surrounding land is landscaped with native plants that are watered with roof and stormwater runoff.

The **Princeton–Mercer County Chamber of Commerce** (304-487-1502; www .pmccc.com) has a small visitor center located within the McNutt House (see *To See—Historic Home*) at 1522 North Walker St., Princeton 24740. It is open Mon.–Fri. 8:30–4:30 (closed for lunch).

The **Southern West Virginia Convention & Visitor's Bureau** (304-252-2244; 1-800-847-4898; www.visitwv.com), 1406 Harper Rd., Beckley 25801. Not located within this area, this is an umbrella organization that provides information for the entire Southern West Virginia region.

The **Three Rivers Travel Council** (304-466-5332; www.threeriverswv.com), at 200 Ballengee St., Hinton 25951, provides information about attractions and events in Summers County.

The **West Virginia Tourist Information Center** (304-487-2214), located on US 460, just off I-77 exit 5, has information for the entire state as well as a gift shop that features products and arts and crafts made in the state. It is a large facility with a number of picnic tables situated on a knoll that almost always has a cool breeze blowing across it.

GETTING THERE *By bus*: **Greyhound** (1-800-231-2222; www.greyhound.com) has a terminal at 514 Scott St. in Bluefield.

By car: The **West Virginia Turnpike (I-77)** will bring you into this area from the north or south, while **I-64** is the way to come here from the east. **US 460** enters the state from southwestern Virginia. At present, there are no four-lane highways coming into the area from the west, but plans are progressing quickly, and that situation will change sometime in the near future.

By rail: An **AMTRAK** (1-800-872-7245; www.amtrak.com) train, *The Cardinal*, is an east–west train that makes a stop in Hinton three times a week.

GETTING AROUND *By bus*: **Bluefield Area Transit** (304-327-8418; 1-866-759-0978; http://ridethebatbus.com) has routes through and between Princeton, Bluefield, and Welch, and operates Mon.–Fri., with limited service between Princeton and Athens on the weekend. The Welch schedule includes stops in many of the small towns along US 52, including Bluewell, Bramwell, Elkhorn, Northfork, and Kimball.

By taxi: **Cimarron Coach** (276-322-2275) and **Taxi One** (304-431-8294) operate in and around Princeton and Bluefield. **War Taxi** (304-875-2274) services the area near War and Welch.

MEDICAL EMERGENCIES

Bluefield
Bluefield Regional Medical Center (304-327-1100; www.bluefield.org), 500 Cherry St.

Hinton
Summers County Appalachian Regional Healthcare Hospital (304-466-1000; www.arh.org/SummersCo), Terrace St.

Princeton
Princeton Community Hospital (304-487-7000; www.pchonline.org), 12th St.

Welch
Welch Community Hospital (304-436-8461), 454 McDowell St.

✳ To See

COLLEGE Concord University (304-384-5317; 1-800-344-6679; www.concord .edu), P.O. Box 100, Athens 24712. Chartered in 1872, Concord University has been called the "Campus Beautiful" for its scenic location on a knoll overlooking the mountains of Southern West Virginia. A liberal arts school, it is the cultural center of the area, with its arts center offering exhibits, plays, concerts, and live theater open to the general public. Every day a small recital of about 15 minutes resounds throughout the surrounding landscape as the university's 48-bell carillon plays a variety of music, from classical to popular, with religious and seasonal favorites. Former university president Joseph F. Marsh donated the entire cost ($750,000) for the carillon.

DRIVING TOURS, SCENIC & HISTORIC I highly recommend traveling the **Coal Heritage Trail National Scenic Byway** (304-256-6941; www.coalheritage .org). It is one of the best ways to introduce yourself to the industry that has shaped and affected nearly every aspect of life in West Virginia. Starting on US 60 in Ansted, it turns south on US 19 to pass through Fayetteville and Beckley before continuing along two-lane WV 16 through Pineville and Welch. It then turns eastward on two-lane US 52 to end in Bluefield.

Crossing rugged mountains and following the twisting routes of rivers and creeks, the byway will take you into many former mining towns and camps, such as Coalwood, Elkhorn, Stotesbury, and Itmann. Places like the Gary Cemetery, whose grave markers are etched in a number of different languages, attest to the influx of immigrants who came to work in the mines in the early 1900s. Massive amounts of coal are still extracted every day from Southern West Virginia, but changes in the industry have left behind deserted mine sites with slag heaps and abandoned tipples, communities still clinging to life on steep hillsides, and old company stores (seek out the magnificent porticoed company store on WV 16 in Itmann that was hand built by Italian stonemasons of native stone in the 1920s). A number of interpretive sites, such as the restored train depot in Bramwell, add background information to what you are seeing along the roadways.

As I said, I highly recommend this trip—it is not always pretty or scenic, huge coal and logging trucks may hamper your progress on narrow roads, and services can be few and far between, but what you see here will open your eyes considerably to much of what the heritage of West Virginia is all about. A brochure detailing the route is available from any of the places mentioned in *Guidance*.

If you are able to locate a copy of the ***Wyoming County Points of Interest Tour*** brochure, it details several possible side trips from the Coal Heritage Trail National Byway. The drives are definitely off the beaten path, yet the brochure provides information on current mines, points out the evidence of old mining operations, and gives snippets of history that I've not found available anywhere else.

The **Lower Greenbrier River Byway** (www.lowergreenbrierriver.org; mailing address: P.O. Box 277, Alderson 25910) follows the last 30 miles of the eastern United States' longest untamed river as it drops from the high plateau of the Greenbrier River Valley to empty into the New River Gorge. Starting in Fort Spring on WV 63, it passes through historic Alderson, where it picks up WV 12/WV 3 to enter Talcott, home of the John Henry Historical Park near the mouth of the Great Bend Tunnel. (Make a stop at Dillon's Superette Grocery Store to peruse the items in their Talcott Area Memorabilia Room.)

CONCORD UNIVERSITY

The byway rises high above the river to go by the John Henry Statue and Tunnel Overlook. Was there ever really a John Henry, the "steel-drivin' man"? Although there does seem to be a lot of legend around the story, it is known that there was a man named John Henry who worked for the C&O Railroad during the time the mile-long Great Bend Tunnel was built in the 1870s. Did he compete with a steam drill? Again, there is some evidence that he did. What is not known is if he died from exhaustion after the competition, was killed by a rock blast in the tunnel, or passed away at a later date. I guess it really doesn't matter now; it's a great tale, one that has been told and embraced by generations.

The Lower Greenbrier River Byway drops quickly from the statue and overlook to return to the river, which it follows into Hinton.

For an alternate route, you could turn onto WV 15 in Pence Springs, cross the Greenbrier River, and follow the **Lowell Backway** on one-lane paved roads (WV 15 and WV 17) to go by farmlands and summer camps before turning right onto WV 12 to rejoin the Lower Greenbrier River Byway at WV 3.

There are more than 200 buildings in Bluefield that are listed on the National Register of Historic Places, and the *Bluefield Historical Society Historic Homes Driving Tour* pamphlet (available from the Mercer County Convention and Visitors Bureau—see *Guidance*) takes you along residential streets to view dozens of palatial 1920s and 1930s Colonial Revival and neoclassical homes. A large percentage of them were residences for bank presidents, architects, merchants, and mine owners. By far, the most interesting is the Sydney Kwass house at 730 Parkway Ave. Built in 1935, it resembles a ship, complete with porthole windows and a shiplike interior.

HISTORIC CHURCH Concord United Methodist Church (304-384-7922; http://cumcathens.org), 109 Vermillion St., Athens. The church can trace its origins to 1858, and the present building was constructed in 1901. Of interest to the general traveler, though, are the 18 stained-glass windows. Produced with intricate cuts and scrolling by an unknown artist, they depict various scenes and symbols, two of which have a large eye in the center, representing the eye of God. A number of the windows were presented to the church by organizations, such as the Concord Philomethean Literary Society, that are no longer in existence. A protective outdoor layer makes it hard to truly appreciate the beauty of the windows from outside the church; go inside to revel in their rich colors and artistry.

HISTORIC HOME McNutt House (304-487-1502; www.pmccc.com), 1522 North Walker St., Princeton. Open Mon.–Fri. 8:30–4:30 (closed for lunch). Free. Confederate soldiers burned Princeton as they fled superior Union forces, and the McNutt House, built in 1840 with a foundation of 15-inch logs, is the town's only standing pre–Civil War home. A half-spiral staircase greets visitors to the house, log beams in the basement still have bark on them, and the original wooden pegs hold the windows together. New flooring covers the bloodstains of Civil War soldiers who were cared for in the house, which is currently the home of the Princeton–Mercer County Chamber of Commerce (see *Guidance*).

HISTORIC SITES

Kimball

Kimball World War I Memorial (304-436-3096), on US 52. The memorial is a stop on the state's African American Heritage Trail, so do not just pass by this columned building as you go driving along US 52. Constructed in 1928, it is believed to be the first (and maybe the only) monument dedicated to black veterans. At the time of World War I, black citizens comprised more than one-third of McDowell County's population, and more than 1,500 of them participated in America's overseas efforts during the conflict. Sadly, the building caught fire in the 1990s, but a concerted effort by local volunteers has returned it to its former self.

Lowell

Graham House (304-466-2520; mailing address for the Graham House Preservation Society: P.O. Box 218, Pence Springs 24962), on WV 3 a short distance south of Pence Springs. Open Fri.–Sat. from Memorial Day to Labor Day. Small admission fee. The two-story log cabin was constructed by Col. James Graham in the 1770s and is believed to be the oldest log structure still at its original location in West Virginia. The cabin served as much as a fort as it did a home, being attacked in 1777 by Shawnee Indians, who killed two people and kidnapped Graham's 7-year-old daughter. He spent eight years searching for her and finally found her in Kentucky. Such was the life of isolated frontier families, and the Graham House gives you a good picture of what is was like to live here at that time.

Also on the property is the 1800s Saunders one-room schoolhouse, filled with memorabilia from educational days gone by.

Welch

McDowell County Courthouse (304-436-3113), Court and Wyoming streets. Constructed of hand-cut Berea stone in 1895, the four-story Romanesque Gothic courthouse, with a peaked bell tower, almost looks like a medieval castle as it stands on a knoll overlooking the town. As impressive as the architecture is, the structure is most noted as the site where guards hired by mine operators murdered union supporters Sid Hatfield and Ed Chambers in 1921. (A plaque marks the spot where this took place.) Although it was just one more incident in the ongoing miners' struggles in the early 1900s, it led to the Battle of Blair Mountain in Logan County, where thousands of armed miners gathered to protest their conditions. Federal forces were called in, and a number of lives were lost.

MCDOWELL COUNTY COURTHOUSE

LAKES

Justice
R. D. Bailey Lake (304-664-3229; www.lrh.usace.army.mil). Most easily accessed from WV 97 and US 52 several miles west of Pineville. The U.S Army Corps of Engineers Visitor Center sits close to 400 feet above the lake, providing an excellent vantage point to look across the 630 acres of water. Exhibits supply an overview of why the

dam was built and how it operates. Around the lake are a marina, campground (spread out along a 6-mile stretch of shoreline), picnic facilities, and hiking opportunities. Anglers know the lake to be a hot spot for largemouth, smallmouth, and striped bass, but you may also be able to hook catfish, walleye, crappie, tiger muskie, and panfish.

The shoreline, steep hillside, and narrow valleys around the lake attract a large number of breeding birds, such as eastern kingbirds, sparrows, chickadees, Carolina wrens, blue-gray gnatcatchers, indigo buntings, Acadian flycatchers, Baltimore orioles, and dozens of other species.

R. D. BAILEY LAKE

Because of the many miles of winding roadways that must be negotiated to reach the lake, it is agreeably underused and provides one of the least-crowded lake experiences in the entire state.

Hinton

Bluestone Lake (304-466-1234; www.lrh.usace.army.mil). Most easily accessed from WV 20 south of Hinton. Long and narrow, 2,040-acre Bluestone Lake was created by an executive order from President Franklin D. Roosevelt as a means to control flooding, provide recreational opportunities, and protect fish and wildlife. A visitor center provides a good overview of the many opportunities on and around the lake, such as swimming, camping, picnicking, boat rentals, and hunting. The lake has consistently yielded warm river citation game fish such as smallmouth and largemouth bass, catfish, crappie, hybrid striped bass, and muskellunge.

MUSEUMS

Bluewell

Buddy's Country Store & Museum (304-589-5659), Old US 52. Open May–Sept. No admission fee. One of the rules I made for myself when putting this book together was that if an attraction is not readily available to the general public, I would leave it out. I had to make an exception for this privately owned museum. You need to make an appointment to see it, but the extra effort is worth it. There are thousands of pieces of memorabilia from years gone by crammed into a small space. There's a 1926 Model T Ford, a package of 1913 ground roasted rye coffee substitute, and a part of the plane that crashed with World War II hero Audie Murphy aboard. The back room is one of the most complete representations of an early coal camp home you will find anywhere in the state. Come here as soon as you can. The owner is getting up in years, and, truly, he is the real reason to visit the museum. His stories (ask about how margarine is made) will sadly be lost when he is gone.

Hinton

Hinton Railroad Museum (304-466-5420), 206 Temple St. Open Tue.–Sat. Donations accepted. Appropriate for a town that pretty much owes its existence to railroads, the Hinton Railroad Museum displays a number of artifacts from the early days of the C&O Railroad. Not to dismiss this fine collection, but the real reason to come here is to see the more than 100 pieces of wood sculpture relating to railroading by folk artist Charlie Permelia of nearby Lester. One display has figurines that represent every job that existed on the railroad in 1870—and every one of them has a different facial expression! It took Mr. Permelia more than three years, and 20 kinds of wood, to complete the collection.

Princeton

The Mercer County War/Those Who Served Museum (304-487-8328), 1500 West Main St. Open Mon.–Fri. 10–4. Free. The building that houses the museum was constructed in 1928 as a memorial to veterans, and it now contains multiple rooms of memorabilia dating from the Civil War. There are many items to see, such as weaponry, uniforms, and medals and awards, but more than the exhibits, what will most stick with you after you leave is meeting the veterans who serve as volunteer docents and having the opportunity to listen to their stories.

SCENIC VIEWS **East River Mountain Overlook Park** is on WV 598 in Bluefield, which is accessed from US 460. It's a bit of a drive from downtown Bluefield, but the view overlooking the city and out to mountains on the West Virginia–Virginia border from the observation deck at 3,500 feet above sea level makes the twisting and winding car ride worth it. The park is the site of West Virginia's first visitors information center (no longer in operation) and has restrooms, picnic facilities, and short hiking trails leading to the top of the mountain.

WV 20 is a twisting two-lane roadway that parallels the New River from Hinton to I-64 near Sandstone. At one point, there is a designated overlook with a trail just a

THE VIEW FROM THE OBSERVATION DECK AT EAST RIVER MOUNTAIN OVERLOOK PARK

SANDSTONE FALLS

couple of hundred feet long that leads to a soaring view of **Sandstone Falls** (see *Waterfalls*) churning and roaring more than 600 feet below.

WATERFALLS Just north of Hinton are three waterfalls that should not be missed, especially since they are located within a few miles of each other along the same road:

From the west side of the New River on WV 20 at Hinton, turn northward onto WV 26 and follow it 3.9 miles to the **Brooks Falls** parking lot. A platform just a few feet from the car lets you watch the New River tumble 2 to 4 feet down a set of rocks. Directly across the road is the 1.9-mile **Big Branch Loop Trail,** which steeply ascends the mountain to pass by small but scenic cascades.

For the area's best waterfall, continue driving northward from the Brooks Falls parking lot for 4 miles to the parking lot for the very impressive **Sandstone Falls**. Spanning the full width of the New River, the falls are 1,500 feet wide (the widest in the state) and, divided by a number of islands, drop 10 to 25 feet. Anglers wade the waters below the falls in the hope of hooking smallmouth bass and catfish.

A 1-mile circuit trail takes you across bridges and observation decks for a close-up view of the falls and an ambulation of the significant Flatrock Community environment around them. Plants include arrowhead, water willow, fringe tree, lizard's tail, and more than 50 different composite plants. Among the animals are great blue herons, kingfishers, mussels, hellgrammites, crayfish, mallards, bullfrogs, eastern river cooters, and other turtles.

OTHER SITES

Bluefield
Eastern Regional Coal Archives (304-325-3943), 600 Commerce St. Open Mon.–Thurs. It is primarily a repository of materials for those who are doing intensive research about the coal industry, but the general public is welcome to browse through the artifacts, diaries, old equipment, photographs, and movies.

Mullens
Murals are a thing of the past in many towns across America, but tiny **Mullens** is a showcase for them and

A MURAL IN MULLENS

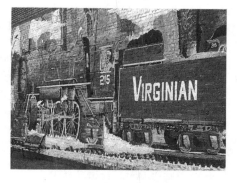

provides ample evidence of how they can add interest and beauty to a municipal landscape. The 35-by-56-foot 1918 *Homecoming* mural on the back of City Hall represents the return of soldiers from World War I, and, on Howard Ave., a 20 by 90-foot mural depicts the Old Virginian Railway steam engine roaring by as it pulls mail, baggage, and passenger cars. Walk around town, and you will find one showing how Mullens looked in 1912 and another highlighting a cabin of the late 1800s. Also in town is the restored Virginian Railway Company's Caboose #307, which was used in a rail yard in town. It now serves as the Railroad and Mullens Area Historic Museum, open on special occasions.

✴ To Do

AERIAL TRAMWAY Pipestem Resort State Park (304-466-1800; www.pipe stemresort.com; mailing address: P.O. Box 150, Pipestem 25979), located on WV 20 approximately 14 miles north of Princeton and 12 miles south of Hinton. Small fee; free to Mountain Creek Lodge guests. The park's aerial tramway, which operates daily May–Oct., is used by guests of Mountain Creek Lodge to reach their riverside accommodations, but it is also open to the general public. Enclosed gondolas take you 1,000 feet from the canyon rim to the Bluestone River far below. In addition to getting an up-close view of the gorge, you will travel above flowing waterfalls, lush growths of wildflowers, and, if you're lucky, a few deer rambling along the deep gorge walls.

ATV RIDES AND TRAILS Close to 200 miles of the **Hatfield-McCoy ATV Trails** (1-800-592-2217; www.trailsheaven.com) are located in this area.

I have been on other sections, but not the 100-mile **Pinnacle Creek Trail System**, so I can't personally verify it, but according to several locals I spoke with, this is the most scenic section of the Hatfield-McCoy ATV Trails. Close to half of it is rated easiest, with about one-third rated more difficult, and 20 percent most difficult.

The major access for this section is the **Castle Rock Trailhead**, reached by driving 1 mile south of Pineville on WV 10, turning right on WV 16, going another 0.5 mile to make a left at the sign for the trail, and continuing another 2.8 miles to the trailhead.

The **Indian Ridge Trail System** is located near Ashland and provides access to the towns of Northfork and Keystone. With 63 miles of trail, 30 percent of it is rated easiest, 41 percent more difficult, 20 percent most difficult, and the remainder considered most difficult single-track or extreme difficulty. To reach the 2-acre parking area (with restrooms) at the trailhead, follow US 52 for more than 26 miles from Bluefield to Northfork, turn right onto WV 17, and continue for another 6.5 miles. Find more background information about the Hatfield-McCoy ATV Trails in "What's Where in West Virginia" at the front of this book. Remember, you must purchase a permit before making use of the trails.

Note: If plans fall into place as they should, some new sections of connector trails, enabling even longer rides, should be open by the time this book goes to press. Plans also call for a Hatfield-McCoys Trails ATV Trails visitor center to be constructed somewhere in Mercer County.

Happy Trails ATV Rentals (304-732-6096; 1-877-498-2887; www.happytrailsatv

.com; mailing address: P.O. Box 549, Pineville 24874), in Pineville, offers ATV rentals, shuttle service, and lodging facilities with a swimming pool and picnic area.

BICYCLING See the "If Y'all Are Real Men" and the "You Should Come Here" sidebars later in the chapter.

BIRDING Berwind Lake Wildlife Management Area (304-875-2577; www .berwindlake.com; mailing address: Rte. 16, Box 38, Warriormine 24894). From War follow WV 12/4 for 3.6 miles. Maybe it is because of its isolation from large population centers, or maybe because it is a green oasis in an area of active mountain top–removal mining, but Berwind Lake Wildlife Management Area (see *Green Space—Wildlife Management Area* for more background information) has become a haven for dozens of species of birds. Spotted sandpipers can be seen scampering along the lake shoreline, while wood ducks, pied-billed grebes, blue-winged teals, buffleheads, scaups, hooded mergansers, and ruddy ducks have been spotted resting on the waters of the lake. An abundance of warblers—such as worm-eating, yellow, Tennessee, black and white, and northern parula—stop by during spring migrations. Other species that have been observed in the spring include rose-breasted grosbeaks, yellow-breasted chats, and white-eyed and solitary vireos. Winter brings juncos, pine siskins, evening grosbeaks, and purple finches.

Also see *To See—Lakes*, the "You Should Come Here" sidebar later in the chapter, and *Green Space—Wildlife Refuge*.

BOWLING

Bluefield

☙ **Green Valley Bowling Center** (304-327-0481), Airport Rd. Magic scorers keep track of what is happening on the 24 lanes. There are also concessions, a billiard room, an indoor mini golf course, and a game room.

☙ **Mountaineer Family Entertainment** (304-325-7037), 3224 Cumberland Rd. Bowling alley and arcade games.

Welch

☙ **Landmark Lanes** (304-436-4097), 909 Stewart St.

FAMILY ACTIVITIES ☙ **Wildwater Express Waterslide** (304-466-1600), 206 Temple St., Hinton. Open Memorial Day to mid-Aug. A downtown water park that features wave pools and 267 feet of water slides.

FISHING The Bluestone Turnpike Trail runs for about 10 miles along the **Bluestone River** in the National Park Service's Bluestone National Scenic River between Pipestem Resort State Park and Bluestone State Park (see *Green Space— Parks*) to give you access to some good smallmouth bass fishing. The stream is shallow enough that you can wade it pretty much the entire length of the trail. For a full day's worth of hiking and fishing, take Pipestem's Aerial Tramway down to the river and have someone meet you at the other end in Bluestone State Park.

Appalachian Backcountry Expeditions (304-228-7048; www.appalachianback country.com; mailing address: P.O. Box 67, Daniels 25832), on WV 26 about 2 miles downstream from Sandstone Falls. In business for more than a decade, this outfitter provides half-day ($150), full-day ($295), and overnight ($750) float fishing trips on the New River and other nearby streams in search of smallmouth bass, muskie, and catfish. There are cabin accommodations at their base camp.

For other fishing opportunities, also see *To See—Lakes*, *To See—Waterfalls*, and *Green Space—Parks*.

GOLF

Anawalt
Blackwolf Links (304-383-4615; mailing address: 92 McDowell St., Welch 24801), at the intersection of WV 103 and WV 161 several miles south of Welch. The nine-hole course at Blackwolf Links just may be one of the lowest-cost games of golf you will ever play; a round and a cart will probably cost you less than $20. It's an interesting course on a bit of narrow, flat land with railroad tracks running through the middle of it. How's that for a hazard? Tee off at the wrong moment, and your ball may be taken out of state along with tons of coal.

Bluefield
Bluefield Elks Country Club (304-327-6511), 1501 Whitehorn St. The nine-hole semiprivate course was built in 1911.

Oceana
Clearfork Valley Golf Course (304-682-6209), on WV 971 several miles south of Oceana. The 18-hole, par 70, Bermuda grass course opened in 1958 and is 5,753 yards from the longest tees.

Princeton
Princeton Elks Golf Course (304-425-3273), Maple Acres Rd. Opened in 1921, the nine-hole, par 36 course is 3,036 yards.

Also see the "You Should Come Here" sidebar later in the chapter.

GOLF, MINIATURE See Glenwood Recreational Park under *Green Space—Parks* and the "You Should Come Here" sidebar later in the chapter.

HIKING Panther State Forest (304-938-2252; www.pantherstateforest.com; mailing address: P.O. Box 287, Panther 24872). From US 52 about 1 mile north of Iaegar, turn at the forest sign to Panther. At the Panther Post Office, turn left at the sign and follow the road approximately 3.5 miles to the state forest entrance. Established in the 1940s, Panther State Forest's charms lie in the fact that it is quite primitive. This is not a place where you will be mollycoddled with a luxury lodge to stay in or have warm showers in a campground's heated bathhouse. There is no lodge, and the small campground and picnic area have only pit toilets.

Looking at it another way, this lack of overblown, unnatural attractions and facilities keeps away the large numbers of people who need such things to have a good time, and it ensures that the 7,810-acre state forest remains a relatively quiet place for those who enjoy the outdoors for its simple pleasures. (There is a swimming pool that is a favorite of local children on hot summer days, however.)

A trail network, lined with an amazing abundance of wildflowers in the spring, will take you to a lookout tower on the state forest's highest point (2,065 feet) for a grandstand view into three states. Like national forests, state forests are managed under the multiple-use philosophy, which means that the extraction of timber and other natural resources, such as gas, are permitted. Much of your hiking will be on unsigned roads that were built for these activities, so you will have to pay attention to the map you can pick up at the state forest office. The hiking trails are signed but are not blazed.

For other hiking opportunities, also see *To See—Lakes*, *To See—Waterfalls*, *Fishing*, the "If Y'all Are Real Men" sidebar later in the chapter, and *Green Space—Parks*.

HORSEBACK RIDING See the "If Y'all Are Real Men" and "You Should Come Here" sidebars later in the chapter.

KAYAKING & CANOEING See *To See—Lakes* and *Green Space—Parks*.

SKATING Skatetown Green Valley (304-327-8175; www.skatetowngreen valley.com), Airport Rd., Bluefield. You can bring your own or rent skates to go around the rink.

SKIING, CROSS-COUNTRY See Twin Falls Resort State Park under *Green Space—Parks*.

SWIMMING See *To See—Lakes* and *Green Space—Parks*.

SWIMMIN' HOLE It may not have the prettiest of names, but locals know that **Suck Creek** has a nice swimmin' hole at the base of a small cascade close to where gravel WV 27/1 intersects WV 27 a little less than 5 miles south of Nimitz.

WALKING TOURS Most of the architecture in downtown Bluefield dates from the boom era of 1921–25, when the tonnage of coal shipped from the town increased dramatically. The **Downtown Bluefield Walking Tour** pamphlet (available from the Mercer County Convention and Visitors Bureau—see *Guidance*) provides information about eight of the most interesting buildings. Starting at the 1924 Classical Revival–style Old City Hall, you will be directed to the 1919 Peery Building, with a cornice of gargoyles, and the 1923 ashlar limestone West Virginia Hotel, which, at 12 stories, is still the tallest building in the city.

✳ Green Space
PARKS

Bramwell
Pinnacle Rock State Park (304-248-8565; www.pinnaclerockstatepark.com; mailing address: RR 1, P.O. Box 1,

> **ON AN EARLY-MORNING WALK**
> I came upon an eerie scene when I decided to take the Sled Run Trail on one of my visits to Panther State Forest. It was early morning, and the fog was still settled on the hillside when I came around the corner to the small family cemetery at the trail's end. I had been told the cemetery had not been used for decades, but there, barely discernible through the mist, was a large, plain pine casket sitting beside the gaping hole of an open grave.

Bramwell 24715), on US 52 a short distance east of Bramwell. It would be easy to miss this small state park as you go zipping by it on US 52. It is only about 400 acres in size, and the only part of it visible from the highway is a large stone picnic shelter constructed in the 1930s and a parking lot. Make a stop, get out of the car, and take the short trail to the top of the huge sandstone formation for which the park was named, and you will be treated to a grandstand view of mountain ridges along the Virginia–West Virginia border. Another pathway, the Homestead Trail, descends hundreds of feet in 2 miles to Jimmy Lewis Lake (also accessible from WV 52/6), where you can fish for largemouth bass, catfish, and bluegill.

IF Y'ALL ARE REAL MEN

"If y'all are real men, y'all will be willin' to take a dip in that creek when ya get to it." The ranger's challenge to a buddy and me from several Aprils ago came coursing back through my thoughts. Yet I held back, watching the water drop down a 10-foot cascade into what surely had to be an icy-cold pool.

I was on my way home and had pulled into Camp Creek State Forest and Park (304-425-9481; www.campcreekstatepark; mailing address: P.O. Box 119, Camp Creek 25280) for a few moments of escape from the knuckle-whitening truck traffic of I-77. I was tired of repeatedly passing the same semi on the uphills only to have it barrel toward me on the descents, its chrome grille molded into a sinister sneer and filling up every bit of space in my rearview mirror. My wife and I have dubbed this phenomenon "truggling," to indicate that you are struggling with, and unable to escape from, a truck.

Located off I-77 exit 20 between Beckley and Princeton, Camp Creek State Forest and Park encompasses close to 6,000 acres in Southern West Virginia. The park segment contains basketball, volleyball, and badminton courts; playgrounds; picnic areas; two separate campgrounds, and a third known as the Double C Horse and Rider Campground (sites are by reservation only) specifically for equestrians. The forest portion is managed for timber harvest and multiple-use recreation. Several trails and close to 60 miles of dirt roads (open to hikers, mountain bikers, and horseback riders) wander through the remote hillsides.

I drove aimlessly through the park—enjoying its greenness—and eventually found myself at a gated dirt road next to a waterfall on Marsh Fork. I hadn't thought about taking a swim when I pulled off the interstate, but now that the opportunity presented itself, the idea seemed irresistible.

Yet, I stared at the waterfall and its pool for a long time, reflecting on other late-April plunges I had taken into mountain streams. I stuck my arm in up to the elbow and recoiled at how chilly it was. This led to more minutes of hesitation—until the ranger's challenge came back to me.

So, okay, no more pussyfooting around. The cold be damned; today I'm going to be a real man!

Bluestone State Park (304-466-2805; www.bluestonesp.com), on WV 20, only a few miles south of Hinton and approximately 22 miles north of I-77 exit 14 north of Princeton. After 2,040-acre Bluestone Lake and Dam were completed under the direction of the U.S. Army Corps of Engineers in the 1940s, Bluestone State Park was established in the 1950s as a recreational site to draw tourism dollars into an economically depressed area. Located along the western arm of the lake, the 2,000-acre park became remarkably popular, and, to keep up with growing

Shoes, socks, and shirt came off, and I entered the water at a full body run. WHAM! The cold hit me like a fifth-grade bully's punch to the chest. I was immediately winded, and my heart skipped a couple of beats before racing and pounding against my rib cage as if I was on the last leg of a marathon. The sharp pain in my forehead was reminiscent of what happens from eating too much ice cream too fast.

I beat back the reaction to escape and took a few quick strokes to an overhanging rock. I crawled underneath it, watching the water of the falls crash down in front of me and sparkle in the sunlight of early afternoon. A few more strokes and I was out of the liquid ice and putting my clothes back on.

Hoping to warm up a bit, I began walking a dirt road, following the creek upstream into one of the prettiest Appalachian Mountain hollows around. Shiny, leathery-skinned rhododendron leaves filled in the spaces below the evergreen boughs of towering hemlocks; deer tracks and turkey scratchings spoke of abundant wildlife; and trout lily, bluets, and a few spring beauties added scatterings of color to the forest floor.

About 30 minutes into the walk, I spied a perfectly smooth rock in the stream, which tilted into the edge of a large pool. I just couldn't resist. The clothes came off again, and I spent the next quarter-hour acting like a river otter at play: slide down the rock, splash into the pool, swim around a few moments, climb back to the top of the rock, repeat, repeat, and repeat some more.

Camp Creek abounds with such swimming opportunities. Bearing right at the main park intersection leads to the primitive tent sites in the Blue Jay Campground. From there it is a 15-minute walk to a waterfall and pool on Deer Branch. A 1-mile round-trip jaunt on the park's principal hiking trail will deliver you to the area's most impressive cascade and adjoining swimmin' holes on Farley Branch. Just about every stream in the park and forest—and there is an abundance of them—has a spot big enough to immerse your body.

Maneuvering the car back onto the four-lane highway, I felt relaxed, rejuvenated, and ready to once again truggle with the tractor-trailers. Every interstate exit should have its own swimmin' hole.

THE HUGE SANDSTONE FORMATION FOR WHICH PINNACLE ROCK STATE PARK IS NAMED

numbers of visitors, amenities and attractions were added through the years.

Today, it offers two campgrounds with dump station and warm showers, a primitive campsite accessible only by boat, and modern cabins with heat that may be rented year-round. A variety of paddle and motorized boats are available for rent, or you may use park facilities to launch your own craft. Picnic areas, a swimming pool, children's playground, game courts, an activities building, and seasonal nature/recreation programs bring many families to the park for day, weekend, or weeklong visits. Other folks come for the warmwater fishing of muskellunge, channel catfish, crappie, and largemouth, smallmouth, and striped bass.

A hike in the park will not deliver you to any roaring waterfalls nor open up any grand vistas of the surrounding countryside. What it will do is provide you with the opportunity to escape the activity in the developed part of the park and meander through a quiet woodlands, surveying the different small parts of the forest that come together to make up the whole. Redbud, comfrey, and rattlesnake weed grow under the deciduous forest canopy of buckeye, locust, maple, poplar, and ash. Beside the small streams are sycamore and cardinal flower, while you may see cattails and hooded mergansers when walking beside the lake. In addition, there is the possibility of coming in close contact with a box turtle, deer, wild turkey, red fox, bobcat, mink, skunk, squirrel, chipmunk, or black bear.

Mullens

Twin Falls Resort State Park (304-294-4000; www.twinfallsresort.com; mailing address: P.O. Box 667, Mullens 25882). From the intersection of WV 54 and WV 97 in Maben, drive westward on WV 97 for 5.5 miles and turn left onto Bear Hole Rd. at the sign for the state park. Of the resort state parks in West Virginia, Twin Falls is one of the least developed, which is good. The golf courses in the other parks occupy so much land that they can be

BLUESTONE STATE PARK

intrusive, and their lodges and banquet facilities are so large that you may feel like you are attending a convention with hundreds of other people instead of visiting a quiet place in the outdoors. The lodge at Twin Falls, perched upon a knoll with pleasant views, has less than 50 rooms, and the 18-hole golf course is confined to the narrow Black Fork Valley.

However, the 3,776-acre park does not lack amenities. There is a full-service restaurant, small café open seasonally, gift shop, swimming pool, game courts, and picnic areas. The campground has electric hookups, laundry facilities, and hot showers, while fully equipped cottages have fireplaces and electric heat to make them available for rent every month of the year. The staff at the nature center conducts educational activities and special programs year-round, and a small museum and Pioneer Farm provide insight to the area's past. Also, located at 2,400 feet above sea level on the Allegheny Plateau, the park receives a significant amount of snow and is a favorite place for local cross-country skiers.

Hiking trails wind onto hillsides, into narrow hollows, past nice viewpoints, and next to the two waterfalls for which the park is named. Compared to some of the high, crashing, roaring waterfalls found in other parts of the state, the twin falls are rather meek and mild, but their settings are just as attractive and fit in well with the understated atmosphere and beauty of the park.

Princeton

Glenwood Recreational Park (304-425-1681), 1823 Glenwood Park Rd., on WV 20 about 5 miles west of Princeton. As a quick escape from busy downtown Princeton, the 325-acre park offers picnic facilities, walking and hiking trails, a miniature golf course, and paddleboat rentals so that you can glide along the surface of the 55-acre lake.

WILDLIFE MANAGEMENT AREA Berwind Lake Wildlife Management Area (304-875-2577; www.berwindlake.com; mailing address: Rte. 16, Box 38, Warriormine 24894). From War, follow WV 12/4 for 3.6 miles. The largest percentage of state wildlife management areas have very few amenities, but 18,000-acre Berwind has a small campground with electricity and water; a 20-acre lake for the fishing of largemouth bass, trout, and catfish; three trails that are officially designated and named; and a swimming pool usually open from Memorial Day to Labor Day. This is the southernmost piece of land owned by the state for outdoor recreation and is so isolated that you are almost guaranteed to be one of the few people who actually make use of it. (This situation changes during hunting season, a time when you should avoid the area anyway—unless, of course, you are a hunter.) It is also home to what seems to be more than its fair share of bird life (see *To Do—Birding*).

WILDLIFE REFUGE Three Rivers Avian Center (304-466-4683; www.tracwv .org; mailing address: HC 74, Box 279, Brooks 25951), Brooks Mountain Rd., Brooks. This is not a wildlife refuge in the usual sense that you would think of such a place as having acres and acres of protected land. Rather, the employees and volunteers provide veterinary and rehabilitative care for threatened wild birds. The center's primary contact with the public is through outreach programs presented for schools, civic groups, state parks, and colleges However, tours are usually given about once a month from May–Oct., or you can arrange a private tour for your

YOU SHOULD COME HERE

Pipestem Resort State Park (304-466-1800; www.pipestemresort.com; mailing address: P.O. Box 150, Pipestem 25979), located on WV 20 approximately 14 miles north of Princeton and 12 miles south of Hinton. Through the years, many people, including West Virginia attorney general Howard B. Lee and Hinton newspaper publisher John Faulconer, had stated that the beauty of the Bluestone River Canyon and the land around it was worthy of being preserved as a park. The reality would have to wait until the 1960s, when the federal government provided funds for economic development in West Virginia's pockets of low employment and income.

Dedicated on Memorial Day 1970, Pipestem Resort State Park, with rolling lands upon the Allegheny Plateau, steep canyon walls, and a narrow strip of bottomland beside the Bluestone River, has become a premier destination in Southern West Virginia. There is something here for just about everyone: two golf courses, driving range, and pro shop; miniature golf; tennis and basketball courts; swimming pools; a Mountain Artisans' Shop with resident artists and craftspeople present during the summer; two gift shops; and several restaurants and snack bars. The year-round campground has full hookups, heated bathhouses, laundry facilities, and a playground. Fully equipped rental cottages provide electric heat and fireplaces. Seven-story McKeever Lodge (open year-round) sits on the lip of the canyon (make sure to ask for a room with a canyon view when making reservations), while Mountain Creek Lodge (which has a dining room—see *Dining Out*), open

group if you call in advance. It's a good way to learn more about the nature of the state you are living in or visiting, and it gives you the chance to get up close with owls, eagles, hawks, and other winged beings.

✱ Lodging

RESORTS See the "You Should Come Here" sidebar earlier in the chapter.

MOTELS & HOTELS

Bluefield 24701
Quality Hotel & Conference Center (304-325-6170; www.bluefield hotelonthehill.com), 3350 Big Laurel Highway. Fitness room, outdoor pool, wireless Internet, restaurant, 24-hour business center, and a lounge with occasional live entertainment. $89–139.

Pineville 24874
Cowshed Motel (304-732-7000; www .cowshedmotel.com; mailing address: P.O. Box 639), 1.5 miles from Pineville on WV 10. Low-key, low-cost motel rooms that have become popular with Hatfield-McCoy ATV Trails riders. $46–51.

Princeton 24740
Comfort Inn (304-487-6101; www .comfortinn.com) 136 Ambrose Ln. A short distance from I-77, the inn offers free continental breakfast, Wi-Fi, and

seasonally and accessible by the Aerial Tramway, is located on the canyon floor, with guest rooms next to the river.

The park's amphitheater, which can accommodate 2,000 people, hosts movies, concerts, nature events, evening programs, and theatrical productions. A nature center is open year-round (with a varying schedule), overnight horseback camping is available seasonally, and trail and pony rides and hayrides are scheduled. Constructed Long Branch Lake tempts anglers to try their luck for trout and largemouth bass.

All of this development and activity makes it sound like there couldn't be much left of the natural world. Yet the park encompasses more than 4,000 acres, and numerous pathways wind into its more remote places. The more-than-1,000-foot difference in elevation—with deep, moist hollows and dry, rocky sandstone outcrops—provides many different environments for a diverse assemblage of plants and animals.

Almost 100 species of trees and shrubs grow above so many wildflowers that it takes an eight-page pamphlet just to list them. More than 160 kinds of birds have been recorded here, with wild turkeys, chickadees, titmice, and nuthatches living year-round, and warblers, vireos, and flycatchers flying south for the colder months. Among the many animals are salamanders, toads, frogs, turtles, snakes, bats, beavers, red foxes, weasels, otters, deer, bobcats, and black bears.

A network of trails, some open to mountain bikes, takes visitors through all of the regions of the park.

an outdoor hot tub. Convenient to the area's attractions. Rooms start at $85.

INNS

Langraff 24829
Elkhorn Inn (304-862-2031; 1-800-708-2040; www.elkhorninnwv.com), on US 52 west of Keystone. The Elkhorn Coal & Coke Company built the Elkhorn Inn as a miners' clubhouse in 1922. Since that time it has served as a rooming house for mining families, a state police barracks, and an office building. When Dan and Elisse Clark purchased it in 2002, it had more than 4 feet of mud on the first floor from a recent flood. In restoring it, they have uncovered turn-of-the-20th-century tile floors in the two-tub bathroom, transom windows, and the original hemlock banister. Elkhorn Creek (good trout fishing) is a scant few feet from the back of the inn, US 52 is a scant few feet from the front, and busy railroad tracks (a real attraction for rail fans) are a scant few feet away from the highway.

The inn has 13 guest rooms (some shared bath, some private bath) filled with 1930s period furnishings. Since there are few restaurants anywhere nearby, take Dan up on his offer to cook you a gourmet dinner. (He made a delicious Cornish hen the last time I visited.)

Dan and Elisse do a bit of everything

at the inn. There's a gift shop with handcrafted West Virginia items, a small museum of coal and locally relevant memorabilia, and a studio for visiting artists. Maybe the most interesting thing is the Elkhorn Theater, on the hill behind the inn. It is a copy of Shakespeare's Globe Theatre and is used for weddings, concerts, and other events. It's worth stopping by just to see it. $99–120.

Pipestem 25979
Nostalgia Inn (304-466-0470; www.nostalgiainn.com; mailing address: Rock Ridge Resort, Box 13). About 0.25 mile north of the Pipestem Resort State Park entrance on WV 20, turn right onto Indian Ridge Rd. and go 0.25 mile. After a 30-year career of teaching in Florida, native West Virginians Jim and Ellie White returned home to open the Nostalgia Inn. In a quiet wooded area, the inn is luxuriously rustic (or maybe it's rustically luxurious). Constructed of wood and with an imposing central stone fireplace, it has six suites that have access to the main part of the house, where you can play the baby grand piano, watch TV, browse through the array of nostalgic antique items, or relax on the veranda. $110–135.

NOSTALGIA INN

BED & BREAKFASTS
Athens 24712
 The View B and B (304-384-9754; 1-866-766-7690; www.theviewbb.com; mailing address: P.O. Box 876). Take I-77 to Athens exit 14, follow signs to WV 20, turn left, and go 1 mile. Although this B&B sits just a few yards from busy WV 20, the view from the back deck and breakfast area takes in the large, green expanse of the deep ravine leading to Athens Lake and open meadows of rolling farmland. Cheerful host Elizabeth Muldoon welcomes guests, including children, with afternoon refreshments (nice hot drinks for those arriving from Winterplace—see *To Do—Skiing* in the "Along the New and Gauley Rivers— Beckley, Fayetteville, and Summersville" chapter). Three rooms are available, each with private bath. Also a good choice for those visiting Concord University or taking in the sites of Pipestem Resort State Park. $79–99.

Bluefield 24701
Dian-Lee House (304-327-6370; 1-800-225-5982; www.dianlee.com), 2109 Jefferson St. The Dian-Lee House is, without a doubt, the most gracious and refined B&B in Bluefield. Owner Sandra Hancock has captured the essence and formality of a Southern mansion with rich furnishings— such as a baby grand piano, crystal chandelier, leather upholstery, and Italian veined marble mantel—and guest bedrooms that Scarlett O'Hara would have been accustomed to. Gardens and walkways surround the house, and a bright, sunlit veranda with a swing and handcrafted chairs provides a vantage point overlooking the quiet residential neighborhood. You also get to choose a breakfast from a menu that has included stuffed French toast, homemade waffles, and eggs Benedict. President Woodrow Wilson appeared to enjoy his

stay in this house in the early 1900s; it's a good bet you will, too. $85; corporate rates available.

Bramwell 24715
Sugar Hill Bed and Breakfast (304-248-8240; www.sugarhillbandb.com), 414 Durhing St. As befits a town that at one time had more millionaires per capita than any other place in the country, prepare to be pampered here. Gilded mirrors, Egyptian cotton linens, antiques-filled common areas and three suites, and views that overlook the town from the home's perch on the hill make for a relaxing and rejuvenating break from your daily life. $95; discounts for multinight stays.

CABINS & VACATION RENTALS

Bluefield 24701
Hidden Path Cabins (304-327-3429; www.hiddenpathcabins.com), on WV 7 between Bluefield and Princeton. Log cabins that can accommodate up to six people, with heating and air-conditioning and fully equipped kitchens, sit on eight acres with a pond. $89–99, two-night minimum.

Bramwell 24715
Main Street Suites (813-748-9403; 813-748-9402. www.bramwellwvvaca tionrentals.com), Each suite offers two bedrooms, one full bath, living and dining room, kitchen, and large foyer. Children and pets are welcome. $100.

Pineville 24874
Southern Trails ATVs Dawghouse (304-682-5447; www.southerntrails atvs.com). 62 Rush St. It is just a modestly furnished, small frame house in a residential neighborhood, but it's a real deal for large groups coming to the area to take a ride on the Hatfield-McCoy ATV Trails. There are two large bedrooms that can accommodate up to 11 people, two bathrooms, and a full kitchen. $125.

Sandstone 25985
🦐 🐾 🏚 **Richmond's Rustic Almost Heaven Vacation Hide-Away** (304-466-0874; 466-4150; mailing address: P.O. Box 2), on Falls View Lane, a short distance downstream from Sandstone Falls on WV 26 north of Hinton. Open Apr.–Nov. These vacation log cabins, which sit in a small residential area, are constructed from native trees logged from the property and are decorated so masterfully that you truly feel as if you are staying on a working mountain farm of the 1800s. Everything is furnished, including linens, all kitchen items (even some incidentals such as flour and cornmeal, coffee, and cooking oil), and wood-burning stoves. The cabins can accommodate four to eight people; for the most privacy, ask for the one that sits off by itself. $70–90.

For other cabin accommodations, also see *Green Space—Parks*.

CAMPGROUNDS

Ashland 24868
Ashland West Virginia ATV Resort (304-862-2322; 1-888-862-2322; www .atvresort.com; mailing address: HC 76, Box 681, Northfork 24868). From the intersection of US 52 and WV 17 in Northfork, follow WV 17 for 6.8 miles. Many campgrounds offer cabins and cottages, sites with all hookups for

RICHMOND'S RUSTIC ALMOST HEAVEN VACATION HIDE-AWAY

RVs, modern restrooms with hot showers, and free cable TV and wireless Internet throughout the campground. What sets this 1,800-acre facility apart is that much money has been lavished on making it attractive to the many ATV riders attracted to the area's Hatfield-McCoy ATV Trails, including ATV rentals with groomed trails adjacent to the campground; a quiet trail for dog walking, and a camp store.

Pineville 24874

Pinnacle Creek Village (304-732-8346; www.pinnaclecreekvillage.com; mailing address: P.O. Box 1379), on WV 10/WV 16 at the south end of Pineville. Open year-round. There is no doubt about it—this enclave exists to cater to ATV riders. It is located 2.5 miles from the Castle Rock Trailhead of the Pinnacle Creek Trail and has a campground, small lodge, convenience store, and café (see the Whistlestop Café under *Eating Out*). The campground, with sites for RVs, trailers, and tents situated close together, has modern restrooms with hot showers, and hookups for electricity, water, sewer, and cable TV.

For other camping options, also see *To See—Lakes*, the "If Y'all Are Real Men" sidebar earlier in the chapter, and *Green Space—Parks*.

✳ Where to Eat

DINING OUT

Bluefield

David's at the Club (304-327-9822), in the Elks Lodge golf course, 1501 Whitehorn St. Tasteful surroundings accompany meals of lamb chops, crab cakes, ahi tuna, and duckling, while windows overlook the golf course. Entrées $11.95–25.95.

Pipestem

Mountain Creek Dining Room at Pipestem Resort State Park (304-466-1800, ext. 387; www.pipestem resort.com), located on WV 20 approximately 14 miles north of Princeton and 12 miles south of Hinton. Reservations required. Most state park restaurants, whether in West Virginia or other states, have a reputation for serving food that is adequately good but certainly not outstanding. Mountain Creek Dining Room is the exception. Located in the park's lodge deep in Bluestone Canyon and reached only by the Aerial Tramway, its chef is a graduate of the Greenbrier Culinary Arts Center. It's a dining adventure, accompanied by an adventurous tram ride into the gorge. Entrées $17.95–26.95.

🍴 **The Oak Supper Club** (304-466-4800; www.oaksupperclub.com), on Indian Ridge Rd. about 20 miles north of Princeton via WV 20. Open for dinner in the summer Tue.–Sat., and in the winter Fri.–Sat.; closed Jan. Reservations recommended. For decades, The Oak Supper Club has been *the* place to dine in this area. Named for the 300-year-old oak tree in the front yard, it is in a serenely rustic setting where you can look out the windows and see horses grazing in the meadows.

On my last visit, my meal started with escargot in butter sauce, moved on to fruit-stuffed roast duckling, and finished with homemade blackberry ice cream (my notes from that evening read "very blackerryish and outrageously creamy"). As with many good restaurants, the menu changes every so often, but you will almost always be able to choose fresh West Virginia rainbow trout, lamb chops, barbecue ("smoked, oh so slowly over crackling hickory"), steak, and seafood. My commendations also go to the wait staff, who are attentive, friendly, and knowledgeable. Entrées $12.95–28.95.

EATING OUT

Bluefield

Valley Country Restaurant (304-325-8556), on Bluefield/Princeton Rd. in Green Valley between Bluefield and Princeton. Open daily for breakfast, lunch, and dinner. The name should give you a clue as to the type of meal you can obtain here—country dinners of fried chicken, ham, breaded flounder, baskets of shrimp, and bowls of brown beans served in a common-folks atmosphere with vinyl booths and chairs. My experiences here have never included lunch or dinner, but I can say that whenever I'm nearby, this is the place I come to for a hearty country breakfast at a reasonable price. The homemade desserts look tempting, but I have always been too full after my meal. Breakfast $2.50–7.25, dinner $5–9.

Hinton

Kirk's (304-466-4600), in the business area on WV 20 between the WV 3 and WV 20 bridges. Open for breakfast, lunch, and dinner daily. The big draw to Kirk's is the outdoor patio built directly over the New River. Good breakfasts and burgers; the most expensive dinner is usually less than $10.

Kimball

Ya' Sou Deli (304-585-7959; www.wv grocery.com), 138 Main St. Open for breakfast, lunch, and dinner; closed Sun. Authentic Greek dishes (pastitsio, spanakopita, dolmathes), with a few American items also on the menu. Entrées $3.49–6.95.

Mullens

Twin Falls Resort State Park (304-294-4000; www.twinfallsresort.com). From the intersection of WV 54 and WV 97 in Maben, drive westward on WV 97 for 5.5 miles and turn left onto Bear Hole Rd. at the sign for the state park. The park's restaurant has large windows overlooking the golf course and serves the expected pastas, turkey and dressing, chicken, and other country meals. Especially good is the rainbow trout with lemon and a special seasoning, and you better be really hungry if you order the ham and beans served with corn muffins and fried potatoes. If this doesn't give you enough carbohydrates, order the pecan cobbler with ice cream. Entrées $8.95–18.95.

Pineville

Whistlestop Café (304-732-8346; www.pinnaclecreekvillage.com), on WV 10/16 at the south end of Pineville. Open daily for breakfast, lunch, and dinner. The Whistlestop Café is inside a gas station/convenience store at the Pinnacle Creek Village campground (see *Lodging*), but it is large enough to accommodate close to two dozen diners. The offerings are what you would expect in a place like this—burgers, sandwiches, fried entrées, and salads. I come here for the low-cost breakfasts, such as two eggs, meat, and biscuit for less than $4.

Pipestem

Brandon's at Nostalgia Inn (304-466-9110; 1-877-890-9110; www.brandonsbbq.com). About 0.25 mile north of the Pipestem Resort State Park entrance on WV 20, turn right onto Indian Ridge Rd. and go 0.25 mile. Open for lunch and dinner, but hours and days change seasonally. Not long after Jim and Ellie White opened the Nostalgia Inn (see *Lodging*), their son, Brandon, constructed his adjacent restaurant. Set amid towering shade trees, the restaurant reminds me of a summer camp dining hall, except it is certainly a bit more luxurious, with a stone fireplace, open beams, hardwood floors, and lots of barn wood. If the weather is nice, dine on the screened porch. Brandon's specialty is barbecue in its many forms: ribs, pulled pork, chicken, shrimp, and sandwiches. Other entrées include steak and seafood. Entrées $9.95–18.95.

COFFEE BAR Sisters' Coffee House (304-487-8701), 1606 W. Main St., Princeton. Gwen Ramey spends the early-morning hours baking muffins, scones, and other goodies for her customers. Homemade soups, salads, and sandwiches are available later in the day. With somnolent couches serving as seating and works of local artists adorning the walls, the coffeehouse is dissimilar to any other business in downtown Princeton. Check the Web site for special dinners and for the timing of appearances of local and national music acts.

✳ Entertainment
FILM
Bluefield
Cinema 8 (304-325-6530), Mercer Mall. First-run movies.

Hinton
Ritz Theater (304-466-6684; www.ritzwv.com), 211 Ballengee St. Opened in 1929, and renovated in 2009, this downtown theater is still showing first-run movies.

Speedway
Pipestem Drive-In Theater (304-384-7382). Open Apr.–Oct. Of the few remaining state drive-in theaters, Pipestem is the youngest, having been built in 1972. Double features are shown every night between Memorial Day and Labor Day and on the weekends in the spring and fall.

Welch
Marquees Cinema McDowell Cinemas 3 (304-436-3456), 60 McDowell St. A modern downtown theater showing first-run movies.

MUSIC
Brushfork
♪ **Blue Top Bluegrass** (304-589-3457; www.bluetopbluegrass.com), on WV 123. Local, regional, and even national bluegrass musicians perform in a what was once a church. No smoking and no alcohol permitted makes this a good place to introduce the kids to this kind of music.

Glenwood
♪ **The Little Opry** (304-487-6075), at the intersection of Glenwood Park and Maple Acres roads. You might pass this place up because, quite frankly, it doesn't look all that inviting from the outside. Yet, this is a family-friendly business that does not serve any alcohol, but it does offer some of the best in local and regional traditional bluegrass and old-time music. Thursday nights are jam sessions, Friday has open mike, and Saturday nights are band concerts. No matter what is happening on the stage, the huge dance floor is filled with children, parents, and other adults flat-foot, line, or square dancing.

SPORTS
Bluefield
Bluefield Blue Jays (276-326-1326; www.bluefieldorioles.net), Bowen Field. Bowen Field, built in 1939, has been the home of the Bluefield Orioles, an Appalachian League affiliate of the Toronto Blue Jays, for decades. Throughout the regular baseball season you can watch minor-league players give their all in the hope of becoming called up to the majors. Those who have played here and did reach their dream include Cal Ripkin Jr., Boog Powell, and Don Baylor.

Princeton
PrincetonRays (304-487-2000; http://web.minorleaguebaseball.com/),

Hunnicutt Field. At a time when major U.S. cities are having a hard time attracting and keeping professional baseball teams, it is amazing that there are two in this area—and located just a few miles apart. And how's this for a rivalry? The Princeton Rays and the Bluefield Orioles are in the same league and play each other a number of times throughout the season.

THEATER

Bluefield

Bluefield Area Arts Center (304-325-8000; www.bluefieldareaarts center.org), 500 Bland St. Housed within the 1924 three-story Classical Revival Old City Hall, the Bluefield Arts Center has ever-changing exhibits and the Summit Theatre has a number of plays each year.

Princeton

Chuck Mathena Center (304-425-5128; 1-877-425-5128; www.chuck mathenacenter.org), 2 Stafford Commons. A variety of local, regional, and national cultural, educational, and theatrical events are presented in the impressive venue with good seating and great acoustics.

Welch

Terror of the Tug at the McArts Amphitheatre (304-585-7107; www .mcartswv.org), Mountain View High School, off US 52 about halfway between Kimball and Welch. Adults $10, children under 12 years of age $6. Usually presented in July and/or August. *Terror of the Tug* was written by West Virginian Jean Battlo and is a depiction of events in the state's "coal-mining wars" of the early 1900s. By concentrating on the murders of Sid Hatfield and Ed Chambers outside the McDowell County Courthouse in Welch, the play is an excellent introduction to events that continue to shape life in Southern West Virginia.

ANTIQUES

Bluefield

Landmark Antique Mall (304-327-9686), 200 Federal St. A large selection of clocks, dolls, coins, furniture, toys, and Norfolk and Western Railroad memorabilia from a number of dealers.

Princeton

Four Seasons Antiques and Appraisals (304-0898-8369), Harmon Branch Rd. A 10,000-square-foot, multidealer mall, with certified appraisal services available.

ART GALLERY RiffRaff Arts Collective (304-425-6425; www.theriff raff.net), 869 Mercer St. Princeton. This collective of artists, craftspersons, and musicians is spread across several storefronts and upstairs studios in the downtown area. There is an ever-changing array of artwork in the gallery and at least one concert a week (but many, many impromptu performances). Stop by to see what is happening.

CRAFTS Wakerobin Gallery (304-466-2227, mailing address: HC 65, Box 112-C, Forest Hill 24935), at the intersection of WV 12 and Seminole Rd., Forest Hill. Open Mon.–Tue. and Thurs.–Sat. Along with the work of other artists and craftspersons, blind potter Marcia Springston displays and sells her hand-thrown wares.

FARMERS' MARKETS

Princeton

From June through Oct., more than a dozen vendors bring produce and other items to the **Mercer County Tailgate Produce Market** (304-487-1405) on South Second St. Open on Wed. and Sat. 7–1.

Princeton

The Bronze Look (304-425-5005; www.thebronzelook.com), 311 Mercer St. A gallery with a little bit of everything including items from some of West Virginia's finest art glass manufacturers, mass-produced collectibles, coins, and works by regional artists.

Elizabeth's Boutique (304-425-0425), 901 Mercer St. Elizabeth's has small selections of women's fine dresses and apparel, picture frames, an assortment of bric-a-brac, and items for ladies of the Red Hat Society.

✳ Special Events

May: **Bramwell Mansion & Historic Homes Tour** (304-248-8381), Bramwell. **Bluefield Mountain Festival** (304-327-7148; www.bluefield chamber.com), Bluefield. Carnival, helicopter rides, and fun and games.

July: **John Henry Days** , Talcott. Inner-tube races, live entertainment at the Great Bend Tunnel, food and crafts, and John Henry memorabilia.

July/August: **West Virginia Water Festival** (304-466-53422), Hinton.

Bass fishing tournament and the crowning of Miss Mermaid.

September: **Culturefest** (304-425-6425; www.culturefestwv.com), Appalachian South Folklife Center, Pipestem. Music acts and dance performances from around the world, ethnic food and art, educational demonstrations, and workshops. On-site camping. **Princeton Autumn Fest** (304-487-1502), Princeton. Pumpkin painting, food and crafts, apple butter making, and music.

October: **Italian Heritage Festival** (304-589-3317; www.sonsofitalywv .com), Bluefield Auditorium, Bluefield. Dinner, dance, and vendors. **Railroad Days** (304-466-5420), Hinton. A scenic train ride originates in Huntington, West Virginia, and passengers disembark in Hinton, where the streets are lined with homemade-crafts and food vendors.

November: **Pocahontas NRHS Train Show** (304-431-2593), 1780 Stadium Sr., Bluefield. Model trains and more.

December: **Bramwell Mansion & Historic Homes Tour** (304-248-8381), Bramwell.

ALONG THE NEW AND GAULEY RIVERS— BECKLEY, FAYETTEVILLE, AND SUMMERSVILLE

In the not-too-distant past, West Virginia's New River Gorge was known for two things: the spectacular view from Hawk's Nest State Park and the interminably twisting two-lane mountain roads that had to be negotiated to reach it. Woe unto you if you got behind a coal truck crawling uphill. Terror unto you if one came barreling downhill, inches from your back bumper.

The views and the trucks are still around, but construction of four-lane US 19 and I-77/I-64, and the establishment of the New River Gorge National River, changed the area's image. The gorge is now known for great rock climbing, BASE jumping from the world's second-longest arch bridge (on the third Saturday in October), and arguably the country's best whitewater rafting on the New and Gauley rivers.

Those who want their experiences on the water to include motorized movement of some kind or another head upstream to the state's largest body of water, Summersville Lake. High cliffs and boulders tower above the water, creating some of the country's most interesting settings for rock climbing. (You can only reach these spots by boat.)

With the New River Gorge National River, Gauley River National Recreation Area, Monongahela National Forest, state parks, wildlife management areas, and county parks, there are more than 150,000 acres of public land in this area on which to hike, bike, canoe, kayak, climb, fish, and camp.

Beckley, the area's largest city, is located on a high plateau 2,400 feet above sea level. Like other places in the state, coal is still important, but it does not play as big a role as it once did. Yet, its location at the intersection of I-77/I-64 with US 19 has helped the city hold on to some of its economic vitality. Tamarack, the state-operated arts-and-crafts center, attracts tens of thousands of visitors annually, while the Beckley Exhibition Coal Mine takes them underground to witness a part of history.

Sitting almost on the lip of the New River Gorge, tiny Fayetteville has become the hub of whitewater rafting, kayaking, and rock climbing in West Virginia. Once

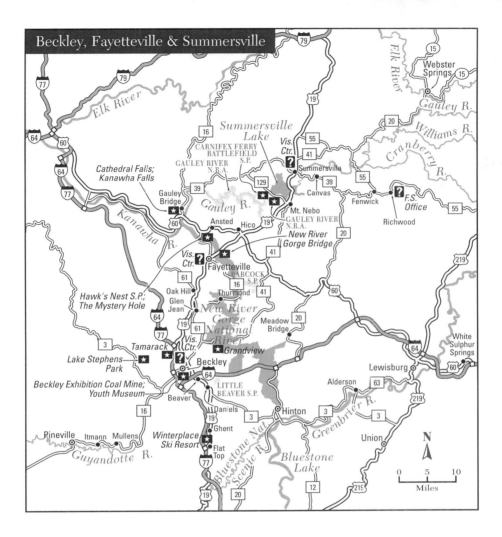

a sleepy town often bypassed by travelers, it is now what one person described as "the Boulder, Colorado, of the East." Although that is bit of hyperbole, as the town is nowhere as big as Boulder, it is certainly teeming with outdoor types who frequent the paddling, hiking, climbing, and bicycling outfitters. Restaurants that serve a fare not seen here several decades ago, such as gourmet pizzas, Cajun dinners, specialty coffees, and quesadillas and panini, are thriving.

Summersville was established around 1820 and remained an out-of-the-way town until the construction of Summersville Lake and four-lane US 19. The lake is a major outdoor-recreation attraction, and the highway, which connects I-79 with I-77/I-64, is a popular shortcut for north–south travelers. All of this traffic has generated miles of commercial development along the highway. (*Insider's tip*: Make sure you pay strict heed to the speed limits along US 19 in and around Summersville; it is heavily patrolled.)

> **A LITTLE-KNOWN FACT**
> Thomas Batts and Robert Fallam were the first white men to pass through the New River Gorge when they reached Kanawha Falls in 1671.

COMMUNITIES Oak Hill has a couple of blocks of shops in its downtown district that are worth investigating.

Located at the confluence of the North and South forks of the Cherry River, **Richwood** was founded as a sawmill town to take advantage of the area's abundant timber. It was booming in the early part of the 20th century with the world's largest clothespin factory and largest sole-leather tannery. The population hit a high of more than 7,000, but as hard times hit, it dwindled to its present 2,400. Services and businesses are now few and far between, but Richwood is the western gateway to the outdoor playground of the Monongahela National Forest's Cranberry Backcountry and Wilderness, and the city fathers are working hard to let the rest of the world know that.

Thurmond is located within a few feet of the New River, deep inside the gorge. During the coal boom days, the town boasted opera houses, hotels, saloons, and more than 400 residents. Today, it only has a population of fewer than 10 and a park service visitor center inside a restored train depot. (The movie *Matewan* was filmed here. Check out the video—it's an excellent portrayal of miners' struggles in the early 1900s.)

GUIDANCE A visitor center on US 19, the home of the **Fayette County Chamber of Commerce and New River Convention and Visitors Bureau** (304-465-5617; 1-800-927-0263; www.newrivergorgecvb.com; mailing address: 310 Oyler Ave., Oak Hill 25901), is open daily and is a font of information about what to see, do, eat, and buy in and around the New River area.

Located downtown, the **Fayetteville Historic Landmark Commission and Convention & Visitors Bureau** (304-574-1500; 1-888-574-1500), 306 North Court St., Fayetteville 25840, will answer questions you may have about the town and surrounding area.

Personnel in the **Gauley Ranger District** office (304-846-2695), 932 North Fork Cherry Rd., Richwood 26261, can help you with information about the portion of the Monongahela National Forest that is under their jurisdiction.

The **New River Gorge National River** (www.nps.gov/neri) has a number of places you may obtain information: **The Canyon Rim Visitor Center** (304-574-2115), open year-round, is on US 19 only 2 miles north of Fayetteville and has exhibits, auditorium programs, and trails leading to overlooks of the New River Gorge Bridge. The visitor center at **Grandview** (304-763-3715) is open seasonally and may be reached from I-64 exit 129. On WV 25 in **Thurmond**, the park service has a visitor center (304-465-8550) that is open seasonally in the restored train depot. Visitor services are limited at the **Park Headquarters** (304-465-0508) in Glen Jean, but the lobby has some brochures and maps; personnel will try to help as time permits.

The **Southern West Virginia Convention & Visitors Bureau** (304-252-2244; 1-800-847-4898; www.visitwv.com), 1406 Harper Rd., Beckley 25801, is an umbrella organization that provides information for the entire Southern West Virginia region. They also maintain a small visitor center in Tamarack (see *Selective Shopping*) off I-77/I-64 exits 45 and 44.

The **Summersville Convention and Visitors Bureau** (304-872-3722; 1-866-716-0448; www.summersvillecvb.com) is located at 3 Amory Way, Summersville 26651.

GETTING THERE *By air*: The **Raleigh County Memorial Airport** (304-255-0476; www.flybeckley.com) in Beckley has commuter flights connecting to other airports.

By bus: **Greyhound** (1-800-231-2222; www.greyhound.com) has a terminal at 105 Third Ave. in Beckley.

By car: **US 19** is a north–south shortcut that connects I-79 with **I-77** and **I-64**. The latter two interstates share the same route from Charleston to Beckley, where they split, with I-64 running in an east–west direction toward Lewisburg and I-77 heading in a north–south direction to Bluefield. From Charleston to Bluefield, the highway is the **West Virginia Turnpike**, with three tollbooths along its full length.

Note: A major four-lane highway is currently being constructed that will run southward from Beckley through the Southern West Virginia area and into Virginia.

By rail: An **AMTRAK** (1-800-872-7245; www.amtrak.com) train, *The Cardinal*, is an east–west train that makes a stop in Prince (a few miles northeast of Beckley) three times a week. The small, historic town of Thurmond is also on this route as a flag stop, which means the train will only stop on a signal or with advance notice to the conductor.

GETTING AROUND *By bus*: The **Mountain Transit Authority** (304-872-5872; 1-877-712-9432; www.mtawv.com) has scheduled routes that have stops in the more northern portion of this area, including Summersville, Richwood, Gauley Bridge, Fayetteville, Oak Hill, and many points in between.

By taxi: **City Cab** (304-469-2100) operates in Oak Hill and vicinity.

MEDICAL EMERGENCIES

Beckley
Beckley Appalachian Regional Hospital (304-255-3000; www.arh.org/beckley), 306 Stanaford Rd.

Raleigh General Hospital (304-256-4100; www.raleighgeneral.com), 1710 Harper Rd.

Oak Hill
Plateau Medical Center (304-469-8600; www.plateaumedicalcenter.com), 430 Main St.

Richwood
Richwood Area Community Hospital (304-846-2573), 75 Avenue B Riverside Addition.

Summersville
Summersville Memorial Hospital (304-872-2891; www.summersvillememorial .org), 400 Fairview Heights Rd.

DRIVING TOURS, SCENIC & HISTORIC US 60 has been designated the **Midland Trail National Scenic Byway** (see *To See—Driving* Tours, Scenic & Historic in the "Old Towns, Surviving and Alive—Lewisburg, White Sulphur Springs, and Union" chapter for background information). The twisting, two-lane road (an old local saying states that you can see your taillights in your rearview mirror as you go around some of the curves) enters this area by crossing over 3,170-foot Sewell Mountain and going past the turnoff to Babcock State Park. If you have the time and are feeling a bit adventurous, take extremely scenic WV 82 to Winona and follow it all of the way into the New River Gorge.

US 60 continues westward, crossing four-lane US 19 and climbing to the small mountain town of Ansted and Hawks Nest State Park. Beyond the park, there are some spectacular views of the gorge, but look at them only if you are a passenger; the driver really needs to keep his eyes on the winding highway as it descends past Cathedral Falls and into the small town of Gauley Bridge, where the Gauley and New rivers meet to form the Kanawha River. (This reminds me of a bad joke from my childhood: Do you know how the New and Gauley rivers got their names? Well, many years ago some Native Americans were paddling up the Kanawha River when they came to a confluence, and one of them shouted out, "Golly, a new river!")

Running just a few hundred yards from the Kanawha River, the scenic byway passes Kanawha Falls and three other cascades dropping down side streams before it leaves this area near the town of Boomer.

The **Coal Heritage Trail National Scenic Byway** (304-256-6941; www.coal heritage.org) is one of the best introductions to the industry that has shaped and affected nearly every aspect of life in West Virginia. Starting on US 60 in Ansted, it turns south on US 19 to pass through Fayetteville and Beckley before continuing along two-lane WV 16 through Pineville and Welch. It then heads eastward on two-lane US 52 to end in Bluefield. More background information about it may be found in *To See—Driving Tours, Scenic & Historic* in the "The Southern Border—Bluefield, Hinton, Pineville, Princeton, and Welch" chapter.

The **Paint Bank Scenic Trail** (www.paintcreekscenictrail.com: P. O. Box 402, Pax 25904). Heading northward from Tamarack (see "The Best of West Virginia" sidebar later in the chapter) in Beckley, the scenic byway follows Dry Hill, Sweenysburg, and Paint Bank roads to Hansford, a few miles east of Charleston. As an alternative, albeit slower, drive between the two cities, the route passes through an area more often associated with coal mining than tourism, presenting visitors with a glimpse into the heritage of coal, but maybe more important, opening up scenic wonders, such as Westerly Falls and Plum Orchard Lake. There is a surprising diversity of hiking, biking, fishing, kayaking, and camping along the way.

GUIDED TOUR ✐ ♿ ✪ **The Beckley Exhibition Coal Mine** (304-256-1747; www.beckleymine.com; mailing address: P.O. Box 2514, Beckley 25802). Take I-77/I-64 exit 44, turn east on Harper Rd. (WV 3), go 1.5 miles, turn left onto Ewart Ave., and continue an additional mile. Open daily Apr. 1–Nov. 1. Adults $20, seniors $15, children $12. If you have never been in a coal mine, here is your chance to go underground. Authentic "man cars" rumble 1,500 feet into a 36-inch-seam mine that was active until the mid-1950s. Guides, who are former miners, narrate the trip, which takes you from the earliest days of mining before mechanization to some of the first machines that made extracting the coal a somewhat easier task.

Every citizen of the state, along with the most casual of visitors, should take this tour. Coal is such an integral part of West Virginia, yet so few of us really understand how, for generations, it has provided the fuel for much of the world's power generators and industrial plants. On this trip you will see the rock duster used to keep coal dust from exploding deep in the mine, how roof bolts are put in to prevent cave-ins, and learn how pumps were used to pull water out of the mine to keep it from flooding (yet many times miners worked knee-deep in the black liquid). While an entertaining trip, this is not an amusement-park ride, but one that will truly educate. My only regret is that you are not permitted to get out of the car and crawl into the 18-inch-high old drift mine shaft that miners used to work in for hours. Can you imagine lying on your stomach using a pick and shovel to extract tons of coal each day?

Included in the price of admission is a tour of reconstructed buildings that provide a glimpse into what life was like in a coal camp of the early 1900s. Interpreters stationed in the Pemberton Coal Camp Church, Helen Coal Camp School, a coal company house, and other buildings provide additional background information.

RULES OF CONDUCT FOR TEACHERS (1915)
(Courtesy of Helen Coal Camp School)

You will not marry during the term of your contract.
You are not to keep company with men.
You must be home between the hours of 8 PM and 6 AM unless attending a school function.
You may not loiter downtown in ice-cream stores.
You may not travel beyond the city limits unless you have permission of the chairman of the board.
You may not ride in a carriage or automobile with any man unless he is your father or brother.
You may not smoke cigarettes.
You may not dress in bright colors.
You may under no circumstances dye your hair.
You must wear at least two petticoats.
Your dresses must not be any shorter than 2 inches above the ankle.

To keep the schoolroom neat and clean you must:
• Sweep the floor at least once a day.
• Scrub the floor at least once a week with hot, soapy water.
• Clean the blackboards at least once a day.
• Start the fire at 7 AM so the room will be warm at 8 AM.

The gift shop, where you purchase your ticket, has a small coal-mining museum with old equipment and some very enlightening photographs. Adjacent is a small RV camp with power, water, and sewage.

Next door to all of this are the Youth Museum of Southern West Virginia with its Mountain Homestead (see *Museums*) and the New River City Park (see *To Do— Swimming*).

HISTORIC SITE See Carnifex Ferry Battlefield State Park under *Green Space— Parks*.

LAKE With a surface area of 2,790 acres, **Summersville Lake** (304-872-3412; www.lrh.usace.army.mil; mailing address: Rte. 2, Box 470, Summerville 26651) is the state's largest body of water. Constructed by the U.S. Army Corps of Engineers in 1966 as a flood-control project, it has become a major recreation destination. Marinas rent boats and other watercraft, campgrounds are within site of the lake, trails wander into the woods, public beaches attract swimmers, and the exceptional clarity of the water enables an enjoyable level of scuba diving not often found in the state. Anglers may spend days casting on the lake for smallmouth and large-mouth bass, crappie, and bluegill, while rock climbers can scramble onto the miles of cliffs surrounding the lake. A pullout on WV 129 provides a panoramic view of the lake, while the

> **GAD DAM?**
> It is a tradition for the U.S. Army Corps of Engineers to name a dam after the town that is closest to it. In this case, the closest town (once located near the present site of the Long Point Marina) was Gad. The traditional way of naming the dam was considered for just a short while before administrators decided it would be better to call it the Summersville Dam.

SUMMERSVILLE LAKE

nearby visitor center has displays and information about the dam and recreational opportunities.

MUSEUMS

Ansted
⚓ **Contentment** (304-658-4809; 304-658-5695), on US 60 in Ansted. Open Tue.–Sat. from June through Aug. Donations accepted. Docents are on hand to answer questions you may have about Contentment, which was built in 1830 and became the post-war home of Confederate Col. George W. Imboden. Very little has changed since that time. The door panels and rolled-glass windowpanes are original, as are the three walnut mantels. Antiques from the period are in each room. Take a close look at the 1870s quilt—no two stitches are alike. Also on the grounds are the Fayette County Historical Society Museum and a one-room schoolhouse.

Beckley
Raleigh County "All Wars" Museum (304-253-1775), 1557 Harper Rd. Open Wed. and Fri.–Sun. from Apr. through Oct. Very small admission fee. Originally started by eight local veterans, the museum is a tribute to all veterans and is a repository for donated items and memorabilia.

⚓ **Wildwood House Museum** (304-252-3730), 121 Laurel Terrace. Open Sat. and Sun. from May through Sept. Small admission fee. Built in the 1830s, Wildwood was the home of the town's founder, Gen. Alfred Beckley. On the National Register of Historic Places, the restored home is filled with period antiques, many of them once owned by the Beckley family.

✍ **Youth Museum of Southern West Virginia and the Mountain Homestead** (304-252-3730; www.beckleymine.com; mailing address: P.O. Box 2514, Beckley 25802). Take I-77/I-64 exit 44, turn east on Harper Rd. (WV 3), go 1.5 miles, turn left onto Ewart Ave., and continue an additional mile. Open daily Apr. 1–Nov. 1; Tue.–Sat. the rest of the year. Small admission fee, or included in the ticket price for the adjacent Beckley Exhibition Coal Mine (see To See—Guided Tour). The small museum entertains the kids as much as it educates them with hands-on exhibits about nature, history, art, and culture. The Mountain Homestead is a re-created Appalachian settlement of the 1800s, with interpreters providing information on the lifestyle of the times. It's small compared to other similar places, but that just means you can learn and see more in a shorter amount of time.

Also see Hawks Nest State Park under *Green Space—Parks*.

SCENIC VIEWS See *To See—Lake*, and Hawks Nest State Park under *Green Space—Parks*.

WATERFALLS Because it tumbles down a narrow grotto about 100 feet from the highway, it would be easy to miss **Cathedral Falls** as you go zipping by it on US 60 about a mile east of the bridge over the Gauley River. Make sure you don't; this is one of the state's prettiest falls. It tumbles 60 feet down rock walls and into a small roadside park with picnic tables and a small wooden bridge over the stream. Kudos to those responsible for creating and maintaining the little park. For decades this spot was so desecrated with trash and broken beer bottles that you

CATHEDRAL FALLS

didn't want to stop. Now it is a jewel of a place and well worth a few minutes of your travel time.

The same praise goes for the creation of the public fishing area 2 miles downstream at **Kanawha Falls**. It, too, was a dank, muddy trash pit for many decades. Today, it has a designated parking area, picnic tables, and a manicured lawn. Kanawha Falls are not very high, but they stretch across the length of the river, which is more than 100 yards wide at this point.

ZOO See Good Evening Ranch under *Lodging*.

OTHER SITES

Ansted

 🦆 🌱 **The Mystery Hole** (304-658-9101; www.mysteryhole.com; mailing address: HC 65, Box 86, Ansted 25812), on US 60 a short distance east of Hawks Nest State Park (see *Green Space—Parks*). Open days and hours change with the season, but usually open daily, except Tue. during the summer months. Small admission fee. The sign says, WOW! SEE THE UNBELIEVABLE MYSTERY HOLE, and for more than three decades travelers have been doing just that and experiencing what has to be the ultimate kitschy roadside attraction. A VW Beetle is wrecked into the side of the maladroitly painted Quonset hut that you enter to pay the small admission fee. Inside is a gift shop straight out of the 1950s, with souvenirs and kids' toys that are sure to bring back memories of childhood.

The entertainment begins as you descend stairs into a narrow hallway lined by funhouse mirrors that make you appear skinny, tall, fat, or short. Step into the slanted room of The Mystery Hole, and everything you were taught about gravity becomes untrue. Water and balls run uphill, a chair that you can sit in is on the wall instead of the floor, and when you think you are standing straight up it looks as if you are leaning sideways. Is it truly nature gone mad, or are you the victim of a grand deception? Who cares? It's a hoot—and a lot of fun.

THE MYSTERY HOLE

Fayetteville

Built in 1977, the **New River Gorge Bridge** is the Western Hemisphere's longest steel arch span bridge. At a height of 876 feet, it carries US 19 across the deep chasm and has become such an icon that it is featured on the West Virginia commemorative U.S. quarter. Sadly, you can't really experience its architectural and scenic beauty as you drive across it, but a couple of short trails close to the New River Gorge National River Canyon Rim Visitor Center (see *Guidance*) take you to some good vantage points. You can walk across it once a year on Bridge Day (see the "New River Gorge Bridge Day" sidebar later in the chapter).

For an exciting, twisting, and winding driving trip into the gorge directly below the bridge, follow Fayette Station Rd. (WV 82) from the visitor center. As you drive along the narrow route and go over the small bridge across the New River, keep in mind that this was the main thoroughfare before the construction of the gorge bridge. The park service has placed a number of interpretive signs along the way, and a driving-tour brochure is available from the Canyon Rim Visitor Center (see *Guidance*).

✳ To Do

BICYCLING

Beckley

& Beckley's **Lewis McMannus Memorial Honor Rail Trail** follows the former route of a CSX railroad line for 3.6 miles from Mabscott to the Cranberry Creek Shopping Area. At 12 feet across, it is one of the widest paved rail trails I've ever seen. It is also definitely an urban route, using culverts to go under the four-lane highways that it is often located next to, and passing through warehouse and business districts. Yet, it also winds into quiet residential areas, with plenty of shade trees, songbirds, and wildflowers. A number of access points are on WV 16 (Robert C. Byrd Dr.) and US 19 (Eisenhower Dr.).

Fayetteville

New River Bike & Touring Company (304-574-2453; 1-866-301-2453; www .newriverbikes.com), 103 Keller Ave. When you read that a particular whitewater rafting company offers guided mountain bike trips, it is a good bet that what they are really doing is hooking you up with these folks. All of their guides are certified in first aid and CPR, and they will take you on half- or full-day trips, or customize an outing based on your time and skill level. Tours are offered during the usual tourist months, but the shop is open year-round to rent, sell, or repair bikes.

Richwood

Depending on which source you consult, the **Cranberry/Tri-Rivers Trail** is anywhere from 13.5 miles to 16 miles long. Whatever the distance, it is a superb rail trail that follows the twisting courses of the Gauley and Cherry rivers and crosses the Cranberry River on a railroad trestle along the western edge of the Monongahela National Forest. Near the northern end, it passes through the curving 640-foot Sarah's Tunnel, which local lore says is haunted by a woman who was murdered a short distance downstream. The southern trailhead is at the intersection of Oakford and Railroad avenues in Richwood, but many people start at the Holcomb Trailhead (about 6 miles west of Richwood on WV 55/WV 20) to miss riding or hiking through town. Currently, there is no road access to the northern terminus of the trail.

Summersville/MuddletyWalking/Bicycle Trail. This pathway is a nice gift the local citizens have given to themselves to enhance the quality of their lives and the experiences of visitors. It is hard to say how long it is, as portions of it were still being developed as I wrote this, but there will be at least 3 miles or more that parallel the tremendously scenic Muddlety Creek as it flows from WV 41 a short distance north of Summersville to empty into Summersville Lake close to WV 39. The well-designed and easy-to-follow pathway goes through a mature forest, over attractive bridges, and by several series of small cascades, swimmin' holes, picnic areas, and a number of historic sites, including the Campbell Electric Company and the Starbuck Mill, both of which harnessed the movement of the creek for power. As one of the area's nicest walking/biking trails, this is a great resource and one that I highly recommend you make use of. The easiest access is off US 19 on West Webster Rd., which delivers you to the Jones Hole Trailhead.

Also see *Hiking*, Four Seasons Outfitter under *Outdoors Outfitters*, and Lake Stephens Park under *Green Space—Parks*.

BIRDING The **New River Birding & Nature Festival** (www.birding-wv.com) is held each spring in April and/or May in and around the New River Gorge National River. This component of the national park system has been recognized as a crucial stopover habitat for species such as golden-winged, blue-winged, and Swainson's warblers, as well as the scarlet tanager. The weeklong event features wildflower walks, bird-watching trips, and lectures and classes from noted and well-known speakers.

If you are not able to attend the festival, the organizers have identified several areas that are especially good for birding. Take **Fayette Station Rd.** (WV 82), which drops to the river from near the New River Gorge National River Canyon Rim Visitor Center (see *Guidance*), and you may see a wood thrush, kingfisher, indigo bunting, or Cerulean, worm-eating, yellow-throated, or yellow warbler. Golden-winged, black-throated blue, Cape May, and Carolina warblers have been seen in **Babcock State Park** (see *Green Space—Parks*). The area around Kanawha Falls (see *To See—Waterfalls*) on US 60 near Gauley Bridge attracts great blue herons, American kestrels, killdeer, scaups, and hooded mergansers.

The town of **Ansted** is a designated bird sanctuary where you may spot a ruby-throated hummingbird, yellow-billed cuckoo, or northern parula. The hiking trails at **Grandview** may yield a rose-breasted grosbeak, blue-headed vireo, and yellow-billed cuckoo, along with yellow-throated, black-throated green, and Blackburnian warblers.

BOAT EXCURSIONS ✪ **New River Jet Boats** (304-479-2525; www.newriverjet boats.com), in Hawks Nest State Park (see *Green Space—Parks*), Ansted. Open daily (except Wed.) from Memorial Day to Labor Day and in Oct.; Sat. and Sun. in May and Sept. Adults $25; seniors $23; children (ages 5–16) $10. All tickets include a round-trip ride on the state park's aerial tram (the only easy way to reach the jet boats). This is the ride to opt for if you want to get close to the New River, but the idea of whitewater rafting is more of an adrenaline rush than you wish to experience. The covered, 12-seat *Miss M. Rocks* takes passengers 3 miles upstream for one of the area's best views of the New River Gorge Bridge. Along the way, you will pass by some cabins that amazingly cling to the bank just a few feet above the water. Some are in well-kept condition, others much less so, but all were here before the stream became a part of the New River Gorge National River. (I hope you get the same captain I did—he was a crusty old river man who fit his role perfectly and was full of some great tales concerning the area.)

BOAT RENTALS West Virginia Water Sports (304-872-6907; www.wvweb sites.com/West-Virginia-Watersports), Salmon Run Rd., Summersville. Pontoon boat rentals from mid-May to mid-Sept.

BOWLING ♂ **Leisure Lanes** (304-253-7328; www.leisurelaneswv.com), 700 Johnstown Rd., Beckley. There are 24 lanes that the management sometimes bathes in lights, music, and fog for what they call "futuristic bowling."

CLIMBING With close to 1,500 established routes going over extremely hard and featured sandstone rock with lots of cracks and face routes, the **New River Gorge National River** has become one of the most popular climbing areas in the country. Most of the routes are 5.9 or harder, meaning they are for advanced and expert climbers, but there are some good beginner spots, too, such as the Bridge Buttress and Junkyard Wall. The climbing season runs Apr.–Nov., with the park service recommending late Apr. to mid-June and mid-Sept. to late Oct. as the best times. *New River Rock* by Rick Thompson and *New River Gorge Rock Climbs* by Mike Williams contain information on almost every route in the gorge.

The rock cliffs surrounding **Summersville Lake**, especially those close to the US 19 bridge, and those rising above the **Meadow River** are also popular climbing places. *New River Gorge, Meadow River and Summersville Lake Rock Climbers' Guidebook* by Steve Cater covers these routes.

ALONG ONE OF THE TRAILS IN THE NEW RIVER GORGE NATIONAL RIVER

Hard Rock Climbing (304-574-0735; www.hardrockclimbing.com), 131 South Court St., Fayetteville. For more than two decades, Hard Rock Climbing has been taking beginning, intermediate, and advanced climbers on climbing and rappelling trips to the New River Gorge and Summersville Lake. They also do retail sales of equipment and have a bouldering room in the store.

New River Mountain Guides (304-574-3872; www.newriverclimbing.com), 101 East Wiseman St. (inside Water Stone Outdoors), Fayetteville. New River Mountain Guides has been providing the same services as Hard Rock Climbing since 1994.

FISHING The **New River** is famous for its quality of bass fishing, especially smallmouth bass. Anglers also come here in the hope of landing walleye, bluegill, catfish, muskie, and more. Three of the most popular spots are Stone Cliff near Thurmond, and McCreery and Glade Creek close to Prince.

If you would like to have the expertise of a local guide, contact **New River Outfitters** (304-255-4769; 304-254-9587; www.small-mouth.com; mailing address: P.O. Box 968, Crab Orchard 25827) or **Mountain State Anglers** (1-800-545-7238; www.mountainstateanglers; mailing address: P.O. Box 360, Fayetteville 25840).

New River Dories (304-465-3332; www.newriverdories.com; mailing address: P.O. Box 504, Mount Hope 25580) uses McKenzie drift boats that can take you into the rapids and around the rocks and deepest pools where the biggest fish are.

Cranberry Wilderness Outfitters (304-846-6805; http://wvoutfitters.com; mailing address: P.O. Box 263, Fenwick 26202). Guided wading trips in search of smallmouth bass, and wild rainbow, brown, and native brook trout on the Cranberry, Elk, Williams, and Greenbrier rivers and their tributaries. They also offer guided bike/fishing trips.

Also see *Whitewater Rafting* and *Green Space—Parks*.

GOLF

Beaver
Grandview Country Club (304-763-2520), 1500 Scott Ridge Rd. Par 71 with 6,834 yards.

Fayetteville
Bridge Haven Golf Club (304-574-2120; http://wvweb.com/bridgehaven), Salem-Gatewood Rd. Open daily year-round. The front nine holes have very few obstacles, while the back nine have sloped greens and some par 5s.

Also see Hawks Nest State Park under *Green Space—Parks* and The Resort at Glade Springs under *Lodging*.

HIKING With all of the publicity about its world-class rock climbing and whitewater rafting, the 50-plus miles of trails coursing through the **New River Gorge National River's** tens of thousands of acres are often overlooked. I explored most of the routes and am going to direct you to some of the most scenic.

Begin at the Canyon Rim Visitor Center (see *Guidance*), north of Fayetteville off US 19, to obtain maps, brochures, and other information. Close by, the 2.5-mile **Endless Wall Trail** and two short, accessible pathways lead to overlooks of the bridge spanning the 1,000-foot-deep gorge.

Across the river near Fayetteville, the **Kaymoor Miner's Trail** drops from the rim almost straight down to the river, passing old mining machinery and coming to a spot that looks like a Tarzan "Lost City" setting. Cement blocks, tipple, valves, old equipment, and buildings have trees and vines growing over, and sometimes through, them.

Upstream, the 6-mile **Brooklyn-Southside Junction Trail** emanates from the Thurmond depot and passes through once bustling, but now abandoned, mining communities. The 3.4-mile **Thurmond-Minden Trail** crosses five railroad trestles, providing views of the river and Thurmond. The **Stone Cliff Trail** runs above the river for 2.7 miles. All three of these routes are also open to mountain bikes.

Hike the trails farther upriver for ruggedness and isolation. You stay in the highlands along the **Kates Plateau** and **Polls Plateau** trails (both are more than 6 miles), where routes may not always be obvious and the park service recommends using topographic maps and a compass. If you fear getting lost, take the 6-mile **Glade Creek Trail** descending the trout-stocked stream to the river's southern bank. A bonus is the deep and wide swimmin' hole at the base of Glade Creek Falls.

Grandview. Bona Vista. Buena Vista. With today's contractors usurping such romantic-sounding names, it is a good probability that there is a "Grandview" housing development somewhere close to where you live. This place, however, is the real deal. Overlooks in the Grandview section of the New River Gorge National River treat visitors to some of the gorge's most spectacular vistas, and the **Canyon Rim** (1.6 miles) and **Castle Rock** (0.5 mile) trails skirt the gorge's edge to deliver you to each one. The Main Overlook, which is just a few feet from the parking area, rewards you with a view from the national river's highest point. The overlook stands at 2,500 feet above sea level, and your eyes can take in 7 miles of the gorge, with the river flowing close to 1,100 feet below you.

In the northeastern part of this area, the Monongahela National Forest's **Cranberry Backcountry** (officially designated a part of the Cranberry Wilderness in 2009) will take you deep into isolated woodlands, and it is a viable and rewarding alternative to hiking on the more remote and less maintained trails of the Cranberry Wilderness (see *To Do—Hiking* in the "Reaching for the Sky—Spruce Knob, Seneca Rocks, and Cranberry Glades" chapter).

The backcountry's 26,000 acres are closed to public motorized vehicles, but bicycles, horses, and handcarts are allowed. Even though the wilderness receives more visitors, these activities sometimes make the backcountry appear to be busier, with people carrying more and moving about faster than just feet alone would permit.

From the stoplight at the intersection of WV 55/WV 39 and Oakford Ave. in the center of Richwood, drive WV 55/WV 39 East for 1 mile, turn left onto Cranberry Rd. (WV 6), and make another left onto FSR 76 in an additional 2.4 miles. Passing by Big Rock Campground, FSR 81, and FSR 101, stay on FSR 76 for 10.7 miles and come to the trailhead at the far end of the Cranberry Campground. The trash cans encircled by a chain-link fence should give some idea of how active the black bears are. Camping is permitted anywhere in the Cranberry Backcountry, but if you prefer a bit of civilization, you can stay in the two mentioned campgrounds from mid-Mar. to early Dec. Both are somewhat primitive sites with vault toilets and drinking water from hand pumps.

The **Ansted–Hawks Nest Rail Trail** winds down the side of the New River Gorge for 2.5 miles from the trailhead off US 60 in Ansted to the churning waters of the river. The pathway follows the route of a railroad once used to haul coal from mines around the town. Open to hikers and bicyclists, it descends at a gentle grade, making it possibly the easiest trail into the gorge. There is no doubt it is one of the most scenic; it passes by two waterfalls, precipitous cliffs, interesting rock formations, and across two reconstructed wooden trestles. You can obtain more information by writing or calling Town of Ansted, P.O. Box 798, Ansted 25812; 304-658-5901.

Feeling lazy? Don't want to walk down *and* up the Ansted–Hawks Nest Rail Trail? Hawks Nest State Park's Canyon Tramway (see *Green Space—Parks*) can deliver you to—or take you from—the trail's lower end at the base of the gorge. You could also take in the arts, crafts, entertainment, and food at the park's Country Roads Festival during the third weekend of September.

Also see *Bicycling*, Four Seasons Outfitter under *Outdoors Outfitters*, and *Green Space—Parks*.

HORSEBACK RIDING

Hico

☙ **Horseshoe Creek Riding Stables** (304-658-3218; www.horseshoecreek.com; mailing address: P.O. Box 264, Hico 25854), on Smales Branch Rd. about 0.25 mile from US 19. Rides, for those as young as 6 years of age, are given from two hours to overnight on 500 private acres, where you can also hike, or camp in the provided tepees. Rides start at $30.

Oak Hill

New River Trail Rides (304-465-4819; 1-888-743-3982; www.ridewva.com; mailing address: P.O. Box 67, Oak Hill 25901). From East Main St. in Oak Hill, take Gatewood Rd., go 3.9 miles, bear right onto Wonderland Rd., and continue another 0.6 mile. Open year-round; all trips go rain or shine. Rides of two hours to overnight trips take you into the gorge to a private overlook and waterfall. Trips start at $55.

Also see Babcock State Park under *Green Space—Parks* and The Resort at Glade Springs under *Lodging*.

MINIATURE GOLF ☙ **Mountain State Miniature Golf** (304-253-7242; www.mtstgolf.com), 1818 Harper Rd., Beckley. Kevin Traube was mowing the steep hillside behind his gift shop (see The Little Brick House Gift Shop under *Selective Shopping*) when he decided he had had enough and was going to utilize the yard in a different way. The result is possibly the most interesting miniature golf course I have ever played. Each hole is based upon something famous in the state, with small plaques providing tidbits of information. You have to cross a narrow replica of the New River Gorge Bridge, drive the ball uphill toward Seneca Rocks, go through one of the lanes of a West Virginia Turnpike tollbooth, and across the Philippi Covered Bridge. You'll know the game is over when your ball drops into a coal mine on hole 18 and does not reappear. It's a challenging course that is a lot of fun, and highly recommended.

OUTDOORS OUTFITTERS

Fayetteville

Water Stone Outdoors (304-574-2425; www.waterstoneoutdoors.com), 101 East Wiseman St. This is the place to shop if you have forgotten, or need to purchase, just about anything to do with hiking, camping, caving, or climbing.

Richwood

Four Seasons Outfitter (304-846-2862; www.fourseasonsoutfitter.com), 190 Middletown Rd., on the western edge of town on WV 39/WV 55. In addition to having a retail store with hiking, camping, hunting, archery, paddling, and biking equipment, Four Seasons Outfitter rents snowshoes, cross-country skis, and mountain bikes (and will repair yours). They also have a shuttle service available for hikers, bikers, and others, even if you don't rent from them. This is a great boon for those who want to explore the nearby Monongahela National Forest but don't have two cars available to shuttle themselves.

SCUBA DIVING Sarge's Dive Shop (304-872-1782; www.sarges.net), Airport Rd., Summersville. A full-service dive shop that also rents pontoon boats at its Summersville Lake location (304-872-1331).

SKATING ✔ Freedom Skate Park, Eisenhower Dr., Beckley. Operated by Beckley Parks and Recreation, Freedom Skate Park is open to anyone who wishes to hone their skills on grinding rails, ramps, and the like.

Also see The Resort at Glade Springs under *Lodging*.

SKIING ✔ Winterplace Ski Resort (304-787-3221; 1-800-607-7669; www.winterplace.com), 100 Old Flat Top Mountain Rd., Ghent. Winterplace is less than a five-minute drive from I-77 exit 28, making it the state's most accessible ski resort. It is also one of the smallest, but don't let that deter you from coming here. There are 28 trails, the bulk of them geared toward beginner and intermediate skiers; nine lifts; a 16-lane snowtubing park; and a terrain park with hits, rails, and jumps for snowboarding. Lights extend the fun well into the night, and 100 percent snowmaking capability ensures that every trail will always be available. Ski lessons are given for adults and children, and there is day care for the little ones who will not be hitting the slopes. Several restaurants offer casual to upscale dining, and condominiums provide slopeside accommodations.

SPA See The Resort at Glade Springs under *Lodging*.

SWIMMING ✔ New River City Park (304-256-1747). Take I-77/I-64 exit 44, turn east on Harper Rd. (WV 3), go 1.5 miles, turn left onto Ewart Ave., and continue an additional mile. Adjacent to The Beckley Exhibition Coal Mine in Beckley (see *To See—Guided Tour*), the park has a fitness trail, basketball and tennis courts, and picnic facilities. The real draw, though, is the seasonal pool with a great water slide.

Also see *Green Space—Parks*, and The Resort at Glade Springs under *Lodging*.

SWIMMIN' HOLE Summersville Lake in Summersville is the state's largest body of water, so you are not going to find a bigger swimmin' hole than this. Swimming is permitted anywhere on the lake, but go to the Battle Run area if you want a developed sandy beach (no lifeguards).

Also see Glade Creek Trail under *Hiking*.

TENNIS See The Resort at Glade Springs under *Lodging*.

WHITEWATER RAFTING The whitewater rafting season on the New and Gauley rivers usually starts in April and ends in October. Rafting on the New River

HE STARTED IT

Just as Gil and Mary Willis of the Elk River Touring Company, Inn, Restaurant, and Guide Service in Slatyfork can be credited with making West Virginia a mountain biking destination, and John Markwell of the Seneca Rocks Climbing School can be considered the one person who focused the attentions of rock climbers on the state, it is no doubt that Jon Dragan is the father of West Virginia whitewater rafting. After he and some friends did their own raft trip down the New River in 1964, he and his two brothers started the state's first commercial rafting enterprise, Wildwater Expeditions.

State newspapers and residents scoffed at the idea that people would actually travel and then pay money just to ride a rubber raft down the river. Dragan proved all of them wrong. Today, close to a quarter of a million people flock to the state, and dozens of commercial rafters provide trips on a number of the state's rivers, helping to generate more than $40 million in annual tourism revenue. As more and more people came to appreciate the gorge's scenic wonders, and politicians realized the economic benefits, the New River Gorge National River, Bluestone National Scenic River, and Gauley River National Recreation Area were established to protect these natural resources.

Jon passed away in 2005, but Wildwater Expeditions continues to provide thrills and chills. It is not as big or as flashy as several of the other businesses that have come after it, but it does provide some of the area's most authentic, perceptive, and supportive trips. So, the next time you are whooping and hollering as you shoot an adrenaline-producing rapid, you just might want to utter a word of thanks to the man who started it all.

takes place on a 53-mile stretch between Hinton and Fayetteville. The upper New River is quite gentle, with only Class I and II rapids, and can easily be rafted or kayaked by just about anyone. With Class III to V rapids, the lower New River is certainly more challenging, but most rafting companies have guides with enough expertise that the general public can safely run it. The Gauley River is considered to be one of the country's most challenging commercially rafted whitewater rivers, and companies will ask for some assurance that you have a degree of experience before they let you sign on for a trip. When the Summersville Dam is releasing water in the fall, the upper Gauley has 60 rapids that include five consecutive Class V rapids, while the lower Gauley is only slightly less demanding.

More than two dozen companies run the two rivers. All of them are certified, but some are quite family oriented, while others tend to have more of a party atmosphere. Several of them are major concerns with camping, cabins, restaurants, and amusements such as miniature golf and swimming pools. Many also provide or arrange guided services for other activities, including hiking, mountain biking, horseback riding, climbing, and fishing.

Since it is impossible to describe every one of them in this book, I have listed a number of the ones that have been around for many years. I suggest you contact the West Virginia Professional River Outfitters Association (304-574-2343; www .americasbestwhitewater.com; mailing address: P.O. Box 32, Fayetteville 25840); it is an umbrella organization that oversees the industry, and employees there should be able to steer you to the company that will best provide the experience you are looking for. There are many different types of trips, including half day, full day, and overnight, and a wide variety of packages available that may save you time and money. Be sure to inquire about all of this.

Lansing

Class VI River Runners (304-574-0704; 1-800-252-7784; www.class-vi.com), Ames Heights Rd. Class VI is one of the largest rafting companies and says it will take you on a trip if you are 6 to 86 years old. Besides the rafting trips, they can provide you with kayaking lessons and guided hiking and fishing trips, along with other outdoor activities. Their canyon rim base camp has cabin rentals and one of the New River area's best restaurants, Smokey's on the Gorge (see *Dining Out*). Their campground, which also has cabin rentals, is less than a mile away.

Minden

North American River Runners (304-658-5276; 1-800-950-2585; www.narr .com), 80 Beachside Dr. North American River Runners was one of the first companies to raft the New River. Open since 1975, they have a campground, cabin tents, bunkhouses, climbing wall, and mountain bike rentals. They also conduct team-building courses and guided climbing, rappelling, and fishing trips.

Wildwater Expeditions (304-658-4007; 1-800-982-7238; www.wvaraft.com; mailing address is P. O. Box 1161, Oak Hill, 25901). Wildwater Expeditions is the state's oldest commercial rafter, started by Jon Dragan and his brothers in 1968 (see the "He Started It" sidebar earlier in the chapter). The company concentrates on providing guests with the personal touch and an authentic river experience. They also have expert guides for kayaking, rock climbing, and rappelling instruction.

Oak Hill

Ace Adventure Center (304-469-2651; 1-800-787-3982; www.aceraft.com; mailing address: P.O. Box 1168, Oak Hill 25901). Ace is one of the largest rafting companies in this area and has a huge, 1,400-acre complex that includes deluxe cabins with hot tubs, bunkhouses, rental tents, a 40-acre campground, outfitting store, restaurant, lounge, massage therapies, and a plethora of other outdoor activities. The company has its own takeout on the Gauley River, which saves you from paddling 3 miles of flatwater. It claims to have the lowest guest-to-guide ratio (7:1).

✳ Green Space

PARKS

Ansted

⅃ **Hawks Nest State Park** (304-658-5212; www.hawksnestsp.com; mailing address: P.O. Box 857, Ansted 25812), on US 60 about 8 miles west of the US 60 intersection with US 19. Decades before the construction of four-lane highways and the advent of rock climbing and whitewater rafting in the New River Gorge, the view from Hawks Nest was one of Southern West Virginia's major attractions. People would drive for hours to walk the 100-yard trail out to the overlook constructed by the Civilian Conservation Corps (CCC) in the 1930s. This is still one of the state's most photographed scenes, and rightfully so. The vista takes in a several miles of one of the widest bends in the New River, which flows hundreds of feet below. It is a sight worth driving a fair distance to behold.

Across US 60, and up a short pathway, is the **Hawks Nest Museum** (open Apr. 1–Nov. 1 whenever the nearby gift shop is open). Housed in a stone structure also built by the CCC, it has displays about Native Americans, early settlers, the Civil War, and "modern" West Virginia. (I put *modern* in quotes because most of the exhibits date from the mid-1900s, making them of historical interest in their own right.) The nearby restrooms are also historic in nature in that they are housed in a circular stone turret also built by the CCC.

All of these features were incorporated into the state park when it was established in the 1960s. The lodge has guest rooms with balconies overlooking the gorge, as does the restaurant. Several trails run along the lip of the gorge or deliver you to the river, where you can take a jetboat journey upstream (see *To Do—Boat Excursions*). An easier way down is to ride the enclosed gondolas of the Canyon Tramway. Other park amenities include a swimming pool, tennis courts, golf course, and a full schedule of events, including plays, concerts, and naturalist programs.

Beaver
Little Beaver State Park (304-763-2494; www.littlebeaverstatepark.com), 1402 Grandview Rd. The history of Little Beaver State Park begins in the 1930s, when members of the Civilian Conservation Corps built roads and prepared the land for the lake, which was completed in 1941. It was operated as a 4-H camp by Raleigh County until 1971, when it was sold to the state for $1. Today, the 562-acre day-use park has picnic areas, paddle- and rowboat rentals, a pretty 300-foot swimming beach, and close to 10 miles of hiking trails that wander beside the lake and onto hillsides of rhododendron. Anglers come here for the bass, catfish, crappie, bluegill, and stocked trout. The park is just a short drive from downtown Beckley, and I often use it as a quick escape from the noise and traffic.

Beckley
Lake Stephens Park (304-934-5323; 1-800-786-8430; www.lakestephenswv.com), 350 Lake Stephens Rd. Operated by the Raleigh County Recreation Authority, 300-acre Lake Stephens is surrounded by 2,000 acres of hardwood forest and offers picnic facilities, dozens of miles of hiking and biking trails, game courts, a skate park, and boating, fishing, and swimming in the lake. Since it is situated only 8 miles west of Beckley, the campground (open Apr. 15–Oct. 15), with full hookups and modern restrooms, is a low-cost option as a place to stay while exploring the area.

Clifftop
Babcock State Park (304-438-3004; www.babcocksp.com), 486 Babcock Rd. From the US 60 intersection with US 19, follow US 60 east for 10 miles, turn right onto WV 41, go 2 miles to the park's campground and another 2 miles to the main park entrance. Whereas the view from Hawks Nest is one of the state's most

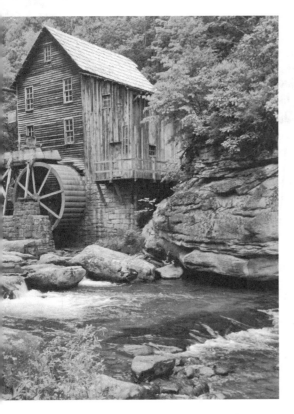

GLADE CREEK GRIST MILL, BABCOCK STATE PARK

photographed scenes, the Glade Creek Grist Mill in Babcock State Park is one of the most photographed buildings. Of course, it is not just the structure that attracts all these shutterbugs. It is the setting, with Glade Creek tumbling over rocks in the stream and forestland vegetation framing the entire scene. The mill is actually a re-creation that was constructed by combining parts of several other mills once found in the state. It is operational, and visitors can purchase the cornmeal and buckwheat flour that it has ground.

The park is also known for the beauty of its many miles of streams and hiking trails that are lined by luxuriant growths of Catawba and great rhododendron. (The prettiest is the Manns Creek Gorge Trail.) Also within the 4,127-acre park are rental cabins and a campground (both open mid-Mar. through Oct.), a swimming pool, boat rentals and fishing on Boley Lake, guided horseback rides from early May to late Oct. (304-438-5046), and a summer naturalist program.

Summersville

🖋 **Carnifex Ferry Battlefield State Park** (304-872-0825; www.carnifexferry battlefieldstatepark.com), 1194 Carnifex Ferry Rd. From the intersection of US 19 and WV 129 a few miles south of Summersville, drive WV 129 West, come to an overlook of Summersville Lake in 1.2 miles, cross Summersville Dam in another 1.3 miles, and turn left onto Carnifex Ferry Rd. (WV 23) in an additional 2.7 miles. Enter the park 0.7 mile later. It became obvious during the early days of the Civil War that the western part of Virginia wanted to break away from the state and remain a part of the Union. To occupy territory and prevent this from happening, Confederate troops were sent into the area. The clash with Federal soldiers on July 3, 1861, at Phillipi is considered by many to be the first land battle of the war. Various other conflicts that occurred during the following months, in which the Confederates were kept out of the northern part of present-day West Virginia, set the stage for what would happen at Carnifex Ferry.

Land was traded back and forth between the two forces in the southern part of the region, with a former Virginia governor, Confederate Brig. Gen. John B. Floyd, establishing a camp on the Patterson farm overlooking Carnifex Ferry on the Gauley River. On September 10, 1861, soldiers under the command of Union Brig. Gen. William S. Rosecrans attacked the encamped Southern troops. Although Confederate casualties were far fewer than those inflicted upon the opposing

NATURE'S THERMOMETERS

If you are outdoors in winter, you can use rhododendron leaves to determine the temperature. To protect their soft undersides from the desiccating effects of cool breezes, the leaves begin to droop and curl under. The tighter the curl, the colder it is. When the leaves are wrapped around themselves to about the size of a choice cigar, the temperature is hovering around freezing; the diameter of a cheap cigar means that it is getting into the 20s and the teens. If you are outside when the leaves have become no larger than a cigarette, you'd better be wearing lots of layers—the temperature is mighty close to zero.

forces. Floyd decided to give in to superior numbers and retreated across the ferry during the night.

Western Virginia continued to experience skirmishes throughout the next few years, but the Union retained virtual control during the remainder of the war, ensuring the safety of delegates meeting in Wheeling and enabling the statehood movement to proceed without any serious threats.

Carnifex Ferry Battlefield State Park preserves 156 acres of land on which the battle took place. A monument, gravesite, replica cannon, wooden fences, and a museum in the refurbished Patterson Farmhouse help visitors recall earlier days. Established in the 1930s, the park is a day-use area with picnic shelters and facilities (open seasonally), game courts, softball field, and playground. There is no campground or backcountry camping permitted, but on the drive to the park, you will pass by a Summersville Lake/U.S. Army Corps of Engineers campground.

The 2-mile Patterson Trail weaves in and out of forest and meadow and by several important battle sites. It traverses a moderate terrain, with just a few very short, steep sections, making it an ideal hike for children. There is enough variety to keep them interested—lots of deer, squirrels, and rabbits; several impressive views of the Gauley River; and a modest water run in which they can search for small aquatic creatures. The playground is located in the middle of the hike, so if the little ones lose interest, one adult can stay with them while they swing and slide, and the rest of your group continues with the hike. If the kids get so tired that the entire trip has to be called off, your car will be parked just a few hundred feet from the playground.

WALKS *The Historic Beckley West Virginia Guide to Courthouse Square National Historic District*, available from the Southern West Virginia Convention & Visitors Bureau (see *Guidance*), describes a walking tour through the streets of the downtown Beckley commercial and office-building district, where a large percentage of the structures were built in the early 1900s.

SOUTHERN WEST VIRGINIA

✳ Lodging

RESORTS

Canvas 26662

❧ **Good Evening Ranch** (304-872-1603; 1-877-595-5448; www.good eveningranch.net; mailing address: P.O. Box 390). From US 19 in Summersville, drive WV 39 East approximately 5 miles and follow Groves Rd. (not Groves Ford Rd.!) for 3 miles. Whereas Glade Springs is a bustling upscale resort with cars traveling miles of paved roadways between hundreds of guest rooms, the Good Evening Ranch provides more of a laid-back, typical West Virginia experience, with only one gravel road taking guests to luxury cabins with outdoor hot tubs nestled in the woods. However, like all good resorts, this one offers so many things to do that you may want to stay here for days without ever leaving the grounds.

Take a guided horseback ride (by reservation), travel the marked hiking and biking trails that wander through the 650 acres, or take a dip in the swimming pool. The on-site Animal Farm not only contains beasts you would expect to see in West Virginia, but it permits you to get quite close to

ONE OF THE SURPRISES THAT AWAIT AT GOOD EVENING RANCH

lions, tigers, zebras, camels, monkeys, kangaroos, and a whole host of other exotic animals. A restaurant and "saloon" can supply your daily requirement of calories. The ranch is also the site of numerous concerts and championship rodeos throughout the year.

Rates for the cabins start at $165. A few RV sites with hookups are also available.

Daniels 25832

♿ **The Resort at Glade Springs** (304-763-2000; 1-800-634-5233; www.gladesprings.com), 255 Resort Dr., off US 19. Within its 4,100 acres, Glade Springs offers many of the same facilities and amenities as The Greenbrier in nearby White Sulphur Springs, and does so at a much lower cost to you. The Stonehaven golf course is a pretty dramatic one, with rock outcroppings and cart paths through a rich forest of rhododendron, while the Cobb course has a more than 200-foot elevation change, 54 sand bunkers, and eight lakes. The Woodhaven course follows a path though rock outcroppings and overlooks Glade Creek Gorge. Tennis players have a choice of two clay courts, three hard ones, and three indoor courts, along with a racquetball club. Miles of challenging trails open to hikers and bikers wander through the acreage (the easy Little Beaver Trail is popular for early-morning and evening walks), and the heated indoor pool is open year-round, as is an equestrian center. The spa offers a variety of massages, scrubs, and treatments.

Glades Grill and Bar (304-763-3033), open daily for breakfast, lunch, and dinner, is a relaxed *Dining Out* experience with picture windows overlooking the fairways. If it is available, I suggest starting your evening meal with the yellow tomato gazpacho with basil pesto and crème fraîche. Dinner choices have included corn crusted quail breast, veal scaloppine with rosemary polenta, lamb chops, and spinach- and goat cheese-stuffed chicken breast. Entrées $14.95–27.95. **The Small Talk Café** (304-763-0814) is primarily a coffee bar with a good selection of fresh-baked pastries, ice cream, and sandwiches.

The resort's accommodations range from stylish rooms in the grand Glade Springs Hotel to suites, villas, lodges, and stand-alone homes. There are also many packages available, such as deals that include skiing at Winterplace. Because of this wide range of choices, rates are also widely varied. As a reference point: Hotel rooms start at about $230.

MOTELS & HOTELS

Beckley 25801
Country Inn & Suites (304-252-5100; www.countryinns.com), 2120 Harper Rd. One of the closest accommodations to Tamarack (see "The Best of West Virginia" sidebar later in the chapter), this national chain offers a heated indoor/outdoor pool, whirlpool, exercise room, and guest laundry. $125–145 includes a complimentary breakfast.

Summersville 26651
Comfort Inn (304-872-6500), 903 Industrial Dr. (off US 19). The Comfort Inn has close to 100 rooms, each with an iron and hair dryer. Other amenities include swimming and wading pools, exercise room, and guest laundry. Small pets are permitted for an extra fee. $89–160 includes a continental breakfast.

BED & BREAKFASTS

Beaver 25813
Cedarwood Cottage B&B (304-253-0618; www.bbonline.com/wv/cedar

wood), 150 Sally Lane. Argle and Reeda Cook have been inviting travelers into their modest, modern home for more than a decade. The two guest rooms share a bath, while a fully equipped one-room apartment is available for those who want more privacy. Located just a few minutes from I-64, the B&B has a quiet rural/suburban setting and hosts who make you feel at home. Breakfasts can be sinfully indulgent, but the Cooks are conscious about their own well-being, so if you are, too, ask them to prepare a healthy, but still tasty, meal for you. $65–100.

Fayetteville 25840
Historic White Horse Bed & Breakfast (304-574-1400; www.historicwhitehorse.net), 120 Fayette Ave. Situated in a residential area of Fayetteville and just minutes from the New River Gorge, the 22-room mansion was built in 1906 by the county sheriff. The current owners have modestly remodeled and restored the house, and they offer superb buffet breakfasts. $105–125; a cottage (can accommodate 8 for the bargain rate of $175) is available for large groups or those who desire a bit more privacy. Pets may be permitted with prior approval.

Flat Top 25841
Foxwood (304-466-5514; www.foxwoodwv.com; mailing address: P.O.

FOXWOOD

Box 5). Take I-77 exit 28, drive south on US 19 for almost 3 miles, and turn left onto Ellison Ridge Rd. Continue for 9 miles and bear right onto Bolen Rd. Go less than 1 mile, bear right again, and continue for 1 more mile. Class, style, grace. Any, or all, of these words could be used to describe Foxwood, a 12,000-square-foot home that sits on hundreds of acres with a picturesque pond beside it and a grand view of the mountains of Southern West Virginia. Each guest room is a suite with décor fitting in with the rest of the house, which has a double fireplace in the dining room, winding staircase to the second floor, and so many other rooms that you could spend your entire time here just looking through them. Breakfast is a grand affair, too, and if offered a choice, I suggest having the stuffed French toast. The rate of $99 is a real deal.

Two other houses, just as regally constructed and appointed, are available for large groups or those who want more privacy. $395–795.

Summersville 26651

♪ **100 Inn & Antiques** (304-872-4944; www.bbonline.com/wv/wildwood), 100 Wildwood Inn Dr. On 7 acres of quiet hillside property, 100 Inn & Antiques sits on a small knoll just minutes from US 19 and Summersville. Built in 1972, it was the first B&B to open in Nicholas County, and two of the three guest rooms share a bath. Breakfast is served from an antique sideboard in a dining room full of Victorian antiques, and small gazebos let you enjoy the breezes outdoors. Children are permitted, but facilities for them are somewhat limited. $80.

CABINS & VACATION RENTALS

Ansted 25812

Mountain Memories (304-658-5800; www.wvmountainmemories.com), on

US 60 about 0.25 mile west of Hawks Nest State Park (see *Green Space— Parks*). The prefabricated cabins, which can accommodate up to eight, sit a short distance back from the highway and have screened porches, central heat and air, and fully equipped kitchens. The rate for two people is $120.

Hico 25854

Country Roads Cabins (1-888-712-2246; www.wvcabins.com; mailing address: P.O. Box 44), on Sunday Rd., which is off US 60 about 100 yards west of the US 60 intersection with US 19. Open year-round. With a fair amount of green space between them, this cluster of luxury cabins, built with logs from West Virginia, maintains a family atmosphere. The one- to four-bedroom cabins have fully equipped kitchens, TVs, decks with hot tubs, and central heat and air. The owners purchase supplies as locally as possible— even the mattresses are manufactured in the state. Rates start at $225 for a one-bedroom cabin; many rafting, climbing, golfing, and other package deals available.

Lansing 25862

Mill Creek Cabins (304-685-5005; 1-800-692-5005; www.millcreekcabins.com; mailing address: P.O. Box 148), off US 19. Built by the owner, these luxury cabins are individually different, but they are fully equipped to accommodate eight to 14 guests. They have complete kitchens, two bedrooms downstairs, two queen beds in the loft, a stone fireplace in the living room, and an outdoor hot tub on the deck. The rate for the smaller cabins is $310.

Opossum Creek Retreat (1-888-488-4836; www.opossumcreek.com; mailing address: P.O. Box 221), off US 19. Open year-round. These are luxury cabins that are spaced in the woods along a one-lane country road. The owner has built them in an environmentally friendly way, using trees that were cut from the property. All are fully furnished with kitchen, baths, and hot tub. Some will accommodate four; others will sleep as many as 20. The rate for the smallest is $180.

Mount Nebo 26679
Carnifex Ferry Cabins (304-872-4442; 1-800-701-0809; www.westvirginiacabins.com), 42 Lakeview Heights. These extremely deluxe cabins are located just before the entrance of Carnifex Ferry Battlefield State Park (see *Green Space—Parks*). They are spacious, well built, and located in the woods far enough apart from each other to give you a semblance of privacy. The hot tubs are welcome after a long day's worth of outdoor activities. Rates start at $145.

CAMPGROUNDS Five small, free primitive sites (with no drinking water) operated by the New River Gorge National River allow you to spend the night close to the rolling waters. The **Army Camp, Grandview Sandbar**, and **Glade Creek** sites can all be accessed from WV 41 near Prince. The **Stone Cliff** site is off WV 25 near Thurmond, and the **War Ridge /Backus Mountain** site is accessed via Backus Rd. All are operated on a first-come, first-served basis and can fill up quickly on nice weekends. For more information, call 304-465-0508 or log onto www.nps.gov/neri/planyourvisit /campgrounds.htm.

Fayetteville 25840
Rifrafters Campground (304-574-1065; www.rifrafters.com; mailing address: Rte. 2, Box 140-A). Two miles south of the New River Bridge, turn off US 19 onto Laurel Creek Rd. Tent and RV sites with hookups. The rental cabins are what the owners call "economy"—they do have electricity, but

there is no kitchen or bathroom. For $40 per night for two people, they're a good deal if want to save money yet still be able to sleep on a bed indoors.

Mount Nebo 26679
Summersville Lake Retreat (304-872-5975; 1-888-872-5580; www.summersvillelakeretreat.com), 278 Summersville Lake Rd. Open meadow and wooded sites with hookups on 60 acres close to the lake. The A-frame rental chalets are tucked into the woods by themselves and rent for $189 per night. Canoe and kayak rentals are also available.

Summersville 26651
🐾 **Mountain Lake Campground** (304-872-4220; 1-800-624-0440; www.mountainlakecampground.com), 1898 Airport Rd. Along with campsites with full hookups, the campground offers hiking trails, miniature golf, and other amenities. Lakeside cabins ($175) are also available. This is the closest commercial campground to the lake.

✳ Where to Eat
DINING OUT

Lansing
✪ **Smokey's On The Gorge** (1-800-252-7784; www.class-vi.com), Ames Heights Rd. I have eaten at restaurants operated by other rafting companies and would give them just an okay rating, but that is not the case with Smokey's, which is inside the Class VI River Runner complex (see *To Do— Whitewater Rafting*). Despite being served buffet style (which I find usually makes the food taste like cafeteria fare), everything here was absolutely delicious and fresh, with the inventive menu always changing to take advantage of what is available. The last time I was here you could eat all you wanted of beef tenders with portobello

ragout, quail with butternut squash and mushroom risotto, grilled catfish with olive caper butter, and buffalo-style chicken with Gorgonzola cheese. Imported cheeses and homemade ramp vinaigrette dressing were on the salad bar. Desserts are on par with those I've eaten at The Greenbrier. It's *Dining Out* fare, but since many of the patrons have been rafting, dress is very, very casual. This is one of the area's best restaurants; do not miss it. $24.95.

Summersville

Café Acropolis (304-872-0254), 331 McMillion Dr. Open for lunch and dinner Mon.–Fri; dinner Sat. It's sometimes quite serendipitous how life takes its many twists and turns so that you and I can enjoy a wonderful meal in a pleasant setting. Peter Kudurogianis was a chef on cruise ships for many years before working in restaurants in New York and Washington, DC. A friend invited him to visit the Summersville area, and he liked it so much that he moved here. Sitting all by itself on a knoll overlooking the town, the café has captured the distinct flavor of the Mediterranean, complete with an outdoor seating area covered by the shade of a thick grape arbor.

Italian and Greek dishes are the specialty here, and I can recommend the eggplant parmigiana. So often this is cooked to an unappetizing fried glop. Not here; it was fresh, crunchy, and tasty. Entrées $9–24.

Also see The Resort at Glade Springs under *Lodging*.

EATING OUT

Beckley

Pasquale Mira's Italian Restaurant (304-255-5253; http://beckleyitalian.com), 224 Harper Park Dr. Open for lunch and dinner daily. Pasquale Mira left his native Sicily in 1954 to join his father and brothers in the restaurant business in Beckley. His sauce and salad dressing (I had not experienced this wonderful taste since my Italian mother had passed away) soon garnered a loyal local following. After working with him for close to a decade, Brian Williams took over operations when Pasquale retired, but he has kept the same recipes and food quality. (Seafood is brought in from the Virginia coast, and all sauces, doughs, and house dressings are homemade.) I enjoy the spicy spaghetti diavolo and always finish a meal with the freshly made tiramisu. Entrées $7.95–21.95.

Brian Williams also operates **The Char** (304-253-1760; www.the-char .com), 100 Char Dr., known for the quality of its steaks. Try the house specialty, brascioli, a fillet with bread crumbs and cheese. Seafood and some Italian dishes are also served, and the décor includes portraits of wildlife hanging on the walls. Entrées $9–39.

Young Chow's (304-253-2469), 219 Pikeview Dr. When I asked where to go for Chinese food, several people suggested Young Chow's. The menu contains the usual items—chow mein, egg foo yong, wonton soup, and egg rolls—along with some not-often-found dishes, such as prawns with pineapple, tofu vegetable soup, and a large selection of sushi. Entrées $5.95–13.95.

Cranberry

Southern Red's Bar-B-Que (304-255-4227; http://southernreds.wvweb sites.com), 4631 Robert C. Byrd Dr. Young entrepreneurship is alive and well in West Virginia, and you smell its aroma rising in the smoke from the outdoor barbecue pits as soon as you pull into the parking lot. Micah Seavers was only 16 years old when he opened his first restaurant based upon his family's recipe. The cooking method is a well-guarded secret, but he does let it be known that only the pork shoulder is used to ensure a moist sandwich. Ribs and smoked chicken are also available. The few small tables and sparse décor are proof that people come here for the food and not the atmosphere. Entrées $2.99–16.99.

Fayetteville
Cathedral Café (304-574-0202; www.cathedralcafe.com), 134 South Court St. Open for breakfast and lunch daily. It would be a mistake to pass through Fayetteville and not stop at the Cathedral Café. Inside an early-20th-century church with cathedral ceilings and stained-glass windows, the restaurant's tone is a cross between a bit of a bohemia and a modern cybercafé. Free computers are available for you to check e-mail as you enjoy one of the area's best breakfasts (the breakfast burrito is my choice), or a lunch of a quesadilla, panino, or sandwich with a wide variety of ingredients. Specialty coffees (this is the sixth-largest dealer of equal-exchange coffee on the East Coast) and homemade desserts (the carrot cake has won awards) are the other reasons to make sure you visit. Entrées $5.50–8.75. The café is the most popular hangout for the outdoorsy types that flock to this area, and you may get a chance to meet some of the world's best, and most well-known, rock climbers and kayakers.

Gumbo's (304-574-4704), 103 South Court St. Open for lunch and dinner; closed Mon. and Tue. Gumbo's is a bit of Louisiana in West Virginia. Start a meal with crawfish and white bean ya-ya soup and choose from Cajun andouille sausage, filé gumbo, shrimp étouffée, or Gullah rice as an entrée. There are too many other low-country items available for me to list here; suffice it to say that this is a popular place. Entrées $5.95–18.

🐟 **Pies and Pints** (304-574-2200; www.piesandpints.net), 219 W. Maple Ave. Open daily for lunch and dinner. Winter hours vary. Very popular during the whitewater rafting season. David Bailey grew up eating pizza on Long Island; Kimberly Shingledecker was the original owner of the Cathedral Café. Their combined forces enable you to enjoy Southern West Virginia's finest gourmet pizzas. Sure, you can get one with pepperoni and cheese, but how often can you chow down on a bacon, spinach, tomato, and aioli pie? Or one with roasted eggplant, red peppers, pesto, and goat cheese? Kimberly suggested the pie with grapes, Gorgonzola, and rosemary; despite my initial skepticism, I found it thoroughly enjoyable. A wide choice of beers helps the pies go down easily, while the in-house-made peanut butter brownie terrine is reason enough to stop by here for dessert if you made the mistake of eating dinner somewhere else. Entrées $9–22.

Oak Hill
Chico's (304-469-6505), 2027 East Main St., on US 19 in the old Skyline Plaza Shopping Center. Reasonably good Tex-Mex food and reasonable prices.

✳ Entertainment
FILM

Beckley
Cinemas–Galleria 14 (304-252-5565), 200 Galleria Plaza. Operated by Marquee Cinemas.

Meadow Bridge
🎞 **Meadow Bridge Drive-In** (304-484-7878; www.mbdrivein.com), on WV 20. The state's smallest drive-in, Meadow Bridge was built in 1953 and shows double features on the weekends May–Sept.

Summersville
Marquee Cinemas (304-872-2470), 300 Merchants Walk. First-run movies in Summersville.

THEATER

Beckley
✔ **Theatre West Virginia** (304-256-6800; 1-800-666-9142; www.theatre westvirginia.com; mailing address: P.O. Box 1205, Beckley 25802), in the Cliffside Amphitheater at Grandview. For decades, Theatre West Virginia has been presenting two excellent outdoor musical dramas during the summer months. *Honey in the Rock* is a dramatization of West Virginia's birth during the Civil War, and *Hatfields and McCoys* is an account of the state's most famous feud.

Fayetteville
Historic Fayette Theatre (304-574-4655; www.historicfayettetheatre.com), 115 South Court St. Musical and dramatic productions with Appalachian themes are presented throughout the year.

Summersville
Ivy & Stone Council for the Arts (www.ivyandstone.org). The council sponsors a series of concerts and performing-arts presentations, with most of them taking place in the Nicholas County High School Auditorium.

✳ Selective Shopping
FARMERS' MARKETS

Beckley
Produce and more may be found at the Beckley **Uptown Farmers' Market** (304-255-9321) on Wed. and Fri., July–Sept., at the Neville St. City Parking Lot.

Summersville
The **Summersville Farmers' Market** (304-872-4121) is open Mon.–Fri. 7:30–1, June–Sep., at the intersection of Broad St. and US 19.

SPECIAL SHOPS

Beckley
✔ **The Little Brick House Gift Shop** (304-253-7242; 1-800-733-7242; www.mtstgolf.com), 1818 Harper Rd. Open daily. Owner Kevin Traube was one of the first individuals in and around Beckley to recognize the value of arts and crafts produced by West Virginians, and he opened his gift shop to feature such items. He did a good business until Tamarack opened nearby with thousands of West Virginia–made items, so he added quality mass-produced items such as Tom Clark Gnomes and Cat's Meow Villages. It's a homey little shop worth visiting—and behind the shop is one of the best miniature golf courses (see *To Do—Miniature Golf*) you will ever play.

WINERIES

Glen View
Daniel Vineyards (304-252-9750; 1-877-378-1990; www.danielvineyards .com), 200 Twin Oaks Rd. Closed Mon. and major holidays. Tours of the vineyards and winery, along with sales and tastings of wines produced from French hybrid, Swenson hybrid, and North American varietal grapes.

Summersville
Kirkwood Winery and Isaiah Morgan Distillery (304-872-7332; 1-888-498-9463; www.kirkwood-wine.com), 1350 Pillips Run Rd. Open daily; closed Sun. Jan.–Mar. Rodney Facemire was working in the coal industry when he planted a few grape vines. When I asked him if he knew anything about making wine when he planted those vines, he replied, "They were making wine thousands of years ago, so it can't be that hard." He read books on winemaking and talked to other vintners, and evidently taught himself well, as the winery now makes

more than 40 different wines. From his experiences of making the country's only distilled grape wine, he established the Isaiah Morgan Distillery (named after his son), which produces rye and corn whiskey and a variety of brandies. Sadly, Rodney passed away in 2006, but his family is operating the winery and keeping it open for all to enjoy.

The tasting house, built from timber cut from the property, is open daily, and a fun grape-stomping wine festival (you can stomp some grapes if you wish) is held the third weekend in September.

THE BEST OF WEST VIRGINIA

✪ Take I-77/I-64 exits 44 or 45 at Beckley, and you will arrive at **Tamarack** (304-256-6843; 1-888-262-7225; www.tamarackwv.com; 1 Tamarack Park), a huge, modern, circular building whose roof is a series of triangles thrusting upward. Charleston architect Clint Bryan says he was emulating the star pattern often found on quilts. Go inside the building and you will find quilts, pottery, glassware, furniture, sculpture, paintings, textiles, jewelry, baskets, and more from close to 2,000 of West Virginia's most highly regarded and talented artists and craftspersons. It truly is the best that the state has to offer, as all of the work must pass a panel of jurors, which rejects about two-thirds of the items submitted. Some of the works are priced in the thousands of dollars, yet I'm willing to bet that you will still find something, if none other than a book or jar of jam, that will catch your eye, and you will end up taking it home.

This is not just a retail shop, though. Studios are available for visiting artists to demonstrate their skills. One day you may see a basket maker and a sculptor at work, the next it might be a wood turner or a glassblower. Also, on any given day you may be privileged to hear one of the state's finest fiddlers, enjoy a lap dulcimer concert, witness folk dancing, or see an audiovisual program in the auditorium. Next to the auditorium is a fine-arts gallery displaying works not for sale.

Don't feel rich enough to dine at The Greenbrier Resort in nearby White Sulphur Springs? Then have a meal at Tamarack's The Taste of West Virginia, managed by the staff of the world-famous resort. Served cafeteria style are samples of chicken potpie, barbecue, fried green tomato sandwiches, corn pudding, and, when the season is right, a number of dishes made with ramps.

West Virginia has always had a reputation for the quality of its arts and crafts, and Tamarack has helped reinforce and enhance it. In fact, in my travels around the state, I have conversed with a number of talented people who decided to call the state home primarily because of the impact Tamarack has made in attracting arts-and-crafts lovers, not just to Beckley, but to the entire state.

✳ Special Events

April: **Feast of the Ramson** (304-846-6790; www.richwoodwv.com), Richwood. Wild ramps are featured in a variety of hometown country-cooking dishes, along with arts, crafts, and music and dance.

May: **The New River Birding and Nature Festival** (www.birding-wv.com), various locations. A week of birding by van, foot, and boat, along with lectures and art exhibits.

June: **Annual Wine Festival** (304-252-9750; www.danielvineyards.com), Daniel Vineyard, Glen View. Wines from a number of state vineyards, along with music, artists, and food from local restaurants. **Annual Music in the Mountains Bluegrass Festival** (304-872-3145), Music Park, Summersville. Features top acts in bluegrass and country music.

July: **Summersville Lake Festival** (304-872-3722), Summersville. Concerts, fireworks, boat parade, and the always-fun (and funny) "Anything That Floats" contest.

August: **Appalachian String Band Music Festival** (304-438-3005; www.wvculture.org), Camp Washington Carver, Clifftop. Five days of string band music from around the world. Primitive camping on-site.

NEW RIVER GORGE BRIDGE DAY
The New Ridge Gorge Bridge is closed for six hours for the annual **Bridge Day Festival** (www.official bridgeday.com) on the last Saturday in October, and more than 250,000 people show up to walk across the bridge, taste food, look over arts and crafts from scores of vendors, and watch hundreds of BASE jumpers hurl themselves off the bridge and parachute to a landing zone located along the river's edge. (This is also the largest gathering of BASE jumpers in the country, complete with classes, trade show, and film festival.)

September: **Country Roads Festival** (304-658-5212; www.hawksnestsp.com), Hawks Nest State Park, Ansted. Food, artisans, and entertainment.

December: **Appalachian Coal Town Christmas and Light Festival** (304-256-1747), Beckley. Go underground to see the season's light display in The Beckley Exhibition Coal Mine. The adjoining miners' village is also decorated, and some nights there is music, a bonfire, and vendors.

The Hatfield-
McCoy Mountains

4

JOHNSON
WM. A.
ROBERT L.
NANCY
ELLIOTT R.
MARY
ELIZABETH
ELIAS
TROY
JOSEPH D.
ROSE
WILLIS E.
TENNIS S.
THEIR CHILDREN

HATFIELD

THE HATFIELD-MCCOY MOUNTAINS

Indian wars. A feud so intense that it became known nationwide. A bloody struggle to secure the dignity of hard-working miners that claimed dozens of innocent lives. Such is the legacy of the Hatfield-McCoy Mountains region, and the attractions here echo this turbulent history.

A county, town, and state park all bear the name of a leader of the Mingo Indians. Chief Logan was a friend to the early settlers until his family was murdered in a cowardly raid.

In and around the Tug Fork River Valley along the West Virginia–Kentucky border are sites associated with the Hatfield-McCoy feud, such as the Hatfield Family Museum and the grave of family patriarch Devil Anse Hatfield.

Coal mining is a dirty business, literally and figuratively, and the Hatfield-McCoy Mountains have seen more than their fair share. The Bituminous Coal Heritage Foundation Museum in Madison explores the nuts and bolts of the industry with displays showing how mining has changed through the years. The excellent Matewan Depot Replica Museum not only provides background on how coal is mined and transported to faraway markets, but also paints a vivid and accurate picture of the struggles miners faced in trying to form a union in the early part of the 20th century. The entire town of Matewan is a museum, having been named a National Historic Landmark. It was here that miners and guards hired by operators met in a gun battle on the town's streets, which have changed little from those days.

However, not all is about strife. There is some great beauty here, too. Chief Logan State Park is on the site of an old coal mine and camp, but you would never know it, as a lush forest now covers a land known for its wonderful display of wildflowers throughout the spring and summer. Twisted Gun Golf Club is built upon a former strip mine that provides soaring vistas of three states.

The region's most recent innovation is the Hatfield-McCoy ATV Trails, with hundreds of miles of routes open to hikers and those riding ATVs, motorcycles, horses, and mountain bikes. The trail system has won a number of awards, not only for its design, but also for the fact that almost all of it is on a patchwork of private property.

Please note: The West Virginia Division of Tourism includes sites in Wayne County—such as Beech Fork State Park, Cabwaylingo State Forest, and East Lynn

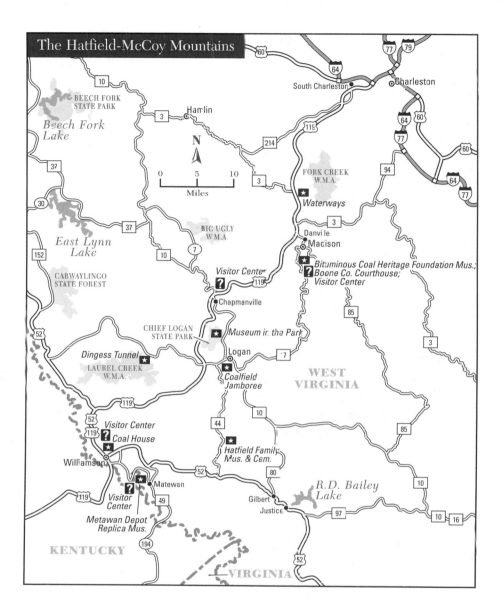

The Hatfield-McCoy Mountains

Lake—in the Hatfield-McCoy Mountains region. However, I have included them in the "River Towns—Huntington and Point Pleasant" chapter within the Metro Valley region because, in my experience, locals and travelers tend to visit them on forays from Huntington more often than from within the Hatfield-McCoy Mountains region.

COMMUNITIES Gilbert is a small community along the Guyandotte River.

The sleepy little town of **Hamlin**, the county seat of Lincoln County, is near the place where Chuck Yeager, the first man to fly faster than the speed of sound, grew up. It is also where my father was born and raised.

Logan came into prominence when railroads arrived in the late 1800s to transport coal out of the region. It was also a center of controversy in the early 1900s, when miners marched on the town in an effort to form a union. The strife resulted in President Harding sending in federal troops to protect property. It remains one of the largest towns in the region.

Williamson, incorporated in 1892, is the southern gateway into the region from Kentucky, and, despite the loss of population due to cutbacks in mining jobs, it remains a major coal transportation hub. Railroading buffs could spend hours watching trains do their thing here.

GUIDANCE The **Boone County Community and Economic Development Office** (304-369-9118; www.boonecountywv.org), Suite 101, Ave. C Building, Madison 25130, can help you with tourism opportunities in its county.

The **Hatfield-McCoy Convention and Visitors Bureau** (304-753-6020; www .hatfieldmccoycvb.com), 214 Stratton St., Logan 25601, provides information for Logan County and much of the entire Hatfield-McCoy Mountains region.

THE REAL STORY

The feud between the Hatfield family of West Virginia and the McCoys of Kentucky has been parodied in cartoons, satirized in television situation comedies, and wrongly portrayed by journalists for so many decades that the true story has almost become lost. It is a tale with as many twists, turns, misunderstandings, and revenges as a classic Greek tragedy, with a bit of William Shakespeare's *Romeo and Juliet* mixed in:

• **1860s**: Many researchers believe the ill feelings between the families start during the Civil War when the body of Asa McCoy, a Union sympathizer and Ranel (Randolph) McCoy's brother, is found in a cave. He is thought to have been killed by a group of Confederates under the command of Devil Anse (Anderson) Hatfield or Devil Anse's uncle, Jim Vance.

• **1878**: Floyd Hatfield, cousin of Devil Anse, is tried and acquitted of charges of stealing hogs belonging to Ranel McCoy.

• **1879**: Sam and Paris McCoy, Ranel's nephews, kill William Stanton, who testified in favor of Floyd Hatfield during the trial. Tried in West Virginia by a judge who is Devil Anse's brother, they are acquitted on self-defense grounds.

• **1880**: Rosanna McCoy falls in love with, and becomes pregnant by, Johnse Hatfield, Devil Anse's son. They never marry, as both fathers oppose the union, and Johnse marries Nancy McCoy, Rosanna's 16-year-old cousin, a year later. (In later years, some people accuse Johnse of having been an abusive husband.)

• **1882**: Ellison Hatfield is stabbed by Tolbert McCoy, Ranel's son, during an argument over an overdue debt. Tolbert's brothers intervene, and one of

The **Gilbert Convention and Visitors Bureau** (304-664-34770; www.visitgilbert wv.com) in the Gilbert Municipal Building on Main St., can help you with destinations within the town and surrounding area.

Although it is primarily concerned with economic development, the **Matewan Development Center** (304-426-4239; www.matewan.com), P.O. Box 368, Matewan 25678, provides tourist information through its Web site, mail requests, and in the visitor center at the **Matewan Depot Replica Museum** (see *To See— Museums*) in downtown Matewan.

Located within **The Coal House** (see *To See—Other Sites*) in downtown Williamson, the **Tug Valley Chamber of Commerce** (304-235-5240; mailing address: P.O. Box 376, Williamson 25661) is on the corner of Second Ave. and Court St. Check with them to learn more about the counties along the West Virginia–Kentucky border.

GETTING THERE *By air*: The closest airports with scheduled flights are **Yeager Airport** (304-344-8033; www.yeagerairport.com) in Charleston and **Tri-State Airport** (304-453-6165; www.tristateairport.com) in Huntington.

them, Pharmer, shoots Ellison but does not kill him. The McCoy brothers are arrested, but before they can be taken to jail in Pikeville, Kentucky, a posse organized by Devil Anse overtakes them and forces them into West Virginia. Ellison Hatfield dies two days later, and the Hatfields tie the McCoy brothers to a pawpaw tree in Kentucky and execute them in retaliation. Devil Anse and 20 of his supporters are indicted in Kentucky for the murders, but no further official action is taken. Bounty hunters conduct raids into West Virginia hoping to capture the Hatfields.

• **1888**: Tired of the raids, a group of Hatfields burns the McCoy home, killing two of Ranel's children, Alifair and Calvin, and beating his wife, "Aunt" Sally. Ranel survives by hiding in the pigpen. Newspapers pick up and run the story across the United States. A posse of Kentucky constables conducts a series of raids into West Virginia, killing Jim Vance and capturing several Hatfield supporters. Valentine Hatfield surrenders, but Devil Anse escapes. A battle between a posse from West Virginia and the posse from Kentucky results in the death of two West Virginia law enforcement officials.

• **1889**: Eight Hatfield supporters are convicted of murder and sentenced to life imprisonment. Ellison Mounts is convicted of the murder of Alifair McCoy and hanged the following February. Although most people think Devil Anse will seek revenge, he never does, and the feud comes to an end. He dies of pneumonia in 1921 at the age of 83. Ranel McCoy is 85 when he passes away in 1901.

• **2000**: The descendants of Devil Anse and Ranel meet in a friendly family reunion to demonstrate that the feud is a thing of the past. The gathering is now an annual event.

By bus: **Greyhound** (1-800-231-2222; www.greyhound.com) will drop you off in Charleston or Huntington. From those cities, you need to take a taxi to the South-ridge Shopping Center in South Charleston or the Barboursville Mall east of Huntington and catch a **Tri-River Transit** (304-824-2944; 1-877-212-0815; www .tririver.org) bus into the Hatfield-McCoy Mountains region.

By car: The four-lane highway entering the region from the north and south is **US 119**, also known as Corridor G, which links most of the larger communities, such as Madison, Logan, and Williamson. The other major route, **US 52**, is a two-lane roadway that follows the twisting route of the Tug Fork and Big Sandy rivers along the West Virginia–Kentucky border.

GETTING AROUND *By bus:* **Tri-River Transit** (304-824-2944; 1-877-212-0815; www.tririver.org) has a number of routes in the region that link most of the major communities together.

MEDICAL EMERGENCIES

Logan
Logan Regional Medical Center (304-831-1101; www.loganregionalmedical center.com), 20 Hospital Dr.

Madison
Boone Memorial Hospital (304-269-1230; www.bmh.org), 701 Madison Ave.

Williamson
Williamson Memorial Hospital (304-235-2500; www.williamsonmemorial.net), 859 Alderson St. Just across the Tug River from Williamson is the **South Williamson ARH Hospital** (606-237-1700; www.arh.org), 260 Hospital Dr., South Williamson, in Kentucky.

✴ To See

DRIVING TOURS, SCENIC & HISTORIC A small pamphlet available from the **Tug Valley Chamber of Commerce** or the visitor center at the **Matewan Depot Replica Museum** (see *Guidance*) details a driving tour that takes in close to a dozen sites in West Virginia and nearby Kentucky pertaining to the Hatfield-McCoy feud. It's interesting to see how close Devil Anse Hatfield and Ranel McCoy actually lived to each other and to other historical locations. Be sure to allow ample time for the tour, as you will be driving exclusively on two-lane road-ways. Also, a number of the sites take some searching to find.

HISTORIC SITES

Dingess
Dingess Tunnel. You might say, "It's just a tunnel. What's the big deal?" Well, how about this? It is approximately ½-mile long and was built more than 100 years ago on the Twelve-Pole line of the Norfolk & Western Railway between Lenore and Wayne. It's now a part of the state highway system (WV 3/5), and it is only one lane wide but open to two-way traffic—and that makes it an unforgettable experi-ence. Turn your lights on as you approach the entrance. Stop and peer into it, look for lights coming from the other direction, and proceed if all looks safe. Soon dark-

ness blocks out most of the light, and water drips from rocks overhead. Hopefully, you will make it through before someone comes at you from the far end. What a thrill—and a cheap one at that.

Lenore

Dingess Petroglyphs in **Laurel Lake Wildlife Management Area** (304-475-2823; www.laurellakewma .com), located northeast of Lenore off WV 65. The Dingess Petroglyphs were found on a nearby strip mine in a rock shelter that could have been occupied by humans. Although the markings look like scratches on the rock to a layperson, some historians say they resemble the Ogam alphabet, Irish or Celtic writing by priests and scholars of past centuries. Other people claim Native Americans made the markings. Still others claim it is a superb hoax. Visit the wildlife management area's parking lot and decide for yourself.

DINGESS PETROGLYPHS

Madison

Boone County Courthouse (304-369-7301), 206 Court St. Listed on the National Register of Historic Places and built in the Classical Renaissance style with Roman Keystone windows and Corinthian columns, the courthouse sits on a low knoll overlooking the small town. Be sure to get out of the car and walk around so that you can also see the **Coal Miner's Monument** on the grounds.

Sarah Ann

The **grave of Anderson "Devil Anse" Hatfield**, Hatfield family patriarch, is situated in a cemetery overlooking narrow Island Creek Valley. Devil Anse ordered the life-size marble statue of himself carved in Italy and had mules pull it up the hillside to the gravesite. He picked the spot because he said it was a "nice and dry" place. Located off WV 44 in Sarah Ann, several miles south of Logan, the dirt road up to the cemetery is steep and rutted, so it's best to leave your car at the bottom and walk the few hundred yards to the grave. More information may be obtained from the **Hatfield Family Museum and Information Center** (see *Museums*).

LAKE The very western tip of **R. D. Bailey Lake** is located in the Hatfield-McCoy Mountains region. For more information see *To See—Lakes* in the "The Southern Border—Bluefield, Hinton, Pineville, Princeton, and Welch" chapter.

MUSEUMS & ART GALLERIES

Logan

Museum in the Park (304-792-7229), located in Chief Logan State Park (304-792-7125; www.chiefloganstatepark.com; mailing address: General Delivery, Logan 25601). Open weekends (and some weekdays, but best to call ahead). Free. It is always a mystery as to what you may find here, as the museum has ever-changing exhibits and displays that feature historical items and artwork on loan from the

West Virginia State Museum and State Archives. Other exhibits will help you learn more about local and regional history.

Madison

Bituminous Coal Heritage Foundation Museum (304-369-5180), 347 Main St. Mon.–Fri. noon–4. Sadly, I have never found this small museum open when I'm in town, but looking through the windows it looks like it gives a quick overview of coal mining. Call ahead if you wish to visit.

Matewan

Matewan Depot Replica Museum (304-426-5744; www.matewan.org; mailing address: P.O. Box 368, Matewan 25678). Open daily; donations accepted. Located in downtown Matewan, the museum is the place to go if you are unfamiliar with West Virginia's history of the Hatfield-McCoy feud, railroading, coal mining, and the strife related to each. In what some people have called "Smithsonian-quality" exhibits and displays, you will learn about the coal mine wars and miners' struggles to form a union.

The building is a replica of the depot that stood here near the turn of the 20th century (note the curvature of the rear waiting room, designed for clearance of the railroad tracks), and much of the money for construction was provided by a modern-day coal company—which may account for a lack of displays about issues in today's coalfields.

Sarah Ann

Hatfield Family Museum and Information Center (304-946-2760), on WV 44 in Sarah Ann, a few miles south of Logan. Donations accepted. The museum is a private endeavor by Jean Hatfield, the granddaughter-in-law of Devil Anse, and is located in a trailer that also serves as the office for her grave-monument business. There is not a lot here, but what is, is fascinating—certificates of death, photos, and artifacts from the days of the feud. For sale are an assortment of books and films about the family. Jean, the museum, and its setting are experiences not found anywhere else.

THE COAL HOUSE

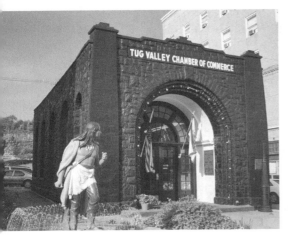

ZOO 🐾 Wildlife Exhibit (304-792-7125; www.chiefloganstatepark.com), Chief Logan State Park, Logan. It is really too small to be called a zoo, but the park's wildlife exhibit is sure to be a treat for children and adults. On a short walk you will see live animals native to the state—bear, bobcat, wild boar (a nonnative), birds of prey, and reptiles, including a rattlesnake. All are in small enclosures, so you are almost assured of seeing them.

OTHER SITES The Coal House (304-235-5240) is on the corner of Second Ave. and Court St., Williamson. As the name implies, this really is a house made out of coal. Sixty-five tons of coal blocks make up the outside walls and pilasters of the building, constructed in 1933. After all of these years, the building is in remarkably good shape, thanks to weatherproof varnish that is applied every two years, making the exterior shine when the sun hits it at the correct angle. At present, the building houses the Tug Valley Chamber of Commerce (see *Guidance*).

✶ To Do

ATV TRAILS As stands to reason, close to 400 miles of the more than 500 miles of the **Hatfield-McCoy ATV Trails** (304-752-3255; 1-800-592-2217; www.trails heaven.com;) are located within the Hatfield-McCoy Mountains region. After all, it was more the trail system than the famous feud that prompted the West Virginia Division of Tourism to give the area its name and keep it from being included, as it once was, in the Metro Valley region. Find more background information about the trail system in "What's Where in West Virginia" at the front of this book. Remember, you must purchase a permit before making use of the trails.

The four sections of the Hatfield-McCoy ATV Trails within this region are:

The **Little Coal River Trail**, which is approximately 60 miles long and has the highest percentage of easy trails. The main access, known as the **Waterways Trailhead**, is located on Little Coal River Rd. (WV 119/67), which is off US 119 near Julian (a little more than 20 miles south of Charleston). A trails visitor center (304-369-9342), usually open daily, is located close to the Little Coal River Trail.

Dingess Run has a little more than 100 miles of trails, and possibly the most evenly distributed difficulties of routes. There's even some single track in the mix. The main access, the **Bear Wallow Trailhead**, is on WV 17, about a 20-minute drive east of Logan.

There are also more than 100 miles of trails on the **Browning Fork**, which has direct access to all of the amenities in the small town of Gilbert. The primary trailhead, with ample trailer parking, is just south of Man off WV 80 near **Rockhouse Creek**.

I am most familiar with the **Buffalo Mountain** section, which has about 95 miles of trail. With direct access from the town of Matewan, the trail system rises high above the Tug Fork River, providing some special views into Kentucky and of the stream coursing its way through the narrow valley. Be aware that this system has the largest percentage of routes considered to be most difficult. Additional access is at the **Reverend Compton Park**, less than 10 miles east of Williamson on US 52.

ATV RENTALS

Matewan
Hatfield-McCoy West Virginia Outback ATV (304-426-5152; www.wvoutback atv.com), on WV 49 just west of downtown. Outback ATV rents ATVs and will work on yours if you happen to be having problems with it. In addition, they rent cabins and offer package deals (see *Lodging*).

BIKING, MOUNTAIN See *Hiking*.

BOWLING ✐ **Plaza Lanes** (304-752-1162), Water St., Logan. Automatic scoring and, just for the fun of it, glow-in-the-dark bowling.

FAMILY ACTIVITIES ✐ **Waterways** (304-369-1235; 304-369-6125; www.water wayspark.com), located on US 119 close to Julian and just south of the Boone County line. Open Memorial Day to Labor Day. Admission $12; children age 5 and under free with paying adult. Float on inner tubes on the Lazy River, slide down the double flume water slides, or splash down the Rapid River Ride at this water park. The children's pool features a life-size elephant slide and gorilla swings. Miniature golf and go-carts are also available for kids with a bit of maturity.

FISHING Laurel Lake Wildlife Management Area (304-475-2823; www.laurel lakewma.com), located northeast of Lenore off WV 65. At 29 acres, Laurel Lake may be small by some standards, but it still yields anglers good fishing for channel catfish, largemouth bass, and bluegill. Trout is stocked monthly Feb.–May.

GOLF

Madison
Riverview Country Club (304-369-9835), WV 17. Built in 1970, the Bob Plant–designed 18-hole course has challenging, small greens, while the well-known 16th hole is a 314-yard with a par 4 with an approach shot over water onto a green surrounded by sand bunkers.

Sprigg
Tug Valley Country Club (304-235-2106), 282 Country Club Rd. Nine holes, with part of the course in West Virginia and the other portion in Kentucky.

Wharncliffe
Twisted Gun Golf Club (304-664-9100; www.twistedgungc.com), 2000 Twisted Gun Ave. West Virginia has acres upon acres of old strip-mine sites, and the Twisted Gun Golf Club is one way to reclaim these areas for recreational use. It has far-reaching views into West Virginia, Virginia, and Kentucky, so you may find it hard to keep your concentration on the game.

HIKING

Lenore
Laurel Lake Wildlife Management Area (304-475-2823; www.laurellakewma .com), located northeast of Lenore off WV 65. Like most wildlife management areas, 12,854-acre Laurel Lake is primarily managed for hunting and fishing, but it does have three short pathways that will get you into the woods if you are in this part of the state. The 2-mile **Lakeside Trail** runs above the waters of 29-acre Laurel Lake, the 2-mile **Sleepy Hollow Trail** takes you into more isolated areas, and the **Flying Squirrel Trail** is just a short leg stretcher at 0.25 mile. Be aware that maintenance and markings may be spotty.

Logan
Chief Logan State Park (304-792-7125; www.chiefloganstatepark.com; mailing address: General Delivery, Logan 25601). More than 20 miles of pathways, also open to mountain bikers and equestrians, wander to the outer reaches of the park,

taking you onto the jumbled mountains and ridgelines that make up the Hatfield-McCoy Mountains region and past old mine openings and other reminders of former industrial days.

277

THE HATFIELD-MCCOY MOUNTAINS

The **Backbone, Interpretive Nature, Buffalo**, and **Cliffside** trails join together to make a 5.6-mile, moderate loop that from spring to fall is lined with a profusion of wildflowers. There are also a couple of nice views along the way.

In May, the difficult, 1.1-mile **Guyandotte Beauty Trail** is a sure bet to see the endangered Guyandotte Beauty flower as well as abandoned coal mines. The moderate, 1-mile **Coal Mine Trail** follows an old mine tram road to a former coal tipple site and to a junction with the **Wilderness Trail**, which makes a quick climb to a ridgeline and then gradually descends to the Wildlife Exhibit (see *To Do—Zoo*) in 6 miles.

Several other, shorter pathways enable you to visit a small waterfall and walk in the woods while remaining close to the main park roadway.

Also see *Green Space—Wildlife Management Areas*.

SWIMMING
Gilbert
Larry Joe Harless Community Center (304-664-2500; www.ljhcc.com), 202 Larry Joe Harless Dr. Open daily. In addition to a gymnasium, walking track, fitness equipment, outdoor tennis courts, dance studio, movie theaters, and a playground, the community center has an Olympic-size indoor pool.

Logan
Chief Logan State Park (304-792-7125; www.chiefloganstatepark.com), on WV 10 about 4 miles north of Logan. The state park's swimming pool, open from Memorial Day to Labor Day, is popular with local children because it has a long water slide and a kiddie pool with a fountain.

TENNIS See Larry Joe Harless Community Center under *Swimming*.

WALKING TOURS A small pamphlet available from the **Matewan Development Center Visitors Center** (see *Guidance*) directs you to sites in Matewan that played varying roles in the feud between the Hatfields and McCoys and the gunfight between miners and the Baldwin-Felts detectives hired by mine owners. Seven detectives and two miners were killed, and bullet holes are still visible in the bricks of the Old Matewan National Bank Building.

Also see *Green Space—Walks*.

✳ Green Space
PARKS Chief Logan State Park (304-792-7125; www.chiefloganstatepark.com), on WV 10 about 4 miles north of Logan. Named for the leader of a Mingo Indian tribe whose territories once included this area, the state park is built upon an old coal mine and camp. The land is well reclaimed, and, unless you hike some of the trails, you would be hard pressed to recognize it as such. Manicured lawns make up the lower elevations, and lush forest covers the jumbled slopes onto which a network of hiking trails meanders.

Chief Logan is one of West Virginia's most popular state parks, and with good reason. First, it is located in an area that does not have as much public land as other parts of the state. Moreover, it has something to offer just about everyone. There are picnic areas, a campground, swimming pool, small fishing lake, horseback rides, an amphitheater with seasonal presentations of *The Aracoma Story* (see *Entertainment—Theater*), and a wildlife exhibit with live animals native to West Virginia (see *To See—Zoo*). Playgrounds, miniature golf, and tennis, basketball, and bocce courts are located throughout the park, with equipment rentals available.

Bringing a bit of the arts and culture to the outdoors is the **Museum in the Park** (see *To See—Museums & Art Galleries*), while a statue honors the park's namesake, and a restored C&O steam locomotive is a reminder of its coal history.

In spring, the park's 4,000 acres become a veritable garden of wildflowers. There are so many species, ranging from the delicate Dutchman's breeches to the 9-foot-tall cow parsnip, that even the most casual of wildflower enthusiasts could spend hours studying and enjoying them. Of particular interest is the Guyandotte Beauty, a rare member of the mint family, which blooms in May and June, and grows both in the middle and along the edges of the trails.

The 1-inch flowers, which spring from the axils of the leaves on the upper part of the 1-foot stem, are some of the prettiest in the forest. The upper lip is a yellowish white, while the lower lip, with three tiny lobes, has lavender lines running along its length. The flower is found from Illinois to Alabama, but it never grows in any great numbers and is listed as rare, threatened, or endangered in every state it occurs. Consider yourself lucky if you see it, as Chief Logan State Park is one of the few places that Guyandotte Beauty grows in West Virginia.

The park sponsors an annual guided wildflower pilgrimage every April if you want to gain more expertise.

WALKS

Matewan's location on a horseshoe bend of the Tug Fork of the Big Sandy made the town susceptible to repeated devastating floods, sometimes as many as four in just a few months. Finally, after decades of discussion, a 0.5-mile floodwall that protects the town was completed in 1996. Most structures of this type are ugly behemoths, but thanks to graphics imbedded in the concrete, this flood wall has

MATEWAN FLOODWALL

become a work of art. Walking upriver, you get to trace the town's history, from the formation of coal millions of years ago, through the Native American occupation of the valley, to the days of railroading and coal mining. It's also a pleasant, scenic outing along the northern bank of the river.

A small pamphlet available from the visitor center in the Matewan Depot Replica Museum in town (see *Guidance*) provides interesting tidbits about the wall's graphics and the history of the floods.

CHIEF LOGAN

Chief Logan, the leader of a Mingo tribe, was known to be friendly to white settlers moving into the area that would become West Virginia and Ohio. However, his feelings changed when his family and other tribe members were brutally murdered in 1774. Vowing revenge, he led a Native American uprising, referred to by historians as Lord Dunmore's War, which resulted in scores of deaths on both sides.

Eventually defeated, he refused to meet with the English to sign a peace treaty, but he sent a message, which came to be known as Logan's Lament, which is printed on the plaque below his statue in Chief Logan State Park:

> I appeal to any white man to say, if ever he entered Logan's cabin hungry, and he gave him not meat; if ever he came cold and naked, and he clothed him not. During the course of the last long and bloody war, Logan remained idle in his cabin, an advocate for peace. Such was my love for the whites, that my countrymen pointed as they passed, and said, Logan is the friend of the white men. I have even thought to live with you but for the injuries of one man. Col. Cresap, the last spring, in cold blood, and unprovoked, murdered all the relations of Logan, not sparing even my women and children. There runs not a drop of my blood in the veins of any living creature. This has called on me for revenge. I have sought it: I have killed many: I have fully glutted my vengeance. For my country, I rejoice at the beams of peace. But do not harbour a thought that mine is the joy of fear. Logan never felt fear. He will not turn on his heel to save his life. Who is there to mourn for Logan? Not one.

CHIEF LOGAN MEMORIAL

WILDLIFE MANAGEMENT AREAS Big Ugly Wildlife Management Area
(304-675-0871). Located 25 miles south of Hamlin off WV 46, or 15 miles north-west of Logan off WV 7 near the town of Leet. In a part of the state that is lacking in public lands on which to hike or walk, the Big Ugly provides a place to get out and stretch your legs in a mature upland hardwood forest. Be aware the terrain is steep, and trails are unmarked and rarely, if ever, maintained. However, if you come here when it is not hunting season, chances are you may be the only person on the entire 6,421 acres. There is the very real possibility of spotting deer, squir-rels, turkeys, grouse, and raccoons.

✳ Lodging

MOTELS & HOTELS

Chapmanville 25508

Best Western Logan Inn (304-831-2345; 1-866-700-7293), 2 Central Ave. Modern rooms with nice amenities; indoor heated pool and exercise room. $79–109.

Rodeway Inn (304-855-7182), WV 10 and US 199. Close to the Hatfield-McCoy ATV Trails, the motel has a guest laundry, free continental break-fast, and Wi-Fi. $60–90.

Williamson 25661

Mountaineer Hotel (304-235-2222; www.mountaineerhotel.com), 31 East Second Ave. The Mountaineer Hotel has been offering accommodations in downtown Williamson since 1925. With extensive and expensive renova-tions completed in 2006, it is now, once again, a historic and comfortable place to stay. As to be expected in a facility with this much age, rooms vary in size and class; ask to see a couple before you make the decision on which one you want. $60–100.

♿ **Sycamore Inn** (1-800-446-6865; www.sycamoreinn.com), 201 West Sec-ond St. The Sycamore Inn is within a few blocks of the downtown business district and has well-kept king or dou-ble rooms. What I find to be the most pleasant, though, is that given the lack of bookstores in the Hatfield-McCoy Mountains region, the inn's gift shop has a good selection of local-interest

books. Also operated by the inn is one of the town's more satisfying dining experiences, the Rivers Edge (see *Eat-ing Out*). $79–89.

BED & BREAKFASTS

Matewan 25678

The Historic Matewan House Bed and Breakfast (304-426-5607; 1-866-878-8178; www.historicmatewanhouse .com), Mate and Farrell streets. I can't imagine finding a friendlier place in the Hatfield-McCoy Mountains region. During my stay, hosts Sharon and Pat Garland invited me to a cookout on the front porch with their family and friends. Not only did I enjoy a wonder-fully grilled dinner, but I was made to feel a part of the group as I was readily drawn into the evening's conversations. I understand this happens regularly to their guests. If a cookout is not planned, you can make arrangements for them to make a special dinner just for you.

A Hatfield-McCoy Trailhead is located only 200 yards from the front door, meaning the Garlands are quite knowl-edgeable about the trail—and even have parking space for guests who bring their own ATVs and trailers.

Located on Matewan's main street and believed to be the town's oldest home, the B&B has a hot tub, modern rooms with private baths (if modest, be sure to ask for a room with an enclosed toilet and tub), and full country breakfasts. $80.

Williamson 25661
Linkous House Bed & Breakfast
(304-235-3174; www.thelinkoushouse
.com), 1 West Fifth Ave. Built in 1896,
the house was home to Mrs. Linkous
for more than 90 years. Renovated
with seven new bathrooms and six
guest rooms, the three-story house is
believed to be the oldest wood home
in Williamson. Within walking distance
of everything in town, the B&B provides free long-distance phone calls in
the United States, TVs in each guest
room, and a huge country breakfast of
pancakes, eggs, sausage, and biscuits
with gravy. Rates start at $70.

CABINS & VACATION RENTALS

Gilbert 25621
Fox ATV Lodge (304-664-3867; mailing address: P.O. Box 1781), on US 52
in Gilbert. Several two-story buildings
for rent are situated on the bank of the
Guyandotte River (you can fish directly
from the property) and less than ¼
mile from the Browning Fork section
of the Hatfield-McCoy ATV Trails.
$115 for up to eight people.

Big Bear Lodge (304-664-9515;
www.bigbearlodgewv.com), close to
US 52 in town. Three structures, all
with bathrooms, full kitchens, and
laundry facilities, may be rented by
the day and may accommodate up to
12 people. Rates start at $130 for
three people.

Livingood Lodging (304-664-8051;
www.livingoodlodging.com), Fourth
Ave. and Guyan St. You have the
choice of five different units ranging
from a five-bedroom home (that
accommodates up to 16 people) to a
two-bedroom cabin. All of them have
full kitchens (or kitchenettes with at
least a microwave oven and small

refrigerator) and porches or decks
overlooking the town's main street,
allowing you to watch how many offroad enthusiasts there really are that
take the town up on its statement of
being "ATV friendly." Rates start at
$100 per night for two people.

Madison 25130
Kathryn's Kabins (304-369-2627;
www.kathryns-kabins.com; mailing
address: P.O. Box 162, Julian 25529),
Little Coal River Rd. (WV 119/67), off
US 119 near Julian. Definitely built
with Hatfield-McCoy ATV Trails
patrons in mind, the small, 12 by 16-
foot cabins are clustered close together, and each has two sets of bunk beds,
a small refrigerator, microwave, and
bathroom. The real draw is that they
are only 1 mile from the Hatfield-
McCoy ATV Waterways trailhead. An
added benefit is the Little Coal River,
located across the road and stocked on
a regular basis by the Department of
Natural Resources. $100.

Matewan 25678
Outback ATV (304-426-5152; www
.wvoutbackatv.com; mailing address:
Box 574), on WV 49 just west of downtown. Several small cabins, complete
with bathroom, microwave, and refrigerator, are located within a few hundred feet of the Buffalo Mountain
portion of the Hatfield-McCoy ATV
Trails. $75 for two people, slightly
higher for additional persons.

CAMPGROUNDS

Gilbert 25621
**Twin Hollow Campground and
Cabins** (304-664-8864; mailing
address: P.O. Box 248), 1.7 miles north
of Gilbert on US 52. With direct access
to the Browning Fork section of the
Hatfield-McCoy ATV Trails, the campground has cabins as well as the usual
campground amenities.

Julian 25529

Big Earl's Campground (304-369-1290; www.bigearlscampground.com; mailing address: P.O. Box 85, Foster 25081), 182 Adams Rd. The campground, a large open area next to the Little Coal River, has tent and RV sites. Canoe rentals, also.

Logan 25601

Chief Logan State Park (304-792-7125; www.chiefloganstatepark.com; mailing address: General Delivery). Open Mar.–Nov., the state park campground is tremendously popular and fills up quickly on nice weekends. Sites, some with electrical hookups, are large and clustered around a centrally located bathhouse with hot showers.

Devil Anse Campground and Cabin Rentals (304-752-1841; www.devilansecampground.com; mailing address: P.O. Box 1942, Logan, 25601). With direct access to the Hatfield McCoy Bear Wallow Trailhead, the campground has restrooms and shower facilities, hook ups, and sites large enough to handle 55-foot RVs. Small, primitive cabins (no electricity or running water) are also available.

✳ Where to Eat

EATING OUT

Chapmanville

Surrey House (304-855-5770), 62 Shae Ave. The restaurant is located within one of the town's oldest houses, adding the proper ambience to the home-cooked meals. $7–18.

Logan

𝒮 **Morrison's Drive-Inn** (304-752-9872), east of Logan on WV 10 in the small settlement of Stollings. Morrison's has been a true drive-in (meaning food is served on a tray that attaches to your automobile window) for more than a half century. You can make your choice before the carhop arrives, as the menu is painted on a plywood billboard at the back of the parking lot. I always have a couple of hot dogs because they are served traditional style, with a bun steamed to perfect softness and topped by chopped onions, a meat sauce, and coleslaw.

Reno's Roadhouse (304-752-9336; www.renosroadhouse.com) 105 Nick Savas Dr. Reno's is a regional chain that serves typical American chain restaurant fare—burgers, wings, salads, ribs, and a wide assortment of beef selections, their specialty. $8.95–20.

Matewan

Hatfield & McCoy Vittles (304-426-5152; www.wvoutbackatv.com), on WV 49 just west of downtown. Open daily for breakfast, lunch, and dinner. Operated in conjunction with Outback ATV (see *To Do—ATV Rentals*). There are some good country cooking items on the menu. Pinto beans and corn bread are perfect for a cold day, while the Oreo puddin' is something you don't find in very many places. With three eggs, fried apples, hash browns, biscuits, gravy, and choice of meat, the Reverend Garret breakfast has enough calories to keep you going well into the afternoon. Menu items are in the $2.50–7.95 range.

Wingo's Grill (304-426-4700; www.hatfield-mccoyresort.com; mailing address: P. O. Box 725, 25678). Part of the Hatfield-McCoy Resort, which has rooms to rent, Wingo's specialties are wings and barbecue served with their own homemade sauce. $5–12.

Williamson

The Rivers Edge (304-235-0811), 101 Prichard St. Open daily for lunch and dinner. Operated by the Sycamore Inn (see *Lodging*), it has a family atmosphere, but also boasts a good beer and wine list. A popular place for business meetings and special occasions for families or groups. Entrées $5–25.

Starters (304-235-8600; www.starters sportsrestaurant.com), 116 East Second Ave. Starters is a sports bar that is able, to some degree, to maintain a family dining atmosphere. Multiple TVs ensure that you will never miss any kind of game or sporting event. Barbecue ribs, steaks, sandwiches, and much more. $4–23.95.

✳ Entertainment

FILM

Gilbert

Larry Joe Harless Community Center (304-664-2500; www.ljhcc .com), Gilbert. Inside the publicly funded community center is a three-screen theater showing first-run movies.

Logan

Fountain Place Cinema 8 (304-831-3450), 102 George Kostas Dr. First-run movies in a area almost devoid of movie theaters.

MUSIC Coalfield Jamboree (304-752-2900), 308 Main St., Logan. The renovated Old Logan Theater is the site of many community events and gospel sings, but most amazingly it plays host, on a regular basis, to some of the biggest names in country music. Past performers have included Marty Stuart, Sammy Kershaw, Connie Smith, and Tracy Byrd.

THEATER ⏺ **Chief Logan State Park** (304-792-7125; www.chieflogan statepark.com). On WV 10, about 4 miles north of Logan. For decades, local and regional thespians have presented *The Aracoma Story* (www.the aracomastory.com) in the park's amphitheater. Staged each year in

August, it is the tragic true tale of a Shawnee woman, Aracoma, and her ill-fated love for a captured British soldier, Boling Baker. Performances such as this are always fun, educational, and a nice way to spend a summer evening with the family.

✳ Selective Shopping

FARMERS' MARKET Logan Farmers' Market (304-792-7017), junction of US 119 and Old Logan Rd., Logan. Open Mon.–Sat. year-round. Along with locally grown produce, flowers and plants, there is a selection of West Virginia jams, honey, sauces, and a mix of arts-and-crafts items.

✳ Special Events

May: **Matewan Massacre Anniversary** (304-426-4239), Matewan. An event for true history buffs, as it commemorates the gunfight between union miners and Baldwin-Felts detectives on May 19, 1920.

June: **West Virginia Coal Festival** (304-369-9118), Madison. Parades, entertainment, and a memorial to coal miners accompany commercial displays of coal-mining equipment.

July: **West Virginia Freedom Festival** (304-752-4044; www.wvfreedom festival.com), Logan. Past festivals have included all manner of entertainment including parades, musicians, petting zoo, motorcycle shows, fireworks, and an alligator show.

August: **Big Coal River Festival** (304-854-2658), Whitesville. Three days of music, entertainment, amusement rides, and food to celebrate the town's birthday. **Boone County Fair** (304-369-9118), Danville. Livestock and produce exhibits and competitions, plus amusement rides and arts and crafts. **Logan County Fair** (304-752-1324), Memorial Fieldhouse, Logan.

September: **Rebellion in the Hills Civil War Reenactment** (304-752-2900), Chief Logan State Park, Logan. Reenactments and living-history demonstrations. **King Coal Festival** (304-235-5560), Williamson. Games, entertainment, and the crowning of a local miner as King Coal.

October: **Apple Butter Festival** (304-855-4582), Chapmanville. Apple butter is made and sold, along with arts and crafts. There's also gospel singing and more. **Shawnee Living History Trail** (304-752-7044), Chief Logan State Park, Logan. Reenactors relate the historic events and ways of life from the 1780s.

December: **Winterfest** (304-824-5500), Hamlin. The Lion's Field is aglow with lights throughout the month.

Central West Virginia

5

SHIMMERING LAKES, TUMBLING
WATERS, SPARKLING GLASS, AND
EASYGOING TOWNS

CENTRAL WEST VIRGINIA— SHIMMERING LAKES, TUMBLING WATERS, SPARKLING GLASS, AND EASYGOING TOWNS

There is no doubt that the Potomac Highlands region receives the most press as the place to go for outdoor activities in the state, which, unfortunately, makes it easy to overlook Central West Virginia. Yet here, at the geographic center of the state, dozens of streams have cut across the Allegheny Plateau, creating deep ravines perfect for canoeing and kayaking. Numerous cascades (five major falls and many smaller ones in Holly River State Park alone) attract waterfalls lovers and anglers who come here in search of the abundant game fish.

The West Fork, Elk, and Little Kanawha rivers have been dammed to form four large lakes, with close to 6,000 acres of water, which are destinations for motor-boating, waterskiing, sailing, swimming, and quiet appreciation of their scenic beauty.

State wildlife management areas surround each of the lakes, with more than 60,000 acres of land on which to hunt, fish, hike, and mountain bike, while three state parks encompass additional public lands to roam.

Holly River and Cedar Creek state parks are quiet places with modest amenities, but Stonewall Jackson Lake State Park is, by far, the swankiest of the state's resort parks. A huge, multistory Adirondack-style lodge, sitting on a knoll overlooking the lake, has first-class accommodations, one of the region's finest dining experiences, and a full-service spa. Rental cottages line the shore of the lake, and houseboats are available for those who would like to spend the night floating on the water.

The region is not just about the outdoors, as reflected in its historical and cultural attractions. Jackson's Mill, the boyhood home of Thomas Jonathan "Stonewall" Jackson, provides a glimpse of what life was like for him as he was growing up. As has been seen when visiting other regions of the state, West Virginia was a hotbed of activity during the Civil War, and sites around Burnsville Lake have preserved fortifications and other reminders of the 1863 Battle of Bulltown.

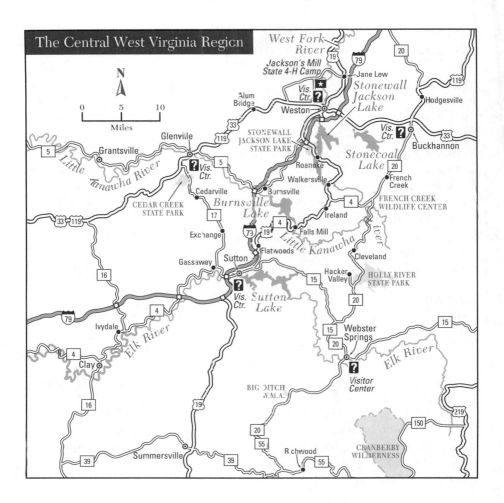

The Central West Virginia Region

Most of West Virginia's large glass factories are no more, but the art of making, blowing, decorating, and etching glass is being kept alive by individual artists, and many of them live and work in Central West Virginia. You could spend a number of days visiting their studios to watch them work their magic.

There are no large cities in Central West Virginia, just towns whose pace of life reflects the easygoing spirit of their inhabitants.

COMMUNITIES Buckhannon is the home of the 1,400-student West Virginia Wesleyan College, founded in 1890 and the cultural center of the town. It's a pleasure to walk the campus and admire the Georgian-style architecture and the huge Greek Revival Wesley Chapel, which seats 1,600 people. The school's auditorium brings in regional, national, and international performing artists, and its art gallery has a continually changing succession of exhibits. Despite large national retailers located a few miles west of the town near I-79, there are several blocks of the downtown area that remain vibrant and alive with restaurants, bookstores, and quite a number of historic buildings, including the courthouse.

A college, Glenville State College, is also the cultural center of small **Glenville**. The school sits on the hillside above the town, and one of its professors helped put it on the map by establishing one of the state's first folk festivals in the 1950s. The town is not much more than a few blocks wide, having ceded land it once occupied to the floods of the Little Kanawha River.

Sutton was a bustling place during the timber-industry boom at the turn of the 20th century, but today it is a sleepy little town several miles removed from I-79. Yet, it has one of the state's best restaurants, an active arts community, and a small historic district. Many of the visitors who pass through it are on their way to nearby Sutton Lake, whose dam towers above the town barely a mile away.

Weston has the region's best-preserved downtown district, with scores of antebellum, Victorian, and early-20th-century homes, churches, schools, and government buildings reflecting its heyday as one of the major glass producers in the state.

GUIDANCE The **Addison Visitors Center** (304-847-5404; http://websterartists .com/addison/index.html), 110 Main St., Webster Springs 26288, is not only a place to obtain travel information, but also one of the region's best shops for locally made arts and crafts, including baskets, furniture, pottery, books, and more. Closed Sun.

Located within the Flatwoods Factory Stores outlet at I-79 exit 67, the **Braxton County Convention and Visitors Bureau** (304-765-6533; 1-877-408-5692; www.braxtonwv.org), 245 Skidmore Lane, Sutton 26601, has the knowledge to direct you to local attractions.

Buckhannon-Upshur Chamber of Commerce/Convention and Visitors Bureau (304-472-1722; www.buchamber.com), 16 Kanawha St., Buckhannon 26201. Open Mon.–Fri.

IT CAME FROM OUTER SPACE?
America was awash with rumors and sightings of unidentified flying objects and space aliens in the 1950s, and West Virginia was no exception. On the evening of September 12, 1952, several boys were playing football when they were startled by a fireball's falling from the sky and landing on a hill not far from the present-day I-79 exit 67 at Flatwoods. Racing to the site, they reported seeing a manlike form almost 12 feet high and 4 feet wide. Dressed in bright green clothing, it had a red face and a spade-shaped head. When it started silently floating toward them, the group quickly ran away. Later, investigators could only find skid marks, disturbed grass, and a metallic odor. The **Braxton County Monster**, as it was dubbed, was never seen again, but newspaper stories fired the imaginations of so many people that more than 10,000 were moved to travel to the county and have a look for themselves.

Find out information about Jackson's Mill, Stonewall Jackson Lake State Park, and other regional attractions from the **Lewis County Convention and Visitors Bureau** (304-269-7328; www.stonewallcountry.com), 499 US 33 East, Weston 26452, which is also the location of Appalachian Glass (see *To See—Glass Artisans*).

The **Sutton Historic District Information Center** (304-765-5581) is within the town hall at 450 Fourth St., Sutton 26601.

GETTING THERE *By air*: **Charleston's Yeager Airport** (304-344-8033; www .yeagerairport.com) is only about an hour away from the southern section of this region, while the **North Central West Virginia Airport** (304-842-3400; www.fly ckb.com) near Clarksburg is less than 30 miles from the northern section.

By car: There is no doubt that **I-79** is the best and fastest way to drive into this region. **US 33** will bring you in from Virginia, but it is a two-lane highway much of the way. Just a bit to the north, four-lane **US 50** will deliver you from Ohio to Clarksburg, where you can then drive south on I-79.

By rail: **AMTRAK** (1-800-872-7245; www.amtrak.com) has an east–west train that stops in Charleston three times a week.

MEDICAL EMERGENCIES

Buckhannon
St. Joseph's Hospital (304-473-2000; www.stj.net), 1 Amalia Dr.

Gassaway
Braxton County Memorial Hospital (304-645-5156; www.braxtonmemorial.org), 100 Hoylman Dr.

Webster Springs
Webster County Memorial Hospital (304-847-5682), 324 Miller Mountain Dr.

Weston
Stonewall Jackson Memorial Hospital (304-69-8000; www.stonewallhospital .com), 230 Hospital Plaza.

✳ To See

COLLEGE ♟ **Glenville State College** (304-462-7361; 1-800-924-2010; www .glenville.edu), 200 High St., Glenville. Sitting on a hillside overlooking the town, Glenville State College was founded in 1872 and, although small, is known for its quality elementary and secondary education majors, as well as the strength of its forestry programs. There's an art gallery and theater for the performing arts, but of greatest interest to visitors is the collection of carved wooden birds by alumnus Claude Kemper. "The Birds of My Hollow" is a display of 45 bird species found near his boyhood home in Gilmer County. Mr. Kemper was self-taught, yet his birds are carved so intricately and painted so accurately that I have seen them sell for hundreds of dollars on Internet auction sites. Look closely and you will see he used nails and bits of hangers for the birds' feet, and mounted them on driftwood found at lakes in Central West Virginia.

COVERED BRIDGE Spanning the Right Fork of the West Fork River, the **Walkersville Covered Bridge**, a 39-foot queenpost truss structure, was built in 1903 at a cost of $567. It was restored in 2003, is still in use, and can be reached by driving US 19 south from Walkersville for about 1 mile.

DRIVING TOURS, SCENIC & HISTORIC Available from the Lewis County Convention and Visitors Bureau (see *Guidance*), the ***Around & About Historic Lewis & Upshur Counties*** pamphlet outlines a 63-mile driving tour that takes you by many of the sites and attractions described in this chapter, in addition to describing historic buildings and sites that are no longer in existence.

The **Mountain Parkway Byway and Backway** (www.mountainparkway.net) forms a loop of more than 30 miles (with spurs) that passes through the northern end of Webster County near Holly River State Park, following twisting two- and one-lane paved roadways through one of the least populated areas of the state. It is a complicated route that is described in detail on the Web site, which points out scenic, historic, and cultural sites, as well as the studios of a number of artists and craftspersons.

The **Cedar Creek Road Backway** parallels the route of its namesake stream for more than 40 miles from I-79 near Flatwoods to WV 5 northwest of Glenville. Sometimes on gravel roads, sometimes on two-lane paved, and often on one-lane asphalt routes, it passes by farms, forests, and many homes from the 1800s, as well as Cedar Creek State Park and the small towns of Exchange and Cedar.

As an alternative to interstate travel, give the **Little Kanawha Parkway Byway** a try. It parallels the Little Kanawha River on WV 5 for more than 77 miles from Burnsville to Parkersburg. As rivers are wont to do, this is a winding route that will take a minimum of two to three hours to drive, but you won't have to put up with interstate traffic, you'll have view after view of the river, and you'll pass through towns that have not changed much for many, many years.

GLASS ARTISANS

Alum Bridge
Willow Creek Glass (304-269-5187; http://community-2.webtv.net/car1942/willow creekglass/page6.html), 1541 Walnut Fork Rd. These craftspersons specialize in artwork made from 95 percent recycled glass, including hand-painted art pieces, flowers, marbles, perfume bottles, animals, and a line from recycled Budweiser bottles. *Please note:* Call before visiting because there was some discussion among the owners about stopping production as this book went to press.

Buckhannon
Catherine Miller Designs (304-472-3331; www.catherinemillerdesigns.com), 7 Cloverleaf Lane. Open Tues.–Sat. When you first watch Catherine Miller use a stone wheel to etch designs into glass, it looks like easy work. Then you realize how much muscle power it takes to keep the glass from slipping off the wheel that is moving 30 miles per hour. Sometimes, the elaborate designs will require a number of different-size wheels. (Former employees of Princess Glass build all of her equipment.) You also see that the design, from her perspective, is backwards as she works on it. The process is known as intaglio engraving, and she is such a recognized talent that orders have come from, among others, governors, diplomats, Mel Gibson, Oprah Winfrey, and Arnold Palmer. Her designs have graced White House Christmas tree ornaments and have been the ceremonial glassware for a

number of U.S. presidents. Of course, in my opinion, her nicest work is the butter-fly she engraved as a gift for my wife.

Jane Lew

⚐ **Masterpiece Crystal** (304-884-7841; 1-800-624-3114; www.masterpiececrystal .com), 96 Trolley St. Sometimes you have to see a product being made to truly appreciate it. At Masterpiece Crystal it takes no less than 10 processes and 10 glassworkers to make just one glass, pitcher, or piece of stemware, many of which are used in table settings at The Greenbrier and the White House. Workers are so meticulous in crafting the products that they make their own tools. Tours are provided Mon.–Fri., and the gift shop, which includes Fenton Glass and items made by local glass artisans, is also open on Sat.

Weston

⚐ **Appalachian Glass** (304-269-1030; www.appglass.com), 499 US 33 East. Chip Turner and his father, Matt, spent decades working in glass factories before using their experience and talents in their own glass-producing business. Chip strongly believes in the preservation of the Appalachian crafts that are dying out, and whenever visitors stop by his shop he will don a microphone and give a complete demonstration on the art of handcrafted, hand-blown glass. Although they produce more than 500 objects, the Turners' specialty is the historic friendship ball. Chip explained to me, "Friendship balls are multicolored globes that were passed from friend to friend as gifts. The sentiment was that they have no beginning or end and would eventually return to the giver." This is the place to come if you only have time to visit one glass artisan in this region.

A GLASSBLOWER AT APPALACHIAN GLASS

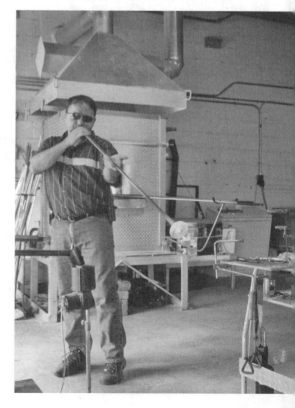

HISTORIC SITES

Weston

The Citizen's Bank (304-269-2862; www.citizensbankweston.com), 201 Main Ave., is still in operation, but welcomes noncustomer visitors to step inside to take a gander at the tallest one-story building in the eastern United States. With India limestone, Vermont granite, Pyrenees marble, French burl marble, Tiffany chandeliers, and a huge wall tapestry, it is quite a magnificent place. Be sure to look up at the ceiling, where a plaster rendition of the Great Seal of West Virginia is covered in precious metals, including 24-carat gold.

Jackson's Mill Farmstead (304-269-5100; 1-800-287-8206; www.jacksons mill.wvu.edu), 160 Jackson Mill Rd.

Closed Mon. from Memorial Day to Labor Day; open Thurs.–Sun. in Apr.–May and Sept.–Oct. Small admission fee. The history of Jackson's Mill goes back to the early 1800s, when three generations of the Jackson family, most notably Thomas "Stonewall" Jackson, lived and worked here. The old gristmill is the last standing structure from the Jackson homestead. Other buildings from the same time period, including a blacksmith shop, a 1790 working gristmill, and several cabins, have been moved here from other sites. A self-guided tour will take you by the sites and, depending on the availability of personal, some living history demonstrations. There is also the Mountain State General Store & Heritage Center, filled with local handcrafted items and foods.

JACKSON'S MILL

The Stonewall Jackson Heritage Arts and Crafts Jubilee, one of the state's largest festivals, is held here every Labor Day weekend and includes Civil War reenactments.

LOUIS BENNETT PUBLIC LIBRARY

Weston's Louis Bennett Public Library (304-269-5151; http://louis bennett.lib.wv.us), 148 Court St., is housed in what has to be the grandest structure of any of the state's libraries. The Jonathan McCally Mansion, constructed in the 1870s by local craftsmen using materials brought in by horse cart from nearby sources, has a huge three-story tower and employs what has been called "riverboat Gothic design." A brochure available at the checkout desk gives complete details of the opulent home.

The Trans-Allegheny Lunatic Asylum (304-269-5070; http://trans -alleghenylunaticasylum.com); 71 Asylum Dr. is that monolithic structure that sits across the West Fork River from the downtown area. Originally known as the Trans-Allegheny Asylum for the Insane when it opened in 1864, it is believed to be the largest hand-cut sandstone (from the river bank) building in the country. More than a quarter of a mile long, it has close to 9 acres of floor space. Sadly, the distinguished building, with a 200-foot central clock tower and acres of parklike grounds, has been abandoned since the state opened a new mental-health hospital in 1994. However, thanks to the media attention brought by the Travel Channel's *Ghost Adventures* and SyFy Channel's *Ghost Hunters*, which "discovered and confirmed" apparitions, there are now historic and ghost tours of the hospital. If you are nervous about the ghosts, sign up for the historic day tours. If not easily frightened, take the two-hour evening tour, or be really brave and go ghost hunting for eight hours all through the night. Times and prices vary; call or check the Web site for the schedule.

Weston Colored School, 345 Center Ave. When constructed in 1881, the brick school was considered a gem, as most schools were wooden frame or log structures. It served as a school for African Americans, many the children of former slaves. In operation from 1882 to 1954 (when the U.S. Supreme Court outlawed segregated education), it now serves, somewhat incongruously it would seem, as the **Mountaineer Military Museum** (304-472-3943; 1-800-296-7329), operated by the local American Legion. Open Fri.–Sun.

Also see Burnsville Lake under *Lakes*.

LAKES

Between Buckhannon and Weston
At 550 acres, **Stonecoal Lake** is Central West Virginia's smallest major lake. Unlike the region's other lakes, which were constructed primarily for flood control, Stonecoal was built by Allegheny Energy to provide water for a nearby power plant. Also unlike the other lakes, it is privately owned (waterfront housing developments are starting to appear), but visitors are permitted to boat (10-horsepower motor limit) and fish for walleye, bass, trout, carp, and catfish. The waters have yielded two state records (one for weight, the other for length) for muskellunge.

Burnsville
&. The U.S. Army Corps of Engineers, which constructed and maintains 968-acre **Burnsville Lake** (304-853-2398; www.lrh.usace.army.mil; mailing address: HC 10, Box 24, Burnsville 26335), reports it plays host to close to half a million people every year. Behind the earthen fill dam on the Little Kanawha River, the lake is long and narrow, with 30 miles of forested and farmland shoreline. The visitor center, reached from I-79 exit 79, provides information on the activities available, including swimming beaches at the Bulltown Day Use Area, and Burnsville Marina (304-853-2822), where you can rent boats. The Riffle Run (304-853-2583) and Bulltown (304-452-8006) campgrounds have hookups, sewage dump stations, showers, and playgrounds. Living within the water are a number of species of game fish, including largemouth and smallmouth bass, rock bass, bluegill,

BURNSVILLE LAKE

sunfish, walleye, saugeye, crappie, muskellunge, channel catfish, flathead catfish, long-nosed gar, and carp. Trout are stocked in the tailwaters during the spring.

Not everything about the lake has to do with outdoor activities. On October 13, 1863, the 12-hour Battle of Bulltown occurred close to Union trenches overlooking the Little Kanawha River on the Weston & Gauley Bridge Turnpike. The present-day Confederate Overlook site has a 0.3-mile paved trail with plaques providing an excellent overview of the battle. Nearby, the Bulltown Historical Area (www.lrh .usace.army.mil/projects/lakes/bus/bulltown) includes a visitor center (open daily during the summer months) and a self-guided trail taking visitors by old Union trenches and the buildings of the reconstructed turn-of-the-20th-century Cunningham Farm. Most of the log structures would have been inundated by the construction of Burnsville Lake and were relocated here to help preserve a bit of the area's history. It's a very worthwhile place to visit, and a reenactment of the Battle of Bulltown takes place at the battlefield each fall.

The land around the lake is owned by the state as the 12,579-acre **Burnsville Lake Wildlife Management Area**. Primarily operated for hunting and fishing, the area is laced with scores of unmarked trails and dirt roads that are open to hiking, biking, and horseback riding. If you are feeling adventurous, the Weston & Gauley Bridge Turnpike runs for 10 miles between Burnsville and Stonewall Jackson lakes. I say "adventurous" because, despite it being listed on the National Register of Historic Places, the last time I hiked the trail, it appeared that there had been no maintenance for a number of years. The route was obvious, but there were many blowdowns and areas where vegetation was overhanging the pathway.

Sutton

& Designed as a flood-control project on the Elk River, whose headwaters are in the Potomac Highlands, 1,440-acre **Sutton Lake** (304-765-2816; 304-725-2705; www.lrp.usace.army.mil; mailing address: P.O. Box 426, Sutton 26601) was authorized by Congress in 1938, but it was not completed until 1961 at a cost of $35 million. This is one of the busiest bodies of water in Central West Virginia, with more than 500,000 people visiting annually. Less than a mile from US 19, the dam visitor center provides a panoramic view of the motorboats, water-skiers, and Jet Skiers zipping across the water, as well as being the place to obtain information about the many opportunities here. Two marinas rent several types of watercraft, and swimming beaches are close to the dam and at the Bee Run Day Use Area. The Gerald R. Freeman (304-765-7756) and Bakers Run–Mill Creek (304-765-5631) campgrounds are open late May to early Dec. and have heated shower houses, dump stations, water fountains, playgrounds, boat launch ramps, and some electric hookups. Open year-round, the Bee Run Campground (304-765-2816)

SUTTON LAKE DAM

is a primitive area with limited facilities. Bass, crappie, bluegill, and muskie are found in the lake, and walleye, northern pike, and stocked trout are in the dam tailwaters. The 18,225-acre **Elk River Wildlife Management Area** surrounds the lake and provides additional outdoor opportunities.

MUSEUMS

Buckhannon

Upshur County Historical Society's History Center and Museum (www .upshurcountyhistoricalsociety.com), 81 West Main St. Open Sun. afternoons May–Sept. Donations accepted. Housed in an 1850s church building, the museum features a number of changing exhibits throughout the summer months. The society also maintains **The Repository** in the Tennerton Public Library, south of Buckhannon, with a variety of materials pertaining to the county's history.

Weston

West Virginia Museum of American Glass (304-269-5006; http://wvmag .bglances.com), 230 Main St. Open noon–4; closed Wed. and Sun. In addition to its extensive displays of handmade glass (primarily from 1900 to the 1970s), the museum also has an area for changing exhibits that often concentrate on one factory or particular artisan.

WATERFALLS The waterfall at **Falls Mill**, Burnsville, only drops about 5 feet, but it is located at a very scenic spot where the Little Kanawha River is more than 50 feet wide. The pool at its base is a popular fishing spot and swimmin' hole. There's an overlook a few feet from the US 19 crossing of the river, but to get close to the falls, turn onto Green Hill Rd. to a large parking area with picnic tables and restrooms.

Also see *Green Space—Park*.

WILDLIFE CENTER ✇ ♿ ✪ **West Virginia Wildlife Center** (304-924-6211; www.wvdnr.gov/wildlife/wildlifecenter.shtm; mailing address: Box 38, French Creek 26218). On WV 20 approximately 12 miles south of Buckhannon. Open daily; very small admission fee. Although operated by the Division of Natural Resources and called a wildlife center, this more closely resembles a zoo—and one that is well run. It presents a realistic and factual look at wildlife by displaying animals in their own habitat in fairly spacious enclosures. You are able to get so close to the animals that you can watch a bobcat family play with its young and purr like housecats, see black bears forage for acorns dropped from oak trees, and marvel at how gray foxes climb trees. You also are privileged to hear the sounds of animals that have not been seen in the state for decades, such as the haunting howling of timber wolves, the stirring bugling of elk, and the chilling cry of a mountain lion. Signs provide tidbits about the natural world: Bison are North America's largest animals; raccoons "wash" their food because water heightens their sense of touch; only one in 10 rabbits survives its first year; and skunks benefit humans by feeding on bees' nests.

A paved pathway of 1.25 miles takes you by the animals, but remember, this is West Virginia: The terrain is hilly, with a number of small ups and downs. I would rate it as a moderate walk, made more enjoyable by the abundance of shade trees.

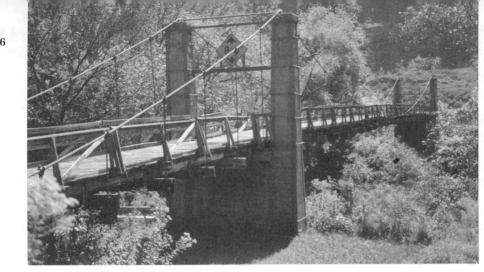

DUCK RUN SUSPENSION BRIDGE

The 1.3-mile Old Oak Trail is an unpaved interpretive route for those who want to do a bit more walking.

The wildlife center is one of the best day outings a family can do. In addition to the exhibits, there are picnic facilities, a small pond where you are permitted to fish, and a gift shop with souvenirs and refreshments.

OTHER SITES If you have never had the opportunity to closely observe a "swinging bridge," here is your chance. Nearby residents, using locally obtained wood, built the **Duck Run Suspension Bridge**, on WV 5/WV 30 about 3 miles east of Glenville, in 1922. The cables, hangers, and anchors were brought downriver by boat.

✻ To Do

BALLOONING Mountain Air Balloons (304-472-0792; www.mountainair balloons.com), 100 Woodall Lane, Buckhannon. Mountain Air Balloons lets you take a silent early-morning or late-afternoon glide through the air over Central West Virginia's green farm fields, deep valleys, mountain ridges, and shimmering lakes. $250 per person, with a minimum of two people.

BICYCLING Fat Tire Cycle (304-472-5882; www.fattirecycle.com), 33 Main St., Buckhannon. In addition to bicycle sales and service, Fat Tire Cycle sponsors mountain bike rides and road trips that everyone is invited to join.

Also see *Green Space–Park* and *Lodging—Resort*.

BIRDING See Cedar Creek State Park under *Hiking*.

BOAT EXCURSIONS ♫ **Little Sorrel Cruises**, offered by the Stonewall Resort (304-269-7400; 1-888-278-8150; www.stonewallresort.com; 940 Resort Dr.) in Stonewall Jackson Lake State Park, Roanoke, are aboard a 100-passenger boat that

takes registered guests out on the lake for a one-hour "Fun in the Sun" cruise.
Included with lodging and operates daily from spring into early fall.

BOAT RENTALS See *To See—Lakes* and *Lodging—Resort.*

BOWLING

Buckhannon
♫ ↑ **Buckhannon Lanes** (304-472-50700, 199 Elkins Rd.

Sutton
♫ ↑ **Mid-Mountain Lanes** (304-765-2811), just off I-79 exit 67.

FISHING In the area around **Holly River State Park** (see *Green Space—Park*), head to the upper **Elk** and **Holly rivers, Sugar Creek, Fall Run**, and **Desert Fork** for some good brook, rainbow, and golden trout fishing. The **Little Kanawha River** and the **Elk River** below Webster Springs are the places to catch smallmouth bass and channel catfish. ♿ Handicapped access is available on the 55-acre lake in the **Big Ditch Wildlife Management Area**, where you can cast for warm-water fish, such as bass, crappie, bluegill, and catfish.

Also see *To See—Lakes* and Cedar Creek State Park under *Hiking*.

GOLF See *Lodging—Resort.*

HIKING Cedar Creek State Park (304-462-7158; www.cedarcreeksp.com), 2947 Cedar Creek Rd. From the intersection of WV 5 and US 33/US 119 in Glenville, drive southward on US 33/US 119 for 4.6 miles, turn left onto WV 17 (Cedar Creek Rd.), and continue for another 4.2 miles. Cedar Creek State Park is situated in the western foothills of the Allegheny Mountains, and the highest point is only 1,448 feet, but that does not mean the hiking will be easy. The terrain is a jumbled mass of narrow valleys and twisting ridgelines that may only be reached by ascending steep hillsides dominated by oak and poplar trees. The lack of far-reaching views is more than compensated for by the opportunity to walk pathways that appear to be rarely trod. On a gorgeous summer weekend when the campground was filled to capacity and every table in the picnic area occupied, I did not see one other hiker as I explored every trail in the park.

On the other hand, wildlife is abundant on the 2,483 acres. Watch for rabbits, chipmunks, grouse, quail, and groundhogs in the lower elevations and edges between field and forest. Raccoons, deer, opossums, squirrels, wild turkeys, and an occasional black bear are likely to be seen anywhere in the park. There is also a variety of butterflies, amphibians, and reptiles, and among the many birds that have been spotted are black and white warbler, American redstart, Canada goose, northern parula, yellow warbler, waterthrush, ovenbird, prothonotary warbler, red-eyed vireo, and orchard oriole.

Recreational facilities within the park include picnic sites and shelters, game courts, miniature golf, a swimming pool, three trout-stocked fishing ponds, and paddleboat rentals. The campground (which is open from early Apr. to mid-Oct. and is extremely popular) has electric hookups, hot showers, laundry facilities, and a camp store, and nature/recreational programs are offered from Memorial Day to Labor Day.

The Park View/Fisherman's Trails take you onto a ridgeline and beside Cedar Creek so that you may experience most of the environments the park has to offer. Its variety and fairly short distance also make it a good choice for an outing with children. Just be sure the kids (and maybe even you) are up to tackling the first portion of the trip. It only lasts for a little more than a half mile, but is it ever steep!

A second trail system, on which there are many loop options, emanates from the campground to follow a number of creeks, rises onto the hillside for scenic views, and passes an interesting watering trough, which was hand carved from solid rock and is believed to be more than 100 years old.

On another historical note, it is thought that the log cabin that currently serves as the campground check-in office was originally built in nearby Troy around the turn of the 20th century. What is known for sure is that it was moved to Glenville in 1928 and served as a gas station for 54 years before being moved once more in 1982 to be rebuilt in the park. Also on park grounds is a reconstructed one-room schoolhouse authentically furnished with a potbellied stove, student desks, and inkwells. Guided tours are offered on Sat. during the summer.

Also see *To See—Lakes*, *Green Space—Park*, and *Lodging—Resort*.

KAYAKING & CANOEING The rivers and streams of this region are barely known to anyone other than local paddlers. Yet, they can provide days of fun on the water. Passing through a quiet country landscape, the 6.6 miles of the **Right Fork** from Cleveland to the Little Kanawha River has Class II–III rapids and an average drop of 50 feet per mile. From Holly Grove to Ingo, the secluded **Little Kanawha River** provides 11 miles of Class I–IV. There's more than 37 miles of good water on the **Elk River** from Elk Springs to WV 7 near Clifton Ford that include Class II–IV and a fun drop on Whittaker Falls. Scenic and remote, but almost always within sound of railroad tracks, the 10.8 miles of Class I–IV on the **Buckhannon River** see very few paddlers, providing you with lots of room and a quiet and uncrowded experience.

Also see *To See—Lakes* and *Lodging—Resort*.

MINIATURE GOLF See Cedar Creek State Park under *Hiking*.

THE PONDS THAT BURPED

The fishing ponds in Cedar Creek State Park were constructed in the 1960s on land that had been used for agricultural purposes, but they wouldn't hold water because of the loamy soil. To keep the water from seeping into the ground, a large plastic sheet covered with clay was placed at the bottom of each pond. What designers had not anticipated was that the natural decomposition of gases under the liner would result in its rising to the surface and falling back down again as the gas bubble escaped. It was such an interesting, and entertaining, sight that crowds of visitors came out on weekends just to watch it happen.

SWIMMING See *To See—Lakes*, Cedar Creek State Park under *Hiking*, and *Lodging—Resort*.

SWIMMIN' HOLES See *To See—Waterfalls* and *Green Space—Park*.

WALKING TOURS

Sutton

The small **Sutton Historic District Walking Tour** brochure (available inside the town hall—see *Guidance*) points out more than a dozen structures in the downtown area and provides a brief description of a few of them.

Weston

Available from the Lewis County Convention and Visitors Bureau (see *Guidance*), the **Weston Walking Tour Map** guides you on a long and extensive discovery of close to 60 sites in town, providing succinct descriptions of each place. You will learn tidbits of history, such as when Virginia's western counties seceded from the state during the Civil War in 1861, $27,000 in gold specie was taken from the vault of the Exchange Bank of Virginia by Union troops and used by the Restored Government of Virginia as the initial treasury of the fledgling state of West Virginia.

✳ Green Space

PARK Holly River State Park (304-493-6353; www.hollyriver.com), 680 State Park Rd. On WV 20, close to 20 miles north of Webster Springs. At 8,101 acres, Holly River is West Virginia's second-largest state park. Located close to the western edge of the Potomac Highlands, its many streams receive a large amount of rain each year, creating deep, narrow valleys with several named waterfalls, numerous smaller cascades, and a rich, lush vegetative environment full of rhododendron bushes and scores of wildflowers.

As the park is miles removed from any large population center or four-lane highway, visitation is lighter than in many other state parks, although it offers a host of amenities, such as rental cabins (see *Lodging*), a large campground with hookups and modern restrooms (cabins and campground are open Apr.–Nov.), a swimming pool, small restaurant, game courts, and a seasonal recreation/natural-history program.

An extensive trail system winds into all corners of the park, most notably taking you by several good views and the park's five named waterfalls. It's about a 2-mile round-trip hike on the Reverie Trail to Tecumseh Falls, named after the famous Shawnee chief. You can walk below the overhang to be behind the falls as it drops about 20 feet. You can also stand behind Tenskwatawa Falls, named for Tecumseh's brother, on a tributary of the Left Fork of the Holly River. The best and most easily reached falls are located along Potato Knob Trail off WV 3. The Lower Falls, which has several drops, flows over a bed of coal; the Upper Falls has a nice wading pool. The best of the lot is Shupe's Chute, where rocks squeeze the stream into a narrow, 4-foot-wide defile and the water goes roaring through it. The pool at the bottom is a popular swimmin' hole.

The park's trail system is closed to mountain bikes, but the large number of unimproved roads open to riders attracts many fat-tire devotees.

Insider's tip: Bring along a rod and reel on any of the waterfall hikes. All of the streams are cooled by the shade of hemlock trees and rhododendron thickets, providing the perfect environment for the abundant trout that congregate in the many small pools.

Also see Cedar Creek State Park under *Hiking* and *Lodging—Resort*.

✳ Lodging
RESORT

Roanoke 26447
Stonewall Jackson Lake State Park (304-269-0523; www.stonewalljackson sp.com), 149 State Park Trail, does not have the word resort in its official name, but if any place ever deserved the moniker, this is it. Within its 2,000-plus acres, and operated by a concessionaire as the Stonewall Resort (304-269-8887; 1-888-278-8150; www .stonewallresort.com; 940 Resort Dr.), are a sprawlingly huge, 198-room lodge ($170–200; many packages available), lakeside cottages (only rented by the week during the summer; by the day the rest of the year), three restaurants, a golf course designed by Arnold Palmer, indoor and outdoor pools, fitness center, bicycle rentals, and a spa

THE LODGE AT STONEWALL JACKSON LAKE STATE PARK

complete with massage therapy, facial treatments, body therapies, and sun deck. There is also a marina with close to 400 slips and a bait shop, with fishing, pontoon, houseboat ($600 per night for first two nights, $150 additional nights), and kayak rentals, along with boat cruises (see *To Do—Boat Excursions*). The campground has full hookups, hot showers, and a playground.

Named for the famous Civil War Confederate general who was born nearby, the lake was completed in the mid-1980s when the West Fork River was dammed for the purposes of flood protection, water quality control and supply, and recreation. The park was created soon afterward. There is an entrance fee, which is a rare thing in the West Virginia state park system and hopefully not a harbinger of fees being imposed for other places. As to be expected for a place on the edge of a 2,650-acre lake, emphasis is on water activities, but a few trails have been built to let you explore the land.

An excellent way to spend a day here would be to rise early enough to take the 2-mile roundtrip Autumn Laurel Trail, on such easy terrain that small children should have little trouble making it to the farthest point to watch the sun rise over the lake. Go to the lodge for a leisurely lunch, spend the afternoon watching for osprey as you kayak along the edge of the lake, and spend the evening swimming in the pool—or better yet—having a full massage.

In the resort's main dining area is **Stillwaters**, possibly the best fine-dining venue in this region. Open for breakfast, lunch, and dinner, it has a menu that is always changing and features items from around the world. The last time I was there I dined on arctic char, raised in cold spring waters in Southern West Virginia. The following month, the chef was going to feature the foods of Germany. Items that are almost always on the menu, and what the chef calls "New Appalachia" cuisine, include entrées of fish, chicken, pork, and beef whose various recipes incorporate interesting and great-tasting sauces and/or spices. I highly recommend having at least one meal here. Entrées $12–34.

The lake was constructed and is maintained by the U.S. Army Corps of Engineers (304-269-4588; www.lrp .usace.army.mil; mailing address: P.O. Box 806, Weston 26452), which also maintains a visitor center near the dam that has an excellent diorama that puts the lake into an easy-to-understand 3-D perspective. Fishing is especially good for largemouth bass and other species, including crappie, walleye, bluegill, yellow perch, muskellunge, channel catfish, bullhead, and carp. The tailwaters contain stocked trout.

MOTELS & HOTELS

Sutton 26601
♿ **Days Hotel** (304-765-5055; 1-866-700-7284; www.flatwoods.com), 2000 Sutton Lane. Within sight of I-79 exit 67, the hotel (actually a Days Inn) is a convenient stopping point. One of the region's best-maintained motels, it has more of the feel of an elaborate hotel. The large lobby has overstuffed chairs, art décor, and fresh coffee available all the time. Its conference facilities are in demand by groups who find its location in the geographic center of the state to be convenient. You are the winner, as management keeps things, such as the swimming pool and exercise room, in top shape so they are always ready to be shown to conference planners. $108–125.

The motel's **Visions Restaurant** offers extensive breakfast and dinner buffets, featuring prime rib and shrimp cocktail with daily specials.

BED & BREAKFASTS

Buckhannon 26201
A Governor's Inn (304-472-2516), 76 East Main St. A Governor's Inn received its name because the Queen Anne home with a wraparound veranda was the home of West Virginia's second governor. Befitting a three-story brick mansion from the Victorian era, there is a stately feel to the B&B. The four guest rooms and two suites are lavishly furnished with period furniture, and frescos painted on the ceiling and walls (done by local college students) add to the atmosphere of stay-

A GOVERNOR'S INN

ing in a not-so-ordinary home. Caramel French toast, casseroles, seasonal drinks, and bread pudding with amaretto sauce are often served for breakfast, and desserts and flavored coffees are offered each evening. My time was spent sitting on the second-floor turret porch watching the comings and goings of life in Buckhannon. $76–99.

Riverside Bed and Breakfast (304-472-0796; www.riversidewv.com), 113 Island Ave. The 1895 home has a great setting—it's on four acres of a peninsula that juts into the Buckhannon River, meaning water runs along three sides of the property. A well-kept yard, three guest rooms (all with private bath), and a nice restoration of the home that retains the original floors, pocket doors, and woodwork make this a place to relax and forget any cares you may have brought with you. $75–115.

Sir Charles Inn Bed & Breakfast and Restaurant (304-472-1415; www.sircharlesinn.com), 85 West Main St. Dee Heater and her mother, Helen, spent many months renovating the Sir Charles Inn after its use as an office building. Shag carpets and false dropped ceilings were removed, and you now get to enjoy the original molding, hardwood floors, and family-heirloom furniture. Each guest room has a gas fireplace and private bath. Possibly the nicest part of staying here is that you just have to walk downstairs to enjoy Dee's wonderful cooking (see *Dining Out*). $90.

Sutton 26601

Café Cimino Country Inn (304-765-2913; www.cafeciminocountryinn .com), 616 Main St. The Colonial Revival mansion, more than 100 years old, has a 500-foot frontage along the Elk River, inviting anglers to cast a line. Hosts Melody and Tim Urbanic,

along with family and staff, renovated the house and have decorated it well.

Furnished with antiques appropriate to the period, the main house has four guest rooms, with four others in the more private carriage house. Two suites are in the separate brick cottage. All accommodations have private baths, and almost all overlook the river. The house is near the center of town, but besides the luxurious feel of the rooms, the best reason I can give you for staying here is that, as at the Sir Charles Inn Bed and Breakfast and Restaurant in Buckhannon, you only have to walk down the steps to sample the owner's wonderful cooking skills offered at breakfast and, again, in the evening in the café (see *Dining Out*). $145–185.

Weston 26452

✿ **Natural Seasons Bed & Breakfast** (304-269-7902; www.wvbnbs.com /inns/68.html), 17 Center Ave. Within easy walking distance of downtown Weston, Natural Seasons B&B is operated in one of the most environmentally friendly ways you may ever encounter. The landscaping, which is designed to provide cooling shade for the house, is also edible, containing blueberry bushes, grapevines, and fruit trees. Furniture in the four guest rooms (private baths) of the unpretentious early-20th-century Federal-style home is made locally from reprocessed wood, and the full breakfast, made with and stored in energy-efficient appliances, includes seasonal fruits and vegetables from the garden. $75.

Relax Inn and Getaway (304-269-2345; www.relaxinnandgetaway.com), 915 Grass Run Rd. Located just two miles from I-79, the large log lodge, with three guest rooms (one is a suite), sits on a 350-acre farm on which you are permitted to roam and walk the hiking trails. With an in-ground swimming pool, exercise room, pool table, fishing pond, 300-yard golf driving range, and horseshoe pit, you'll feel like you are at your own personal resort. $90–125.

CABINS & VACATION RENTALS

Hacker Valley 26222

&. **Holly River State Park** (304-493-6353; www.hollyriver.com; State Park Rd.), on WV 20, close to 20 miles north of Webster Springs. Throughout most of this book, if a state park has rental cabins, I make mention of that only in my description of the park. However, the cabins at Holly River are in such a beautiful setting that they deserve a description of their own. Surrounded by a thicket of some of the state's most lush growths of rhododendron, the cabins are in a quiet part of the park (Number 1 has the most privacy) just a few feet above the inviting wading pools and burbling water of Laurel Fork. Open Apr.–Nov., they are built of native stone or logs and have wood-burning inserts, full kitchens, and all linens, and they can sleep two to five people. $91–140. From the second Mon. in June to Labor Day, the cabins are rented only on a weekly basis and are $462–756 for the week.

A CABIN IN HOLLY RIVER STATE PARK

Weston 26452

Hillbilly Haven Log Cabin Rentals (304-269-3459; 1-866-652-3379; www .hillbillyhavenwv.com), 235 Haven Ln. Situated less than two minutes from Stonewall Jackson Lake State Park, the modern cabins are arranged in a row along 30 acres in a narrow, sloping hollow with its own small brook. Sleeping from two to eight guests, the cabins have kitchens, TVs, and all linens, and some come with a whirlpool tub and washer and dryer. *Insider's tip*: If you are an avid angler, ask for cabin Number 1 or Number 2; you can cast a line into the small pond from the cabins' porches. $120–235.

&. **Lake View Cabins** (304-269-5813; mailing address: 42 Mill St.). From I-79 exit 96, drive WV 30 for 5.5 miles, turn left onto Little Skin Creek Rd., and continue another 0.8 mile. Open all year, weather permitting. These two-bedroom cabins live up to their name, as they sit in an open field just a few hundred feet above the Little Skin Creek section of Stonewall Jackson Lake and only 100 yards from the Georgetown boat ramp. Kitchens are fully equipped, and there are TVs, barbecue grills, and heat and air-conditioning. All bed linens are prov-ided, but you must bring your own towels. $110 per night with a two-night minimum.

Also see *Resort*.

CAMPGROUNDS

Roanoke 26647

Whisper Mountain Campground and RV Park (304-452-9723; www .whispermountaincampground.com), 4897 Three Lick Rd. Open Apr.–Oct. Hookups, dump stations, modern restrooms, and laundry facilities, along with a fishing pond, hiking trails, playground, and an interesting boat-shaped swimming pool.

Sutton 26601

Flatwoods KOA Park (304-765-7284; 1-866-700-7284), behind the Days Inn, which is within sight of I-79 exit 67. In addition to dozens of shaded pull-through sites with full hookups, wide, paved roads, and a few enjoyable hiking trails on the property, the campground's guests are permitted to use the amenities of the adjacent Days Hotel, which include an exercise room and indoor-outdoor pool.

Weston 26452

Broken Wheel Campground (304-269-6097; www.brokenwheelcamp ground.net), 2060 Skin Creek Rd. Open all year. RV (water and electric hookups and dump station) and primitive tent sites less than 2 miles from I-79 exit 96 and Stonewall Jackson Lake State Park. The campground is horse-friendly and even permits you to ride on its trails. The country store has fishing supplies, crafts, groceries, and propane exchange.

Also see *To See—Lakes*, Cedar Creek State Park under *To Do—Hiking*, and *Resort*.

❈ Where to Eat

DINING OUT

Buckhannon

Sir Charles Inn Bed & Breakfast and Restaurant (304-472-1415; www .sircharlesinn.com), 85 West Main St. Open for lunch Wed.–Fri., dinner Wed.–Sat., and brunch on Sun. It seems like there is always something special about a restaurant located in a former home, and Sir Charles is no exception. The menu changes as chef-owner Dee Heater searches for the freshest seasonal ingredients. The orange-walnut salad is refreshing on a hot summer afternoon, and the beef and pineapple skewers will warm you on winter days. The broccoli bundles (tilapia wrapped around broccoli and jack cheese and baked in lemon sauce) was the choice for my dinner, while my dining companion chose the steak pizzaiola (rib-eye steak with sautéed peppers, onions, tomatoes, and pepperoni with a red wine sauce). Currently my favorite Buckhannon restaurant. Entrées $9–18.50.

Sutton

❂ **Café Cimino** (304-765-2913; www.cafeciminocountryinn.com), 616 Main St. Many people consider Café Cimino to be one of the state's finest restaurants and think nothing of driving hours just to have a meal here. The restaurant is named for chef-owner Tim Urbanic's Italian-immigrant grandparents, who taught him the value of good ingredients (from as many local sources as possible) and quality cooking. The menu changes, but to give you an idea of what you may find, the Southern Italian and European cuisine has included shellfish with prosciutto, tuna Gorgonzola, goat cheese and roasted red pepper lasagna, and saltimbocca. You can have the imported linguine with a choice of sauces, such as spinach and anchovy with feta cheese, or creamy mushroom. Save room so that you can end your meal with the Italian mascarpone with fruit.

The setting is just as pleasant as the food, as the restaurant is in the refurbished turn-of-the-20th-century **Café Cimino Country Inn** (see *Lodging*). The antiques and paintings and photographs by West Virginia artists add to the milieu created by the sumptuous smells emanating from the kitchen and the eye-pleasing presentations of the entrées. Entrées $12–42.

Also see *Lodging—Resort*.

Buckhannon

Market Bistro (304-472-3758), 15 East Main St. Open for lunch Mon.–Tues. and lunch and dinner Wed.–Sat. Take a look at the offerings of new books in **The Bookstore** (304-472-1840) as you walk by them to the back of the store, where the bistro is located. Using locally available produce and other products, the chefs create some good soups and sandwiches (with fresh baked breads) and entrées, such as steelhead trout, veggie lasagna, Swedish meatballs over basmati rice, and chilled strawberry soup for dinner. $8.95–17.95.

Webster Springs

✎ **The Custard Stand** (304-847-2942; www.custardstand.com), 364 Webster Rd. Open daily except Thanksgiving, Christmas Eve, and Christmas Day. There is no doubt that the ice-cream treats (try a raspberry or peanut butter milk shake) are popular, but what gets locals and visitors to stop by is the famous hot dog chili, a family recipe that has been available in Webster Springs for more than 80 years. In fact, the owners had so many requests just for the chili that it is now packaged and available in more than 200 grocery stores in several states. Along with the hot dogs, you could order sandwiches, salads, gyros, pizza, French fries, onion rings, cheese sticks, and jalapeño "bottle caps" to eat on picnic tables under the shade of the wooden pavilion (no indoor seating). Entrées $1–6.95.

✎ **Main Street Café** (304-847-2360), 2111 Main St. Open daily for breakfast, lunch, and dinner. The biscuits I had with my breakfast were just like the ones my grandmother used to make—toasty and crunchy on the outside, soft and flaky inside. The most expensive breakfast is around $4, and all the country-cooking dinners are less than $7.

Weston

✎ **Second and Center Café** (304-517-1151), 139 East Second Ave. Open 11–4 Mon.–Fri. The ambience of the Second and Center Café is one of the nicest you will find in this region. Located in a lovingly renovated 1914 building, it retains the original tin ceiling and wooden floors, and is adorned with bits and pieces of items that have been rescued from other older buildings in town that no longer exist. Soups, sandwiches, and wraps prepared fresh. Most items less than $10.

Hickory House (304-269-7373), 1137 US 19 North. Open daily for lunch and dinner. Famous for its barbecue and slaw, the Hickory House has also been known to serve some interesting items such as tilapia parmigiano, Louisiana shrimp sandwich, and a pork-loaded baked potato. Most entrées around $10.

Kathy's Riverside Restaurant (304-269-2112), Water St. Open daily for breakfast, lunch, and dinner. Located inside a former hardware store next to the West Fork River (sadly, the large

THE CUSTARD STAND

picture windows overlook the street and not the river), Kathy's is the place to come for sandwiches for lunch or a simple home-cooked meal for dinner. Entrées $4.95–11.95.

COFFEE BARS

Buckhannon

The Daily Grind Gourmet Coffee House (304-471-2218), 3A East Main St. Closed Sun. The entrance, via an alleyway, belies the pleasant atmosphere, where you can enjoy coffee in its many varieties and the light breakfast and lunch menu.

✳ Entertainment

FILM

Buckhannon

⬆ **Upshur Cinema 6** (304-473-0060; www.upshurcinema6.com), Brushy Fork Rd. First-run movies and self-serve butter for your popcorn. (The management once told me they don't care "if your popcorn is swimming in butter.")

Sutton

⬆ **The Elk Theatre** (304-765-2519) is a one-screen theater located in downtown Sutton that shows current movie releases each weekend.

MUSIC ⬆ **Jerry Run Summer Theater** (304-493-6574; http://members .citynet.net/jerryrun), 22 Soggy Bottom Rd., Cleveland. You can enjoy bluegrass and other traditional music in the indoor auditorium with festival seating every Sat. (and sometimes Fri.) night from late Apr. to early Oct.

THEATER Landmark Studio for the Arts (304-765-3166; www.land markstudio.org), Fourth and Main streets, Sutton. The nonprofit visual- and performing-arts group is located in a converted historic Victorian-era

---

AS AUTHENTIC AS IT GETS
The **West Virginia State Folk Festival** (www.wvfolkfestival.org) grew out of an Appalachian culture class taught by Glenville State College professor Patrick Gainer. It was first held in 1950, which makes it, by far, one of the oldest of the state's music festivals. It is a celebration of true mountain music, with only acoustic instruments permitted. Enjoy historical songs, ballads, and instrumentals played on hammered and lap dulcimers, autoharps, banjos, guitars, fiddles, and mandolins. It's held in June and is one of the state's best events; don't miss it.

---

church, which is also home to the West Virginia Landmark Players and the Landmark Youth Theatre Project.

Mountain Lakes Amphitheater (304-765-2032, ext. 101; 1-866-700-7284; www.mountainlakesamphitheater .com), 2000 Sutton Lane, Sutton. The amphitheater is another undertaking of local entrepreneur John K. Skidmore II (he is also instrumental in the Days Hotel, Flatwoods KOA, Flatwoods Factory Stores, and other businesses). Built in 2005, it is a small but deluxe outdoor venue for theater groups, concerts, and events featuring regional and national acts.

✳ Selective Shopping

ANTIQUES

Buckhannon

Main Street Antiques & Collectibles (304-473-1101), 14 East Main St. Closed Sun. In addition to the usual items found in antiques shops, this large store has fireplace mantels, chandeliers, columns, and pocket doors, along with a seemingly endless supply of oak furniture.

Sutton

Sisters Antique Mall (304-765-5533), 1954 Sutton Lane. The chances to browse for antiques are few and far between in this region, so it is worth it to spend some time here.

BOOKSTORES

Buckhannon

Books • Books • Books (304-473-0011), 47 East Main St. Closed Sun. A good selection of more than 20,000 new and used books.

Glenville

Towne Bookstore and Video Club (304-462-8055), 102 East Main St. One of the smallest bookstores in the state, but also the only one for many miles around where you can pick up bestsellers, local-interest, and children's books in both hardback and paperback. Video and game rentals, too.

Also see Market Bistro under *Coffee Bars*.

FARMERS' MARKETS

Buckhannon

Upshur County Tailgate Market (304-473-4208), Madison St. Operates June–Oct., Tues. and Fri. 6–1.

Weston

The Weston Farmers' Market (304-269-4660), West Second St. Operates July–Dec., Wed. and Sat. 8–noon. Also located in Weston (on US 33), the **Farmers' Market** (304-269-2667) is an indoor business located at the Appalachian Glass Market (see *Special Shops*) and open daily year-round.

OUTLETS Flatwoods Factory Stores (304-765-3300; www.flatwoods

factorystores.com), 2500 Skidmore Lane, Sutton. Although it is within sight of I-79 exit 67, this will be one of the least crowded outlet malls you may ever visit. That's good, because you can browse unharried for bargains from companies such as Tommy Hilfiger, The Paper Factory, CorningWare, Playtex, Dress Barn, and others. Two shops of particular note are the Fenton Art Glass and Fiesta Dinnerware outlets.

SPECIAL SHOPS

Alum Bridge

La Paix Herb Farm (304-269-7681; www.lapaixherbfarm.com), 3052 Crooked Run Rd. La Paix has its own essential-oil distillery to manufacture a full line of natural health products, including lip balms, salves, creams, and fragrances. Yet this is more than just a place to purchase these items. Customers are welcome to wander about the farm, which is on the National Register of Historic Places, relax in the herb and vegetable gardens, become Zen-like by walking the course of the labyrinth, or enjoy the shade of the surrounding forest. La Paix's annual Lavender Fair in June features workshops and demonstrations on essential-oil distillation, lavender-soap making, yoga, wild edibles, and growing mushrooms and medicinal herbs.

Weston

Appalachian Glass Market (304-269-3906), 499 US 33 East. Home to Appalachian Glass and the Central West Virginia Farmers' Market, this building also features the small working galleries of a number of artists, such as a wooden toy maker, basket weaver, painter, and quilter.

WINERY Lamberts' Vintage Wines (304-269-4903; www.lambertsvintage wine.com), 190 Vineyard Dr., Weston.

LAMBERTS' VINTAGE WINES

Open daily. With vineyards surrounding it, the winery (constructed with huge stone blocks collected locally—some weighing more than a ton—and rounded top doors of solid two-by-fours) is an impressive structure flanked by a meticulously maintained flower garden. The tasting room has a 3-inch-thick bar counter made of wood cut in Canada in the 1950s.

Jim and Debbie Lambert, who are in the timber business, started making wine as a hobby, but they got serious about it in 1992. Most of their wines are made from French hybrid and American varietal grapes (my favorite is the Seyval). I'm not a real fan of berry wines, so I was really surprised when I enjoyed the flavor of the blueberry wine.

✳ Special Events

March: **Annual Culinary Classic** (304-269-7400; www.stonewallresort .com), Stonewall Resort at Stonewall Jackson Lake State Park. West Virginia chefs presenting their best in taste testings, demonstrations, and a five-course dinner.

April: **Webster Wildwater Weekend River Festival** (www.websterwv.com /whitewater.html), various rivers. A downriver race on the Class II–III Elk River, with fun trips on the Williams, Cranberry, Gauley, Elk, and Back Fork of Elk rivers.

May: **West Virginia Strawberry Festival** (304-472-9036; www.wvstraw berryfestival.com), Buckhannon. Showing the best of the local harvest for more than six decades. **Webster County Nature Tour** (304-226-3888; www.proseandphotos.com/wv_spring _in_the_mountain_park.htm), Camp Caesar, Cowen. If you enjoy the outdoors, do not miss this annual event, which has, among others, tours to the top of Elk Mountain (difficult hike), an easier walk to 30-foot-tall Leatherwood Falls, and a medium jaunt along the Williams River. Sponsored by the Webster Springs Garden Club and the West Virginia Division of Natural Resources and Department of Agriculture. Dormitory-style accommodations are available. **Native American Gathering** (304-462-5333), Glenville.

Memorial Day weekend: **Annual Webster County Woodchopping Festival** (304-847-7776; www.woodchop pingfestival.com), Baker's Island Recreation Area, Webster Springs. This event has grown so popular, attracting participants from a number of foreign countries, that the finals have been featured on ESPN. Along with the woodchopping and sawing contests are car, truck, and motorcycle shows; the state firemen's rodeo championship; arts and crafts; the state turkey-calling championship; and music concerts.

July: **Lewis County Fair** (304-269-7328), Jackson's Mill.

Labor Day weekend: **Jane Lew Fireman's Arts & Crafts Festival** (304-

IRISH ROAD BOWLING

The annual Irish Spring Festival, held in, naturally, Ireland, West Virginia, includes Irish Road Bowling, a 300- to 400-year-old game primarily played in southern Ireland. To play, you use an underhanded throw to hurl an iron-and-steel ball as far as you can down a country road. The course is usually 1 to 2 miles long and includes all of the roadway's twists, turns, curves, ups, and downs. The fewest number of throws from the beginning to end wins. Don't be shy if you've never played; there is such a merry atmosphere that everyone is invited to give it a try. The festival also includes an Irish jig, leprechaun contest, stew cooking, harp workshop, and other "Irish" events. Head to Ireland in March around St. Patrick's Day to enjoy the weeklong happening. If you do attend, you can also join in on the "Pledge of Weather Regardless":

I pledge allegiance to the flag
Of the Irish Spring Festival.
I will attend all events,
Regardless of the weather.
Rain or shine, snow or fine,
May we all be Irish for the time,
And spring be in our hearts forever.

The Web site www.angelfire.com/wv/irishspringfestival contains information about the festival, and www.wvirishroadbowling.com provides details on other Irish Bowling events in the state.

269-7328), Jane Lew. More than 200 contemporary and heritage artisans participate to benefit the volunteer fire department. **Stonewall Jackson Heritage Arts and Crafts Jubilee** (1-800-296-1863), Jackson's Mill. One of the largest, and most prestigious because it is juried, arts-and-crafts festivals in the state.

September: **Golden Delicious Festival** (www.claygoldendeliciousfestival.com), Clay. Clay County is where the golden delicious apple originated, and the festival pays tribute to it by crowning Miss Golden Delicious and serving up myriad treats containing the fruit.

October: **International Burgoo Cook-off** (304-847-7291), Baker's Island Recreation Area, Webster Springs. Features the famous "Burgoo" stew cook-off, apple pie contest, live music, arts and crafts, kids' contests, and a kids' pot of "Burgoo." What is Burgoo? Any kind of stew cooked in a pot over an open flame outdoors. Come here and taste some concoctions that you never would have imagined.

Mountaineer Country

6

MORGANTOWN AND VICINITY

THE CLARKSBURG/FAIRMONT
ENVIRONS

MOUNTAINEER COUNTRY

M ountaineer Country is named for the West Virginia University (WVU) football team, the Mountaineers, and on game weekends the state's highways are crowded by the migration of fans headed to Morgantown. The team is consistently ranked high nationally and is almost always invited to a bowl game.

Mountaineer Country is more than football, though; it is one of the state's most ethnically diverse regions. Scots-Irish, Welsh, Italian, Polish, and other European immigrants, as well as African Americans, poured into the region in the early 1900s, attracted to jobs in the booming oil, gas, coal, and timber industries. Their heritage and influences remain strong and are celebrated with festivals throughout the year. Clarksburg and Fairmont are home to a myriad of the state's finest Italian restaurants, while Morgantown offers dining pleasures from Europe, Latin America, Asia, and the Pacific Rim.

The New and Gauley rivers in the southern part of the state may be more famous, but Mountaineer Country's Cheat and Tygart Valley rivers have rapids that are just as challenging to kayakers and whitewater rafters, while state parks, state forests, and an abundance of rail trails open the countryside to hikers and bikers.

MORGANTOWN AND VICINITY

Morgantown is West Virginia's trendiest and liveliest city. More than 24,000 students arrive every year to attend West Virginia University, bringing with them fresh, young views that become dispersed throughout the school and the community. Other new ideas come out of the university from the scores of researchers working on dozens of innovative projects, many of them funded by government and industry.

Cultural events take place every day. The McQuain Park Amphitheatre and WVU Coliseum host national and regional acts, the West Virginia Public Theatre books Broadway plays, and, just by itself, the WVU Creative Arts Center sponsors more than 500 performing- and visual-arts presentations annually. Many are by students and professors, whereas others are national and international stars, such as Emmylou Harris, the Moscow Ballet, and Tony winner Patti LuPone.

Despite the usual big-box store and mall developments on the edge of town (and horrendous inner-city traffic congestion), the historic downtown area is alive and vibrant with an eclectic mix of more than 90 upscale clothing stores, coffee bars, art galleries, alternative and funky eateries, clubs, and restaurants. The Wharf District along the Monongahela River, a former warehouse area, has been reborn with many of the city's finest shops and restaurants. Indeed, Morgantown has some of the state's best culinary establishments and just about any kind of ethnic food you could be craving.

This is also a place that embraces the outdoors in a big way. There are close to 50 miles of rail trails—available to hikers, bikers, cross-country skiers, and skaters—that parallel local streams, with many of those miles being located within city limits. Kayakers and canoeists paddle the placid waters of the Monongahela River and Cheat Lake or go for thrills on the churning cascades of Deckers and Big Sandy creeks, while whitewater rafters shoot the rapids on nearby Cheat River. The multiple miles of mountain-biking trails at Big Bear Lake Campland are so challenging and such a thrill that they have been used for a number of races and competitions

The view of the New River from Hawks Nest State Park in Southern West Virginia may get better press coverage, but the overlook into the Cheat River in Coopers Rock State Forest is equally awe-inspiring. Miles of old logging roads and railroad beds left over from former iron-ore mines open the state forest to exploration by hikers, mountain bikers, and cross-country skiers.

Morgantown is such an inviting and exciting place to visit and to live that it is

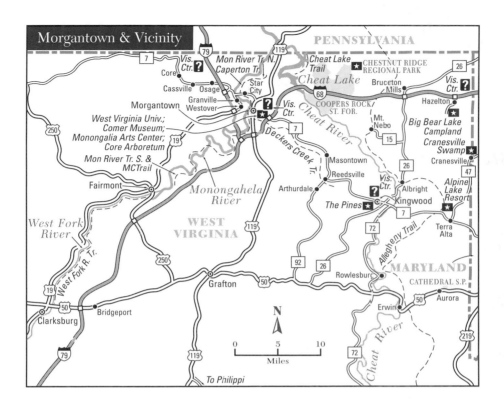

one of the state's fastest growing communities, and many people predict it may soon be West Virginia's largest city. (If you were to figure the WVU students into the population, it already is.)

COMMUNITIES **Kingwood** is the seat of Preston County and has a number of impressive historic buildings, including The Pines—the 1840s home of one of the earliest supporters of West Virginia statehood—and the 1930s art deco courthouse constructed of locally obtained pink sandstone.

It can get rather confusing when you move from one place to another in and around Morgantown, as **Star City** and **Westover**, despite having some of the same zip codes as Morgantown, are separate entities with their own municipal governments. **Sabraton** is a community of Morgantown, and not a separate municipality.

GUIDANCE Located within the downtown area, the **Greater Morgantown Convention and Visitors Bureau** (304-292-5081; 1-800-458-7373; www.tour morgantown.com) is at 68 Donley St., Morgantown 26501.

Preston County Visitors Center (304-329-4660; www.tourpreston.com), 200 West Main St., Kingwood 26537.

West Virginia Welcome Centers, which can provide information on the entire state as well as this area, are located on the southbound lanes of I-79 mile marker 159 (304-328-5261) near Morgantown and the westbound lanes of I-68 mile marker 31 (304-379-2649) close to Bruceton Mills.

GETTING THERE *By air*: The **Morgantown Municipal Airport** (304-291-7461; www.morgantownairport.com), 100 Hart Field Rd., has daily flights that connect to Washington Dulles International Airport (703-572-2700; www.metwashairports .com/dulles) near Washington, DC. You might be better off just flying into **Pittsburgh International Airport** (412-472-3525; www.pitairport.com), which is only about an hour's drive from Morgantown and will usually save you a few dollars.

By bus: Following the termination of Greyhound bus service to Morgantown in 2005, Mountain Line Transit Authority started **The Grey Line**, which serves as a Greyhound connector between Clarksburg, Fairmont, Morgantown, the downtown Pittsburgh Greyhound terminal, and Pittsburgh International Airport. Reservations are available by logging onto www.busride.org or calling 304-296-3869.

By car: The north–south route of **I-79** runs along the western edge of this area. **I-68** enters the eastern part of the area at the West Virginia–Maryland border, about 30 miles east of Morgantown.

By rail: The **AMTRAK** (1-800-872-7245; www.amtrak.com) *Capitol Limited* makes stops daily in Connellsville and Pittsburgh, Pennsylvania, on its east–west Chicago to Washington, DC, route.

GETTING AROUND *By bus*: The **Buckwheat Express** (304-329-0464; www .busride.org/Kingwood.htm) has routes in Preston County, east of Morgantown, that enable you to use public transportation between the small towns of Kingwood, Reedsville, Masontown, Deslow, Terra Alta, Cadell, Bruceton Mills, Newburg, Rowlesburg, and Tunnelton. Not all lines run every day.

The **Mountain Line Transit Authority** (304-291-7433; www.busride.org) has buses that operate throughout Morgantown and most of the nearby towns and areas. It also has routes to and from Fairmont, Clarksburg, and Pittsburgh, Pennsylvania.

By taxi: The **Yellow Cab Company** (304-292-3336) will take you to places in and around Morgantown.

MEDICAL EMERGENCIES

Kingwood
Preston Memorial Hospital (304-329-1400; www.prestonmemorial.org), 300 South Price St.

Morgantown
Monongalia General Hospital (304-598-1200; www.monhealthsys.org), 1200 J. D. Anderson Dr.

Ruby Memorial Hospital (304-598-4400; http://health.wvu.edu/hospitals/ruby .aspx), Elmer Prince Dr., in the Robert C. Byrd Health Sciences Center.

✷ To See

COLLEGE The **WVU Visitors Resource Center** (304-293-3489; 1-800-344-9881; www.wvu.edu), 1 Waterfront Place, Morgantown, is the place to come to for information about the university—and to experience the innovative electronic interactive displays. Video diaries from students give glimpses of daily life, recordings of the marching band accompany a tracing of the route of the school's

PUBLIC TRANSPORTATION OF THE FUTURE THAT HAS BEEN AROUND SINCE THE MID-1970S

WVU's **Personal Rapid Transit** (304-293-5011) is as much of an attraction as it is a public transportation system, and it is as innovative today as when it was completed in 1975. From a distance, it resembles Disney's monorail, but once you get on one of the individual passenger cars, powered by electric motors and running on quiet rubber tires, you will see that they move on an elevated steel guideway, connecting Morgantown with the Evansdale and Health Sciences campuses. Stations are located at Walnut St., Beechurst Ave., Engineering Sciences, Evansdale residential complex, and Health Sciences, so park the car and let the PRT take you around. Heck, this is such an interesting and innovative mode of transportation (and the fare is next to nothing) that you should take a ride just for the experience, fun, scenic views of the Monongahela River, and all of the public/private conversations of students who appear to have cell phones permanently attached to their hands and ears. You would pay multiple dollars at an amusement park to take a similar ride. Closed Sun. and WVU holidays.

Personal Rapid Transit system, and a most interesting exhibit enables you to look over the city from a satellite's point of view. You may also obtain details about the university's many opportunities for the general public, such as museums, art galleries, and hundreds of cultural events. The university dominates the city, so if you are visiting Morgantown, you should at least learn a little bit about the school.

COVERED BRIDGE The 40-foot-long **Dent's Run Covered Bridge** was constructed in 1889 and is still in use over its namesake stream. It is the last remaining covered bridge in Monongalia County and may be reached by taking US 19 south from Westover, turning right onto WV 43, driving another 0.7 mile, bearing left onto WV 43/3, and coming to the bridge in a short distance.

DRIVING TOURS, SCENIC & HISTORIC Running eastward from Morgantown to the West Virginia–Maryland border, the 43-mile **Old Rte. 7 Byway** parallels the tumbling waters of Decker Creek. From Masontown, it passes through rural and forested countryside before going through Kingwood, crossing the Cheat River, and entering Maryland near Terra Alta. Along the way, the two-lane highway gives you access to Deckers Creek Trail (see *To Do—Rail Trails*), Arthurdale (see *Historic Sites*), and Alpine Lake Resort (see *Lodging—Resort*).

The **Northwestern Turnpike Byway** follows the route of US 50 for 54 miles from the West Virginia–Maryland border to Clarksburg. Once a major thoroughfare known as the George Washington Highway, the two-lane road still sees quite a bit of traffic as it winds its way over Cheat Mountain at a 9 percent grade (with 28 curves in 3 miles), and Laurel Mountain at an 8 percent grade. Highlights include the scenic valley between the two mountains, virgin forests in Cathedral State Park (see the "Holy Ground" sidebar later in the chapter), Grafton, and Tygart Lake.

Connecting with the above two byways and passing through Rowlesburg, the 14-mile **Cheat River Byway** on WV 72 is the most scenic of the three, running deep inside the Cheat River Canyon and within yards of the waterway. Frequent pull-outs let you pause to get a better look at Buckhorn Run Waterfall and rafters bouncing up and down in the rapids.

HISTORIC CHURCH Our Lady of the Pines, on US 219 in Horse Shoe Run, is believed to be the smallest Catholic church in the contiguous United States. Barely 20 feet long and only a dozen feet wide, it has a small altar, six pews, and a number of stained-glass windows made in West Virginia. It's open daily from spring to fall (donations accepted). Pick up one of the postcards and mail it to a friend from the adjacent post office, which must surely be one of the country's smallest, too.

HISTORIC HOME The Pines (304-329-0884), 109 East Main St., Kingwood. It is best to call ahead as open times vary; donations accepted. The Pines, the 1841 home of James C. and Persis Hagens McGrew, has been adopted by the Society for the Preservation of McGrew House and is being restored and furnished to reflect its historic significance. James was instrumental in the establishment of the state of West Virginia, serving in its first and second Legislatures, and later for two terms in the U.S. Congress. Because this is a work in progress, it's hard to say what you will find when you visit. The last time I was here, one room featured photographs of early Kingwood and another told the story of one of Preston County's best-known veterinarians.

HISTORIC SITES

Arthurdale

The community of Arthurdale was established by the federal government during the Great Depression as an experimental agricultural community for displaced miners, and it served as the prototype for close to 100 other similar places throughout the United States. Eleanor Roosevelt was the driving force behind the movement and came to visit Arthurdale a number of times, dining with the people and taking part in social and academic events. The Arthurdale Heritage Foundation (304-864-3959; www.arthurdaleheritage.org; mailing address: P.O. Box 850, Arthurdale 26520) maintains a visitor center and a number of the original buildings (forge and furniture factory, gas station, blacksmith shop, and some of the original homes) that you may tour for a very small admission fee. A driving-tour brochure will take you by many of the still-occupied homes, all of which originally had about 4 acres around them that enabled families to have a small garden and some livestock so as to be as self-sufficient as possible.

AN OLD-TIME GAS STATION IN THE HISTORIC COMMUNITY OF ARTHURDALE

Arthurdale was a grand experiment in community living that worked and proved what government can do when those in power are truly looking out for the best interests of the citizenry.

Bruceton Mills

The **Virginia Iron Furnace** is located in a roadside park on WV 26 about 4 miles south of Bruceton Mills. Constructed around 1850, it was the second blast furnace in Preston County, but it remained in operation long after other such sites in nearby counties. A wooden raceway brought water from Muddy Creek to turn a wheel that pumped the bellows. It stands close to 30 feet high with a square base of 34 feet, and currently it reminds me of a Mayan ruin, with ferns and other vegetation growing out of it. There's a nice waterfall next to it, but its beauty is marred somewhat by the water that runs orange from acid mine drainage.

Core

Mason-Dixon Historical Park (304-879-4101; www.masondixonhistoricalpark .com), 79 Buckeye Rd. This small park, with picnic facilities, amphitheater, playground, and ball courts, celebrates its location at the western end of the famous Mason-Dixon Line with a museum and gift shop.

LAKE Cheat Lake, in Pierpont, was created in the 1920s to supply electricity for what is now Allegheny Energy (1-800-255-3443), which oversees and maintains the 1,800-acre body of water. Along the scenic eastern edge of the lake, the company has built Cheat Lake Park, with picnic facilities, restrooms, boat dock facilities, and a 4.5-mile accessible rail trail (see *To Do—Rail Trails*). You are permitted to swim in the lake on Sunset Beach, where you can also rent a variety of watercraft from Sunset Beach Marina (304-594-0050; 117 Sunset Beach Rd., Morgantown).

VIRGINIA IRON FURNACE

MUSEUMS & ART GALLERIES

Morgantown
Comer Museum (304-293-4211), Mineral Resources Building on the WVU Evansdale Campus. Open by appointment. Free. Located in a very small room, the museum showcases a few items from the engineering and mineral-resources industries, including a few fossils, drill bits, and some scale models of drilling rigs expertly crafted by Burl Eddy.

☂ **Monongalia Arts Center** (304-292-3325; www.monarts.bizland.com), 107 High St. Located in a 1913 stone and marble neoclassical building with

Doric columns and pilasters, the MAC (as it is known) contains the Benedum Gallery, with ongoing exhibits by regional and national artists, and the Tanner Theatre, with performing-arts presentations by local talent and organizations.

Osage

Scott's Run Museum (304-599-1931; www.as.wvu.edu/clcold/museum; mailing address: P.O. Box 264, Osage 26543), or WV 7/19 off I-79 exit 155. Open afternoons on Sat. and Sun. Donations accepted. It's small, but it provides an excellent glimpse into coal miners' lives of the late 1800s and early 1900s.

Terra Alta

↑ History House Museum (304-789-8688; www.hhs.net/sss/preston/pchs.htm), 109 East Washington St. Open Sun. afternoon from mid-May through Sept. Donations accepted. Operated by the Preston County Historical Society and housed in the impressive 1892 former Terra Alta Bank, the museum has three floors and 13 rooms with so many items of historical interest that you could easily spend most of a day here and not really get to look at it all.

Also see *Selective Shopping—Mall*.

ZOO 🐾 **Hovatters Wildlife Zoo** (304-329-3122; www.westvirginiazoo.com; mailing address: Rte. 1, Box 2650, Kingwood 26537). On Herring Rd., off WV 7 west of Kingwood. Open daily (except Mon.) Apr.–Oct.; weekends only in Nov. Small admission fee. Set within a residential area, the 8-acre zoo is licensed by the state and federal governments and has native West Virginia animals along with many exotic ones, such as lions, tigers, and cougars. Because it is so small, you and the kids won't have to walk miles to see all of the attractions like you have to in larger zoos. You are also able to get much closer to the animals (which are in fenced areas).

OTHER SITES

Morgantown

West Virginia Regional History Collection (304-293-3536; www.libraries.wvu.edu/wvcollection), on the sixth floor of the Charles C. Wise Jr. Library, accessible through the Downtown Campus Library. With the largest collection of West Virginia materials in existence, this library has data bases in which you can search for articles and books; recordings of folk music made in West Virginia from the 1930s to the 1980s; genealogical research; West Virginia history, arranged by county and subject; state historical newspapers; photographic archives; and public records. There are also some rare items of interest, such as maps and books more than 500 years old, clay tablets believed to be at least 5,000 years old, and a first-edition Shakespeare. You should stop by here even if you have no interest in the archives. The grand architecture, marble highlights, chandeliers, sculptures, and paintings in the library make it a work of art that should be seen.

✳ To Do

BICYCLING Wamsley Cycles (304-296-2447; www.wamsleycycles.com), 709 Beechurst Ave., Morgantown. Closed Sun. Chip Wamsley has more than 30 years of experience with selling and servicing bicycles, and he uses his knowledge to go so far as building custom frames. Best of all, he will rent you a bicycle for the hour, day, or week, and his shop in the Seneca Center is a mere few feet from the Caperton Trail.

Also see *To Do—Rail Trails*, *Green Space—State Forest*, and Big Bear Lake Campland under *Lodging*.

BIRDING See Upper Monongahela Water Trail under *Kayaking & Canoeing*, *Green Space—Arboretum*, *Green Space—Nature Preserve*, and the "Holy Ground" sidebar later in the chapter.

BOAT RENTALS See *To See—Lake*.

BOWLING

Morgantown
🐾 **Suburban Lanes** (304-599-3522), 735 Chestnut Ridge Rd. The 24 lanes open early in the morning six days a week and by noon on Sun.

Westover
🐾 **Sycamore Lanes** (304-292-0504), Fairmont Rd. Open for bowling, pool, arcade games, and food in the evenings Tues.–Sun.

FISHING See Upper Monongahela Water Trail under *Kayaking & Canoeing*.

GOLF

Cassville
Meadow Ponds Golf Course (304-328-5570; www.meadowponds.com; mailing address: P.O. Box 309, Cassville 28527), WV 7 West. Meadow Ponds claims to be Morgantown's best golfing value. The management certainly works hard at keeping the facility in good shape: It has a computerized tee-to-green irrigation system, a fleet of 60 carts, and several million dollars' worth of course improvements.

Kingwood
Preston Country Club (304-329-3502; www.prestoncc.info; mailing address: P.O. Box 2020, Kingwood 26537). From I-68 exit 23, drive WV 26 South to Albright and St. Joe's Rd., which you follow to Camp Dawson Rd. and the course. Rebuilt after a major 1985 flood, the par 72 course sits in a wide, flat, bottomland area and is one of the region's longest, with 7,001 yards from the men's blue tees.

Morgantown
Lakeview Golf Resort & Spa (304-594-1111; 1-800-624-8300; www.lakeview resort.com), 1 Lakeview Dr. (off I-68 exit 10). High on the plateau above Cheat Lake, the resort has two courses, both of which have been played by Sam Snead, Arnold Palmer, and Jack Nicklaus (who set a course record). The Lakeview Course was completed in 1954, while the Mountainview Course, which winds through the property's foothills, opened in 1985. This is more than a golf resort; amenities include guest rooms ($149 and up) and condominiums (starting at $250); a fine-dining restaurant, lounge, and sports bar; a full-service spa (www.sparoma.com); and pool, hot tub, and fitness center. The last time I visited, the outside parts of the resort were showing their age, but inside things were neat, clean, and maintained.

Mountaineer Golf and Country Club (304-328-5520), 212 Brand Rd. The 18-hole, par 72 course, along with a driving range, is open to the public.

HIKING Having wound its way from its southern terminus in Southern West Virginia, the final 70 miles of the state's premier hiking route, the **Allegheny Trail** (see "What's Where in West Virginia" at the front of this book for background information) enters this area close to Sell (really not a community so much as a place name). Following country lanes, the trail continues northward, getting to within a mile of Rowlesburg before turning northeastward to come close to Terra Alta, and then swinging to the northwest to enter Albright. Heading almost due north, sometimes on a railroad grade and most often on roadways, the trail comes to its northern terminus at the West Virginia–Pennsylvania border on WV 4. Although much of this section is on roadways, most of them are either dirt or lightly traveled paved roads through a beautiful rural landscape of narrow creek valleys, high open farmlands providing 360-degree views, and extremely small communities of just a few dwellings.

Also see *Rail Trails, Green Space—Arboretum, Green Space—Nature Preserve, Green Space—Parks*, and *Green Space—State Forest*.

KAYAKING & CANOEING Big Sandy Creek, with 5.5 miles from the put-in at the Rockville Bridge north of Hudson to the takeout near the Jenkinsburg Bridge across the Cheat River east of Masontown, is steep, with almost continuous rapids and waterfalls requiring frequent scouting and portages over difficult terrain. It is a good challenge, but only for those with a great amount of experience.

Deckers Creek has many miles of water to paddle, all of the way from Masontown to Morgantown. The eastern third is relatively mild with a few easy thrills, while the middle third drops at a more rapid pace over a number of rapids and obstacles that need to be negotiated. The creek becomes placid again as it emerges out of its narrow canyon and gets closer to Morgantown.

The **Upper Monongahela Water Trail** takes in about 65 miles of the Monongahela River from Fairmont to Rices Landing in Pennsylvania. Thanks to dams and locks (there are three in West Virginia that the trail takes you through), most of the river is slack water, providing a moderately easy outing for those just learning how to paddle. The forested riparian zone is home to herons, kingfishers, owls, and a plethora of songbirds. It is not uncommon for canoeists and kayakers to be privileged to watch an osprey swoop down from the sky to grab a fish out of the water. Beaver and muskrat leave V-shaped trails in the water as they swim back to homes on the riverbanks, while catfish, drum, musky, sauger, white bass, and more glide below the surface. A pamphlet and map available from the Greater Morgantown Convention and Visitors Bureau (see *Guidance*) or online at www.monriver summit.org provides information about access points, services, and communities along the way.

✒ ✪ **Adventures on Magic River** (304-276-8306; www.magicriverwv.com), Morgantown. Tim Terman is an avid kayaker who shares his love of the water by conducting tours on the Upper Monongahela Water Trail. The easy trips (open to all ages) are about two and a half hours long and are a relaxing journey not only on the water, but back into time as Tim shares stories of early settlers' lives, navigation on what was known at the time as "the western waters," and the years when coal wars and mine disasters were common occurrences. Instruction and all equipment are included. $30 per person (children under age 12 are half price with an adult), minimum of four people. Tim has other tours or will arrange a custom trip for you. Also see *To See—Lake*.

OUTDOORS OUTFITTERS Adventure's Edge (304-296-9007; www.adventures edge.org), 131 Pleasant St., Morgantown. Outdoor gear, Army gear, skateboards, snowboards, and scouting equipment.
Pathfinder (304-296-0076; www.pathfinderwv.com), 235 High St. Pathfinder has outfitted generations of hikers, campers, bikers, kayakers, canoeists, climbers, and skiers.

RAIL TRAILS Mountaineer Country is laced by a number of rail trails, most of which are linked in some fashion and have a total distance of approximately 50 miles through urban, forested, and riverside landscapes. The paved portions of the trails are popular with skaters, while all of the routes see cross-country skiers when enough snow falls. The Mon River Trails Conservancy (www.montrails.org; P.O. Box 282, Morgantown 26507) maintains the eastern 16 miles of the Deckers Creek Trail and the Mon River Trail North and South, while BOPARC—Board of Parks and Recreation Commissioners—oversees the Caperton Trail and the western 3 miles of the Deckers Creek Trail. A map of all of the trails is available from the Greater Morgantown Convention and Visitors Bureau (see *Guidance*).

Stretching for 19 miles from Morgantown to east of Reedsville, the **Deckers Creek Trail** is the longest. Paralleling its namesake stream, it starts beside the Monongahela River at Hazel Ruby McQuain Riverfront Park, where the first 2.5 miles through Morgantown are paved, providing an ideal surface for skaters and access to Morilla Park for a swimming diversion in the pool and water slides. Beyond the urban landscape, the creek, whose foaming rapids are a destination for expert kayakers, is lined by the cool shade of a hardwood forest with a rhododendron understory and interesting rock outcroppings. With its urban, field, forest, and wetland environments, the pathway harbors more than 60 species of wildflowers and 20 ferns. Trailhead parking is available at Ruby Hazel McQuain Riverfront and Marilla parks, and in Masontown and Reedsville. *Insider's tip*: There is a difference of almost 1,000 feet in elevation between the trail's termini, so for an almost continuously downhill outing, do it from Reedsville to Morgantown.

The crushed limestone **Mon River Trail North** begins at the West Virginia–Pennsylvania border. Meandering along the Monongahela River for 6 miles, it meets up with the paved Caperton Trail.

About 6 miles in length, the **Caperton Trail** has a more urban flavor to it, providing access to the two WVU campuses, shopping centers, restaurants, and bicycle- and kayak-rental establishments. Yet, it is also a scenic outing, as it stays next to the river, passing through Edith Barill and Hazel Ruby McQuain Riverfront parks and the Core Arboretum before ending at the Mon River Trail South. Parking is at Ruby Hazel McQuain Riverfront Park, the Seneca Center, the Wharf District, and Edith Barill Riverfront Park.

Leaving the urban area behind, the crushed limestone, 17.7-mile **Mon River Trail South** is an unexpected gem. There are few roads paralleling the trail as it wanders through the quiet, wooded stream valley, passing a number of waterfalls, scenic river views, and an abundance of wildflowers, such as Queen Anne's lace, sunflower, purple-flowering raspberry, and milkweed. The trail comes to an end a short distance north of Fairmont at Prickett's Fort (see *To See—Museums* in "The Clarksburg/Fairmont Environs" chapter), where you could then take the MCTrail (see *To Do—Rail Trails* in "The Clarksburg/Fairmont Environs" chapter) into Fairmont. Parking is available along the Caperton Trail, at the Uffington boat dock off WV 73, and in Prickett's Fort State Park.

Currently not connected to the above trails (but it will be if plans become reality), the 4.5-mile **Cheat Lake Trail** (see *To See—Lake*) is a handicapped-accessible route along the lake shoreline. Following an abandoned railroad right-of-way, it has access to fishing piers, lake overlooks, and nature-viewing platforms. This one is the least crowded of all the region's rail trails.

SKATING ❧ **Marilla Skate Park** (304-296-8356), East Brockway Ave., Morgantown, is an outdoor skateboard and BMX bike facility with a half-pipe, pyramid with a rail, and other events. Open daily from daylight to dusk.

❧ **Morgantown Ice Arena** (304-292-6865), Mississippi St., Morgantown. The regulation hockey–size arena, which has a pro shop, skate rentals, and a warming room, is open Sept.–late Mar.

Also see *To Do—Rail Trails*.

SKIING, CROSS-COUNTRY See *To Do—Rail Trails* and *Lodging—Resort*.

SPA See Lakeview Golf Resort & Spa under *To Do—Golf* and Waterfront Place Hotel under *Lodging*.

SWIMMING ❧ Public swimming pools, open during the usual summer season, are located in Morgantown's **Krepp's Park** (304-296-8356), near the WVU Coliseum, and **Marillia Park** (304-296-8356), East Brockway Ave.

Also see *To See—Lake*.

SWIMMIN' HOLE Because it is popular with the college crowd, you should expect some possible skinny dipping and drinking when you arrive to take a swim in **Big Sandy Creek** where it empties into the Cheat River. If you don't mind those distractions, this is a great swimmin' hole with a good-size beach. Follow WV 23 from Masontown for several miles, turn left onto WV 21 for close to 5 miles, turn onto dirt WV 14/4, and continue on it to cross the Cheat River. Park on the far side of the bridge, and you'll see a short pathway leading to the creek.

WALKING TOURS Obtained from the Greater Morgantown Convention and Visitors Bureau (see *Guidance*), the **Suncrest Walking Tour** brochure directs you to 13 sites in the Suncrest neighborhood of Morgantown that developed in the early 1900s. Unlike the cookie-cutter developments of today, the neighborhood has a wide variety of architectural styles and sizes of homes.

WHITEWATER RAFTING The **Cheat River** has its headwaters in the Potomac Highlands region, and by the time it reaches Mountaineer Country, it has become a major whitewater rafting stream. Because it is a naturally flowing stream without any dams, water levels are at their most challenging in the spring, but there is at least some portion of the river that can usually be run throughout much of the year.

The river, during more than 11 miles in the remote **Cheat Canyon** from Albright to the Jenkinsburg bridge, drops close to 300 feet, with challenging undercuts, big holes, lots of boulders, and Class III–V rapids with such names as Big Nasty and Swimmers Rapids.

Upstream, from Rowlesburg to Albright, which includes a stretch known as the **Cheat Narrows**, are about 14 miles of river that are some of the most popular for family trips. In the spring, there are Class II–IV rapids, while the flow drops enough in the summer that it can be a nice, easy float trip.

Many of the same outfitters that raft the New and Gauley rivers in Southern West Virginia (see *To Do—Whitewater Rafting* in the "Along the New and Gauley Rivers—Beckley, Fayetteville, and Summersville" chapter) also raft on the Cheat. However, **Cheat River Outfitters** (304-329-2024; 1-888-99-RIVER; www.cheat riveroutfitters.com, 2764 N. Preston Highway, Albright 26519) has headquarters right next to the Cheat River. In addition to whitewater rafting, Cheat River Outfitters offers guided wild caving and rock-climbing trips (at nearby Coopers Rock State Forest).

CORE ARBORETUM

✷ Green Space

ARBORETUM Core Arboretum (304-293-5201; www.as.wvu.edu /biology/facility/arboretum.html), off Monongahela Blvd., at the WVU Coliseum, Morgantown. Open dawn to dusk; no admission fee. The 91-acre arboretum drops close to 200 feet in elevation from the boulevard to bottomland along the Monongahela River, providing you with a restful place to escape the hustle, bustle, and traffic of town. Approximately 3 miles of pathways, with interpretive signs to help you learn as you explore, wind by 300 species of trees (some more than 200 years old) and 300 kinds of herbaceous plants. The grounds are especially known for the vast array of wildflowers that pop up in the spring, as well as the 180 species of birds that have been observed here. By the river you may see northern pintails, ruddy ducks, great blue herons, tundra swans, and lesser scaups. Bank, barn, and cliff swallows have also been seen, as well as 35 species of warblers.

GARDEN West Virginia Botanic Garden (304-376-2717; www.wvbg.org), Morgantown. From I-68 exit 4, drive WV 7 eastward, turn right onto Tyrone Rd., and continue 1.8 miles. The 82-acre botanic garden was established in 2000 and is still a work in progress, yet you can already wander miles of trails through old-growth hemlock and deciduous forests, wetlands, meadows, and a bottomland area. It's a nice place to escape the modern world and promises to be even more so when all of the plans of the nonprofit West Virginia Botanic Garden, Inc., become reality.

NATURE PRESERVE Located along the West Virginia–Maryland border, The Nature Conservancy's **Cranesville Swamp** (304-637-0160; www.nature.org) is a relic of the Ice Age, having changed little since the glaciers receded. Situated within a depression, the swamp is a "frost pocket," a place in which cold air is trapped by the surrounding mountains. When the rest of the area is experiencing a relatively mild spring or fall day, there may be a heavy frost in the swamp.

Because of its microclimate, the plants that inhabit the swamp are more typical of those found far to the north in boreal Canada. Spiny woodfern, rose pogonia, hoary alder, creeping snowberry, yellowfringe orchis, and the carnivorous round-leaf sundew all make their homes here. In addition, the swamp is where the tamarack tree (also commonly called the American larch) comes close to its southernmost point. Northern saw-whet owls nest here, as do red-eyed vireos, hooded warblers, and golden-winged warblers.

Cranesville Swamp can be reached by driving eastward from the small Cranesville community, turning south on unpaved Burnside Camp Rd., and continuing for 1 mile to The Nature Conservancy signs. A 1-mile trail, part of which is a boardwalk across wet areas, permits you to explore the area by foot.

PARKS

Bruceton Mills
Chestnut Ridge Regional Park and Campground (304-594-1773; 1-888-594-3111; www.chestnutridgepark.com; mailing address: Rte. 1, Box 267, Bruceton Mills 26525). Take I-68 exit 15 and drive on WV 73/73 for a short distance to turn left and follow WV 69/3 to the campground. Close to Coopers Rock State Forest and operated by Monongalia County, the park has RV and tent sites, rustic and modern cabins, sports fields, swimming, two fishing lakes (no license required), hiking trails, and, during the winter, a lighted 400-foot hill for sledding and tubing.

Morgantown
❅ Stanley's Spot Dog Park (304-296-8356) is located along the Deckers Creek Trail and has fenced areas for dogs, all of whom love being able to socialize, play, and run free. It's a shame more communities don't have such facilities.

STATE FOREST Coopers Rock State Forest (304-594-1561; www.coopersrock stateforest.com), 61 County Line Dr., Bruceton Mills 26525. From I-68 exit 15, drive southward on WV 73/16 to enter the state forest. The view into Cheat River Canyon is so spectacular and breathtaking that it consistently draws hundreds of people into 12,713-acre Coopers Rock State Forest every week throughout the year. Locals bring visiting friends to see it, travelers routinely pull off I-68 to stretch their legs and gaze onto the geological wonder, and the outing has almost

HOLY GROUND

✪ **Cathedral State Park** (304-737-3771; www.cathedralstatepark.com; 12 Cathedral Way, Aurora 26705). About a mile east of Aurora on US 50. Open daily during daylight hours. Many people have likened the Appalachian forests to cathedrals, and this state park will help you understand how such places can be seen as monuments to the wonders of creation. The park's 133 acres contain one of the few remaining virgin forests in West Virginia, and easy trails (the terrain is nearly flat) take you by towering hemlock and hardwood trees within a cool, moist environment where rhododendron, partridgeberry, and hemlock keep things looking green throughout the year, and wildflowers flourish in the spring.

The wonder of this place really takes hold as you walk farther away from the road. Trees rise close to 100 feet on bases that measure more than 20 feet in circumference. I am not against logging if done sensibly, but I will no longer be swayed by the argument that a forest needs to be cut to maintain its vitality. This woodland is more alive than any place I've been (although the hemlock wolly adelgid, which has killed almost every hemlock tree in Virginia's Shenandoah National Park, may take its toll). Plants are lush and growing upon every inch of moist and fertile soil. Chipmunks and squirrels scamper over deer tracks. And the birds. Oh, so many birds that my wife and I have become giddy laughing at the many songs filling the air. Thrush and vireo chirps mix with the calls of warbler and wren, while woodpecker staccatos add a backbeat.

Cathedral State Park is what a forest is supposed to be—do not miss it.

A TOWERING TREE IN CATHEDRAL STATE PARK

become a rite of passage for freshman students of nearby WVU. After having come here once and finding out all that the state forest has to offer, a large percentage of people return here time and again to walk, hike, mountain bike, bird-watch, rock climb, cross-country ski, fish, and hunt. The campground (electric hookups and hot showers) and picnic areas have playgrounds for the kids, which makes the facilities popular with families. They fill up quickly on nice weekends.

Iron ore played a large role in the early history of this area. An abundance of limestone and low-grade iron ore was discovered in the late 1700s, and for the next 100 years furnaces dotted the countryside. Vast amounts of timber were cut and turned into charcoal to feed the furnaces' voracious appetites. As coal began to replace charcoal for fuel, and large deposits of ore were discovered in the Great Lakes region, the industry faded away and was replaced by logging for the next half century. Reminders of these days, when natural-resource extraction was the primary use of the land, can still be found, and many of the old road and railroad grades are now part of the state forest's trail system.

A 0.1-mile walkway takes you to a wooden bridge over a cleft and onto Coopers Rock for soaring views into the canyon and of the Cheat River flowing hundreds of feet below. A local legend says the state forest and Coopers Rock were named for a convict who hid out in the rugged area around the overlook. Although a fugitive from the law, he was a cooper by trade and continued to make barrels, which he sold in the communities nearby.

Two other places in the state forest you should not miss are the 1830s Clay Furnace and Rock City. If you let yourself go and be a kid again, Rock City can be the highlight of your visit. I have seen entire families spend hours in here, traversing narrow corridors and climbing in and out of small caves that lead to other passageways.

✳ Lodging

RESORT

Terra Alta 26764

Alpine Lake Resort (304-789-2481; 1-800-752-7179; www.alpinelake.com), 700 West Alpine Dr. Primarily a residential resort community, Alpine Lake Resort has a small motel and offers cabin and vacation rentals for visitors. Guests are permitted to use the indoor pool; swim, fish, or boat on the 150-acre lake; hike or bike a few trails; play miniature golf or tennis; cross-country ski and tube; and work out in the fitness center. The 18-hole golf course is open to the general public. The resort is in a lovely mountain setting with land immediately around the lake having been preserved. As stated, though, this is a residential resort, and most of

BOATS AWAIT GUESTS AT ALPINE LAKE RESORT

the 2,300 acres have been divided into home lots.

Also see Lakeview Golf Resort & Spa under *To Do—Golf*.

MOTELS & HOTELS

Kingwood 26573

Heldreth Motel (304-329-1145; www .heldrethmotel.net), WV 26 South. The Heldreth is an older but well-kept motel. A restaurant and lounge are on premises, and each room has a microwave and refrigerator. $65–80.

Morgantown 26505

☸ **Comfort Inn** (304-296-9364), 22 Comfort Inn Dr., off I-68 exit 1. This Morgantown location of the well-known chain is listed in this book because it is one of the few in the area to permit pets. Outdoor pool, indoor whirlpool, exercise room, and complimentary continental breakfast. $90–150.

Euro-Suites (304-598-1000; 1-800-678-4837; www.euro-suites.com), 501 Chestnut Ridge Rd. All the accommodations in this small-scale hotel, close to hospitals and WVU's Mountaineer Stadium and Coliseum, are spacious two-room arrangements with kitchenettes, large beds, and two TVs. High-speed Internet access and complimentary breakfast and newspaper make it popular with business travelers. $120–199.

Hotel Morgan (304-292-8200; www .clarionhotelmorgan.com), 127 High St. Dozens of grand hotels like the 1925 Hotel Morgan once stood in many of West Virginia's cities. Unlike the others, the Morgan has survived and has even been refurbished to bring out the grandeur of its earliest days. Original oak panels greet you in the lobby, the first-floor ballroom has magnificent chandeliers, oak pillars rise to the cathedral ceiling, and all accommo-

dations are two-room suites. Eleanor Roosevelt and John F. Kennedy are just a couple of the illustrious past guests. The **Elevation 127 Restaurant**, on the eighth floor, which used to be a private residence, serves some interesting meals that incorporate lamb and kangaroo, and the bar has an expansive view of the town. $100–150.

Waterfront Place Hotel (304-296-1700; www.waterfrontplacehotel.com), 2 Waterfront Place. Overlooking the Monongahela River and next door to the Caperton Trail and the WVU's Visitors Resource Center, the high-rise Waterfront has all the luxuries travelers have come to expect in a top-tier establishment, along with a 1,400-square-foot full-service spa and a free area shuttle service. $130–160.

Unlike many hotel restaurants that should be avoided, the Waterfront's **Regatta Bar & Grille** (304-284-9850; www.regattabarandgrille.com) is a fine-dining establishment you will want to patronize even if you are not staying here. The high-quality lunch buffet (and I usually eschew such things) has a chef-attended station that features rotating specials. Dinners feature seafood, beef, and pasta. The rock shrimp appetizer with sweet Thai sauce is the way to start your meal. Entrées $15–35.

☸ **Ramada Inn** (304-296-3431; www.ramadainnwv.com), 20 Scott Ave., off I-68 exit 1. Close to 150 rooms and an outdoor pool, guest laundry, fitness room, and airport shuttle. Pets permitted. $90–150; includes full breakfast.

INNS

Aurora 26705

Brookside Inn (304-735-6344; 1-800-588-6344; www.brooksideinnwv.com); 25174 George Washington Highway, on US 50 directly across from Cathedral State Park. Sitting on a hillside surrounded by flower gardens and woodlands, the Brookside Inn was built in 1899. A bit on the rustic side, the inn's furnishings and interior are showing their age, but guest rooms are neat and clean, and the mountain breezes are almost always blowing when you sit on the wraparound porch. This is a place to relax and enjoy getting away from it all—no phones or TVs in the guest rooms. $110–125; includes breakfast.

Kingwood 26537

𝒮 **Preston County Inn** (304-329-2220; 1-800-962-6260; www.preston countyinn.com), 112 West Main St. Located in the center of Kingwood, the 1857 Federal brick Preston County Inn offers four suites and four rooms (all with two private baths) that the management says provide "a bed and breakfast atmosphere with the privacy and security of a small hotel." Everything is kept neat and clean, and the swing and chairs on the front porch are a window onto Kingwood's daily life. $75–125.

CABINS & VACATION RENTALS

Bruceton Mills 26525

Mountain Creek Cabins (1-866-379-7548; www.mountaincreekcabins.com; mailing address: Rural Rte. 1, Box 332-K). Open all year. The three- to five-person, fully furnished cabins are situated in a quiet woods just a few steps away from Big Sandy Creek. My favorite thing to do is to take the short trail to the waterfalls, and then relax in the hot tub on the back porch as day turns to night and moonlight filters through the trees. $170–190.

Also see *Resort*, and Big Bear Lake Campland and Pinehill Campground under *Campgrounds*.

Albright 26519

Teter's Campground (304-329-3626; mailing address: Rte. 1, Box 37-B), about 1 mile north of Albright on WV 26. RV and tent sites (with hookups) that are popular with those rafting on the Cheat River.

Bruceton Mills 26525

Sand Springs Camping Area (304-594-2415; www.sandspringscamp ground.com; mailing address: P.O. Box 18143, Morgantown 26507). Take I-68 exit 15 and drive on WV 73/73 for a short distance. Turn left and follow WV 69/3 for 2 miles. Located on the same road as Chestnut Ridge Park, the Good Sampark campground caters to families and those with RVs. There are modern restrooms and showers, laundry, miniature golf, and a snack bar.

Hazelton 26535

Big Bear Lake Campland (304-379-4382; www.bigbearwv.com; 450 Big Bear Lake Rd.), on WV 5/18 about 3 miles south of I-68 exit 29. High on the Allegheny Plateau, with elevations ranging from 2,400 feet to close to 3,100 feet, Big Bear Lake Campland is well known to the mountain-biking crowd. The more than 20 miles of trails (open Jan.–Oct. 1) that traverse the 4,000-acre landscape have attracted so much attention that they have been used for a number of races, including the grueling 24 Hours of Big Bear.

The facility is primarily a resort for RV owners who purchase their own personal lot. (A few home sites are also now being sold.) However, a commercial campground and cabin rentals let visitors take advantage of the many amenities, including a swimming pool, water slide, miniature golf, game courts, snowmobiling, cross-country skiing, and fishing and paddling in 35-acre Big Bear Lake.

Pinehill Campground (304-379-4612; www.pinehillcampground.com), off I-68 exit 29. Open Apr. through mid-Oct. Within 110 acres of forestland are RV (with hookups) and tent sites, camping cabins, bathhouses and showers, a playground, and hiking and biking trails.

Also see Chestnut Ridge Regional Park under *Green Space—Parks*, and *Green Space—State Forest*.

✱ Where to Eat

DINING OUT ✪ ♈ **Café Bacchus** (304-296-9234; www.cafebacchus.net), 76 High St., Morgantown. Open for dinner; closed Sun. Reservations recommended. Within an 1895 house, Heath Finnell has created my favorite Morgantown restaurant. Drawing upon the expertise he gained cooking in England, Germany, and other places, he brings European, American, and Asian influences to the menu, which features seafood flown in from Maine and pork ordered from a company in California. The crab cake is flavored with lemongrass and ginger and served over Japanese seaweed salad. You don't get just a grilled filet mignon—it's covered with green peppercorns and cognac sauce, and the pork chops are marinated in juniper berry brine and served with grilled peaches. My mouth is watering just writing about all the delights to be found here. The food, the décor and ambience of the old home, the opportunity to dine alfresco on the porch, and the attentive and knowledgeable wait staff all combine to make this an experience not to be missed. Entrées $18–34.

Glasshouse Grille (304-296-8460; www.theglasshousegrille.com), 709 Beechurst Ave. (in the Seneca Center), Morgantown. Open for lunch Mon.–Fri. and dinner Mon.–Sat. Reservations recommended. It sometimes seems that the best of restaurants come and go quickly, but the Glasshouse Grille has been serving some of Morgantown's finest food since 1992. Like Café Bacchus, the seafood, beef, chicken, and other items are all adorned with some kind of wonderful sauce, broth, reduction, or vegetable preparation. Something as simple as blackened tilapia is made tasty with the addition of a roasted red pepper sauce. Smoked scallops are sautéed with roasted Roma tomatoes, artichoke hearts, shiitake mushrooms, sweet peppers, and herbs. The raspberry West Coast–style cheesecake is lighter than New York style, the West Virginia peach cobbler is divine, and the Belgian chocolate pâté will make your taste buds think they are tasting heaven. The Glasshouse Grille is high on the do-not-miss list. Entrées $14–30.

Also see Waterfront Place Hotel under *Lodging*.

EATING OUT

Aurora
Melanie's Family Restaurant (304-735-3219). You are miles away from any other restaurant when you find Melanie's, on US 50 directly across from Cathedral State Park, so stop in for some home cooking. The large breakfast menu is served all day, and the most expensive dinner, which includes meat, vegetable, potato, homemade bread, and unlimited soup and salad bar, is only $15.95. Open daily for breakfast, lunch, and dinner.

Bruceton Mills
Little Sandy's (304-379-7200), on WV 26 off I-68 exit 23. Breakfast is served 24 hours a day. Little Sandy's is known for its buckwheat pancakes, but I find myself always ordering their outstand-

ing biscuits and gravy. Other meals are in the country-cooking vein. Entrées $3.95–13.95.

Kingwood

◢ **Monroe's Deli Style Eatery** (304-329-3354), 110 East Main St. In a huge building that has been a lumberyard, livery stable, and automobile dealership, Jim Maier serves a menu that features dishes he, his staff, and local people have developed. Soups are homemade, the Cajun barbecue sandwich is a bestseller, and dinners of chicken, beef, and seafood (good crab cakes) come with a generous portion of pasta. There is an abundance of seating, but don't be surprised if you have to wait for a table at lunchtime. Looking over the locally handcrafted items that adorn the walls can help you pass the time. Entrées $7.95–16.95.

Morgantown

◢ **Black Bear Burritos** (304-296-8696; www.blackbearburritos.com), 132 Pleasant St. Open for lunch and dinner. With wooden slat booths and the definite feel of a college-town business, Black Bear Burritos lets you choose the items you want for your burrito, quesadilla, or nachos. Large portions, and many veggie options. Entrées $4–9. Live music some evenings when the bar stays open late.

Blue Moose Café (304-292-8999; www.thebluemoosecafe.com), 248 Walnut St. Open daily for breakfast, lunch, and dinner. With its alternative-lifestyle milieu, the Blue Moose serves up some great coffee and veggie sandwiches.

Flying Fish and Company Seafood Deli and Market (304-225-FISH), 709 Beechurst Ave. (in the Seneca Center). Open for lunch and dinner; closed Sun. Operated by the same people as the Glasshouse Grille (see *Dining Out*), Flying Fish has a casual atmosphere, where you can pick up

fresh fish to take home or order a meal at the counter and dine in. Prices are very reasonable for the quality and preparation of the food. All the seafood arrives fresh from Baltimore, and you can have the cod, flounder, tuna, and other fillets grilled, blackened, broiled, or pan-seared. The shrimp, oysters, crabs, clams, and mussels are prepared a variety of ways, and the soups and desserts are all made in-house. (The cinnamon spice pecan ice cream is very refreshing.) Entrées $4.95–12.95.

Mediterranean Market & Deli (304-292-3506), 350 High St. Open for lunch and dinner Mon.–Sat. You can choose from a variety of authentic Mediterranean foods—sambusa, tabbouleh, baba ghanoush, falafel, shish kebab, knafa, and baklava—prepared by cooks with a true Mediterranean heritage. Entrées $5.50–9.95.

Mountain People's Kitchen (304-291-6131; www.mountaincoop.com), 1400 University Ave. Open daily for breakfast and lunch. The place in town to get wholesome foods—such as blue corn nachos with black beans and veggies, hummus and pita, tempeh Reuben, or a black bean burrito—made with West Virginia–produced tofu, oils, and other items. The other part of the business is a co-op, so you could purchase many of these same items to prepare at home. Entrées $5–8.

Ⓨ **The Vintage Room** (304-225-9595; www.bwvintageroom.com), 467 Chestnut St. The Vintage Room has an upscale style absent from just about every other Morgantown dining establishment, although I'm not sure it should quite be classified as a restaurant. The emphasis is on fine wines, posh champagnes, choice cigars, gourmet appetizers, and brick-oven pizzas. A strict dress code (collared shirt required and torn, tattered, or offensive clothing prohibited) is enforced.

COFFEE BARS See Zenclay under *Selective Shopping—Art and Crafts Galleries.*

MICROBREWERY Morgantown Brewing Co. (304-292-6959; http://morgantownbrewing.com/), 1291 University Ave., Morgantown. Open for lunch and dinner daily. The state's first brewpub specializes in handcrafted ales, pale ales, stouts, and golds, with seasonal brews such as raspberry wheat, oatmeal stout, and rye brown. Salads, sandwiches, and a small entrée menu complement the brews. Entrées $5.95–14.95. This place really hops, especially on the weekends.

✳ Entertainment
FILM

Granville
Hollywood-Stadium 12 (304-598-3456), 1001 Mountaineer Dr. Easily accessed from I-79.

Morgantown
Carmike Cinema (304-983-6868), Morgantown Mall. First-run movies on 12 screens.

Warner Theater (304-291-3939; www.thewarner.com), 147 High St. Despite having been split into three screens, the Warner Theater's wonderful art deco architectural features have been retained. Along with first-run movies, the Warner also shows art house–type films, too.

THEATER Morgantown Metropolitan Theatre (304-291-4884; www.mettheatre.org), 369 High St., Morgantown. Opened in 1924, the Metropolitan has had quite a few notables, such as Helen Hayes, Bob Hope, and Bing Crosby, perform on its stage. It

was also the site of the first public appearance of Don Knotts, who grew up in Morgantown. Having undergone a restoration, the theater now hosts live theatrical performances, musical and dance presentations, movies, and community events. *Please note:* Supporters of theatre were working on renovating it as this book went to press, but its future was unknown.

M. T. Pockets Theatre (304-284-0049; www.mtpocketstheatre.com), 107 High St., Morgantown. Within the Monongalia Arts Center is a theater where you can witness classic drama, the first presentation of a writer's newest work, or the zany antics of comedians. The venue is so small that you get to see the facial expressions that are impossible to make out when you're sitting in the back of a huge auditorium.

West Virginia Public Theatre (302-291-4122; 1-877-999-WVPT; www.wvpublictheatre.com) is an organization that brings Broadway to Morgantown. Past presentations have included *Miss Saigon*, *Mame*, and *Beauty and the Beast*.

Also see Monongalia Arts Center under *To See—Museums & Art Galleries.*

✳ Selective Shopping
ANTIQUES

Bruceton Mills
Bruceton Antique Mall (304-379-4040), on WV 26, off I-68 exit 23. Open daily. There is a lot to look at here, and I have to hand it to the proprietors, who must have worked in a museum at some time or another, as many of the displays are arranged thematically with historical perspectives.

Morgantown
Antiques Walk at Historical Seneca Center (304-296-8117), 709 Beechurst Ave. Open daily. This is not

a multidealer, run-of-the-mill antiques shop. The owners have a true eye for older treasures, so the furniture is of a high quality, as are the numerous smaller items. Also at the same location is **B. E. F. Collectibles Riverfront Antique and Flea Market**, specializing in Morgantown, Seneca, and Beaumont glass.

Terra Alta

High Mountain Treasures (304-789-5925), on WV 7. Open Fri.–Mon. Unlike many antiques shops that have items set out in a haphazard manner, the displays at High Mountain Treasures are nicely put together, going so far as having place settings on tables. There is a lot of furniture here, much of it quite modern and mixed in with the older offerings.

ART AND CRAFTS GALLERIES

Appalachian Gallery (304-296-0163; www.wvcraft.com), 44 High St., Morgantown. Inside a two-story house is a collection of just about every kind of art and craft you can think of: pottery, wooden items, glass, folk toys, books, cards, lithographs, textiles, ironwork, quilts, photographs, and more. Much of it is from West Virginia artisans.

Brown's Creations in Clay (304-296-6656), 343 Bull Run Rd., Morgantown. Anna Brown is a potter who does not use a wheel; all of her creations are done by coiling, pressing, pinching, and sculpting the clay, giving her pieces a distinction that has won her a loyal following for more than three decades. A visit to her studio includes a walk through the small garden, where she grows the plants whose leaves she uses to make impressions in the pottery (natural minerals are used for color) and whose herbs find their way into her food products, such as ramp biscuit mix and infused vinegars.

Morgantown Art Association Gallery (304-291-6720; www.artsmon.org), 201 High St., Morgantown. The gallery features the artwork of local and regional artists, while the association works to enhance the city's opportunities to experience all kinds of creativity, including the performing arts.

Tanner's Alley (304-292-0707; www.tannersalleyleather.com), 416 High St., Morgantown. Charles McEwuen has been working in leather for more than 30 years, and his experience shows in the items he creates for his shop.

Zenclay (304-599-2069; www.zenclay.com), 2862 University Ave., Morgantown. Susan Ting has turned a three-story building into a place that reflects her passions. The first floor is her studio, where she creates and teaches pottery (there's also a small gallery for the works of other three-dimensional artists). The second floor contains the Zenclay Café, where you can get a great cup of tea or coffee (my Morgantown choice for coffee), healthy light food, and house-made muffins, scones, breads, and biscotti. The top floor is a display space for large two-dimensional works and sculpture. Come here, enjoy a wholesome meal and drink (there's a play space for the kids), and look over art that gets displayed here only after being juried in.

BOOKSTORE The Bookshelf (304-599-4601), 735 Chestnut Rd., Morgantown. Good selection of new and used books.

FARMERS' MARKETS

Kingwood

The **Kingwood Farmers' Market** (304-329-1391) operates 8–11 on Sat. from mid-July until mid-Oct. at the WesBanco parking lot.

Morgantown

Find fruits, vegetables, honey, mushrooms, eggs, herbs, and more at the producer-only **Morgantown Farmers' Market** (304-275-1865; www.morgantownfarmers.org) on the corner of Spruce and Fayette Sts., 8:30–noon Sat. from late May-Oct.

MALL The Seneca Center (1-800-289-7362; www.senecacenter.com), 709 Beechurst Ave., Morgantown, is a restored glass factory (1891–1983) that now houses some of Morgantown's most interesting shops, such as Antiques Walk, The Little Studio (an artists and craftpersons gallery), and Wamsley Cycles. Also here is the Riverfront Museum, which exhibits fine glassware once produced at Seneca and other regional factories.

SPECIAL SHOPS

Bruceton Mills

Hostetler's Country Store (304-379-4910), off I-68 exit 23. You will find many of the usual "gift shop" type of items here—stuffed bears, candles, and so on—but there is also a very good offering of quality West Virginia handmade craft items, such as Anna Brown pottery, Marble King marbles, Fenton glass, and Thistle Dew folk toys, along with West Virginia wines, jams, jellies, and sauces.

Granville

Mannette Steel Drums (1-866-237-3786; www.mannettesteeldrums.com), 166 Dent Runs Rd. Caribbean steel drums made in West Virginia? That's right. You can tour the world's only factory that lets you see, hear, and learn the history, creation, and tuning of steel drums. Buy one, take it home, and let your neighbors mark your practicing progress.

Kingwood

The Calico Cat (304-329-1496), 110½ West Main St. A gift and collectibles shop, located in two former houses, which features many of the usual items, along with some West Virginia handcrafts and a year-round Christmas shop.

Morgantown

Mountaineer Corner (304-292-1423), 732 Beechurst Ave. The place to buy all of your WVU souvenirs, including hats, shirts, cups, pennants, stickers, and glassware.

The Old Stone House (304-296-7825), 313 Chestnut St. Open 10–2 Mon.–Fri., and 11–3 Sat.; hours increase during the holiday season. Inside the oldest stone dwelling in Monongalia County, built circa 1795, the Service League of Morgantown operates a small shop with handcrafted items, interesting gifts, and gently used articles. If you have the urge to buy something to remember your trip to Morgantown, purchase it here, as proceeds are given to local groups, such as a children's theater, school libraries, and charities that provide client emergency assistance.

Slight Indulgence (304-292-3401; 1-888-424-3401; www.slightindulgence.com), 407 High St. A gourmet shop with wines, coffees, teas, food, and fine chocolates.

WINERY Forks of Cheat Winery (304-298-2019; 1-888-WV-WINES; www.wvwines.com), 2811 Stewartstown Rd., Morgantown. Open daily. Even if you are not a wine lover, you can still appreciate the setting of the Forks of Cheat Winery, whose tasting room, koi pond, gardens, and large pavilion overlook the 16 acres of vines growing upon a sloping hillside. Owners Jerry and Susan Deal met as students at WVU and started making wine as a hobby. This is now the state's largest production winery using French hybrid and American varietal grapes, all picked by hand.

✳ Special Events

Late winter to early spring: **Festival of Ideas** (304-293-SHOW; http://festivalofideas.wvu.edu), WVU, Morgantown. A free lecture series featuring some of the most interesting minds of the day. Past speakers have included Julian Bond and Seymour Hersh.

June: **Old Morgantown Glass Show and Sale** (304-594-1111), Lakeview Golf Resort and Spa, Morgantown. Educational seminars and thousands of glass items.

July: **Arts on the River Fest** (www.wvarts.net), McQuain Park, Morgantown. An art festival that also features West Virginia wines and foods.

September: **Buckwheat Festival** (www.buckwheatfest.com), Kingwood. A major annual event with a feast of buckwheat pancakes, carnival, livestock exhibits, parades, and an antique car show. To help you understand just how big an event this is, just one food vendor reported selling more than 6,000 pounds of French fries. **West Virginia Wine and Jazz Festival** (www.wvwineandjazz.com), Camp Muffly, Morgantown.

October: **Mountaineer Balloon Festival** (304-296-8356; www.ummbf.com), Morgantown. It is quite an amazing spectacle to see 50 hot-air balloons launch at the same time and hover over the city.

November: **Mountaineer Week Craft Fair and Quilt Show** (304-293-2702), Morgantown. A juried event with more than 60 artisans. Also features music and other entertainment.

THE CLARKSBURG/FAIRMONT ENVIRONS

There is a hustle and bustle along I-79 in the cities of Clarksburg and Fairmont.
Clarksburg was the birthplace of Confederate Gen. Stonewall Jackson (a plaque
marks the spot at 326–328 Main St.) and served as a Union depot during the war.
Lowndes Park, with a scenic overlook of the city, still has breastwork trenches as a
reminder of those days. Thanks to the early-1900s Italian stonemason immigrants,
the Downtown Historical District, on the National Register of Historic Places, has
an abundance of Italianate, Gothic Revival, Greek Revival, Victorian, and Victorian
Romanesque buildings. An annual Italian Festival honors this heritage, while
famous restaurants like Minard's showcase some of the traditions all year long.

Fairmont sits at the confluence of three rivers. The West Fork and Tygart Valley rivers meet to form the Monongahela River, which flows northward to another
city of three rivers, Pittsburgh, Pennsylvania. The city's main bridge across the
Monongahela was built in 1921 and was one of the country's earliest reinforced
concrete bridges, with three arches and art deco decorations. Below the bridge,
Palatine Park is a peaceful place to take a stroll or launch a canoe. Famous Fair-
monters include Olympian Mary Lou Retton and Johnnie Johnson, a member of
the Rock and Roll Hall of Fame who was the subject of Chuck Berry's *Johnny B.
Goode*.

In recent years, the two cities have joined the high-tech world, with hundreds
of jobs in the National White Collar Crime Center, the FBI's Criminal Justice
Information Services Division, and NASA's Independent Verification and Valida-
tion Facility.

COMMUNITIES Often overlooked and overshadowed by Clarksburg, which is on
the west side of I-79, **Bridgeport** is a fast-growing city along the interstate's eastern side. Many businesses are still located on its main street, but significant housing and commercial development will surely have an impact on the small-town
atmosphere.

Grafton was a major prize during the Civil War because of its location along the
B&O Railroad. The first soldier to be killed during the war at the Battle of Philippi
is buried in town at the Grafton National Cemetery. (Some historians say that the
soldier, Thornsberry Bailey Brown, met his death before the battle so should not

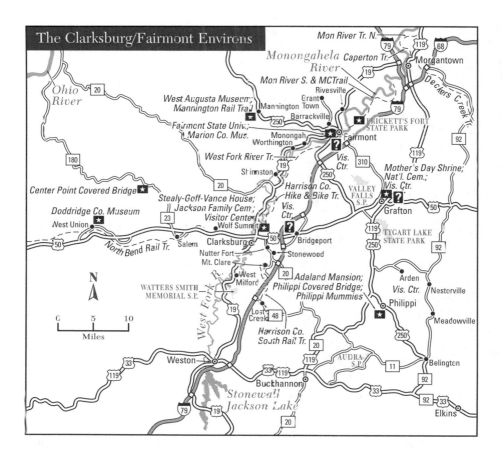

be considered the first to die in the war.) The town gained lasting national fame in 1908 when it became the first place in America to celebrate Mother's Day.

It may not be common knowledge in the rest of America, but by the time every West Virginian graduates from high school, he or she knows that the covered bridge over the Tygart Valley River in the town of **Philippi** was the site of what many historians consider to be the first land battle of the Civil War. On June 2 and 3, 1861, Confederate Col. George Porterfield's troops were occupying the town when Union soldiers captured the bridge and gunfire erupted around the main street and courthouse. Today, there is a newer courthouse, constructed in 1903 of hand-cut Hummelstown stone (be sure to go inside to the impressive courtroom, with a stained-glass ceiling, dome, columns, and ornate woodwork), and a pleasant paved walking trail running along the riverfront. A guided walking tour brochure, available from the Philippi Convention and Visitors Bureau (see *Guidance*), will take you by remarkable Greek Revival, Richardsonian Romanesque, and Italianate homes and buildings.

Salem was founded in 1792 by a group of Seventh-Day Baptist families, and the traditions of Scots-Irish and German immigrant farmers shaped the early part of its history. By the turn of the 20th century, oil, gas, and timber extraction drove its economy. Today, it's a small town located off a major four-lane highway and is home to Salem International University.

Shinnston, with a population of about 2,500, began in 1778 when Levi Shinn built a two-story log cabin that still stands on its original site along US 19. The town's location as the southern terminus of the West Fork River Rail Trail has introduced it to many travelers who would have probably never given the small town a second look as they drove through it. Also of interest to some is the Chapel of Perpetual Adoration, which is open 24 hours a day for people of all faiths.

GUIDANCE The **Convention and Visitors Bureau of Marion County** (304-368-1123; 1-800-834-7365; www.marioncvb.com) can be found at 2 Mountain Park Dr., White Hall, close to I-79.

The **Grafton/Taylor County Convention and Visitors Bureau** (304-265-3938) is at 214 West Main St., Grafton 26354.

The **Greater Bridgeport Convention and Visitors Center** (304-842-7272; 1-800-368-4324; www.greater-bridgeport.com), 164 West Main St., Bridgeport 26330, is also a small museum with items from a locally influential family, the Benedums. Close to the visitor center is the 1924 Bowstring Bridge, used by the Bridgeport Lamp Chimney Company to provide access between its glass plant and warehouse. Look on the ground around the bridge, and you may find bits of glass from this company or rounded pieces of glass from the Master Glass Company, which manufactured marbles from 1940 to 1973.

The **Greater Clarksburg Visitors Bureau** (304-622-2157; www.cityofclarksburg wv.com) is located along a pedestrian walkway at 208 Court St., Clarksburg 26301.

You can obtain information for Philippi and Barbour County from the **Philippi Convention and Visitors Bureau** (304-457-3700; www.philippi.org), 108 North Main St., Philippi 26416.

GETTING THERE *By air:* The **North Central West Virginia Airport** (304-842-3400; www.flyckb.com) near Clarksburg and the **Morgantown Municipal Airport** (304-291-7461; www.morgantownairport.com; 100 Hart Field Rd.) have daily flights that connect to other airports, but you might want to consider flying into **Pittsburgh International Airport** (412-472-3525; www.pitairport.com) or **Yeager Airport** (304-344-8033; www.yeagerairport.com) in Charleston. The latter two are less than a two-hour drive from this area, and fares are usually much less.

By bus: The closest **Greyhound** (1-800-231-2222; www.greyhound.com) will get you is either Pittsburgh, Pennsylvania or Charleston. However, Morgantown's **Mountain Line Transit Authority** (304-291-7433; www.busride.org) operates a Greyhound commuter service to Pittsburgh that makes stops in Fairmont and Clarksburg.

By car: **I-79** is the four-lane highway that will deliver you to this area from the north or south. Coming from Ohio and the west, the most convenient route is four-lane **US 50**. Those coming from the east should follow **I-68** through Maryland and turn southward on **I-79** in Morgantown.

GETTING AROUND *By bus:* & All the vehicles of the **Central West Virginia Transit Authority** (304-623-6002; www.centrabus.com) are ADA accessible.

Bridgeport, Stonewood, Nutter Fort, West Milford, Wolf Summit, Hartland, Salem, and Shinnston.

&. In Fairmont, the **Fairmont/Marion County Transit Authority** (304-366-8177; www.fmcta.com) has routes that take in the city's many communities and the small towns of Carolina, Fairview, Mannington, and Rivesville. You can also take a bus to the area malls and to Clarksburg. All vehicles are ADA accessible.

&. To get around in Clarksburg and Fairmont, call **Royal Cab** (304-622-0590). In Grafton, call **Grafton Taylor Taxi** (304-265-0100).

MEDICAL EMERGENCIES

Clarksburg
United Hospital Center (304-624-2121; www.uhcwv.org), 3 Hospital Plaza.

Fairmont
Fairmont General Hospital (304-367-7100; www.fghi.com), 1325 Locust Ave.

Grafton
Grafton City Hospital (304-265-0400; www.graftonhospital.com), 500 Market St. Grafton.

Philippi
Broaddus Hospital (304-457-1760; www.davishealthsystem.org), Mansfield Hill (US 119, south of Philippi).

✷ To See
COLLEGES

Fairmont
Fairmont State University (304-367-4892; www.fairmontstate.edu), 1201 Locust Ave. Thanks to a plethora of cultural events, there is never a dull moment at the 8,000-student university, founded in 1865. The school of fine arts and its associated fine-arts guild sponsor concerts, visual-arts presentations, plays, and theatrical performances. The Brooks Memorial Gallery, along with the interesting Tower Room (a partially circular room with a circular staircase connecting two levels), has ever-changing art shows from students, faculty, and touring exhibits. There is an intimate feel to productions presented in the school's small 400-seat theater.

Also on campus is the 1871 Snodgrass one-room schoolhouse, now serving as a museum with donated items of McGuffey Readers, a Franklin stove, hand bell, and other memorabilia.

In 1999, the school opened a 36,000-square-foot branch at 501 West Main St. (304-367-4037) in Clarksburg that has more than 1,400 students and whose facilities are used for community cultural events.

Philippi
Alderson-Broaddus College (304-457-1700; www.ab.edu), 101 College Hill Rd. Established in 1932 by the joining together of two existing schools of higher education, the college overlooks the town and is built upon 170 acres that were the site of the Battle of Philippi. With a total student population of less than 1,000, the school adds to the town's cultural life with painting, sculpture, and other artistic

exhibits in the Daywood Gallery, and live theatrical performances in the Funkhouser Theater. The chapel's acoustics are a great complement to the extraordinary pipe organ and the tall windows' wonderful view of the countryside. Also on campus is a one-room-schoolhouse museum.

COVERED BRIDGES

Barrackville

The **Barrackville Covered Bridge** was constructed by Lemuel and Eli Chenoweth (see Lemuel Chenoweth House Museum under *To See—Museums* in the "Reaching for the Sky—Spruce Knob, Seneca Rocks, and Cranberry Glades" chapter) in 1853 as part of the Fairmont and Wheeling Turnpike. At a length of more than 140 feet, it is the state's second-oldest existing covered bridge and is still in use, spanning Buffalo Creek on WV 21 at the junction of WV 250/32, a short distance northwest of Fairmont.

Bridgeport

Built in 1881, the **Simpson Creek Covered Bridge** was washed out in a flood and moved to its present site in 1889. Located on WV 24/2 within 0.2 mile of I-79 exit 121, it is probably the state's most accessible covered bridge.

Carrollton

Built in 1856, the **Carrollton Covered Bridge** was an important link on the Middle Fork Turnpike, permitting traffic to cross the Buckhannon River. More than 140 feet long and 16 feet wide, it is the state's second-longest and third-oldest existing covered bridge. Drive US 119 South from Philippi and turn left onto WV 36.

Center Point

Built in 1888, the **Center Point Covered Bridge** was in use until 1940, when it fell into private hands. It was donated to the Doddridge County Historical Society in 1981, renovated, and turned over to the state of West Virginia. It is located about 300 feet from WV 23 in Center Point.

Philippi

Without a doubt, the **Philippi Covered Bridge** is the state's most famous. It is West Virginia's oldest (built in 1852 by Lemuel and Eli Chenoweth) and longest (285 feet, 10 inches) existing covered bridge. Spanning the Tygart Valley River, it enabled traffic to travel all the way from Norfolk, Virginia, to the Ohio River on the Staunton-Parkersburg Turnpike. Perhaps, though, its real claim to fame is that, in what many consider to be the first land skirmish of the Civil War, Union and Confederate forces fought over the bridge. In 1989, a fire destroyed much of it, but it was rebuilt and is the country's only covered bridge still in use on a federal highway (US 250).

Wolf Summit

Enabling vehicles to cross the Righthand Fork of Ten Mile Creek, the 58-foot-long **Fletcher Creek Covered Bridge** has not been significantly altered since it was built in 1891. Only 12 feet 4 inches wide, the multiple kingpost structure can be reached by driving US 50 West from Wolf Summit, turning right onto WV 5, and continuing to WV 5/29.

DRIVING TOURS, SCENIC & HISTORIC Available from the Anna Jarvis Birthplace Welcome Center (see *Historic Sites*), **Detour into the Past** is a four-page pamphlet directing you on a 50-mile driving tour that takes in eight significant Civil War sites, including the locations of the battles of Philippi and Laurel Hill.

HISTORIC CHURCH Central United Methodist Church (304-366-3351; www.cumcwv.org), 301 Fairmont, Fairmont Ave. The 1922 church is home to the congregation that, at one time, held services in the Williams Memorial Methodist Episcopal Church, where the first Father's Day celebration was held. A mining accident in Monongah had killed more than 350 men, and the pastor of the church held a special service to honor the fathers who had perished.

HISTORIC SITES

Clarksburg

Now a part of the Jackson City Park on East Pike St., the **Jackson Family Cemetery** is the final resting place of Stonewall Jackson's father, Jonathan, and other family members. Also buried here are Dolly Madison's mother and sister.

Grafton

Grafton National Cemetery (304-265-2044), 431 Walnut St. Established in 1867 by Congress for soldiers who died during the Civil War, the national cemetery holds the remains of 1,215 men, both Union and Confederate, with almost half of them being unknown. Standing in places such as this, I can't help but think about how the human race seems to expend so much more energy for hostile actions than for peaceful pursuits.

A short drive from Grafton will bring you to the **West Virginia National Cemetery**, the final resting place for hundreds of members of the Armed Forces of the United States. High on a hillside, it has a 360-degree view.

𝍐 The **International Mother's Day Shrine** (304-265-1589; www.mothersday shrine.com), 11 East Main St. Open Fri.–Sun. (depending on the schedules of volunteers). On May 10, 1908, the first Mother's Day observance was held in Andrews Methodist Church. The idea for such a celebration is credited to Anna M. Jarvis, a teacher who wanted to honor the life of her mother and all other mothers, living and dead. After the celebration in Grafton, she started lobbying to have the day declared a national celebration, which President Woodrow Wilson proclaimed in 1914. The church, which still has its pews, stained-glass windows, and glorious pipe organ, has a few rooms with Jarvis memorabilia, such as the Jarvis Sunday School room and the original proclamation from President Wilson.

WEST VIRGINIA NATIONAL CEMETERY

Sutton, West Virginia, artist William Douglas Hopen Jr. sculpted the *Mother with Children* statue in the plaza next to the church as a tribute to the security children feel when in the arms of their mothers.

Not far from the shrine is the **Anna Jarvis Birthplace** (304-265-5549; www.anna jarvishouse.com), on US 119/US 250 about 4 miles south of Grafton. Looking at it from the outside, it would be hard to believe that the simple restored farmhouse could contain more than 5,000 individual pieces of memorabilia, some pertaining to the Jarvis family, others from the Civil War, and others that help round out what life was like in this part of West Virginia in days gone by. Open Apr.–Oct., Tues.–Sun. Small admission fee.

LAKE Head to **Curtisville Lake**, near Mannington, if you are looking for a quiet time. This has to be one of the most underused bodies of water in the state, sometimes going for days before someone comes along to cast a line for largemouth and smallmouth bass, catfish, bluegill, and trout. Hiking trails (once again, rarely used) and picnic areas are located around the lake. Although there is no official swimming area, local people often take a dip close to the boat launch ramp. From Mannington, stay on Main St. (WV 1) for close to 6 miles, turn left onto WV 7 (Curtisville Pike), and continue an additional mile.

Also see Tygart Lake State Park under *Green Space—Parks*.

MUSEUMS

Clarksburg
Ϯ **Stealy-Goff-Vance House** (304-629-0098), 123 West Main St. Open by appointment. Free; donations accepted. Depending on who the volunteer docent is at the time of your visit, you may get a guided or self-guided tour of this 1807 home with unusual Flemish bond on the brick. Displays are set up as if someone was still living in the home, and the parlor, dining room, bedroom, and other parts of the house contain articles that illustrate the lifestyle of 18th- and 19th-century inhabitants of the area. Of special note are items from Stonewall Jackson and the family of Cyrus Vance (secretary of state under President Jimmy Carter), who were the last private owners of the home.

CURTISVILLE LAKE

Fairmont
Ϯ **Marion County Historical Society Museum** (304-367-5398), 211 Adams St. Open Memorial Day–Labor Day, Mon.–Sat. 10–2; closed Sat. the rest of the year. Free; donations accepted. A project of the Marion County Historical Society, the museum is located in what was the county sheriff's home in

PRICKETT'S FORT STATE PARK

the early part of the 20th century. Still present in the sheriff's office is his ledger, but more importantly, the corridor that provided direct access to the jail and courthouse. The rest of the rooms are thematic, with one devoted to the Civil War, another containing a compass thought to have belonged to George Washington, and one with antique toys, small-scale furniture, and the last Lehman Brothers model train made in Germany.

🐾 ♂ **Prickett's Fort State Park** (304-363-3030; www.prickettsfortstatepark .com; mailing address: Rte. 3, Box 407, Fairmont 26555). Follow signs for 2 miles from I-79 exit 139. Open daily mid-Apr. through Oct. Small admission fee. On a knoll overlooking the meeting of Prickett's Creek and the Monongahela River, the fort is a 110-by-110-foot replica of the original structure built in the 1770s to protect early settlers. As many as 80 families sought refuge here during Indian raids, and close to 100 of these forts were located within a 30-mile radius.

We have all been to sites where costumed interpreters and craftspersons re-create days gone by, but the small size (making it easy to see and do everything) and the quality of the presentations make Prickett's Fort stand out from those other places. You may even get invited to throw a tomahawk or help weave a basket. Outside the fort is the Job Prickett House, built in 1859 by the grandson of Capt. John Prickett and furnished with 85 years' worth of family belongings.

The park has picnic facilities, a boat launch, amphitheater, and a short interpretive nature trail. It is also the trailhead for the MCTrail and the Mon River Trail South (see *To Do—Rail Trails*).

Lost Creek

&. **Watters Smith Memorial State Park** (304-745-3081; www.watterssmithstate park.com; mailing address: P.O. Box 296, Lost Creek 26385). From I-79 exit 110, follow directional signs for about 7 miles to the park. Donations accepted. Like Prickett's Fort, Watters Smith is a state park, but both are more museum than park. A large percentage of its 532 acres were part of a farm that operated until the park opened in the late 1940s, and many structures, most built without nails or wooden pegs and held together only by notched corners, remain to tell the story. Watching the video and looking at historic items in the visitor center will help provide background to your self-guided tour (free brochure available) of the barn, corncrib, hog pen, woodworking shop, and other buildings. The 1876 farmhouse, filled with some original furnishings, is open for tours on certain days (check at the visitor center).

Other park amenities include picnic facilities; playgrounds; a few hiking, biking, and equestrian trails; and a handicapped-accessible swimming pool open from Memorial Day to Labor Day. The Watters Smith Memorial Foundation operates a small mountain crafts shop in the visitor center, which I found to contain some real treasures that are bargains at the prices marked on them.

Mannington

⇞ West Augusta Historical Society Museum and Mannington Round Barn (304-986-1298), Main St. S. Open Tues., Thurs., and Fri. Small donation requested. Housed in the former 1912 Wilson School, the museum contains some remarkable documents, such as original land grant papers; items from Dr. Phoebe Moore, the first woman to study medicine at WVU; an 1898 roller organ; and a kerosene film projector. The log cabin, with spinning wheel, cord bed, and working fireplace, was built in 1870 and moved next to the museum with the help of the local Future Farmers of America.

MANNINGTON ROUND BARN

Located a short distance from the museum on Flaggy Meadow Rd., the 1912 Mannington Round Barn is one of the few remaining examples of its kind. The advantage of such a structure is the large loft, which enabled farmers to store hay directly above the cattle and not have to haul it from another place. In addition to looking over the farm implements, some scale models, and a few other items of interest, be sure to ask about the ingenious automatic livestock watering system that the cattle could turn on and off by themselves.

Philippi

⟁ Adaland Mansion (304-457-1587; www.adaland.org; mailing address: P.O. Box 74), on WV 76 northwest of Philippi. Open Wed., Thurs., Sat., and Sun. May–Dec. Admission $10; children under age 12 are free. The late-1800s mansion sat empty and deteriorating for 20 years before volunteers and the City of Philippi undertook the restoration process. Today, costumed docents take you on a tour of the home, which features the original homemade bricks and walnut woodwork. One room depicts state judge Ira E. Robinson's bedroom of the early 1900s (his death mask is on display), another exhibits life of the Victorian period, the basement is furnished as it would have been in the 1840s, and other rooms have more modern accoutrements. The 1850s barn has been restored and houses a display of early farm tools, and a large flower garden has been created next to the home. All of this sits on a low knoll overlooking the scenic countryside.

Barbour County Historical Society Museum (304-457-4846), 200 North Main St. Open Fri.–Sun. (call ahead; hours may change). Very small admission fee. Located in the restored 1911 train depot at the east end of the Philippi Covered Bridge, the museum not only displays Civil War memorabilia (such as a part of the courthouse flagpole that was split by a bullet during the Battle of Philippi), but is also a place to discover little-known bits of local history: Ida L. Reed, born nearby in 1865, became famous for her religious writings and more than 2,000 hymns, which have been used by 11 denominations in the United States. Ted Cassidy, who played "Lurch" on TV's *Addams Family*, was born in Philippi. It's too long a tale to

THE PHILIPPI MUMMIES

There's no need to go to the pyramids of Egypt or even the Smithsonian in Washington, DC, to see mummified bodies. Within the former restroom of the railroad depot that is now the Barbour County Historical Society Museum are the remains of two unidentified women, whose story after death is surely more colorful than what their lives were. All that is known about them is that, in 1888, Graham Hamrick obtained their corpses from the Hospital for the Insane in Weston. They were preserved using his patented Mummifying Fluid, which he said he invented as an easier and cheaper method of embalming. His fluid evidently worked, as the bodies have survived being traveling curiosities on a tour of Europe with P. T. Barnum, on display in the defunct Mountaineer Hall of Fame in Richwood, and getting washed away in the famous flood of 1985.

You can take a gander at the mummies laid out in glass-covered boxes for a meager $1 per person.

retell here, so be sure to ask for the full story concerning the Dr. Myers' Remedies display.

West Union

Doddridge County Museum (304-873-3050), Main St. Open by appointment only; donations accepted. Housed in a building built in 1937 and used for six decades as the county jail, the museum has items from the 18th through the 20th centuries. The top floor still has the original jail cells open for public viewing.

While in West Union, you should also stop to take a look at the **Doddridge County Courthouse**, constructed at the turn of the 20th century. Stained-glass windows, a carved gargoyle, hand-carved scrollwork on the outer oak doors, marble wainscoted interior walls, and a marble stairway with handmade wrought iron are just a few of the reasons it is on the National Register of Historic Places. Also see *Colleges*.

WATERFALLS Pretty much known only to local residents, a few kayakers, and Alderson-Broaddus College students (who come here to do what college students often do when away from authority figures), **Moatsville Falls** is a scenic 18-foot drop in the Tygart Valley River. In addition to the scenery (there are numerous smaller falls upstream and downstream), you can enjoy drying off in the sun after a swim on the large rocks along the shore. The drive along the river from Arden is so scenic that I recommend you bring your bike and do some riding before or after taking a dip.

✳ To Do

BICYCLING There are a number of nice rides on the quiet country roads, both paved and unpaved, around Philippi. Two of the easiest and certainly most scenic are an out-and-back trip on dirt **WV 52** along the Tygart Valley River south of Belington, and one on paved **Arden Rd.** (about 4 miles south of Philippi) beside the roiling waters of the stream.

You can make a challenging circuit ride of a little more than 13 miles on what is known as the **Moatsville Climb** by riding upstream on Arden Rd., turning right for a steep climb on WV 12, making a left to cross Laurel Fork River on WV 10/13, turning left onto WV 10 at Moatsville, and making one final left to return to the starting point on Arden Rd.

The 10-mile loop on unpaved roads around the **Teter Creek Wildlife Management Area** north of Belington will take you beside pretty Glade Creek, along heavily forested roadways, and up to a mountaintop viewpoint. Start by riding past the wildlife management area's campground on WV 26. Turn right onto WV 42, right onto WV 9 at Meadowville, left onto WV 9/5, right at the sign to Mount Zion Church, left onto WV 26/5, right onto WV 26/7, and another right onto WV 26.

✄ **Marion County BMX Park** (304-363-7037; www.mcparc.com), Fairmont. From I-79 exit 139, follow signs to Prickett's Fort State Park, but soon turn onto WV 73 to Hoult Rd. The National Bicycle League sanctions the track, known as the Poor Farm BMX Track. It has the usual dirt route, but few other facilities.

Also see *Rail Trails* and *Green Space—Parks*.

BOWLING

Clarksburg
✄ **Compton Bowling Lanes** (304-622-1261), 1 Bridgeport Hill Rd. Automatic scoring for the 24 lanes and bumper bowling for the younger children.

THE FUN SLIDE AT VALLEY WORLDS OF FUN

Fairmont
✄ **Fairmont Bowling Center** (304-366-0631), 1 Kirkway Dr. There are 24 lanes for open, league, and cosmic bowling, along with TVs, video games, and a snack bar and lounge.

Grafton
Vintage Lanes (304-903-8229; www.vintagelanes.com; mailing address: Rte. 1, Box 90B, Grafton 26354), 1 Vintage Sq., east of Grafton on US 50.

Also see *Family Activities*.

FAMILY ACTIVITIES ✄ ⊤ **Valley Worlds of Fun** (304-366-2500; 1-877-366-2501; www.valleyworldsoffun.com), 2017 Pleasant Valley Rd., Fairmont. Open daily. Valley Worlds of Fun is a popular place, with many attractions packed into only 2 acres. There are bumper cars, bumper boats (with squirt guns to ensure you get wet), a maze, climbing wall, miniature golf course, and fun slide. The 61,000-square-foot arcade has one of the most colorful bowling alleys you will ever see, along with a huge laser tag room and 50 arcade games from which winners can redeem tickets for trinkets. The Monster Mansion has black lights that make fluorescent paint stand out in relief, giving things a 3-D effect. In addition, there are live humans inside whose job is to scare you as much as possible.

FISHING You can fish for largemouth bass, bluegill, and stocked trout from the shore, in a canoe, or atop a seat on your small boat with an electric motor in the 35-acre lake in **Teter Creek Lake Wildlife Management Area**, north of Belington. The **Middlefork**, **Monongahela**, and **Buckhannon** rivers are where many anglers go in search of smallmouth bass, while the **Tygart Valley River** has smallmouth bass, as well as catfish and bluegill.

Don't like to fish with crowds? Then seek out little-known **Paw Paw Creek** near Grant Town and **Wickwire Run** north of Grafton.

If you want to make almost sure that you will catch something, **Family Fun Fishing and Camping** (304-265-1000; mailing address: Rte. 2, Box 290, Grafton 26354) is the place to be. A number of ponds constructed on sloping ground are filled with channel cats, bass, flathead blues (some up to 70 pounds), and stocked trout. The ponds and campground, with rental cabins and tent and RV sites, are not the most scenic of spots, but the whole operation is very family-friendly, with playgrounds and a watchful management.

Also see *To See—Lake* and *Green Space—Parks*.

GOLF

Bridgeport
Pete Dye Golf Club (304-842-2801; www.petedye.com), 801 Aaron Smith Dr. I have not included other private clubs in this book, but the Pete Dye Golf Club is so interesting that it deserves a mention. The course is built upon a former strip mine and has reminders of that activity, including strip-mined high walls, a rotary car tipple, coal-laden mine cars, a cart path through a once-active deep mine, and waterfalls that originate from old deep mining activity.

Fairmont
Fairmont Field Club (304-366-2321), 1709 Country Club Rd. Established in 1912, the club has a regulation length nine-hole course, swimming pool, and four tennis courts.

Green Hills Country Club (304-287-7439), Everson Rd. The 18-hole course at the Green Hills Country Club facility has 6,056 yards from the longest tees, par 72. It was designed by Edmund B. Ault and opened in 1962.

Grafton
Tygart Lake Golf Course (304-265-3100; www.tygartlakegolfcourse.com; mailing address: Rte. 1, Box 449-B, Grafton 26354), Knoxville Rd. Designed by Edmund B. Ault and opened in the 1960s, the 18-hole course has a par 72 layout, with bentgrass greens, Bermuda grass fairways, and more than 20 sand bunkers. Water comes into play on seven holes, especially on hole number 7, where you have to drive more than 100 yards over the water in front of the tee.

Mount Clare

Bel Meadow Golf Club (304-623-3701; www.belmeadow.com; mailing address: Rte. 1, Box 450, Mount Clare 26408), Bel Meadow Dr. Designed by Robert Trent Jones Sr. and opened in 1965, the course is thought to be one of the most challenging in the state, with 51 sand traps and large rolling greens. It was the site of the West Virginia Open in 1967 and 1971. Both times it was won by Sam Snead, who said about the course, "It's a little tough for the average player, and if I was a local player I would play the front twice. To heck with losing all those balls on the back nine."

Philippi

Barbour Country Club (304-457-2156), off US 119 south of Philippi. Open mid-Mar. to mid-Nov. The semiprivate club has nine holes and is par 70.

GOLF, MINIATURE ✐ **Coal Country Miniature Golf** (304-366-9300; www .coalcountrywv.com), 2200 Country Ln., Fairmont. From I-79 exit 137, drive 0.2 mile on WV 310 and turn left onto Hopewell Rd. Open Apr.–Oct. Actual mining equipment, such as a ventilation culvert or a mining car, make up the obstacles on the course. Adding to the challenge are the PVC pipe railings that cause the balls to react differently than wood railings do. You'll learn a bit about the mining industry from signs that explain what the equipment at each hole was used for. There's also a small mining museum and a long list of those killed in industry accidents. Batting cages are next to the course.

Also see *Family Activities*, and East Marion Park and Wavepool under *Green Space—Parks*.

HIKING The **American Discovery Trail**, a route that runs more than 6,800 miles from the Atlantic Ocean to the Pacific shore, enters this area near the town of Nestorville, comes into contact with Tygart Lake and Valley Falls state parks, and uses the Harrison County Bike and Hike Trail to get near Clarksburg. From here it again uses roadways to connect with the North Bend Rail Trail, which it follows to the rail trail's western terminus near Parkersburg.

For more information about the American Discovery Trail, write to P.O. Box 20155, Washington, DC 20041; call 540-720-5489 or 1-800-663-2387; or log onto www.discoverytrail.org.

Also see *Rail Trails* and *Green Space—Parks*.

KAYAKING & CANOEING The **Tygart Valley River** and its tributaries have some excellent paddling and whitewater rafting opportunities that only a few commercial companies and individual kayakers run—or even know about.

One of the easier trips takes in 6 miles of the **Buckhannon** and **Tygart Valley** rivers. For the put-in, drive US 119 South from Philippi and turn left onto WV 36 to the Carrollton Covered Bridge. Takeout is at the boat ramp above the Philippi Covered Bridge. The first mile is easy Class II, with one hole that should probably be scouted. Once you enter the Tygart Valley River, you'll negotiate some large boulders in Class I–II water (of course, they will be more difficult in high water) before enjoying a fairly easy final 2 miles.

With some spectacular scenery, a 5-mile outing on the **Middle Fork River** starts out somewhat easy from Poe Rd. (about 3 miles from Audra State Park), but it soon enters a Class II–III boulder slalom and an 8-foot drop that should definitely be scouted. Be sure to take out just before the bridge in the state park, or you will be committed to going into the challenging Class III–V waters described in the next paragraph.

A longer, more challenging—and possibly dangerous—Class III–V, which should only be done by very experienced paddlers, begins on **Tygart Valley River** at the bridge in Belington and ends at the Philippi Covered Bridge. The first few of the 16 miles are fairly easy, but that soon changes with a number of 8-foot ledges, lots of boulders, and narrow rapids. Scout often so that you will be aware of the many keepers, pinning hazards, and difficult hydraulics. Things mellow out once you pass the confluence with the Buckhannon River.

Another Class III–V outing on the **Tygart Valley River** passes through some of the stream's most beautiful scenery, but it has one challenge after another. For the put-in, drive US 119 North from Philippi for 5 miles, turn right on Arden Rd., and continue to the first rapids. The takeout is beside Cove Run on Cove Run Rd. north of Moatsville. Again, do not skimp on the scouting as you come to rapids with names such as Deception, Undercut, Classic, Rodeo, and Another Nasty Hole. In between these are the 18-foot Moats Falls and Wells Falls. The first is runnable, but many people decide not to, while the latter has been described as the most powerful runnable rapid in the Monongahela River drainage system.

If all of the aforementioned outings sound too adrenaline producing, or involve more energy than you wish to expend, there are many acres of easy flatwater on **Tygart Valley Lake**, and near-flatwater on the **Monongahela River**.

RAIL TRAILS & As you found out in the "Morgantown and Vicinity" chapter, this region is blessed with an abundance of rail trails, with at least seven (more are planned) running through this area alone. All are handicapped accessible, and many connect to one another in some fashion, providing various opportunities and miles for hiking, biking, horseback riding, and cross-country skiing.

Having paralleled its namesake river for more than 10 miles from Morgantown, the southern terminus for the **Mon River Trail South** (see *To Do— Rail Trails* in the "Morgantown and Vicinity" chapter) is located in Prickett's Fort State Park (see *To See— Museums*). This is also the northern

TYGART VALLEY RIVER

terminus of the 2.5-mile **MCTrail**, which passes through a lighted railroad tunnel on its way to its southern end in northern Fairmont on Winfield St. From here, you can follow the Across Town Link, a signed route that takes you along the city's streets for several miles to meet up with the **West Fork River Rail Trail**.

The 15.5-mile West Fork River Rail Trail crosses three bridges (one is more than 500 feet long), provides access to beaches and swimming areas along the river, and is sometimes wooded and sometimes in small towns. Seek out the old coke ovens near the settlement of Enterprise and an old milldam near Worthington. The trail comes to an end in Shinnston.

The **Mannington** (or **North Marion**) **Rail Trail** is a 2-mile route not connected to any of the aforementioned trails, and it has its trailhead at the original railroad depot in Mannington.

For more information on all the aforementioned trails, call the Marion County Parks and Recreation Commission at 304-363-7037 or log onto www.mcparc.com.

Also not connected to any other trails, or to each other, are the **Harrison County Southern Rail Trail**, an 8-mile route with termini in Lost Creek and Mount Clare (plans are to extend it to Clarksburg), and the 7-mile **Harrison County North Hike and Bike Trail**, which travels along the West Fork River between the North View section of Clarksburg and Spelter. For more information about these two routes, call the Harrison County Parks and Recreation Commission at 304-624-0418 or log onto www.hcparks.org.

The **North Bend Rail Trail** is a part of the West Virginia State Park system and runs 72 miles from I-77 at Parkersburg to Wolf Summit in Harrison County. At present there are only about 5 miles in this area—plans call for it to eventually connect Parkersburg with Clarksburg. See *To Do—Rail Trails* in the "The Mid-Ohio Valley—Beside the Waters of the Ohio and Little Kanawha Rivers" chapter for more information.

SKATING

Bridgeport
Skate World (304-842-4426), corner of Masonic Dr. and Broadway.

Clarksburg
A skate park opened in **Veterans Memorial Park** (304-624-1655; www.cityof clarksburgwv.com) in 2006.

Fairmont
Skate A Way (304-367-9700), 718 Carlone St.

SWIMMING The swimming pools in Clarksburg's **Veterans Memorial Park** (304-624-1655; www.cityofclarksburgwv.com), Grafton's **City Pool** (304-265-0583), Philippi's **Dayton Park** (304-457-3700), Salem's **City Park** (304-782-1318; www .salemwv.com), and Shinnston's **Ferguson Park** (304-592-2126; www.shinnstonwv .com) are usually open from Memorial Day to Labor Day.

Also see East Marion Park and Wavepool under *Green Space—Parks*.

SWIMMIN' HOLES See *To See—Lake, To See—Waterfalls*, and Audra State Park under *Green Space—Parks*.

available from the Convention and Visitors Bureau of Marion County (see *Guidance*), directs you on a 1.3-mile circular tour of downtown Fairmont streets lined by buildings of the late 1800s and early 1900s, with examples of Romanesque Revival, Gothic, and Baroque architectures.

WHITEWATER RAFTING See *Kayaking & Canoeing.*

✳ Green Space

PARKS

Audra
Audra State Park (304-457-1162; www.audrastatepark.com; mailing address: Rte. 4, Box 564, Buckhannon 26201). From Philippi, travel US 119 South to Volga, where a left turn onto WV 11 will bring you to the park. What it lacks in size (it's only 355 acres), Audra State Park makes up in scenic beauty. Located along the small rapids, cascades, and swimmin' holes of the Middle Fork River, the park's landscape is lushly green, with towering hardwood and hemlock trees, rhododendron thickets, and moss-covered rocks. Hiking trails (about 3 miles in total) take you to picnic tables hidden in the rhododendron and out to Alum Cave. The large overhanging rock deep in the forest is most impressive in winter when large icicles form over its entrance. At the designated swimming area in the Middle Fork, you can sit below small waterfalls and have nature's own whirlpool effect ease away any aches and pains. The park's campground is located along a different stretch of the river and is usually open from mid-Apr. to mid-Oct.

Bridgeport
♿ Located on South Virginia Ave. no more than 0.5 mile from the downtown area, **Deegan** and **Hinkle lakes** can be quick escapes from noise and traffic. In addition to being able to fish (handicapped-accessible pier/dock) in the two stocked lakes, you can picnic, hike, play tennis, or launch a small boat.

Fairmont
🚣 **East Marion Park and Wave Pool** (304-363-7037). Take I-79 exit 135 and follow the signs. A lot is packed into this 70-acre hillside park, including tennis courts, horseshoe pits, basketball courts, a softball field, playgrounds, picnic facilities, and a miniature golf course. The main attraction during the summer is the water slide and wave pool, which is almost always crowded, but it is a lot of fun.

Valley Falls State Park (304-367-2719; www.valleyfallsstatepark.com; mailing address: Rte. 6, Box 244, Fairmont 26554). From I-79 exit 137, follow WV 310 southward for 7 miles, turn right at a sign for the park, and continue another 2 miles. Open daily during daylight hours. Within an area that was once a thriving railroad com-

AUDRA STATE PARK

munity, the park's 1,145 acres rise from the Tygart Valley River, with more than 10 miles of trails running along the stream and onto the hillsides. All of the trails interconnect in one way or another, with numerous possibilities for circuits. There is barely a 200-foot difference between the park's low and high points, so the hiking is usually fairly moderate, and a couple of the pathways are open to mountain bikes.

The major draw here is Valley Falls, accessible by a very short walk from the main parking area. The height is not that great, about 12 feet for the upper falls and 15 for the lower one, but the river is quite wide, and rocks along the shore and in the river let you have a close-up view. (The current is strong, so be careful; wading and swimming are prohibited.) Of all the state's easily accessible falls, this is one of the prettiest.

Expert kayakers run the 1.5 miles of Class III–V cascades from the falls to a take-out on WV 86. Be aware that the dam upstream regulates the flow of water, so it will vary greatly. Anglers are often seen casting a line from the shore or a canoe in hopes of landing a walleye or the abundant smallmouth and largemouth bass, and families arrive in droves to enjoy the picnic facilities close to the river.

Grafton

Tygart Lake State Park (304-265-6144; www.tygartlake.com; mailing address: Rte. 1, Box 260, Grafton 26354), off US 119 south of Grafton There is no doubt that the main focus of the 2,134-acre park is 10-mile-long Tygart Lake. There are four boat launching ramps; a marina with pontoon- and fishing-boat rentals; fishing for bass, walleye, perch, bluegill, muskie, and catfish; and a swimming area open from Memorial Day to Labor Day. The park's restaurant, 20-room lodge, and cabins (all usually open from about mid-Apr. through Oct.) overlook the water. (*Insider's tip*: All rooms have a view, but for the best water vistas, ask for one near the center of the lodge. If staying in a cabin, ask for numbers 6 through 9; they are closest to the water.)

A small trail system of about 5 miles wanders through forested lands on the hillside, with only the Tygart Dam Trail, which goes from the lodge to the dam, running along the shoreline.

The dam and the lake were constructed in the 1930s as a flood control project, and it's estimated that in the 1985 flood alone, it prevented more than $195 million in damages. Operated by the U.S. Army Corps of Engineers, a small visitor center close to the dam provides an overview of the lake and its amenities. Below the dam, anglers fish for rainbow and golden trout, and campers set up a tent or RV in Grafton City Park (304-265-1412). More rustic camping is available in the Pleasant Creek Wildlife Management Area (304-457-5144) on the lake's western shore.

Salem

Depot Park (304-782-1318), downtown. The last transcontinental train to pass through Salem ran in 1985, and the depot fell into disrepair. Now revitalized, it has the North Bend Rail Trail running beside it, a restored caboose, and a pavilion used for civic events, such as the annual Apple Butter Festival (see *Special Events*).

Dog Run Nature Preserve (304-782-1318), on US 50 less than a mile east of Salem. Dog Run is a 362-acre area with a 22-acre lake, picnic facilities, and hiking trails that can be a welcome sight if you have been traveling for a while and need to stretch your legs or the dog needs to take a walk. Facilities are really quite limited, but the preserve is just a moment off US 50. If you brought your tackle along, you can cast for trout, crappie, bluegill, catfish, and bass.

Also see Prickett's Fort State Park under *To See—Museums*.

WALKS A moderately easy walking trail in the **Bridgeport City Park** (304-842-8200), Bridgeport, goes from the parking area, over a small knoll, by sports fields, and into a nicely secluded wooded area with some interesting boulders and a small brook.

✴ Lodging

RESORTS See Tygart Lake State Park under *Green Space—Parks*.

MOTELS & HOTELS

Bridgeport 26330
☀ ♿ **Holiday Inn** (304-842-5411), 100 Lodgeville Rd., just east of I-79 exit 119. The two-story (no elevators) motel offers high-speed Internet access, an outdoor pool, and a restaurant. Small pets permitted. $100–135.

☀ **Travelodge** (304-842-7115), 1235 West Main St., on US 50 about 0.3 mile east of I-79 exit 119. Some of the region's lowest rates. Outdoor pool. Pets permitted. $70–90.

Clarksburg 26330
Days Inn & Suites (304-842-7371), 112 Tolley Dr., east of I-79 exit 119. Clarksburg's only lodging facility with an indoor pool. Free deluxe continental breakfast. $75–135.

☀ **Sleep Inn** (304-842-1919), 115 Tolley Dr., east of I-79 exit 119. The two-story motel (no elevator) permits pets and serves a free continental breakfast. $89.

Fairmont 26554
☀ ♿ **Holiday Inn** (304-366-5500), 930 East Grafton Rd., within sight of I-79 exit 137. More than 100 standard motel rooms, restaurant, and outdoor pool. Small pets permitted. $79–120.

☀ **Red Roof Inn** (304-366-6800), 50 Middletown Rd., close to I-79 exit 132.

No pool, no restaurant, but nice standard rooms, and pets are permitted. Low cost at about $60–90.

Philippi 26416
☀ ♿ **Budget Inn** (304-457-5888; mailing address: Rte. 4, Box 155), on US 250 about 2.5 miles south of Philippi. Nothing fancy, but it is clean and is about the only place to stay near Philippi. Small pets permitted. $55–70.

Also see Greenbrier Restaurant and Motel under *Eating Out*.

BED & BREAKFASTS

Mannington 26582
A Nature's Song Bed and Breakfast (304-986-3401; www.anaturessong .com), 274 Forest Lane. One of the nicest ways to spend your time here? Lazily rocking back and forth in the chairs on the front porch that overlooks one of the two ponds on the property. If that's too sedentary for you, explore the 140 acres, possibly coming across the abundant birdlife. Two guest rooms have private baths and a host of amenities. This place is a little off the well-traveled road, but has both a rustic and luxurious charm to it. $125.

Shinnston 26431
Gillum House Bed and Breakfast (304-592-0177; 1-888-592-0177; www .gillumhouse.com), 35 Walnut St. Kathleen Fanek has been inviting guests into her modest home (once the resi-

dence of Shinnston's B&O Railroad station agent, and now decorated with the artwork of her husband, John) for more than a decade. She has also been the president of the state's bed & breakfasts association, so she knows a bit about hospitality. Two of the nicely furnished guest rooms share a bath (there is a chamber pot under every bed—just in case), while the third has its own bath. Using many West Virginia–produced products, she makes all the breads, rolls, and muffins from scratch, and she has adapted the recipes to be as heart-healthy as possible. Chocolate crisp muffins and English muffin bread were a part of breakfast the last time I visited.

Also active in the promotion of the West Fork River Rail Trail (which is only a block from the B&B), Kathleen will arrange for bike rentals, shuttles, and even stable facilities for those who ride the pathway on their horses. Don't know what to do with your vacation time? Just ask, and the Paneks will set up a custom itinerary based on your interests. $95–129.

CABINS & VACATION RENTALS
See Tygart Lake State Park under *Green Space—Park*.

CAMPGROUNDS
Fairmont 26554
Prickett's Creek Campground (304-363-1910; mailing address: Rte. 3, Box 127B). Located a very short distance from I-79 exit 139. Open all year. A small commercial campground with tent and RV sites with hookups.

Also see Audra State Park and Tygart Lake State Park under *Green Space—Parks*.

✳ Where to Eat
DINING OUT
Bridgeport
🍴 **Oliverio's Ristorante** (304-842-7388; www.oliveriosristorante.com), 507 East Main St. Open daily for dinner; Mon.–Fri. for lunch. The descendants of Italian-immigrant grandparents, Sonny and Shirley Oliverio opened their restaurant in a converted Dairy Queen in 1966. The business now seats more than 200 customers who come here to enjoy Shirley's homemade breadsticks and salad dressing. The menu is almost entirely traditional Italian dishes, such as chicken parmigiana, shrimp scampi, lasagna, rigatoni, and fettuccine. Entrées $11.95–36.95.

Clarksburg
Julio's Café (304-622-2592; www.julioscafe.com), 501 Baltimore Ave. Since it opened in 1968, Julio's has been one the area's busiest fine-dining restaurants. In addition to the Italian entrées (excellent marinara sauce and bean soup!), Julio's is known for other dishes, such as New Zealand rack of lamb, salmon with bacon sage cream sauce, and crab cakes served with rémoulade sauce. Homemade desserts and a specialty drink are the way to end your visit here.

Julio's also has a nice setting, with exposed logs, a stone fireplace from the original warehouse days, and a carved bar that is a true work of art. Entrées $20–30.

Fairmont
Aquarium Restaurant and Lounge (304-366-1500), 620 Gaston Ave. Open for lunch and dinner; closed Sun. Do not judge the Aquarium from its drab exterior; the inside is pleasantly decorated and maintained. One of Fairmont's most popular restaurants, it has many nice touches, such as waiting

FRANCE COMES TO BRIDGEPORT

🔖 ⊘ **Provence** (304-848-0911; www.provencemarketcafe.com), 603 South Virginia Ave. (on US 58 about 0.3 mile from the US 50 intersection with US 58), Bridgeport. Open for lunch and dinner Tues.–Sat. Clarksburg native Anne Hart lived in the south of France for close to two decades and has brought the true flavors of that region back to West Virginia. To ensure the best quality, she has contracts with local growers for seasonal vegetables, and the seafood comes in fresh from various sources. There are tastes here that I have not enjoyed since my hike along the full length of the Pyrenees. The Niçoise salad is a signature item, while specials have included blue crab ravioli and a very creamy blue cheese soup. You'll have to come back here often so that you can try the roasted pork with mustard green peppercorn sauce; salmon with Mediterranean salsa and lime butter; and veal with caramelized shallots, thyme butter, and demiglaze. And there are the house-made desserts.

The restaurant's interior is nicely decorated, but for more of a French atmosphere, sit on the outside deck overlooking the small babbling creek. The cost of an entrée ($12.95–29) is about half what you would pay if you were to eat at a comparable French restaurant in the Washington, DC, area. Don't miss this place.

Attached to the restaurant are a wine and cheese shop and an espresso bar.

DINING ALFRESCO AT PROVENCE

until you walk through the door before putting your serving of garlic and/or honey cinnamon butter bread into the oven. It's hard to decide from the large choice of steaks, seafood, chicken, pork, and pasta entrées, but whatever you choose, start your meal with the delicious roasted red pepper chicken soup. Entrées $12.99–24.99.

EATING OUT

Bridgeport
Philip's La Pasta Cucina (304-623-6400), 128 Thompson Dr. Open for lunch and dinner. Philip Podesta's mother was a Muriale (of Muriale's in Fairmont), and she must have taught him well, as all of the traditional Italian dishes he serves have the same taste that my Italian mother used to serve me. If you can't decide among all the offerings, go for the lunch buffet, which lets you try a sampling of just about everything. Although the interior is nice enough, opt for the pleasant outdoor brick plaza in good weather. Entrées $8.59–17.79.

Clarksburg
Bluebird Restaurant/Deli/Store (304-624-7429), 332 West Main St. The Bluebird is the downtown location to grab a quick breakfast, sandwich

PLEASANT OUTDOOR DINING AT PHILIP'S LA PASTA CUCINA

lunch, or a complete meal for less than $5.

*✏ **Greenbrier Restaurant and Motel** (304-624-5518; www.green brierclarksburg.com), 200 Buckhannon Pike (WV 20). Open for dinner daily. When Frank and Victoria Loria opened their business in 1967, WV 20 was a major travel route. The construction of I-79 took most of the traffic away, and Frank and Victoria are gone, but daughters Terri and Mary continue the tradition of hand-making the pasta (one of the few places I have found that still do this), bread, sauces, and desserts. Although it seems like a tavern when you first walk in, this is a family restaurant that does so many things the right way. Entrées $9.95–21.95 (with a few extra special meals costing up to $39.95).

Speaking of doing things right: From the outside, the motel looks like any other built in the mid-1900s. However, the sisters have added their special touches to it, and you will almost feel like you're in a B&B, with spacious rooms, terry-cloth robes and slippers, and a Jacuzzi (in some rooms). Good value at $75.

*✏ **Minard's Spaghetti Inn** (304-623-1711), 813 East Pike St. Michael and Rose (Oliverio) Minard served their first plate of spaghetti in the dining room of their home in 1937. (The home and the dining room table are still part of the restaurant.) Michael's brother Samuel, and his wife, Agnes (Oliverio) Minard, joined the business a year later, and they all lived in the home where they worked. (The china cabinet is original to the home and contains a number of family items; if not busy, they will be happy to give you a quick tour.)

The dressing on the salads is still the original 1937 recipe, as is the sauce for the spaghetti. The Italian wedding soup is some of the best around. Entrées $9.50–19.95.

Ritzy Lunch (304-622-3600; www .ritzylunchwv.com), 456 West Pike St. Another travel guide once proclaimed this business to have the best hot dog on the East Coast. I have not eaten at every place in the East where hot dogs are available, but I can tell you that Ritzy Lunch's dogs are this area's tastiest. Don't expect much for the restaurant's décor, but do take pleasure in some of the lowest-cost breakfasts and lunches around. Entrées $2.50–6.50.

Vito's Pizza and Restaurant (304-622-4023), 104 Park Blvd. Local residents consistently vote Vito and Tony Gialone's pizza the town's "best pizza by the slice." Entrées $8–16.

Fairmont

Colasessano's (304-363-9713; www .colasessanospizza.com), 506 Pennsylvania Ave. Closed Sun. and Mon. John and Josephine Colasessano lived upstairs when his father opened this pizza shop more than 50 years ago, serving square, thick dough pizza with more cheese than you have ever seen on a pizza. The new owners have kept the same recipes, and the business is open early in the morning for those who wish to pick up some pepperoni rolls for breakfast or lunch. It certainly does not have the same atmosphere, but another location is at 9705 Mall Loop Road (304-363-0571) Pizzas are $10–12.50.

☞ **DJ's Diner** (304-366-8110), 1181 Airport Rd. Open daily for breakfast, lunch, and dinner. Re-creating the atmosphere of a 1950s and 1960s diner, DJ's serves good sandwiches, large-portioned dinners, and breakfast all day. The old-fashioned floats are nice to have with your meal or as a dessert. Entrées $7.99–11.99.

☞ **Muriale's** (304-363-3190; www .murialesrestaurant.com), 1742 Fairmont Ave. Open daily for lunch and dinner. Talk about Fairmont with a West Virginian, and it's almost assured that Muriale's will be part of the conversation. Frank and Sam Muriale opened the 39-seat (it now seats 230) restaurant in 1969, using recipes from their grandfather, father, and uncle. As is so often the case, it's the little things that make a big difference in taste. Many places serve bruschetta with tomato, olive oil, basil, and onion, but Muriale's has a touch of sweetness, thanks to a balsamic vinegar reduction. The house salad is served with roasted red peppers and caramelized onions, and the marinara sauce (the best in this area) is chunky and full of flavor. All desserts are made in-house, so save room for the wonderful Italian amaretto cream. Entrées $9.95–29.95.

☞ **Poky Dot** (304-366-3271; www.the pokydot.com), 1111 Fairmont Ave. Under various names and ownerships, the Poky Dot has been a Fairmont fixture since the mid-1900s. The décor, artwork, and life-size dolls sitting in some of the booths and on counter stools help replicate those early days. The menu mixes the old (country fried steak, pork chops, pot roast) with a bit of the new (wraps, croissants, raspberry walnut chicken salad). The milk shakes are definitely old style—thick and rich with hand-dipped ice cream. Entrées $5.99–12.99.

Philippi

Medallion Restaurant (304-457-3463), 7 South Main St. The Medallion has a small-town atmosphere and simple country cooking, such as hamburger steak, meat loaf, beer-battered cod, and pork chops. The highlight of any meal—other than having a conversation with everyone who comes through the door—is the opportunity to eat one

PEPPERONI ROLLS

A debate rages in the northern part of the Mountain State as to who was the inventor of the pepperoni roll. I'm not sure there was an inventor. When Italian immigrants began going into West Virginia mines, they carried bread and pepperoni in their lunch pails, and to make it easier to eat, they simply wrapped the bread around the meat. Today, there are various versions. Some are baked with sticks of pepperoni, some with sliced pieces or chunks, and some add cheese. Some are narrow and only a couple of inches long, while others are thick and 6 inches or more. All are basically a baked piece of bread wrapped around pieces of pepperoni. As the dough cooks, it soaks up the pepperoni's juices, making a soft, tasty treat. At one time, the rolls were just an uncelebrated part of the local scene, but since the 2002 publication of Jeanne Mozier's book *Way Out in West Virginia*, in which she proclaims the pepperoni roll to be the State Food, they have become an almost gourmet cult item.

MAKING PEPPERONI ROLLS AT COUNTRY CLUB BAKERY IN FAIRMONT

of the homemade cream pies. Entrées $6.75–15.95.

Shinnston

Jimmy's (304-592-0745), 1501 Hood Ave. If you are really hungry after biking or hiking the entire 17 miles of the West Fork River Trail, you should take advantage of Jimmy's offering of all-you-can-eat pasta, served every day for about $8. If you don't feel like gorging, you could order a salad, sandwich, pizza, or other Italian or American dish. Entrées $7.99–11.99.

SNACKS & GOODIES

Bridgeport

À La Carte Fine Chocolates (304-842-4047), 410 East Main St. Closed

Sun., with shortened daily hours during the school year. High school French teacher Diane Wickland is a French pastry chef and chocolatier, having studied and received certification both in Europe and the United States. Using only the best of Belgian and Venezuelan chocolate, she handmakes all of her delicious treats.

Clarksburg

Almost Heaven Desserts (304-622-7641), Wonder Bar Rd. Patti Oliverio Simon, a graduate of the Hyde Park Culinary Institute, oversees the construction of dozens of kinds of cakes, tortes, cookies, cobblers, pastries, biscotti, and truffles. There is another location at 100 West Main St., Bridgeport.

Tomaro's Bakery (304-622-0691), 411 North Fourth St. Oh, the wonderful aromas that waft out of this bakery! It was opened in 1914 and is still operated by the same family. Round breads, rye breads, twists, rolls, and buns have customers lining up early in the day. Local lore claims that this is the site of the invention of the pepperoni roll. They're good—whether they originated here or not.

Fairmont

Country Club Bakery (304-363-5690), 1211 Country Club Rd. Closed Wed. and Sun. Just as those in Clarksburg insist that the pepperoni roll was first created at Tomaro's Bakery, local Fairmont lore claims that Joseph Argiro, a coal miner turned baker, invented the handheld munchies in 1927. What is known for sure is that this bakery still turns out more than 300 dozen handmade pepperoni rolls in the small kitchen every day that it is open. They also make Italian pretzels, biscotti, and some great pecan tassies.

Dairy Creme Corner (304-366-6809), 187 Homewood Ave. Open May–Sept. The largest ice-cream cones

at some of the lowest prices you will find anywhere.

✳ Entertainment

FILM

Bridgeport

Cinemark 10 (304-842-9296), Meadowbrook Rd. Shows most Hollywood movies when, or shortly after, they are released.

Fairmont

Tygart Valley Cinema (304-363-3498), US 250 South. Opened in the 1970s, the cinema is showing a bit of its age, but the owner is, over time, upgrading to compete with the new cineplexes.

Grafton

Grafton Drive-In (304-265-1096), on US 119. Opened in 1949, it shows first-run movies on the weekends Apr.–Oct. *Insider's tip*: The locals rave about the concession stand, especially the chili cheese dogs, barbecue, and hoagies.

Shinnston

Sunset Drive-in (304-592-3909), US 19 north of town. At one time Harrison County had five drive-ins; the Sunset is the only survivor. Built in 1947, it is also the state's second oldest. It is open daily Apr.–Sept. and projects movies on a 70-foot screen.

MUSIC Sagebrush Roundup (304-334-8629; http://billjanoske.tripod .com), 6 miles east of I-79 exit 139 at Bunner Ridge, Fairmont. There are major bluegrass and country music programs here every weekend. Many are local and regional talents, but a good percentage of the concerts are by nationally (or internationally) known performers.

Also see *To See—Colleges*.

THEATER See *To See—Colleges*.

✳ Selective Shopping

ART AND CRAFTS GALLERIES

Bridgeport

Artworks (304-842-7626), Averil Place (on US 58 about 0.3 mile from the US 50 intersection with US 58). Many custom framing shops also sell paintings and prints, but I've found those at Artworks to be more worthy of my browsing time than at other such businesses. The prints of local scenes are first rate.

Clarksburg

Historic Central Storage Gift Shops (304-623-6108; www.giftswv .com), 425-429 North 4th St. The place does not have the most mellifluous name, but it does have the creative works of dozens of artists and craftspersons displayed within a rehabilitated warehouse, and some of them have studios here so you can watch the creative process in person.

Evansville/Thornton

Allegheny Treenware (304-892-5008; 1-866-279-7526; http://allegheny treenware.com; 1922 South Evansville Pike), on US 50 in the community of Evansville, about 10 miles east of Grafton. Stan and Sue Jennings are living examples of the phrase, "When one door closes, another opens." The underground mine they worked in closed in the mid-1980s, and looking for another way to make a living, they turned to West Virginia's abundant timber resources to make treenware (wooden kitchen utensils). Within the last 20 years, they have racked up award after award for the quality of their work. Each piece is hand-shaped and gouged, using West Virginia hardwoods such as cherry, maple, birch, beech, and walnut.

Mount Clare

West Virginia Heritage Crafts (304-622-3304; 1-800-524-4043; mailing address: Rte. 2, Box 215-B), on WV 20 within sight of I-79 exit 115. Housed in a former school building that is on the National Register of Historic Places, this is the outlet of a co-op of close to 50 craftspersons. In addition to selling their work—such as stained glass, pottery, wood products, clothing, books, and specialty foods—they offer classes for those who wish to learn how to do such things on their own.

Philippi

Mountain Treasures (304-457-2030), 1 North Main St. A continually changing stock of West Virginia handmade crafts, food items, and books.

FARMERS' MARKETS

Bridgeport

The vendors of the **Bridgeport Farmers' Market** (304-669-4340; bridgeportfarmersmarket.vpweb.com) held on Sun. 10–2 from May–Oct. at the Bridgeport High School parking lot selling only items that were farmed, raised, or grown in West Virginia.

Fairmont

From July through Oct., come to the corner of Madison Ave. and Adams St. on Tues. at 4 PM and Sat. at 8 AM to see what the **Fairmont Farmers' Market** (304-367-2772) has to offer.

Philippi

The **Community Garden Farmers' Market** (304-457-3816) operates July–Sept. and is open Mon.–Fri.

PICK-YOUR-OWN PRODUCE

FARM West Virginia Fruit & Berry (304-842-8945; 1-888-982-3779; www .wvfruitandberry.com), Bridgeport. From I-79 exit 117, drive into Anmoore, turn left at the UCAR Plant, and continue 4.6 miles. Pick your own berries or purchase a very complete line of West Virginia food products in the quaint-looking cabin.

Bridgeport

The Nest (304-848-2444), Averil Place (on US 58 about 0.3 mile from the US 50 intersection with US 58). I had never considered putting a knitting shop in a travel guide, but the items The Nest carries bring people from all over the United States as well as a few foreign countries. The fibers you'll find here, such as silk, linen, wool, alpaca, cashmere, cotton, synthetic, and various blends, may be hard to find anywhere else. They also carry specialty needles often overlooked by other knitting shops.

Clarksburg

Oliverio's Cash and Carry (1-800-296-4959), 427 Clark St. Open Mon.–Fri. 8–4. Unfortunately, there is no place to sit down and immediately enjoy the food you can buy at this tiny family-owned grocery store, but that just means you can anticipate the taste of the fresh Italian sausage that is hand-ground and stuffed into natural casings behind the butcher's counter. Also made here, and perfect complements to the sausage, are jars of hot and mild roasted peppers, cauliflower salsa, pickled peppers, and hot peppers. It's worth it to come here just to see a kind of grocery store that has almost faded from the American landscape

Fairmont

✎ **Duck Soup Books & Toys** (304-366-2100), 325 Adams St. Are you tired of having to give your children the same toys that are found at all the national chain stores? Duck Soup is the alternative, carrying many items that the big-box stores overlook and that the kids will enjoy playing and using for a long time to come.

Empire Gift Garden (304-363-7908), 327 Adams St. This looks like it could be a run-of-the-mill gift shop from the outside. Walk inside, however, and you will find interesting bird-houses and items made from fibers and straw. Seeing what the owners were able to do in turning an old, dilapidated building into an attractively styled business should be enough to let you trust their judgment in advising you for any project you have in mind.

Friendly Furniture Galleries (304-366-9113; 1-800-794-0406; www .friendlyfurniture.com), 205 Adams St. I don't think I have ever included a furniture store in a travel guide, but Friendly Furniture deserves a mention. To begin with, you can get some of the city's best coffee here. Then you can wander around looking at the selection of fine and sometimes quite different styles of furniture.

✳ Special Events

Late April/early May: **Annual Bird Walk** (304-363-3030; www.pricketts fortstatepark.com), Prickett's Fort State Park, Fairmont. **Scottish Festival & Celtic Gathering** (www.scots -westvirginia.org), various locations in Clarksburg and Bridgeport. Music, Highland dance, parades of the clans, herding demonstrations, traditional "heavy" athletics, and crafts.

May: **Three River Festival** (304-363-2625), Fairmont. Entertainment, parade, Civil War reenactment, carnival, and games.

June: **Annual Car Show** (304-986-2560), Mannington fairgrounds. Cars, cars, cars; music; food; and cars. **Blue and Grey Reunion** (304-457-3700), Philippi. Encampments and reenactments of the Battle of Philippi. **Greek Food Festival** (304-624-5331), St. Spyridon Greek Orthodox Church, Clarksburg.

July: **Battle of Laurel Hill Civil War Reenactment** (304-823-2557; www .battleoflaurelhill.org), Belington. **Johnnie Johnson's Blues Festival** (304-363-5377; www.johnniejohnson bluesandjazz.com), Fairmont. Three days of music honoring the Fairmont native, considered by some to be a founding father of rock 'n' roll.

August: **Blackberry Festival** (304-622-3206; www.wvblackberry.com), Clarksburg. Enjoy blackberries in myriad dishes, along with arts and crafts, fireworks, and free entertainment. **Mannington Fair** (304-986-2155; www.manningtondistrictfair.org), Mannington. Parades; carnival; farm stock, produce, and baked-goods judging; live entertainment; and many events for children. **Pasta Cook-off** (304-622-7314), Clarksburg. Open to amateurs and professionals.

September: **Italian Heritage Festival** (304-622-7314; www.wvihf.com), Clarksburg. All things Italian, including delicious foods, grand parade, three stages of entertainment, and cultural events. **Black Heritage Festival** (304-623-2335), Clarksburg. A street festival with great food, entertainment, and cultural events.

October: **Apple Butter Festival** (304-782-1318), Depot Park, Salem. A chance to watch this traditional treat be made in copper kettles suspended over slow-burning wood fires. Music, crafts, talent contests, car show, and children's activities. **Octoberfest** (304-986-1700), Mannington. The October celebration has been taking place for more than two decades in this small village. **18th Century Fall Rendezvous** (304-363-3030; www.pricketts fortstatepark.com), Prickett's Fort State Park, Fairmont. Encampments and reenactments of 18th-century life.

November: **Annual Historic Houses Tour** (304-367-5398), Fairmont.

The Metro Valley 7

LIFE ALONG THE KANAWHA RIVER—
THE STATE CAPITAL AND
SURROUNDING AREA

RIVER TOWNS—HUNTINGTON AND
POINT PLEASANT

THE METRO VALLEY

The Metro Valley is West Virginia's most populated region and includes Charleston and Huntington, the state's two largest cities. Just like many other places in America, these two cities are growing toward each other, transforming the land between them from an agrarian landscape to one of housing developments, business parks, office buildings, and dozens of malls and shopping centers. Town lines have blurred, and it is often hard to tell where one ends and another begins.

This can be a good thing for travelers and explorers, however. Many of the region's best restaurants, museums, and other attractions are located close to each other, reducing the time you have to spend driving. In fact, almost all the places described in this section are easily reached within an hour or so drive from Charleston or Huntington.

It is not all suburbs, chemical plants, and urban sprawl, however. Take a short detour off the four-lane highways, and you will find inviting small towns like Point Pleasant on the Ohio River. The quaint downtown area of Barboursville is located barely more than a mile from an interstate. Escaping to woodlands is also easy, with Coonskin Park and Kanawha State Forest no more than 15-minute drives from downtown Charleston, and Beech Fork State Park and East Lynn Lake reached by quick trips from Huntington.

LIFE ALONG THE KANAWHA RIVER—THE STATE CAPITAL AND SURROUNDING AREA

In the springtime, when tens of thousands of pink, purple, and white crabapple-tree blossoms are reflected in the waters of the Kanawha River and thousands more daffodils dot the banks, Charleston, the state capital, may be West Virginia's prettiest large city. A bilevel walkway—one alongside Kanawha Boulevard's stately early-1900s homes and the other within a few feet of the river—runs the length of the city, providing greenwaylike access to quiet neighborhoods, riverfront parks, the Capitol Complex, and the downtown area.

Thanks to a major revitalization effort in the 1970s and 1980s, the downtown area has come back from the brink of being deserted and is now a thriving mixture of art galleries, fine restaurants, bookstores, shopping experiences, farmers' markets, and business offices. Trees planted more than 20 years ago on Capitol Street have spreading branches and lush foliage that cover the sidewalks and roadway in a deep shade and give the city center a tranquil manifestation not often found in large cities. Revitalization also brought a rediscovery of the river, and the Haddad Riverfront and Magic Island parks bring people into town to walk easy pathways or attend concerts, festivals, and other special events.

The city's population of a little more than 50,000 has the choice of a wide range of cultural activities. An active schedule of concerts, plays, and theatrical performances are presented year-round by the **Appalachian Children's Chorus** (302-343-1111; www.wvacc.org), **Charleston Ballet** (304-342-6541; www.thecharlestonballet.com), **Charleston Chamber Music Society** (304-344-5389; www.charlestonchambermusic.org), **Charleston Light Opera Guild** (304-343-2287; http://charlestonlightoperaguild.org), **Children's Theatre of Charleston** (304-346-0164; www.ctoc.org), **Kanawha Players** (304-343-7529; www.kanawhaplayers.org), **West Virginia Symphony** (304-561-3500; www.wvsymphony.org), and others. The 234,000-square-foot Clay Center is a combination museum and performance venue.

The East End Historic District is rich with august homes built from the late 1800s to the mid-1900s and links downtown with the State Capitol Complex. In addition to being the heart of state government, the complex contains the

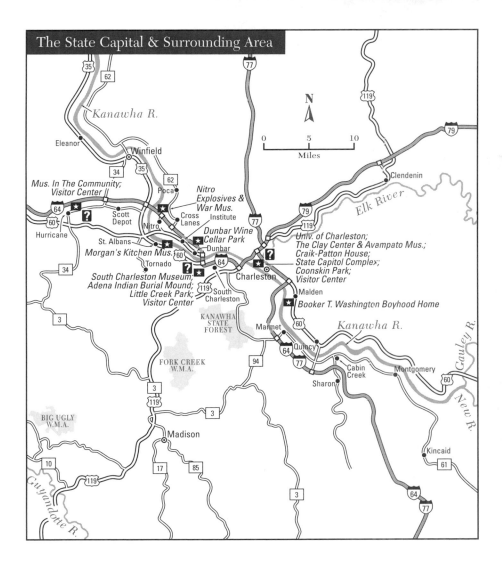

Kanawha R.

Eleanor
Winfield

N

0   5   10
Miles

Clendenin

Mus. In The Community;
Visitor Center
Poca
Nitro
Explosives &
War Mus.

Elk River

Scott
Depot
Cross
Lanes
Institute
Hurricane
Nitro
St. Albans
Morgan's Kitchen Mus.
Dunbar Wine
Cellar Park
Dunbar

Univ. of Charleston;
The Clay Center & Avampato Mus.;
Craik-Patton House;
State Capitol Complex;
Coonskin Park;
Visitor Center

Tornado
South Charleston Museum;
Adena Indian Burial Mound;
Little Creek Park;
Visitor Center
South
Charleston
Charleston

Malden
Booker T. Washington Boyhood Home

KANAWHA
STATE
FOREST

Marmet
Kanawha R.

FORK CREEK
W.M.A.
Quincy
Cabin
Creek
Montgomery

Gauley R.

Sharon

New R.

BIG UGLY
W.M.A.
Madison

Guyandotte R.

Kincaid

gold-domed capitol building, governor's mansion, and cultural center—all open for tours by the public.

Many of the factories that had earned this area the nickname "the Chemical Valley" have closed or greatly curtailed production. The once-polluted river and air that had a palpable taste are now fresher and cleaner, inviting boaters onto the river, and families, hikers, and bikers into great parks located just a few minutes from downtown.

COMMUNITIES The bituminous coal underlying the mountain lands along WV 61 and WV 79/3 gave rise to many coal-mining communities. These settlements, the largest of which are **Cabin Creek** and **Sharon**, retain much of the look they had when first established.

In 1774, a group commissioned by George Washington to scout along the Kanawha River came to a place where all the trees were pushed over in the same direction, and they noted in their journal, "the place of the hurricane." The name stuck, and by 1811 a small town had been chartered. The construction of I-64 has brought the usual commercial development to the outskirts of **Hurricane**, but its downtown remains a place of interesting independently owned shops and special murals depicting local history. Stop by to see the Maiden in the Rock petroglyph. Some say it is of ancient origin—others say it was a prank carved in the early 1900s.

Before King Coal, salt production was western Virginia's largest economic engine. First called Kanawha Salines, **Malden** later became the boyhood home of Booker T. Washington.

Situated at the confluence of the Coal and Kanawha rivers, **St. Albans** is a residential community whose historic downtown district contains a number of fine homes and buildings from the early 1900s. Be sure to seek out the palatial 1900 Mohler House at 819 Pennsylvania Ave., built for a prominent lumberman, and the interesting 1910 Old First National Bank building, with a half-round arch above the three-door entry.

A small area of green space decorated by a few pieces of public art has been preserved in the business district of **South Charleston** to protect the state's second-largest (35 feet high and 175 feet in diameter at the base) Adena Indian Burial Mound. A number of finely crafted murals depict the city's history and civic pride.

GUIDANCE The **Charleston Convention and Visitors Bureau** (304-344-5075; 1-800-733-5469; www.charlestonwv.com), 200 Civic Center Dr., Charleston 25301, is downtown, inside the Civic Center.

Located amid the small shops of the downtown area, the **City of Hurricane Convention and Visitors Bureau** (304-562-5896; 1-877-487-7982; www.hurricane wv.com) is at 3255 Teays Valley Rd., Hurricane 25526.

The **Putnam County Convention and Visitors Bureau** (304-562-0518; www .putnamcounty.org/tourism), 1 Valley Park Dr., Hurricane 25526, is within a few steps of the Museum in the Community (see *To See—Museums*) and Waves of Fun pool in Valley Park (see *Green Space—Parks*).

You can find the **South Charleston Convention and Visitors Bureau** (304-746-5552; 1-800-238-9488; www.south charlestonwv.org) at 311 D St., South Charleston 25303, just a couple of blocks from the city's famous Adena Indian Burial Mound.

GETTING THERE *By air*: Flying into West Virginia's largest air facility, **Yeager Airport** (304-344-8033; www .yeagerairport), may be one of the most exciting things you do while visiting West Virginia. It is located atop several mountains whose summits have

A LITTLE-KNOWN FACT
On October 23, 1870, Charleston became the site of the world's first brick street, which was constructed on Summers St. between Kanawha Blvd. and Virginia St. In addition, the 1500 block of Virginia St. is believed to be the world's longest city block.

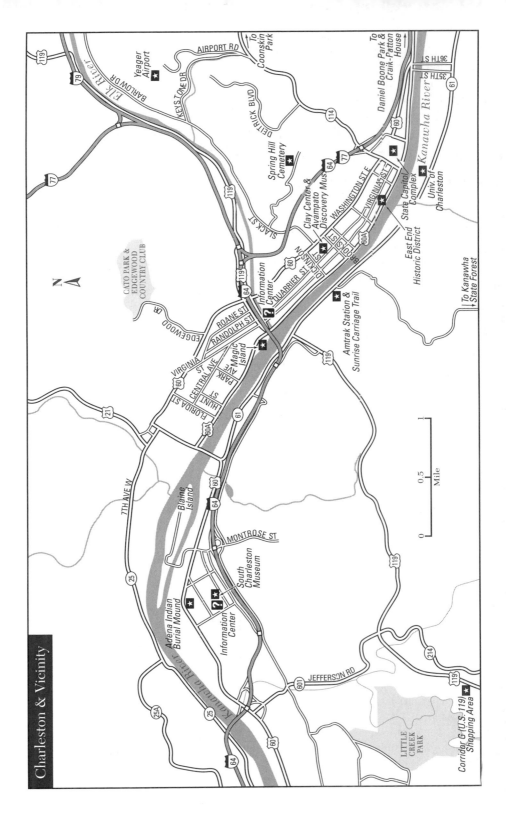

Charleston & Vicinity

been shaved off to fill in the valleys between them. As you feel the plane touch down and the engines go into reverse, you can't help wondering if your plane will stop before it reaches the end of the runway. Don't worry; no commercial passenger plane has ever fallen off.

By bus: The **Greyhound** (1-800-231-2222; www.greyhound.com) terminal is located in Charleston's downtown area at 300 Reynolds St.

By car: Charleston is the meeting place of four four-lane highways. **I-64** enters the state on the east near Covington, Virginia, and in the west from Ashland, Kentucky. Travelers from the southeast may reach this area on **I-77** as it enters the state near Bluefield, Virginia, while those coming from the northwest will be arriving on the same interstate after crossing the Ohio River at Marietta, Ohio. From Pittsburgh, Pennsylvania, and other points in the northeast, **I-79** is the most convenient access. **US 119** traverses the southwest part of the state and provides access from Kentucky.

By rail: An **AMTRAK** (304-342-6766; 1-800-872-7245; www.Amtrak.com) train, *The Cardinal*, is an east–west train that you may take to Charleston from as far away as New York and Chicago. *Insider's tip*: AMTRAK does not publicize it as a scenic excursion, but you can enjoy a daytrip by getting on the morning eastbound train at the station at 350 MacCorkle Ave. SE and traveling through the stunning New River Gorge before getting off in White Sulphur Springs. You will have more than five hours to explore the town and maybe have dinner at The Greenbrier resort before catching the westbound *Cardinal* and returning to Charleston around 10 PM. The colors of the leaves in the gorge make this an especially beautiful outing in the fall.

GETTING AROUND *By bus:* The **Kanawha Valley Regional Transportation Authority** (304-343-7586; www.rideonkrt.com) is one of the state's most extensive public transportation systems. In addition to passing through every Charleston neighborhood, buses reach far into the county, enabling you to visit South Charleston, St. Albans, Nitro, Cross Lanes, Sissonville, Clendenin, Cabin Creek, Malden, Montgomery, and more. For a very small fare, you can ride a trolley from downtown, through the historic East End, and to the State Capitol Complex.

By taxi: **C&H Taxi** (304-344-4902) provides personal transportation in and around Charleston.

MEDICAL EMERGENCIES

Charleston
Charleston Area Medical Center, General Division (304-388-6037; www.camc.org), Morris and Washington streets.

Charleston Area Medical Center, Memorial Division (304-388-5432; www.camc.org), 3200 MacCorkle Ave. SE.

St. Francis Hospital (304-347-6500; www.stfrancishospital.com), 333 Laidley St.

Montgomery
Montgomery General Hospital (304-442-5151; www.mghwv.com), 401 Sixth Ave.

South Charleston

Thomas Memorial Hospital (304-766-3600; www.thomaswv.org), 4605 MacCorkle Ave. SW.

UNIVERSITY OF CHARLESTON

✳ To See

COLLEGES

Charleston

University of Charleston (304-357-4800; www.ucwv.edu), 2300 Mac-Corkle Ave. SE. My alma mater sits on the south bank of the Kanawha River, directly across from the State Capitol. With close to 1,000 students, it sponsors the University Speaker Series, featuring some of the most prominent figures of our time, including Erin Brockovich, Peter Arnett, and Dr. Myles Brand, NCAA president. Although small, the Frankenberger Gallery of Art sponsors quality exhibits throughout the year. One of the most exciting times is when rowing teams from other colleges converge on the school to compete in the Governor's Cup Regatta by racing on the Kanawha River.

Institute

West Virginia State University (1-800-987-2112; www.wvstateu.edu; mailing address: P.O. Box 1000, Institute 25112). Founded in 1891 as the West Virginia Colored Institute, one of 17 black land grant colleges established by the sale of U.S. public lands, West Virginia State University has evolved into a fully accessible, racially diverse, and multigenerational institution offering baccalaureate, associate, and graduate degrees. Events open to the general public include an art gallery, special lecture events, and movie showings.

DRIVING TOURS, SCENIC & HISTORIC US 60 has been designated the **Midland Trail National Scenic Byway** (see *To See—Driving Tours, Scenic & Historic* in the "Old Towns, Surviving and Alive—Lewisburg, White Sulphur Springs, and Union" chapter for background information). Having traversed the mountains of eastern West Virginia, US 60 enters this area along the Kanawha River, passing small towns and industrial plants before going through the center of Charleston and running along the business areas of South Charleston and St. Albans. The scenery becomes a little more rural as the roadway takes its leave of the Kanawha River to continue westward toward Huntington.

HISTORIC HOME Craik-Patton House (304-925-5341; www.craik-patton.com), 2809 Kanawha Blvd. E, Charleston. Open Tues.–Thurs. 8:30-4:30 (but be aware open dates have changed often in the past). Small admission fee. The 1834 American Greek Revival home, once owned by the grandfather of World War II's Gen. George Patton and moved from its original location on Virginia St., has been restored and authentically furnished with time-appropriate items.

HISTORIC SITE Booker T. Washington Boyhood Home, Malden Dr., Malden. Tours are free, but they must be arranged in advance by contacting West

Virginia State University (304-766-3020) or Larry L. Rowe (304-533-0672), who has taken a special interest in the site. Based on historical photographs, the cabin that Booker T. Washington, author of *Up From Slavery* and a founder of Alabama's Tuskegee Institute, grew up in is reconstructed behind the 1872 African Zion Baptist Church. After graduating from Hampton University, Washington returned here to teach Sunday school in the church, which was the first African American Baptist church constructed in the western part of the state.

MUSEUMS & ART GALLERIES

Charleston

✿ ✐ ⟰ ✪ **The Clay Center and Avampato Discovery Museum**, 300 Leon Sullivan Way. Completed in 2003, The Clay Center (304-561-3570; www.theclay center.org) is one of the most exciting developments in Charleston in recent times. The 234,000-square-foot arts and sciences center contains the 1,883-seat Maier Foundation Hall, home of the West Virginia Symphony (304-561-3500; www.wv symphony.org) and site of theatrical and musical presentations by national and international performers. (Past acts have included Vince Gill, Bill Cosby, and the Count Basie Orchestra.)

The first-class Avampato Discovery Museum (www.avampatoart.com) includes two floors of interactive exhibits that adults and kids will find stimulating and educational. (I spent many minutes playing the electronic laser harp.) The 9,000-square-foot Juliet Museum of Art is a state-of-the-art gallery with movable walls that can accommodate anything that the curators decide to display during the schedule of changing exhibits. The Electric Sky Theater features a huge tilted dome for large-format films and planetarium shows. There is also a gift shop and a small café.

Open Wed.–Sun. Admission to the museum, gallery, and a film is $13.50 for adults, $11 for seniors and children (ages 2–18), and free for children under age 2. Individual-attraction and other combination tickets are also available.

Hurricane

Museum in the Community (304-562-0484; www.musueminthecommunity.org), 3 Valley Park Dr. Open Tues.–Sat. While this is a place to visit to see changing art exhibits or take classes, the modern building is an architectural attraction in itself. It is a large, open space with exposed pipes, meters mounted over electrical switches so you can see how much power is being used, and transparent walls so that wiring can be seen. Even design features, such as soffits, are labeled.

Nitro

Nitro Explosives and War Museum (304-755-0619), Nitro Community Center, 21st St. Donations accepted. As befitting a town established to manufacture nitro tetroxide and other armaments for America's use in World War I, the museum is a memorial to the town's early history and efforts in subsequent wars. *Please note*: It seems as if the museum is almost constantly in a state of flux, and open hours (and even sometimes its location) change often. Call in advance.

St. Albans

Morgan's Kitchen (304-727-5972), Walnut St. at MacCorkle Ave. Open Sun. afternoon from Memorial Day to Labor Day. Donations accepted. John Morgan Jr. and his family moved into the area near St. Albans in 1846, and this log cabin served as their home until they completed a 14-room plantation mansion. The cabin then became their kitchen, and in later years it was used by the Union army as a kitchen, hospital, and headquarters to plan the Battle of Scary Creek. Moved to this site in the late 1900s, it is furnished as it would have been when the Morgans used it as a kitchen, complete with a few family belongings, including Mr. Morgan's bear trap.

South Charleston
&. **South Charleston Museum** (304-744-9711), 311 D St. Open Mon.–Fri.; call ahead for Sat. hours. No admission fee. The small museum is located inside the historic LaBelle Theatre and has displays that change frequently. The museum often sponsors special events to coincide with the exhibits.

MORGAN'S KITCHEN

STATE CAPITOL COMPLEX ⬆ ✪ Completed in 1932 and designed by Cass Gilbert, a leading architect of his time, West Virginia's **State Capitol** building is generally regarded as one of the country's most beautiful state capitols. From its gold dome to its sculpted mythological gods and goddesses above entrance doors, the building has such an abundance of details that it could take weeks to seek out and enjoy all of them. The best way to see as much as possible in a relatively short time is to take one of the free tours (304-558-4839; no reservations required) that are given Mon.–Sat. Originating on the first floor of the rotunda, where a 4,000-pound, 10,080-piece Czechoslovakian crystal chandelier hangs from the top of the dome, the tours provide historical perspective and point out some of the building's most interesting features. The second-floor ceiling, decorated with intricately carved panels depicting leaves of the state's native trees, has always impressed me.

There are also free tours of the adjacent **Governor's Mansion**, but you must call 304-558-4839 to make reservations. Built at the same time as the capitol building, the 30-room Georgian home, which overlooks the Kanawha River, is equally impressive, with Corinthian columns, a mahogany double staircase, a black Belgian and white Tennessee marble floor, and walls of butternut paneling from West Virginia forests.

You don't need reservations to take a self-guided tour of the **West Virginia Cultural Center** (304-558-0162; www.wvculture.org) next door to the mansion. Completed in 1972, the modern building is a repository of the

INSIDE THE CULTURAL CENTER

state's artistic, cultural, and historical heritage. A gallery showcases contemporary art (and has more than 800 pieces in its collection), and the state archives are open to anyone wanting to do research. There is almost always something being presented in the 500-seat theater, from lectures to movies, dances to plays, and traditional music concerts to the weekly performances of public radio's *Mountain Stage* (see *Entertainment—Music*).

Don't overlook taking a restful stroll along the capitol complex grounds. Not only will you be entertained by dozens of squirrels scampering in and around decades-old trees, but you will also walk by more than a dozen pieces of statuary related to the state's history. Stonewall Jackson riding upon his horse, Little Sorrel, was the first one erected on the grounds. One of the most inspiring is *Lincoln Walks at Midnight*, created by West Virginian's Vachel Lindsay and Bernie Wiepper; it depicts Lincoln pondering if he should grant statehood to West Virginia. Evocative of the Vietnam Memorial in Washington, DC, the Veterans Memorial records the names of 10,000 West Virginians who gave their lives in 20th-century wars.

OTHER SITES Spring Hill Cemetery Park (304-348-8010; www.cityof charleston.org/government/city-departments/spring-hill-cemetery), 1555 Farnsworth Dr., Charleston. I have always thought cemeteries were parklike places to take quiet, meditative walks, and that is exactly what the designers intended when the Spring Hill Cemetery was dedicated in 1869. It would be possible to spend hours, and even days, walking the 150 acres of Gothic-, art deco–, Romanesque-, and neoclassical revival–style memorials. The graves of some of the city's most famous families— Quarrier, Hale, Lewis, Summers, Ruffner, and others—are here, as well as those of Governors Atkinson, MacCorkle, and Wilkinson. Veterans of the Civil War are interred in various places, and a monument pays tribute to a number of them who are unknown.

Note that the word *park* is in the cemetery's name, and it lives up to this designation by providing soaring panoramic views of the city. Also, the *Birds of Spring Hill Cemetery Park* and *Spring Hill Cemetery Park and Arboretum Tree Identification Guide* pamphlets are available from the office. More than 120 species of birds, including raptors, woodpeckers, and dozens of warblers, have been seen here, while there are literally hundreds of trees many decades old.

Spring Hill Cemetery is also my parents' final resting place.

SPRING HILL CEMETERY PARK

ARCADE & GO-CARTS ✎ ♟ **Southridge Grand Prix Family Fun Center** (304-720-4FUN; www.southridgegrandprix.com), 500 Southridge Blvd., Charleston. It can get a little noisy, but that just adds to the excitement of three indoor go-cart tracks, laser tag, a video game arcade, and a miniature golf course.

BICYCLING

Charleston
Charleston Bicycle Center (304-925-8348), 409 53rd St. Sales and service of mountain, road, children's, BMX, and freestyle bikes.

The **Elk River Rail-Trail** is a 1-mile, packed gravel, multiuse trail along the Elk River with termini in Coonskin Park and Barlow Dr., just a short distance from downtown.

The **Kanawha City Bike Route** is one of the state's few designated road rides within a city. Starting near the University of Charleston, the 7-mile route has signs directing riders along a meandering course of quiet, tree-shaded residential streets with occasional views of the Kanawha River. As a bonus, there are few cars, and the ride is about as flat as you can get.

St. Albans
John's Cyclery (304-727-2180), 309 MacCorkle Ave. Reported to have the area's largest in-stock selection of bicycles and accessories.

Also see Little Creek Park under *Hiking*, Coonskin Park under *Green Space—Parks*, and *Green Space—State Forest*.

BIRDING See Little Creek Park under *Hiking* and *Green Space—State Forest*.

BOWLING

Charleston
Galaxy Lanes (304-925-1156), 6545 MacCorkle Ave.

Dunbar
Dunbar Bowling Center (304-768-2191), 1212 Ohio Ave. Bowling, games, and food.

Nitro
Towne 'N Country Lanes (304-727-2259), 409 First St.

St. Albans
Venture Lanes (304-768-7307), 6300 MacCorkle Ave.

FISHING Cast a line just about anywhere into the **Kanawha River**, and you are likely to hook smallmouth and white bass, catfish, and drum. It is not unusual for a 40-pound catfish to be taken from the **Coal River**.

Also see Coonskin Park and Dunbar Wine Cellar Park under *Green Space—Parks*.

GAMING AND DOG RACING Mardi Gras Casino and Resort (304-776-1000; 1-800-224-9683; www.tristateracetrack.com), 1 Greyhound Dr., Cross Lanes. Sparky is off, and they're out of the gate! Which dog will win the race, and who—if

GOLF

Charleston

Cato Golf Course (304-348-6859), Edgewood Dr. and Baker Lane. Closed Mon. Located within a residential area, this is the only public course within Charleston city limits. The nine-hole par 3 course also has some of the lowest fees in the state—it is less than $10 (!) to play a full 18-hole round.

Clendenin

Sandy Brae Golf Course (304-965-6800), 9 Osborne Mills Rd. Open all year. Sandy Brae is built on hilly ground, making for some uneven lays. There are water hazards on three holes, and number 16 is probably the most difficult, with a narrow dogleg fairway.

Institute

Shawnee Golf Course (304-341-8030), Shawnee Regional Park. The opposite of Sandy Brae, Shawnee is on flat ground, but it presents challenges with water hazards and a dogleg fairway beside a river.

South Charleston

Little Creek Country Club (304-744-9646), 99 Fairway Dr. Opened in 1921, the par 70 course is located just a short distance from downtown South Charleston and features 6,096 yards. Slope rating is 109.

Tornado

Big Bend Golf Course (304-722-0400), 150 Riverview Dr. Open all year. The scenic Coal River runs beside the course, trees line the fairway, water comes into play on three holes, and sloping greens may test your putting skills.

Also see Coonskin Park under *Green Space—Parks*.

GOLF, MINIATURE See *Arcade & Go-Carts*, and Coonskin Park under *Green Space—Parks*.

HIKING Little Creek Park (304-768-1909), 1 Little Creek Park Rd., South Charleston. Hikers (and mountain bikers) take note! For you, Little Creek Park is a treasure of a place. The park's trail system is almost unknown to locals, leaving the routes blessedly underused and often deserted. Close to 20 miles of pathways traverse the rugged terrain, winding onto hillsides of hemlocks and into deep and narrow creek valleys such as Trace Fork Canyon. You can walk by interesting rock formations (one is known as the "Devil's Tea Table"), historic sawmill ruins, caves, and a waterfall. Birders have identified eight species of wood warblers, and, in winter, kinglets and pine siskins seek refuge in the evergreen boughs of the hemlock trees. Five kinds of salamanders, two species of toads, and 240 different plants exist in this amazing bit of backwoods, located just a short distance from the sprawling commercial development on Corridor G (US 119). In fact, one of the trailheads is in the Shops at Trace Fork parking lot.

The park also has picnic facilities and game courts.

KAYAKING & CANOEING At one time, the **Coal River** was a recognized recreation site with fishing, paddling, and swimming opportunities. Decades of mining activity and other pollution eventually gave the river an undesirable reputation. However, many of the industrial activities have ceased, and the river is on the rebound. A group of dedicated volunteers is working to spread the word and let people know how scenic the stream has become once again. Their Web site, www .coalrivergroup.com, provides information on places to put in and what stretches offer the best paddling and fishing. The Web site also has information about the **Walhonde River Trail**, an 88-mile route that the group developed taking in portions of the Big Coal, Little Coal, and Coal rivers.

A QUICK ESCAPE INTO THE NATURAL WORLD

Across the Kanawha River from the downtown area is one of those little hidden gems that every city has but is known to only a handful of residents. William A. MacCorkle, who was a governor of the state, had the **Sunrise Carriage Trail** constructed in 1905 as a way to reach his palatial home overlooking Charleston without having to use an existing steeply rising roadway. Now owned by the city, the 0.65-mile route gently switchbacks along the hillside and is a quick escape into the natural world to walk through a forest of beech, buckeye, tulip poplar, magnolia, oak, walnut, and pawpaw trees. Native and planted flowers add to the beauty of the walk in the springtime. There's also artwork and history. Matching gateposts frame the upper and lower entrances, a small cave is carved out of a stone bank, and massive stone benches invite you to take a breather at opportune spots. An arched stone shrine containing a religious figure with outstretched arms is in memory of MacCorkle's daughter, who died in an automobile accident in 1926. Perhaps the most interesting thing along the pathway is a stone marker erected to honor two women whose skeletal remains were found during the construction of the carriage trail. Although the story has never been verified, MacCorkle had the stone inscribed with the words:

IN THE SECOND YEAR OF THE CIVIL WAR

TWO WOMEN CONVICTED AS SPIES BY

DRUMHEAD COURT MARTIAL WERE

BROUGHT TO THIS SPOT, SHOT, AND

HERE BURIED. IN 1905 WHEN BUILDING

THIS ROAD TO SUNRISE, THEIR REMAINS

WERE DISINTERRED AND REBURIED

OPPOSITE THIS STONE.

W. A. M.

SCUBA DIVING **Divers Training and Supply** (304-545-2125; www.dtsdiving .com), 4142 MacCorkle Ave. SE, Charleston. In addition to being a dive shop (sometimes only open by appointment) where you can get supplies and tanks filled, they also offer evening and weekend instruction and put together trips to exotic locales.

SKATING

Charleston
Skateland of Campbells Creek (304-925-4939), 421 Campbells Creek Dr. The indoor rink was founded in 2002 and is open Tues., Fri., and Sat., during the school year, for public skating.

South Charleston
South Charleston Memorial Ice Arena (304-744-4423; www.cityofsouth charleston.com/memorialice.php), 20 RHL Blvd., in Trace Fork Plaza (on Corridor G, US 119). Indoor ice skating year-round with a heated spectator area.

Also see Coonskin Park under *Green Space—Parks*.

SWIMMING Charleston's **Cato Park**, Dunbar's **City Park**, Eleanor's **County Park**, and the **St. Albans City Park** all have public pools usually open from Memorial Day to Labor Day.

Also see Coonskin Park and Valley Park under *Green Space—Parks*, and *Green Space—State Forest*.

TRAIN EXCURSIONS See *Getting There—By Rail*.

✳ Green Space
PARKS

Charleston
✐ ⅙ ♂ **Coonskin Park** (304-341-8000; www.kcprc.com), 200 Coonskin Dr. Coonskin Park is a gift that the people of Kanawha County gave to themselves by passing a $200,000 bond levy in 1948. It may have the distinction of being the only park in the state, and possibly the entire country, that was built in just two days. With more than a million dollars' worth of equipment, materials, and labor that were donated to the effort, two lakes, an access road, picnic shelters, comfort stations, and a dance pavilion were built on June 27–28, 1950.

The park has continued to develop and now has so many offerings that appeal to so many people that it sometimes

COONSKIN PARK

hosts several thousand visitors on a single weekend. Within an easy 15-minute drive of downtown Charleston are picnic areas and shelters, a handicapped-accessible 18-hole golf course, swimming pool, concessions, game courts and playing fields, children's playgrounds, miniature golf, skate park, fitness trail, fishing, canoe/boat ramp, bicycle and pedal boat rentals, and even a wedding garden. A 2,000-seat soccer stadium and modern amphitheater attract crowds for games, concerts, and other special events.

The park has a small network of trails, and the setting for its 1.5-mile Nature Trail is so enchanting that it was featured in a full-color, multipage article in *Wonderful West Virginia* magazine. Winding along a pathway that clings to the hillside of a deeply shaded ravine, the trail passes through a lush forest of mixed hardwood and hemlock trees, runs under interesting sandstone rock formations and overhangs, comes into contact with a small brook, and is lined by dozens of ferns and scores of springtime wildflowers. The temperature is usually a few degrees cooler than surrounding areas thanks to the lush forest canopy blocking much of the sunlight. Those same leaves make this a colorful walk in the fall, and icicles clinging to the rock overhangs turn the ravine into a sparkling wonderland in winter. Its short length and many little delights make it a good choice for families with children—just be aware that the pathway is narrow and can be slippery in places.

& **Daniel Boone Park** (304-348-6860), Kanawha Blvd. E. Long and narrow, with picnic facilities, a boat ramp, and a handicapped-accessible pier for fishing in the Kanawha River, the park is named for the famous frontiersman who lived for a while in a cave on a mountainside overlooking the river. Unfortunately, the cave was destroyed by construction of a four-lane highway.

Dunbar

& **Dunbar Wine Cellar Park** (304-766-0223), Dutch Hollow Rd. The park's name comes from three stone cellars constructed into the side of mountain that were part of a vineyard in production from 1855 to about 1863. Some historians say it was the strife of the Civil War that caused the demise of the vineyard; others say the owners stopped the wine production so that the cellars could be used as part of the Underground Railroad.

THE THREE STONE CELLARS THAT GAVE DUNBAR WINE CELLAR PARK ITS NAME

In addition to the cellars, the park has picnic facilities, a few short hiking routes, and a paved, handicapped-accessible nature trail leading to 7-acre Laura Anderson Lake, where you can fish for stocked bass, trout, catfish, and bluegill.

Hurricane

✈ & **Valley Park and Waves of Fun** (304-562-2355; http://putnamcounty parks.com/wavesoffun.htm), 1 Valley Dr. In addition to the usual picnic areas, game fields and courts, short hiking trails, and a miniature golf course, this county park has the Waves of Fun swimming pool (open from

Memorial Day to Labor Day). The giant pool produces waves as big as those you would find on any Atlantic shoreline, and three spiraling water slides will keep the kids busy for hours while you work on your tan on the "beach."

STATE FOREST Kanawha State Forest (304-558-3500; www.kanawhastate forest.com; 7500 Kanawha State Forest Dr., Charleston 25314), Charleston. From I-64 exit 58A, drive south on US 119, turn left onto Oakwood Road in 1 mile, and make a right onto Bridge Rd in another mile. Keep straight, driving onto Louden Heights Rd. About 0.4 mile later, make a right onto Connell Road in an additional 0.2 mile, and negotiate a hard left turn onto Kanawha Forest Rd. 2.2 miles later. Another 2.5 miles brings you into the state forest.

Being so close to the large population of the greater Charleston area, Kanawha State Forest has come to be viewed by its neighbors as more akin to a regional or municipal park than the typical state forest. Because amenities often associated with such facilities are quite absent in this portion of West Virginia, the state forest is a magnet for those looking for outdoor recreation. Contained within its 9,300 acres are picnic grounds and shelters, a swimming pool, several children's playgrounds, and a shooting range. A developed campground provides a modern bathhouse with hot showers, laundry facilities, and electric and water hookups. (Backcountry camping is not permitted.)

Almost all of these facilities are located within the narrow valley created by Davis Creek, which leaves the rest of the state forest undeveloped—except for a system of fire and gas well roads. These roads are for authorized vehicles only, so traffic is basically nonexistent, and the routes can be used in conjunction with more than 25 miles of trails to create some very long and adventurous loop hikes and mountain bike rides. The terrain is steep and rugged, but all of the pathways are blazed and signed at trailheads, and they are often in a better state of repair and maintenance than those in other state forests.

The state forest has such an abundance and variety of flora and fauna that it is beginning to garner international acclaim. In fact, some birdwatchers maintain more birds may be seen in Kanawha State Forest than in any other place in the state. So many species of wood warblers have been identified (at least 19) that it is now attracting birdwatchers from other countries. Also within the forest boundaries is just about every other type of wildlife found in the state, including deer, bobcat, fox, coyote, black bear, rabbit, chipmunk, squirrel, mice, vole, raccoon, muskrat, opossum, groundhog, snake, turtle, salamander, lizard, skink, frog, toad, and bat.

More than 1,000 species of flora have been identified here. All of the cove hardwoods—including basswood, cherry, beech, maple, and poplar—grow here and intermingle with trees, such as the tamarack, more often associated with forests farther north. Of all its natural wonders, it may be wildflowers that attract the most attention and visitors. More than 20 species of wild orchids have been seen, and springtime bursts forth with bluet, hepatica, mayapple, bloodroot, trillium, spring beauty, lady's slipper, trout lily, and more. Wintergreen, rattlesnake plantain, jewelweed, Indian pipe, and joe-pye weed appear during the warmest months of the year, whereas goldenrod, aster, and other composites persist into the cool temperatures of autumn.

✳ Lodging

MOTELS & HOTELS

Charleston 25301

Ġ **Embassy Suites** (304-347-8700), 300 Court St. Located directly across from the Charleston Town Center Mall and only a block away from the Civic Center. Heated indoor pool, sauna, whirlpool, exercise room, and free newspaper and full breakfast. $145–240.

🐾 **Holiday Inn Express Civic Center** (304-345-0600), 100 Civic Center Dr. With approximately 200 standard rooms, this is one of the few downtown motels to permit pets. $110–135.

Marriott Town Center (304-345-6500; 1-800-228-9220), 200 Lee St. E. Located directly across from the Charleston Town Center Mall and Civic Center, the Marriott has more than 350 rooms and suites. Amenities include an indoor pool, tennis, health club, whirlpool, sauna, and restaurant. Complimentary airport shuttle. Considered by many to be the city's swankiest motel. $120–195.

Ġ **Best Western Charleston Plaza** (304-345-9779), 1010 Washington St. E. With an outdoor pool, the Best Western has some of the downtown area's lowest rates. $75–90.

Charleston 25304

🐾 **Charleston Comfort Suites** (304-925-1171), 107 Alex Lane, within sight of I-77 exit 95. Heated pool, whirlpool, exercise room, in-room refrigerators and microwaves, and complimentary hot breakfast. $120–170.

🐾 Ġ **Red Roof Inn** (304-925-6953), 6305 MacCorkle Ave. SE. It is located almost on top of I-79 exit 95, but you are compensated by the fact that it permits pets and, of all of the city's motels that offer clean and comfortable rooms, has some of the lowest rates. $50–70.

Charleston 25309

♪ 🐾 Ġ **Hampton Inn—Southridge** (304-746-4646), 1 Preferred Plaza, off Corridor G (US 119). Heated indoor pool, exercise room, business center, playground for the kids, complimentary continental breakfast, and airport shuttles. $120–220.

Hurricane 25526

🐾 Ġ **Red Roof Inn** (304-757-6392), 500 Putnam Village Dr. Within sight of I-64 exit 39, the two-story motel permits small pets. $55–75.

St. Albans 25177

America's Best Value Inn (304-766-6231), 6210 MacCorkle Ave. SW. Located in a commercial area, the 100-room motel has an outdoor pool and a picnic area with barbecue grills overlooking the Kanawha River. $55–80.

South Charleston 25303

🐾 **Ramada Plaza Hotel** (304-744-4641), 400 Second Ave. The Ramada is located in an industrial area next to busy railroad tracks, yet the rooms are inviting, well kept, and have irons and hair dryers. The hotel also offers a fitness room, whirlpool, heated indoor pool, and complimentary full breakfast buffet. $100–170.

BED & BREAKFASTS

Charleston 25311

♪ 🐾 **Brass Pineapple Bed & Breakfast** (304-344-0748; 1-866-344-0748; www.brasspineapple.com), 1611 Virginia St. E. Less than a block from the State Capitol Complex, the early-1900s Brass Pineapple is an excellent representative of the many stately homes in Charleston's historic East End neighborhood. An interesting blend of the Victorian and art nouveau, the house has stained-glass windows and Victorian antiques, and each of the five guest rooms and a suite has a private bath (one with a claw-foot tub, others with marble showers), phone, TV, and work desk. A full breakfast is served in the formal dining room, and business travelers are welcome to make use of the fax/copier, wireless Internet access, and dry cleaning pickup and delivery service. Making as little an impact on the environment as possible, the host uses only biodegradable cleansers and no air fresheners, and organically cultivates the lawn, flowers, and rest of the grounds. Well-behaved children are welcome, and pets can be boarded in the basement washroom, which has a separate heating/cooling system to maintain the B&B's dander-free environment. $100–175.

28 Bradford Street Bed and Breakfast (304-344-0228; 1-888-344-0228; www.28bradfordstreet.com), 28 Bradford St. Built in 1889, the restored Queen Anne–style Victorian home is centrally located between the downtown area and the state capitol complex. The two guest rooms, one a suite with a circular tower bedroom, have private baths. Homemade breads and other baked goods are available for snacking. $120-150.

CAMPGROUNDS

St. Albans 25177
St. Albans Roadside Park (304-722-4625), MacCorkle Ave. This is not really a campground, but it is beside the Kanawha River, and it is a free place (courtesy of the City of St. Albans) to park your RV or pitch a tent. Picnic shelters, a boat ramp, dump station, water, and restrooms are available. Depending on who camped here before you, or who is parked next to you in the very limited number of small spaces, this can be either a littered and depressing experience or one that you enjoy. Best used as a one-night stopover.

Also see *Green Space—State Forest*.

DINING OUT

Charleston
Bridge Road Bistro (304-720-3500; www.thebridgeroadbistro.com), 915 Bridge Rd. Open for lunch and dinner. Say the name Robert Wong to West Virginians serious about food, and you can almost see them begin to salivate. Having established a reputation at other restaurants, he opened his own establishment in the South Hills area of Charleston. Offerings like Caribbean mahi with shrimp grits, pineapple salsa, and lime butter sauce; seared Hudson Valley foie gras with caramelized mangoes and truffle-scented mushrooms; and chicken saltimbocca with country ham and basil accompanied by creamy polenta, sautéed wild mushrooms, and Marsala sauce are quickly turning the bistro into my favorite Charleston restaurant. The wine selection is extensive. Entrées $18–32.

The Chop House (1-888-456-3463; www.thechophouserestaurant.com), 1003 Charleston Town Center Mall. Open daily for dinner. The Chop House serves only graded "Prime" beef that has been aged a minimum of 28 days. It's also a very upscale establishment most often frequented by those wearing coats and ties—and on a company expense account. The meat entrées range from $26–45. If you desire a salad, add another $7–9; a side dish such as a baked potato or grilled asparagus will put another $7–9 on your bill. Appetizers range from $11–50, and handcrafted desserts start at about $9. There is no doubt that The Chop House is a wonderful experience, and everything is delicious and wonderfully prepared—just be ready for a bit of sticker shock. I had a bowl of French onion soup, a small filet mignon, au gratin potatoes, and a glass of wine, and my bill was over $70.

Soho's Italian Restaurant (304-720-7646; www.capitolmarket.net/soho.htm), 800 Smith St., in the Capitol Market. Open noon–5 Sun., and for lunch and dinner Mon.–Sat. Charleston has a long history of good Italian restaurants, and Soho's is keeping the tradition alive. There are the usual pasta dishes, along with some nice soups (try the escarola e fagioli), gourmet pizzas (the gamberi piccanti has spicy shrimp, tomatoes, mozzarella, and goat cheese in pesto), and a house-made ravioli with Maine lobster, sweet corn, and pink crayfish sauce. The quality is so good that I encountered a line of more than 40 people waiting for the restaurant to open at noon on a Sunday. Entrées $12–28.

🦪 ♿ ♈ **Tidewater Grill** (304-345-2622; www.tidewatergrillrestaurant.com), 1060 Charleston Town Center Mall. Open for lunch and dinner daily. My family and I have been coming here for decades and have never been disappointed. In fact, this is one of the state's best seafood restaurants. There is a raw bar, my mother (who was raised in New Jersey) said the Manhattan seafood chowder is authentic, and you can even order a "heap of frog legs" as an entrée. Everything is always freshly prepared, service is as prompt as it can be in a place that is almost always crowded at lunch and dinnertime, and the bar has an extensive wine and beer selection. Make sure to have at least one meal here. Entrées $16.95–29.95.

St. Albans

Aubrey's Yorkshire Pub and Eatery (304-727-7782), 601 Sixth Ave. Open for lunch and dinner Tues.–Fri.; dinner only on Sat. Located in a professional building close to the downtown area, Aubrey's has a plush environment and serves a quality of food not found in St. Albans before this. Like you should at all good restaurants, I suggest you go with a group so that you can sample each other's dishes. A popular entrée is the beef Wellington—a filet mignon topped with foie gras and mushrooms and wrapped in a puff pastry. Hopefully, one of your companions will order the pistachio-encrusted lamb chops served on spinach mashed potatoes and a tomato beurre blanc. Those who enjoy seafood should go for the shrimp, scallops, oysters, and tuna tossed with pasta and a cheese–white wine tomato sauce. Entrées $15.95–29.95. Lunch is a lighter fare of soups, salads, and sandwiches ($4.95–8.95).

EATING OUT

Charleston

Blossom Deli (304-345-2233; www.blossomdeli.com), 904 Quarrier St. Open for breakfast, lunch, and dinner Tues.–Sat., and breakfast and lunch only Mon. (Expect to wait for a table at lunchtime.) Built in the mid-1900s, the Blossom Deli has its original circular booths, gleaming aluminum and metal accents, and mirrors that go from the floor to the ceiling. Sit at the long counter and watch your order being

BLOSSOM DELI

prepared. However, don't be misled by this description and the word *deli* in the name—this is one of Charleston's nicer dining experiences. Lunch sandwiches are freshly made, and dinner entrées range from pork medallions to spinach and goat-cheese stuffed-chicken. Paying homage to the original soda fountain, the deli serves all manner of ice-cream goodies. Lunch entrées $7–12; dinner entrées $19–40.

Cozumel Mexican Restaurant (304-342-0113), 1120 Fledderjohn Rd. Off Corridor G (US 119) in the South Hills area, Cozumel has been my favorite Charleston Mexican restaurant for many years. Although it serves the expected fare, all the dishes—especially the fajitas—are well prepared, fresh, and tasty. Entrées $5.50–13.95.

Practically Delish (304-343—2121), 110 MacFarland St. Open for lunch Mon.–Fri. Despite being located in a small storefront on a narrow side street, Practically Delish is always crowded for lunch. The reason is an ample-portioned menu that draws on a variety of cultures, dishes that use fresh ingredients, and extremely fast service. On the menu have been grilled peach salad with fresh greens and feta; pasta with chickpeas in a red wine vinaigrette; couscous with green onions, black olives, and sautéed vegetables; chipotle-flavored sweet potatoes; chicken and beef kebabs; and a bacon, spinach and tomato lasagna. Here's the real twist: This is a not-for-profit restaurant and all proceeds over operating costs are donated to charities. Another twist: Although the suggested donation was $8 the last time I was there, you are asked to pay whatever you wish, less or more, depending on your income ability. What could be better? Good food for worthy causes.

✒ **Fazio's** (304-344-3071; www.fazios .net), 1008 Bullitt St. Reservations suggested. Fazio's is located in a warehouse district, but that has not kept families from seeking it out for more than five decades. It was one of Charleston's first Italian restaurants and remains many people's favorite. Pizzas are popular items, as are the lasagna and eggplant parmigiana. Entrées $7.95–20.95.

First Watch (304-343-3447; www .firstwatch.com), 164 Summers St. With a large, bright, and airy dining space, this national chain has the feel of a California coffee bar, with gourmet coffee and teas. However, it offers much more, including omelets, waffles, crêpes, burritos, salads, and sandwiches. The atmosphere invites you to linger. Entrées $3.95–8.95.

Fresh Seafood Market and Restaurant (304-343-3134; www.capitolmar ket.net/freshseafood.htm), 800 Smith St., in the Capitol Market. The name says it all—fresh seafood to take home, and some of the lowest-cost and tastiest quick-serve seafood in the city. Entrées $4.99–15.99.

✒ **Leonoro's Spaghetti House** (304-343-1851), 1507 Washington St. E. Open for lunch and dinner; closed Sun. Like Fazio's, Leonoro's has been a Charleston favorite for many decades. Located in the East End neighborhood, the establishment does not try to put on airs, but it is the spaghetti sauce and reasonable prices that bring people back time after time. Many meals under $10.

Main Kwong (304-342-8899), 1407 Washington St. E. Sometimes the most unassuming places can really surprise. Main Kwong has all of four booths and is in one of Charleston's more untidy neighborhoods, but it does some of the city's most brisk take-out business. And with good reason—I would put the quality of the Chinese food they serve up against any establishment offering the same fare at two to three times the cost. Entrées $4.50–12.95.

Sitar of India (304-346-3745), 702 East Lee St. Open for lunch and dinner. Surprisingly, Charleston has a number of Indian restaurants, and Sitar of India is the best of them. Entrées $9.95–20.95.

Sub Shop Downtown (304-345-6700), 807 Quarrier St. Open for breakfast and lunch Mon.–Fri. Good, quick-service sandwiches. $3.90–5.90.

South Charleston

Farm Table Restaurant (304-744-3850), 419 D St. Open daily for breakfast, lunch, and dinner. The area's best place for good country cooking, like country ham with redeye gravy, fried chicken livers, and country-fried steak. Also good breakfasts, which are served all day. Entrées $4.95–11.95.

COFFEE BARS Capitol Roasters Café (304-720-7375; www.capitol market.net/caproasters.htm), 160 Summers St., Charleston. Coffees, teas, desserts, casual cuisine, wine and beer, and live jazz on the weekends. They have another location in the Capitol Market at 800 Smith St.

SNACKS & GOODIES

❧ **Ellen's Homemade Ice Cream** (304-343-6488), 225 Capitol St. It is shops like this that add small-town ambience to walks taken along tree-shaded Capitol St. Gourmet coffees, smoothies, and light lunch fare complement the "super premium home-made ice cream."

❧ **The Peanut Shoppe** (304-342-9493), 126 Capitol St. Closed Sun. Generations of Charlestonians are familiar with the aroma of roasting peanuts that wafts out of this small and narrow shop. The Kimble family is now in its third generation of owner-

ship and is still preparing peanuts in the same roaster that was used when The Peanut Shoppe opened in this location more than 50 years ago. The warm peanuts are a special treat on cold winter days, other nuts and candies by the pound are also available, and cold drinks are welcome during Charleston's long, hot summers. The collection of Planters Mr. Peanut figurines is a nostalgic amusement for those who remember when this memorabilia first appeared.

South Charleston

Spring Hill Pastry Shop (304-768-7397), 600 Chestnut St. Closed Sun. and Mon. Cakes, pies, rolls, dough-nuts, and some great cookies have been made here since 1948.

THE PEANUT SHOPPE

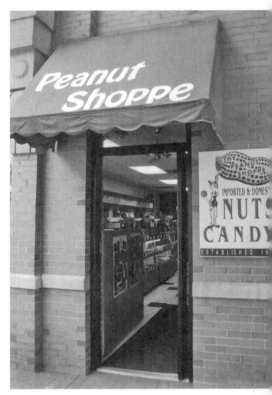

✳ Entertainment

FILM

Charleston

Park Place Stadium Cinemas (304-345-6540), 600 Washington St. E. Has multiple screens and is located in a downtown parking building.

Nitro

Great Escape Nitro 12 (304-769-0405), 12 JW Dr. Multiple screens for multiple showings.

Scott Depot

Teays Valley Cinemas (304-201-7469), 170 Erskine Lane. Close to I-64 exit 39.

South Charleston

Marquee Cinema (304-746-9900), 331 Southridge Blvd., behind Wal-Mart. One of the area's first stadium theater complexes, it is located amid the major development along Corridor G (US 119).

MUSIC Empty Glass (304-345-3914; www.emptyglass.com), 410 Elizabeth St., Charleston. The Empty Glass is just an unassuming bar in the East End neighborhood, yet it is often the place where musicians who have been on Mountain Stage come to after their radio presentations. If a national or international act is not performing on the weekend, you are still assured of hearing some good local and/or regional talent.

Mountain Stage (www.mountainstage.org), in the Cultural Center at 1900 Kanawha Blvd. E, Charleston. West Virginia Public Radio's famous *Mountain Stage*, heard internationally on more than 100 stations, takes place most Sun. evenings beginning at 7. Known for its blend of music from throughout the world, it has featured such diverse acts as the Indigo Girls, Los Lobos, Buckwheat Zydeco, Emmylou Harris, Phish, Sheryl Crow, Joan Baez, Randy Newman, Alison Krauss, and Jerry Jeff Walker. There is also music you would never otherwise hear on the radio, including bands and performers from Ireland, France, Hungary, Japan, Australia, South America, Asia, and Africa. Many acts appeared on Mountain Stage years before they became famous. Plan to attend when you're in Charleston; tickets (1-800-594-TIXX) are usually no more than $20, and you never know what musical wonders you will be exposed to.

Also see Taylor Books in *Bookstores*

NIGHTLIFE Comedy Zone (304-414-2386), 400 Second Ave., South Charleston. Some of the country's funniest stand-up comedians perform every Fri. and Sat. night.

SPORTS The West Virginia Power (304-344-2287; www.wvpower.com), a minor-league affiliate of the Pittsburgh Pirates, play their home games in an interesting stadium. Located at 601 Morris St., Charleston, the playing field is "recessed" into the ground, with the seats rising to a height of not

THE WEST VIRGINIA POWER, WITH A HOME-FIELD ADVANTAGE

much more than street level. Minor-league games are often more entertaining and exciting than those played in the majors, and Charleston has a long history of colorful fans providing some of that entertainment.

✷ Selective Shopping

ANTIQUES

Nitro
Nitro has developed into one of the state's premier concentrations of antiques shops. Among the standouts are **Antiques on the Avenue** (304-755-2078; 1-866-262-6255; 2207 First Ave.), **Nitro Antique Mall** (304-755-5002; 110 21st St.), and **Somewhere in Time** (304-755-0734; 307 21st St.).

South Charleston
South Charleston Antique Mall (304-744-8975), 617 D St. A multidealer mall with close to 18,000 square feet of space to look through.

ART AND CRAFTS GALLERIES
Annex Gallery (304-342-1461; www.taylorbooks.com), 226 Capitol St., Charleston; inside Taylor Books (see *Bookstores*). Ever-changing displays from local and regional artists, and art classes.

The Art Store (304-345-1038), 1013 Bridge Rd., Charleston. Closed Sun. and Mon. I remember when The Art Store was just a framing shop. It still is, but much of its space is now devoted to exhibiting works by some of the region's best artists. I've seen wonderful sculptures, plein air paintings, wool-felt jewelry, and unique folk-art works.

Callen McJunkin Gallery (304-342-5647; www.mcjunkingallery.com), 221 Capitol St., Charleston. One of the state's most well-respected art dealers, the gallery handles the works of artists in every medium you can think of,

from photography to furniture and everything in between. All admirers of fine art should spend a few moments here.

Gallery Eleven (304-342-0083; www.galleryeleven.com), 1033 Quarrier St., Charleston. A cooperative that was started by 11 creative talents that now features other artists who become members by invitation only.

BOOKSTORES Taylor Books (304342-1461; www.taylorbooks.com), 226 Capitol St., Charleston. Of the half dozen or so independent bookstores that once populated the city, Taylor Books is the only one to survive. It's a pleasant place to shop, for in addition to the books, the business has a large magazine selection, small coffee bar, and live entertainment on a regular basis.

FARMERS' MARKETS See Capitol Market under *Special Shops*.

SHOPPING AREAS It is interesting to watch how commercial shopping areas ebb and flow, with one place enjoying favor for a few years, then declining when a new and "improved" development happens. From the early 1900s to the 1960s, **Capitol St.** in downtown Charleston was the place to shop, with a multitude of five-and-dimes, department stores, and men's and women's clothing shops. When the **Charleston Town Center** (304-345-9525; www.charlestontowncenter.com; 3000 Charleston Town Center), a three-story mall located several blocks from Capitol St. opened, Capitol St. went into decline. In the 1990s, big-box national chain stores opened along **Corridor G** (US 119), and this area has now become a major shopping center. Yet, Capitol St. has had a renaissance and is now an inviting tree-lined route bordered by a bookstore, eclectic restaurants, and interesting, locally owned shops.

SPECIAL SHOPS

Charleston
Capitol Market (304-344-1905; www.capitolmarket.com), 800 Smith St. The lands underneath elevated roadways often become abandoned eyesores. Not so in Charleston. Open daily all year, the rehabilitated former Kanawha and Michigan Railroad depot houses some of the city's most appealing shops, including Soho's Italian Restaurant (see *Dining Out*), Holl's Swiss Chocolatier (1-800-842-4512; see *Snacks & Goodies* in "The Mid-Ohio Valley—Beside the Waters of the Ohio and Little Kanawha Rivers" chapter), **Fresh Seafood Market and Restaurant** (see *Eating Out*), **Johnnies Fresh Meats** (304-342-0224), and **Perdue Grocery** (304345-4873), with many West Virginia–produced food items.

The outdoor stalls make up one of the state's largest farmers' markets. To sell here, each stall must have someone who is a farmer, and at least 75 percent of the produce sold must have been grown in West Virginia.

Nitro
Nitro Hobby and Craft Center (304-755-4304), 104 21st St. A first-rate model-railroading selection.

St. Albans
Fret 'n Fiddle (304-722-5212; www.fretnfiddle.com), 809 Pennsylvania Ave. Owner Joe Dobbs is one of the state's most well-respected old-time musicians. His shop is filled with vintage and new instruments and is often the site of impromptu jam sessions. If you can't make it to the shop, you can listen to him on West Virginia Public Radio. His program, Music from the Mountains, has been on the air since

CAPITOL STREET

the 1980s (and was the replacement for my own Down Home Music Show, which I gave up to do a thru-hike of the Appalachian Trail).

✳ Special Events

January: **Martin Luther King Jr. Holiday Celebration** (304-558-0162; www.wvculture.org), Charleston. A celebration of the civil rights leader's life.

February: **Critter Dinner** (304-766-0220), Dunbar. A banquet prepared with wild game.

SHOPPING ON BRIDGE ROAD IN CHARLESTON'S SOUTH HILLS NEIGHBORHOOD
Cornucopia (304-342-7148), **Eggplant** (304-346-3525), and **Geraniums** (304-344-1350) carry interesting fashions and home furnishings, while your children will have fun looking around **Kid Country Toys** (304-342-8697). If all of this shopping makes you hungry, walk over to **The Wheelhouse** (304-720-2477) for a sandwich, or dine at one of the city's finest restaurants, **Bridge Road Bistro** (see *Dining Out*).

CABIN CREEK QUILTS

Generations of West Virginia women have turned scrap material into beautiful quilts that are given to, and prized by, family and friends. In the late 1960s and early 1970s, VISTA volunteers recognized the artistic quality of the quilts produced by a number of women in a coal-mining community of Kanawha County and helped form **Cabin Creek Quilts** (304-382-2685; www.cabin creekquilts.com). The first few quilts sold for just a few dollars—and then Jacqueline Kennedy bought one. The works of art now sell for hundreds, and sometimes thousands, of dollars, and they have been produced for several U.S. presidents, Congress members, and music and movie stars. Others are found in highly acclaimed museums.

Cabin Creek Quilts dissolved as a nonprofit organization in 2007, but many of the same artisans exhibit their works at various galleries and festivals, and their quilts may be ordered through the Web site.

April: **Civil War Reenactment Weekend** (304-562-0518), Valley Park, Hurricane. Commemorates the skirmishes that took place at Scary Creek and Hurricane Bridge. Usually attracts 200–250 reenactors from more than a dozen states. Parade drills, night firing, and a military dance. **International Film Spring Festival** (304-342-6522; www.wviff.org), Charleston. National and international feature films, shorts, documentaries, and animation. A fall festival is held in Nov.

May: **Putnam County Bridge to Ridge Bike Tour** (304-562-0518), Winfield. Choice of a 62- or 32-mile road ride.

June: **Rhododendron State Arts and Crafts Festival** (304-776-4308), Charleston. State and regional artists exhibit their works on the State Capitol Complex grounds. **Smoke on the Water Chili Cook-Off** (www.smoke onthewater.org), Charleston. See if your taste buds can stand up to sampling 80–100 different chilis. **Wine and All that Jazz Festival** (304-345-0775; www.fundfortheartswv.org), Charleston. Sample wines from a multitude of state vineyards while listening

to regional and national jazz bands. **Soap Box Derby Races** (304-746-5552), South Charleston. The country's only lighted course that enables night racing.

July: **Cruise-In and Car Show** (304-562-5896), Hurricane. **Putnam County Fair** (304-586-4001l; www.putnam countyfair-wv.com), Eleanor. **Ribfest** (304-984-2412; www.charlestonwv ribfest.com), Charleston. Vendors from across the country serve barbecue ribs and chicken.

August: **Multifest** (304-421-1585; www.multifestwv.com), Charleston. A celebration in food and music of the state's ethnic diversity.

September: **The Legacy of Mary Ingles** (304-562-0518), Winfield. An annual event with reenactors commemorating early frontier life and the long journey of Mary Draper Ingles, who escaped her Native American captors near what is now Cincinnati, Ohio, and walked through the wilderness to her home at present-day Blacksburg, Virginia.

October: **West Virginia Book Festival** (304-343-4646; wvbookfestival

.org), Charleston. Fast becoming a major event with well-known authors and those who have connections to West Virginia and Appalachia.

November: **Capital City Arts and Crafts Show** (304-345-1500), Charleston. The state's largest arts-and-crafts event.

PURE WEST VIRGINIA

Held annually on the grounds of the State Capitol Complex at the end of May, the three-day **Vandalia Gathering** (304-558-0162; www.wvculture.org) is one of the state's finest venues for true Appalachian music and culture. It attracts hundreds of mountain- and bluegrass-music musicians who present concerts and compete for the titles of best fiddler, banjo player, and so on. To really hear what they are capable of, walk around the grounds, enjoying the sounds of dozens of impromptu performances by musicians who may have just met each other moments before. There are also games for children and demonstrations of old-time activities like apple butter churning, wool spinning, and basketry. Getting to listen to the hilarious tall tales told during the State's Biggest Liar Contest is reason enough to attend.

RIVER TOWNS—HUNTINGTON AND POINT PLEASANT

Located at the meeting point of Ohio, Kentucky, and West Virginia, Huntington is situated at a scenic spot where West Virginia's rolling foothills give way to the flowing waters of the Ohio River.

Recognizing the great shipping potential of a railroad line extending from the East Coast to connect with the vast water transportation network offered by the river, Collis P. Huntington, the president of the C&O Railroad, founded the city that bears his name in 1871. Rufus Cook, the city's designer, understood the tremendous traffic that such a transshipment center would endure. Accordingly, he designed many of the city's streets to be 100 feet wide so that two horse-drawn coaches could pass each other while other coaches were parked along the sides of the streets. These six- to eight-lane roadways are now one of Huntington's most distinctive features.

Its founder's dream proved to be true. At one time, Huntington transferred more freight than any other city its size along the Ohio River. To this day it remains a busy transshipment and industrial center, with 11 miles of floodwalls protecting it from the unpredictable waters of the river.

The city also has a rich and varied cultural life. With more than 16,000 students, Marshall University is one of the state's largest schools of higher learning and keeps close ties with the city through its Marshall Artists Series, Jazz-MU-Tazz Festival, and visual- and performance-arts presentations. Theatrical performances, concerts, and art exhibits are presented throughout the year by groups such as the **First Stage Theater Group** (304-733-4909; www.firststagetheatre.org), **Huntington Symphony Orchestra** (304-535-0670; www.huntingtonsymphony.org), Huntington Dance Theater (304-781-8343; www.huntingtondance.org), and **Huntington Outdoor Theater** (304-523-8080; www.hotwv.org). The Huntington Museum of Art (see *Museums & Art Galleries*) is the largest facility of its kind in the state.

The Harris Riverfront Park attracts walkers and joggers to a paved route along the Ohio, while Ritter Park is a 70-acre green oasis running along the edge of the city's hillside property. Built in 2004, Pullman Square is a $60-million retail, restaurant, and entertainment center that helps keep shoppers and tourist dollars within the downtown area.

While on a surveying trip along the Ohio River in the 1740s, George Washington made an entry into his diary noting a "pleasant point" at the confluence of the Ohio and Kanawha rivers. Several decades later, in 1774, Gen. Andrew Lewis's forces clashed with Native Americans in what many consider to be the opening battle of the American Revolution. Soon afterward, a number of forts were

THE TALE OF A MOTHMAN

In 1966, at a time when West Virginia was in the throes of numerous UFO sightings, a mysterious creature was first seen flying more than 100 miles an hour near a highway close to Point Pleasant. Within the next year, 25 more sightings were reported, with almost every witness giving the same general description of a humanlike creature nearly 7 feet tall, with blazing red eyes and wings that unfolded from its back to be as wide as a two-lane highway. During this same time, other unexplained occurrences were reported. Electrical appliances stopped working, police radio dispatches were interrupted, automobiles failed to start or stopped running for no apparent reason, and the number of UFO sightings increased dramatically. Many people blamed all of these occurrences, and the 1967 collapse of the Silver Bridge across the Ohio that killed 46 people, on the activities of Mothman. (Other people said Mothman and the disaster were part of a 200-year curse Chief Cornstalk placed on the area in retaliation for his murder while in captivity.) Sightings decreased after the bridge's collapse, but the legend gained new life with the 2002 release of *The Mothman Prophesies*, starring Richard Gere. Many people still come to Point Pleasant with the hope of seeing Mothman—and they are not disappointed. A gleaming metal, life-size statue of the creature—with fiery red glass eyes (made by Blenko Glass in Milton), outspread wings, and clawlike hands—is placed in a downtown square. A small museum dedicated to the legend is also located downtown.

THE MOTHMAN STATUE

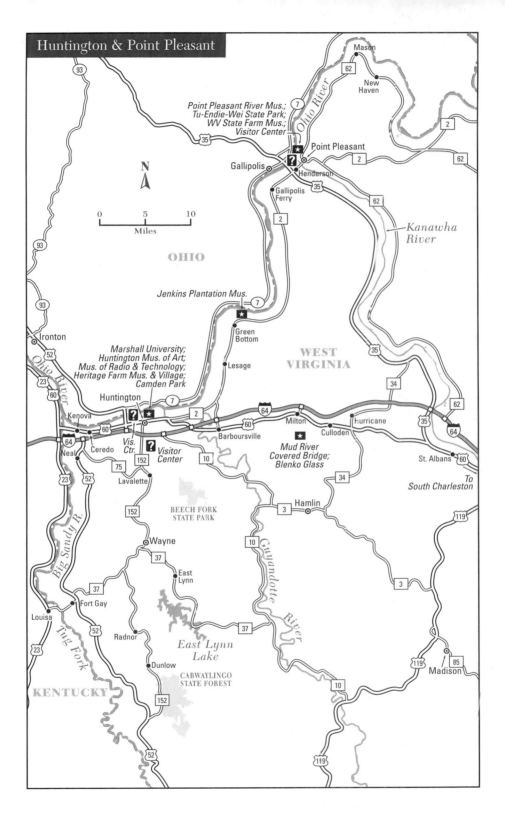

Huntington & Point Pleasant

established in the area, and river transportation and a boat-building industry came to dominate Point Pleasant's economy.

A community of about 5,000, the town preserves much of its history in Tu-Endie-Wei State Park, the West Virginia State Farm Museum, reconstructed Fort Randolph, and the Point Pleasant River Museum.

Please note: The West Virginia Division of Tourism includes sites in Wayne County—such as Beech Fork State Park, Cabwaylingo State Forest, and East Lynn Lake—in the Hatfield-McCoy Mountains region. However, I have included them within the Huntington area because, in my experience, locals and travelers tend to visit them on forays from Huntington more often than from within the Hatfield-McCoy Mountains region.

GUIDANCE The **Cabell-Huntington Convention and Visitors Bureau** (304-525-7333; 1-800-635-6329; www.wvvisit.org), 763 Third Ave., Huntington 25701, is on the western edge of the downtown area.

The **Mason County Convention and Visitors Bureau** (304-675-6788; www.masoncountytourism.org), 210 Viand St., Point Pleasant 25550, is close to the WV 2 bridge over the Kanawha River.

The state **Welcome Center** (304-522-1062) at eastbound I-64, mile marker 10, has information concerning the Huntington area and the entire state.

GETTING THERE *By air*: **Huntington's Tri-State Airport** (304-453-6165; www.tristateairport.com) has flights that connect with major airports in other parts of the country.

By bus: Huntington is one of the few cities in the state that is still serviced by **Greyhound** (1-800-231-2222; www.greyhound.com).

By car: East–west **I-64** is the primary four-lane highway providing access to the area.

By rail: An **AMTRAK** (304-342-6766; 1-800-872-7245; www.amtrak.com) train, *The Cardinal*, is an east–west train that you may take to Huntington from New York or Chicago and points in between.

GETTING AROUND *By bus*: The **Transit Authority** (304-529-RIDE; www.tta-wv.com) has routes throughout Huntington and into the surrounding communities of Barboursville, Culloden, and Milton.

By taxi: In Huntington, you may call **Yellow Cab** (304-529-7131).

MEDICAL EMERGENCIES

Huntington
Cabell Huntington Hospital (304-526-2000; www.cabellhuntington.org), 1340 Hal Greer Blvd.

St. Mary's Medical Center (304-526-1234; www.st-marys.org), 2900 First Ave.

A LITTLE-KNOWN FACT
The world's first electric railroad—built as a commercial business—was constructed between Huntington and Guyandotte.

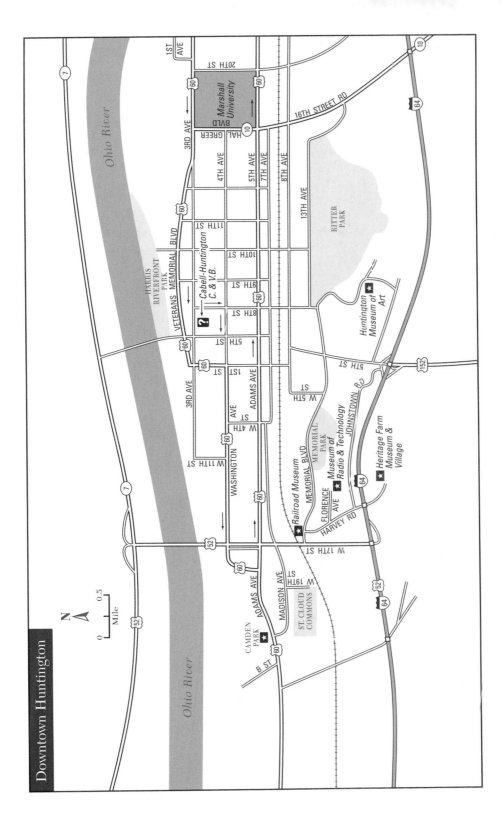

Downtown Huntington

N

0   0.5
Mile

Ohio River

7

52

HARRIS RIVERFRONT PARK

VETERANS MEMORIAL BLVD

60

Cabell-Huntington C. & V.B.

3RD AVE

4TH AVE

5TH AVE

7TH AVE

8TH AVE

13TH AVE

RITTER PARK

11TH ST

10TH ST

9TH ST

8TH ST

5TH ST

1ST ST

60

60

Marshall University

HAL GREER BLVD

1ST AVE

20TH ST

60

60

10

16TH STREET RD

10

64

7

ADAMS AVE

W 4TH AVE

WASHINGTON AVE

60

W 11TH ST

52

60

Railroad Museum

MEMORIAL BLVD

Museum of Radio & Technology

FLORENCE AVE

HARVEY RD

W 17TH ST

5TH ST

W 5TH ST

JOHNSTOWN RD

Huntington Museum of Art

152

Heritage Farm Museum & Village

64

52

64

CAMDEN PARK

60

B ST

ADAMS AVE

MADISON AVE

W 19TH ST

ST. CLOUD COMMONS

Ohio River

Pleasant Valley Hospital (304-675-4340; www.pvalley.org), 2520 Valley Dr.

✳ To See

COLLEGE Marshall University (304-696-6833; 1-800-642-3463; www.marshall
.edu). Visitors center is at 1801 Fifth Ave., Huntington. The world became familiar
with Marshall University through the Hollywood movie *We Are Marshall*, which
starred Matthew McConaughey and chronicled the sad days after a plane crash
claimed the lives of many members of its football team and fans in 1970.

The university is a large part of the community. On game days, of course, traffic
can back up for miles as thousands of fans head to the stadium to watch the Thun-
dering Herd in action. The school also offers a variety of lectures, art exhibits, concerts, and theatrical performances that are open to the public.

COVERED BRIDGE The **Mud River Covered Bridge**, built in 1879, is more
than 100 feet long, 14 feet wide, and was moved to its present site (and rebuilt) in
the Pumpkin Festival Grounds in Milton in 2002. It is the only Howe truss covered bridge in the state.

DRIVING TOURS, SCENIC & HISTORIC US 60 has been designated the
Midland Trail National Scenic Byway (see *To See—Driving Tours, Scenic &
Historic* in the "Old Towns, Surviving and Alive—Lewisburg, White Sulphur
Springs, and Union" chapter for background information). Having traveled
through Charleston and its surrounding area, US 60 enters this area near the small
town of Milton, home of the Blenko glass factory. When you take US 60 through
Barboursville, you may do a double take when you spy a pink elephant by the side
of the road. There seems to be confusion as to its origin, but local lore says it was a

MUD RIVER COVERED BRIDGE

gift from grandparents to a grandchild. It sits beside a storefront whose business has changed over the years, yet the elephant remains in good shape and painted brightly pink. From here, US 60 enters the metro Huntington area, giving access to its many attractions.

GLASS FACTORIES **Blenko Glass** (304-743-9081; 1-877-425-3656; www .blenkoglass.com), 9 Bill Blenko Dr., Milton. Visitor center open daily; craftspersons work 8–3:15 Mon.–Fri. At one time there were hundreds of glass factories in West Virginia; Blenko was one of the first, and it is one of the less than 20 surviving companies. Established in the 1800s, it is now in its fourth generation of the same family, which oversees the production of hand-blown stained glass, art glass, and tableware. Through the years, Blenko has created the Country Music Award, the U.S. Capitol lighting globe, windows in New York's Saint Patrick's Cathedral, and thousands of "thank-you" gifts for public television stations. A small museum lets you peruse the best of what has been produced, and the visitor center offers items at substantial savings.

An observation platform allows you to get close to the teams of craftspersons as they go through the process of turning a molten lump of glass into a work of art. *Insider's tip*: Guided tours are only available to groups, so I usually hang around in the background with the folks who get off a tour bus so that I can get the full story on the history of Blenko—and just exactly what those glassmakers are doing when you watch them from the observation deck.

LAKE **East Lynn Lake** (304-849-2355), located on WV 37 southeast of Wayne. More than 500,000 people visit East Lynn Lake every year. Around the 12-mile-long body of water are a large campground (304-849-5000) with hookups, dump station, showers, and a playground; numerous boat launch sites; a marina; hiking trails; and an environmental interpretive center. Rainbow, brook, and brown trout are stocked in the outflow waters, while the lake contains crappie, walleye, catfish, and a variety of bass.

EAST LYNN LAKE

MUSEUMS & ART GALLERIES

Huntington

🐾 🍎 **Heritage Farm Museum and Village** (304-522-1244; www.heritage farmmuseum.com), 3300 Harvey Rd. Open Mon.–Sat. 10–3. Admission for a three museum tour $8 for adults (ages 13–64), $7 for seniors, and $6 for children (ages 3–12). Admission for two additional museums is an additional $4. Petting zoo admission is $5.

Lawyer, banker, and college president Mike Perry's passion to make sure future generations understand where they come from has led him to create the Heritage Farm Museum and Village. As you walk from one of the more than 16 buildings to another, you will not only learn about blacksmithing, flour milling, and older medical practices, but you will be amazed that it was only one man who collected all of these items. The 1800s log barn houses three floors of exhibits, while the Progress Building depicts the changes in home life—such as from candles to electric lights, open fireplaces to gas stoves, and outside wells to running water. The Transportation Building contains so many different vehicles—Conestoga wagon, stagecoach, 1908 electric truck, Model T cars, and railroad engines—that it could stand as a museum on its own.

This is an outstanding place, made all the more remarkable by the fact that Perry has received no outside funds. I highly recommend that you plan on devoting at least a couple of hours to touring here. You may enjoy it so much that you'll want to spend the night in one of the village's deluxe cabins (see *Lodging*).

⬧ **Huntington Museum of Art** (304-529-2701; www.hmoa.org), 2033 McCoy Rd. Closed Mon. Very small admission fee. The Huntington Museum of Art is nationally acclaimed and is the largest such facility in the state, so once you get inside and see what it has to offer, you'll find that you will be tempted to spend quite a bit of time here. It is easy for minutes to slip away while you look over Appalachian folk art, sculptures, 19th- and 20th-century American and European paintings, glass produced primarily in the Ohio Valley, Islamic prayer rugs, Georgian silver, and more. The Dean Firearms Collection contains hundreds of items, from powder horns to rifles, made in Harpers Ferry. The C. Fred Edwards Conservatory is the only plant conservatory in the state and has year-round displays of palms, shrubs, and herbs. There is also a short hiking trail that wanders through some of the museum's more isolated grounds (see the "An Urban Oasis" sidebar later in the chapter).

⬧ **Museum of Radio & Technology** (304-525-8990; www.mrtwv.org), 1640 Florence Ave. Open Sat. and Sun. all year, and also on Fri. during the summer. Free; donations accepted. Called the largest of its kind in the country, the museum collection fills all the rooms and hallways of a former elementary school. Those who delight in the technological progress of communication will be wowed by the hundreds of radios from the 1920s to the 1950s; early phonographs, TVs, and computers; ether dyne crystal, citizen band, and ham radios; and a re-creation of a 1920s radio sales and service shop. The gift shop is full of replicas that you can purchase to re-create earlier days in your own home.

⬧ **Railroad Museum** (304-736-7349; www.newrivertrain.com), corner of West 14th St. and Memorial Blvd. Open Sun. 2–5 Memorial Day–Labor Day and on Sun. in Sept. if a volunteer is available. Free; donations accepted. The small, outdoor Railroad Museum has a 1949 freight locomotive, a steam engine once used to haul coal, a couple of cabooses, and a working crossing light. Unlike many such museums, which prohibit you from touching and looking, here a docent will take you inside the engines and the cabooses—

AT THE HUNTINGTON MUSEUM OF ART

and the kids (and you, too, I bet) will get a kick out of being able to run an old wood-frame handcar along 100 feet of track.

Lesage

Jenkins Plantation Museum (304-762-1059; www.wvculture.org), 8814 Ohio River Rd. (WV 2). Open Tues.–Sat. (Open days have been known to change; it is best to call ahead.) The home of Virginia merchant William Jenkins and his son, Confederate Gen. Albert Gallatin Jenkins, was built in the 1830s by slave labor. Once part of a 4,400-acre plantation worked by more than 80 slaves, the house, which has walls that are four bricks thick, played host to such luminaries as Buchanan and Lincoln. Docents take visitors through the house and some of the grounds, providing a glimpse into the lives of those who lived and died here.

Point Pleasant

✿ ⅃ ⚓ **Point Pleasant River Museum** (304-674-0144; www.pprivermuseum .com), 28 Main St. Closed Mon. Very small admission fee. West Virginia's only river museum is the result of a collaboration of former riverboat captains who worked diligently to preserve a part of the state's history that was quickly becoming lost. And they have done an excellent job.

The museum has displays and videos concerning boat construction, stern-wheelers, towboats, historic floods, industries along the state's waterways, an aquarium with fish from the Ohio River, and an amazing collection of more than 10,000 boat photographs. Rarely can you gain such a thorough understanding of an important aspect of the state while visiting just one place. A highly recommended stop.

Tu-Endie-Wei State Park (304-675-0869; www.tu-endie-weistatepark.com), 1 Main St. Situated on 4 acres overlooking the confluence of the Ohio and Kanawha rivers, the state park's focus is an 84-foot granite obelisk honoring the men who lost their lives during the 1774 Battle of Point Pleasant. By defeating the Shawnee Indians and forcing them to give up claims to land in what would become West Virginia, the militiamen opened the frontier to settlement and prevented the Indians from forming alliances with the British during the Revolutionary War.

Also on-site is the **Mansion House** (open May–Oct.), erected as a log tavern in 1796. Among the many articles on display are an original letter from Daniel Boone, Colonel Lewis's surgical kit, artwork made from "Mad" Ann Bailey's hair, and a newspaper ad placed by George Washington urging settlers to move into the area. The cases on the third floor that house Native American artifacts are museum pieces in themselves.

OTHER SITES

Gallipolis Ferry

Robert C. Byrd Locks (304-576-2272), accessed from WV 2. A small visitor center has a few displays explaining how the locks enable vessels to travel up and down the Ohio River safely. Other exhibits contain archeological items found during the locks' construction. The real draw, though, is the observation platform from which you can watch the process huge barges go through when they enter the lock system.

Huntington

With more than a score of houses of worship located within a few city blocks,

A LOOK INTO THE AGRARIAN LIFE OF THE PAST

◇ ઇ **West Virginia State Farm Museum** (304-675-5737; www.pointpleasant
.org; mailing address: Rte. 1, Box 479, Point Pleasant 25550), off WV 62 on
Fairgrounds Rd., about 4 miles north of Point Pleasant. Open Apr.–Nov. 15,
Tues.–Sat. Donations accepted. At one time it was almost a universal experience for Americans to wander through the fields and woodlots of cultivated
farmlands. If we did not live on a farm ourselves, we at least knew and visited someone who did. As we have become increasingly urbanized, however,
fewer and fewer of us have maintained ties with those in the country, and
rural landowners are more reluctant than ever to allow people on their land.

Thankfully, the 120 acres and more than 30 buildings of the West Virginia
State Farm Museum have preserved many aspects of this disappearing way of
life. Thousands of items that shaped farm life—such as threshing machines,
cultivators, tractors, gas and steam engines, looms, and blacksmith's tools—
are on display, and some are still in use in the plowed fields of the farm. Log
cabins, farmhouses, a country doctor's office, a barbershop, one-room schoolhouse, and other buildings provide further insight into 1800s rural life.

Also on site is the **Morgan Museum**, which contains the life work of
taxidermist Sidney Morgan. Hundreds of expertly preserved birds, mam-
mals, and reptiles that Mr. Morgan collected on river trips to the Gulf of
Mexico are displayed in natural poses. I visited this museum a number of
years ago when Mr. Morgan was still alive. Sadly, he is no longer here to
add his personal touch with a guided tour.

Also see *To Do—Hiking*.

WEST VIRGINIA STATE FARM MUSEUM

Huntington's Fifth Ave. has been called the **Avenue of Churches**. Most were built in the late 1800s, and, while all of them are architecturally interesting, there are a few that are real standouts.

Completed in 1884, the Gothic English chapel **Trinity Episcopal Church** (304-529-6084; http://wvtrinitychurch.org), on the corner of Fifth Ave. and 11th St., has lancet-shaped stained-glass windows designed by Louis C. Tiffany and a two-story Gothic arch with recessed oak doors. **Johnson Memorial United Methodist Church** (304-525-8116; www.johnsonmemorialumc.com), built in 1892 and located on the corner of Fifth Ave. and 10th St., is a Roman Gothic Revival structure built with red rusticated brownstone. Its embellished gable facade has battlement towers, while a number of Tudor arches add interesting lines.

The **First Presbyterian Church** (304-523-6476; www.firstpreshuntington.org), on Fifth Ave. between 10th and 11th streets, is considered by many to be the city's finest Gothic building. The central stone facade ends in a Gothic arch, the Renaissance battlement towers have parapets and lancet openings, and an upper Gothic arched stained-glass window is flanked by lancet windows. The **First United Methodist Church** (304-522-0357; www.firstunitedmethodist.com), on the corner of Fifth Ave. and 12th St., was completed in 1914 and has two massive, 100-foot-tall gray sandstone towers that are reproductions of the Magdaline towers of Oxford. Inside, a Gothic stairway leads to an auditorium with Corinthian pillars underneath large arches.

It is not a house of worship, but you should still seek out the impressive **Cabell County Court House** (304-526-9899), near the center of the city at 750 Fifth Ave. Its smooth ashlar sandstone has numerous pillars and arches placed upon the elaborated stone foundation, and European domes with cupolas mark the east and west entrances. A clock tower rises from the middle of the building, but be sure to go inside to take a look at the rotunda, with its hemispherical roof, mosaic floors, Greek key borders, and Tennessee rose marble wainscoting.

You should also make a stop at the **Memorial Arch** on the 1300 block of Memorial Ave. Dedicated to those who lost their lives in World War I, the neoclassical revival arch is reminiscent of L'Arc de Triomphe in Paris and has what many scholars believe to be some of the country's best large-scale bas-relief stone carvings. The wonderfully large trees that provide shade as they curve over Memorial Ave. are living tributes to soldiers of World War I, and each had a plaque attached to it (sadly, now long gone) commemorating the individual in whose memory it was planted in the late 1920s.

✴ To Do

AMUSEMENT PARK ✐ **Camden Park** (304-429-4321; 1-866-8CAMDEN; www.camdenpark.com; 5000 Waverly Rd., Huntington 25704), Huntington. From I-64 exit 6, drive west on US 60. Open late Apr. through Oct., but days and times change each month. Adults $20.99; seniors and children $14.99. Many generations of West Virginians have fond memories of Camden Park, which opened to the public at the end of a trolley line in 1903. It may not be a Six Flags or a Kings Dominion, but it packs a lot into its 26 acres, with 26 rides, miniature golf, food vendors, an arcade, and yearly special attractions and concerts. Roller coaster fans come from around the world to ride the Big Dipper, one of the few wooden coasters left in the country. Little children will especially enjoy the variety of rides that mimic the rides older children can take.

Camden Park is a lot of fun, and, unlike larger amusement parks, you won't have to mortgage the house just so that the family can enjoy a day here.

BALLOONING Fox Fire Resort (304-743-4588; www.foxfirewv.com; 660 Fox Fire Rd., Milton 25541), on US 60 between Milton and Barboursville. One of the best (and most romantic) ways to start the day is to make reservations for a balloon ride to

RIDING THE BIG DIPPER AT CAMDEN PARK

take you on an early-morning flight over Teays Valley. Floating along—almost as silently as a drifting fog—you will be above the rest of the world, able to watch cattle, deer, and other creatures wake to greet the sun as it rises over rolling hills. Rates for two people start at $500. Evening flights are also available.

BICYCLING Jeff's Bike Shop (304-522-2453; www.jeffsbikeshop.com), 740 Sixth Ave., Huntington. Jeff's has been servicing and selling bicycles to Marshall University students and the general public since 1989. They can supply you with maps to plan your own trip, or you can join one of their free scheduled rides and meet some local riders.

Also see Beech Fork State Park under *Green Space—Parks*.

BIRDING See Beech Fork State Park under *Green Space—Parks*.

BOWLING ✍ **Colonial Lanes** (304-697-7100; www.coloniallaneswv.com), 626 Fifth St. W, Huntington. Colonial Lanes has been in business since 1959, and it has 34 wooden lanes and an automatic scoring system. This is quite the deluxe place, with columns on the outside porch and a huge brass chandelier inside.

✍ **Strike Zone Bowling Center** (304-733-2695), 141 Eastern Heights Shopping Center, Huntington.

FAMILY ACTIVITIES ✍ **Milton Corn Maze** (302-634-MAZE; www.cornfield maze.com; mailing address: Rte. 3, Box A156, Milton 25541), Milton. From I-64 exit 28, follow US 60 West and park behind the Milton Middle School. Open Fri. evening and Sat. and Sun. afternoon and evening Sept.–Oct. Adults $7; children (ages 5–11) $6.50. A fun way to spend an afternoon or evening. Miles of trails twist, turn, and befuddle as the maze takes you through acres of tall, living cornstalks. After making your way through the labyrinth (some folks have had to be rescued!), you can reward the kids by taking a hayride or grabbing a snack.

FISHING On the edge of Point Pleasant, **Krodel Lake**, with a one-mile trail around it, contains brook, brown, and rainbow trout along with largemouth bass

ROLLING INTO THE GLORIES OF A WEST VIRGINIA AUTUMN

The C. P. Huntington Railroad Historical Society sponsors scenic **New River Train Excursions** (1-866-639-7487; www.newrivertrain.com) on two weekends in Oct. every year. The daylong trips, which originate in Huntington and stop to pick up passengers in St. Albans and Montgomery, travel into the New River Gorge at the height of the leaf-color season. The thousand-foot gorge walls are bathed in the yellow leaves of hickory trees, the reds and browns of oaks and maples, and the brilliant crimsons of dogwoods and sassafras. A three-hour layover in historic Hinton allows passengers a chance to enjoy the town's annual Railroad Days street fair before returning to Huntington. Prices start at $139 for adults and $90 for children (ages 3–12). Tickets usually sell out quickly, so purchase them as early as possible.

and catfish. Head to where the **Kanawha River** meets the **Ohio** in Point Pleasant, and you will most likely be landing a variety of bass in addition to catfish and northern pike.

Also see *To See—Lake*, Beech Fork State Park under *Green Space—Parks*, and *Green Space—State Forest*.

GOLF There is an abundance of courses within short drives of downtown Huntington. In Lavalette, just 5–6 miles south of the city, are the **Twin Silos at Lavelette Golf Club** (304-525-7405), a hilly course with many trees, sand bunkers, and water hazards, and the **Sugarwood Golf Course** (304-523-6500), which is more level but has a number of creek and pond water hazards. In Barboursville east of Huntington, you can enjoy the wide fairways and large greens of the **Esquire Golf Course** (304-736-1476) or the nine holes and tree-lined fairways of the **Orchard Hills Golf and Country Club** (304-736-8225). About 6 miles north of Huntington on WV 2 is the **Riviera Golf Course** (304-736-7778), with wide, flat fairways and a back nine that borders the Ohio River. North of Point Pleasant on US 33, the **Riverside Golf Course** (304-773-5354) has water that comes into play on 10 holes.

HIKING The **Old TNT Trail** at the **West Virginia State Farm Museum** (304-675-5737; mailing address: Rte. 1, Box 479, Point Pleasant 25550), off WV 62 on Fairgrounds Rd., about 4 miles north of Point Pleasant. (See the "A Look into the Agrarian Life of the Past" sidebar earlier in this chapter.) A facility near Point Pleasant produced explosives during World War II. Within the 7,000-acre site were 10 TNT-manufacturing lines, acid-producing areas, pumping stations and holding ponds, and 100 dome-shaped, grass-covered concrete storage buildings. Most of these facilities are now gone, but a few of them—gradually being overtaken by nature—can still be seen on the 2-mile (round-trip) trail that follows an old paved roadbed. Definitely a unique, and somewhat eerie, hiking experience.

Also see *To See—Lake*, Beech Fork State Park under *Green Space—Parks*, and *Green Space—State Forest*.

SKATING ♿ **Roll-A-Rama** (304-529-0909), 137 Seventh Ave., Huntington. Opened in 1961, the facility is handicapped accessible, and the management permits those in wheelchairs access to the rink. The concession stand sells pizza, popcorn, nachos, and other goodies.

SWIMMING You can practice your strokes, have fun, and get exercise from Memorial Day to Labor Day at the **Barboursville Swimming Pool** (304-736-2715), and **Huntington's A. D. Lewis Pool** (304-696-5908). You will be jumping into history when you take a dip in the **Dreamland Pool** (304-453-6288) west of Huntington; it is close to 100 years old.

Also see Beech Fork State Park under *Green Space—Parks*, and *Green Space—State Forest*.

✳ Green Space

PARKS

Barboursville

Beech Fork State Park (304-528-5794; www.beechforksp.com), 5601 Long Branch Rd. Whereas Chief Logan State Park (see *Green Space—Parks* in the "The

AN URBAN OASIS

In 1948, years before the urban trails/greenway movement began to attract advocates, the founders of the **Huntington Museum of Art** (see *To See—Museums*) resolved that the greater part of its 50-plus acres would remain in its naturally forested state so that the institution would "enrich the lives of all people." It took a few years, but in 1964, a small trail network was established on the property's western slope. Steps, railings, and wooden bridges blend in well with their surroundings and make it easier to negotiate the pathways' steeper portions. One of the nicest hikes you could take within the limits of any of West Virginia's cities, this is a great place to start a walking/exercise program for yourself or introduce young children to the joys and wonders of the outdoors.

Maintained by museum staff and several groups and individual volunteers, the network provides the citizens of Huntington with an easily accessible place in which to recreate in the outdoors. It is short enough that you could walk it during your workday lunch break, but it is interesting enough to be worth a drive from some distant place to enjoy its plants, animals, and rejuvenating atmosphere. Despite being located next to an interstate and surrounded by houses, the trails travel through a forest of large oak, poplar, ash, hickory, beech, black locust, and maple that is home to squirrels, chipmunks, turtles, woodpeckers, and others. In spring, the unfolding fronds of a variety of ferns are joined on the forest floor by mayapple, trillium, sweet cicely, and jack-in-the-pulpit.

Hatfield-McCoy Mountains" chapter) can be a wildflower lover's springtime paradise, Beech Fork State Park can fill a birdwatcher with excitement year-round. It certainly has its fair share of flowers—just a few of them include mayapple, trillium, sweet William, larkspur, live forever, twinleaf, and bloodroot—but it is its wide mix of habitats and environments that attracts such a variety of birds.

Be on the watch for swallows, flickers, hummingbirds, meadowlarks, killdeer, and chickadees in the meadows and mowed areas. Among those you may see in the forest are warblers, owls, thrushes, and woodpeckers; the border areas between woods and fields tend to be favored by kingbirds, thrashers, and sparrows. Floating upon Beech Fork Lake may be mallards, wood ducks, coots, and Canada geese, while the backwater areas and small creeks harbor herons and kingfishers.

In the low-lying hills that make up West Virginia's topography less than 10 miles from the Ohio River, Beech Fork State Park occupies 3,144 acres along the upper end of Beech Fork Lake. The U.S. Army Corps of Engineers developed the 760-acre lake in the 1970s primarily as a flood-control measure that would also provide fish and wildlife conservation and recreational opportunities.

Within the park are picnic areas and shelters, game courts, ball fields, a 50-meter swimming pool, and deluxe year-round rental cottages fully equipped with all the amenities you would find in your own home (heating and air-conditioning, fireplace, microwave, telephone, and television). The huge campground, with 275 deluxe sites—80 of which are located on the lakefront—sprawls over several hundred acres and offers full hookups, laundry facilities, modern restrooms, and hot showers. One portion of the campground is open year-round.

There is no doubt that the recreational opportunities on the minds of most of the park's visitors are on the lake. Rowboats and pedal boats may be rented, and a boat launch is available for those who bring their own watercraft (motors limited to those of 10 horsepower or less). The lake is stocked on a regular basis with a variety of warm-water fish, and from a short time before sunrise to the darkening hours of dusk on almost every day of the year, there will be someone, if not many someones, sending a hook and line splashing into the water. Bluegill, channel catfish, tiger muskie, saugeye, and largemouth bass are what these folks are hoping to catch.

All of this emphasis on the lake means that you may be the only person taking advantage of the park's small network of pathways—except on nice weekends. With its proximity to the population of the greater Huntington area, the park is a lure for local mountain bikers. Although most devotees of the activity I have met have been courteous, you should be prepared to quickly step aside at any moment as an unannounced biker goes zipping by you.

Huntington

🐾 ☀ ♿ **Ritter Park** (304-696-5954), along Eighth to 12th streets and 13th Ave. Ritter Park may well be one of the state's most utilized urban parks. If it is not walkers, joggers, cyclists, pet owners, and families with baby strollers making use of its 70 acres underneath 39 species of trees, then it is concert or live-theater fans attending a performance in the amphitheater. The park's award-winning playground is cut into the hillside and is always filled with young children climbing onto the arches, pillars, triangles, and other forms—all built out of stone. Those

RITTER PARK

who just want to enjoy a few moments in the outdoors can relax on benches while watching the dancing waters of the fountain at the 10th St. entrance.

On the hillside portion of the park is its famous Rose Garden, which has more than 1,500 bushes and is at its most colorful from late June through July. Even the garden walls are a work of art; Civilian Conservation Corps stonemasons built most of them in the 1930s.

Point Pleasant

🦢 Located near town on WV 2, **Krodel Park** (304-765-1068) is a 44-acre family-oriented site operated by the city with camping, fishing, miniature golf, and a one-mile trail around the lake. An excellent replica of the 1700s Fort Randolph (304-675-6788) was constructed in the park in the 1970s and is open to visitors on Sat.

STATE FOREST Cabwaylingo State Forest (304-385-4255; www.cabwaylingo .com; mailing address: Rte. 1, Box 85, Dunlow 25511). Follow US 52 south from Huntington for 42 miles. Cabwaylingo State Forest occupies 8,123 wooded acres in a remote part of the state less than 10 miles from the Ohio River. Developed by the Civilian Conservation Corps in the 1930s, the park offers fully equipped vacation cabins (open mid-Apr. through late Oct.), two shaded hilltop campgrounds (open through Nov.), a swimming pool, picnic area, and fishing in trout-stocked Twelvepole Creek. The trail system, which includes about 12 miles of pathways, is well marked and signed, but it is very underutilized, so you may be the only person hiking on the easy to moderate routes

WALKS Befitting a river town, **Riverfront Park** in Point Pleasant extends for more than a mile along the Ohio River, with a walking path lined by the waterway on one side and historical murals on the other. The park becomes a hotbed of activity during the July Sternwheel Regatta and September's Tribute to the River events.

THE METRO VALLEY

❋ Lodging

MOTELS & HOTELS

Barboursville 25504

& **Best Western** (304-736-9772), 3441 US 60 East. All of the more than 100 rooms have a coffeemaker, iron, hair dryer, and large work desk. Fitness center, outdoor pool, and complimentary continental breakfast. $70–100.

🐾 & **Comfort Inn** (304-733-2122), 249 Mall Rd. The three-story Comfort Inn is close to the Huntington Mall, has an indoor pool, and permits pets for an additional fee. Complimentary continental breakfast. $85–100.

Huntington 25701

& **Holiday Inn Hotel & Suites** (304-523-8880), 800 Third Ave. In the heart of downtown, and just a block away from the shopping and entertainment of Pullman Square and the open space of Harris Riverfront Park. Heated indoor pool and exercise room. $89–129.

& **Pullman Plaza Hotel** (304-525-1001; 1-866-613-3611; www.pullman plaza.com), 1001 Third Ave. In the downtown area, the Pullman is an 11-story facility with more than 200 rooms, two restaurants, a fitness center, and a heated outdoor pool. $115–150.

& **Ramada Limited & Conference Center** (304-523-4242), 3094 Hal Greer Blvd. Close to Marshall University, the Ramada has a heated indoor pool and exercise room. Complimentary continental breakfast. $100–150.

🐾 **Red Roof Inn** (304-733-3737), 5190 US 60 East, within sight of I-64 exit 15. The Red Roof Inn is one of the few major chain motels in the Huntington area to permit pets. It also has some of the lowest rates. $60–70.

Point Pleasant 25550

Lowe Hotel (304-675-2260; www.the lowehotel.com), Main and Fourth streets. Located in the heart of the Point Pleasant Historic District, the Lowe Hotel has been in continuous operation since it opened in 1901. Restored and continually being upgraded, it offers two-room, family, and Jacuzzi suites, along with one- or two-bed rooms. The lobby retains the charm and simple elegance of its turn-of-the-20th-century origins. $70–109.

CABINS & VACATION RENTALS

Huntington 25704

✍ **Heritage Farm Museum and Village** (304-522-1244; www.heritage farmmuseum.com), 3300 Harvey Rd. After having stepped back in time at the museum (see *To See—Museums*), you can continue the illusion by spending the night in one of the log cabins or the farmhouse. Yet, you don't have to give up modern conveniences. Each includes multiple bedrooms, baths, full kitchen, washer/dryer, heating, air-conditioning, and a wood-burning fireplace. (One cabin even comes with a swimming pool.) If you wish, a conti-

HERITAGE FARM MUSEUM AND VILLAGE

nental breakfast can be provided for an additional $10 per person. $225.

CAMPGROUNDS

Gallipolis Ferry 25515
Shady Waters Campground (304-576-4006; mailing address: Rte. 1, Box 91), 10 miles south of Point Pleasant. With boat-ramp access to the Ohio River, Shady Waters offers a laundry facility, hot showers, and city water.

Milton 25541
Fox Fire Resort (304-743-5622; www.foxfirewv.com; mailing address: Rte. 2, Box 655), on US 60 between Milton and Barboursville. Fox Fire is one of the state's most deluxe camping facilities. There is an extensive list of amenities and things to do on its 60 acres: complete hookups, laundry facilities, multiple swimming pools, 240-foot water slide, hot tub and sauna, miniature golf, lake fishing and swimming, playgrounds, boat rentals, hiking and biking trails, and planned activities. Sorry, tent campers, there are no facilities for you—RVs only.

The resort owner is also a hot-air balloon enthusiast who has many hours of experience taking passengers for a ride. (See *To Do—Ballooning*.) *Please note:* There was no camping available as this book went to press, and there was some question as to whether there would be in the future.

Point Pleasant 25550
Oldtown Campground (304-675-3095), 859 Old Town Campground Rd. This commercial campground is situated on 118 acres and has hookups, tent sites, modern restrooms, dump station, and laundry facilities.

Also see *To See—Lake*, Beech Fork State Park and Krodel Park under *Green Space—Parks*, and *Green Space—State Forest*.

✳ Where to Eat

DINING OUT

Barboursville
Black Hawk Grill (304-736-9494), 646 Central Ave. Open for dinner Tues.–Sat. Reservation recommended, especially on the weekend or special occasions. Located in the quaint downtown area, the Black Hawk Grill has one of the area's best fine-dining reputations. Entrées have included sautéed salmon over saffron risotto, peach and corn-bread-stuffed chicken with a five-onion cream sauce, and pork chops topped with pineapple and a sweet-and-sour sauce. Entrées $15–28.

Ceredo
Rocco's Ristorante (304-453-3000; www.roccosristorante.com), 252 Main St. Open for dinner Tues.–Sun. Very popular; expect to wait to be seated. The Huntington area's finest Italian restaurant has dishes that most Americans will recognize—lasagna, rigatoni, chicken cacciatore, and the like—but since the owner travels often to keep abreast of the latest in food innovations, you may also find gnocchi verde (cheese and spinach mixed into the flour) or lobster ravioli (with cream and a roasted sun-dried tomato pesto sauce) on the menu. All the pastas and sauces are made in-house, and Rocco's mother and aunt create the desserts. A most pleasurable dining experience. Entrées $13.95–28.95.

Huntington
Savannah's (304-529-0919; www.savannahsmenu.com), 1208 Sixth Ave. Open for dinner Tues.–Sat.; reservations recommended. A 1903 Victorian mansion is the setting for Huntington's finest dining experience. Owner Ava Bicknell told me she opened the restaurant as a result of a midlife crisis and career change. We are the lucky recipients of her decision. All chefs are

culinary school–trained, and, to ensure freshness, many items are grown in a small garden in the backyard. The menu changes at least two times a year, so there will always be something new each time you visit. Past offerings have included honey mustard–glazed sautéed salmon with crème fraîche Dijon aioli; raspberry marinated maple-leaf duck breast stuffed with Boursin cheese and cherries and wrapped in a puff pastry; and filet mignon with an herb and Gorgonzola crust and finished with a green peppercorn demiglaze. Tasty appetizers, such as southern cheese puffs with spinach balls and oysters Rockefeller, along with freshly prepared desserts, like rich pecan pie with caramel sauce or a lemon tart with raspberry coulis, ensure that you will have a happy tummy by the time you finish dining at my favorite Huntington restaurant. Entrées $18–40.

EATING OUT

Barboursville

✦ **Tascali's Pasta & Grill** (304-736-0504), 6700 US 60 East. Tascali's is an interesting combination of a theme diner (rooms are decorated in memorabilia, one from the 1940s and '50s, another from the 1960s and '70s, and a third from the 1980s and '90s) and an Italian restaurant. Diner offerings include sandwiches, meat loaf, steak, and chicken. Among the Italian dishes is a traditional item that many long-time Huntington residents will recognize: the spaghetti sauce with ground beef, which had been a staple for many decades at the old 29th Street Wiggins's restaurant. Entrées $8.95–18.95.

Huntington

Central City Café (304-522-6142), 529 West 14th St. Open for lunch and dinner. A first glance of the menu leads you to believe this is a typical sandwich and country-cooking establishment, but then you notice that they also offer ostrich, buffalo, and garden burgers, along with a portobello mushroom sandwich, bowls of French onion soup, and a smoked swordfish dinner. You can entertain yourself while waiting for your order to arrive by looking over the artwork on the walls, which ranges from religious items to newspaper front pages, and from a photo of Ernest Hemmingway enjoying a drink in Key West to Norman Rockwell scenes. Entrées $5.99–8.99.

Frostop Drive-In (304-523-6851), 1449 Hal Greer Blvd. Foot-long hot dogs and great root beer. $2.50–8.95.

✦ **Jim's Steak & Spaghetti House** (304-696-9788), 920 Fifth Ave. Closed Sun. and Mon. Since 1938, Jim's has been known as the place to go when you are hungering for a fine piece of beef. Homemade pies for dessert. Entrées $10.95–29.95.

Nana's County Kitchen (304-736-5268), 4801 US 60. Open for breakfast, lunch, and dinner. It's a good bet that you won't be dining with many other travelers in Nana's. The restaurant is located inside a doublewide trailer, and each room has only a couple of tables and chairs. Frequented almost exclusively by locals, Nana's may just be the best place in all of Huntington to get a good, low-cost breakfast. Entrées, $3.95–11.95, are in the country-cooking vein, with hamburger steak, liver and onions, chicken and dumplings, and catfish being some of the most popular offerings. Call ahead, the owner was experiencing health problems as this book went to press.

Stewart's Original Hot Dogs (304-529-3647; www.stewartshotdogs.com), 2445 Fifth Ave. Stewart's has had carhops delivering hot dogs (with their famous secret sauce) to patrons' automobiles in this same location since

HILLBILLY HOT DOGS

1932. A visit to Huntington is not complete without making a stop here. 99¢–$5.99

Lesage
Hillbilly Hot Dogs (304-762-2458; www.hillbillyhotdogs.com), 6951 Ohio River Rd. (WV 2). Open daily. Hillbilly Hot Dogs is an experience. It's really just a roadside ramshackle hut with a carryout window and a few picnic tables crammed onto the edge of the dirt parking lot. If it is raining or too cold, you can seek refuge inside an old school bus with a few seats and tables. You can take all of this in while you chow down on your choice of more than 20 kinds of hot dogs, with names like Buckeye Dog, Snuffy Dog, Stacy's Flu Shot, Chuck's Junk Yard Dog, and Ol' Yeller Dog. If you are on a quest to see how much fat and cholesterol you can consume in just one bite, order the Hillbilly Hot Dog—a deep-fried dog smothered in chili, mustard, and onions. This place is a hoot—and a must-visit site! Dogs run $1.29–4.99.

Point Pleasant
Emma's Galley (304-675-5151), 509 Main St. A good choice for breakfast, lunch, and dinner. If you can be satisfied with good country cooking, you'll enjoy Emma's Galley. Homemade

desserts, too. Most items in the $6–12 range.

COFFEE BARS See The Old Village Roaster under *Snacks & Goodies*.

SNACKS & GOODIES

Ceredo
Austin's Homemade Ice Cream (304-453-2071), 1103 C St. Open daily. Austin's has been producing its own homemade ice cream for more than five decades. There's no inside seating, but that's okay, because your car is the perfect place to enjoy this traditional summertime treat.

Huntington
Francois Pastry Shop (304-697-4151), 817 Eighth St. Nothing short of traveling to France will enable you to enjoy a better pastry. Francois, without a doubt, makes the state's best and most authentic French baked goods; do not miss this place.

The Old Village Roaster (304-697-1944), 919 Fourth Ave. Closed Sun. The Old Village Roaster uses machines from the late 1800s to roast the peanuts and coffees they serve to you. They also offer bulk coffees, teas, chocolates, and caramel corn.

The Peanut Shoppe (304-522-4621), 941 Fourth Ave. Closed Sun.

INSIDE OLD VILLAGE ROASTER

It's a good bet that the aroma will entice you into this store even if you originally had no intention of getting a snack. The décor and ambience definitely recall the era when The Peanut Shoppe first began roasting peanuts at this location in the 1920s.

Kenova

♪ **Griffth & Feil** (304-453-5227), 1405 Chestnut St. Much care has been taken to retain the authenticity of this pharmacy/soda fountain, which opened its doors in 1892. The hardwood floors, tin ceiling, wood and tile counter, and even the soda dispenser are all original. The sodas—or phosphates, as they were once called—are all hand mixed, and you get to choose what flavor you would like. Shakes, floats, and malteds are hand dipped. This is a fun atmosphere where you could spend quite a few minutes looking over the historical pictures that line the walls. They also have a light breakfast and lunch menu.

✷ Entertainment

FILM

Barboursville

Located at the Huntington Mall in Barboursville, the **Cinemamark** (304-733-3984) has multiple screens.

Huntington

The **Cinema 4 Theatre Huntington** (304-525-4440), 401 11th St., was built in the early 1900s.

Giving this older theater a lot of competition, the **Marquee Pullman Square 16** (304-525-7469), 26 Pullman Square, opened soon after the turn of the 21st century.

MUSIC

Huntington

Huntington Symphony Orchestra (304-781-8343; www.huntington symphony.org; mailing address: P.O.

Box 2434, Huntington 25725). The orchestra, which has been around in one form or another since the 1930s, performs indoor classical concerts during the fall and winter season, and outdoor pops concerts in the summer.

Milton

Mountaineer Opry House (304-743-5749; www.mountaineeropry.com), I-64 exit 28. The Mountaineer Opry House has been bringing the best in bluegrass and country music to the Huntington area for many decades. It is a family-friendly atmosphere with no smoking or alcohol, and a place where you may see local, regional, or national talent. Just a few of the people who have performed here include Ralph Stanley, Bill Monroe, the Country Gentlemen, Jim & Jesse, Doyle Lawson, Rhonda Vincent, Mountain Heart, Lonesome River Band, the Seldom Scene, Blue Highway, the Lewis Family, Lynn Morris, Eddie Adcock, Larry Sparks, the Goins Brothers, and the Lily Brothers.

THEATER Huntington Outdoor Theatre (www.hotwv.org), 660 North Blvd., Huntington. Founded in 1990, the regional theater group stages outdoor presentations in the Ritter Park (see *Green Space—Parks*) amphitheater that run for a four-week period during July and usually attract more than 10,000 spectators. Past presentations have included *Beauty and the Beast, Footloose, Annie Get Your Gun*, and *My Fair Lady*.

✷ Selective Shopping

ANTIQUES

Huntington

Old Central City in the western part of Huntington bills itself as the "Antiques Capital of West Virginia," and with more than a dozen individual shops and malls, it may be right. The **Black Cat Antiques & Antique Center** (304-523-7887; www.black catantiques.com; 610/612 West 14th St.) is also the home of **Brassmaster**, where copper and brass are polished and old lamps are restored. Don't go looking for flea market items in **Hattie and Nan's Antiques** (304-523-8844; 521 West 14th St.); this is a true antiques store with quality furniture and other merchandise. The wares of **Grandmother's Attic** (304-525-4880 444 West 14th St.) center on glassware, pottery, and some other interesting antiques. The specialty of the **Old Central Auction** (304-544-4880; 304-654-2067; 1404 Adams Ave.) is complete estate liquidations.

Point Pleasant

The Mason Jar Antique and Craft Mall (304-675-4477), 408 Main St. Open daily. Multiple dealers here sell as many new items as they do antiques.

BOOKSTORE Empire Books & News (304-529-7323; www.empire booksandnews.com), 30 Pullman Square, Huntington. Open daily. The Huntington location of what was once a small regional chain is one of the area's most complete bookstores. Not only do they have an excellent and large selection of books, but they also carry a hefty sampling of magazines from around the world.

FARMERS' MARKETS

Huntington

With stalls located both indoors and outdoors, **Huntington's Central City Market** (304-555-1500; www.central citymarket.com), 555 West 14th St. is open late June into Oct. (closed Sun.) with offerings that include locally produced fresh produce, while pumpkins and other late harvests are on display in Oct.

New Haven

The **Big Bend Farmers' Market** (304-675-2067) is open on Tues. 10–3 across from Field's Hardware.

Point Pleasant

The **Mason County Farmers' Co-op** (304-675-2067) may be found operating June–Oct., Wed. and Sat. 8–2 on First St. under the Bartow-Jones Bridge.

✳ Special Events

April: **Dogwood Arts & Crafts Festival** (304-696-5990), Huntington. Indoor demonstrations and sales of traditional arts and crafts, plus ethnic foods.

May: **Steam and Gas Engine Show** (304-675-5737), West Virginia State Farm Museum, Point Pleasant.

June: **Jazz-MU-Tazz** (304-696-6656), Huntington. Marshall University's summer festival features live jazz and outdoor family activities. **Juneteenth Festival** (304-696-5908), Huntington. Food, music, and crafts in celebration of the freedom from slavery for African Americans. **Woodland Indian Gathering** (304-675-7933), Krodel Park, Point Pleasant. Eastern Woodland Indian village recreation and reenactors.

July: **Cabell County Fair** (www .cabellcountyfair.org), Milton.

August: **Mason County Fair** (304-675-5737), Point Pleasant. **Riverfront Ribfest & Jet Ski Races** (304-696-5990), Huntington. Four days of ribs, barbecue, live entertainment, and family activities at Harris Riverfront Park.

September: **Chilifest** (304-529-4857; www.chilifestwv.com), Huntington. Chili cooks from West Virginia and surrounding states vie for the honor of being state champion and moving on to compete in the World Chili

Championship. **Pilot Club of Huntington's Antiques Show and Sale** (304-886-5851), Huntington. More than 50 dealers arrive with wares to sell in one of the tri-state's largest antiques events. **Annual Mothman Festival** (www.mothmanfestival.com), Riverfront Park, Point Pleasant.

October: **Battle Days** (304-675-3844), Point Pleasant. Historical reenactors, sutlers, and crafters meet to re-create the 1774 Battle of Point Pleasant. **West Virginia Pumpkin Festival** (304-683-1633; www.wvpumpkinpark.com), Milton. Fifty thousand people attend this four-day festival to participate in pumpkin decorating, a horse show, border collie demonstrations, petting zoo, juried arts and crafts, and many other events.

November: **Guyandotte Civil War Days** (www.guyandottecivilwardays.com), Guyandotte. Reenactment of the Confederate raid on Guyandotte and the subsequent Union reprisal. Period music, crafts, displays, and living histories.

The Mid-Ohio Valley

8

THE MID-OHIO VALLEY

BESIDE THE WATERS OF THE OHIO AND LITTLE KANAWHA RIVERS

The Mid-Ohio Valley is a blend of early frontier history, Victorian homes built with the riches of the country's first oil and gas boom, and a modern-day economy bolstered by transportation on rail, four-lane highways, and the Ohio River.

Looking at the waters of the Ohio today, it is hard to imagine that when settlers first appeared along its banks it was a temperamental, free-flowing stream that, in any given year, could vary in depth from less than a foot to more than 65 feet. Yet, as all major waterways do, it has influenced life along its banks for thousands of years. Native Americans, French trappers, early settlers, and Colonial armies used it as the region's easiest access to frontier lands.

The U.S. Army Corps of Engineers began dredging sandbars and removing snags in 1825, and they completed the first dam in 1885, enabling glass companies to locate close to the river and take advantage of the country's first oil and gas boom in the late 1800s and early 1900s. The Ohio now carries about 25 percent of the country's total inland waterway traffic.

Beyond the Ohio and the city of Parkersburg, the economic and cultural hub of the region, the Hughes and Little Kanawha rivers flow across rolling hills and farmlands as they wend their way westward. These may not be swift-moving white-water streams, yet canoeists and kayakers who appreciate the easy-flowing waters seek them out, as do anglers who come here to cast a line without having to contend with hordes of others doing the same thing. A dam completed on the North Fork of the Hughes River soon after the turn of the 21st century has added additional water-sports options.

Out in this rural hinterland, there are no big cities—just small, friendly towns with mom-and-pop restaurants, dozens of craftspersons working in unpretentious huts beside their homes, and the 72-mile North Bend Rail Trail, taking hikers, bikers, and equestrians from one tranquil place to another.

COMMUNITIES Cairo was one of the boomtowns of the oil and gas industry around the turn of the 20th century. Today, it has found new life with crafts stores, art galleries, a bicycle-rental shop, and a couple of eateries catering to the scores of

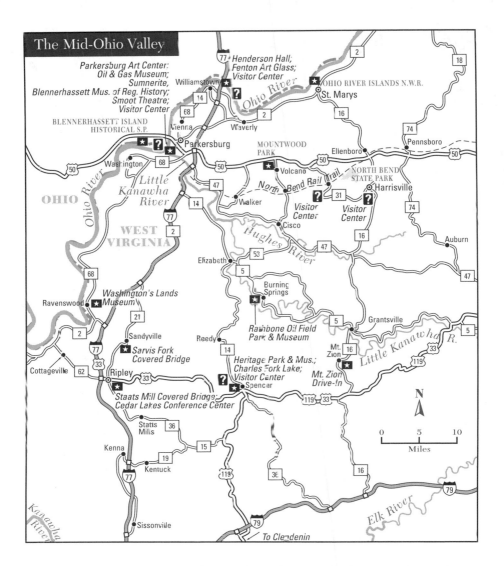

The Mid-Ohio Valley

Parkersburg Art Center;
Oil & Gas Museum;
Sumnerite,
Blennerhassett Mus. of Reg. History;
Smoot Theatre;
Visitor Center

BLENNERHASSETT ISLAND
HISTORICAL S.P.

Henderson Hall;
Fenton Art Glass;
Visitor Center

OHIO RIVER ISLANDS N.W.R.

Williamstown
St. Marys
Ohio River

Vienna
Waverly

Parkersburg
MOUNTWOOD PARK
Ellenboro
Pennsboro

Washington
Volcano
NORTH BEND STATE PARK
Harrisville

Little Kanawha River
North Bend Rail Trail
Visitor Center
Visitor Center

OHIO
Walker
Cisco
Auburn

WEST VIRGINIA
Hughes River

Elizabeth

Burning Springs

Washington's Lands Museum

Ravenswood

Rathbone Oil Field Park & Museum
Grantsville

Sandyville
Reedy
Little Kanawha R.

Sarvis Fork Covered Bridge
Heritage Park & Mus.;
Charles Fork Lake;
Visitor Center
Mt. Zion

Cottageville
Ripley
Mt. Zion Drive-In
Spencer

Staats Mill Covered Bridge;
Cedar Lakes Conference Center

Statts Mills
Kenna
Kentuck

N

0   5   10
Miles

Sissonville

To Clendenin

Kanawha River
Elk River

people who come into town via the North Bend Rail Trail. The post office, still in operation, is almost a museum, and, if you look at the old bank building you can still see the evidence of where a train crashed into it.

Insider's tip: So as to not immediately be marked a visitor, be sure to pronounce the name of the town exactly as it is spelled and not like the famous city in Egypt. Say the word *air* and put a *k* sound on the front and an *o* at the end, and you'll say it correctly.

It may surprise **Parkersburg** visitors that a city whose population is barely more than 30,000 has so many cultural organizations and activities. The **River Cities Symphony Orchestra** and **Parkersburg Choral Society** (www.parkersburg choralsociety.com) offer concerts, theatrical performances are presented in a restored 1920s vaudeville theater, and an arts center sponsors exhibits you would expect to find only in a larger city.

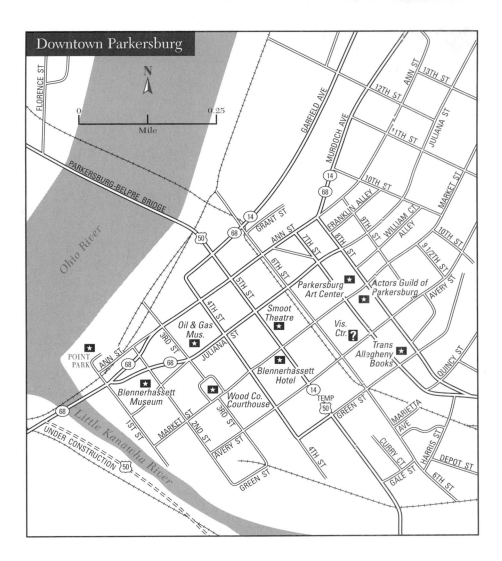

Downtown Parkersburg

One of America's saddest episodes of scandal and possible treason is told through exhibits in the Blennerhassett Museum of Regional History and on the exact land where the story took place—Blennerhassett Island. (For the whole story, see the "A Tragic Story of Riches to Rags" sidebar later in the chapter.) The region's industries are showcased in other museums, and, even though glass manufacturing is greatly diminished from what it once was, Fenton Art Glass is still one of the world's foremost producers of blown art glass—and presents one of the state's best glass factory tours.

Truth or Consequences, New Mexico, can say it was named after a television game show. **Ravenswood**, West Virginia, has the distinction of being named for a fictitious person. Lord Ravenswood was a character in Sir Walter Scott's novel *The Bride of Lammermoor*. A town of about 4,000, its riverfront city park is a good place to have a picnic and watch river barges go chugging along the Ohio River.

Ripley is home to one of the country's longest-running festivals, the Mountain State Art and Craft Fair, as well as the state's largest Fourth of July celebration. Chartered in 1832, the downtown area retains much of a small-town feel with independent businesses clustered around the courthouse square. Like many such places, its outskirts are becoming ever more densely developed with motels, chain restaurants, and big-box retailers.

Like it did in almost every town in this region, the oil boom gave a boost to the economy and population of **Saint Marys**, located on the Ohio River's eastern bank. Cooper shops produced oil barrels, an oil refinery was located next to the river, and two glass factories had scores of employees. All these major industries are gone, and the town has returned to a slower pace of life, providing access to the Ohio River Islands National Wildlife Refuge on Middle Island.

West Virginians of a certain age remember that **Spencer** was once primarily known for the state hospital for the insane and others suffering mental illnesses. The facility closed in 1989, and the town now attracts visitors with its annual Black Walnut Festival and nearby Charles Fork Lake. Spencer was incorporated in 1867 and many buildings from the late 1800s and early 1900s are included in the self-guided walking tour pamphlet, *Historic Buildings in Spencer, West Virginia*, available from the Roane County Chamber of Commerce (see *Guidance*).

GUIDANCE Greater Parkersburg Convention and Visitors Bureau (304-428-1130; 1-800-752-4982; www.greaterparkersburg.com), 350 Seventh St., Parkersburg 26101. Located along the edge of the downtown area, this bureau's employees have a thorough knowledge of the city and surrounding area.

Contact the **Ravenswood Development Authority** (304-273-2621; www.ravenswoodwv.org) before traveling to Ravenswood. If you are passing through, staff at the **City Hall** (304-273-261; 212 Walnut St.) can assist you with your travels.

Ritchie County Economic Development Authority (304-643-2505; www.ritchiecountyeda.com), 217 West Main St., Harrisville 26362. Inside the Thomas H. Harris School Museum, it keeps a full supply of brochures and other information.

The visitor center for the **Ritchie County Tourism & Visitors Bureau** (304-869-4070; www.visitritchiecounty.com; mailing address: P.O. Box 116, Harrisville 26362) is located in Ellenboro.

Like most such organizations, the **Roane County Chamber of Commerce** (304-927-1780; www.roanechamberwv.org), 207 Court St., Spencer 25276, is primarily a business organization, but its employees are also helpful in providing information to visitors.

A **West Virginia Welcome Center** (304-375-2700) is located a few feet from I-77 exit 185 and is one of the largest of these state facilities. Information concerning this region and the entire state is available here.

GETTING THERE *By air*: There are commuter connections from Washington, DC to Parkersburg's **Mid-Ohio Valley Airport** (304-464-5113; www.flymov.com). Charleston's **Yeager Airport** (304-344-8033; www.yeagerairport.com) is barely more than an hour away from Parkersburg, while the **North Central West Virginia Airport** (304-842-3400; www.flyckb.com) near Clarksburg is less than 40 miles from the eastern portion of this region.

By bus: **Greyhound** (1-800-231-2222; www.greyhound.com) stops to deliver and pick up passengers at 520 Juliana St. in Parkersburg.

By car: **I-77** is the most convenient way to enter this region from the north, west, and south. You could follow **WV 2** from I-64 at Huntington for a slower-paced, but certainly more scenic, route along the Ohio River. **US 50** comes into the region from the east and west.

GETTING AROUND *By bus:* The **Mid-Ohio Valley Transit Authority** (304-422-4100; www.easyriderbus.com) has buses that follow routes throughout Parkersburg and into neighboring Vienna.

MEDICAL EMERGENCIES

Grantsville
Minnie Hamilton Healthcare Center (304-354-9244; www.mhhcc.com), 186 Hospital Dr.

Parkersburg
Camden-Clark Memorial Hospital (304-424-2111; www.ccmh.org), 800 Garfield Ave.

St. Joseph's Hospital (304-424-4111; www.stjosephs-hospital.com), 1824 Murdoch Ave.

Ripley
Jackson General Hospital (304-372-2731; www.jacksongeneral.com), 122 Pinell St. Within sight of I-79 exit 138.

Spencer
Roane General Hospital (304-927-4444; www.roanegeneralhospital.com), 200 Hospital Dr.

✳ To See

COVERED BRIDGES

Ripley
The 97-foot-long **Staats Mill Covered Bridge** was constructed in 1888 and saw almost continuous use until it was moved to the Cedar Lakes Conference Center (see *Lodging*) in 1982, where it was restored and opened to pedestrians.

Sandyville
Constructed in 1889 and more than 100 feet long, the **Sarvis Fork Covered Bridge** was dismantled and moved to its present location in 1924. From Sandyville, follow WV 21 north for 1.2 miles and turn right onto WV 21/15.

DRIVING TOURS, SCENIC & HISTORIC The **Little Kanawha Parkway Byway** follows WV 14 and WV 5 for more than 77 miles along the twisting route of its namesake river, providing views of the waterway and access to some of the state's most pastoral scenery and smallest towns. Look for the small Sportsman's Park near Elizabeth if you need a break from driving. It has a short paved walking trail.

Available from the Oil and Gas Museum (see *Museums*) or the Greater Parkersburg Convention and Visitors Bureau (see *Guidance*), the **Oil, Gas & Civil War**

A CRAFTSPERSON HARD AT WORK AT
FENTON ART GLASS

Heritage District brochure provides details on a driving tour taking you to such diverse places as Camp "Big Bend," a place where Confederate "guerrilla" soldiers gathered; Ritchie Mines, whose asphalt paved Pennsylvania Avenue in front of the White House in Washington, DC; and Burning Springs, site of the world's oldest producing oil well.

GUIDED TOURS ↑ ✪ **Fenton Art Glass** (304-375-6122; 1-800-319-7793; www.fentonartglass.com), 700 Elizabeth St., Williamstown. Free tours Mon.–Fri.; last tour begins early afternoon. If you are going to tour only one West Virginia glass factory, this is the one. Yes, Fenton has been making glass for more than 100 years, and their products are considered some of the world's finest, but I say visit here because their tour is one of the best and most complete in the state. From the beginning video in the adjoining museum to the ending in the gift shop, the narrated tours take you into the factory for close contact with every step of the glass-making process, showing you how many skilled craftspersons it takes to produce just one piece of glass.

HISTORIC CHURCH Several miles southeast of Elizabeth, a sign on WV 5 directs you onto a narrow paved, then dirt, road for several miles to the **Ruble Church**. The drive is definitely worth it. The small log building was built in 1835 and is one of the state's oldest attended churches. Kerosene lamps provide light and an old woodstove the heat. Pre–Civil War graves are in the cemetery beside the church, whose sentiments are displayed on a plaque above the door: ALL ARE WELCOME HERE EXCEPT THOSE OF NORTHERN PRINCIPLES.

HISTORIC HOMES

Parkersburg
Cook House (304-422-6961; www.jl parkersburg.org), 1301 Murdock Ave. Built in 1825–29, the Federal-style, T-shaped Cook House, with eight rooms and five fireplaces, is the second-oldest brick home still at its original location in Parkersburg. The Junior League of Parkersburg provides guided tours by request.

Williamstown
Henderson Hall (304-375-2129), on WV 21 about 2 miles south of

COOK HOUSE

Williamstown. Open daily 12–5. Small admission fee. A visit to the Italianate villa–style Henderson Hall is an immersion into one family's history. The mansion was in the Henderson family from the time it was built in the mid-1800s until 2007, when it was willed to the Oil and Gas Museum (see *Museums*), and, other than a few modern conveniences, very little has been changed and much has been saved. There are 100-year-old wool shawls, the original land grant document to the family from Patrick Henry, an 1868 letter from Robert E. Lee to Elizabeth Ann

A TRAGIC STORY OF RICHES TO RAGS

In 1764, Harman Blennerhassett was born into a distinguished family that could trace it roots to England's King John. Living a life of luxury, he inherited his father's fortune but faced scandal for marrying his niece, Margaret. Wishing to leave the outrage behind, they, along with servants, immigrated to the United States, eventually reaching the American frontier and purchasing 169 acres on the fifth-largest Ohio River island. Three years later, their magnificent mansion, costing a staggering $60,000, was completed, and the couple lived a happy life.

That is, until Aaron Burr visited and convinced Blennerhassett to become part of a plan to invade Mexican territory. Historians disagree as to just exactly what the men's intent was, but at the time President Thomas Jefferson concluded the two planned to establish their own country, and he issued warrants of treason for them. Leaving the island, and eventually acquitted of the charge, Harman and Margaret failed in an attempt at a cotton plantation and sailed for England. More or less penniless, he died on the island of Guernsey in 1831, and Margaret lived out the rest of her days in poverty in New York.

The mansion burned to the ground in 1811, but archaeological research enabled its reconstruction in the late 1900s. You can now get a glimpse of the past by visiting the **Blennerhassett Island Historical State Park** (304-420-4800; www.blennerhassettislandstatepark.com), which can only be reached by a 20-minute, lightly narrated stern-wheeler ride from Parkersburg's Point Park.

Trips to the island really start at the **Blennerhassett Museum of Regional History** (304-420-4800; Second and Juliana streets), where you should devote some time to the video providing background on the island and looking over exhibits of Native American artifacts, items from archaeological digs, and a display devoted to the history of stern-wheelers.

There are so many things to see and do once you're on the island that you should plan to spend several hours. As costumed docents provide an excellent narration about the Blennerhassetts and a tour of the house, remembering that the original structure was built at the turn of the 19th century will make you marvel even more at the magnificent rooms of walnut

Henderson, copious amounts of family correspondence, tableware hand-painted by Rosalie Henderson, and an 1875 rosewood grand piano. I could go on and on. Suffice it to say, the home is a testament to the value of being pack rats—items eventually become old and of historic value.

HISTORIC SITE Sumnerite (304-422-0985; 304-295-9639), 1016 Avery St., Parkersburg. Tours by appointment; donations accepted. Opened in 1862, Sumner

walls, gold trim, plaster moldings done by Italian craftsmen, and extravagant furnishings (some of which belonged to the Blennerhassetts).

If you don't want to walk the trail system that takes you to other parts of the island, you may rent a bicycle or take a horse-drawn wagon ride. (*Insider's tip:* I found that the narration on the wagon ride added greatly to my understanding of the Blennerhassetts' life on the island.) Loaner binoculars are available at the gift shop for those interested in looking for the more than 100 birds seen here, including herons, ducks, gulls, hawks, hummingbirds, and more than a dozen species of warblers. Picnic tables are scattered throughout the island, and a concession stand provides light food and snacks (great lemonade!).

The Blennerhassett Museum of Regional History is closed Mon. from Apr. to late Dec., and only open Sat. and Sun. from Jan.–Apr. The stern-wheeler to the island is closed Mon. from May to early Sept., and it only operates Thurs.–Sun. from early Sept. through Oct. The park and all the island amenities are closed the rest of the year. Adult fees: museum $4, boat ride $8, mansion tour $4. Fees for children (ages 3–12): museum $2, boat ride $7, mansion tour $2.

BLENNERHASSETT ISLAND

School was the nation's first free African American school below the Mason-Dixon Line. The school (actually, its two-story gymnasium; the rest of the school has been demolished) now serves as a museum and community center. Displays consist of information about the Underground Railroad, hundreds of photographs of past teachers and students, and memorabilia from the city's first black families.

MUSEUMS & ART GALLERIES

Burning Springs

Rathbone Oil Field Park and Museum (304-485-5446; www.oilandgasmuseum .com), on WV 5 south of Elizabeth. Operated under the auspices of the Oil and Gas Museum in Parkersburg and open dawn to dusk for self-guided tours; a mini-museum (very small admission fee) is often open Sat. and Sun. Visiting this site during the week when the little museum is closed is almost like stepping into the Twilight Zone. No one is here, yet the park has antique operating equipment, old parts, and an oil derrick that you can wander among at will. The site is next to the Little Kanawha River, so you can also sit on one of the benches and watch the water flow past. If adventurous, traipse into the woods to search for hidden pieces of old equipment.

Harrisville

Thomas M. Harris School Museum (304-643-2505; www.schoolmuseum .ritchiecounty.biz), 217 West Main St. Open Tues.–Thurs. Donations accepted. Local-history displays include school items, veterans' exhibits, and the history of the region's industries.

Parkersburg

⟂ **Oil and Gas Museum** (304-485-5446; www.oilandgasmuseum.com), 119 Third St. Open daily; very small admission fee. Like coal, the oil and gas industries have been major players in the state's history, alternately booming to provide jobs and create personal fortunes and busting to leave behind broken lives and abandoned towns. This museum is the largest in the state to tell the story. Be sure to start with the video that illustrates how the wealth derived from these enterprises greatly influenced the creation of West Virginia. Then allow a minimum of two hours to cover the multiple floors of displays, with authentic pieces from early industry days to the present. There are also exhibits paying homage to other Parkersburg businesses, such as electrical insulation, textiles, glass, and steel. Outside are pieces of equipment much too large to put into the building and a nicely painted mural of the city's history.

OIL AND GAS MUSEUM

🌿 ✎ ♿ ⟂ **Parkersburg Art Center** (304-485-3859; www.parkersburgart center.org), 725 Market St. Open Wed.–Sat. Very small admission fee; children free. The center's Federal-style building has more than 35,000 square feet of exhibition, office, and classroom space, including a large gallery whose exhibit changes every two months. A smaller gallery has monthly exhibits, and a third one features the works of local teenagers. Special events—such as Christmas trees decorated as if famous artists had done them—take place year-round. The center is one of Parkersburg's most outstanding features and can easily stand up to comparison with other such places found in much larger cities.

Ravenswood

Washington's Lands Museum and Sayre Log House (304-273-2621; 304-372-5343; www.museumsofwv.org), on WV 2 south of downtown Ravenswood. Open Sun. afternoon May–Sept. (times and dates have been known to change). Donations accepted. It seems that no matter where you go in West Virginia, George Washington was there before you—and probably owned some of the land, too. He camped here on the Great Bend of the Ohio River in 1770, eventually bringing thousands of acres into his possession. Having said that, George is only a small part of this museum, housed on the two floors of what was once the powerhouse for locks on the Ohio River. The Jackson County Historical Society operates the museum, and the emphasis is on local history, with displays concerning pioneer, Civil War, and Victorian times. The adjacent Sayre Log House has been restored to the 1840–1880 period.

Spencer

Heritage Park and Museum (304-927-1640; www.cityofspencer.com), downtown. Open 10–2 on the first Fri. of the month, May–Oct., and for special events. (Open times and dates seem to change frequently; call ahead.) Donations accepted. Items of local interest in this former train depot include an old dentist's office, displays about veterans from the region, and a barrel made from a hollow tree trunk. To fully appreciate what is here, you should ask the docent to accompany you and explain things. Next door is a one-room schoolhouse (with a kitchen!) and an oil derrick left over from the boom days.

While here, ask directions to the **Tanner Homeplace** (it's a short walk away). The site is actually a small cave created by an overhanging rock that the town's first settlers, Samuel and Sudna Tanner, lived in for several months while building a more permanent home.

Also see Parkersburg City Park under *Green Space—Parks*.

SCENIC VIEWS Quincy Park, 13th St., Parkersburg, looks like an average residential neighborhood park with a playground and picnic facilities—until you get out of the car. Take just a few steps into the park and the ground drops dramatically, opening up a panoramic view of downtown Parkersburg, the Ohio River, and Blennerhassett Island.

For more intimate contact with the river, take a walk or sit on one of the benches in **Point Park** at the foot of

THE TANNER HOMEPLACE

Second St. in Parkersburg. Here, at the confluence of the Little Kanawha and Ohio rivers, you can laze away a few hours watching barges and other river traffic, imagining what this landscape must have looked like when George Washington stopped here on a trip down the Ohio in 1770.

✳ To Do

BICYCLING

Cairo

The Cairo Supply Company/Country Trail Bikes, LLC (304-628-3100), Town Square. Open daily. Make a stop at this shop, within inches of the North Bend Rail Trail, to rent a bike or have yours serviced. Also take time to look around the old-style general store, with grocery items, local-history books, a small memorabilia display, and proprietors who have a vast knowledge of the history of this region.

Spencer

Charles Fork Lake (304-927-1640; www.charlesfork.org; www.cityofspencer .com). From Spencer drive south on US 119 to WV 36, turn left, and look for the sign for the lake. Local volunteers have built one of the state's best mountain biking venues, with more than 25 miles of trails on 1,700 acres of land surrounding a mile-long lake. Most of the routes are single track, and there are many ups and downs and roots and rocks. Just about the time you feel you can move a bit faster, there's a sharp turn or a stiff uphill—but there is such a variety that there's something here for every skill level. (An obstacle I hadn't anticipated is the abundant wildlife. More than once I had to swerve to miss a kamikaze squirrel or wildly flapping turkey.) The Web site www.charlesfork.org contains very detailed descriptions of each of the pathways, which are also open to hikers.

Primitive camping is permitted in a meadow close to the trailhead, and canoeists and anglers are encouraged to make use of the lake, which is stocked by the Division of Natural Resources. Things are really busy here when scores of bike riders show up for the annual Tour de Lake Race in May.

Vienna

Vienna Bicycle Shop (304-295-5469), 2910 Grand Central Ave. Sales and service.

Also see *Rail Trails*, and Mountwood Park under *Green Space—Parks*.

BIRDING See *Green Space—Wildlife Refuges*.

BOAT RENTALS See Mountwood Park under *Green Space—Parks*.

BOWLING

Parkersburg

Emerson Bowling Lanes (304-485-7406), 1501 36th St. Forty-six lanes with computerized scoring.

Pike Street Lanes (304-485-6000), 2605 Pike St. Bowl on one of the 32 lanes.

Ravenswood

Raven Lanes (304-273-4475), 241 Washington St. Bowling, pool tables, games, and a restaurant.

Spencer Lanes (304-927-6521), Arnoldsburg Rd. Bowling, pool tables, and games.

FISHING The Eastern Panhandle and Potomac Highlands receive the most press about fishing opportunities in West Virginia. However, the Mid-Ohio Valley's waterways should not be overlooked or discounted. Fishing from a boat or along the banks of the **Ohio River** can net you largemouth bass, catfish, sauger, crappie, and walleye.

Located 3 miles northwest of Pennsboro, 300-acre **Tracy Lake Park** contains an 11-acre lake stocked with trout in Jan. and Mar. Used almost exclusively by locals, the park is one of the least crowded and quietest places to cast a line that you will find anywhere.

The Division of Natural Resources says the **Little Kanawha River** is one of state's best smallmouth bass and muskie waters, along with the **Hughes River** and its **South Fork** and **North Fork**.

In addition, the division stocks trout, largemouth and smallmouth bass, bluegill, crappie, and channel catfish in a number of small lakes in the southern portion of this region. Being in a part of the state not all that well known for its fishing, you may be the only person casting a line in 41-acre **Rollins Lake**, west of Ripley; 72-acre **Charles Fork Lake**, south of Spencer; 15-acre **Turkey Run Lake**, on the northern edge of Ravenswood; or 224-acre **Woodrum Lake**, near Kentuck.

If you want some river fishing, there are boat ramps giving access to **Mill Creek** at the intersection of US 33 and WV 2 near Millwood, and at the Jackson County Fairground east of Cottageville. Another one in Ravenswood provides access to hundreds of miles of the **Ohio River** and is large enough to handle any size fishing boat.

Angler's Xstream (304-485-6911; 1-877-909-6911; www.anglersxstream.com), 2109 Camden Ave., Parkersburg. Angler's Xstream is an authorized Orvis dealer if you need any tackle or specialized equipment and clothing.

Also see Charles Fork Lake under *Bicycling* and Mountwood Park under *Green Space—Parks*.

GOLF

Harrisville
North Bend Golf Course (304-643-2206), 945 West High St. A nine-hole course open to the public a short distance from North Bend State Park.

Mineral Wells
New Woodridge Plantation Golf Club (304-489-1800; 1-800-869-1001; www .woodbridgegolfclub.com), 301 Woodridge Dr. Several sources have said that the Bermuda fairways, bent-grass greens, pro shop, PGA-qualified instructional staff, and tiered driving range with varied distance greens rank this course within the state's top five.

Parkersburg
Worthington Golf Club (304-428-4297), 34124 Roseland Ave. The Worthington was constructed in 1941 on flat terrain for easy walking. A creek flows throughout

the entire course, requiring shots across the stream at six holes from men's tees and four holes from women's tees.

Ravenswood

Greenhills Golf Club (304-273-3396; 304-273-4121; www.greenhillsgolfclub .com; mailing address: P.O. Box 206, Ravenswood 26164), on WV 56. The front nine are long and hilly; the back nine are shorter.

GOLF, MINIATURE See Parkersburg City Park and Mountwood Park under *Green Space—Parks*, and *Lodging—Resort*.

HIKING See Charles Fork Lake under *Bicycling, Rail Trails*, and Mountwood Park under *Green Space—Parks*.

KAYAKING & CANOEING The slow-moving waters of the **Little Kanawha** and **Hughes rivers** and their tributaries attract paddlers who are not looking for the thrill of whitewater. For the most part, these streams offer easy float trips, most often passing by banks thick with lush vegetation and trees that shade the streams, but remember to always be on the lookout for obstacles, such as old dams and many, many fallen trees.

The Division of Natural Resources has constructed a number of access points, including a ramp into the Little Kanawha River at Sportsman's Park in Elizabeth, and one into the Hughes River on WV 47 about 1 mile east of Casco.

Also see Charles Fork Lake under *Bicycling*.

OUTDOOR ADVENTURE ✇ ♿ **Adventure Pursuit** (304-485-0911; mailing address: P.O. Box 431, Parkersburg 26102). This has to be one of the most distinctive outdoors outfitters in the state—and maybe the country. It is a nonprofit organization that will advise you on area outdoor activities, arrange guided trips, and provide rental bicycles, kayaks, and other outdoor equipment. Although the services are available to anyone, Adventure Pursuit is dedicated to helping those with special needs enjoy these recreational opportunities. There is a lift on their boat dock, and employees are well versed in working with those who have physical or mental challenges.

RAIL TRAILS Never underestimate the power of a group of citizens banding together to achieve a common goal, as the **North Bend Rail Trail**, administered by North Bend State Park (see *Green Space—Parks*), is the result of one man's vision and hard work and many people's collaborative efforts. After the CSX Corporation abandoned its rail line between Clarksburg and Parkersburg, Dick Bias dedicated himself to the development of a rail trail. Upon establishing the North Bend Rails to Trails Foundation, he led negotiations with CSX to purchase the corridor and is credited with raising the majority of the $350,000 that funded the initial phase of the project.

The line was built in the 1850s as the Northwestern Virginia Railroad and was soon incorporated into the Baltimore and Ohio Railroad's main line, which stretched westward to St. Louis. More than 30 bridges and 12 tunnels were constructed to enable the line to pass through the hills and rolling terrain of western West Virginia. Used for both freight and passengers, the line serviced the region's booming oil and gas industry and helped establish many of the small towns that still exist. The number of passengers began to decline in the 1950s as Americans became enamored with the automobile to supply their transportation needs, while the freight train made its final run in 1984.

Today, the North Bend Rail Trail is part of the West Virginia State Park system and runs 72 miles from I-77 at Parkersburg to Wolf Summit in Harrison County. (Plans call for it to eventually connect Parkersburg and Clarksburg.) Incorporated into the coast-to-coast American Discovery Trail, the route goes into small communities, through 10 tunnels (bring a flashlight) and over 36 bridges, while providing options for sight-seeing, dining, lodging, or camping (in designated sites) without venturing far from the trail.

Walking through the darkness of one of the tunnels, you may not really want to hear the story of the Ghost of Silver Run. A local legend states that the shadowy figure of a young woman dressed in a flowing white gown occasionally appears to those traveling through the tunnel. One account says a passing train struck her many years ago, while another version holds that she disappeared one night while riding the train to meet her beau in Parkersburg.

Like the Greenbrier River Trail (see *To Do—Bicycling* in the "Reaching for the Sky—Spruce Knob, Seneca Rocks, and Cranberry Glades" chapter), the North Bend Rail Trail is a great place to introduce friends to the joys of hiking, biking, or horseback riding without subjecting them to harsh or isolated terrain. The pathway has barely perceptible little ups and downs, picnic areas and vault toilets located at convenient intervals, and frequent road crossings if the need for help should arise.

Major access points include the towns of Wolf Summit, West Union, Pennsboro, Ellenboro, and Cairo. The western terminus may be reached by taking I-79 exit 174 and turning east on WV 47, but almost immediately making a right onto old WV 47. Continue 0.7 mile, turn right onto Happy Valley Rd., and go another 0.4 mile.

SKATING

Parkersburg
Skate Country (304-422-6600), Sixth Ave. and Gladstone St. The rink is open on a very irregular schedule that seems to vary from month to month. Call ahead.

Spencer
Roane Recreational Center (304-927-3385), 130 Steele Hollow Rd. Open Fri. and Sat. evenings; only Sat. evening during the summer. In addition to the rink, patrons can play video arcade games, pool, and air hockey.

SWIMMING The swimming pools in Vienna's **Jackson Park** (304-494-2531) on 34th St., Parkersburg's **Southwood Park** (304-424-8572) on Blizzard Dr., Ripley's **City Park** (304-372-8543) on Second Ave., Ravenswood's **North Park** (304-273-2621), and Spencer's **Washington Park and Municipal Pool** (304-927-3152) are open during the usual summer months.

Also see North Bend State Park and Parkersburg City Park under *Green Space—Parks*.

WAGON RIDES Wagon master John Smith hand builds the wagons and carriages you will be riding in if you take trips with the **Hardly Able Carriage Company** (304-869-3051; 1-877-564-8074; www.hardlyablecarriage.com; mailing address: P. O. Box 81, Ellenboro 26346) in either North Bend or Blennerhassett Island state parks. The short ride at North Bend takes you on a spur trail of the North Bend Rail Trail, while those on the island are narrated to provide historical information. Longer three-hour trips include many miles along the rail trail, but to really enjoy the earlier days of wagon riding, join one of the company's three-day camping trips, where you'll partake in a cowboy cookout under the stars. You can either take part in a scheduled trip or get a group of six together and have your own outing.

A WAGON RIDE WITH THE HARDLY ABLE CARRIAGE COMPANY IN NORTH BEND STATE PARK

When I asked John how he came up with the company name, he said, "I was hardly able to think of a name, so that became it."

WALKING TOURS A number of Parkersburg residents amassed large fortunes during the region's oil and gas boom in the late 1800s, and many used their wealth to build palatial homes just north of downtown in an area now known as the **Julia-Ann Square Historic District**. More than 30 homes in the quiet, tree-lined residential neighborhood are featured in a walking-tour brochure available from the Greater Parkersburg Convention and Visitors Bureau (see *Guidance*). Among the many outstanding houses, the 16-room, 1868 Second Empire home at 904 Juliana St. and the 1855 "castle" at 1209 Ann St. impressed me the most.

A CLOSE-UP OF THE DETAIL ON PARKERSBURG'S RICHARDSON-ROMANESQUE COURTHOUSE

A separate pamphlet has the details of a **Historical Walking Tour of Parkersburg** in the downtown area, where most of the buildings described were constructed from 1870 to 1915. Be sure to seek out the Richardson-Romanesque Courthouse. Walk around it, and you'll be amazed at the quantity and quality of artwork and figurines done by Italian stonemasons. Along the exterior walls are a ram's head, gargoyles, winged angels' faces, two pairs of miners, and more. See if you can pick out the two lions and identify how they are different.

Susan Shepherd leads the **Ghost Tours of Parkersburg** (304-428-7978; www .hauntedparkersburg.com) that take place on Fri. and Sat. nights from late Sept. to early Nov. Beginning from The Blennerhassett hotel (see *Lodging*) at 7:30, the tours (and Ms. Shepherd) have gained such fame that they have been featured on ABC Family's *Scariest Places on Earth*.

✳ Green Space

ARBORETUM ♿ The **John Bloomberg Arboretum** is really just a small plot of land next to the Parkersburg Library at 31st St. and Jefferson Ave. in Parkersburg. Yet, this little bit of green space has a lot packed into it. Numbered posts are keyed to a brochure available at the information kiosk, and you can find out tidbits of information on more than 30 trees and close to 50 types of native grasses, in addition to enjoying the fluttering of butterflies and melodies of songbirds.

PARKS

Cairo
♿ **North Bend State Park** (304-643-2931; www.northbendsp.com; 202 North Bend Park Road, Cairo 26337), off WV 14 east of Cairo. North Bend State Park is not officially one of West Virginia's "resort" state parks, yet it has many of the amenities often offered by such a place. Guest rooms ($65–99) in the lodge have nice views of the park, the restaurant (entrées $7.95–18.95) is one of the better ones found within the state park system, deluxe cottages (open year-round) with heat and TVs are on a ridgeline nicely secluded from park traffic, and the campground (open mid-Apr. through Nov.) has hookups, a dump station, and a central bathhouse. An outdoor pool is open Memorial Day to Labor Day; nature and recreation programs are offered all year; there is a miniature golf course; and the trail system, which connects with the 72-mile North Bend Rail Trail, includes the handicapped-accessible Extra-Mile Trail. Don't want to walk or bike? Take a horse-drawn wagon ride (see *To Do—Wagon Rides*).

The completion of a 300-acre lake on the North Fork of the Hughes River in 2003 has added even more things to do in the park, such as fishing for bass, channel catfish, and muskie. On Fri., Sat., and Sun., North Bend Outfitters (304-299-1768; 643-2931; www.northbendoutfitters.com) offers kayak, canoe, johnboat, and bicycle rentals. Volunteers are at work on a 25-mile multiuse trail that will encircle the lake, and additional camping opportunities close to the body of water have been constructed.

Parkersburg
Parkersburg City Park (304-424-8572), Park Ave. between 18th and 23rd streets. Much more than the typical small municipal park, Parkersburg City Park is a large green space in a residential neighborhood. Come here to stretch your legs on the walking trail (heavily used in the early morning), take a swim in the pool, make use of various game courts, glide across the lake in a rented paddleboat, play miniature golf, or wander from one piece of public art to another. When it's time for a break, sit in the Gossip Corner gazebo and join in on the lively conversations.

Also within the park, the small **Cooper Log Cabin Museum** (open Sun. afternoon Memorial Day–Labor Day) is one of the state's few two-story log cabins still in existence from the pioneer days (built circa 1805). Operated by the Daughters of American Pioneers, its exhibits provide a quick overview of the region's history. The days of the Civil War are here (complete with a skull damaged by a bullet hole), as are surveyors' tools from the oil and gas boom days. Upstairs, the items are more Victorian in nature, with clothing, dolls, and bedroom furniture. The museum is so small that you can see everything somewhat quickly, which is good for those who want to learn about the area they are visiting but are limited on time.

PARKERSBURG CITY PARK

Volcano

Mountwood Park (304-679-3611; 1-877-1688; www.mountwoodpark.org; 1014 Waverly Rd., Waverly 26184), on US 50 east of Parkersburg. Sometimes, a lack of money can be a good thing, especially for those of us who like our parks more on the natural side. Due to funding cutbacks, many of the expansive outdoor recreational facilities originally proposed for Mountwood Park in the 1970s were never built. This is not to say that there is a lack of activities to engage in. A launch is available for those who bring their own boat to the 50-acre lake, decks and platforms provide barrier-free access for fishing for trout and bass, and a marina rents paddleboats, canoes, johnboats, and kayaks. Miniature golf, game courts, ball fields, and a disc-golf course cater to the competitive-minded. Picnic shelters and more than 200 tables enable families to enjoy outdoor gatherings. A campground, located on a disjunct portion of the park a short distance away, has full hookups, modern restrooms, and hot showers. Two "beach" houses next to lake are also available for rent.

It may sound like a lot, but all of these activities and facilities are located on a relatively small portion of the park, leaving the rest of the 2,600 acres undisturbed. Several years ago, a dedicated group of local mountain bikers worked with officials to rehabilitate and expand the park's network of trails, creating some of the most environmentally sound biking and hiking pathways I have ever seen volunteers build. Sidehill sections are banked and shored up correctly, switchbacks are long and wide, and extremely steep sections are kept to a minimum. Their superb construction should keep the routes in good shape for years to come.

On rolling topography located less than 20 miles from the Ohio River, the 35-mile trail system starts with an initial short, quick rise from the lake, but it continues with just minor changes in elevation before gradually descending back to the starting point. In addition to going through deciduous forestland populated by squirrels, rabbits, foxes, chipmunks, and turkeys, it can be a lesson in the region's oil and natural-gas industry history, with interpretive placards placed at strategic locations. One such spot is the ruins of the Stiles Mansion. The huge house, known as Thornhill, was built in the shape of a Maltese Cross in 1874 by William Cooper Stiles. As you go around its foundation, grown over by honeysuckle and other vegetation, you can get only a small idea of how large it was. With three stories and 25 rooms, it contained Wood County's first bathtub and was adorned by a rambling porch reached by steep stone steps. Stiles was born in Philadelphia, Pennsylvania, and was one of the first and most successful of the investors and operators in the oil fields of the region.

WILDLIFE REFUGES

St. Marys

Ohio River Islands National Wildlife Refuge (304-375-2923; www.fws.gov /northeast/ohioriverislands; 3983 Waverly Rd., Willliamstown 26187), access from George St. in St. Marys. Established in 1990, the Ohio River Islands National Wildlife Refuge currently consists of more than 20 islands and several mainland tracts in Pennsylvania, West Virginia, and Kentucky. Eventually, the refuge will include islands along the length of the Ohio River to where it empties into the Mississippi, helping to protect, restore, and enhance habitat for wildlife native to the river's floodplain. Close to 200 species of birds use refuge lands and surrounding waters, including prothonotary warblers, bald eagles, and osprey. Mallards, wood ducks, and Canada geese are some of the most common waterfowl seen here, while buffleheads, mergansers, and scaups are frequent winter visitors. Deer, squirrels, raccoons, opossums, groundhogs, cottontail rabbits, foxes, frogs, toads, and snakes are frequently seen, and muskrats and beavers swim along the water's edge. Smallmouth and largemouth bass, white bass, and catfish are just a few of the 50 or so species found in refuge waters, as well as more than 40 species of freshwater mussels.

Unbeknown to many people, the Ohio River (up to the low-water mark on its western shore) is part of West Virginia, which enables the refuge to be included in a guide to the state. The island is one of only two in the refuge that are currently accessible by automobile. A nature trail on level terrain takes visitors through several different types of vegetative cover and wildlife habitats. The island is the perfect spot to bring city-bound children who have never been delighted by a rabbit hopping from the underbrush, the cry of an osprey flying overhead with a fish grasped in its talons, or the bark of a red fox calling out to its young.

Vienna

❦ ♿ **McDonough Wildlife Refuge** (304-295-4473). From 1-77 exit 179, follow WV 68 for 3 miles, turn right onto Rosemar Ave., and continue another 5.2 miles. (The entranceway is one of the fanciest I've ever seen for a wildlife refuge—stone pillars topped by a sculpted deer and turkey.) Administered by the Vienna Department of Parks and Recreation, the McDonough Wildlife Refuge is a favorite hiking spot for locals and a hidden gem for visitors, as it is a quick and easy escape from urban noises. Pets (on leashes) are permitted, too. Within its 277 acres is a well-marked and well-maintained trail system passing through a surprisingly scenic and diverse landscape of ponds, wetlands, meadows, bottomland forests, and wooded ridgelines populated by deer, coyote, fox, geese, and turkey.

✳ Lodging

RESORT

Ripley 25271

Cedar Lakes Conference Center
(304-372-7860; www.cedarlakes.com;
mailing address: HC 88, Box 21).
From I-77 exit 132, follow WV 21
North, turn right onto Cedar Lakes
Dr., and continue 3.5 miles. Home of
the Mountain State Art and Craft Fair
and weeklong arts classes (see "The
Granddaddy of Them All" sidebar later
in the chapter), the 450-acre conference center is not a luxury resort, but
rather a low-key place where you can
hike, mountain bike, take a swim in the
pool, and play miniature golf. It's popular with area residents who come
here to picnic or have a family
reunion. Again, lodging options are not
lavish, but there is a choice of motel-
type rooms, cabins, cottages, and dormitory rooms. Lodging rates start at
about $50.

MOTELS & HOTELS

Parkersburg 26101

&. **The Blennerhassett** (304-422-
3131; 1-800-262-2536; www.theblen
nerhassett.com), 320 Market St. A five-
story turret, palladium windows, and
other architectural features from the
late 1800s blend with modern amenities like wireless Internet access, exercise facilities, and first-class dining to
maintain The Blennerhassett's reputation for grace, sophistication, and service that it had when it was built in
1889. Rich wood accentuates the lobby
and hallways, rooms are furnished with
Chippendale reproductions, triple-
sheeted beds have feather and synthetic pillows and padded headboards, and
oversized bathrooms (the one in my
room was almost as large as my own
home's living room) have glass-
enclosed corner showers with rain-
shower heads. Be sure to have at least

MCDONOUGH WILDLIFE REFUGE

one of your meals in the hotel's restaurant, Spats (see *Dining Out*).
$119–250.

INNS

Harrisville 26362

Heritage Inn (304-643-2938; 1-800-
528-7944), 315 West Main St. Constructed from 1926 to 1933, the inn was
known for many years as "the stone
building" for its 18-inch-thick walls.
Refurbished in the 1990s, all the guest
accommodations are now suites, so
there is the luxury of space. Each room
has a private bath, different decorating
scheme, and modest antique furnishings. Close to North Bend State Park
and its adjoining lake. Rates start at $75.

Pennsboro 26415

The Legacy Inn (304-659-3551; www
.thelegacyinn.com), 203 Broadway St.
Directly across from the North Bend
Rail Trail, the inn is inside a converted
warehouse. Don't let this deter you, as
the owners (and volunteers) have done
a nice job with the conversion and
there are now 14 rooms, some with
whirlpool tubs and all with a private
bath. Great rates, too. $59–99.

BED & BREAKFASTS

Cairo 26337

✤ **The Log House Homestead Bed
& Breakfast** (304-628-3249; www.log

househomestead.com; mailing address: Homestead Cove Lane, Rte. 1, Box 223B), off US 50. A stay at The Log House Homestead is more than a retreat to a quiet country house where you can rock the hours away on the front porch beside a pond surrounded by lush vegetation. It is a chance to admire the handiwork of Dick and Martha Hartley, who, almost all by themselves, cut, hauled, hand-hewed, and built (using old-style tools and construction techniques) this replica of an early-1800s two-story house. The result is true rustic luxury. There are all the old things—dovetailed logs, blacksmith-fashioned thumb latches and door hinges, a stone fireplace, and hand-split roof shingles—mixed with modern bathrooms, air-conditioning, refrigerator, microwave, and a Jacuzzi for two. The whole house is yours, and you'll get to meet the Hartleys (who live in the home across the pond) when they prepare a full country breakfast for you. The B&B is just 0.25 mile from the North Bend Rail Trail, can accommodate up to five people, and accepts children age 12 and older. Smoke free and no pets permitted. $105–140.

Parkersburg 26101

Old Carriage House (304-428-9588; www.oldcarriagehouse.com), 118 12th St. The Old Carriage House B&B is surrounded by the other homes of the historic Julia-Ann Square district. Built around 1895, it's a three-story brick home with an oak staircase and floors, curved ceilings, and cherry and oak woodwork. Each guest room has a sitting area and a four-poster bed, and period antiques and art are found throughout the house. After a long day of traveling, I found the patio, with its lovingly cared-for flowers, to be the place to relax and have an easy conversation with other guests. Joseph H. Diss Debar, the designer of the West

THE LOG HOUSE HOMESTEAD BED & BREAKFAST

Virginia state seal, lived in the original carriage house beside the patio. $110–120.

Ravenswood 26164

Chestnut Acres Bed & Breakfast (304-273-9824), 1 Chestnut Lane. A stay at Chestnut Acres is a chance to live, at least for a short time, the

OLD CARRIAGE HOUSE

romance of a genteel life on the Ohio River in the mid-1800s. The Robert Park House was constructed in 1839 with bricks made on the property, and the 32 acres it sits on are a parklike enclave that permits visitors to take a walk down to the riverbank. In addition, you can play a game on the tennis court, canoe the small creek running through the grounds, cast a line from the boat dock, or do nothing more than watch the sunset from the gazebo. Four guest rooms, each with its own decorating scheme (kids will enjoy staying in The Secret Garden Room), have private baths complete with plush robes and towels, and a large country breakfast is served on the porch. A separate cottage is available if you desire a bit more privacy. $79–89.

Spencer 25276
Cunningham House (304-927-2022; www.cunninghamhouseinn.com), 224 Chapman Ave. The Cunningham House was built in 1900 and remained in the same family until it was purchased in 1993 by Sonny and Sherry Truman. Sonny and a couple of friends spent several years refurbishing it and installing modern conveniences and amenities. Guests can now sit on the porch to have quiet conversations or watch the neighborhood children ride bikes. Most of Spencer's attractions are within short walking distances. $70–109.

The Arnott House Bed and Breakfast (304-519-5166; 304-377-8733; www.thearnotthouse.com), 103 Locust Ave. Within this Victorian B&B are six guest rooms, two of which are suites, named for members of the Rex Arnott family, the original owners. All of the accommodations have a private bath. $79–99.

CAMPGROUNDS

Cottageville 25239
Jackson County Fairground (304-

372-8199; 304-373-2286; mailing address: Rte. 2, Box 280). on US 33 about 7 miles west of Ripley at I-79 exit 138. Open all year. More than 100 sites with water, electric. and sewer, along with two modern bathhouses and all the amenities of the fairground, such as picnic areas, ball fields, and a boat ramp on Mill Creek.

Sandyville 25275
Ruby Lake (304-273-3427; 4 Ruby Lake Lane), WV 21 east of Ravenswood. Open Mar. 1–Nov. 1.

Also see Mountwood Park under *Green Space—Parks.*

✷ Where to Eat
DINING OUT

Parkersburg
Colombo's Restaurant (304-428-5472; 304-428-9370), 1236 Seventh St. Open for lunch and dinner. Closed Mon. If you've read other portions of this book, you know that the Clarksburg/Fairmont area is West Virginia's epicenter of Italian dining. James B. Colombo opened his original restaurant in Clarksburg in 1949 before moving to Parkersburg to open this establishment in 1954. Traditional recipes and ingredients (they have been using the same brand of flour all these years) have built a loyal following that often fills all 400 seats. Steaks, seafood, and pork entrées are also available. Entrées $8.95–16.95.

&. **Spats** (304-422-3131; 1-800-262-2536; www.theblennerhassett.com), 320 Market St. Reservations recommended. Spats, in The Blennerhassett (see *Lodging*), is the place to come for Parkersburg's finest dining. All the hallmarks of an excellent restaurant are here: Fish is flown in from Florida or Hawaii, the daily specials are dependent on what fresh ingredients are available, the wine list offers $17 to $1,000 bottles, and the wait staff are attentive without being intrusive. The marlin I had the last time here was firm, but soft and succulent. My dining companion almost wanted to lick the plate after finishing her duck à l'orange, and we agreed the crème brûlée was the best we had ever had in West Virginia. Soft piano music complements the meals, but sometimes the amplified live music in the adjoining lounge has much higher decibels. Entrées $18–33.

Williamstown

da Vinci's (304-375-3633; www.villa davinci.com), 215 Highland Ave. Open for lunch and dinner; closed Mon. (Very popular, so plan on possibly waiting for a table.) da Vinci's started out serving just pizza and salad in a converted service station. It has grown and been added onto so much that you may require a guide just to find your way around its many twists, turns, hallways, and dining areas. Traditional Italian entrées and pizzas are the restaurant's forte, but, interestingly, one of its most popular items is the German pizza. Made with corned beef, sauerkraut, cheese, and a horseradish sauce, it tastes like a gourmet Reuben sandwich. Entrées $7.95–16.95.

EATING OUT

Ellenboro

Happy Trails Café (304-869-3635; www.happytrailscafe.com), 133 Washington Ave. E. Hours vary. The creative talents of Mary Ann and Gary Schoeny have turned the café into an unexpected pleasure, located on a country road just a few feet from the North Bend Rail Trail. One side of the café invites you to relax on couches and stuffed chairs while enjoying a cup of gourmet coffee. They roast the coffee (one of the few state establishments to do so) and have such a range of choices that the drink menu is four

pages long. All breads, pastries, cakes, pies, cookies, and biscotti are homemade—and there is not one item on the menu that is fried. Breakfast is served anytime. Get the blueberry Belgian waffles or the gourmet French toast—you won't regret ordering either one. Happy Trails Café may just be the best dining experience between Clarksburg and Parkersburg. Entrées $2.55–7.95. *Please Note*: Sadly, the owners were experiencing some difficulties as this book went to press; be sure to call ahead.

Parkersburg

J. P. Henry's (304-485-9390; www .jphenrys.com), 5106 Emerson Ave. Open daily at 2. Part family restaurant, part sports bar (large-screen TVs with surround sound and eight beers on tap), and part entertainment venue with music and a dance floor, J. P. Henry's has been a Parkersburg favorite since 1991. Fresh fish, hand-cut Angus steaks, pasta, and slow-roasted prime rib are the primary menu offerings. Entrées $12.95–22.95.

Third St. Deli (304-422-0003), 343 Third St. Open Mon.–Sat. for lunch 10–3. Gerald and Marty Moore make everything from scratch in their deli,

HAPPY TRAILS CAFÉ

which was a lumber company office in the 1880s. (Check out the pressed tin wainscoting.) Different soups are made each day—the Aztec chowder, with chicken and white beans, was drawing a multitude of customers on a Thursday—and there are more than two dozen sandwiches and salads from which to choose. Prices are nice, too. Entrées $5.75–8.95.

✎ **Tim's Root Beer** (304-422-2958), 1401 Staunton Ave. Open daily; really busy at lunch during the week. Their slogan is "We at Tim's believe in Dessert first!" So, start with a triple-scoop banana split or root beer float. Then order one of the famous all-beef hot dogs with homemade sauce, a hot Virginia ham and cheese, or a Poor Man's steak (grilled bologna). Full dinners are also served, and the kids have not been forgotten. They can order items made just for them, such as grilled cheese, corn dogs, and peanut butter and jelly sandwiches. Entrées $2.50–8.99.

Pennsboro

✎ ⅙ **P & H Family Restaurant** (304-659-3241), across from the depot. Named for the former Pennsboro & Harrisville Railroad, the P & H is the kind of place where people invite other people to sit at their table if the place is crowded and seats are at a premium. The mural above the kitchen pays homage to the past and present by showing a train entering a tunnel and hikers, bikers, and equestrians coming out to enjoy the North Bend Rail Trail. Sandwiches, such as grilled turkey and mozzarella or ground chuck with cheese and Italian pepperoni, and country-cooking entrées (roast beef, chicken, fried shrimp, and ham) figure prominently on the menu. Entrées $3.50–10.95. In the same building, Vogt's Ice Cream is a nice treat after a few miles on the trail.

MICROBREWERY North End Tavern & Brewery (304-428-5854; www.netbrewery.com), 3500 Emerson Ave., Parkersburg. Proprietor Joe Roedershimer has been associated with this tavern, which locals refer to as the NET, for more than three decades. With equipment purchased from a defunct Charleston brewery, he and his staff create reds, porters, wheats, stouts, and what they call a NET light. Known for its burgers (which are really good), NET's food is definitely "tavern" fare—sandwiches, salads, and fried appetizers. I felt like I was on the set of Cheers during my meal here. Other than me, it seemed that everybody knew the name of each person who came through the front door. Entrées $3.95–8.50.

SNACKS & GOODIES

Cairo

The Double Scoop (304-628-3828), Main St. Open daily Labor Day–Memorial Day and weekends in Sept. The Double Scoop is a nice place to take a break from a journey on the North Bend Rail Trail. The décor and atmosphere recapture the days of 1950s ice-cream parlors with an art deco bar, jukebox, hand-dipped ice cream, and all manner of ice-cream goodies. Hot dogs, hamburgers, and salads are also available if you want something less sweet.

Vienna

Holl's Swiss Chocolatier (304-295-6576; 1-800-842-4512; www.holls.com), 2001 Grand Central Ave. What a treat! Founder Fritz Holl worked as an apprentice at a *conditorei* (a pastry and chocolate shop inside a café) in Switzerland during the 1930s, and all the expertise he gained goes into his company's handcrafted chocolates (at least 1.3 million pieces annually). The raw chocolate is produced in Switzerland using a formula that is unique to Holl's. No preservatives or artificial flavors are used in any of the candy, all nuts are roasted in-house, and the truffles are created with fresh dairy cream. Yum. The retail space, which also has coffees and boutique wines, is a pleasure to walk into. It's very open and reflects a modern European design.

✳ Entertainment

FILM

Mount Zion

Mount Zion Drive-In (304-354-9405; www.mountziondrivein.com), on WV 6. Opened in 1945, this is the state's oldest remaining drive-in. With a giant 85-foot screen, it usually shows double features most often on Fri., Sat., and Sun. June–Sept. Some people come here just for the snack bar, which serves hand-formed hamburgers, and the hot dog sauce, pizza, and coleslaw are all homemade. If you lose interest in the movies, you can come inside to play a game of pool.

Parkersburg

Jungle Drive-In (304-464-4063; www.jungmovies.com; 6600 Old St. Marys Pike), about 6 miles north of Parkersburg on WV 2. Not much has changed at the Jungle since it first opened in 1952. It still has a playground for kids, the Jungle Boy burgers are still a popular item at the concession stand, and sound is via the traditional pole speakers, not broadcast on AM radio as many drive-ins do today. Double features are shown nightly, except Thurs., when the kids are out of school and on weekends only when school is in session Apr.–Oct.

Regal Grand Central Mall 12 (304-483-3376), 700 Grand Central Mall. Take in a new movie when shopping at the mall's more than 100 stores tires you out.

A Family Cinema (304-372-8206), 126 Academy Dr., Hecks Shopping Center.

Spencer

The Robey Theatre (304-927-1390; www.robeytheatre.com), 318 Main St. The Robey claims to be America's longest-running movie house. It certainly has the history and legacy. Even though it has been located in a number of places in Spencer, it has never shut down—even going so far as to project movies inside a large tent when it was displaced for a short while. There is no doubt the Robey is showing its age, but even if you don't want to see a movie, you can still purchase some popcorn from outside the theater, as the concession stand has a window overlooking the sidewalk.

MUSIC The River Cities Symphony Orchestra (304-424-3457; 304-485-7068; www.rcso.us; mailing address: P.O. Box 477, Parkersburg 26102). The professional orchestra, comprised of about 60 regional musicians, presents concerts at various locations in and around the city.

THEATER ⅙ **Actors' Guild of Parkersburg** (304-485-1300; www.actors guildonline.com), Eighth and Market streets, Parkersburg. Local and regional thespians stage a variety of live performances throughout the year inside a refurbished 1920s movie house. Past performances have included *Fiddler on the Roof*, *Ten Little Indians*, *Nunsense*, and *A Little Night Music*. The theater is handicapped accessible and has a sound system for the hearing impaired.

✍ ⅙ **Smoot Theatre** (304-422-7529; www.smoottheatre.com), 213 Fifth St., Parkersburg. The Smoot started life as a 1926 vaudeville theater, but it fell into disrepair. Three weeks before it was slated to be demolished in 1986, it was saved by a group of volunteers and has been restored to its former glory, with the original 1928 organ, mahogany doors, chandelier, and a marquee that is a replica of the original. With performances throughout the year, the Smoot has shows ranging from big band concerts to musical acts (regional to international), plays, dance, and children's events. Like the Parkersburg Art Center (see *To See—Museums*), the Smoot has a class that you would expect to find only in larger cities.

West Virginia University at Parkersburg Performing Arts Events (304-424-8000; 1-800-982-9887; www.wvup.edu), 300 Campus Dr., Parkersburg. The college sponsors some very innovative live performances of music, dance, and theatrical works, along with some traditional presentations. The season mirrors the school year.

✱ Selective Shopping
ANTIQUES
Harrisville
Arlo's Antique Flea Market (304-643-4247), 413 South Spring St. Open most days. Arlo's has 10,000 square feet of antiques, collectibles, glassware, tools, and, as their business card says, "anything and everything."

Spencer
Spencer Antique Mall (304-927-8066), 207 Main St. Open daily. Individual dealers offer a mix of the old, new, and country crafts in a heated and air-conditioned 8,000-square-foot building.

Williamstown
Williamstown Antique Mall (304-375-6315), 801 Highland Ave. Located a short distance from the Fenton Art Glass factory, the mall is full of items

from Fenton, plus other antiques and collectibles.

ART AND CRAFTS GALLERIES
Ellenboro
Sammy L. Hogue (304-869-3146; mailing address: Rte. 83, Box 1, Ellenboro 26346), off US 50. Mr. Hogue had more than 40 years of experience in glass factories before opening his own handmade-marble shop in a small building next to his home. If you're lucky, he'll be producing some marbles when you stop by.

West Virginia Glass Specialty (304-869-3374), on WV 16 close to the North Bend Rail Trail. The company's six to eight employees specialize in luster coloring, silk screening, frosting, and hand painting glass.

Harrisville
Colonial Retrospectives: A Gallery (304-643-5154), 307 South Spring St. Open Fri.–Sun. Works of West Virginia and Ohio Valley artists along with some Country Cabinetmaker furniture.

Main Street Crafter and Artisans (304-643-5446), Main Street. A consignment shop showing the handmade items of painters, quilters, potters, basket makers, jewelers, sculptors, woodworkers, and more.

Pennsboro
Davis Handmade Marbles (304-659-2537; 304-659-0225; www.davismarbles.com), Main St. and Collins Ave. It is now the second generation of the Davis family that is crafting beautiful crystal spheres out of molten glass. The storefront is a marble collector's dream, with row upon row of the shiny orbs displayed in such a way that you can see each one's small nuances.

BOOKSTORES The selection of books is limited in **Peoples News**, a regional chain, but I wanted to tell you about it because of the remarkable number of magazines the stores carry. I had no idea there were so many, and I mean dozens and dozens, of special-interest publications. Stores in Parkersburg are located at 1624 Blizzard Dr. (304-422-7500) and in the North Plaza (304-485-5403). Another Peoples News is in St. Marys at 301 Second Street (304-684-7822).

Trans Allegheny Books (304-422-4499; 1-800-371-1283; www.transalleghenybooks.com), 725 Green St., Parkersburg. Browsing through 500,000 used and 1,000 new West Virginia titles is a visual as well as an intellectual treat. The store is inside the 1905 Carnegie Library building, with such wonderful architectural features as a wrought-iron and brass spiral staircase, stained-glass windows, glass-tiled floors, and vintage wooden bookcases. You also get to pet the resident cats. *Please note:* The owner passed away as this book went to press, and the family stated that there were some questions about its future.

FARMERS' MARKETS

Parkersburg
The best of the season may be found Tues.–Fri. 10-2 May-Oct. at the **Downtown Farmers' Market** at #1 Government Square on the corner of 3rd and Market streets.

Ripley
In addition to fresh produce, visitors to the **Jackson County Farmers' Market** (304-372-3965) in New Stone Square near I-77 Exit 138 may purchase eggs, baked goods, plants, and local crafts on Sat. May–Oct.

SPECIAL SHOPS

Cairo
Dinah's Truly West Virginia (304-916-1053; www.dinahsgoatmilksoaps .com), Main St. Using only natural ingredients, including fresh unpasteurized goat's milk, Dinah Monast makes soaps useful in treating psoriasis, eczema, and other skin problems. Products are not limited to soaps, and the shop is full of powders, lotions, shampoos, and other items by Ms. Monast, in addition to some West Virginia artisan-made products.

Rail Trail Pantry (304-628-3700), in the Historic Cairo Theater, Main St. Closed Mon. With bulk offerings of snacks, spices, soups, baking supplies, and Amish Cheeses and other food items, this is the place to stock up on supplies for your next camping trip or put together your own mixture of gorp for a ride on the nearby North Bend Rail Trail.

Harrisville
✄ ☂ **Berdines 5 & Dime** (304-643-2217; www.berdinesdimestore.com), 106 North Court St. Closed Sun. Berdines claims to be the country's oldest dime store. It certainly looks the

DINAH MONAST CREATING MILK SOAPS

part, with tin ceilings, old-fashioned display cases, individual spools of thread for sale, and bulk candy in shapes and tastes that have not been sold for decades in other stores. It could take you a good bit of time to look over the vast array of toys from yesteryear (nothing in the store is made in China). Be sure to ask for a demonstration of the nose flute!

Ravenswood

Sandy Creek Farms (304-273-2569; 1-800-487-2569; www.sandycreek farms.com; mailing address: Rte. 2, Box 40, Ravenswood 26164), on Silverton Rd. about 0.3 mile from its junction with the WV 2 Bypass. Meat lovers, take notice: The cattle on Sandy Creek Farms are raised only on natural feeds, such as corn, soybean meal, molasses, and oats, producing a superior lean and tasty beef. In addition to choice beef and smoked meats, the retail store, which is on the farm, carries lamb and Amish cheese and butter.

WINERY Roane Vineyards Farm Winery (304-927-3200; 304-927-1939; 1-866-927-WINE; www.roanevine yards.com), 1585 Reedyville Rd., Spencer. Call for times and dates of tours and tastings. The vineyard's first vines were planted in 1996, and the winery now offers more than a dozen red, white, blush, and seasonal wines. In summer, sit on the deck overlooking the property; in winter stay warm next to the tasting room's fireplace.

✴ Special Events

May: **West Virginia Marble Festival** (304-628-3321), Cairo. Games, exhibits, lectures, and marble history. **Heritage Days Festival** (304-927-1640; www.cityofspencer.com), Spencer. Celebrates the olden days with music, dance, crafts, and historic buildings tours. **Tour de Lake Moun-**

TRUE WEST VIRGINIA COUNTRY KINDNESS (AND DARN GOOD FOOD, TOO)

Sunny Hollow Farms (304-349-2589; www.sunnyhollowfarms.com; mailing address: Rte. 1, Box 50, Auburn 26235). Call for directions. The country food products Jill Brookover and a few employees make at her rural farm are available by Internet and mail order. However, she also welcomes you to stop by the farm to see her operation and pick out the items you want in person. She will also probably invite you to have a sit-down meal with her— for free! I'm sure she hopes you will purchase some of her products, but she told me that for most people it is going to be a long drive to her place, and she feels that it's only right that she feed them. And, made from the products she produces, what a meal you will get. I was served ribs with barbecue sauce, salad with poppy-seed dressing, several kinds of pickles (all crispy and tasty), and chocolate–peanut butter cookies. When I asked if she was sure she wanted me to tell the readers of a travel book about her offer, she said she would be disappointed if I didn't.

So, take the drive into rural West Virginia and discover one of the state's foremost resources—its genuinely friendly people.

THE GRANDDADDY OF THEM ALL

The **Mountain State Art and Craft Fair** (304-372-3247; www.msacf.com) is recognized by most people as being one of the first art and craft fairs in the state—and the one that other such events pattern themselves after. Started in 1963, the festival draws more than 20,000 people to the Cedar Lakes Conference Center (see *Lodging*) near Ripley during the four-day Fourth of July celebration. They come to see at least 250 of the state's best (and juried) artisans at work and to purchase their wares. Among the many items available are handwoven baskets, paintings, handmade glass, jewelry, leather goods from notebooks to saddles, musical instruments, heritage toys, silk and wool wearables, and woodwork.

Within the Heritage Village you can see lye soap, brooms, shingles, quilts, and apple butter being made. There are also demonstrations on beekeeping, sheepshearing, blacksmithing, and bookbinding and paper marbling.

If you have time to visit only one of the state's art and craft fairs, this is the one to attend.

Throughout the rest of the year, many of these same artisans hold weeklong classes at the conference center for those of you wanting to become more creative. Just a small sampling from the schedule includes instructions on pottery, weaving, painting, fiddle playing, spinning, photography, chair making, and hand-forged cutlery.

---

tain Bike Race (304-927-1790; www.charlesfork.org), Charles Fork Lake. 15K and 30K mountain bike races with free food and camping.

May–September: **Movies in the Park** (304-273-2621), Ravenswood. Bring a blanket or a lawn chair to the Riverfront Park on a Saturday evening, and enjoy a free, family-fare movie under the stars.

June: **Mid-Ohio Valley Multi-Cultural Festival** (304-428-5554; www.movmcf.org), City Park, Parkersburg. A large celebration of the valley's cultural diversity, with folk artists, ethnic foods, dance and musical performances, an international marketplace, and children's activities.

July: **Fourth of July** (304-372-3482), Ripley. The town claims to have the state's largest holiday celebration, which includes a two-hour parade, carnival, live music, flea markets, and fireworks. **West Virginia Interstate Fair & Exposition** (304-489-1301; www.wvinterstatefair.org), Mineral Wells. Six days of livestock judging, country-music concerts, a carnival, and watermelon-eating, pretty-baby, horseshoe-pitching, spitting, and garden-tractor-pulling contests.

August: **Parkersburg Homecoming Festival** (www.parkersburg-homecoming.com), various sites in Parkersburg. Entertainment, a rubber-ducky derby, antique car show, square dancing, and children's events. **West Virginia Honey Festival** (www.wvhoneyfestival.org), City Park, Parkersburg. Honey and beeswax contests, along with entertainment, food, and a classic car show.

September: **Harvest Moon Arts & Crafts Festival** (304-424-7311), City Park, Parkersburg. Close to 250 booths of artists (all juried) in all manner of media. **Volcano Days Antique Engine Show & Festival** (304-679-3611; www.mountwoodpark.org), Mountwood Park, Volcano. Exhibits, lectures, and demonstrations that revisit the heady days of the oil and gas boom of the late 1800s and early 1900s. Also entertainment, food, fireworks, and arts and crafts.

October: **West Virginia Black Walnut Festival** (304-927-5616; www.wvblackwalnutfestival.org), Spencer. Since 1955, this five-day festival, which started out as a celebration of the abundant black walnut harvest, has grown in size and the number of people it attracts. As organizers say, there is something here for everyone. Children and teenagers come for the carnival, kids' day parade and activities, band and majorette contest, and tons of food. Everybody comes for live music concerts, juried crafts, agricultural exhibits and competitions, a golf scramble, 5K Nut Run, classic car show, and parade of floats. Named one of America's Top Ten Fall Festivals by the Society of American Travel Writers.

November: **Holiday in the Park** (304-428-1130; 1-800-752-4982), Southwood and City parks, Parkersburg. A festival of lights so large it has to be located in two parks.

Northern
Panhandle

9

NORTHERN PANHANDLE

J utting almost as far north as New York City, West Virginia becomes barely more than 3 miles wide at some points in the Northern Panhandle. There are no real mountains here, and the land immediately beside the Ohio River is level, but the Northern Panhandle's terrain is certainly not flat. Elevation changes are never much more than 200 to 300 feet, but here on the western edge of the Allegheny Mountains, ridgelines run in all directions, sometimes so close together that towns (and even colleges) had no choice but to build upon them. Other than Wheeling and Weirton, this is a decidedly rural area, somewhat of a surprise in this day and age since it is within an easy hour's drive of the sprawling metropolis of Pittsburgh, Pennsylvania. Countryside rides still enable travelers to take in lush farmlands or restful views of the Ohio River.

Reminders of days gone by are around the many twists and curves of these country roads. More than 2,000 years ago, the Adena people built mounds to honor their dead, while construction of the National Road in the 1700s brought settlers from the urbanized East Coast to prosper, with businesses utilizing the road, railroads, and the Ohio River. During the Civil War, delegates came to Wheeling via those same travel routes to declare that the western counties of Virginia wished to secede from that state and remain loyal to the Union. Abundant gas and oil fields fueled the steel mills and glass and pottery factories, spawning another period of prosperity, evident in the many large Victorian homes found in Wheeling, Sistersville, and other towns.

COMMUNITIES The small town of **Bethany**, with just a few businesses, is dominated by Bethany College, a liberal-arts school established in 1840.

Moundsville has a surprising number of worthwhile attractions located within its small-town borders. For more than a century, it was known to West Virginians as the place where the state's most hardened criminals were incarcerated. The penitentiary was closed in the late 1900s, and you can take tours to see what life was like behind bars. Glass and toy museums provide glimpses into 20th-century life, while the Grave Creek Mound takes you back a couple thousand years.

Orchards were the first economic base for what was to become **Newell**, developed and constructed by the Homer Laughlin China Company as a complement to its mile-long factory.

Until 1889, **Sistersville** was a small town servicing local farmers and steamboat

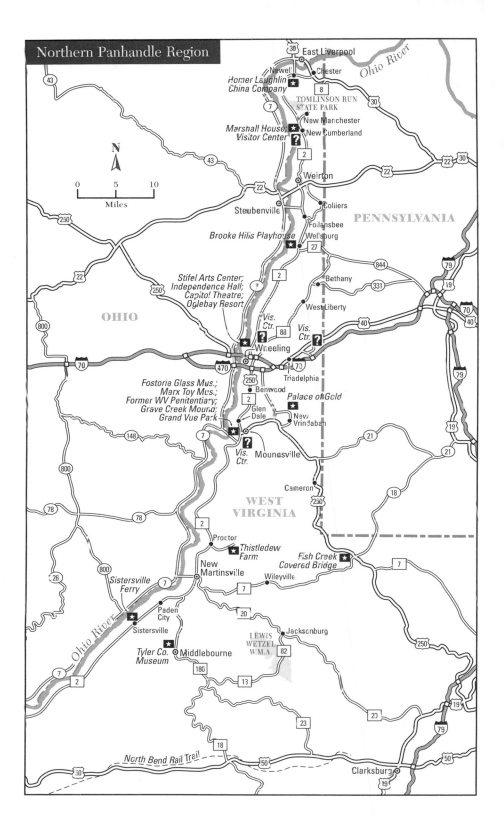

Northern Panhandle Region

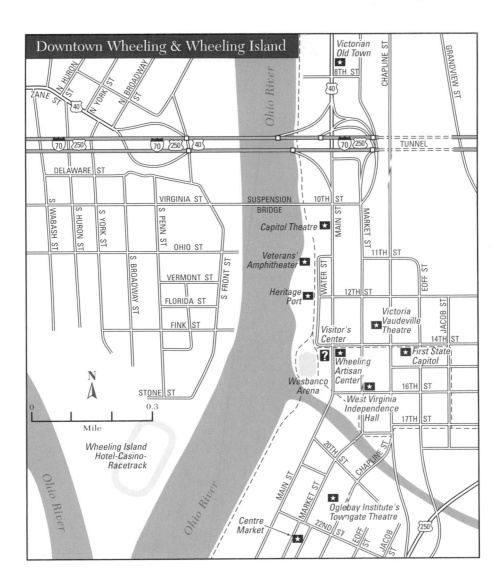

Downtown Wheeling & Wheeling Island

Victorian Old Town
8TH ST
CHAPLINE ST
GRANDVIEW ST
ZANE ST
N HURON ST
N YORK ST
N BROADWAY ST
Ohio River
40
DELAWARE ST
70 250
70 250 40
70 250
TUNNEL
S WABASH ST
S HURON ST
S YORK ST
S PENN ST
S BROADWAY ST
VIRGINIA ST
OHIO ST
S FRONT ST
SUSPENSION BRIDGE
10TH ST
MAIN ST
MARKET ST
Capitol Theatre
11TH ST
EOFF ST
Veterans' Amphitheater
WATER ST
12TH ST
VERMONT ST
FLORIDA ST
Heritage Port
Victoria Vaudeville Theatre
JACOB ST
FINK ST
Visitor's Center
14TH ST
First State Capitol
Wheeling Artisan Center
STONE ST
Wesbanco Arena
16TH ST
West Virginia Independence Hall
17TH ST
N
0   0.3
Mile
Wheeling Island Hotel-Casino-Racetrack
Ohio River
Ohio River
20TH ST
CHAPLINE ST
MAIN ST
MARKET ST
Oglebay Institute's Towngate Theatre
Centre Market
22ND ST
EOFF ST
JACOB ST
250

traffic on the Ohio River. The discovery of oil in that year drew speculators and laborers to the town, which soon had derricks churning away along city streets, in backyards, and on the hillsides. The riches from this boom financed hotels, casinos, theaters, opera houses, and dozens of palatial Victorian homes and business buildings. The boom went bust in 1915 and the population dwindled, but many of the homes and other structures remain in the town's historic district. A walking-tour brochure (available from the Wells Inn—see *Lodging*) directs you to more than a dozen sites, including the Little Sister oil well and derrick, operated every September during the West Virginia Oil and Gas Festival.

Land around what became **Weirton** was settled as early as 1770, but the town truly began to develop in 1909, when E. T. Weir and Associates constructed a steel-manufacturing plant beside the Ohio River. Many other companies soon followed. Steel is not as important as it once was, but the city now stretches from the river to the Pennsylvania border.

Established in 1791, **Wellsburg** once rivaled Wheeling as an Ohio River transshipment center. Its historic district contains the Wellsburg Wharf, where flatboats were loaded with goods; the 1798 Millers Tavern; and the 1848 Brooke County Courthouse.

It seems that cities are always touting the plans they have to save their historic buildings and heritage, while at the same time modernizing themselves by creating new and exciting attractions and activities for the citizens of today. **Wheeling** doesn't have to proclaim such nebulous plans; it has already accomplished what those other places are hoping to do.

Many of the city's structures from days past continue to be used. The Wheeling suspension bridge was the longest (1,010 feet) wire cable suspension bridge in the world when it was built in 1849. It's now the world's oldest such bridge, taking gamblers over the Ohio River to the **Wheeling Island Hotel-Casino-Racetrack**.

When delegates met inside a federal customs house in the 1860s, they passed a resolution dissolving the western counties' bonds with Virginia—and the state of West Virginia was born. A museum in this "Independence Hall" tells the story, while just a few blocks away is the state's first capitol building.

Wheeling's zenith as a transshipment and industrial center is reflected in the dozens of well-preserved Victorian homes in the North Wheeling, Chapline Street Row, and Monroe Street East historic districts.

As stated, though, not everything is focused on the past. Erected in 1853 and added onto in 1890, Centre Market was the place German, English, Scots, Irish, Lebanese, and Greek immigrants came to purchase the daily needs of life. (Be sure to look at the Doric columns on the Upper Market Building. They serve as rain spouts!) Today, the market is alive once again with restaurants, shops, and an art gallery. Another downtown art venue is housed in a former 1891 industrial building.

Just as Charleston, Huntington, and Morgantown have, Wheeling has rediscovered its waterfront, and the Wheeling Heritage Port plays host to outdoor theatrical presentations, concerts, and festivals within a few feet of the Ohio River. Classical-music lovers keep coming back year after year to the historic Capitol Theatre to enjoy the full schedule of the Wheeling Symphony.

Having left behind its mid-1900s reputation as a tired, somewhat gritty industrial municipality, Wheeling may well be West Virginia's most unheralded city. Go visit, find out for yourself what a vibrant place it is, and pass the word on to others.

GUIDANCE The Information Center of the **Marshall County Tourism and Chamber of Commerce** (304-845-2773; www.marshallcountychamber.com), 609 Jefferson Ave.,

A LITTLE-KNOWN FACT
The world's largest shipment of matches (210 million) was shipped from Wheeling to Memphis, Tennessee, in 1933.

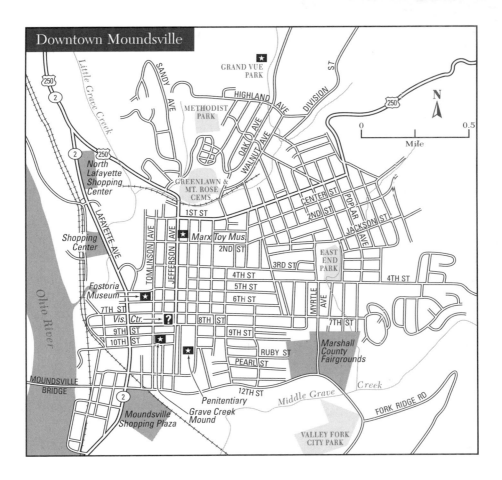

Downtown Moundsville

Moundsville 26041, is located inside the historic 1877 Italianate-style brick Kirkside building.

The **Top of West Virginia Convention and Visitors Bureau** (304-797-7001; 1-877-723-7114; www.topofwv.com), which provides information about attractions in Brooke and Hancock counties, shares space with the Weirton Area Museum and Cultural Center (see *Museums*) at 3393 Main St., Weirton 26062.

Volunteers operate the **Visitors Center** in the **Brooke County Public Library** (304-737-1551; http://wellsburg.lib.wv.us), 945 Main St., Wellsburg 26070, so it may not be staffed when you stop in, but you can always pick up brochures from a rack.

The state **Welcome Center** (304-547-0660) near I-70 mile marker 13 can help you plan excursions in this region as well as the entire state.

The **Wheeling Convention and Visitors Bureau** (304-233-7709; 1-800-828-3097; www.wheelingcvb.com), 1401 Main St., Wheeling 26003, is in the downtown area and has free curbside parking.

A CORNUCOPIA OF CIVIC STATUARY

Every city has its share of public art, but my walks in Wheeling have uncovered an abundance of sculpted pieces, many of them easily overlooked when you're driving by and need to pay attention to the traffic around you.

Located along US 40 near the Wheeling Park entrance, the *Madonna of the Trail* is one of 12 such statues placed along the route of the "National Old Trails" from Washington, DC, to Los Angeles. Commissioned by the Daughters of the American Revolution, the base of the one in Wheeling is dedicated To the pioneer mothers of our Mountain State whose courage, optimism, love and sacrifice made possible the national highway that united the East and West.

At the top of Wheeling Hill on US 40 is a statue erected in the early 1900s that pays tribute to the **Mingo Indians**. I've always thought it ironic that a plaque that reads The Mingo, original inhabitants of this valley extends greetings and peace to all wayfarers is placed at this particular spot. It's also the exact site of "McColloch's Leap," where Samuel McColloch and his horse were forced to jump more than 150 feet down the mountainside to escape a band of Native Americans who were intent on killing him in 1777.

Traffic goes zipping by the statue honoring **Labor Unions** located next to a busy intersection on Main St., while it would be very easy to miss the eagle perched above the entrance of the **Scottish Rite Cathedral** on 14th St.

The city's most famous statue is *The Aviator*, on the Linsly School campus located off US 40. It is believed to be the country's first monument to a pilot—Weston, West Virginia, native Louis Bennett, who was shot down during World War I. The mythological Icarus, who fell from the sky after a glorious flight, inspired the stirring work.

GETTING THERE *By air*: **Pittsburgh International Airport** (412-472-3525; www.pitairport.com) is the closest major airport, and it's not more than an hour away from many places in this region.

By bus: There is a **Greyhound** (1-800-231-2222; 304-232-1500; www.greyhound .com) terminal on Main St. in downtown Wheeling.

By car: East–west **I-70** goes through downtown Wheeling, while east–west **US 22** comes directly from Pittsburgh into Weirton. **WV 2**, sometimes four-lane, sometimes two-lane, parallels the Ohio River in a north–south direction and is the road you will probably travel, at least some distance, to reach many of the attractions in this region. The roadway alternates between being a scenic drive along the Ohio River and passing through industrial and business districts.

By rail: An **AMTRAK** (1-800-872-7245; www.amtrak.com) train, the *Capitol Limited*, makes stops daily in Pittsburgh, Pennsylvania, on its east–west Chicago to Washington, DC, route.

GETTING AROUND *By bus*: The **Weirton Transit Company** (304-797-8597; www.bhjmpc.org/Transportation/Transit/wtc.htm) operates a bus line completely within the city of Weirton, while the **Ohio Valley Regional Transportation Authority** (304-232-2190, www.ovrta.org) has routes in and around Wheeling.

By taxi: In and around Weirton, it is **Weir-Cove Taxi** (304-748-1515) that provides transportation services. **Yellow Cab** (304-232-5151) and **Moundsville Cab** (304-232-8798) operate in and around Wheeling.

Insider's Tip: Pick up the "Passport of Savings" at the Wheeling Convention and Visitors Bureau and save some money, such as dollars off admissions to the Museums of Oglebay, West Virginia Penitentiary Tour, and other attractions. You can also save on dining and lodging. The best part is that the passport is free.

MEDICAL EMERGENCIES

Glen Dale
Reynolds Memorial Hospital (304-845-3211; www.reynoldsmemorial.com), 800 Wheeling Ave.

New Martinsville
Wetzel County Hospital (304-455-8000; www.wetzelcountyhospital.com), 3 East Benjamin Dr.

Sistersville
Sistersville General Hospital (304-652-2611; www.sistersvillehospital.com), 314 South Wells St.

Weirton
Weirton Medical Center (304-797-6000; www.weirtonmedical.com), 601 Colliers Way.

Wheeling
Ohio Valley Medical Center (304-234-0123; www.ovmc-online.com), 2000 Eoff St.

Wheeling Hospital (304-243-3000; www.wheelinghospital.com), 1 Medical Park.

✳ To See

COLLEGES

Bethany
Bethany College (304-829-7000; www.bethanywv.edu). The redbrick Gothic buildings of Bethany College sit on a hillside overlooking the quiet, tree-lined streets of the small town. The school was established in 1840 by Alexander Campbell, a leader in an American religious movement that led to the creation of the Disciples of Christ, Churches of Christ, and the Christian Church.

It's a pleasant walk around campus to see the fountain and Gresham Garden in front of the 142-foot tower of Old Main, whose look was inspired by a building at the University of Glasgow, Scotland.

After the campus tour, take the short drive to the 24-room **Campbell Mansion**

(304-829-4258), built in four stages between 1792 and 1840. (Small admission fee; usually open Mon.–Fri. Apr.–Oct., but hours and days have been known to change.) This was one popular place, with so many friends and dignitaries, such as Henry Clay, Jefferson Davis, and James Garfield, stopping by so often and in such large numbers that the dining table was always at the ready with more than 30 chairs. Rooms are furnished in original family belongings, including a cradle and quilt from early family days, Campbell's bed, and a bust made from his death mask.

CAMPBELL MANSION

God's Acre, the Campbell family cemetery, is on the hillside overlooking the mansion. Also nearby is the plain brick 1852 **Old Meeting House**, which remains practically unchanged from the way Campbell had it constructed. (Ask what the wedge of wood in one of the pews was used for.)

West Liberty

West Liberty University (304-366-8013; http://westliberty.edu). Established in 1837, West Liberty is one of the state's oldest institutions of higher learning. The 450-seat Helen Pierce Elbin Auditorium has a great-sounding Moeller pipe organ and sponsors concerts and lectures open to the public. Within the Hall of Fine Arts is another theater and an art gallery also open to the public.

Wheeling

Wheeling Jesuit University (304-243-2000; 1-800-624-6992; www.wju.edu), 316 Washington Ave. The 1,500-student university, which offers undergraduate and graduate degrees, sits on 65 acres on the eastern end of Wheeling. The school is on the cutting edge with its Center for Educational Technology and National Technology Center, but it also keeps students aware of the human condition with the Appalachian Institute and Mother Jones House. An active arts program opens its productions to the public (exhibits and live theater), and there is even a Picasso sketch in the library building. Incidentally, the university is the alma mater of my sister's two sons, my nephews.

Also on campus is the **Challenger Learning Center** (304-243-8740), a most interesting place geared toward teachers and students, but it is open to any group that makes reservations. Through extremely realistic simulations, you and your group will fly a mission in the Space Station—complete with its Operations Deck and rows of monitors at Mission Control back on Earth. All I can say is, get a group together; this is the closest you will probably ever get to being in space.

COVERED BRIDGE Still in use, the 36-foot, kingpost truss **Fish Creek Covered Bridge** was built around 1880 and renovated in 2001. Follow US 250 east from Hundred and turn right onto WV 13.

DRIVING TOURS, SCENIC & HISTORIC In 1775, British forces under Gen. Edward Braddock, accompanied by a young George Washington, widened a Native American trail to facilitate their march westward. With funds provided by the state of Maryland in 1806, the route was improved, extended from Baltimore to Cumberland, Maryland, and named the National Pike. At the same time, the U.S. Congress also authorized federal funds for another road, this one to begin in Cumberland and head westward. Eventually the two roads came to be known as

PRABHUPADA'S PALACE OF GOLD

"AMERICA'S TAJ MAHAL"

Prabhupada's Palace of Gold (304-843-1812; www.palaceofgold.com; mailing address: Road 1, NBU# 23, Moundsville 26041). Drive US 250 eastward from Moundsville for about 8 miles, turn left onto WV 7 (Limestone Ridge/Palace Rd.), and, when you go around a curve a few miles later, spectacular golden domes rising high above the treetops may make you think you have somehow left West Virginia and traveled to India.

A reporter from the *Washington Post* once wrote, "The magnificence of the Palace of Gold would be hard to exaggerate," and I agree. In the 1970s, Hare Krishna devotees of Swami Prabhupada started out to simply build a house for him, so that he could write books and enjoy West Virginia's fresh country air. Yet, somehow (devotees say Lord Krishna guided them) plans became grander and grander as volunteer builders, who had little construction experience and actually read "how-to" and "do-it-yourself" books, went from one phase of the construction to another. The result is an 8,000-square-foot palace covered by pounds of gold leaf and with so many intricate and outstanding features that it would take a full book to describe and days on end to take it all in.

the **National Road** (www.historicwvnationalroad.org). It was one of the major thoroughfares of the day, and such luminaries as Daniel Webster, Henry Clay, and Presidents Lincoln, Jackson, William Henry Harrison, Polk, Taylor, and Van Buren traveled it.

In the Northern Panhandle, **US 40** follows the route of what was once the National Road. As you explore the region, take a break from the interstate to travel the roadway and discover historic sites you might have otherwise passed by.

Given year-round, guided tours (small fee required) take you through 10 rooms where sunlight filters through 31 stained-glass windows to shine upon antique French crystal chandeliers. The palace is built with more than 254 tons of marble, some of it columns that are topped with gold, other portions intricately inlaid with 50 varieties of marble and onyx. Hand-painted murals, many in the tradition of Renaissance masters that call to mind the Sistine Chapel, cover walls and ceilings. Details on Swami Prabhupada's bedroom walls and ceiling are so complex that one person spent more than six months painting them. I could go on and on—a gold-plated lion's head, carved teakwood furniture from India, and four royal peacock windows with more than 1,500 pieces of hand-shaped stained glass—but you will see it all on the tour.

The palace is just a part of the New Vrindaban Hare Krishna complex. Two levels of terraces bordered by hundreds of ornate fountains and flower gardens overlook the hills of West Virginia, Ohio, and Pennsylvania. Sculptures of lions lead into the Garden of Time, full of colorful blossoms from spring into late fall. Visitors are permitted to freely wander around all the grounds. There are also some interesting and low-cost lodging options if you are interested in spending more time here.

You will probably hear chanting sometime during your visit, but don't worry about devotees trying to convert or lecture you with doctrine. While happy to explain the tenets of their religion, guides are quite restrained in promoting their views to visitors.

Also in the area is **Lewis Wetzel's Grave and McCreary Cemetery**, a historic cemetery located just 0.25 mile past the Palace of Gold. It contains the graves of Revolutionary War, War of 1812, and Civil War veterans. Also buried here is Lewis Wetzel, one of West Virginia's earliest citizens, whose skill as a hunter and marksman have had him compared to Daniel Boone and Simon Kenton. Wetzel's fame was such that numerous songs and stories were written to tell of his exploits. After Native Americans killed one of his brothers in 1777, he gained another reputation—and the name Death Wind. Depending on which source you read, he became "a defender of the feeble settlers" or a ruthless "killer of Indians with only vengeance on his mind."

Newell

☂ **Homer Laughlin China Co.** (304-387-1300; 1-800-452-4462; www.hlchina .com), Sixth and Harrison streets. Free tours Mon.–Fri. at 10:30 and 12:30—reservations required. Factory store open daily. Homer Laughlin has been producing china since the 1870s and is considered by many to be the world's largest producer of china for both home and commercial use. It currently has more than 1,000 employees working in the 37-acre plant. The White House, Colonial Williamsburg, Biltmore Estate, Disney World, and national food chains like P. F. Chang's use the company's products. (It claims to have made one-third of all the china ever produced in America.) Its most recognized line is the colorful Fiesta dinnerware, introduced in 1936 and still popular today.

PADEN CITY

✐ **Marble King** (304-337-2264; 1-800-672-5564; www.marbleking.com), First Ave. In operation seven days a week, all year long, Marble King produces 1 million marbles a day. The office is open Mon.–Fri., and, if workloads permit, someone will be happy to take you on a tour of the manufacturing process.

HISTORIC HOME The Eckhart House (304-232-5439; 1-888-700-0118;

www.eckharthouse.com), 810 Main St., Wheeling. Gloria Figaretti inherited the 1892 Queen Anne town house, and she and her husband, Joe, have done a commendable job in keeping one of Wheeling's most magnificent Victorian-era homes in great shape. By retaining original features, such as the lincrusta and fretwork (made in Wheeling), they have embraced the home's historic aspects. On Wed.–Sat. afternoons, Joe takes visitors on a guided tour and paints a vivid picture of how the home played an important role in the city's social and business scenes. You will learn little-known facts—such as Wheeling had a water system as early as 1834, it was the fourth city in the country to have electricity, Louis Comfort Tiffany came to the Wheeling area to learn his trade, and the house was one of the first to have an indoor toilet and bath.

Also in the home, Gloria has a gift shop full of interesting items and serves parlor teas Wed.–Sat. afternoons.

HISTORIC SITES

Chester

Is it a historic site or a historic oddity? Whichever it is, the **World's Largest Teapot** (14 feet high and 14 feet in diameter) has been attracting people since it was erected in 1938 as an outdoor advertisement for the area's locally manufactured china and pottery. (Some people say it really started out as a gigantic wooden barrel advertising Hire's Root Beer.) You can see it at the intersection of WV 2 and US 30.

Moundsville

Grave Creek Mound Archaeological Complex (304-843-4128), 801 Jefferson Ave. Let your mind wander back to life a little more than 2,000 years ago. The Adena people—who lived in well-organized groups and farmed, hunted, and fished—inhabited land from the Atlantic Ocean to the Mississippi River. Known to us today as "Mound Builders," they buried their dead in large earthen mounds,

PETER TAPR FURNACE

with the largest one located close to the Ohio River in present-day Moundsville.

The Adena had no horses and did not use the wheel, so imagine the labor it must have taken to move and carry 60,000 tons of earth and put it into a pile almost 70 feet high and 295 feet in diameter at the base. Access to the mound closes at 4:30.

Next to the mound, the **Delf Norona Museum** (closed Mon.; free) has exhibits, displays, and artifacts found in the mound (which had multiple burial chambers, indicating it was in use for generations).

Weirton

The **Peter Tarr Furnace**, constructed in 1794, was the first iron furnace west of the Allegheny Mountains. It was normally used to make cooking utensils and iron gates, but it was put into action to cast the cannonballs used by Commodore Perry during the Battle of Lake Erie in 1813. Rebuilt in 1968, the structure is in excellent condition, and today it sits, somewhat incongruously, on a corner lot in a housing subdivision on Kings Creek Rd. east of Weirton.

Wheeling

First State Capitol (304-232-2576; www.firststatecapitol.com), 1413 Eoff St. Built as a part of the Linsly Institute, this neoclassical building served as the first state capitol of West Virginia from the state's inception in 1863 to 1870, and again from 1875 to 1876. Although it is currently home to private offices, you are permitted to step inside to look at a couple of the historic rooms and *Wheeling Heroes* by local artist Jamie Lester.

🐾 ↑ **Independence Hall** (304-238-1300; www.wvculture.org), 1528 Market St. Closed Sun. Very small admission fee; admission is sometimes free. When delegates from western counties gathered in 1861 to discuss and pass a resolution seceding from Virginia, they met in this 1859 customs house, which also served as the capitol of the "Restored Government of Virginia." The Renaissance Revival building has been renovated (complete with faux painting on the plaster and steel shutters) and houses exhibits and displays that, more than any other place I have visited, provide excellent information on the differences between the populations of eastern and western Virginia. Start your tour with the short film; look over the original 1861 document that made the case for secession; continue to the second floor to see the first U.S. flag to have 35 stars; and, as you sit on the benches of the restored third-floor courtroom, imagine the heated arguments that must have taken place between the delegates as they hammered out the reasons to form a new state.

SCARE YOUR CHILDREN (AND YOURSELF) STRAIGHT

✎ Former West Virginia Penitentiary (304-845-6200; www.wvpentours.com), 818 Jefferson Ave., Moundsville. Open Tues.–Sun. Apr.–Nov. Adults $10; seniors $8; children $5; under age 5 are free; last tour leaves at 4. You know those old prison movies where the cell door closes behind the prisoners and the clang! clang! sound echoes through the halls? You can experience the same thing by being locked into one of the 5 by 7-foot cells of the former West Virginia Penitentiary. (Think about spending close to 20 hours a day with two other men in this tiny space.) The tours are interesting and entertaining, but after going through here and seeing what prison life could be like, I vowed to never even think about speeding up when a traffic light turns yellow.

FORMER WEST VIRGINIA PENITENTIARY

Much of the imposing Gothic-style prison, which looks exactly like something out of a horror movie, was built by prisoners shortly after the Civil War. It was used until 1986, when the state Supreme Court ruled the 5 by 7-foot cells were cruel and unusual punishment. The men incarcerated here were considered the state's most violent, and many of them died at the hands of fellow inmates.

Tours take you through the dark and dank halls where inmate graffiti and artwork adorn almost every cell. Old Sparky, the electric chair constructed by an inmate and used to carry out nine executions, looks like it is ready to handle another prisoner at any moment. And you can't help but be frightened—and amazed—at the ingenuity prisoners used in creating grisly weapons from whatever kind of materials they could get their hands on.

If the 90-minute tour is not long enough, there are all-night ghost tours held once a month that can be so scary they were featured on MTV.

MUSEUMS & ART GALLERIES

Middlebourne

🐾 ↑ **Tyler County Museum** (304-758-2100; www.tylercountymuseum.com), Dodd St. Open Sun., Tues., and Thurs. afternoons. Donations accepted. It is phenomenal the amount of material that is on display in this local museum, conceived and operated by volunteers. Plan to spend a number of hours on three floors of themed rooms in West Virginia's first county school, which operated from 1908 to 1993. Some pretty amazing things are here: a sheepskin deed from before the Revolutionary War, an 1863 flag from before West Virginia became a state, a dog-powered (!) butter churn, and a display of all the patterns produced by the now-defunct Paden City Pottery company. Also on the premises are a one-room schoolhouse and a log cabin from the 1700s. Do not miss this place if you have even the slightest interest in days gone by.

Moundsville

T **Fostoria Glass Museum** (304-845-9188), Sixth and Tomlinson. Open in the afternoon Wed.–Sat. Mar.–Nov. Small admission fee. During its nearly 100 years of existence, the Fostoria Glass Company became the largest maker of handmade glassware in the country, producing blown stemware, crystal dinner services, and etched and pressed patterns of such high quality that they were ordered by presidents from Eisenhower through Reagan. A small brochure guides you through the museum, providing commentary on the 37,000 pieces displayed (quite artistically, I must say) to show their best features.

Marshall County Historical Society Museum (304-845-5996; 304-845-3692; www.marshallcountyhistorical.com), 13th St. and Lockwood Ave. Open Thurs. 10–3 Apr.–Oct. and other times by appointment. Donations accepted. Coal mining, farming, glass, pottery, and household items provide a look back to see how the region's earlier populations lived.

✐ T **Marx Toy Museum** (304-845-6022; www.marxtoymuseum.com), 915 Second St. Open Tues.–Sat. Apr.–Dec. Small admission fee. At one time, Louis Marx and Co. was the world's biggest toy manufacturer. During the 1950s, Marx sold more toys than its two closest competitors, and its largest factory was located in nearby Glen Dale, which produced 75 percent of the toys found in the museum. Here you can relive your childhood, especially if you grew up anytime from the 1940s to the 1970s. Remember Robin Hood, Alamo, and Ben-Hur play sets? How about Big Wheel tricycles, Story Book Village, and Rock 'Em Sock 'Em Robots? They're all here, waiting to teach you about the man who started the company and the employees whose labors sparked the imaginations of generations of children.

New Cumberland

The Hancock County Historical Museum at the Marshall House (304-564-4800), 1008 Ridge Ave. Open by appointment. The Marshall House has some outstanding features, including a winding stairway that extends from the first floor to the attic three floors above; oak, walnut, and cherry woodwork and ornately carved fireplace mantels; door hinges with intricate patterns; and all but one window facing the Ohio River. Some of the furniture is from the Marshall family, whose patriarch had the home built of local brick in 1887.

Weirton

Weirton Area Museum and Cultural Center (304-479-7226; 304-797-7001; 1-877-723-7114; www.weirtonmuseum.com), 3393 Main St. Open Mon.–Fri. With an emphasis on the area's steel industry, the small museum has permanent and changing exhibits along with sponsoring many special events such as films and cultural festivals.

Wheeling

✐ T **Kruger Street Toy and Train Museum** (304-242-8133; 1-877-242-8133; www.toyandtrain.com), 144 Kruger St. Open daily Memorial Day–Dec.; only open

Sat.–Sun. Jan.–Memorial Day. Small admission fee. The museum started out as hobby for Allan Robert Miller and his son, Allan Raymond Miller. Now housed in a restored 1906 Victorian school, the collection has grown into what the Millers claim to be the country's largest toy museum. Allocate a minimum of two hours to walk through the two floors of model trains, 1950s play sets, dolls and dollhouses, Mr. Potato Heads (the first toy to ever be advertised on TV), cars, trucks, and more. There is no doubt that hundreds of childhood memories will be rekindled. One of the most fascinating displays is the prototype room, where there are hundreds of pieces of memorabilia related to the process of designing and manufacturing toys.

☝ **Stifel Fine Arts Center** (304-242-7700; www.oionline.com), 1530 National Rd. Open on somewhat of an irregular basis; call for hours. Admission is free. Operated by the Oglebay Institute, the center is housed in the grand former home of the Edward W. Stifel Sr. family. The entire building is made of concrete (which does not sound all that appealing—until you see the impressive columns, porches, and other small, artistic features, such as an interior stained-glass window, that have been incorporated into the design).

The center features changing art exhibits, special events, and classes, along with an overview of the family that built and inhabited the home.

Wheeling-Ohio County Airport (304-234-3865; mailing address: Rte. 5, Box 5, Wheeling 26003). Take WV 2 north of Wheeling and follow signs. A museum in an airport? That's right, but just about everything concerning this airport is a museum. It was built in 1946, and not much has changed. The original wood doors are still here, as are the period urinals in the men's restroom and the original fixtures in the ladies'. It is the lobby, though, that is the main attraction. Airport manager Thomas Tominack and staff started the small museum by saving items that played a role in the airport's history. You will see the chairs that John F. and Jacqueline Kennedy sat in while waiting for a car during his 1960 presidential campaign. There are photos of Jimmy Doolittle and Charles Lindbergh; items relating to the "American Girl," Ruth Elden, who almost flew across the Atlantic in 1927; and a propeller from one of the Fokker planes that used to be manufactured nearby.

Also see Bethany College under *Colleges* and the "More than Just a Park" sidebar later in the chapter.

ZOO See the "More than Just a Park" sidebar later in the chapter.

✳ To Do

BICYCLING Wheelcraft (304-242-2100; www.wheelcraft.us), 2187 National Rd. (US 40), Wheeling. Wheelcraft is a full-service shop that can perform maintenance or repairs on your bicycle, or sell you a new one, along with clothing and accessories.

Also see *Rail Trails*, and Grand Vue Park under *Green Space—Parks*.

BIRDING Hillcrest Wildlife Management Area (304-825-6787), Middle Run Rd., off WV 8 east of New Manchester. The WMA's open meadows, bottomland, and rolling hills are habitat for a variety birds. In spring, look for ring-necked pheasants in the low brush, while open fields are home to Henslow's sparrows, bluebirds, and bobolinks. Meadowlarks and Baltimore orioles are often seen in the orchard areas.

Also see *Green Space—Wildlife Refuge*.

FERRY In continuous operation (in one form or another) since 1808, the **Sistersville Ferry** is the last of many such boats to ply the waters of the Ohio River between West Virginia and Ohio. The current boat has a pilothouse that swings around so that the pilot can face forward no matter which direction the boat is going. Although it's primarily a utilitarian boat that operates Apr.–Oct., the ride across the river can be a scenic and enjoyable one as you watch waterfowl and other birds wing their way above the water. You will also get a chance to look at the river from the same perspective as the folks who took the ferry in the 1800s.

FISHING See Tomlinson Run State Park under *Green Space—Parks*, and the "More than Just a Park" sidebar later in the chapter.

GAMING AND DOG RACING ♻ **Wheeling Island Hotel-Casino-Racetrack** (304-231-1831; 1-877-943-4536; www.wheelingisland.com), 1 South Stone St., Wheeling. You can place bets on live greyhound racing (closed Tues. and Thurs.), play a variety of table games, or feed thousands of slot machines that are available for play 21 hours a day. I'm not much of a gambler, but as you have seen throughout this book, I do like to eat—and this place has Wheeling's best dining experience, The Pointe (see *Dining Out*). For a less formal and decidedly lower-cost meal, the **Islander Buffet** (about $15 for lunch, $20 for dinner) is one of the state's better buffets, with more than 130 well-prepared all-you-can-eat items, including steak, pork chops, chicken Kiev, pasta, Asian dishes, and ribs made to order. The dessert island has chocolate fountains, fresh fruit for dipping, and a vast array of calorie-laden goodies. Also on location are a couple of other restaurants, a

SISTERSVILLE FERRY

150-plus-room hotel, and live entertainment (often with national music acts and professional boxing).

GAMING AND HORSE RACING ♿ The **Mountaineer Casino Racetrack and Resort** (304-387-8300; 1-800-80-40-HOT; www.mtrgaming.com: mailing address: P.O. Box 358, Chester 26034), a short distance south of Newell on WV 2. All of the amenities of The Mountaineer, including the gaming area with thousands of slot machines and table games, are a bit more upscale than those at Wheeling Island. The Grande Hotel offers deluxe guest rooms and suites ($180–250; many packages available), fine dining (see La Bonne Vie under *Dining Out*), a full-service spa with Swedish massages and European facials, indoor and outdoor pools, and a fitness center.

Thoroughbred racing usually takes place year-round (sometimes there is no racing in Jan. and Feb.), live entertainment (regional and national acts, boxing, and more) is offered on a regular basis, and the resort's 18-hole, par 72 Woodview Golf Course is a short drive away.

GOLF

New Manchester
Pleasant Hills Golf Club (304-387-0068), on WV 8. The nine-hole public course was designed by Red Baily and was opened in 1961. Built on heavily wooded, hilly terrain, the greens are bent grass, while the fairways have winter rye. Cost to play 18 holes is only $20 on weekends—and less during the week.

Sistersville
Sistersville Golf Course (304-652-3005), RR 2. The par 35, nine-hole course was opened in 1919 and has 3,098 feet.

Wellsburg
Highland Springs Golf Course (304-737-2201), 1600 Washington Pike. This par 72, 18-hole regulation public course has 6,853 yards from the longest tees.

Also see *Gaming and Horse Racing*, Brooke Hills Park under *Green Space—Parks*, and the "More than Just a Park" sidebar later in the chapter.

GOLF, MINIATURE ⚓ **Foggy Bottom Country Club** (304-242-7888; www .foggybottom.net), 68 Cove Ave., Wheeling. Foggy Bottom has some of the longest holes you will ever find on a miniature golf course. With streams, ponds, fountains, waterfalls, and sand traps, the course's average hole is 75 feet long, while the par 5, 17th hole measures 125 feet. There are also batting cages, video arcade games, a laser tag maze, and a café.

Also see Grand Vue Park, Tomlinson Run State Park, Brooke Hills Park, and Wheeling Park under *Green Space—Parks*, and the "More than Just a Park" sidebar later in the chapter.

HIKING Lewis Wetzel Wildlife Management Area (304-889-3497; mailing address: HC 62, Box 8, Jacksonburg 26377). From Jacksonburg, follow Buffalo Run (WV 82); soon after entering the WMA, come to an intersection, where you want to turn left toward the campground. The small trailhead parking turnout is 1.1 miles later, just before you would enter the campground.

In an area of the state where large tracts of public land available for outdoor recreation are somewhat slight, 12,448-acre Lewis Wetzel Wildlife Management Area provides the opportunity to enjoy the beauty of foothills located on the western edge of the Allegheny Plateau and along the eastern reaches of the Ohio River Valley. The rugged terrain ranges in elevation from 736 feet to 1,560 feet. Wildlife includes squirrel, ruffed grouse, deer, turkey, raccoon, mink, muskrat, fox, groundhog, coyote, black bear, skunk, opossum, rabbit, and rattlesnake. Of the 13 species of bats that have been confirmed to be in West Virginia, the little brown myotis, eastern pipistrelle, and red bat have been seen in the wildlife management area. You might want to shout a word of thanks to them: It is estimated that a single little brown myotis will consume more than 500 mosquitoes per hour, or more than 2,000 during the course of one night's feeding.

As with most of the state's WMAs, the forest road-and-trail system is rarely maintained, routes are not blazed, and intersections may not be signed. It is suggested that you save this outing until you have a fair amount of outdoors experience and are comfortable with the feeling of not knowing exactly where you may be at any given moment. With this in mind, the wildlife management area can provide one of the most primitive hiking experiences you will find. Backcountry camping is not permitted; a small campground with pit toilets is located near the trailhead.

Also see *Rail Trails*, Grand Vue Park and Tomlinson Run State Park under *Green Space—Parks*, and the "More than Just a Park" sidebar later in the chapter.

HORSEBACK RIDING Peace Point Equestrian Center (304-829-4800; www
.peacepointfarms.com), Peace Point Rd., Bethany. A part of Bethany College's equestrian program, Peace Point is open to the public for guided rides on more than 20 miles of trail passing through thousands of acres of gently rolling countryside. A 24-hour notice is requested for reservations.

Also see the "More than Just a Park" sidebar later in the chapter.

RAIL TRAILS At one time, as many as seven different railroad companies serviced Wheeling. Today, not a single locomotive passes through the city, but hikers, bikers, and skaters are the winners, as the city has developed two rail trails along the former rights-of-way.

The **Ohio River Trail** (www.wheelingheritagetrail.com) starts at the parking lot on 48th St. in the southern part of Wheeling and stays within sight of the waterway for 8.5 miles. With historical interpretive signs to help you appreciate the area you are going through, it passes by a number of industrial sites and warehouse districts and goes under the Wheeling Suspension Bridge before coming to an end at the Pike Island Dam, where you can watch huge barges work their way through the lock system. Along the way, the trail provides access to the downtown area, Wheeling Heritage Port, and dozens of Victorian homes.

The **Wheeling Creek Trail** (www.wheelingheritagetrail.com) branches off the Ohio River Trail at 14th St. Approximately 5 miles in length, it climbs a small knoll beside commercial and residential streets in the original part of Wheeling before descending to make use of the Hempfield Viaduct high above Wheeling Creek. Passing through the Hempfield Tunnel is one of the trail's highlights, just before it parallels I-70 and comes to an end at Lava Ave. in Wheeling's Elk Grove neighborhood.

Other rail trails, most about 3 miles or so in length, have been constructed in other parts of this region. Head to Wellsburg to hike, ride, or skate next to the Ohio River on the paved **Brooke Pioneer Trail** (304-737-0506; http://brookepioneer trail.org), which connects with the 1.1-mile **Yankee Trail**. Just south of Weirton, near Colliers, is the **Panhandle Trail** (www.panhandletrail.org), most easily accessed from US 22 exit 3, and stretching for 29 miles from this terminus to Collier Township, Pennsylvania. In the more southern part of the region, the **Marshall County Inter-Modal Rail Trail** runs for 3 miles from Riverfront Park in Moundsville to a trailhead behind the old Marx Toy factory in Glen Dale. Located at Hundred in Wetzel County, the 1.5-mile **East Wetzel Rail-Trail** has an asphalt and packed-sand surface. Access is on WV 7 and US 250.

SCUBA DIVING Velas T Diving & Supply (304-242-3676; 1-800-362-1962; www.velasdiving.com), 1201 Valley Ave., Wheeling. Open daily. More than 20 years of experience providing lessons, equipment, and trips.

SKATING See Wheeling Park under *Green Space—Parks*.

SWIMMING The **Starvaggi Memorial Pool** (304-723-1040; http://mcc-weir .tripod.com/smp.html), 136 Starvaggi Dr., Weirton, has an outdoor pool open during the warmer months and an indoor head pool open year-round.

Also see Tomlinson Run State Park, Brooke Hills Park, and Wheeling Park under *Green Space—Parks* and the "More than Just a Park" sidebar later in the chapter.

SWIMMIN' HOLES Local families use a small park and dock next to 12th St. in Wellsburg as a place to take a dip in the Ohio River. Just be sure to pay attention to currents (do not even think of swimming here in high water), and don't swim out too far, or you may have a collision with a river barge!

TRAIN EXCURSIONS See the "More than Just a Park" sidebar later in the chapter.

WALKING TOURS As with many cities of today, the main roadway in Moundsville has become a long stretch of food chains, businesses, and office buildings. However, take a few steps onto the less-traveled streets, and you discover a historically rich town. The *Moundsville Historical Walking Tour* pamphlet (available from Marshall County Tourism and Chamber of Commerce—see *Guidance*) directs you to more than a dozen buildings and sites dating from the late 1800s and early 1900s, including the homes of W. F. Dalzell, founder of Fostoria Glass, and Davis Grubb, author of *Night of the Hunter* and *Fool's Parade*.

OHIO RIVER SWIMMIN' HOLE

PARKS

Moundsville

🐾 **Grand Vue Park** (304-845-9810; 1-800-705-6171; www.grandvuepark.com), 250 Trail Dr. With a view that takes in West Virginia and Ohio, this is one of the region's nicest (and most underutilized) parks. There's an 18-hole, par 3 golf course; miniature golf; disc golf course; an outdoor heated pool; picnic facilities; and more than 6 miles of hiking, biking, and cross-country skiing trails (with mountain bike and ski rentals). Pet-friendly rental cabins with heat, air-conditioning, kitchens, and fireplaces are open year-round ($80 daily; weekend and weekly rates available).

Valley Fork Park (304-845-7733), 12th St. and Fork Ridge Rd. In addition to ball courts and restrooms, the small municipal park has a nice walking trail if you need to stretch your legs.

New Manchester

Tomlinson Run State Park (304-564-3651; www.tomlinsonrunsp.com; 84 Osage Rd., New Manchester 26506). From New Cumberland drive north on WV 2 for 0.8 mile, turn right on WV 8, and continue another 3.3 miles. This is it: This is as far north as you can go to hike on public land and still be in West Virginia. In fact, Tomlinson Run State Park is farther north than Pittsburgh, Pennsylvania, and is on the same latitude as Staten Island, New York.

The 1,398-acre park is administratively divided into two areas. Within the larger Activity Area are picnic sites and shelters, a playground, courts for various sports, and miniature golf. Tomlinson Run Lake (rowboat and paddleboat rentals available during the season) and three smaller fishing ponds attract anglers, while the swimming pool, with a 182-foot figure-eight water slide, is popular with children. The campground (open Apr.–Oct.) has electric hookups, a dump station, camp store, laundry facilities, and bathhouses with hot showers. If you don't own your own equipment, opt for the Rent-A-Camp, which supplies you with a six-person tent, cooler, propane stove, lantern, and cookware.

The focus of the smaller Wilderness Area is Tomlinson Run, which flows to the northwest and empties into the Ohio River less than a mile from the park's boundary. Although it is an easy-moving river, it has carved a gorge into the rolling landscape, whose elevation ranges from 700 feet to 1,200 feet above sea level. During the 1800s, several mills were built along the stream's length to take advantage of

TOMLINSON RUN STATE PARK

MORE THAN JUST A PARK

✂ ♿ ⚲ ✪ **Oglebay Resort** (304-243-4000; 1-800-624-6988; www.oglebay -resort.com), on WV 88 about 3 miles from I-70 exit 2A. In the 1920s, Earl W. Oglebay willed his 700-acre summer estate of "splendid drives, magnificent shade trees, beautiful gardens, lawns, and rolling meadows" to the citizens of Wheeling for "as long as the people shall operate it for purposes of public education and recreation." Since then, Oglebay Resort has become one of the top tourist attractions in West Virginia, with more than 3.5 million visitors annually. And, according to the City of Wheeling, it is the only major self-sustaining public park system in America.

One of the things that makes Oglebay Resort so much more than the usual municipal parks—which often bring to mind a small area with a few sports fields, several picnic tables, possibly an exercise trail, and a couple of pit toilets—is its size. New York's Central Park has only 843 acres, and the City Park of New Orleans encompasses 1,500 acres, while additions to Mr. Oglebay's gift have brought Oglebay Resort, now at 1,650 acres, the distinction of being one of the largest municipal parks in the country.

ALL ABOARD THE OGLBAY RESORT'S MINIATURE TRAIN

Yet, size alone is not enough to draw people to a place. Perched atop low knolls and rolling terrain, Oglebay's attraction is that its many facilities appeal to a wide range of people. History and art lovers can wander through the Carriage House Glass Museum, with more than 3,000 pieces of Wheeling glass, or take in the period-decorated Mansion Museum. Those who have trouble pulling themselves away from malls have seven distinct shops to browse in. The glass gift shop is sure to wow collectors.

Golf addicts can tee off on a choice of courses, equestrians may participate in guided trail rides, and gourmets have given the Ihlenfeld Dining Room (with a panoramic view of the manicured grounds) a number of awards for its presentations of regional specialties. Birdwatchers have open spaces and forested lands in which to pursue their activity, and wildflower lovers can seek out the more than 180 species of blossoms that have been identified in the park.

With the ambience of a mountain inn, Wilson Lodge has hundreds of guest rooms ($175–275), an indoor pool, fitness center, and massage therapy. For those wanting a place of their own, close to 50 fully equipped cottages can accommodate 8 to 26 people ($215–935). (*Insider's tip*: There are many package deals, with a wide variety of themes, that will save you a great deal of money over renting a cabin or room just by itself; be sure to ask about these when making a reservation.) Other attractions include miniature golf, fishing, skiing and snowboarding, pedal boat rentals, playgrounds, picnic areas, tennis courts, and a heated outdoor pool. Of the many special events, the Winter Festival of Lights, which covers more than 300 acres, is the country's largest holiday-season light show and attracts more than 1 million visitors. Paved and unpaved walking and hiking trails take you into every part of the park.

Oglebay's real forte is how well it can introduce small children to the natural world. Playgrounds and picnic areas are located next to many different environments so the kids will see and experience a variety of plants and animals, the 30-acre Good Zoo features exotic species that don't live in West Virginia, and the Benedum Planetarium opens young eyes to the wonder of the night sky. A miniature train ride pulled by a gasoline-powered engine takes you along a narrow-gauge track, through the zoo, and into the woods. It even goes clickety-clack like its larger relatives. The $2 million Schrader Environmental Education Center has a number of excellent displays, a hands-on children's area, and a staff eager to pass on their knowledge. The model-train layout is a replica of a village in days gone by, complete with an amusement park, industrial area, and moving water. (It took 15,500 volunteer hours to construct!) Seasonal day camps provide a fun and educational time in the outdoors.

THE PETTING ZOO OF THE GOOD ZOO AT OGLEBAY RESORT

You could spend an entire vacation here, doing something new every day, and never have the need to leave the park. If you do get an urge to venture outward, all of Wheeling's attractions are not much more than a 10-minute drive away.

the power created by a drop of 100 feet per mile. The forest vegetation that covers the park today appears to be so healthy and profuse that it may be hard to believe that the land had been abused by coal mining, clear-cut timbering, and unsound agricultural practices before it was purchased for the state park in the early 1900s. It is a lesson in what nature is capable of doing if left alone and permitted to work its magic.

A system of connecting hiking trails meanders through both areas of the park.

Wellsburg
Brooke Hills Park (304-737-1236; www.brookehillspark.com), 140 Gist Dr. The park has a multiplicity of facilities, including an 18-hole golf course, miniature golf, paddleboat rentals, heated swimming pool, and primitive campsites (with showers).

Wheeling
*✏ **Wheeling Park*** (304-243-4085; 1-800-624-6988-wheeling-park.com), 1801 National Rd. The 406-acre park has been a place of outdoor recreation since 1925. Facilities include indoor and outdoor tennis, miniature golf, pedal boats, ice skating, picnic facilities, and an outdoor pool with a huge water slide.

WILDLIFE REFUGE PPG Natrium Wildlife Management Area (304-455-2200), Natrium. On WV 2, about 18 miles south of the WV 2 intersection with US 250 in Moundsville. What a delightful surprise it is to find this bit of green tucked next to an industrial plant along the Ohio River. This is not a state WMA that is managed primarily for game animals; rather, it is a preserve set aside by PPG Industries, Inc. So, get out of the car, stretch your legs, walk the dog (on a leash), and keep an eye out for groundhogs, skunks, deer, raccoons, beavers, coyotes, muskrats, and squirrels. The backwater area is home to herons, ducks, Canada geese, and shorebirds. If you're feeling lazy and don't want to walk, you can often spot a number of these animals from the observation platform next to the parking area—especially if you are here in early morning or early evening.

✳ Lodging

RESORT See the "More than Just a Park" sidebar earlier in the chapter.

MOTELS & HOTELS

New Martinsville 26155
♿ **Travelers Inn** (304-455-3355), 519 North State Rte. 2. This inn has pretty basic rooms, but each does have a refrigerator, microwave, hair dryer, and iron. It also has some great low rates. $45–55.

Sistersville 26175
Wells Inn (304-652-1312; 1-800-935-5746; www.hotelwells.com), 316 Charles St. During the oil boom of the late 1800s, there were many boarding-houses for roustabouts and laborers, but no accommodations for more genteel travelers. Ephraim Wells opened his hotel in 1894 to remedy the situation. The hotel has alternately flourished and diminished through its more than 100 years of history, but the present owners have thoroughly renovated it (although it retains the feel of a place with a long history). Each room is decorated differently, and the wallpaper is a replica of the original. An indoor swimming pool and Internet access are acknowledgments of the 21st century. $79–89. *Please note*: The Wells Inn was closed for a complete renovation once again as this book went to press. Call ahead.

Tridelphia 26059

🐾 **Comfort Inn** (304-547-0610), 675 Fort Henry Rd., I-70 exit 11. Some of the more than 100 standard motel rooms have whirlpools. All guests get to use the indoor swimming pool and exercise room. Pets permitted with the payment of a fee. Close to Cabela's (see *Selective Shopping*) and Wheeling. $99–120.

🐾 **Holiday Inn Express** (304-547-1380), 87 Jenkins Lane, I-70 exit 11. Outdoor pool, exercise room, guest laundry, and free expanded continental breakfast. Pets permitted with payment of a small fee. Close to Cabela's (see *Selective Shopping*) and Wheeling. $105–190.

Weirton 26062

Baymont Inn & Suites (304-723-0050; 1-877-229-6668; www.baymont inns.com), 1 Amerihost Dr., within sight of US 22 exit 4. Some of the rooms have whirlpools; all have irons and hair dryers. You also have access to the heated indoor pool and exercise room, and receive a free continental breakfast and newspaper. $95–169.

🐾 ♿ **Holiday Inn** (304-723-5522), 350 Three Springs Dr. There are more than 100 rooms (and a few suites), along with an outdoor pool, exercise room, and restaurant. Pets are permitted, but only with an additional $50 fee added to your room bill. $119–150.

Wheeling 26003

🐾 **McClure City Center Hotel** (304-232-0300; www.mclurehotel.com), 1200 Market St. Opened in 1852, it has hosted many dignitaries, including Ulysses S. Grant, William Howard Taft, Theodore Roosevelt, Woodrow Wilson, William McKinley, Chester A. Arthur, Dwight Eisenhower, and John F. Kennedy. Located within walking distance of downtown attractions, the seven-story McClure has a refrigerator and microwave in some of the rooms.

Wi-Fi is available throughout the hotel; pets permitted with an additional $25 fee. $109.

🐾 ♿ **Super 8** (304-243-9400), 2400 National Rd., off I-70 exit 5. The Super 8 is a basic motel with an exercise room, guest laundry, and some of the lower-cost accommodations in Wheeling. Pets permitted with an additional fee. $65–105.

Also see *To Do—Gaming and Horse Racing*.

BED & BREAKFASTS

Glen Dale 26038

Bonnie Dwaine Bed and Breakfast (304-845-7250; 1-888-507-4569; www.bonnie-dwaine.com), 505 Wheeling Ave. The Bonnie Dwaine House astounds with the sheer number and volume of Victorian-era and Victorian-style furnishings found in every room. In addition, the collection of artwork, sculptures, and Fostoria glass is so extensive you could occupy a full afternoon trying to take it all in. The renovated late-1800s home has five guest rooms, each decorated differently and with a private bath and whirlpool tub. The weekend gourmet breakfasts are served in the formal dining room; an extended continental breakfast is provided in the kitchen during the week. Bonnie keeps snacks and a refrigerator stocked with soft drinks that guests are welcome to help themselves to at any time. $89–125.

New Martinsville 26155

Magnolia House Bed & Breakfast (304-455-4440; www.magnoliahouse bnb.com), 757 Maple Ave. Like the Bonnie Dwaine, the Magnolia House was built around the turn of the 20th century, but the owner of this home has decided to be frugal with the furnishings, keeping things simple and with more open space. The guest rooms are large (one has a private

MAGNOLIA HOUSE BED & BREAKFAST

bath), and the homemade sticky buns served to me at breakfast are some of the best I've had. Because of the B&B's relaxed atmosphere, guests tend to mingle and converse in the parlor or on the porch swing overlooking a quiet residential neighborhood. $70–115; rent the entire house for $150.

West Liberty 26074

&. **Liberty Oaks Alumni House Bed & Breakfast** (304-336-8079; 1-800-732-6204; http://www.libertyoaksbb .com/), Rte. 88N. Located on the edge of the West Liberty State University campus, the B&B was the school's president's residence from 1937 to 1997. The large, columned home features a number of guest rooms (all with private bath, TV, phone, and Internet access), desktop computer, and laundry room. Students enrolled in the university's Hospitality and Tourism Management program provide the services. You will also have easy access to all the university's amenities, such as the fitness center, tennis courts, and swimming pool. $89–129.

CABINS & VACATION RENTALS

Wheeling 26003

✐ **Park View Chalets** (304-233-7055; 1-866-241-8171; www.cabins.com), Waddles Run Rd. These two cabins (one sleeps 10, the other eight) are in a nicely wooded area only 0.2 mile from Oglebay Resort's back entrance. Each cabin is fully equipped with two bathrooms, kitchens, laundry facilities, and other amenities. Only rented by the weekend (Fri., Sat., and Sun. for $797.50–897.50) or week (call for rates).

Also see Grand Vue Park under *Green Space—Parks* and the "More than Just a Park" sidebar earlier in the chapter.

CAMPGROUND

Cameron 26033

🐾 **Fish Creek Campground** (304-686-2471), Rural Rte. 5. Open all year; pets permitted. The creekside sites in this small campground are large, flat, and grassy, with modern restrooms. Fishing and swimming in Fish Creek.

Also see Tomlinson Run State Park and Brooke Hills Park under *Green Space—Parks*.

✳ Where to Eat
DINING OUT

Chester

La Bonne Vie Steakhouse (304-387-8250; www.mtrgaming.com/dining /labonnevie.html), in the Mountaineer Casino Racetrack and Resort (see *To Do—Gaming and Horse Racing*), a short distance south of Newell on WV 2. Closed Mon. and Tues. Reservations suggested; resort casual attire requested. High-quality steaks prepared well and offered with a tantalizing array of toppings and sauces are the hallmark of La Bonne Vie's à la carte menu. My East Meets West dish had shrimp with coconut cream dipping sauce and two fillets accompanied by chocolate dipping sauce, an odd-sounding but surprisingly wonderful combination. All sauces, reductions, dressings, and desserts are prepared fresh in-house. (The raisin-bread toast served at the beginning of the meal is sweet enough to be a dessert.) Everything I saw come out of the kitchen was nicely arranged and presented on the plate. Next time I intend to try the white chocolate prawns.

Be prepared to spend a few dollars. I had been given a $50 certificate and just had a soda, appetizer, and main dish, and spent almost every cent. Some entrées alone were in the $40–47 range.

Wheeling
The Pointe (304-231-1831; 1-877-946-4373; www.wheelingisland.com), 1 South Stone St. Reservations recommended (304-232-5050). Since it opened a number of years ago in the Wheeling Island Hotel-Casino-Racetrack (see *To Do—Gaming and Dog Racing*), The Pointe has become the city's special-occasion restaurant. For me, it is currently my favorite Wheeling fine-dining experience. The wait staff are impeccable, wine offerings are nice, and all the food is prepared and presented with a touch of flair and elegance. The bread and the sun-dried tomato vinaigrette dressing are right on the mark, the gazpacho is spicy, and the Chilean sea bass moist and delicious. Other people have raved about the prime rib. The lowest-cost entrée is $22; if you add an appetizer, drink, and dessert, expect to pay a minimum of $50 per person.

Stratford Springs Restaurant (304-233-5100; www.stratfordsprings restaurant.com), 100 Kensington Dr. Within an inn built in 1906 and listed on the National Register of Historic Places, the Stratford Springs Restau-

rant is a fine-dining experience located close to Oglebay Resort. Some evenings it is amazingly uncrowded; other nights you will probably only be able to get in if you have made a reservation. A covered outdoor bar and terrace overlook the grounds and feature live entertainment. The menu includes chicken, steak, seafood, and lamb. Entrées $18–28.

Also see the "More than Just a Park" sidebar earlier in the chapter.

EATING OUT

Benwood
Undo's (304-233-0560; www.undos .com), 753 Main St. Benwood is the original location of a small regional chain that started when Undo and Jenny Sparachane opened their first restaurant in 1953. It's in an old industrial neighborhood with the iron girders of a bridge towering above it, but you don't see this once you're inside and enjoying the large portions of traditional Italian entrées. All meals come with unlimited salad and garlic cheese pizza bread (delicious, filling, and precludes any reason to order a pizza). Entrées $5.95–17.95.

Moundsville
Acapulco Mexican Restaurant (304-843-0111), 800 Lafayette Ave. The same menu you will find in hundreds of other Mexican restaurants operating in the mid-Atlantic states, but the food is fresher and better prepared here. Entrées $4.95–15.95.

Alexander's on 7th (304-845-0582; www.alexanderson7th.com), 508 Seventh St. Open Mon.–Fri. for lunch and dinner. Within a 1907 former bank building, the restaurant's ornate ceilings, marble wainscoting, and vault sitting behind the coffee bar provide a glimpse of what life was like around the turn of the 20th century. During the day, a menu of light lunch items is served (the Mediterranean, a grilled veggie sandwich, is especially good), whereas on Fri. night full dinners are served. The ambience and the quality of the food are refreshingly different from many of the average restaurants of this region. Lunch $5.95–8.95; dinner $9.95–17.95.

New Martinsville

Barista's Café (304-455-5410; www .baristascafe-pub.com), 326 Main St. Open for breakfast, lunch, and dinner; closed Sun. Such a nice find in a town almost bereft of an alternative to country cooking. Barista's serves chicken enchilada quiches; artichoke, mushroom, and banana pepper panini; and wood-fired oven pizzas. Home-baked goods and coffee are the reasons to stop by in the morning, while the pub is the reason to hang around at night. Most entrées less than $10.

Quinet's Court Restaurant (304-455-2110), Main St. Open for breakfast, lunch, and dinner daily; open at 11 on Sun. Quinet's has been around for about a century, and close to a thousand photographs of celebrities and locals who have dined here line the walls. (They have almost 5,000 pictures that are rotated every so often.) There are no factory-produced foods here; everything is made from scratch, from the bread, soups, and desserts to the 75 items on the buffet ($8.95 lunch; $9.95 after 4 and all day Sat. and Sun.). Many of the entrées, which include meat loaf, ham, liver, and fried chicken, are based on recipes from local "hobby" chefs. Entrées $7.95–8.95.

Tridelphia

Cabela's (304-238-0120), 1 Cabela Drive (I-70 exit 10). The cafeteria in Cabela's (see *Selective Shopping*) offers some of the most interesting and diverse meat sandwiches you will prob-

ably ever find in one place. You can choose to have bear, ostrich, elk, buffalo, or other wild-game meats stacked high on a variety of breads. Don't want a sandwich? Then go for the elk stroganoff or soup. Sandwiches $5.95–10.95.

Wellsburg

✎ ℉ **Drovers Inn** (304-737-0188; www.droversinn.net), 1001 Washington Pike. Open for dinner Wed.–Sat; open Sun. noon–7. Reservations suggested. The log Drovers Inn, in one form or another, has been providing food and lodging since the 1850s. With a fireplace and other reminders of the earlier days, the inn serves an American menu of sandwiches, roasted chicken, steak, and seafood ($9.99–15.99). The tavern in the basement gets really busy, especially on the weekends.

✎ ℉ **Pier 12 Restaurant and Lounge** (304-737-3280), 12th and River. Open daily for lunch and dinner. The menu of pasta, steak, chicken, and seafood is almost secondary to the pleasant view of the Ohio River from the dining room and outside deck. The restaurant also owns the 40-slip marina, so it can get quite crowded with pleasure boaters stopping in for lunch or dinner on a nice day. Entrées $7.95–16.95.

PIER 12 RESTAURANT AND LOUNGE

Staffileno's on the River (304-737-0064), 801 Main St. Open for lunch and dinner daily. The grandson of immigrants from Guilianova, Italy, Ron Staffileno uses many of his ancestors' traditions in preparing the pasta dishes he serves. The menu contains more than that, though. You can order liver and onions, sirloin, country-fried steak, or ribs while enjoying a view of the Ohio River from the dining room. Entrées $8.95–26.95.

Wheeling

Abbey's Restaurant and Lounge (304-233-0729), 145 Zane St. Located on Wheeling Island, Abbey's is a nice alternative to the hustle and bustle that often accompanies dining at the Wheeling Island Hotel-Casino-Racetrack. Unlike a number of establishments that serve liquor in the northern part of the state, Abbey's has a clean, well-kept, brightly lit atmosphere with a friendly staff. It's also a true family-run business. Father Abbey Maroon owns it, mother Kathy does the cooking, son Joey is manager, and daughters Vanessa, Angie, and Lenora wait tables. Servings are more than ample, and I enjoyed the light touch that went into preparing my fish stuffed with crab, shrimp, and scallops. The chicken orzo soup was good, too. Entrées $7.95–25.95.

Bella Via (304-242-8181), #1 Burkham Court. Open daily for lunch and dinner. For more than six decades, Bella Via has been serving up large portions of homemade Italian and American dishes. Whatever you do, make sure you order something with the homemade marinara sauce; it is the best the city has to offer. Entrées $8.95–17.50.

Coleman's Fish Market (304-232-8510; www.centremarket.net), 2226 Market St. Open until 5:30 Mon.–Thurs. and Sat., open until 7. Closed Sun. Located inside Centre Market, Coleman's fish sandwiches are renowned throughout the area. Fried in a special canola oil that is 94 percent free of saturated fat, the fish is served on white bread—and is absolutely delicious. It's cheap, too. Don't miss this local tradition. Fresh fish is also available for you to take home and cook. Entrées $4–10.

DeFelice Brothers Pizza (304-232-8999; www.defelicebrospizza.com), 1000 National Rd. (US 40). My sister, who is one of the world's harshest pizza critics, says the DeFelice Brothers make about the best carryout pizza in the city. Others must agree with her, because the small regional chain was named the "Best Traditional Pizza in America" at the World Championship held in Salsomaggiore, Italy. Salads, sandwiches, and pizzas range from $2.99 to $16.99. (My mother's maiden name was DeFelice.)

Figaretti's (304-243-5625; www.figarettisrestaurant.com), 1035 Mount DeChantal Rd. Open for lunch and dinner. Figaretti's is a Wheeling institution, serving a loyal following since 1948. In fact, the restaurant has crowds of regulars who show up on their own respective nights (in other words, the Monday people are different from the Friday folks, and the Tuesday group is here every Tuesday, and so on, with very little mixing of the crowds). Expect to wait for a table. Although the restaurant is known for its Italian dishes, the regulars I talked with recommended the ribs, steaks, and seafood. Very few places still make their own spumoni, so save room for dessert. Entrées $9–19.

Honest to Goodness Salsa Café (304-232-2468; www.honesttogoodnesssalsacafe.com), 56 Carmel Rd. Open Mon.–Sat.; closed Sun. So often, if you want to eat a healthy meal, you have to settle for some second-rate flavors. Not so here. The breakfast, bean spinach, beef, or chicken burritos are all tasty and served with some of the best freshly made salsa you will find in the state. Portions are big, too; don't order the large unless you are really hungry. Entrées $4.95–7.50.

Uncle Pete's (304-234-6701), 753 Main St. Open daily for breakfast, lunch, and dinner. Uncle Pete's is housed in an 1880s Victorian home with a back deck overlooking the Ohio River. Owner Robert Conniff trained at the Stratford Springs Culinary School and offers daily specials of his own design featuring a variety of meats and seafoods. Lunches are sandwiches and salads. Entrées $9.95–39.95.

✒ **Ye Old Alpha** (304-242-1090; http://yeoldealpha.com), 50 Carmel Rd. Open daily for breakfast, lunch and dinner. Weekend reservations suggested. Established in 1932, Ye Old Alpha has been through a number of owners, but it has always been a landmark neighborhood family restaurant that prides itself in its "dead animals [trophy animals line the walls], cold beer, and classic American food." Most of the patrons know at least several other patrons, and the wait staff acts as if they know everyone (whether they do or not). Entrées $8.95–21.95.

COFFEE BAR Wheeling Coffee and Spice Company (304-243-0141; www.wheelingcoffeeco.com), 13 14th St., Wheeling. Across the street from the Wheeling Convention and Visitors Bureau (see *Guidance*). This is the original location of the wholesale and retail outlet (a couple of rooms full of couches and chairs) for the company that, for more than 100 years, has roasted and packed the Paramount brand of coffee for institutional food service. The Burns coffee roasters, manufactured by the Blaw-Knox Company in 1884, are still operational and are used for single-batch roasting.

SNACKS & GOODIES

Chester
Frank's Pastry Shop (304-387-0136), 430 Carolina St. Closed Sun. and Mon. Doughnuts, cookies, and cream horns baked fresh daily.

Moundsville
Quality Bakery (304-845-3452), 1004 Second St. Quality Bakery has been turning out pies, cakes, doughnuts, and cookies for decades.

Weirton
Gus's Goodies (304-748-2870; www.gussgoodies.com), 3972 Main St. Relatives of the original Gus, who immigrated from Greece in 1912 and opened a bakery in 1935, still operate the bakery, most well-known for its foam and wedding cakes.

Wheeling
Suzie-Q Bakery (304-277-3131), 1261 Warwood Ave., in the Warwood Shopping Center. Known for good pastries and breads.

Valley Cheese (304-232-0882; www.centremarket.net), in the Centre Market. Closed Sun. Three generations of the same family have sold this establishment's Amish cheeses, meats, jams, jellies, chocolates, and more.

✳ Entertainment
FILM

Chester
Hilltop Drive-In (304-387-1611), at the intersection of WV 8 and WV 208 south of Chester. Having been open on and off since 1950, the Hilltop shows double features nightly from Memorial Day to Labor Day and on weekends during the spring and fall.

Glen Dale

Glen Dale Drive-In (304-845-2064, on WV 2, about 1 mile north of Moundsville. With movie screens few and far between in the more southern portion of this region, the Glen Dale Drive-In fills the void by showing double features from Apr. through Sept. Opened in 1948, it's one of the state's oldest drive-ins.

New Martinsville

Valley Cinema 3 (304-455-5866; www.valleycinema3wv.com), 3 Martinsville Plaza. Three screens showing mainstream movies.

Tridelphia

Marquee Cinemas—The Highlands (304-547-1290), 150 Sims Circle. First-run movies in the Cabela's shopping area east of Wheeling.

MUSIC The Capitol Theatre (304-233-7000; 1-800-828-3097; www .capitoltheatrewheeling.com), 1015 Main St., Wheeling. Mention Wheeling to country-music fans, and they will almost invariably start waxing reverently about what was one of America's longest-running country-music radio shows—second only to Nashville's Grand Ole Opry. Since 1933, Wheeling's Jamboree USA had featured—often when they were undiscovered—some of the genre's most famous and best-loved talents, including Merle Haggard, Loretta Lynn, Johnny Cash and June Carter, Sammy Kershaw, Ronnie Milsap, Willie Nelson, Tanya Tucker, and the Oak Ridge Boys. Sadly, the music hall was purchased by the nationwide Clear Channel Radio company, and, in what surely has to have been a very short-sighted move, they closed the music hall in 2005. Decades of tradition killed by an organization that obviously had no idea what it was purchasing.

However, I'm happy to report that later that year, a consortium, spearheaded by the Wheeling Convention and Visitors Bureau took over operations and renovated the structure. Reopened in 2009 as the Capitol Theatre, it walls once again reverberate with the sounds of plays, concerts, and other performance arts. Thank you, far-sighted citizens of Wheeling.

SPORTS Wheeling Nailers (304-234-GOAL; 1-877-NAIL-TIX; www .wheelingnailers.com). The Nailers, members of the ECH League and affiliates of the NHL Pittsburgh Penguins, play their home games at the WesBanco Arena in Wheeling.

THEATER

Wellsburg

Brooke Hills Playhouse (304-737-3344; www.brookehillsplayhouse.com), in Brooke Hills Park (see *Green Space—Parks*). Brooke Hills Playhouse is the oldest community summer theater in West Virginia and presents its productions in a refurbished barn. Past presentations have included comedies, farces, dramas, and musical productions such as *Charlotte's Web*: *Come Blow Your Horn*: *Natalie Needs a Nightie*: *Little Shop of Horrors*; and *A Bad Year for Tomatoes*.

Wheeling

Towngate Theatre and Cinema (304-242-7700; 1-88TOWNGATE; www.oionline.com), 2118 Market St. Located close to Centre Market, the Towngate is operated by the Oglebay Institute as a venue for live plays presented throughout the year. Movies are shown on weekends when no live performance is scheduled.

Victoria Vaudeville Theater (304-223-SING; 1-800-505-SING; www .Victoria-theater.com), 1228 Market St.

Presented in the 1904 Victoria Theater, the variety show is a throwback to the past, with country, bluegrass, gospel, rock 'n' roll, popular, and Elvis music of the 1940s and '50s mixed in with humor patterned after that found in early-1900s vaudeville shows. The theater has been restored, and there is not a bad seat in the house. The grand columns, box seats, and raised-relief features recall the great opera theaters of old.

✳ Selective Shopping

ANTIQUES Christy's (304-455-1900), 172 Main St., New Martinsville. Antiques and collectibles along with arts and crafts created by local talent.

ART AND CRAFTS GALLERIES

Sistersville
Tyler Artisan Co-op (304-652-1006), 315 Charles St. Open daily. Handmade by local and regional residents, most of the items are what I refer to as folk or primitive art.

Wheeling
Artworks Around Town Gallery and Art Center (304-233-7540; www.artworksaroundtown.org), 200 Market St. Closed Sun. Artworks Around Town is a nonprofit organization whose gallery is a multipurpose space hosting monthly exhibits and sales by local and regional artists, and live performances featuring music, theater, poetry, and author readings. It's a nicely renovated space in the historic Centre Market with some excellent track lighting that helps highlight all the little nuances to be found in creative artwork. The organization also has a full schedule of classes for those who wish to learn more.

Wheeling Artisan Center (304-232-1810), 1400 Main St. Shop for a nice mix of arts and crafts by West Virginia

and regional artists inside a renovated 1891 industrial building. A three-story atrium provides an airy and open space for the products to be displayed. Alongside the artwork are the Made in Wheeling exhibits—interactive, walk-through displays that showcase the town's strong industrial past. All the artwork and exhibits are museum quality, and there is no admission fee, so there is no excuse not to spend a few minutes here.

BOOKSTORE The Book Store (304-447-2200), 161 North St., New Martinsville. New and used books and a few art items.

FARMERS' MARKETS

Moundsville
The indoor **Marshall County Farmers' Market** (304-635-1402) is located on the Marshall County Fairgrounds and opens on Sat. at 9 May–Oct.

Weirton
You can find locally grown produce and home-baked goods in the **Weirton Farmers' Market** (304-564-3805) every Mon. beginning at 3:30 July–Oct. in the Wal-Mart parking lot on Three Springs Dr.

Wheeling
The **Wheeling Farmers' Market I** operates July–Oct. at the St. Michael's Parish parking lot on Sat. 9–1. If you miss the Saturday opportunity, you have another chance during the same months at the **Wheeling Farmers' Market II** on Wed. in the Elk Grove Pizza Hut parking lot from 2 to 6. For more information about either location, call 304-635-1402.

SPECIAL SHOPS

Proctor
ThistleDew Farm (304-455-1728; 1-800-854-6639; www.thistledewfarm

.com; mailing address: Rural Rte. 1, Box 122, Proctor 26055). From Proctor drive eastward on WV 89. Open Mon.–Fri. Apiarists Ellie and Steve Conlin have so many bees—more than 50,000—that the hives are spread across a three-county area. I had never really thought about it before, but my stop at their shop in the old Grandview Schoolhouse revealed the many color variances and flavor nuances that honey can have. The couple showed, and had me taste, the differences between the products that the same bees can produce during the spring, summer, and fall. Besides honey, Ellie and Steve manufacture beeswax candles, honey mustard, honey chutney, honey-filled candy, and more.

Also located in the same retail space is the **Mountain Craft Shop** (304-455-3570; 1-877-FOLKTOYS; www.folk toys.com), with traditional Appalachian toys (like whimmydiddles, flipperdingers, limberjacks, and corncob dolls) handmade by local craftspersons.

Tridelphia
Cabela's (304-238-0120), 1 Cabela Dr. (I-70 exit 10). Is this a retail store or a museum? Before I visited, I was only going to write a few lines about the outdoor gear, clothing, and provisions that this mail-order company is known for. Yet, the 175,000-square-foot store has almost as much nonretail as retail space. The centerpiece is a 30-foot-tall mountain replica with close to 100 wild-game mounts depicted in native habitats. In the African safari display, lions protect a zebra kill from hyenas, and an elephant (which is dwarfed in this huge store) has its trunk upraised. The trophy-deer museum seems to be about the size of a typical Wal-Mart, and hundreds of live fish swim through the walk-through freshwater aquariums. Don't miss (as if you could) the magnificent 20-foot bear and eagle sculpture at the front entrance. A very worthwhile visit even if you are not into hunting or fishing. There's also the opportunity to dine on game meats (see *Eating Out*).

Wheeling
Imperial Teachers Store (304-233-0711; 1-800-947-9701; www.imperial teachersstore.com), 2347 Main St. There is an entire warehouse floor full of materials that teachers, students, parents, and even collectors will find interesting. Puzzles, games, puppets, science project ideas, books, and school supplies—it is almost staggering. Also in the store is a year-round Christmas shop.

Patrick's Trains (304-232-0714; www .patstrains.com), 142 29th St. It's a small shop, but model-train enthusiasts will be delighted with the amount of merchandise packed into it. The selection includes items from Williams, Lionel, Weaver, K-Line, MTH, and Dept. 56. The staff is enthusiastic about their avocation and will help you with information on types of gauges, from N to O.

The Pepper Posse (304-233-2330; 304-233-1285; www.pepperpossee

CABELA'S

.com), 2200 Market St., in the Centre Market. Dozens and dozens of chili sauces (from mild to hot 'n spicy) manufactured in the United States and abroad, with some of the most interesting labels you will ever see. Also a variety of marinades and cutlery.

✳ Special Events

January: **Regional Student Art Exhibit** (304-242-7700), Stifel Fine Arts Center, Wheeling. Works from local school students.

March: **Wheeling Celtic Celebration** (304-232-3087), Wheeling Artisan Center. Hours of music and all things Celtic.

April: **Annual Antique Show** (304-242-7272), Oglebay Resort, Wheeling. The sales of antiques and collectibles from more than 50 selected dealers benefit the resort's museums.

May: **Elizabethtown Festival** (304-845-6200), Moundsville. An early-1800s Heritage Festival.

June: **Marx Toy & Train Collectors Convention** (304-242-8133), Kruger Street Toy and Train Museum, Wheel-ing. Lectures by former Marx employees, toy swaps, and repairs of old toys.

August: **Heritage Blues Fest** (304-238-6064; http://heritagemusicfest .com), Heritage Port, Wheeling.

September: **Brooke County Fair** (304-737-1236), Brooke Hills Park, Wellsburg. **Hancock County Old Time Fair** (304-564-3805; www .hancockcountyoldtimefair.org), Tomlinson Run State Park, New Manchester. **West Virginia Oil & Gas Festival** (304-652-2939), Sistersville. Honors the industry that was the area's major economic engine in the early 1900s. Oil and gas exhibits, gas-engine shows, entertainment, and crafts. **Sistersville Marble Festival** (304-652-4030), Sistersville. The entire downtown area becomes a place where you can watch marbles being made; attend marble auctions; and buy, sell, or trade marbles.

November–January: **Winter Festival of Lights** (304-234-4066), Oglebay Resort. The country's largest display of holiday lights attracts a million visitors annually.

INDEX

C